Praise for Sven Beckert's

EMPIRE OF COTTON

"Too little present-day academic history is written for the general public. *Empire of Cotton* transcends this barrier and should be devoured eagerly, not only by scholars and students but also by the intelligent reading public. The book is rich and diverse in the treatment of its subject. . . . Beckert's book made me wish for a sequel."   —Daniel Walker Howe,
The Washington Post

"Deeply researched and eminently readable, *Empire of Cotton* gives new insight into the relentless expansion of global capitalism. . . . With graceful prose and a clear and compelling argument, [Beckert] not only charts the expansion of cotton capitalism, . . . but also addresses the conditions of enslaved workers in the fields and wage workers in the factories."
     —Thomas Bender, *The New York Times*

"A masterpiece of the historian's craft: combining a global scope with concern for the nuances of individual experience, Beckert tracks the fortunes of a single commodity, cotton, across six continents and thousands of years."   —Timothy Shenk, *The Nation*

"[Beckert's] detailed narrative never scants the rich complexity of the cotton trade's impact on many different societies."   —Wendy Smith,
The Boston Globe

"Beckert is a big-order thinker. His book offers a masterly picture of the empire of cotton as an economic system that held together myriad different parts. . . . Impressive indeed."   —Stephanie McCurry,
The Times Literary Supplement

Sven Beckert

EMPIRE of COTTON

Sven Beckert is the Laird Bell Professor of American History at Harvard University. He received his PhD from Columbia University and has written widely on the economic, social, and political history of capitalism. He has been the recipient of numerous awards and fellowships, including from Harvard Business School, the Dorothy and Lewis B. Cullman Center for Scholars and Writers at the New York Public Library, and the Charles Warren Center for Studies in American History. He was also a fellow of the American Council of Learned Societies and the John Simon Guggenheim Memorial Foundation. He lives in Cambridge, Massachusetts.

svenbeckert.com

ALSO BY SVEN BECKERT

The Monied Metropolis: New York City and
the Consolidation of the American Bourgeoisie, 1850–1896

EMPIRE of COTTON

A Global History

Sven Beckert

VINTAGE BOOKS

A DIVISION OF PENGUIN RANDOM HOUSE LLC

NEW YORK

FIRST VINTAGE BOOKS EDITION, NOVEMBER 2015

Copyright © 2014 by Sven Beckert

The Library of Congress has cataloged the Knopf edition as follows:
Beckert, Sven.
Empire of cotton : a global history / Sven Beckert.—First edition.
pages cm
1. Cotton textile industry—History.   2. Cotton trade—History.
3. Cotton plantation workers—History.   4. Slavery—Economic aspects.   5. Slaves.
6. Textile workers.   7. Capitalism—History.   8. Labor—History.   I. Title.
HD9870.5 .B43   2014
338.4'767721—dc23   2014009320

Vintage Books Trade Paperback ISBN: 978-0-375-71396-5
eBook ISBN: 978-0-385-35325-0

Maps by Mapping Specialists

www.vintagebooks.com

Printed in the United States of America
10   9   8   7   6   5   4   3   2   1

For Lisa

Contents

Introduction

Edgar Degas views the empire of cotton: merchants
in New Orleans, 1873.

In late January 1860, the members of the Manchester Chamber of Commerce assembled in that city's town hall for their annual meeting. Prominent among the sixty-eight men who gathered in the center of what was then the most industrialized city in the world were cotton merchants and manufacturers. In the previous eighty years, these men had transformed the surrounding countryside into the hub of something never before seen—a global web of agriculture, commerce, and industrial production. Merchants bought raw cotton from around the world and took it to British factories, home to two-thirds of the world's cotton spindles. An army of workers spun that cotton into thread and wove it into finished fabrics; then dealers sent those wares out to the world's markets.

The assembled gentlemen were in a celebratory mood. President

Edmund Potter reminded his audience of the "amazing increase" of their industry and "the general prosperity of the whole country, and more particularly of this district." Their discussions were expansive, touching on the affairs of Manchester, Great Britain, Europe, the United States, China, India, South America, and Africa. Cotton manufacturer Henry Ashworth added superlatives of his own, celebrating "a degree of prosperity in business which has probably been unequalled in any previous time."[1]

These self-satisfied cotton manufacturers and merchants had reason to be smug: They stood at the center of a world-spanning empire—the empire of cotton. They ruled over factories in which tens of thousands of workers operated huge spinning machines and noisy power looms. They acquired cotton from the slave plantations of the Americas and sold the products of their mills to markets in the most distant corners of the world. The cotton men debated the affairs of the world with surprising nonchalance, even though their own occupations were almost banal—making and hawking cotton thread and cloth. They owned noisy, dirty, crowded, and decidedly unrefined factories; they lived in cities black with soot from coal-fueled steam engines; they breathed the stench of human sweat and human waste. They ran an empire, but hardly seemed like emperors.

Only a hundred years earlier, the ancestors of these cotton men would have laughed at the thought of a cotton empire. Cotton was grown in small batches and worked up by the hearth; the cotton industry played a marginal role at best in the United Kingdom. To be sure, some Europeans knew of beautiful Indian muslins, chintzes, and calicoes, what the French called *indiennes*, arriving in the ports of London, Barcelona, Le Havre, Hamburg, and Trieste. Women and men in the European countryside spun and wove cottons, modest competitors to the finery of the East. In the Americas, in Africa, and especially in Asia, people sowed cotton among their yam, corn, and jowar. They spun the fiber and wove it into the fabrics that their households needed or their rulers demanded. As they had for centuries, even millennia, people in Dhaka, Kano, and Teotihuacán, among many other places, made cotton cloth and applied beautiful colors to it. Some of these fabrics were traded globally. Some were of such extraordinary fineness that contemporaries called them "woven wind."

Instead of women on low stools spinning on small wooden wheels in their cottages, or using a distaff and spinning bowl in front of their hut, in 1860 millions of mechanical spindles—powered by steam engines and operated by wage workers, many of them children—turned for up to fourteen hours a day, producing millions of pounds of yarn. Instead of householders growing cotton and turning it into homespun thread and hand-loomed cloth, millions of slaves labored on plantations in the Americas, thousands of miles away from the hungry factories they supplied, factories that in turn were thousands of miles removed from eventual consumers of the cloth. Instead of caravans carrying West African cloth across the Sahara on camels, steamships plied the world's oceans, loaded with cotton from the American South or with British-made cotton fabrics. By 1860, the cotton capitalists who assembled to celebrate their accomplishments took as a fact of nature history's first globally integrated cotton manufacturing complex, even though the world they had helped create was of very recent vintage.

But in 1860, the future was nearly as unimaginable as the past. Manufacturers and merchants alike would have scoffed if told how radically the world of cotton would change in the following century. By 1960, most raw cotton came again from Asia, China, the Soviet Union, and India, as did the bulk of cotton yarn and cloth. In Britain, as well as in the rest of Europe and New England, few cotton factories remained. The former centers of cotton manufacturing—Manchester, Mulhouse, Barmen, and Lowell among them—were littered with abandoned mills and haunted by unemployed workers. Indeed, in 1963 the Liverpool Cotton Association, once one of cotton's most important trade associations, sold its furniture at auction.[2] The empire of cotton, at least the part dominated by Europe, had come crashing down.

This book is the story of the rise and fall of the European-dominated empire of cotton. But because of the centrality of cotton, its story is also the story of the making and remaking of global capitalism and with it of the modern world. Foregrounding a global scale of analysis we will learn how, in a remarkably brief period, enterprising entrepreneurs and powerful statesmen in Europe recast the world's most significant manufacturing industry by combining imperial expansion and slave labor with new machines and wage workers. The very particular organization of trade, production, and consumption they created exploded the disparate worlds of cotton that had existed for millennia. They animated cotton, invested it with world-changing energy, and then used it as a lever to transform the world. Capturing the biological bounty of an ancient plant, and the skills and huge markets of an old industry in Asia, Africa, and the Americas, European entrepreneurs and statesmen built an empire of cotton of tremendous scope and energy. Ironically, their shocking success also awakened the very forces that eventually would marginalize them within the empire they had created.

Along the way, millions of people spent their lives working the acres of cotton that slowly spread across the world, plucking billions of bolls from resistant cotton plants, carrying bales of cotton from cart to boat and from boat to train, and working, often at very young ages, at "satanic mills" from New England to China. Countries fought wars for access to these fertile fields, planters put untold numbers of people into shackles, employers abbreviated the childhoods of their operatives, the introduction of new machines led to the depopulation of ancient industrial centers, and workers, both slave and free, struggled for freedom and a living wage. Men and women who had long sustained themselves through small plots of land, growing cotton alongside their food, saw their way of life end. They left behind their agricultural tools and headed to the factory. In other parts of the world, many who had worked at their looms and who wore clothing that they themselves had woven found their products overwhelmed by the ceaseless output of machines. They left their spinning wheels and moved into the fields, now trapped in a cycle of endless pressure and endless debt. The empire of cotton was, from the beginning, a site of constant global struggle between slaves and planters, merchants and statesmen, farmers and merchants, workers and factory owners. In this as in so many other ways, the empire of cotton ushered in the modern world.

Today cotton is so ubiquitous that it is hard to see it for what it is: one of mankind's great achievements. As you read this sentence, chances are you are wearing something woven from cotton. And it is just as likely that you have never plucked a cotton boll from its stem, seen a wispy strand of raw cotton fiber, or heard the deafening noise of a spinning mule and a power loom. Cotton is as familiar as it is unknown. We take its perpetual presence for granted. We wear it close to our skin. We sleep under it. We swaddle our newborns in it. Cotton is in the banknotes we use, the coffee filters that help us awaken in the morning, the vegetable oil we use for cooking, the soap we wash with, and the gunpowder that fights our wars (indeed, Alfred Nobel won a British patent for his invention of "guncotton"). Cotton is even a component of the book you hold in your hands.

For about nine hundred years, from 1000 to 1900 CE, cotton was the world's most important manufacturing industry. Though it now has been surpassed by other industries, cotton remains important in terms of employment and global trade. It is so ubiquitous that in 2013 the world produced at least 123 million cotton bales, each weighing about four hundred pounds—enough to produce twenty T-shirts for each living person. Stacked on top of one another, the bales would create a tower forty thousand miles high; laid horizontally the bales would circle the globe one and a half times. Huge cotton plantations dot the earth, from China to India and the United States, from West Africa to Central Asia. The raw strands they produce, tightly packed in bales, are still shipped around the globe, to factories employing hundreds of thousands of workers. The finished pieces are then sold everywhere, from remote village stores to Walmart. Indeed, cotton might be one of the very few human-made goods that is available virtually anywhere, testifying both to cotton's utility and to capitalism's awe-inspiring increases in human productivity and consumption. As a recent advertising campaign in the United States announced, quite accurately, "Cotton is the fabric of our lives." [3]

Take a moment and imagine, if you can, a world without cotton. You wake up in the morning on a bed covered in fur or straw. You dress in woolens or, depending on the climate and your wealth, in linens or even silks. Because it is hard to wash your clothes, and because they are expensive or, if you make your own, labor-intensive, you change them irregularly. They smell and scratch. They are largely monochromatic, since, unlike cottons, wool and other natural fibers do not take colors very well. And you are surrounded by sheep: it would take approximately 7 billion sheep to produce a quantity of wool equivalent to the world's current cotton crop. Those 7 billion sheep would need 700 million hectares of land for grazing, about 1.6 times the surface area of today's European Union. [4]

Hard to imagine. But in a patch of land on the westernmost edge of the Eurasian landmass, such a world without cotton was long the norm. That land was Europe. Until the nineteenth century, cotton, while not unknown, was marginal to European textile production and consumption.

Why was it that the part of the world that had the least to do with cotton—Europe—created and came to dominate the empire of cotton? Any reasonable observer in, say, 1700, would have expected the world's cotton production to remain centered in India, or perhaps in China. And indeed, until 1780 these countries produced vastly more raw cotton and cotton textiles than Europe and North America. But then things changed. European capitalists and states, with startling swiftness, moved to the center of the cotton industry. They used their new position to ignite an Industrial Revolution. China and India, along with many other parts of the world, became ever more subservient to the Europe-centered empire of cotton. These Europeans then used their dynamic cotton industry as a platform to create other industries; indeed, cotton became the launching pad for the broader Industrial Revolution.

Edward Baines, a newspaper proprietor in Leeds, called cotton in 1835 a "spectacle unparalleled in the annals of industry." He argued that analyzing this spectacle was "more worthy the pains of the student" than the study of "wars and dynasties." I agree. Following cotton, as we shall see, will lead us to the origins of the modern world, industrialization, rapid and continuous economic growth, enormous productivity increase, and staggering social inequality. Historians, social scientists, policy makers, and ideologues of all stripes have tried to disentangle these origins. Particularly vexing is the question of why, after many millennia of slow economic growth, a few strands of humanity in the late eighteenth century suddenly got much richer. Scholars now refer to these few decades as the "great divergence"—the beginning of the vast divides that still structure today's world, the divide between those countries that industrialized and those that did not, between colonizers and colonized, between the global North and the global South. Grand arguments are easily made, some deeply pessimistic, some hopeful. In this book, however, I take a global and fundamentally historical approach to this puzzle: I begin by investigating the industry that stood at the very beginning of the "great divergence."[5]

A focus on cotton and its very concrete and often brutal development, casts doubt on several explanations that all too many observers tend to take for granted: that Europe's explosive economic development can be explained by Europeans' more rational religious beliefs, their Enlightenment traditions, the climate in which they live, the continent's geography, or benign institutions such as the Bank of England or the rule of law. Such essential and all too often unchangeable attributes, however, cannot account for the history of the cotton empire or explain the constantly shifting structure of capitalism. And they are often also wrong. The first industrial nation, Great Britain, was hardly a liberal, lean state with dependable but impartial institutions as it is often portrayed. Instead it was an imperial nation characterized by enormous military expenditures, a nearly constant state of war, a powerful and interventionist bureaucracy, high taxes, skyrocketing government debt, and protectionist tariffs—and it was certainly not democratic. Accounts of the "great divergence" that focus exclusively on conflicts between social classes within particular regions or countries are just as flawed. This book, in contrast, embraces a global perspective to show how Europeans united the power of capital and the power of the state to forge, often violently, a global production complex, and then used the capital, skills, networks, and institutions of cotton to embark upon the upswing in technology and wealth that defines the modern world. By looking at capitalism's past, this book offers a history of capitalism in action.[6]

Unlike much of what has been written on the history of capitalism, *Empire of Cotton* does not search for explanations in just one part of the world. It understands capitalism in the only way it can be properly understood—in a global frame. The movement of capital, people, goods, and raw materials around the globe and the connections forged between distant areas of the world are at the very core of the grand transformation of capitalism and they are at the core of this book.

Such a thorough and rapid re-creation of the world was possible only because of the emergence of new ways of organizing production, trade, and consumption. Slavery, the expropriation of indigenous peoples, imperial expansion, armed trade, and the assertion of sovereignty over people and land by entrepreneurs were at its core. I call this system *war capitalism.*

We usually think of capitalism, at least the globalized, mass-production type that we recognize today, as emerging around 1780 with the Industrial Revolution. But war capitalism, which began to develop in the sixteenth century, came long before machines and factories. War capitalism flourished not in the factory but in the field; it was not mechanized but land- and labor-intensive, resting on the violent expropriation of land and labor in Africa and the Americas. From these expropriations came great wealth and new knowledge, and these in turn strengthened European institutions and states—all crucial preconditions for Europe's extraordinary economic development by the nineteeth century and beyond.

Many historians have called this the age of "merchant" or "mercantile" capitalism, but "war capitalism" better expresses its rawness and violence as well as its intimate connection to European imperial expansion. War capitalism, a particularly important but often unrecognized phase in the development of capitalism, unfolded in a constantly shifting set of places embedded within constantly changing relationships. In some parts of the world it lasted well into the nineteenth century.

When we think of capitalism, we think of wage workers, yet this prior phase of capitalism was based not on free labor but on slavery. We associate industrial capitalism with contracts and markets, but early capitalism was based as often as not on violence and bodily coercion. Modern capitalism privileges property rights, but this earlier moment was characterized just as much by massive expropriations as by secure ownership. Latter-day capitalism rests upon the rule of law and powerful institutions backed by the state, but capitalism's early phase, although ultimately requiring state power to create world-spanning empires, was frequently based on the unrestrained actions of private individuals—the domination of masters over slaves and of frontier capitalists over indigenous inhabitants. The cumulative result of this highly aggressive, outwardly oriented capitalism was that Europeans came to dominate the centuries-old worlds of cotton, merge them into a single empire centered in Manchester, and invent the global economy we take for granted today.

War capitalism, then, was the foundation from which evolved the more familiar industrial capitalism, a capitalism characterized by powerful states with enormous administrative, military, judicial, and infrastructural capacities. At first, industrial capitalism remained tightly linked to slavery and expropriated lands, but as its institutions—everything from wage labor to property rights—gained strength, they enabled a new and different form of integration of the labor, raw materials, markets, and capital in huge swaths of the world.[7] These new forms of integration drove the revolutions of capitalism into ever more corners of the world.

As the modern world came of age, cotton came to dominate world trade. Cotton factories towered above all other forms of European and North American manufacturing. Cotton growing dominated the U.S. economy throughout much of the nineteenth century. It was in cottons that new modes of manufacturing first came about. The factory itself was an invention of the cotton industry. So was the connection between slave agriculture in the Americas and manufacturing across Europe. Because for many decades cotton was the most important European industry, it was the source of huge profits that eventually fed into other segments of the European economy. Cotton also was the cradle of industrialization in virtually every other part of the world—the United States and Egypt, Mexico and Brazil, Japan and China. At the same time, Europe's domination of the world's cotton industry resulted in a wave of deindustrialization throughout much of the rest of the world, enabling a new and different kind of integration into the global economy.

Yet even as the construction of industrial capitalism, beginning in the United Kingdom in the 1780s and then spreading to continental Europe and the United States in the early decades of the nineteenth century, gave enormous power to the states that embraced it and to capitalists within them, it planted the seeds of further transformation in the empire of cotton. As industrial capitalism spread, capital itself became tied to particular states. And as the state assumed an ever more central role and emerged as the most durable, powerful, and rapidly expanding institution of all, labor also grew in size and power. The dependence of capitalists on the state, and the state's dependence on its people, empowered the workers who produced that capital, day in and day out, on the factory floor. By the second half of the nineteenth century, workers organized collectively, both in unions and political parties, and slowly, over multiple decades, improved their wages and working conditions. This, in turn, increased production costs, creating openings for lower-cost producers in other parts of the world. By the turn of the twentieth century, the model of industrial capitalism had traveled to other countries and was embraced by their modernizing elites. As a result, the cotton industry left Europe and New England and returned to it origins in the global South.

Some may wonder why the claims made here for the empire of cotton do not apply to other commodities. After all, before 1760, Europeans had traded extensively in many commodities in the tropical and semitropical areas of the world, including sugar, rice, rubber, and indigo. Unlike these commodities, cotton, however, has two labor-intensive stages—one in the fields, the other in factories. Sugar and tobacco did not create large industrial proletariats in Europe. Cotton did. Tobacco did not result in the rise of vast new manufacturing enterprises. Cotton did. Indigo growing and processing did not create huge new markets for European manufacturers. Cotton did. Rice cultivation in the Americas did not lead to an explosion of *both* slavery and wage labor. Cotton did. As a result, cotton spanned the globe unlike any other industry. Because of the new ways it wove continents together, cotton provides the key to understanding the modern world, the great inequalities that characterize it, the long history of globalization, and the ever-changing political economy of capitalism.

One reason it is hard to see cotton's importance is because it has often been overshadowed in our collective memory by images of coal mines, railroads, and giant steelworks—industrial capitalism's more tangible, more massive manifestations. Too often, we ignore the countryside to focus on the city and the miracles of modern industry in Europe and North America while ignoring that very industry's connection to raw material producers and markets in all corners of the world. Too often, we prefer to erase the realities of slavery, expropriation, and colonialism from the history of capitalism, craving a nobler, cleaner capitalism. We tend to recall industrial capitalism as male-dominated, whereas women's labor largely created the empire of cotton. Capitalism was in many ways a liberating force, the foundation of much of contemporary life; we are invested in it, not just economically but emotionally and ideologically. Uncomfortable truths are sometimes easier to ignore.

Nineteenth-century observers, in contrast, were cognizant of cotton's role in reshaping the world. Some celebrated the amazing transformative power of the new global economy. As a Manchester *Cotton Supply Reporter* put it in 1860, rather breathlessly, "Cotton seems to have been destined to take the lead among the numerous and vast agencies of the present century, set in motion for human civilization. . . . Cotton with its commerce has become one of the many modern 'wonders of the world.' "[8]

When you look at the cotton plant, it seems an unlikely candidate for one of the wonders of the world. Humble and unremarkable, it grows in many shapes and sizes. Prior to Europe's creation of the empire of cotton, different peoples in different parts of the world cultivated plants quite unlike one another. South Americans tended to grow *G. barbadense*, a small bushy tree that sprouted yellow flowers and produced long-staple cotton. In India, by contrast, farmers grew *G. arboretum*, a shrub about six feet in height, with yellow or purple flowers, producing a short-staple fiber, while in Africa the very similar *G. herbaceum* thrived. By the mid-nineteenth century, one type dominated the empire of cotton— *G. hirsutum*—also known as American upland. Originating in Central America, this variant, as described by Andrew Ure in 1836, "rises to the height of two or three feet, and then divaricates into boughs, which bristle with hairs. The leaves are also hairy on their inferior surfaces, and are three- or five-lobed. The upper leaves are entire and heart-shaped; the petioles are velvety. The flowers near the extremities of the boughs are large, and somewhat dingy in colour. The capsules are ovate, four-celled, nearly as large as an apple, and yield a very fine silky cotton wool, much esteemed in commerce."[9]

This fluffy white fiber is at the center of this book. The plant itself does not make history, but if we listen carefully, it will tell us of people all over the world who spent their lives with cotton: Indian weavers, slaves in Alabama, Greek merchants in the Nile Delta towns, highly organized craft workers in Lancashire. The empire of cotton was built with their labor, imagination, and skills. By 1900 about 1.5 percent of the human population—millions of men, women, and children—were engaged in the industry, either growing, transporting, or manufacturing cotton. Edward Atkinson, a mid-nineteenth-century Massachusetts cotton manufacturer, was essentially correct when he pointed out that "there is no other product that has had so potent and malign an influence in the past upon the history and institutions of the land; and perhaps no other on which its future material welfare may more depend." Atkinson was speaking of the United States and its history of slavery, but his argument could be applied to the world as a whole.[10]

This book follows cotton from fields to boats, from merchant houses to factories, from pickers to spinners to weavers to consumers. It does not separate the cotton history of Brazil from that of the United States, Great Britain's from Togo's, or Egypt's from Japan's. The empire of cotton, and with it the modern world, is only understood by connecting, rather than separating, the many places and people who shaped and were in turn shaped by that empire.[11]

I am centrally concerned with the unity of the diverse. Cotton, the nineteenth century's chief global commodity, brought seeming opposites together, turning them almost by alchemy into wealth: slavery and free labor, states and markets, colonialism and free trade, industrialization and deindustrialization. The cotton empire depended on plantation and factory, slavery and wage labor, colonizers and colonized, railroads and steamships—in short, on a global network of land, labor, transport, manufacture, and sale. The Liverpool Cotton Exchange had an enormous impact on Mississippi cotton planters, the Alsatian spinning mills were tightly linked to those of Lancashire, and the future of handloom weavers in New Hampshire or Dhaka depended on such diverse factors as the construction of a railroad between Manchester and Liverpool, investment decisions of Boston merchants, and tariff policies made in Washington and London. The power of the Ottoman state over its countryside affected the development of slavery in the West Indies; the political activities of recently freed slaves in the United States affected the lives of rural cultivators in India.[12]

From these volatile opposites, we see how cotton made possible both the birth of capitalism and its subsequent reinvention. As we explore the twinned paths of cotton and capitalism across the world, and the centuries, we are reminded again and again that no state of capitalism is ever permanent or stable. Each new moment in capitalism's history produces new instabilities, and even contradictions, prompting vast spatial, social, and political rearrangements.

Writing about cotton has a long history. Indeed, cotton might be the most fully researched of all human industries. Libraries are filled with accounts of slave plantations in the Americas, the beginnings of cotton manufacturing in Britain, France, the German lands, and Japan, and the merchants who connected one to the other. Much less common are efforts to link these diverse histories; in fact, what is perhaps the most successful such effort is now nearly two centuries old. When Edward Baines penned his *History of the Cotton Manufacture in Great Britain* in 1835, he concluded that "the author may be permitted to express . . . that his subject derives interest not merely from the magnitude of the branch of industry he has attempted to describe, but from the wonderful extent of intercourse which it has established between this country and every part of the globe."[13] I share Baines's enthusiasm and his global perspective, if not all of his conclusions.

As a Leeds newspaper editor living close to the center of the empire of cotton, Baines could not help but take a global perspective on these matters.[14] However, when professional historians turned to cotton, they almost always focused on local, regional, and national aspects of this history. Yet only a global viewpoint allows us to understand the great realignment that each of these local stories was part of—the huge global shifts in labor regimes in agriculture, the spread of state-strengthening projects by nationalist elites, and the impact of working-class collective action, among others.

This book draws on the vast literature on cotton, but places it in a new framework. As a result, it contributes to a vibrant but often stultifyingly presentist conversation on globalization. *Empire of Cotton* challenges excited discoveries of an allegedly new, global phase in the history of capitalism. It shows that capitalism has been globe-spanning since its inception and that fluid spatial configurations of the world economy have been a common feature of the last three hundred years. The book argues also that for most of capitalism's history the process of globalization and the needs of nation-states were not conflicting, as is often believed, but instead mutually reinforced one another. If our allegedly new global age is truly a revolutionary departure from the past, the departure is not the degree of global connection but the fact that capitalists are for the first time able to emancipate themselves from particular nation-states, the very institutions that in the past enabled their rise.

As its subtitle suggests, *Empire of Cotton* is also part of a larger conversation among historians trying to rethink history by looking at it within a transnational, even global, spatial frame. History as a profession emerged hand in hand with the nation-state, and played an important part in its constitution. But by assuming national perspectives, historians have often underemphasized connections that transcend state borders, settling for explanations that can be drawn from events, people, and processes within particular national territories. This book is intended as a contribution to efforts to balance such "national" perspectives with a broader focus on the networks, identities, and processes that transcend political boundaries.[15]

By focusing on one specific commodity—cotton—and tracing how it was grown, transported, financed, manufactured, sold, and consumed, we are able to see connections between peoples and places that would remain on the margins if we embarked upon a more traditional study bounded by national borders. Instead of focusing on the history of a particular event, such as the American Civil War, or place, such as the cotton factories of Osaka, or group of people, such as West Indian slaves growing cotton, or process, such as rural cultivators turning into industrial wage workers, this book uses the biography of one product as a window into some of the most significant questions we can ask about the history of our world and to reinterpret a history of huge consequence: the history of capitalism.[16]

We are about to embark on a journey through five thousand years of human history. Throughout this book, we will look at a single, seemingly inconsequential item—cotton—to solve a vast mystery: Where does the modern world originate? Let's begin by traveling to a small farming village in what is today Mexico, where cotton plants bloom in a world utterly unlike our own.

Empire of Cotton

Chapter One

The Rise of a Global Commodity

Aztec woman spinning cotton

Half a millennium ago, in a dozen small villages along the Pacific coast of what is today called Mexico, people spent their days growing maize, beans, squash, and chiles. There, between the Río Santiago to the north and the Río Balsas to the south, they fished, gathered oysters and clams, and collected honey and beeswax. Alongside this subsistence agriculture and the modest crafts they produced by hand—small painted ceramic vessels decorated with geometric motifs were their most renowned creation—these men and women also grew a plant that sprouted small tufted white bolls. The plant was inedible. It was also the most valuable thing they grew. They called it *ichcatl*: cotton.

The cotton plant thrived among the maize, and each fall, after they harvested their food crops, the villagers plucked the soft wads of fiber from the pyramidally shaped, waist-high plants, gathering the numerous bolls in baskets or sacks, then carrying them to their mud-and-wattle huts. There they painstakingly removed the many seeds by hand, then beat the cotton on a palm mat to make it smooth, before combing out the fibers into strands several inches long. Using a thin wooden spindle fitted with a ceramic disk and a spinning bowl to support the spindle as it twirled, they twisted the strands together into fine white thread. Then they created cloth on a backstrap loom, a simple tool consisting of two sticks attached by the warp threads; one stick was hung from a tree, the other on the weaver herself, who stretched the warp with the weight of her own body and then wove the contrasting thread (the weft) in and out between the warps in an unending dance. The result was a cloth as strong as it was supple. They dyed the cloth with indigo and cochineal, creating a rich variety of blue-blacks and crimsons. Some of the cloth they wore themselves, sewn into shirts, skirts, and trousers. The rest they sent to Teotihuacán as part of an annual tribute owed to their distant Aztec rulers. In 1518 alone, the people of these twelve coastal villages provided the emperor Moctezuma II with eight hundred bales of raw cotton (each weighing 115 pounds), thirty-two hundred colored cotton cloths, and forty-eight hundred large white cloths, the product of thousands of hours of backbreaking and highly skilled labor.[1]

For hundreds of years both before and after, similar scenes unfolded across vast stretches of the world's inhabited land. From Gujarat to Sulawesi, along the banks of the Upper Volta to the Rio Grande, from the valleys of Nubia to the plains of Yucatán, people on three continents had grown cotton in their fields, and then manufactured cotton textiles in the houses next door, just as their ancestors had done for generations prior. The plant is stubborn, seemingly able to thrive with little help from farmers, given the right natural conditions. It grows in a wide range of environments thanks to its "morphological plasticity," that is, in the words of plant scientists, its ability to "adapt to diverse growing conditions by shortening, lengthening, or even interrupting its effective bloom period."[2]

The many peoples who grew cotton remained for thousands of years unaware that their efforts were being replicated by other peoples around the globe, all of whom lived in a geographic band roughly from 32–35 degrees south to 37 degrees north. These areas offered a climate suitable for the growing of cotton. As a subtropical plant, it needs temperatures not dipping below 50 degrees Fahrenheit during its growth period and usually remaining above 60 degrees. Cotton, we now know, thrives in areas in which no frost occurs for around 200 days, and in which it rains from twenty to twenty-five inches a year, concentrated in the middle of the growing period, a common climate zone that explains its abundance across multiple continents. Seeds are put in trenches about three feet apart and then covered with soil. It takes from 160 to 200 days for the cotton to mature.[3]

By themselves or through encounters with other peoples, each of these cotton cultivators had discovered that the fluffy white fiber that quelled out of the cotton boll was superbly suited to the production of thread. This thread in turn could be woven into a cloth that was easy to wash, pleasant against the skin, and effective as protection from the sun's burning rays—and to some degree from the cold. As early as a thousand years ago, the production of cotton textiles in Asia, Africa, and the Americas was the world's largest manufacturing industry; sophisticated trade networks, mostly local but a few regional, connected growers, spinners, weavers, and consumers.

The history of clothing is difficult to reconstruct, because most cloth has not survived the ravages of time. We know that ever since *Homo sapiens* moved from the African savanna into colder climes, about one hundred thousand years ago, they had to protect themselves from the elements. The spotty archaeological record that we have tells us that humans first used furs and skins to clothe themselves. There is evidence that they spun and wove flax as early as thirty thousand years ago. Such cloth production expanded significantly about twelve thousand years ago, once humans settled down and began to engage in agriculture and animal husbandry. Then men and women began to experiment more widely with different fibers to spin and to weave cloth for protection against the cold and the sun.[4]

The methods for transforming plants into cloth were invented independently in various parts of the world. In Europe, people began to weave various grasses and also linen during the Neolithic Era, starting about twelve thousand years ago. About eight thousand years later, during the Bronze Age, they also began to harvest wool from animals. In the Middle East and North Africa, for seven millennia before the Common Era, societies spun and wove various kinds of wool and flax as well. Over the same millennia, Chinese peasants and artisans manufactured clothing from ramie and silk. As societies became more stratified, cloth emerged as an important marker of social rank.[5]

In this world of linen, wool, ramie, and silk, cotton's importance gradually grew. About five thousand years ago, on the Indian subcontinent, people, as far as we know, first discovered the possibility of making thread out of cotton fibers. Almost simultaneously, people living on the coast of what today is Peru, ignorant of developments in South Asia, followed suit. A few thousand years later, societies in eastern Africa developed techniques for the spinning and weaving of cotton as well. In each of these regions cotton quickly became the dominant fiber for the spinning of thread, its properties for most uses clearly superior to those of flax and ramie and other fibers. For these first millennia of the plant's cultivation, the production of cotton goods rarely expanded beyond cotton's natural growing zone, but all who encountered it saw it as a remarkable material for the production of clothing: soft, durable, and light, easy to dye and easy to clean.

Evidence of cotton's essential role in early societies can be found in the foundational myths and sacred texts of many peoples. In Hindu scripture, cotton appears frequently and prominently. Vishnu, Hindus believe, wove "the rays of the sun into a garment for himself." People across West Africa attributed their spinning skills to Ananse, a spider deity. In North America, a Hopi spider goddess was believed to spin and weave cotton. The Navajo believed that Begochiddy, one of the four sons of Ray of Sunlight and Daylight, had created and planted cotton after making the mountains and insects. According to a Navajo belief, "When a baby girl is born to your tribe you shall go and find a spider web . . . and rub it on the baby's hand and arm. Thus, when she grows up she will weave, and her fingers and arms will not tire from the weaving." In China, according to a 1637 text from the late Ming dynasty, clothing, including cottons, distinguished humans from beasts, and among humans it "distinguished between the rulers and the ruled." Moreover, the idea of fate as either spun or woven was central to many diverse cultures, including those, not surprisingly, in which cotton played a dominant role.[6]

Modern plant scientists have looked beyond cotton as a gift of the gods, but are no less impressed. Biologists think cotton plants have grown on earth for 10 to 20 million years. Four genetically different species of cotton have developed since—the Mesoamerican *G. hirsutum*, the South American *G. barbadense*, the African *G. herbaceum*, and the Asian *G. arboretum*. These four species, in turn, have sprouted hundreds of further variations, of which only a few would come to dominate commercial cotton production. Today, more than 90 percent of the world's cotton crop is *G. hirsutum* cultivars, also known as American upland. Human domestication has changed the plant even further. Over a five-thousand-year period, according to one expert, our forebears transformed it "from undisciplined perennial shrubs and small trees with small impermeable seeds sparsely covered by coarse, poorly differentiated seed hairs, to short, compact, annualized plants with copious amounts of long, white lint borne on large seeds that germinate readily." Cotton growers carefully experimented with the plant, gradually forging it into something that supported their growing need for cloth. They adapted the plant to particular environmental niches, transported it over long distances, spread its reach, and increased its diversity. As with so many other pieces of the natural world, human cultivation radically accelerated and altered the biological history of cotton—a capacity that would quicken during the nineteenth century and become of great importance to the empire of cotton.[7]

Farmers in the Indus valley were the first to spin and weave cotton. In 1929, archaeologists recovered fragments of cotton textiles at Mohenjo-Daro, in what is now Pakistan, dating to between 3250 and 2750 BCE. Cottonseeds found at nearby Mehrgarh have been dated to 5000 BCE. Literary references further point to the ancient nature of the subcontinent's cotton industry. The Vedic scriptures, composed between 1500 and 1200 BCE, allude to cotton spinning and weaving. The very first reports by foreign travelers to South Asia similarly mention cotton: The ancient Greek historian Herodotus (484–425 BCE) was familiar with India's fine cotton clothing, observing in 445 BCE that in the subcontinent "wild trees bear fleeces for their fruit surpassing those of the sheep in beauty and excellence, and the natives clothe themselves in cloths made therefrom."[8]

From the earliest time until well into the nineteenth century—that is, for several millennia—the people of the Indian subcontinent were the world's leading cotton manufacturers. Peasants in what are today India, Pakistan, and Bangladesh cultivated small quantities of cotton alongside their food crops. They spun and wove cotton for their own use and for sale in local and regional markets. Most regions within South Asia produced all the textiles they consumed well into the nineteenth century. They harvested the crop by hand, employed a roller gin to remove the seeds, removed dirt and knots with the help of a bow (a wooden tool with string attached that vibrates if struck with a piece of wood), spun the fiber on a distaff (a tool holding the unspun cotton) and a spindle into thread, and wove this thread into fabric using looms hung between trees.[9]

The quality of the top tier of Indian cotton fabrics was legendary: In the thirteenth century, the European traveler Marco Polo elaborated on Herotodus's observations of nearly nine hundred years earlier, noting on the coast of Coromandel "the finest and most beautiful cottons that are to be found in any part of the world." Six hundred years later, Edward Baines, a newspaper proprietor and cotton expert from Leeds, reported the best Indian cloth was of "almost incredible perfection. . . . Some of their muslins might be thought the work of fairies, or of insects, rather than of men." They were, in effect, "webs of woven wind."[10]

The subcontinent, however, was far from alone. Cotton was plentiful and cotton cloth ubiquitous in the Americas, long before Europeans arrived in the New World. In a four-thousand-mile arc through Mesoamerica and the Caribbean to South America, cotton was the most important manufacturing industry. Perhaps the oldest center of cotton manufacture was located in present-day Peru. There, archaeologists have excavated cotton fishing nets dated to 2400 BCE and textile fragments from 1600–1500 BCE. When Francisco Pizarro attacked the Inca Empire in 1532, he marveled at the quality and quantity of cotton fabrics he saw. At the Incan city of Cajamarca, the conquistadores found stores filled with huge quantities of cotton textiles "far superior to any they had seen, for fineness of texture, and the skill with which the various colors were blended."[11]

Several thousand miles to the north and a decade earlier, Europeans were just as surprised when they penetrated the Aztec Empire and encountered extraordinary cottons. In addition to gold and other treasure, Hernán Cortés sent to Charles V cotton cloth brilliantly dyed with indigo and cochineal. The Mesoamerican cotton industry, like its South American counterpart, had a long history. Cotton was planted throughout what is today central Mexico as early as 3400 BCE, and the earliest thread found in archaeological excavations has been dated to between 1200 and 1500 BCE. Cotton use by the Mayas has been documented as early as 632 BCE, and in the lowlands of modern-day Veracruz, a cotton industry probably emerged between 100 BCE and 300 CE. As the wearing of cotton spread from elites to commoners, production increased, especially with the rise of the Aztecs' military and economic empire after 1350. And as more people wore cotton, its processing became ever more important. Techniques in weaving and dying all became more and more refined, not least to display social difference through distinctive clothing.[12]

Indigenous production continued after the conquest of Central America by Spanish colonists in the sixteenth century. One late-seventeenth-century colonial Spanish administrator, Don Juan de Villagutierre Soto-Mayor, praised the Indian women of the former realm of the Maya who "spin cotton and weave their cloths with energy and ability, giving them perfect colors." In addition to clothing, cotton was used for religious offerings, as gifts, a medium of exchange, for decorative hangings, for wrapping mummies, as armor, and even for medicinal uses. An estimated 116 million pounds of cotton were produced annually in pre-Columbian Mexico, equaling the cotton crop of the United States in 1816. As the rulers of Teotihuacán expanded the reach of their power, they drew tribute and trade from cotton-growing and -manufacturing regions. Places within the Aztec Empire that were particularly prominent growers of cotton had Nahuatl names that meant "on the cotton temple," "in the river of cotton," and "on the hill of cotton."[13]

Mexico and Peru were the centers of the pre-Columbian cotton industry, but the production of cotton textiles also spread to other parts of the continent. In what is today Brazil, cotton fibers gathered from wild plants were used to manufacture cloth. In what later became the southwestern United States, Native Americans became avid cotton producers, especially the Navajos and Hopi, perhaps as early as 300 BCE. Knowledge about cotton had traveled up the west coast of Mexico from Central America. When Spanish settlers came into contact with Indians north of the Rio Grande, they noticed that "the Indians spin cotton and weave cloth" and that they "wear Campeche-type cotton blankets for they have large cotton fields." For some Native Americans, cotton also had important religious uses: The Hopi utilized it to symbolize clouds in ceremonies in which they prayed for rain, and placed it over the faces of the dead "with the idea of making the spiritual body light, like a cloud." In the Caribbean, as well, cotton growing was widespread. Indeed, one of the reasons why Christopher Columbus believed that he had reached India was that he encountered great quantities of cotton in the Caribbean; he recounted islands "full of . . . cotton."[14]

Cotton growing and manufacturing also has a long history in Africa. It was probably first cultivated by Nubians in what today is eastern Sudan. Some claim that the fiber was cultivated, spun, and woven there as early as 5000 BCE, though archaeological finds at Meroë, a former city on the east bank of the Nile, confirm the presence of cotton textiles only for the years between 500 BCE and 300 CE. From Sudan, cotton spread north to Egypt. While cotton textiles played no significant role in ancient Egyptian civilizations, we know that cottonseed was used as animal fodder as early as 2600–2400 BCE, and depictions on the Karnak Temple in Luxor show cotton bushes. Yet cotton cultivation and the manufacturing of cotton textiles only took off in Egypt between 332 BCE and 395 CE. In 70 CE, Pliny the Elder observed that "the upper part of Egypt, in the vicinity of Arabia, produces a shrub, known by some as gossypium. The shrub is small, and bears a fruit similar in appearance to a nut with a beard, and containing in the inside a silky substance, the down of which is spun into threads. There is no tissue known that is superior to those made from this thread, either for whiteness, softness, or dressing . . ." After 800 CE, the spread of cotton, and its attendant production, accelerated further on the wings of Islam.[15]

Knowledge about how to grow and process cotton then traveled to western Africa. How exactly cotton came there is still unclear, but it is possible that itinerant weavers and merchants brought it from East Africa sometime around the beginning of the Common Era. With the arrival of Islam in the eighth century CE, the cotton industry expanded significantly, as Islamic teachers taught girls to spin and boys to weave, while advocating a previously unimagined modesty of dress to peoples whose environmental conditions demanded little clothing. Excavations have found cotton cloth dated to the tenth century. Literary sources and archaeological finds testify to cotton spinning and weaving in West Africa in the late eleventh century, by which time it had spread as far south as present-day Togo. By the early fifteenth century, Leo Africanus reported on the "great abundance" of cotton in the "kingdome of Melli" and the wealth of cotton merchants in the "kingdome of Tombuto," meaning the great West African empires of Mali and Timbuktu.[16]

The domestication, spinning, and weaving of cotton, to the best of our knowledge, evolved independently in these three regions of the world.[17] From South Asia, Central America, and eastern Africa, however, knowledge spread rapidly along existing trade and migration routes—from Mesoamerica to the north, for example, and from East Africa to the west. Central to these movements of the cotton industry was India. From there, cotton growing and manufacturing skills moved west, east, and south, placing Asia at the center of the global cotton industry, where it would remain until well into the nineteenth century, and return again in the late twentieth century. India's location, and skill with cotton, was most consequential to the plant's prominent role in our world, since a group of Europeans, clothed no doubt in fur, wool, and linen, was most impressed when they stumbled more than two thousand years ago upon these wondrous new fabrics arriving from a mythical "East."

But prior to its discovery by Europeans, cotton was busy altering the lives of others. Cotton moved westward, from India via Turkestan into the Middle East and later into the Mediterranean. Even before the Common Era, we have evidence of cotton being grown in Persia, Mesopotamia, and Palestine. Cotton clothing dated to around 1100 BCE was found in Nineveh (in present-day Iraq), and an Assyrian cylinder dated to the seventh century BCE speaks of a tree that bears wool. A few hundred years later, during the first centuries of the Common Era, Anatolian peasants had taken up cotton cultivation. Just as in Africa, the spread of Islam played a major role in transmitting the skills to grow, spin, and weave cotton across the Middle East, as religious demands for modesty made cotton an "ordinary article of clothing." Ninth- and tenth-century Iran saw a "cotton boom" to supply urban markets, especially at Baghdad. In the thirteenth century, Marco Polo encountered cotton and cotton cloth everywhere from Armenia to Persia, and the "abundance" of cotton across Asia became a major motif of his reporting.[18]

Just as cotton cultivation moved farther west, the knowledge of cotton also spread from India east through Asia, and especially into China. While China eventually became one of the most significant producers of cotton and cotton textiles worldwide, and is the center of the world's cotton industry today, the plant is not indigenous there. Indeed, the Chinese word for cotton and cotton fiber is borrowed from Sanskrit and other Indian languages.[19] By 200 BCE, cotton was known in China, but for the next millennium it did not spread much beyond the southwestern border regions where it had originally been introduced.

Cotton became a major presence in the Chinese countryside during the Yuan dynasty (1271–1368). During those years, it effectively replaced ramie, which, with silk, had traditionally served the Chinese as a fiber for making cloth. By 1433, Chinese subjects could pay taxes in cotton, which enabled the state to clothe its soldiers and officials in the fiber. As we will see, the connection between the crop and taxation was one of many

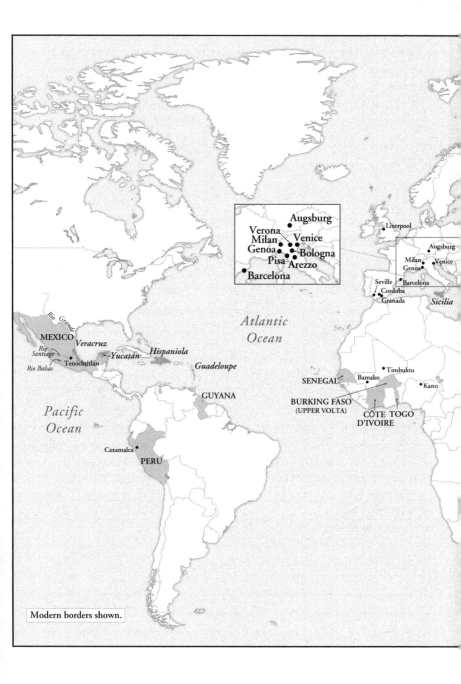

Augsburg
Verona
Milan   Venice
Genoa   Bologna
Pisa   Arezzo
Barcelona

Liverpool

Augsburg
Milan   Venice
Genoa
Seville   Barcelona
Cordoba
Granada   Sicilia

Rio Grande
MEXICO   Veracruz
Rio Santiago   Yucatán   Hispaniola
Rio Balsas   Tenochtitlan   Guadeloupe

Atlantic Ocean

SENEGAL   Timbuktu
Bamako   Kano
BURKING FASO
(UPPER VOLTA)
CÔTE TOGO
D'IVOIRE

GUYANA

Pacific Ocean

Caxamalca
PERU

Modern borders shown.

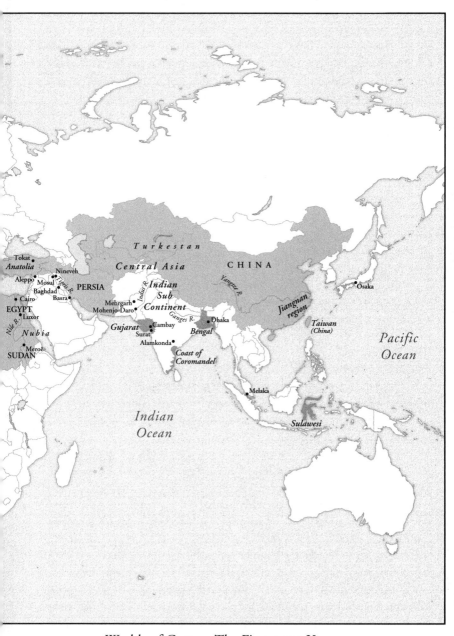

Worlds of Cotton: The First 5,000 Years

instances of political authorities taking an interest in the cotton industry. During the expansionary Ming dynasty (1368–1644), cotton production spread throughout China's new conquests. At the end of the Ming, the Chinese produced an estimated 20 million cotton cloth bales annually. A geographical division of labor had emerged in which northern farmers shipped raw cotton south to the lower Yangtze, where farmers used it, along with their own homegrown cotton, to manufacture textiles, some of which they sold back to the north. So vibrant was this interregional trade that cotton cloth accounted for one-fourth of the empire's commerce. By the seventeenth century, nearly all Chinese men, women, and children wore cotton clothing. Not surprisingly, when China's population doubled over the course of the eighteenth century, to 400 million people, its cotton industry became the second largest in the world after India's, growing an estimated 1.5 billion pounds of cotton in 1750, roughly equal to U.S. production as its planters ramped up production in the decade prior to the Civil War.[20]

Indian cotton technology also spread into Southeast Asia. As production skills advanced, cotton cloth emerged as the region's most valuable manufactured product after foodstuffs. Buddhist monks brought it to Java sometime between the third and fifth centuries CE. Much later, between 1525 and 1550, cotton cultivation expanded into Japan. By the seventeenth century it had become an important commercial crop there, as small farmers grew cotton to earn extra income for tax payments, often in rotation with rice.[21] With cotton's arrival in Japan, the original Indian cotton culture had now spread over most of Asia.

Fashioned by African, American, and Asian peasants, spinners, weavers, and merchants over at least five millennia, this cotton world was vibrant and expanding. Despite its diversity across three continents, the centers of this huge manufacturing industry had many things in common. Most important, cotton growing and manufacturing almost always remained small-scale and focused on households. While some growers sold their raw cotton into markets, including long-distance markets, and many rulers forced cultivators to part with some of their crop as tribute, no growers depended on their cotton crops alone; instead they diversified their economic opportunities, hoping to lessen risk to the best of their ability. In a large swath of Africa, and parts of South Asia and Central America, such patterns persisted until well into the twentieth century.

For millennia, then, households planted cotton in a delicate equilibrium with other crops. Families grew cotton alongside their food crops, balancing their own and their community's need for food and fiber with their rulers' demands for tribute. In Veracruz, for example, double cropping of food grains and cotton was common, providing subsistence both for those who grew cotton and those who spun and wove. In the Yucatán, Mayan peasants grew cotton in fields that also produced maize and beans. In West Africa, cotton was "interplanted with food crops," such as sorghum, in present-day Ivory Coast, or with yams, as in the area that is now Togo. In Gujarat, "the [cotton] shrubs are planted between the rows of rice." In the cotton-growing areas of Central Asia, peasants grew the fiber alongside not only rice, but also wheat and millet, and in Korea alongside beans. No significant cotton monoculture emerged before the eighteenth century, and yet when that monoculture appeared so too did the hunger for ever more land and labor.[22]

Like cotton growing, cotton manufacturing throughout the world began in households, and, with few exceptions, stayed there until the nineteenth century. In areas controlled by the Aztecs, for example, all cotton manufacturing was organized within households. In Africa as well, "in many cases the production of cotton goods was purely a family industry, each social unit being entirely self-sufficient." We have similar testimony for India, China, Southeast Asia, Central Asia, and the Ottoman Empire. Household production enabled a family to produce the cloth they needed, but it also allowed production for markets. Since labor needs in most agricultural societies varied enormously by the season, and since picked cotton could be stored for months, peasants could focus on textile production intermittently and seasonally, during slack times. This was especially the case for women, whose activities focused on the house, with some of their labor available for the homebound production of yarn and cloth.[23]

In every society a definite gender division of labor emerged, with a particularly strong association between women and textile production. Indeed, there was a premodern saying in China that "men till the soil and women weave." Except among the Navajo, Hopi, and some peoples in Southeast Asia, women throughout the world have had a virtual monopoly on spinning. Because spinning can be done intermittently, and enables a simultaneous commitment to other activities, such as watching young children and cooking, women's roles within households usually led them to be in charge of spinning as well. So close was the association of women and cloth production that in some cultures women were buried with their spinning tools. With weaving, on the other hand, no such stark gender divisions emerged. While men tended to dominate the weaving industry in places such as India and southeast Africa, there were many cultures in which women wove as well, such as in Southeast Asia, China, and North and West Africa. Yet even in societies in which both women and men wove, they usually specialized in different designs, produced distinct qualities, and worked on different types of looms. This gendered division of labor was reproduced in the emerging factory system as well, making gender relations in the household an important factor in the emergence of factory production.[24]

Embedded within households and their particular strategies for survival, this premodern cotton industry was also characterized by slow technological change in ginning, spinning, or weaving. As late as the eighteenth century, a woman in Southeast Asia, for example, needed a month to spin a pound of cotton and another month to weave a piece of cloth ten yards long.[25] This enormous time requirement was partly the result of what economists call "low opportunity costs" for the labor that went into spinning and weaving, and partly of a world in which rulers taxed their subjects' production to the maximum extent possible. Moreover, since many households were self-sufficient in textiles, markets were of a limited scale, again reducing incentives to improve production techniques.

Yet slow technological change was also related to constraints on the supply of raw materials. In most regions of the world, raw cotton could not be transported efficiently very far. Beasts of burden or humans sometimes carried raw cotton over relatively short distances. In the Aztec Empire, raw cotton was transported into highland areas to be manufactured, at distances of perhaps a hundred miles. More efficient and common was the waterborne cotton trade. In the second millennium CE, for example, observers reported hundreds if not thousands of boats floating cotton down the Yangtze to the region of Jiangnan. Gujarati and central Indian cotton was similarly shipped on the Ganges and along the coast to South India and Bengal. Nonetheless, until the nineteenth century the overwhelming bulk of raw cotton was spun and woven within a few miles from where it was grown.[26]

So many people in so many parts of the world grew cotton, spun it, and wove it into fabrics that it was very likely the world's most important manufacturing industry. And while household production for household consumption would remain until the nineteenth century its most important sector, there was significant change before the Industrial Revolution of the 1780s. Most importantly, cotton goods—partly because they were so labor-intensive to produce—became an important store of value and a medium of exchange. Rulers everywhere demanded cotton cloth as tribute or taxes, and indeed it might be said that cotton was present at the birth of political economy as such. Among the Aztecs, for example, it was the most important medium for tribute payments. In China, beginning in the fifteenth century, households were required to pay some of their taxes in cotton cloth. And in Africa the payment of tribute in cloth was common. Practical as a means to pay taxes, cotton cloth was also used as currency in China, throughout Africa, in Southeast Asia, and in Mesoamerica. Cloth was an ideal medium of exchange because unlike raw cotton it could be easily transported over long distances, was not perishable, and was valuable. Nearly everywhere in the premodern world, a piece of cotton cloth could buy needed things: food, manufactured goods, even protection.[27]

Cotton's use as proto-money illuminates the fact that not all cotton textiles, with their favorable ratio of value to weight, were used in the immediate vicinity of their production. Indeed, the cotton centers that had emerged separately in the Americas, Africa, and Asia all developed increasingly sophisticated networks of trade, connecting growers, manufacturers, and consumers over long, eventually even transcontinental distances. In Iran, the ninth- and tenth-century cotton industry led to significant urbanization, drawing raw cotton from the surrounding countryside, spinning, weaving, and tailoring it to sell into long-distance markets, especially in what is today Iraq. In precolonial Burkina Faso one author finds that "cotton was at the center of trade." Gujarati cotton cloth, as early as the fourth century BCE, came to play a very significant role in the trade between the various lands bordered by the Indian Ocean, and large quantities were sold along the East African coast, to be traded far into the African hinterland. In all of these exchanges, traders, especially if far removed from the polities they originated from, had to adjust to local tastes, and had to offer their products at prices attractive to local consumers.[28]

In Mesoamerica, cloth was traded over many hundreds of miles, including to neighboring states, as, for example, when merchants brought cloth from Teotitlán (in modern-day Oaxaca) to Guatemala. In the Southwest of what is now the United States, yarn and cloth were also important trade items. Cotton goods have been found in excavations far from regions in which cotton could grow. Since the thirteenth century, Chinese merchants imported cotton yarn and cloth to supplement domestic production from as far away as Vietnam, Luzon, and Java. In similar ways, African merchants traded cotton textiles over long distances, as for example when they exchanged Malinese cotton cloth for salt brought in by desert nomads. Ottoman cotton textiles found their way to places as distant as western Europe, while cotton goods were already being imported into Japan in the thirteenth century.[29]

India, at the center of this increasingly global reach, traded with the Roman Empire, Southeast Asia, China, the Arab world, North Africa, and East Africa. Indian cottons crisscrossed South Asia on the backs of people and bullocks. They crossed the seas in Arab dhows, traversed the great Arabian Desert to Aleppo on the backs of camels, moved down the Nile to the great cotton mart of Cairo, and filled the bottoms of junks on their way to Java. Already in the sixth century BCE Indian cotton was traded to Egypt, as merchants brought Indian cotton to Red Sea and Persian Gulf ports. Greek merchants then took it from Egypt and also Persia to Europe. Roman merchants eventually participated in this trade as well, making cotton a coveted luxury good among the imperial elites. Throughout eastern Africa, Indian cottons were an important presence as well. And throughout the Arab world and Europe, India remained a major supplier until the nineteenth century, with Gujarati merchants, among others, unloading huge quantities of cloth. As an Ottoman official complained in 1647, "So much cash treasury goes for Indian merchandise that . . . the world's wealth accumulates in India."[30]

Indian cloth also traded eastwards into other parts of Asia. Merchants sold it in the marts of China in very ancient times. Huge quantities of Indian cloth also found their way to Southeast Asia to clothe the local elite: Imports to Malacca in the early sixteenth century, it has been estimated, filled the holds of fifteen ships that arrived annually from Gujarat, Coromandel, and Bengal. So dominant was Indian cloth on world markets that around 1503 the Italian merchant Lodovico de Varthema observed about the Gujarati port town of Cambay, "This city supplies all Persia, Tartary, Turkey, Syria, Barbary, i.e., Arabia Felix, Africa, Ethiopia, India and a multitude of inhabited islands, with silk and cotton stuff." The Sanskrit word for cotton goods (*karpasi*) entered into Hebrew, Greek, Latin, Persian, Arabic, Armenian, Malay, Uigur, Mongolian, and Chinese. Even the names of particular fabrics became global brand names—chintz and jackonet, for example, are corruptions of terms in Indian languages that eventually came to describe a particular style throughout the world. Beginning in the seventeenth century, Indian cottons, in fact, were what historian Beverly Lemire has called the "first global consumer commodity."[31]

As demand grew, cotton took its first tentative steps out of the home. During the second millennium CE, production in cotton workshops became more common, especially in Asia. Professional weavers emerged in India; they focused on supplying the long-distance trade, providing rulers and wealthy merchants both at home and abroad with cotton cloth. In Dhaka, weavers labored under tight supervision to produce muslins for the Mughal court, "forced to work only for the Government which paid them ill and kept them in a sort of captivity." Workshops containing more than one loom are also reported to have been located in Alamkonda, in modern-day Andhra Pradesh, as early as the fifteenth century. In contrast to the subsistence weavers, the long-distance trades-men were geographically concentrated: Bengal was known for its fine muslins, the Coromandel coast for its chintzes and calicoes, and Surat for its strong but inexpensive fabrics of every kind. Though weavers could occupy very different positions within India's caste system, in some parts of the subcontinent they found themselves in the upper reaches of social hierarchies, prosperous enough to be among the leading donors to local temples. Groups of full-time cotton manufacturers emerged in other parts of the world as well: In fourteenth-century Ming China, for example, higher-quality textiles were worked up in "urban loom houses," which collectively employed many thousands of workers. In the Otto-man city of Tokat, highly skilled weavers produced significant quanti-ties of cotton textiles. Baghdad, Mosul, and Basra, among other cities in the Islamic world, had large cotton workshops, and indeed the word *muslin* for fine cottons derives from Musil, the Kurdish name for Mosul. In Bamako, the capital of present-day Mali, up to six hundred weavers plied their trade, while in Kano, the "Manchester of West Africa," a large weaving industry arose, supplying the people of the Sahara with cloth. In Timbuktu, already in the 1590s twenty-six cotton-producing workshops plied their trade, each with fifty or more workers. In Osaka as well, thousands of workers wove cotton textiles; workshops spread throughout the region employing thirty to forty thousand people by the early eighteenth century.[32]

As the workshop became more common, so too did a new type of weaver: an individual, usually male, who produced specifically for sale in a market. Yet even as workshops emerged, this specialized production for markets typically took place in the countryside, not towns, and in homes, not workshops. What set these rural market producers apart from those who produced for subsistence only was their reliance on an emerging force in global commerce: putting-out networks held together by merchant capital. In these networks, which would form the nuclei of nineteenth-century mechanized cotton production, spinners and weavers worked up cotton thread and cloth for urban merchants who would collect the products of the spinners and weavers and then sell them on distant markets. The particular ways merchant capitalists and producers related to one another varied widely. On the Indian subcontinent, for example, rural weavers relied on merchants for the capital needed to purchase sufficient yarn, and for the food they needed to subsist while weaving, yet these weavers generally owned their own tools, worked without supervision, and enjoyed some control over the disposal of their products. In other parts of the world, rural weavers enjoyed considerably less power. In the Ottoman Empire, for example, merchants advanced cotton and yarn to peasants, who spun and wove it, then returned the product to the merchants for a small profit. Unlike weavers in India, they did not have any control over disposal of the product. In China merchants also enjoyed great control over production. "They bought up raw cotton, put it out at local markets for peasant women to spin and to weave, had the cloth dyed and calendared in town or city workshops and then exported it all over China for sale." Merchants, in fact, controlled every stage of production, foreshadowing their central role in the nineteenth-century construction of a globe-spanning empire of cotton.[33]

With expanding markets, cotton technology changed as well. While the basic principles of cotton processing were quite similar throughout the world, and productivity was dramatically lower before the invention of the novel gins, spinning machines, and looms of the late eighteenth and early nineteenth centuries, there were some significant innovations. In Mesoamerica, for example, spinning was improved by the introduction of "specially formed ceramic spindle whorls." After 1200 CE, Mesoamericans also used specifically designed spinning bowls, which increased the productivity of spinners, enabling them, among other things, to feed the voracious appetite for tribute of their rulers. The center of technological innovation, however, was Asia: The roller gin (to remove seeds), the bow (to clean and disentangle ginned cotton), the spinning wheel, and new kinds of looms, including the upright warper, all originated in Asia. The spinning wheel, invented in the eleventh century, was an especially significant innovation as it allowed peasants to spin cotton much faster. Weavers in the same regions also invented a novel kind of loom—the treadle loom. While its exact origins are uncertain, it was introduced into India sometime between 500 BCE and 750 CE, and into China (where it was first used in silk manufacturing) in the third century CE.[34]

The greatest innovations occurred in the domestication of the cotton plant itself, indeed so much so that the cotton picked by slaves in the nineteenth century would be nearly unrecognizable to Indian farmers of two thousand years earlier. Human selection made cotton compatible with highly varied environmental conditions and rendered its fiber ever more applicable to the production of textiles. Rural cultivators in China, Japan, Southeast Asia, North and South America, western Africa, and Anatolia brought cottonseeds from adjacent territories and added cotton to their crop mix. Through the centuries, this process of domestication drastically altered the physical properties of cotton, creating plants that produced longer and brighter fibers (later-day cotton experts would refer to the length of the fiber as "staple"), ever more plentiful and easier to remove from the filbertlike shell. Moreover, advances in irrigation techniques and agronomy allowed for the expansion of production into new regions. Through seed selection and improved technology, the cotton plant flourished in drier and colder parts of Africa, Asia, and the Americas, including the mostly arid soils of the Islamic world. In Iran, for example, investments in irrigation systems as early as the ninth century enabled a significant extension of cotton agriculture. Nonetheless, compared to eighteenth- and nineteenth-century changes, overall productivity increases in the two thousand years prior to the Industrial Revolution were small. For much of its history, the world's cotton industry expanded primarily because ever-increasing numbers of people spent ever more time growing, spinning, and weaving cotton.[35]

These manufacturing networks connecting rural spinners and weavers with urban merchant capital, especially in Asia, created a gradual but significant expansion of output for markets. They did so, however, largely without exploding older social structures, without altering production as it had been organized for centuries. The household, and the technology associated with it, remained at their center. This premodern world was safe behind two bulkheads: first, the markets for finished goods, which were growing but, compared to the world after 1780, only at a modest pace, and second, the great obstacles to sourcing raw cotton across long distances. A great countervailing force would be needed to break through those ancient constraints.

For a very long time, in this remarkably diverse, fabulously vibrant, and economically important world of cotton, Europe was nowhere to be found. Europeans had remained marginal to networks of cotton growing, manufacturing, and consumption. Even after they began importing small quantities of cotton cloth during Greek and Roman times, they remained of little importance to the global cotton industry as a whole. People dressed, as they had since the Bronze Age, in clothing made from flax and wool. As Mahatma Gandhi put it, while India supplied Europe with cottons, Europeans themselves "were submerged in barbarism, ignorance and a state of wilderness."[36]

Cotton, quite simply, was exotic to Europe. The fiber grew in faraway lands, and many Europeans reportedly imagined cotton as a mixture of a plant and an animal—a "vegetable lamb." Stories circulated in medieval Europe about little sheep growing on plants, and bending down at night to drink water; other fables told of sheep attached to the ground by low stems.[37]

Cotton's first serious incursion into Europe, as in West Africa, was the result of the spread of Islam. By 950 CE, cotton was manufactured in such Islamic cities as Seville, Córdoba, Granada, and Barcelona, as well as Sicily; some of those textiles were exported to the rest of Europe. During the twelfth century, the Seville botanist Abu Zacaria Ebn el Awam published a treatise on agriculture that included a detailed description of how to cultivate cotton.[38] So tight was the association between Islam and cotton that most western European languages borrowed their words for the fiber from the Arabic *qutun*. French *coton*, English *cotton*, Spanish *algodón*, Portugese *algodão*, Dutch *katoen*, and Italian *cotone* all derive from the Arabic root. (The German *Baumwolle* and the Czech *bavlna*—

The vegetable lamb: Europeans imagine the
cotton plant.

translated roughly as "tree wool"—are the exceptions that prove the rule.) While the Christian Reconquista of Iberia in the first half of the second millennium seriously contracted the region's cotton production, the centuries-long exposure to Arab technology and culture left behind a familiarity with and appreciation for cotton textiles in large areas of Europe.

By the twelfth century, small pockets of Europe—particularly northern Italy—returned to the world of cotton production, and this time to stay. While Europe's climate was largely unsuited for cotton growing, the Crusaders had extended European power into the Arab world, and thereby into areas where cotton grew naturally.[39] The first endeavors to manufacture cotton were modest, but the beginning of a trend that would alter the continent's history, and the world's economy.

The first center of a non-Islamic cotton industry in Europe emerged in northern Italy, in cities such as Milan, Arezzo, Bologna, Venice, and Verona. The industry grew quickly, starting in the late twelfth century, and came to play a vital role in these urban economies. In Milan, for example, by 1450 the cotton industry employed a full six thousand workers making fustians, fabrics using both cotton and linen.[40] These northern Italians became the dominant producers in Europe, and they retained their position for about three centuries.[41]

Cotton manufacturing blossomed in northern Italy for two reasons. First, these cities looked back on a long history of still vibrant wool production, which had left them with skilled workers, capital-rich merchants, and expertise in long-distance trade. Once entrepreneurs decided to engage in cotton manufacturing, they could draw on those resources. They advanced raw cotton to women in the surrounding countryside to have it spun. They contracted with urban artisans, organized in guilds, to weave the yarn. They branded and standardized their goods, and drew upon their long-distance trade networks to export goods to foreign markets throughout the Mediterranean, the Middle East, Germany, Austria, Bohemia, and Hungary.[42]

Second, northern Italy had easy access to raw cotton. Indeed, the northern Italian industry was from the beginning entirely dependent on eastern Mediterranean cotton from such places as western Anatolia and what today is Syria. Already in the eleventh century, cotton yarn and cotton cloth had been imported into the ports of Venice, Genoa, and Pisa, giving people a taste for cottons. Raw cotton imports followed in the wake of the Crusades, with the first such trade documented for the year 1125.[43]

As improvements in shipping allowed for the cheaper transportation of bulk commodities, Venice became Europe's first cotton entrepôt, the Liverpool of the twelfth century. Some traders became dedicated cotton merchants, buying low-grade raw cotton from Anatolia, while procuring better-quality fiber from Syria. This supply was supplemented by Genovese imports from Anatolia, Sicily, and Egypt. But despite importing large quantities, European merchants had little if any impact on the specific ways in which raw cotton was grown in the Levant: They bought cotton from local merchants, loaded it on their ships, and transported it across the sea. Nevertheless, Venice's ability to insert itself into and eventually dominate Mediterranean trade was crucial to the success of the northern Italian cotton industry. Moreover, it was a harbinger of the wedge that European states and capitalists would later drive into the heart of the ancient cotton centers.[44]

Not only did the Mediterranean networks give Italian manufacturers relatively easy access to raw cotton, but they also provided them with access to "Eastern" technologies. Northern Italian entrepreneurs appropriated technologies from the Islamic world—some of which had in turn come from India and China. The twelfth century witnessed a "massive infusion of outside technology into the European textile industry"— most importantly the spinning wheel. Before the spinning wheel was introduced into Europe in the middle of the thirteenth century, Europeans, like Americans and Africans, had spun with hand spindles. It was a slow process: A skilled spinner produced about 120 meters of thread per hour. At that rate, it took about eleven hours to spin enough yarn for one blouse. The spinning wheel increased the output of European spinners tremendously, tripling productivity. Thus the availability of a new material—cotton—led to the embrace of the new manufacturing technique, which is why in medieval Europe the spinning wheel was also called the "cotton wheel." If less dramatic than the spinning wheel, improvement also came to weaving with the horizontal treadle loom. First used in Europe in the eleventh century, it enabled the weaver to change the sheds—the device that separates some of the warp threads to allow the shuttle to pass through—with his feet, freeing the hands to insert the weft, and thus allowing for the production of finer-quality textiles. It came to Europe from India or China via the Islamic world.[45]

The growth of the northern Italian cotton industry rested principally on its access to raw cotton and manufacturing technology from the Islamic world. Yet these linkages and dependencies would become Italy's principal vulnerabilities; the industry remained distant from the sources of raw materials, and lacked control over the growing of cotton. Northern Italy's industry eventually suffered both from the strengthening of the Islamic cotton industry and the marginalization of its own trade networks with the Islamic world.[46]

Yet even before the disruption of these crucial networks, the Italian industry faced another challenge: the rise of nimbler competitors north of the Alps, in the cities of southern Germany. They drew, like their Italian counterparts, on cotton from the Levant. But while Italian manufacturers faced high taxes, high wages, well-organized urban weavers, and guild restrictions, German producers enjoyed the advantage of the more tractable German countryside, where they gained access to cheap labor. By the early fifteenth century, German manufacturers had used this cost differential not only to capture many of the Italian export markets, including eastern and northern Europe, Spain, the Baltic region, the Netherlands, and England, but to make inroads even into the Italian market itself.[47]

Horizontal treadle loom, Milan,
middle of the fourteenth century

One such enterprising manufacturer arrived in the southern German town of Augsburg in 1367. The young weaver Hans Fugger at first tried to sell his father's cotton fabrics, but in due course set up as a master weaver himself. In the next decades, he expanded his investments, eventually employing a hundred weavers in Augsburg to supply the long-distance trade. By the time of his death, he was among the fifty wealthiest citizens of Augsburg, and had laid the foundation for the rise of one of the wealthiest merchant and banking families of medieval Europe.[48]

Hans Fugger furthered the rapid establishment of a dynamic cotton industry in southern Germany in the span of just one generation. Between 1363 and 1383, the output of German weavers effectively supplanted Lombardy fustians on European markets. Fugger and others like him succeeded because they had access to skilled textile workers, capital, and trade networks. With its long history of linen production, southern Germany had powerful long-distance traders with sufficient capital to fund a new industry. But these traders also had access to cheap labor, northern European markets, and the ability to enforce regulations guaranteeing the quality of their products. As a result, cities such as Ulm, Augsburg, Memmingen, and Nuremberg became major centers of fustian production. The industry eventually spread east along the Danube and south to Switzerland.[49]

The control of a rural workforce was crucial. In Ulm, for example, one of the most important manufacturing centers, only about two thousand people were busy with cotton production in the city itself, while eighteen thousand workers labored on cottons in the hinterland. Indeed, most of the weaving was done in the countryside, not the city, as merchants provided money, raw materials, and even tools to spinners and weavers—another putting-out network like the ones that characterized the Indian countryside. This organization of production was much more flexible than urban production, since no guilds regulated it and since rural weavers continued to have access to their own land and thus grew their own food.[50]

With the emergence of a cotton industry in northern Italy and southern Germany, small regions of Europe for the first time became a minor part of the global cotton economy. Yet within Europe, the industry was not yet particularly prominent. Europeans still largely dressed in linen and woolens, not cottons. And hardly any European cotton goods were consumed outside the continent itself. Moreover, after the early sixteenth century, the Venice-dependent European industry declined, as the Thirty Years War disrupted the industry and trade shifted away from the Mediterranean and toward the Atlantic. In the sixteenth century, indeed, Venice lost control over the Mediterranean trade to a strengthened Ottoman Empire, which was encouraging domestic industries and restricted the export of raw cotton. When Ottoman troops consolidated their hold on the realm in the 1560s, the effects were felt in distant German cotton textile towns. The rise of the Ottoman Empire, a powerful state capable of controlling raw and manufactured cotton flows, ruined the northern Italian and German cotton industries. To make matters worse for the once dominant Venetians, by the end of the sixteenth century British ships called ever more frequently in ports such as Izmir (Ottoman Smyrna); in 1589 the sultan granted the English merchants far-reaching trading privileges.[51]

Some shrewd observers surely noted that the first European cotton producers, both the northern Italians and the southern Germans, failed

at least in part because they had not subjugated those people who supplied them with cotton. It was a lesson that would not be forgotten. As
the sixteenth century came to a close, an entirely new cotton industry
arose that focused on the Atlantic, not the Mediterranean. Europeans
took for granted that only the projection of state power would ensure
success in these new trade zones.[52]

Chapter Two

Building War Capitalism

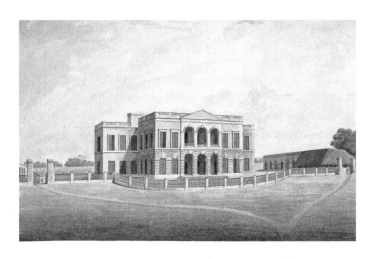

Capturing global cotton networks: the British East India Company
"factory" in Cossimbazar, West Bengal, c. 1795

Though impressive, the emergence of cotton production in twelfth-century northern Italy, and later in fifteenth-century southern Germany, did not seem world-altering. In each instance, boom was followed by bust. And the larger cotton industry, already well established on three continents, continued to hum along as it had for centuries. World production still centered on India and China, and intercontinental trade was still dominated by the products of Indian weavers. No significant technological or organizational departures characterized the European industry: Asian producers remained at the cutting edge of textile technology. To be sure, Europe's new manufacturing endeavors produced an unprecedented quantity of cotton cloth for that continent, spread a taste for cotton fabrics, and established widespread knowledge about the principles of cotton manufacturing—all factors that eventually became exceedingly important. But for now those small shifts were irrelevant to the global cotton industry, because Europeans lacked the ability to compete in transoceanic markets, not least because the quality of their output was much inferior to that of India. Unlike Indian or Chinese producers, moreover, Europeans depended on the import of raw cotton from distant regions of the world—regions over which they enjoyed little control. And in 1600, most Europeans continued to clothe themselves in linens and woolens.

Over the next two hundred years, however, all that was to change. The change was slow, at first hardly perceptible, but the momentum built, faster and faster and then exponentially. The ultimate result was a radical reorganization of the world's leading manufacturing industry: an explosion in how and where cotton was grown and manufactured, and a shocking vision of how the crop could yoke the world together. This recasting of cotton did not at first derive from technical advances, nor from organizational advantages, but instead from a far simpler source: the ability and willingness to project capital and power across vast oceans. With increasing frequency, Europeans inserted themselves, often violently, into the global networks of the cotton trade—within Asia as well as between Asia and the rest of the world—before using that same power to create entirely novel networks between Africa, the Americas, and Europe.[1] Europe's first incursion into the world of cotton had collapsed in the face of superior power; new generations of European capitalists and statesmen took heed and built a comparative advantage with a willingness and ability to use force to extend their interests. Europeans became important to the worlds of cotton not because of new inventions or superior technologies, but because of their ability to reshape and then dominate global cotton networks.

European capitalists and rulers altered global networks through multiple means. The muscle of armed trade enabled the creation of a complex, Eurocentric maritime trade web; the forging of a military-fiscal state allowed for the projection of power into the far-flung corners of the world; the invention of financial instruments—from marine insurance to bills of lading—allowed for the transfer of capital and goods over long distances; the development of a legal system gave a modicum of security to global investments; the construction of alliances with distant capitalists and rulers provided access to local weavers and cotton growers; the expropriation of land and the deportation of Africans created flourishing plantations. Unbeknownst to contemporaries, these alterations were the first steps toward the Industrial Revolution. Centuries before the "great divergence" of per capita economic output between Europe and East Asia, a small group of Europeans seized control of the heretofore episodic and gradual process of forging global economic connections, with dramatic consequences not only for the cotton industry but for human societies across the globe. The "great divergence" was at first a divergence of state power as well as a peculiar relationship between these states and capital owners. In the process, the many worlds of cotton became a European-centered empire of cotton.

Christopher Columbus's landing in the Americas in 1492 marked the first momentous event in this recasting of global connections. That journey set off the world's greatest land grab, with Hernán Cortés attacking the Aztec Empire in 1518 and establishing vast territorial claims for the Spaniards in America, spreading into South America and also farther north. By the mid-sixteenth century, Portugal had followed suit and acquired what is today Brazil. The French set out to the Americas in 1605 and acquired Quebec; parts of the modern-day midwestern and southern United States, which were grouped into a French administrative unit called Louisiana; and a number of Caribbean islands, including, in 1695, Saint-Domingue, the western third of Hispaniola. England established its first successful American settlement in Jamestown, which became a part of the colony of Virginia, in 1607, soon to be expanded with further colonies in North America and also the Caribbean. Eventually, as we will see, controlling huge territories in the Americas allowed, among other things, the monocultural growing of large quantities of cotton.

The second momentous event in the history of cotton came five years later, in 1497, when Vasco da Gama sailed triumphantly into the port of Calicut, having pioneered a sea route from Europe to India around the Cape of Good Hope. Now Europeans could for the first time access the products of Indian weavers—the world's dominant producers—without having to rely on the numerous middlemen who had transported Indian cloth by ship across the Indian Ocean, by camel across Arabia, and then by boat to European ports. Europeans began establishing formal trade relations on the Indian subcontinent when da Gama obtained permission from local rulers to trade in Calicut in 1498. By the early sixteenth century, the Portuguese had established a series of trading outposts on India's west coast, most enduringly in Goa. At the end of the sixteenth century, the Netherlands and Great Britain began to challenge Portugal's monopoly on trade with Asia by chartering joint-stock companies, hoping to catch a share of the highly profitable spice trade. After a series of Anglo-Dutch wars, the Dutch and the British agreed to divide their spheres of interest in Asia, with the Indian textile trade falling mostly into British hands.

That expansion into South Asia, at first, was the most momentous intervention of European merchants and statesmen into the networks of the global cotton industry. With it, Europeans began to play a role in the transoceanic trade of Indian textiles, pioneered by the Portuguese, who brought large quantities of such cloth to Europe. They also tried to assert their dominance over the important trade between Gujarat and both the Arabian Peninsula and eastern Africa—first by violently restricting the access of Gujarati merchants to those traditional markets (with mixed success), and in the second half of the sixteenth century by regulating the trade. Other European merchants later joined in: In 1600, merchants established the British East India Company, in 1602 the Dutch Vereenigde Oost-Indische Compagnie, and in 1616 the Danish Dansk Ostindiske Kompagni. By the early seventeenth century, the Dutch and British were replacing the Portuguese in violently regulating the trade in Gujarati textiles, seizing Gujarati ships, and limiting local merchants' access to the markets of Arabia and, increasingly, Southeast Asia, which were supplied from factories in southern India, along the Coromandel coast, with Madras at its center.[2] France was the last of the great European powers to launch trade with the East. In 1664, French traders founded the Compagnie des Indes Française and brought the first of what the French called *indiennes*—colorfully printed cotton cloth—into France. These companies tried to assert monopoly rights in certain areas, but facing each other as well as competing independent merchants, their project never succeeded completely.[3]

What all these European trading companies had in common was that they purchased cotton textiles in India, to trade for spices in Southeast Asia, and also to bring to Europe, whence they might be consumed domestically or shipped to Africa to pay for slaves to work the plantations just beginning to take root in the New World. Cotton textiles, for the first time ever, became entangled in a three-continent-spanning trading system; the consequences of Columbus's and da Gama's momentous journeys fed on one another. European consumers and African traders hungered for the beautiful chintzes, muslins, and calicoes, or the simpler but useful plain cloths, spun and woven by South Asian householders and artisans.

As a result, cotton textiles became central to European expansion into Asia. Already by the early seventeenth century, European traders and merchants played an important role in the trade at the Bengali port of Dhaka, which for centuries had been the source of some of the world's highest-quality cottons. The East India Company as early as 1621 imported an estimated fifty thousand pieces of cotton goods into Britain. Forty years later, this number had increased by a factor of five. Cotton cloths, in fact, became the company's most important trading good; by 1766 that cloth constituted more than 75 percent of the East India Company's total exports. As a result, according to English writer Daniel Defoe—no friend of the imports—cotton "crept into our Houses, our Closets and Bed Chambers, Curtains, Cushions, Chairs, and at last Beds themselves were nothing but Calicoes or Indian stuffs."[4]

Armed European merchants inserted themselves successfully into the transoceanic trade of Indian cotton textiles. In India itself, however, European power was limited. It basically found its end at the outskirts of port cities, or the walls of the forts that these soldier-traders increasingly constructed along the coast. To secure the very large quantities of Indian textiles they exported, European merchants depended on local traders, *banias*, who guarded their crucial relationships with the inland farmers and weavers who grew, spun, and wove these increasingly valuable goods. Europeans set up warehouses—so-called factories—along the coast of India, in cities such as Madras, Surat, Dhaka, Cossimbazar, and Calicut, where their agents placed orders with *banias* for cloth and received the wares ready for shipment. Hundreds of leather-bound books, many of which are still extant, recorded each one of these transactions.[5]

In 1676, the factory of the British East India Company in Dhaka detailed the mechanisms through which cloth was purchased, testifying to its dependence on indigenous traders. The English merchants subcontracted the task of securing cloth to a number of *banias* eight to ten months before the trading ships arrived, specifying the qualities, designs, prices, and delivery dates they desired. African and European consumers of cotton textiles demanded very particular goods at particular prices.

Banias then advanced cash to various middlemen, who would travel from village to village to advance funds and contract for finished cloth with individual weavers.[6] Eventually the cloth traveled the same chain back to the English factory in Dhaka, where merchants graded and prepared it for shipment.

In this system of production, the weavers themselves had control over the rhythm and organization of their work, owned their tools, just as they had for centuries, and even retained the right to sell their products to whomever they pleased. As European demand grew, weavers were able to increase production and raise prices, which was clearly beneficial to them. In fact, the arrival of European traders in the Gujarati town of Broach, just as much as in Orissa and Dhaka, gave a new impetus to the regional cotton industry. Weavers were still poor, yet they could take advantage of competition for their cloth, as did indigenous *banias* and even Indian rulers, who quickly established taxes and duties on the production and export of cotton cloth.[7] The power of European merchants in India was hence significant, but far from all-encompassing: The English complained that the system was frequently disrupted by "Arabians and Moguls who trade in Dacca cloth carrying yearly very considerable quantities of the same overland some so far as the great Turks Dominions," as well as by the "contest, trouble and Charge" of the weavers and local *banias*.[8]

This "factory" system, with its continuing dependence on local traders and local capital, persisted for roughly two centuries. As late as 1800, the British East India Company agreed to purchase piece goods from Pestonjee Jemsatjee and Sorabje Jevangee, two merchants in Bombay, for more than 1 million rupees, while the Surat *bania* Dadabo Monackjee entered into contracts with weavers north of the city to deliver cloth for the British. Indeed, at first, Portuguese, English, Dutch, and French traders were merely the latest arrivals to an old and vibrant market, taking their place alongside hundreds of merchants from all over South Asia and the Arabian Peninsula. In Dhaka, as late as the 1700s, European traders acquired only about one-third of all the cloth traded. And the trading capacity of Europeans in India remained dependent on South Asian bankers and merchants who financed cotton growing and manufacturing.[9]

The insertion of armed European merchants into the Asian trade, however, slowly marginalized these older networks, as they muscled the once dominant Indian and Arab traders out of many intercontinental markets. In 1670, one British observer could still note that Middle Eastern merchants "carried off five times as many calicoes as the English and the Dutch." Yet with bigger, faster, and more reliable boats, and more damaging firepower, "the old pattern of the Indian-Levant trade as the principal artery for world exchange underwent a complete structural change," one historian concludes, with "the Ottoman Empire . . . the chief loser." Gujarati merchants trading with East Africa also began facing European competition. Just as European merchants became increasingly common in India, they also established themselves in the East African markets; as a result, on both sides of the Indian Ocean, Europe's dominance grew. With the eighteenth-century decline of Surat and the rise of British Bombay, merchants in western India became even more dependent on British power.[10]

The growing influence of European merchants and their sponsoring states in India eventually began to have important repercussions in Europe itself. As much larger quantities of Indian cottons traveled to Europe, new markets and fashions emerged. Beautiful chintzes and muslins attracted the attention of the growing class of Europeans who had the money to purchase them and the desire to flaunt their social status by wearing them. As Indian cottons became ever more fashionable in the eighteenth century, the desire to replace these imports was a powerful incentive to ramping up cotton production in England and eventually to revolutionize it.[11]

Moreover, domination in Asia dovetailed with expansion into the Americas. As Spanish, Portuguese, French, English, and Dutch powers captured huge territories in the Americas, they took away the continent's movable wealth: gold and silver. It was indeed some of these stolen precious metals that had funded the purchase of cotton fabrics in India in the first place.

Eventually, however, European settlers in the Americas could not discover sufficient gold and silver and they invented a new road to wealth: plantations growing tropical and semitropical crops, sugar in particular, but also rice, tobacco, and indigo. Such plantations needed large numbers of workers, and to secure these workers, Europeans deported at first thousands and then millions of Africans to the Americas. European merchants built fortified trading stations along the western coast of Africa—Goree in present-day Senegal, Elmina in present-day Ghana, Ouidah in present-day Benin. They paid African rulers to go on a hunt

for labor, exchanging captives for the products of Indian weavers. In the
three centuries after 1500, more than 8 million slaves were transported
from Africa to the Americas, first mostly by Spanish and Portuguese traders, to be joined in the seventeenth century by the British, French, Dutch,
Danish, and others. During the eighteenth century alone, they deported
more than 5 million people, mostly from west-central Africa, the Bight
of Benin, the Gold Coast, and the Bight of Biafra.[12] Slaves arrived almost
daily on Caribbean islands, as well as along the coasts of both Americas.

Such trade increased the demand for cotton fabrics, since African
rulers and merchants almost always demanded cotton cloth in exchange
for slaves. Although it is often imagined that the slave trade was animated
by simple exchanges of guns and gewgaws for human export, slaves were
more frequently traded for a far more banal commodity: cotton textiles.
One study of 1,308 barters of British merchant Richard Miles between
1772 and 1780 for 2,218 Gold Coast slaves found that textiles constituted
over half of the value of all traded goods. Portuguese imports to Luanda
in the late eighteenth and early nineteenth centuries tell a similar story:
Woven goods constituted nearly 60 percent of imports.[13]

African consumers became notorious for their discerning and dynamic
tastes, much to the consternation of European merchants. Indeed, one
European traveler observed that African consumer tastes were "most varied and capricious," and that "scarcely two villages concur in their canons
of taste." When the slave ship *Diligent* sailed from its French port in 1731,
it carried in its hold a careful assortment of Indian textiles to cater to the
particular demands at the Guinea coast. In the same way, Richard Miles
sent very specific instructions on what colors and types of textiles were
currently in demand on the Gold Coast to his British suppliers, down to
the very manufacturers that should be utilized. "Mr Kershaw's [manufac-
tures] are by no means equal to [Knipe's]," he told a British contact in
one 1779 letter, "at least not in the eyes of the Black traders here, & it is
them that are to be pleased."[14]

European trade in cotton textiles tied together Asia, the Americas,
Africa, and Europe in a complex commercial web. Never before in the
four millennia of the history of cotton had such a globe-spanning system been invented. Never before had the products of Indian weavers
paid for slaves in Africa to work on the plantations in the Americas to
produce agricultural commodities for European consumers. This was an
awe-inspiring system, speaking clearly to the transformative powers of a

union of capital and state power. What was the most radical was not the particulars of these trades, but the system in which they were embedded and how different parts of the system fed upon one another: Europeans had invented a new way of organizing economic activity.

This expansion of European trade networks into Asia, Africa, and the Americas did not rest primarily on offering superior goods at good prices, but on the military subjugation of competitors and a coercive European mercantile presence in many regions of the world. Depending on the relative balance of social power in particular places, there were variations on this central theme. In Asia and Africa, Europeans settled coastal enclaves and dominated transoceanic commerce, without at first much involvement in cultivation and manufacturing. In other parts of the world, most prominently the Americas, local populations were expropriated and often displaced or killed. Europeans invented the world anew by embarking upon plantation agriculture on a massive scale. Once Europeans became involved in production, they fastened their economic fortunes to slavery. These three moves—imperial expansion, expropriation, and slavery—became central to the forging of a new global economic order and eventually the emergence of capitalism.

They combined with one other feature of this new world: states that backed these merchant and settler ventures, but that only weakly asserted their sovereignty over the places and peoples in distant territories. Instead, private capitalists, often organized in chartered companies (such as the British East India Company) asserted sovereignty over land and people, and structured connections to local rulers. Heavily armed privateering capitalists became the symbol of this new world of European domination, as their cannon-filled boats and their soldier-traders, armed private militias, and settlers captured land and labor and blew competitors, quite literally, out of the water. Privatized violence was one of their core competencies. While European states had envisioned, encouraged, and enabled the creation of vast colonial empires, they remained weak and thin on the ground, providing private actors the space and leeway to forge new modes of trade and production. Not secure property rights but a wave of expropriation of labor and land characterized this moment, testifying to capitalism's illiberal origins.

The beating heart of this new system was slavery. The deportation of many millions of Africans to the Americas intensified connections to India because it increased pressure to secure more cotton cloth. It was that trade that established a more significant European mercantile presence in Africa. And it was that trade that made it possible to give economic value to the vast territories captured in the Americas, and thus to overcome Europe's own resource constraints. This multifaceted system certainly showed variation and changed over time, but it was sufficiently different from the world that came before and the world that would emerge from it in the nineteenth century that it deserves its own name: war capitalism.

War capitalism relied on the capacity of rich and powerful Europeans to divide the world into an "inside" and an "outside." The "inside" encompassed the laws, institutions, and customs of the mother country, where state-enforced order ruled. The "outside," by contrast, was characterized by imperial domination, the expropriation of vast territories, decimation of indigenous peoples, theft of their resources, enslavement, and the domination of vast tracts of land by private capitalists with little effective oversight by distant European states. In these imperial dependencies, the rules of the inside did not apply. There, masters trumped states, violence defied the law, and bold physical coercion by private actors remade markets. While, as Adam Smith argued, such territories advanced "more rapidly to wealth and greatness than any other human society," they did so via a social tabula rasa, which, perhaps ironically, provided the foundation for the emergence of very different societies and states on war capitalism's "inside."[15]

War capitalism had an unprecedented transformative potential. At the root of the emergence of the modern world of sustained economic growth, it created unfathomable suffering, but also a consequential transformation of the organization of economic space: A multipolar world increasingly became unipolar. Power long spread across multiple continents and through numerous networks increasingly became centralized through a single node, dominated by European capitalists and European states. At the core of this change stood cotton, as the multiple and diverse worlds of the production and distribution of this commodity increasingly lost ground to a hierarchical empire organized on a global scale.

Within Europe itself, this reorganization of economic space had continent-wide repercussions. "Atlantic" powers such as the Netherlands, Great Britain, and France replaced the erstwhile economic powerhouses such as Venice and its northern Italian hinterland. As Atlantic trade superseded Mediterranean trade and as the New World became an important producer of raw materials, cities with links to the Atlantic also rose in prominence in the manufacturing of cotton textiles. Indeed, as early as the sixteenth century, expanded cotton manufacturing in Europe was contingent on a link to the rapidly expanding markets throughout the Atlantic world—from the cloth markets in Africa to the newly emerging sources of raw cotton in the Americas. In Flemish cities such as Bruges (starting in 1513) and Leiden (starting in 1574), cotton manufacturing burgeoned, as Antwerp began to carry a significant trade in raw cotton and overseas expansion that gave access to huge new markets. French manufacturers, for identical reasons, also embarked upon new cotton spinning and weaving ventures in the late sixteenth century.[16]

Amid these seismic geographic shifts, the most significant in the long run was cotton manufacturing's arrival in England. By 1600, Flemish religious refugees began weaving cotton cloth in English towns. The earliest reference to cotton dates to 1601, "when the name of George Arnould, fustian weaver of Bolton, appears in the records of quarter sessions." The industry grew, and by 1620 British cotton manufacturers exported their wares to France, Spain, Holland, and Germany. Cotton manufacturing thrived especially in the northern English county of Lancashire, where both the lack of guild control and the proximity to Liverpool, an important slaving port, became key to producers who supplied the African trade in slaves and plantations in the Americas.[17]

This slowly emerging English cotton industry drew on earlier experiences with the production of linen and woolens. As on the continent, cottons were at first manufactured in the countryside. Merchants, many of them Puritans and other dissenters, advanced raw cotton to peasants, who employed family labor seasonally to spin and weave, before returning the cloth to the merchants who sold it. As cotton cloth demand exploded, spinning and weaving became ever more important to smallholding peasants, and some of them eventually gave up their traditional crops and became entirely dependent on the industry. Some of the merchants who organized domestic cotton production turned into substantial businessmen. As they accumulated capital, they expanded production by providing ever more credit to ever more spinners and weavers, encouraging an "extensification" of production—its geographic dispersal throughout ever larger areas of the countryside. This was the classic putting-out system, quite similar to its incarnations across Asia centuries earlier, or to the British woolens industry. The countryside became ever more industrial and its inhabitants ever more dependent on putting-out work for distant merchants.[18]

Unlike Indian cotton spinners and weavers, the growing class of English cotton workers had no independent access to raw materials or to markets. They were entirely subordinated to the merchants—indeed, they enjoyed less independence and power than their Indian counterparts.[19] British putting-out merchants, as a result, had far more power than Indian *banias*. The British cotton men were part of a rising global power whose navy increasingly dominated the world's oceans, whose territorial possessions in the Americas and in Asia—India foremost among them—grew rapidly, and whose slavers created a plantation complex that rested in various ways on the manufacturing capacity of spinners and weavers thousands of miles away in the remote uplands of Lancashire and the plains of Bengal.

Despite these beginnings, their significance emerged only in retrospect. Throughout the seventeenth and eighteenth centuries, Europe's cotton industry was not particularly prominent. In England, but also elsewhere in Europe, the "manufacture of cotton remained almost stationary." Even after 1697, it grew only slowly; for example, it took sixty-seven years for the amount of raw cotton worked up into thread and cloth to approximately double, to 3.87 million pounds. That was the amount of cotton used in an entire year. By 1858, in contrast, the United States would export this amount of cotton on average on a single *day*. France was similar, and, outside Britain and France, European cotton demand was even less significant.[20]

One reason for the relatively slow growth of European cotton manufacturing was the difficulty of accessing raw cotton. As cotton was not grown in Europe itself, the industry's essential raw material had to be brought from distant locations. The modest demand for raw cotton among European manufacturers of the seventeenth and eighteenth centuries, before the heyday of the new machines that would by 1780 revolutionize cotton manufacturing, was largely met through established and diversified trade channels, in which cotton remained one commodity among many. In 1753, twenty-six ships arrived in the port of Liverpool from Jamaica with cotton, of which twenty-four had less than fifty bags of the fiber on board.[21] There were neither merchants nor ports nor regions of the world that specialized in cotton production for export.

Since the twelfth century the most important source of cotton imports to Europe, as we have seen, was the Ottoman Empire, especially western Anatolia and Macedonia. Throughout the seventeenth century, cotton from Izmir and Thessaloniki (Ottoman Salonica) continued to dominate local markets, arriving in London and Marseille alongside other products of the East, such as silk and mohair yarn. As European demand for raw cotton slowly expanded in the eighteenth century, Ottoman cotton still filled a significant share: one-quarter of all British imports between 1700 and 1745, and a similar quantity shipped to Marseille.[22]

Small quantities of raw cotton also arrived from other regions of the world, such as the Indian cotton that found its way to London in the 1690s, courtesy of the East India Company. Similarly, in the 1720s, the Royal African Company reported selling "At Their House in Leaden-Hall-Street by the Candle, on Thursday the 12th Day of September 1723, at Ten of the Clock in the Forenoon . . . Cotton from Gambia." A year later, they offered "Casks of Fine Silk Cotton . . . from Whyday," and the subsequent year "Bags of Guinea Cotton." But such minor sales paled in comparison to these merchants' more important trade items like elephant tusks.[23]

More important, however, was a new source of cotton: the West Indies. Though cotton remained a marginal crop compared to sugar on these islands, a number of small farmers, with fewer resources to invest than the sugar lords, did grow the "white gold." The production of these *petits blancs*, as they were called on the French islands, remained rather static until 1760. Yet for the British and French cotton industries, even this small amount of West Indian cotton supplied a significant share of their needs. And more important, as we will see, its way of production pointed to the future.[24]

Before 1770, therefore, European merchants secured the valuable fiber through well-established trade networks from a wide variety of locations. With the exception of the West Indies, their influence did not go much beyond the port cities themselves, as they had neither the power to tinker with how cotton was cultivated in the hinterland nor the inclination to advance capital for additional cotton growing. Cotton came to them thanks to the prices they were willing to pay, but they had no influence on how the cotton came into being. Local growers and merchants remained powerful actors within this global raw cotton nexus, not least because they neither specialized in cotton production for export nor in northern European markets.[25]

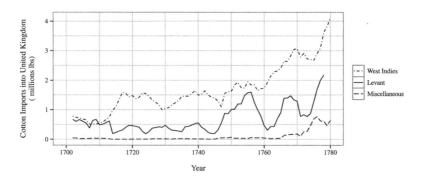

Cotton imports into the UK, 1702–1780, by source,
in millions of pounds, five-year trailing averages

. . .

As small quantities of raw cotton came to Europe to feed the expanding but in global terms still puny European cotton industry, demand for cotton cloth grew in Europe, as well as in Africa and on the slave plantations of the Americas. Yet European production was insufficient to meet it. In response, English, French, Dutch, Danish, and Portuguese traders, all with a similar feverish energy, tried to secure greater quantities of cotton textiles in India under ever more favorable conditions. While in 1614 British merchants had exported 12,500 untailored pieces of cotton cloth, between 1699 and 1701 that number spiked to 877,789 pieces annually. Exports of cloth by the British had increased by a factor of seventy in less than a hundred years.[26]

To obtain these fabulous quantities of textiles from India at favorable prices, representatives for the European East India companies began to insert themselves even more into the production process within India itself. For decades, representatives of the chartered European East India companies had complained about the ability of Indian weavers to sell their goods to competing European companies, competing Indian *banias*, traders from other regions of the world, or even to private European merchants who operated independently of the companies, creating competition that raised prices. Profitability could be increased only if Europeans could force weavers to work for their respective company alone. Monopolizing the market became the way to drive down weavers' incomes and drive up the selling price of particular goods.[27]

European traders were helped in securing cotton cloth in the quantity and quality they needed, and at the price they desired, because their business practices were reinforced with political control of increasingly extensive Indian territories. They came not just as traders, but increasingly as rulers. By the 1730s, the Dhaka factory, for example, hosted a contingent of military personnel and arms to protect the company's interests. Most dramatically, by 1765 the British East India Company—a group of merchants—ruled Bengal, and in the decades thereafter expanded its control over other South Asian territories. Such territorial dreams were furthered by British merchants' increasing investment in the raw cotton trade between India and China by the late eighteenth century, which made them hope for the integration of western Indian cotton tracts into East India Company territories as well. This assertion of private political power by a state-chartered company over distant territories was a revolutionary reconceptualization of economic might. States shared sovereignty over territory and people with private entrepreneurs.[28]

Among many other things, this new combination of economic and political power enabled European merchants to gain greater control over textile manufacturing, especially by increasing control over weavers.[29] Along the Coromandel coast the influential Indian merchants who acted as brokers between Indian weavers and European exporters increasingly were replaced by agents who were under much greater control of the European companies already in the seventeenth century. In Surat, which, like Bengal, would fall under company rule in 1765, the Board of Trade of the governor-general expressed in 1795 its dissatisfaction with

the system in practice hitherto of having a Contractor who has not himself any immediate connection with the manufacturers or weavers, but engages in subordinate contracts with a large number of the Native Merchants of little property or probity and though bound in responsibility, are not competent to pay a penalty if forfeited, and that in fact the goods never came into their possession, and apprehend that the difficulties now existing, will not be removed but with its abolition or very material alteration.[30]

Removing the Indian middlemen promised the foreign merchants better control over production and the ability to secure a greater quantity of piece goods. To that end, the East India Company tried to bypass the independent Indian *banias* who had historically connected them to the weavers by giving that responsibility to Indian "agents" whom they put on their own payroll. The Board of Trade in London instructed the governor-general in great detail how to recast the system of purchasing cotton cloth, hoping thereby to "recover to the Company that genuine knowledge of the business," and thus acquire more cloth at cheaper prices by implementing the "grand Fundamental principle of the Agency System." Through its Indian agents the company now made direct advances to weavers, something the British had not done in earlier years, which was greatly aided by territorial control and the attendant political authority. While weavers had always depended on credit, the novel insertion of Europeans into these credit networks along with the efforts of European merchants to monopolize economic control of particular parts of India made them ever more dependent on the company. Already by the middle of the eighteenth century, European companies sent these agents deep into the manufacturing centers in the countryside near Dhaka, agents who increasingly set the terms of production and thus succeeded in lowering prices. In the 1790s the East India Company even encouraged weavers to relocate to Bombay and produce cloth there—all with the goal of being able to supervise them better "without being extorted by the Servants of the Rajah of Travancore."[31]

The encroachment of British power on the subcontinent meant that weavers increasingly lost their ability to set prices for cloth. According to the historian Sinnappah Arasaratnam "they could not produce for any customer they chose; they had to accept part of their payment in cotton yarn; they were subject to a strict supervision of the process of manufacture by the Company's servants who were located in the village." Weavers were now often compelled to take advances from particular merchants. The ultimate aim, never fully realized, was to make weavers into wage workers—along the lines of what contemporary merchants succeeded in implementing in the English countryside itself.[32]

To further their goal, the company now also employed its coercive powers toward the weavers directly. The company hired large numbers of Indians to supervise and implement new rules and regulations, in effect bureaucratizing the cloth market. Extensive new regulations attached weavers legally to the company, making them unable to sell their cloth on the open market. Company agents now inspected cloth on the loom, and endeavored to ensure that the cloth was, as promised, sold to the company. A new system of taxation penalized those weavers who produced for others.[33]

The company also increasingly resorted to violence, including corporal punishment. When a company agent complained that a weaver was working illegally for a private merchant, "the Company's Gumashta seized him and his son, flogged him severely, painted his face black and white, tied his hands behind his back and marched him through the town escorted by seapoys [*sic*] [Indian soldiers in the employ of the English], announcing 'any weaver found working for private merchants should receive similar punishment.' " Such policies produced their intended results: Indian weavers' income fell. In the late seventeenth century, up to one-third of the price of cloth might have gone to a weaver. By the late eighteenth century, according to historian Om Prakash, the producer's share had fallen to about 6 percent. As income and living standards declined, a lullaby sung by Saliya weavers spoke longingly of a mystical time when their looms contained a silver plank. By 1795, the company itself observed an "unprecedented mortality among the Weavers."[34]

Unsurprisingly, weavers resisted the coercive encroachment of European capital in the production process. Some packed up and moved away from territories controlled by Europeans. Others secretly produced for competitors, but the need to avoid detection made them vulnerable to pressures for lower prices. At times, groups of weavers collectively approached the East India Company to complain about the company's interference with free trade.[35]

Such resistance sometimes reduced the power of European capitalists. Thus despite its wish to eliminate Indian middlemen, the East India Company understood that "it is impossible to do without the subordinate Contractors," whose much denser social networks into weaving villages could never be completely replaced by company agents. The interests of independent European merchants also often worked against the company, as they offered weavers more money for cloth, thus giving weavers an incentive to undermine company policies.[36]

Despite such constraints, aggressive policies succeeded in getting ever more cotton cloth into the stores of European traders. European cloth exports from India amounted to an estimated 30 million yards in 1727, but increased to some 80 million yards annually by the 1790s. British merchants in particular, but also their French counterparts, controlled the acquisition and export of huge quantities of cottons woven for export: In 1776, the district of Dhaka alone counted roughly eighty thousand spinners and twenty-five thousand weavers, while in 1795 the East India Company estimated that the city of Surat alone contained over fifteen thousand looms. And there was pressure for more. A 1765 dispatch from the East India Company office in London to its counterparts in Bombay, reflecting on the possibilities of the peace following the Seven Years War, beautifully summarizes what was at the core of the revolutionary reconceptualization of the global economy.[37]

> Since the Peace the Slaving Trade to the Coast of Africa has greatly encreased, in course the Demand for Goods proper for that Market is very large; & as We are very desirous of contributing so far as lyes in Our Powers to the Encouragement of a Trade on which the well-being of the British plantations in the West Indies so much depends, & considering the same therefore in a National View, We expect & positively direct that you conform as near as possible can, not only to the Provision in general of the several Articles ordered in the abovementioned List of Investment [i.e., cloth], but those marked A which are more immediately for that Trade.[38]

As this message makes clear, cotton from India, slaves from Africa, and sugar from the Caribbean moved across the planet in a complex commercial dance. The huge demand for slaves in the Americas created pressure to secure more cotton cloth from India. Not surprisingly, Francis Baring of the East India Company concluded in 1793 that from Bengal an "astonishing Mass of Wealth has flowed . . . into the Lap of Great Britain."[39]

European merchants' increasing control over the production process in India would seem to threaten Europe's own not particularly important or dynamic infant cotton industry. How could the English, French, Dutch, and other producers possibly compete against India's fabrics, which were both superior in quality and cheaper? And yet it appears that the European industry expanded even as India exported more cloth. Ironically, imports from India helped the European cotton textile industry by creating new markets for cotton fabrics and by continuing Europe's appropriation of relevant technologies from Asia. In the long run, moreover, imports from India influenced Europe's political priorities. As we will see, Great Britain, France, and others emerged as newly powerful states, with a vocal group of capitalists; for states and individuals alike, replacing Indian cotton cloth imports with domestically manufactured cloth became an important, albeit difficult-to-realize priority.

Protectionism played a key role in this process, testifying again to the enormous importance of the state to the "great divergence." By the late seventeenth century, with both cotton imports and domestic cotton manufacturing expanding, Europe's woolen and linen manufacturers pressured their respective governments to protect them from upstart cotton manufacturers in general and Indian imports in particular. Textiles were Europe's most important manufacturing industry: Dislocation of the sector by cotton imports and manufacturing seemed to endanger profits and threaten social stability.[40]

As early as 1621, only a little more than two decades after the creation of the East India Company, London wool merchants protested against the growing importation of cotton cloth. Two years later, in 1623, Parliament debated Indian textile imports, calling them "injurious to the national interests." Indeed, agitation against cotton imports became a constant feature of the English political landscape in the seventeenth and eighteenth centuries. A 1678 pamphlet, "The Ancient Trades Decayed and Repaired Again," warned that the woolen trade was "very much hindered by our own people, who do wear many foreign commodities instead of our own." In 1708, *Defoe's Review* printed a bitter editorial that looked "into the real Decay of our Manufactures," ascribing the decline to the import of ever increasing quantities of "Chints and painted Callicoes" by the East India Company. The result was that "the Bread taken out of [the people's] Mouths, and the East-India Trade carry away the whole Employment of their People." Usually it was woolen and linen manufacturers who agitated against Indian imports, but sometimes cotton manufacturers chimed in as well: In 1779, calico printers, fearful that the East India Company would ruin their business, wrote to the Treasury that "if there is not a Prohibition put to the East India Company's going on with their printing Manufactory in the East Indies a great many more must also leave off this Branch of Business."[41]

Such agitation led to protectionist measures. In 1685, England imposed a 10 percent duty on "all calicoes and other Indian linen and all wrought silks which are manufactures of India." In 1690, the tariff was doubled. In 1701, Parliament outlawed the import of printed cottons, leading to the importation of plain calicoes for further processing in England, giving a huge boost to British calico printing. A 1721 law went so far as to ban people from wearing printed calicoes if the white calicoes themselves originated from India, a measure that gave an impetus to calico fabrication in Britain. Selling Indian cottons was eventually criminalized altogether: In 1772 Robert Gardiner of London rented an apartment to one W. Blair, who "brought illegal goods into his house," namely Indian muslins. He was sent to jail. In 1774, Parliament decreed that cotton cloth for sale in England had to be made exclusively of cotton spun and woven in England. Only goods destined for reexport were permitted from the East Indies. The Indian cotton goods not subject to these bans, such as plain chintz and muslins, were subject to heavy tariffs. In the end, all of these protectionist measures did not help the domestic woolen and linen industry, but did spur domestic cotton manufacture.[42]

Like Britain, France took pains to outlaw the import of Indian cottons. In 1686, in response to pressure from silk and wool industrialists, it outlawed the manufacture, use, and sale of cottons. Over the next seventy years, no fewer than two royal edicts and eighty rulings of the king's council attempted to repress cottons. Penalties were made ever more severe, with imprisonment and, starting in 1726, even the death penalty awaiting offenders. In 1755, France again outlawed the import of Indian printed textiles for consumption in France, and in 1785 the king reconfirmed the prohibitions in order to protect a "national industry." Twenty thousand guards worked on enforcing these laws, sending as many as 50,000 violators to forced labor on French galleys. Explicitly excluded from the long list of prohibited Indian textiles, however, were those destined for Guinée, that is, textiles used in the slave trade. Slaves, after all, could only be gotten by exchanging them for the cottons from India.[43]

Other European countries followed suit: Venice disallowed the import of Indian cottons in 1700, as did Flanders. In Prussia, a 1721 edict of King Friedrich Wilhelm outlawed the wearing of printed or painted chintz and cottons. Spain outlawed the import of Indian textiles in 1717. And in the late eighteenth century, the Ottoman Empire under Sultan Abdulhamid I prohibited subjects from wearing certain Indian cloths.[44]

What began as a policy to protect domestic wool, linen, and silk makers evolved toward an explicit program of encouraging the domestic production of cotton textiles. "The prohibition that the industrial nations imposed on printed textiles in order to encourage their own national production," the French traveler François-Xavier Legoux de Flaix argued in 1807, provided European manufacturers who could not yet freely compete with Indian weavers with a sense of how promising the market for cottons would be. Domestic as well as export markets were potentially huge and extremely elastic. And just as protectionist measures limited access to European textile markets for Indian producers, European states and merchants increasingly dominated global networks that allowed them to capture markets for cotton textiles in other parts of the world. These markets, in fact, provided an outlet for cottons secured in India as well as for domestic producers. Thus Europeans could both increase cloth purchases in India *and* protect their own uncompetitive national industries—a miraculous feat possible only because war capitalism had allowed Europeans to dominate global cotton networks while at the same time constructing new kinds of ever more powerful states whose constant warfare demanded ever greater resources and thus embraced domestic industry.[45]

Imperial expansion and the increasing dominance of Europeans in the global cotton trade allowed, furthermore, for an increasing transfer of Asian knowledge to Europe. Manufacturers in Europe felt more and more pressure to appropriate these technologies in order to compete both on price and on quality with Indian producers. Europe's movement toward manufacturing cotton textiles was based, in fact, on what might be considered one of history's most dramatic instances of industrial espionage.

One reason that Indian textiles were so popular among European and African consumers was their superior design and brilliant colors. In order to match the fabulous qualities of their Indian competitors, European manufacturers, supported by their various national governments, collected and shared knowledge about Indian production techniques. French cotton manufacturers, for example, devoted great effort to copying Indian techniques by closely observing Indian ways of manufacturing. In 1678, Georges Roques, who worked for the French East India Company, wrote what quickly became an invaluable report on Indian woodblock printing techniques, based on his observations in Ahmedabad. Forty years later, in 1718, Le Père Turpin followed suit, and in 1731 Georges de Beaulieu, the second lieutenant on a French East India

Company ship, reached Pondicherry to investigate how Indian artisans produced chintz. As a result of these and other efforts, by 1743 French manufacturers were capable of copying all but the very finest Indian textiles. Yet despite this rapid appropriation of Indian techniques, even in the late eighteenth century cloth from the subcontinent still defined quality. Legoux de Flaix admired in 1807 the qualities of Indian yarn and cloth ("a degree of perfection far beyond what we are familiar with in Europe") and once again reported in minute detail on Indian manufacturing techniques, in the hopes of enabling French artisans to copy them: "All the weaving combs in France should be made according to the model used in Bengal," he advised, among other things. "Then we will succeed in equaling the Indians in the manufacture of their muslin."[46]

Other European manufacturers followed suit. In the late eighteenth century, Danish travelers ventured to India to understand and appropriate Indian technology. And throughout the seventeenth and eighteenth centuries, English cotton printers collected and then copied Indian designs using Indian cotton printing expertise. Publications such as the "Account of the Manufactures carried on at Bangalore, and the Processes employed by the Natives in Dyeing Silk and Cotton," or the similarly oriented "The Genuine Oriental Process for giving to Cotton Yarn, or Stuffs, the fast or ingrained Colour, known by the Name of Turkey or Adrianople-Red," exemplified a persistent interest in technology transfer. Just as was the case with the spinning wheel and the horizontal treadle loom in the centuries prior, Asia from the sixteenth through the eighteenth century remained the most important source of cotton manufacturing and, especially, printing technology. As European domination of the global networks of cotton quickened, so too did the pace of European assimilation of Indian technology.[47]

Replacing Indian cotton cloth with domestic production, both for export markets and for local consumption, became a goal to aspire to. Glasgow cotton manufacturers pressured the government to help them gain access to export markets in 1780, since there was "a surplus of Goods which the Home Consumption cannot exhaust: and therefore a foreign Sale to a much greater extent becomes indispensably necessary, in order to occupy the Machinery (which must otherwise be lost) and also to keep alive the Industry of the People, who have been trained to this business."[48] Imperial expansion, moreover, had acquainted European, and especially British, merchants with global cotton markets. By 1770, it had become clear that markets for cotton textiles in Europe, but even more so in Africa, the Americas, and, of course, Asia, were huge—and the opportunities for profit to anyone able to produce for these markets on a competitive basis virtually limitless. Knowledge of the elasticity and profitability of these markets derived directly from merchants' experience in the world's long-distance cotton trade networks.[49]

Indeed, export markets eventually became central to Europe's cotton textile manufacturers—markets that had been captured, at first, through the export of fabrics from India. "It is of very great importance to our Investment," the London Commercial Department wrote to its counterparts in Bombay, "that we should be enabled to bring regularly to Sale a considerable amount of Surat Goods for the supply of the African Trade in particular." West Africans turned into principal customers for cotton cloth secured by the French from Pondicherry not least because imports into France itself were illegal. As Legoux de Flaix observed in the late eighteenth century, "It was the establishment of colonies [in the West Indies] and the slave trade which gave birth to this branch of commerce with Indoustan. . . . But if the colonies of the Antilles cease to buy slaves, one can say without doubt, that this article will decline more and more."[50]

English manufacturers and merchants had relied early on exports of domestic and Indian fabrics to Africa. This reliance on overseas markets became pronounced after 1750. As historian Joseph E. Inikori has shown, in 1760, Britain exported about one-third of its cotton cloth production. By the end of the eighteenth century the share going abroad had expanded to about two-thirds. Africa and the Americas were the most important markets. By mid-century, 94 percent of all cotton cloth exports from Britain went there. The sheer scale of this market meant that those able to compete there could reap fortunes. Adam Smith saw this clearly when he wrote in 1776 that by "opening a new and inexhaustible market to all the commodities of Europe, it gave occasion to new divisions of labour and improvements of art, which, in the narrow circle of the ancient commerce, could never have taken place for want of a market to take off the greater part of their produce."[51]

Africans' appreciation for these cottons was grounded in their own cotton industry and their much earlier exposure to Indian textiles. European slave merchants at first struggled to deliver exactly the type of cloth for which African demand already existed, especially indigo blue and white cottons. Around 1730 the East India Company remarked that a shortage of Indian cottons had "put people upon making goods in imitation of them here" in England—and European traders even exported cloth under their Indian names, because Africans usually preferred cloth "made in India." In a memorandum for the Board of Trade, Elias Barnes hoped that British weavers could successfully copy Indian cottons. The potential market for such cloth, he believed, was immense: "Besides what is consumed in our Own Dominions, the whole World will be our customer." As late as 1791 the Commercial Department of the East India Company urged Bombay to regularly ship cottons to England "for the supply of the African trade in particular."[52]

Imperial expansion, slavery, and land expropriations—war capitalism—laid the foundations for the still small and technologically backward domestic cotton industry in Europe. It provided dynamic markets and access to technology and to essential raw materials. It also became a significant engine of capital formation. Mercantile cities such as Liverpool, which derived their wealth largely from slavery, became important sources of capital for the emerging cotton industry, and cotton merchants in Liverpool provided ever more credit to manufacturers to enable them to work up the cotton. London merchants, in turn, who sold the yarn and cloth coming from British producers advanced credit to Lancashire manufacturers. In fact, they provided the very important and very significant working capital, as profits from trade were redirected toward manufacturing, "a flow of capital inwards from commerce." Moreover, as these merchants gained wealth in long-distance trade, they could demand political protections from a government increasingly dependent on extracting revenue from them.[53]

Last but not least, war capitalism also nourished the emerging secondary sectors of the economy such as insurance, finance, and shipping, sectors that would become exceedingly important to the emergence of the British cotton industry, but also public institutions such as government credit, money itself, and national defense. These institutions originated in the world of war capitalism "as advanced industrial techniques and commercial practices" migrated from export businesses into the domestic economy.[54]

European—and especially British—merchants, with the willing partnership of the British state, had inserted themselves in unique ways into the global networks of cotton production, between growers and spinners, between spinners and weavers, between producers and consumers. Long before the advent of new cotton-producing technologies, they had in fact already rearranged the global cotton industry and global cotton networks. These networks were dominated by the joint venture of private capital and increasingly robust states. Together their commitment to armed trade, industrial espionage, prohibitions, restrictive trade regulations, domination of territories, capturing of labor, removal of indigenous inhabitants, and the state-sponsored creation of territories that were then left to the far-reaching domination of capitalists had created a new economic order.[55]

From these abundant exertions by merchants, manufacturers, and government bureaucrats alike, Europe by the eighteenth century enjoyed a fundamentally new place in the global networks of cotton. Most of the world's cotton production was still located in Asia, and vibrant cotton industries remained throughout Africa and the Americas, but Europeans now decisively dominated its transoceanic trade. In the New World, they had built a regime for the production of agricultural commodities based on slave labor, a system of production that would ultimately make more and more Europeans into cotton growers, even though little cotton grew on European soil. Strong European states had simultaneously created barriers to the import of foreign textiles just as they built a system for the appropriation of foreign technology. By orchestrating economic processes in Asia, Africa, and the Americas as well as in Europe, Europeans gained the paradoxical ability to direct the global trade in Indian textiles while at the same time keeping Asian cloth increasingly out of Europe, instead trading the products in Africa and elsewhere beyond Europe's shores. A globalized textile industry had emerged and Europeans, for the first time, had grasped the vast scope of the global demand for cotton goods.

What set European statesmen and capitalists apart from their counterparts elsewhere was their ability to dominate these global networks. Whereas trade in Africa, Asia, and the Americas had been characterized by networks fueled by the mutually advantageous exchange of goods, Europeans built transcontinental production systems that exploded existing social relations on their continent and elsewhere. The significance of this early history of global interaction was not global trade as such (which remained of limited quantitative importance to all economies), but instead the reshaping of how things were produced, both in time and in space, and the social and political ramifications of that production.[56] India and China, or, for that matter, the Aztec and Inca empires, had not even come close to such global dominance, and even less so to reinventing how people produced things in the far-flung corners of the globe. And yet starting in the sixteenth century, armed European capitalists and capital-rich European states reorganized the world's cotton industry. It was this early embrace of war capitalism that was the precondition for the Industrial Revolution that eventually created an enormous further push toward global economic integration and continues to shape and reshape our world today.

What happened was a swift transition from the older world of cotton—discontinuous, multifocal, horizontal—to an integrated, centralized, and hierarchical empire of cotton. As late as the mid-eighteenth century, it would have seemed unlikely to contemporary observers that Europe, and especially Britain, would very soon turn into the world's most important cotton manufacturer. Indeed, even in 1860, James A. Mann, a fellow at the Statistical Society of London and a Member of the Royal Asiatic Society, could still remember:

> Our own condition, at a period very recent, would but ill-compare with the then inhabitants of the New World or of India; our moral condition with all the advantages of climate, was absolutely below the latter, and the position of the manufacturing art in America, at the date of its discovery, or in India, surpassed even that of our woolen manufacture; and to this day, with all our appliances, we cannot surpass in fineness the muslins of the East, or the solidity and elegance of the *Hamaca's*, the Brazilians and Carribees were wont to weave. When our people were in primeval darkness, East and West were in comparative light.
>
> India . . . is the source whence we received indirectly our ideas of trade; it was the manufactures of that country, as of China, that inspired the minds of our forefathers with the wish for luxuries according to the received notions of the times. The period in which the manufacture was carried on in India, formed comparatively speaking, the dawning of our day; the sun was then traveling from another and past era in the world's commerce. The Indian manufacture was the forecast of that light, which, intensifying on its road hither, gained the needful warmth

to dispel the early mists of morn, and develop the embryo state; and strengthened by the energy of the European, it has given rise to a new era of commercial splendour never before witnessed.[57]

As the sun was made to rise over a small part of Europe, as enter-prising Europeans sucked the discontinuous, multifocal, and horizontal worlds of cotton slowly into their orbit, they invented tools and methods that enabled them to mobilize land, labor, and markets in the service of a newly and boldly imagined empire. By creating this vast sphere of war capitalism that followed rules so different from the ones in Europe itself, they created not just the conditions for the "great divergence" and the Industrial Revolution but also for a further strengthening of states at home that would in turn become crucial to the creation of the empire of cotton. By 1780, Europe in general, and Britain in particular, had become a hub of the world's cotton networks.

Chapter Three

The Wages of War Capitalism

Spinning mule, Lancashire, 1835

The revolution began in the most unlikely places: a quiet valley in the low hills that surround Manchester, for example. Today just a short bus ride away from the city's bustling international airport, Quarry Bank Mill attracts tourists as much for its well-kept gardens as for its industrial history. Visitors stroll along the banks of the Bollin River, whose waters over the millennia have cut a valley perhaps a hundred feet deep into the surrounding fields.

Two centuries ago that river inspired a British merchant to launch one of the most important experiments in human history. In 1784, on the bank of the stream, Samuel Greg gathered together in a small factory a few newfangled spinning machines, so-called water frames, a collection of orphaned children, putting-out workers from surrounding villages, and a supply of Caribbean cotton. Eschewing the power supply that spinners had been using for hundreds of years—human—Greg put his yarn-spinning machines into motion using the weight of falling water. Though modest in size, Greg's mill was unlike anything the world had seen. By 1784 here and on a handful of riverbanks nearby, for the first time in human history, machines powered by non-animate energy manufactured yarn. Greg and his manufacturing contemporaries, after decades of tinkering, had suddenly increased the productivity of one of mankind's oldest industries, and with it began to choreograph an unprecedentedly grand movement of machines and people.

Samuel Greg's venture was a quintessentially local event. Greg was born in 1758 in Belfast, but grew up in Manchester, and moved to nearby Styal soon after realizing the capacities embedded in its sleepy stream. His workers came from the valleys, hills, and orphanages of Cheshire and nearby Lancashire. Even his machines had recently been invented in nearby towns and cities. Like Silicon Valley's role as the incubator of the late-twentieth-century computer revolution, the idyllic rolling hills around Manchester emerged in the late eighteenth century as the hotbed of that era's cutting-edge industry—cotton textiles. In an area forming an arc of about thirty-five miles around Manchester, the countryside filled with mills, country towns turned into cities, and tens of thousands of people moved from farms into factories.

What at first glance seems like a local, even provincial event, however, could not have occurred without the ideas, materials, and markets provided by the recasting of the worlds of cotton during the previous three centuries. Greg's factory was embedded within globe-spanning networks—and would eventually spark around the world far greater changes than Greg could comprehend. Greg secured the essential raw material for production from his merchant relatives in Liverpool, who had purchased it off boats from places like Jamaica and Brazil. The very idea of cotton fabrics, and the technologies for finishing them, as we know, came from Asia, India in particular, and Greg's desire to produce them was largely motivated by his hope to replace the products of Indian spinners and weavers in domestic as well as international markets. Last but not least, much of Greg's production would leave the United Kingdom for destinations elsewhere—feeding the slave trade on the western coast of Africa, dressing Greg's very own slaves on the island of Dominica, and catering to consumers in continental Europe. Samuel Greg was able to draw upon all of these networks in large part because British merchants had long dominated them.

The actual material contribution made by Greg and his colleagues during the heyday of the Industrial Revolution between 1780 and 1815 would still not come close to matching the volume and the quality of Asian, Latin American, and African spinners and weavers. Yet their mills were the future. These water-powered (and, soon, steam-powered) machines, driven by relentless innovation, animated by wage workers, enabled by significant capital accumulation and the willing encouragement of a new kind of state, seemed almost magical, and they created the central pillar of the empire of cotton. From this local spark, England

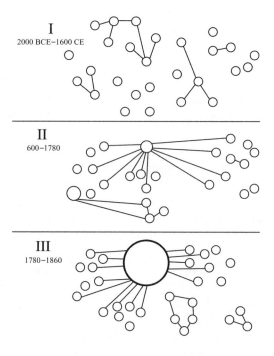

The changing spatial arrangements between growers, manufacturers, and consumers of cotton in the world, 2000 BCE–1860 CE. Phase I: Multipolar, disconnected. Phase II: After 1600, networks focused increasingly on Europe, but production remained dispersed. Phase III: After the Industrial Revolution, production networks focused on Europe, and a multicentric industry became unipolar.

"This Land of Long Chimneys":
The Industrial Revolution in the United Kingdom, 1780–1815

came to dominate a many-pronged world economy, making one of humanity's most important industries its own. From this local spark, industrial capitalism would emerge and eventually spread its wings across the globe. From this local spark, the world as most of us know it emerged.

Samuel Greg was important to this story; he and his contemporaries shaped the future. But like most successful revolutionaries, they relied on the past, on the networks constructed by British merchants, planters, and the state during the previous two hundred years. In other words, the power they harnessed in water was only possible because of the power harnessed by war capitalism. Slavery, colonial domination, militarized trade, and land expropriations provided the fertile soil from which a new kind of capitalism would sprout. Greg's genius lay in realizing that risk-taking English entrepreneurs like him could build upon this material and institutional heritage and generate unprecedented wealth and power by embracing the heretofore ungentlemanly world of manufacturing.

Greg had deep roots in war capitalism, its violent appropriation of territory and slave labor, as well its reliance on the imperial state to secure new technologies and markets. He had secured his part of the family fortune through Hillsborough Estate, a profitable sugar plantation on the Caribbean island of Dominica, where he held hundreds of enslaved Africans until the final abolition of slavery in British territories in 1834. Greg's uncles Robert and Nathaniel Hyde, who had raised him from age nine and also provided much of the capital for the building of Quarry Bank Mill, were also textile manufacturers, West Indian plantation owners, and merchants. Greg's wife, Hannah Lightbody, was born into a family involved in the slave trade, while his sister-in-law's family had moved from the slave trade into the export of cloth to Africa.[1]

Most of Greg's fellow cotton manufacturers came from considerably less prosperous circumstances, without Caribbean slave plantations. They had accumulated only modest amounts of capital, but had a wealth of tinkering spirit and technical aptitude—as well as a hunger for the huge profits that might be generated by manufacturing. Yet they, too, drew their essential raw material—cotton—from slave labor. Even they catered to markets that had first been opened by the trade in Indian cotton textiles, textiles that had been kept out of many European markets in order to protect noncompetitive European producers. And they, too, drew on

Bringing war capitalism home: Hannah Lightbody, Samuel Greg's wife,
and daughter of a Liverpool merchant family

Indian technologies captured through British imperial expansion on that continent. Many, moreover, used capital accumulated via the Atlantic trade and catered to Atlantic markets—especially in Africa and in the Americas, economies fueled almost exclusively by slave labor. And for them, war capitalism had also provided many learning opportunities—how to organize long-distance trade, for example, how to run domestic industries; an understanding of the mechanisms to move capital across oceans—lessons that informed the development of domestic financial instruments. Even modern labor cost accounting had emerged from the world of the slave plantation and only later migrated into modern industry. And British entrepreneurs' incentive and ability to reinvent radically the production of cotton textiles was protected by a powerful imperial state, a state that itself had been the product of war capitalism.[2]

Most crucially, by the second half of the eighteenth century, that heritage allowed British merchants to assume commanding roles at many vital nodes of the global cotton industry—even though British workers produced only a tiny percentage of global output and Britain's farmers grew no cotton whatsoever. England's domination of these global networks, as we will see, was essential to recast production and become the unlikely source of the cotton-fueled Industrial Revolution. While certainly still revolutionary, industrial capitalism was the offspring of war capitalism, the previous centuries' great innovation.[3]

Samuel Greg and his fellow innovators knew that the global reach and power of the British Empire gave them a tremendous advantage over their fellow merchants and artisans in Frankfurt, Calcutta, or Rio de Janeiro. Having started out as a merchant in the employ of his uncles, he had already organized a large putting-out network of cotton spinners and weavers in the Lancashire and Cheshire countryside before investing in his new machines. In addition to the profits and labor from this putting-out network, Greg had easy access to abundant capital from his wife's family. And the Rathbone family, which would become one of the dominant players in the nineteenth-century cotton trade, stood ready in 1780 to supply raw cotton to Greg. He knew firsthand that the market for cotton fabrics—in continental Europe, along the coast of Africa, and in the Americas—was rapidly expanding.[4]

And while the upside was tremendous, the risks of these first ventures were modest. In the 1780s, Greg invested at first a fairly small amount of capital into his Quarry Bank Mill: £3,000, the equivalent of about half a million U.S. dollars today. Then he recruited ninety children between the ages of ten and twelve from nearby poorhouses, attaching them for seven years to his factory as "parish apprentices." By 1800 he supplemented these children with 110 adult workers who received wages. Greg sold his cloth first mostly to Europe and the West Indies, and, after the 1790s, increasingly to Russia and the United States. Thanks to those expanding markets, the new factory, like others, was spectacularly profitable from the beginning, returning annually 18 percent on his original investment, four times as much as UK government bonds.[5]

Contemporary observers as well as modern historians have found many reasons that explain Greg's venture, and with it why the much broader Industrial Revolution, "broke out" in this place, in northern England, and at this time, in the 1780s. The genius of British inventors, the size of the British market and its unusually deep integration, the geography of Britain with its easy access to waterborne transport, the importance of religious dissenters for thinking outside the box, and the creation of a state favorable to entrepreneurial initiative have all been cited.[6] While none of these arguments are unimportant, they omit a core part of the story of the Industrial Revolution: its dependence on the globe-spanning system of war capitalism.

As a result of all these factors, for the first time ever, a new character, the manufacturer, strode onto the scene, an individual who used capital not to enslave labor or conquer territory, though that remained essential, but to organize workers into great orchestras of machine-based production. Manufacturers' efforts to reorganize production rested on new ways of mobilizing land, labor, and resources—and called, among other things, for a new connection between capitalists and the state. It was this nexus of social and political power that together animated industrial capitalism, the transformational invention of the Industrial Revolution. It was that innovation that would, as we will see, eventually take wing and travel to other parts of the world.

Fueled by the wages of war capitalism, Greg and his contemporaries, as one observer remarked in the 1920s, "wrested the empire of cotton from the East within a vigorous generation of invention," rewriting the entire geography of global cotton manufacturing. Their work was revolutionary because it heralded a new institutional form for organizing economic activity and a world economy in which rapid growth and ceaseless reinvention of production became the norm, not the exception. To be sure, important inventions had been made in the past, and there had been moments of accelerated economic growth in various regions of the world before the Industrial Revolution. Yet none of them had created a world in which revolution itself would become a permanent feature of life, a world in which economic growth would, despite periodic collapses, seem to fuel its own expansion. There had been no radical acceleration of economic growth in the thousand years before 1800 in Europe or elsewhere, and any that had occurred had soon foundered on the shoals of resource constraints, a food crisis, or disease. Now industrial capitalism was creating an ever-changing world, and cotton, the world's most important industry, was the mainspring of this unprecedented acceleration of human productivity.[7]

In retrospect, late-eighteenth-century England seemed ripe for a reinvention of cotton manufacturing. British capitalists looked back on two centuries of cotton textile production, had access to investable capital, and employed ever more peasants to spin and weave at home. Also, British textile producers based in households had withstood the pressures of imports from India for decades, an experience that schooled them in the importance of being able to compete with Indian manufacturers to capture their markets. And last but not least, workers were available to staff the new factories, workers who did not have the ability to resist the process of being turned from rural cultivators or artisans into wage laborers. These factors provided the necessary conditions for a radical reimagining of production and the institutions in which it was embedded. Such conditions, however, were hardly unique, in fact they were shared, if not in all aspects, then at least in many particulars, from China to India to continental Europe to Africa. They cannot alone explain why the Industrial Revolution broke out in a small part of the British Isles in the late eighteenth century.[8]

British capitalists, however, in contrast to their counterparts elsewhere, controlled many global cotton networks. They had access to uniquely dynamic markets, they dominated the transoceanic trade in cottons, and they had firsthand knowledge of the fabulous potential wealth that could come from selling cloth. The core problem faced by British cotton manufacturers was the difficulty of competing with high-quality yet cheap Indian products. In the course of the eighteenth century, as we have seen, British producers had largely (though not entirely) solved the quality problem by appropriating Indian technology. Expanding output, and lowering costs, proved more difficult: The putting-out networks that British merchants had built in the countryside proved largely resistant to higher production. Work was performed irregularly, additional workers were difficult to mobilize on short notice, and transportation costs rose with the volume of work. And it was difficult to enforce homogeneous quality in products spun and woven on remote farms. With the existing technology and social organization of production, British outworkers could hardly compete with cotton workers in other parts of the world. Indeed, they succeeded mostly only in the protected domestic and colonial markets.[9]

The main reason for this inability to compete, however, was wage costs. Wages in the United Kingdom were significantly higher than in other parts of the world; indeed, in 1770 Lancashire wages were perhaps as much as six times those in India. Even though by this point improved machinery meant that productivity per cotton worker in Britain was already two to three times higher than in India, that multiplier was still not sufficient to level the playing field. War capitalism had created a fundamentally new set of opportunities for British cotton capitalists, but it had no answer to the question of how to enter cotton cloth markets in a globally significant way. Protectionism had been a workable answer to a point, and was deployed to great success, but the tantalizing possibility of global exports could not be preserved by such prohibitions. What British cotton capitalists needed was a dynamic combination of new technologies to lower costs, the further growth of elastic markets that already had begun to expand on the tails of British expansion, and a supportive state with the ability not just to protect global empire but to transform society in Britain itself.[10]

Since labor costs were the primary obstacle to grasping the new tantalizing opportunities, British merchants, inventors, and budding manufacturers—practical men all—focused on methods to increase the productivity of their high-cost labor. In the process, they effected the most momentous technological change in the history of cotton. Their first noteworthy innovation came in 1733 with John Kay's invention of the flying shuttle. This small wooden tool in the shape of the hull of a ship allowed weavers to attach the weft thread and then propel it to "fly" from one side of the loom to the other through the warp threads. The shuttle doubled the productivity of weavers. At first it spread only slowly, but its spread was unstoppable: After 1745, despite resistance from weavers who feared for their livelihoods, it was widely adopted.[11]

This tiny piece of wood propelled in novel ways prompted a cascade of further innovations that would gradually but permanently change cotton manufacturing. The spread of more productive weaving techniques put huge pressure on spinning, as ever more spinners were needed to supply one weaver with sufficient yarn to keep the looms working. Despite more women in ever more households working longer hours on the spinning wheel, the supply was insufficient. After Kay's invention it took four spinners to supply one weaver. Many artisans tried to find ways to circumvent this bottleneck, and by the 1760s productivity increases became possible with James Hargreaves's invention of the spinning jenny. The jenny consisted of a hand-operated wheel that would rotate a number of spindles within a frame, while the spinner would use her other hand to move a bar back and forth to extend the thread and then to wind it on the spindles themselves. This machine was at first able to spin eight separate threads, later sixteen or more, and as early as 1767 it had tripled a spinner's speed. It spread rapidly, and by 1786 there were about twenty thousand in use in Britain.[12]

As early as 1769, however, spinning was already seeing further improvements thanks to Richard Arkwright's water frame, a machine that anticipated Greg's mill by relying on falling water. Consisting of four rollers that drew out the cotton strands before a spindle twisted them into thread, it allowed for continuous spinning, and unlike the jenny, which had at first been mostly employed in people's homes, the water frame required larger amounts of energy, thus concentrating production in factories. A decade later, in 1779, Samuel Crompton's mule was the capstone of these inventions, combining elements of the jenny with those of the water frame (hence its name). The mule was a long machine with two parallel carriages: Bobbins of roving (lightly twisted cotton fibers) lined one side, and spindles ready to accept spun yarn lined the other. The exterior carriage, mounted on wheels, was pulled out about five feet, stretching multiple lengths of roving simultaneously. The number of rovings spun depended on the number of spindles mounted to the mule: Although two hundred was the norm in the 1790s, the number would climb to more than thirteen hundred over the ensuing century. The stretched roving was then twisted into yarn and wound onto the spindles as the carriage was pushed back in. Unlike with the water frame, which operated continuously, yarn was produced in five-foot bursts, but was stronger and finer than yarn produced on water frames. The mule was first powered by water (which remained the dominant source of power until the 1820s), but later mostly by steam engines (which James Watt patented in 1769).[13]

With spinning no longer a laggard, pressure shifted back to weaving. First came a vast expansion of home-based weaving. With new machines and an abundant supply of thread, this was a golden age for weavers all over the Lancashire and Cheshire countryside, as tens of thousands of cottagers spent endless hours on their looms working up the rapidly increasing output of British spinning factories. While Edmund Cartwright had patented a water-powered loom as early as 1785, productivity improvements in weaving at first proved modest, and technical problems with power looms great.[14]

Britain's growing class of manufacturers, despite issues with looms, were acutely aware that these new machines allowed them to increasingly dominate the one node in the global cotton complex whose control had eluded them: manufacturing. In eighteenth-century India, spinners required 50,000 hours to spin a hundred pounds of raw cotton; their cohorts in 1790 Britain, using a hundred-spindle mule, could spin the same amount in just 1,000 hours. By 1795 they needed just 300 hours with the water frame, or, with Roberts's automated mule after 1825, only 135 hours. In just three decades, productivity had increased 370 times. Labor costs in England were now much lower than in India.[15]

Prices for British yarn fell accordingly, and soon were lower than those manufactured in India. In 1830, British cotton merchant Edward Baines cited the price of one pound of Number 40 yarn (the number reflects the quality of the yarn—the higher the number, the finer the thread) in England as 1 shilling, 2.5 pence, while in India the same quality and quantity of yarn would cost 3 shillings, 7 pence. Manchester spinners McConnel & Kennedy reported that the prices for its high-quality 100-count yarn fell by 50 percent between 1795 and 1811, and, despite various ups and downs, continued to fall further throughout the nineteenth century. While yarn prices, especially of fine yarns, fell the most rapidly, the cost of finished cloth also declined. A piece of muslin in the early 1780s cost (in deflated prices) 116 shillings per piece; fifty years later the same piece could be had for 28 shillings.[16]

The resulting boom in cotton manufacturing was unprecedented. After nearly two centuries of slow growth in Europe, British cotton manufacturing expanded by leaps and bounds. Between 1780 and 1800, output of cotton textiles in Britain grew annually by 10.8 percent, and exports by 14 percent; already in 1797 there were approximately nine hundred cotton factories. In 1788, there had been 50,000 mule spindles, but thirty-three years later that number had increased to 7 million. While it had been cheaper to produce cotton cloth in India before 1780, and its quality had been superior, after that year English manufacturers were able to compete in European and Atlantic markets, and after 1830 they even began to compete with Indian producers in India itself. Once Indians began using British-manufactured yarn and cloth, it signaled to all that the world's cotton industry had been turned on its head.[17]

As ever larger numbers of cotton factories began to dot northern England to accommodate the new spinning and weaving machines, it might come as a surprise that the inventors, who had enabled this departure, had started in distinctly unspectacular ways. They created a world radically different from anything ever seen before without recourse to theoretical science, often even without much education. They were skilled men in tiny workshops, with little formal education. Among the inventors, Kay came from the most prosperous family, as his father was a modestly successful woolens manufacturer. He might have received some formal education in France. Hargreaves, on the other hand, was a handloom weaver from Blackburn, who probably never had any formal schooling—much like Arkwright, the youngest of seven children born to poor parents, who learned how to read first from his uncles and then educated himself. Crompton grew up in dire poverty: After his father died, Crompton began to spin cotton, perhaps as early as age five, while his mother tried to make ends meet by spinning and weaving. All four were tinkerers, people who breathed and lived with their machines, trying to solve practical problems with simple tools and insights that emerged from their day-to-day efforts to improve production.[18]

But they were far from local heroes. Their innovations sometimes even brought down the wrath of their neighbors, who dreaded the job losses the innovators caused. Fear of mob violence drove Kay and Hargreaves away from the places they had made their inventions. Neither translated their inventions into wealth; after losing their efforts to defend their patents, they lived modestly. When Hargreaves died in Nottingham in 1778, he owned little more than a prize from the Society for the Encouragement of Arts and Manufactures, and his children were destitute. Only Arkwright profited from his invention—establishing cotton factories in numerous locations. Yet a rapidly growing number of British manufacturers did embrace the new technologies, a British state valued them so highly that it criminalized their export for nearly half a century after 1786. From then on, technical progress became a constant: Profits were made by increasing the productivity of human labor. This would in fact become a defining feature of industrial capitalism.

These new machines, the "macro inventions" celebrated by historians Joel Mokyr, Patrick O'Brien, and many others, not only accelerated human productivity, but also altered the nature of the production process itself: They began to regulate the pace of human labor.[19] Dependent on central energy sources and requiring large spaces, production moved out of the home and into factories. Along with the machines, workers assembled in unprecedented numbers in central locations. While putting-out merchants had traversed the countryside searching for laborers, now workers sought out manufacturers in search of employment.

The mechanization of cotton spinning created a novel entity: the cotton mill. Although mills could vary tremendously in size, they shared one attribute: a nearby source of running water. To harness its energy, either a dam was constructed or an inlet was cut from a steep section of river and diverted through a waterwheel. The waterwheel drove shafts that ran through the length of the mill, upon which large leather belts could be engaged or disengaged in order to run the various machines. Unlike its predecessors, the mill's primary function was not to simply aggregate and control labor, but to house a complex array of machinery. And by the 1780s, some mills were taking on gargantuan proportions; at two hundred feet long, thirty feet wide, and four to six stories in height, they dominated the surrounding countryside.[20]

Yarn production in these mills entailed three basic steps: willowing, carding, and spinning. The first step had workers, generally women, spread the raw cotton upon meshed tables and beat it with sticks to remove any twigs, leaves, and dirt that the ginning had failed to remove. Since the process pushed so much fire-hazardous cotton dust into the air, it was often completed in adjoining buildings rather than within the main mill complex. After the cotton was cleaned, a series of machines centralized in the bottom floors of the mill would transform the raw cotton into "roving," a thin cord of lightly twisted, parallel fibers ready to be spun. First, the cotton was fed into a carding engine, a spinning cylinder covered in metal teeth fitted into a similarly toothed casing. Through carding, a snarled mess of cotton was turned into an untangled so-called sliver with the fibers running parallel. The cotton was then fed into a draw frame, a set of rollers through which the sliver was passed—stretching, twisting, and drawing it—creating the roving. The cotton strand was then wound into a roving can, from which it could be placed onto a bobbin. Finally, the cotton was ready to be spun. Spinning machines were located across the top floors of the mill, and the machines themselves usually took one of two forms: Arkwright's water frame or, increasingly, Crompton's mule.[21]

To operate all this machinery and to move the cotton through the factory, manufacturers hired hundreds of workers, most of them children and women. And while not all workers arrived at the factory gates voluntarily and received wages, the majority did. This was, as we will see later, another important institutional innovation of industrial capitalism. Outside the slave plantations of the Americas capitalists for the first time organized, supervised, and dominated the production process.[22]

Such domination of labor by capital, embrace of technological revolution, and social innovation did not happen elsewhere, including in the heart of the world's cotton industry, China and India. This was in some ways surprising, since for centuries manufacturing in these parts of the world had defined the cutting edge of global cotton production technology. Way back in 1313, Wang Zhen had written a description of a "machine for spinning hemp thread" that came quite close to Hargreaves's spinning jenny and Arkwright's water frame. Developing new spinning machines was certainly within the grasp of Chinese artisans, or, for that matter, their French or Indian counterparts. Moreover, trade in cotton and cotton textiles was the most important facet of an increasing commercialization of the Chinese economy between the fourteenth and nineteenth centuries.[23]

Despite these promising preconditions, neither China nor India—nor, for that matter, England's closest European competitor in technical education, Prussia—came close to dominating as many nodes within the global cotton production complex as Britain. Nor did any other country embrace war capitalism as effectively. Moreover, in India and China, peasants were more secure on the land than their British counterparts, making it more difficult for eager manufacturers to mobilize large numbers of workers. Because of the different organization of households, especially limitations on women's outside activities, female-dominated spinning had extremely low opportunity costs in India and China, making the embrace of new technologies less likely. Women's labor, in the calculation of peasant households, was inexpensive. In India, addition-

Water-powered ramie spinning wheel, China, 1313

ally, the chain between the weaver and the final consumer was a long one, with many intermediaries. "To break out of this traditional historical institution" proved difficult, as one historian has remarked, and in the minds of many, of little advantage. Many spinners and weavers in the English countryside likely felt similarly to their brethren in India and China; they knew that newer spinning technology would make their home-based manufacturing unsustainable. And yet with few other means of earning income, and with their episodic efforts to organize against the encroachment of technology defeated by a determined state, they had little choice but to capitulate to industrial capitalism.[24]

Embracing new technologies, subduing labor without enslaving it, and finding new ways to organize production emerged in cotton mills first, and as a result the once modest industry scattered along the rivers of Lancashire and neighboring Cheshire grew by leaps and bounds—around the time of Greg's construction of his first mill in 1784, new mills blossomed, and in the decades thereafter existing mills expanded, sometimes quite significantly. Greg himself employed 2,084 workers in five mills in 1833, and the number of spindles at his Quarry Bank Mill had quadrupled, to 10,846. In 1795, cotton manufacturer Robert Peel expanded operations into twenty-three different mills, all owned and managed by him. In other instances, new producers entered the industry, often people with little capital but the right kinds of connections. When Irish merchant William Emerson wanted to help a relative start a spinning mill, he wrote to his business partners McConnel and Kennedy in Manchester, informing them in a letter "that a relation of mine has a desire to acquire a knowledge of Carding and Spinning, and for which purpose, I wd willingly send him to you for Six Mo and pay you any reasonable price for his instruction, you d be so good to say if you could with convenience have him Instructed Either in your own House or any other and on what terms."[25]

As factories multiplied, many remained small and their owners were often not wealthy by the standards of Liverpool merchants, Somerset landowners, or London bankers. In 1812, 70 percent of all firms had fewer than ten thousand spindles and were valued at less than £2,000. The entrepreneurs who entered the industry came from a variety of backgrounds. Many had been merchant-manufacturers, others manufacturers in different industries, while others had started out as well-off farmers, or even as apprentices with unusual mechanical abilities. There were cer-

tainly examples of extraordinary social mobility, such as Elkanah Armitage, who began work at a cotton factory at age eight as a spinner's helper
and fifty-nine years later owned mills that employed 1,650 workers.[26]

Others, however, started with more substantial resources, such
as Samuel Oldknow, who was born in 1756 in Anderton, Lancashire.
His father already owned a successful muslin manufacturing operation
worked entirely by handlooms. Following his father's premature death,
Oldknow was apprenticed to his uncle, a draper, before he returned to
his hometown in 1781 to rebuild the family muslin business. It was aus-
picious timing. The introduction of the spinning mule in 1779 made
high-quality, mass-produced yarn available on an unprecedented scale,
allowing Oldknow to break into a market previously dominated by Indian
manufacturers. Oldknow also partnered with two London firms to secure
wide access to British and overseas markets. As he put it in a draft of a
1783 letter, "The prospect is at present very propitious." By 1786, he was
the most successful muslin manufacturer in Britain. Oldknow continued
to build mills and expand his enterprises, at one point controlling some
twenty-nine mills. By 1790, he was branching out into spinning with the
construction of a steam-powered factory in Stockport; by 1793, an even
larger six-story spinning mill in Mellor began production.[27]

Cotton manufacturing, even if engaged in on a small scale, was aston-
ishingly profitable in the 1780s and 1790s. The firm of Cardwell & Birle
had average annual returns on their capital of 13.1 percent, N. Dugdale
24.8 percent, and McConnel & Kennedy 16 percent. Such profits allowed
them to expand without much recourse to formal capital markets. Indeed,
"the favorite source of capital [for expansion] was retained profits." Yet
such capital was often augmented by merchants who invested in mills
that they did not run themselves, and, more important, by London and
Liverpool merchants' credit for the purchase of raw cotton and the sale of
yarn and cloth. This additional working capital was crucial: While in 1834
fixed capital investments in factories and machines in the British cotton
industry may have amounted to £14.8 million, working capital invested
in raw cotton and wages equaled £7.4 million—a very significant share.
Access to such capital rested often on personal connections, and as the
need to secure significant amounts of circulating capital increased, it
became more difficult for people outside the middle class to join the
ranks of cotton capitalists. High profits from production in turn made
manufacturing an ever more attractive field for further investments.[28]

One example of the rapid growth of cotton mills was the Manchester cotton manufacturers McConnel & Kennedy. They founded their partnership in 1791, focusing on the production of spinning machines, a business that came naturally to machine maker James McConnel. One day, however, McConnel produced two mules that his customer could not pay for, and this seeming bad luck led him to begin using them himself. His partner, John Kennedy, and two other investors expanded both the production of machines and spinning, investing a total capital of £500, an exceedingly modest sum. Calling themselves "machine makers and spinners," they expanded their mills rapidly, focusing on high-quality yarns. In 1797 they operated 7,464 spindles; by 1810 the number of spindles had increased to 78,972, while the number of workers they employed grew from 312 in 1802 to 1,020 in 1816. Like others, they financed that expansion out of retained profits, which had averaged 26.5 percent annually between 1799 and 1804.[29]

The growth of cotton manufacturing soon made it the center of the British economy. In 1770, cotton manufacturing had made up just 2.6 percent of the value added in the economy as a whole. By 1801 it accounted for 17 percent, and by 1831, 22.4 percent. This compared to the iron industry's share of 6.7 percent, coal's 7 percent, and woolens' 14.1 percent. In Britain, as early as 1795, 340,000 people worked in the spinning industry. By 1830, one in six workers in Britain labored in cottons. At the same time, the industry itself became centered on a small part of the British Isles: Lancashire. Seventy percent of all British cotton workers would eventually labor there, while 80.3 percent of all owners of cotton factories originated in that same county.[30]

The explosion of the cotton industry was not a flash in the pan. Instead, as we will see, other industries would be made possible by the rise of cotton: a railroad network, the iron industry, and later in the nineteenth century a new set of industries that would amount to a second industrial revolution. But cotton was the vanguard. As historian Fernand Braudel has argued, the Industrial Revolution in cottons affected the "*entire* national economy."[31] As late as the mid-nineteenth century, the Industrial Revolution was still, numerically, the story of cotton.

The spectacular take off of the British cotton industry allowed British capitalists—along with the British state—to retain even more of the wages of war capitalism. With cheaper production costs thanks to the unprecedented productivity of their new machines and the new organization of production, with wage workers in large factories, British manufacturers, as expected, broke into new markets. Domestic markets expanded as cottons became cheaper and as cotton fabrics became ever more fashionable as their changing designs mattered increasingly to the self-presentation of middle-class consumers.[32]

British cotton manufacturers also moved decisively into the all-important export market. By the 1780s, they came to sell in markets that British merchants previously had served with Indian textiles. Fine muslins that had been the pride of Bengal and "which for some thousands of years stood unequalled" were henceforth produced in the United Kingdom. This was clearly decisive, since the British market, with its 8.66 million people, was quite small, and per capita disposable income grew only modestly. Over the course of the eighteenth century cotton exports from Britain increased two hundred times—yet 94 percent of that increase took place in the two decades after 1780, when exports exploded by a factor greater than sixteen from their 1780 value of £355,060 to £5,854,057 in 1800. By the last years of the eighteenth century, 61.3 percent of all cotton cloth produced on the British Isles was exported. After 1815, thanks to these exports, England had indeed pretty much "eliminated all rivals from the non-European world" in the global trade of cotton yarn and cloth.[33]

The true boom of the British cotton industry was thus an export boom. By 1800 British manufactured cottons had become a major pres-

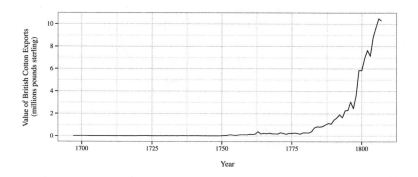

The export explosion: growth of British exports of cotton goods, 1697–1807

ence on world markets—and at the same time thousands of spinners and weavers in newly built factories all over the English countryside, not to mention hundreds of factory owners and merchants and seamen, were newly dependent on such foreign markets. As Edward Baines observed in amazement in 1835, cotton exports "at the present day . . . are three times as large as the woolen exports,—having in so short a period outstripped and distanced a manufacture which has flourished for centuries in England and which for that length of time all writers on trade had justly considered as the grand source of commercial wealth to the country." Indeed, such record trade in cottons influenced the entire British economy: 56 percent of all additional British exports from 1784–86 to 1804–6 were in cottons.[34]

British cottons now rapidly replaced Indian cottons on world markets. While in fiscal year 1800–1801, piece goods valued at £1.4 million were still exported from Bengal to Britain, by 1809–10, only eight years later, cloth exports had been reduced to just a bit more than £330,000—and would continue to fall rapidly thereafter. As a result, Indian weavers, who had dominated global cotton textile markets for centuries, went into free fall. In 1800, commercial resident John Taylor wrote a detailed history of the clothing industry of the Bengali city of Dhaka and reported that the value of cloth exports there had fallen by 50 percent between 1747 and 1797. Spinners especially had been hurt by British competition, and as a result a great number, he reported, "died of famine." The people of the once thriving manufacturing city had been "reduced and impoverished," its houses "ruined and abandoned," and its commercial history become "a melancholy retrospect." The "ancient celebrity" and "great wealth" of Dhaka were all but gone. By 1806, another report on Bengali commerce concluded that "the exports of Piece Goods on the public account, have also very considerably decreased . . .; the consequences are, that the weavers finding no employment for their looms, many of them have been necessitated to quit their homes and seek employment elsewhere; most of them take to the plough, some remain in their own districts, while others migrate into distant parts of the country." One critic of the East India Company, observing that it seemed the goal of British policy to make India into an importer of cotton cloth and an exporter of raw cotton, found it "a policy similar to that which Spain pursued towards the unhappy aborigines of America."[35]

British cottons captured the multifaceted export markets formerly controlled by Indian spinners and weavers, while manufacturers focused at first on selling to parts of the world subject to war capitalism. During the last decades of the eighteenth century, the heyday of the Industrial Revolution, more than two-thirds of British cotton exports went to such places. Exports flowed, in effect, within the same channels of the Atlantic economy that Britain had spent two hundred years and untold treasure building. Slaves on plantations in the Americas, unlike agricultural producers elsewhere, did not produce their own clothing and provided a uniquely rich market despite the low level of their masters' provisioning. In the African trade—mostly in slaves—demand was just as high (and even increasing, as a result of the cotton planting boom in the Americas), as African merchants began to accept British-made cloth as equivalent to Indian cloth in quality and price. After 1806, British cottons were decisively dominating this market that had for so long eluded them.[36]

The ability of merchants and manufacturers to access these markets pointed to the importance of a peculiar and novel form of state, a state that would be the crucial ingredient for industrial capitalism and would eventually travel in quite peculiar patterns around the globe. After all, cotton exports expanded on the strength of British trade networks and the institutions in which they were embedded—from a strong navy creating and protecting market access to bills of lading allowing for the transfer of capital over large distances. This state was capable of forging and protecting global markets, policing its borders, regulating industry, creating and then enforcing private property rights in land, enforcing contracts over large geographical distances, forging fiscal tools to tax populations, and building a social, economic, and legal environment that made the mobilization of labor through wage payments possible.

As one perceptive French observer argued in the early nineteenth century, "England has only arrived at the summit of prosperity by persisting for centuries in the system of protection and prohibition."[37] Indeed, in the end, it was not so much the new machines that revolutionized the world, impressive and important as they were. The truly heroic invention was the economic, social, and political institutions in which these machines were embedded. These institutions came to further define industrial capitalism and increasingly set it apart from its parent, war capitalism.[38]

The creation of such a state at the core of industrial capitalism was a complicated dance between various interests. A rising group of manufacturers pressed for a recognition of their interests, while statesmen and bureaucrats came to understand that their own exalted position in the world rested on Great Britain's rapidly expanding manufacturing capacity. Manufacturers fought competing interests—the East India Company, for example—and competing elites, such as aristocratic landowners. And as merchants and manufacturers accumulated significant resources on which the state came to depend, these capitalists could translate their growing importance to the national economy into political influence.[39] Cotton mill owners became increasingly active politically, culminating in the 1832 Reform Act that extended them the suffrage, allowing many textile entrepreneurs to move into the House of Commons, where they strenuously lobbied for the (global) interests of their industry, from the Corn Laws to British colonial expansion.[40] The argument of the manufacturers for policies conducive to their interests was straightforward and strikingly modern, as this 1789 petition of 103 cotton goods manufacturers from around Glasgow to the Treasury shows:

> That your Petitioners began early to Manufacture British Muslins, and of late years have made great Progress in extending and improving this valuable branch of Trade, as well as the other Articles denominated Callicoes, and Mixed Goods. That the Power of Machinery applied on this Manufactory, joined to the new Facilities, which a more extended Practice has enabled your Petitioners to introduce, occasions a surplus of Goods which the Home Consumption cannot exhaust: and therefore a foreign Sale to a much greater extent becomes indispensably necessary, in order to occupy the Machinery.[41]

Built by newly empowered manufacturers and a state with vastly increased capacity, industrial capitalism found a very different answer to the question of how to mobilize labor, capital, and markets compared to its parent, war capitalism. Labor, unlike in the Americas, could be mobilized because changes in the countryside, including legal changes, had already produced a large group of landless proletarians who were forced to sell their labor power to survive, and did so without being physically coerced. Moreover, unlike for the plantation economy of the Americas, the territorial needs of cotton manufacturing were limited and focused mostly on accessing waterpower. As markets in land had emerged centuries before, and property rights in land were relatively secure and protected by the state, the land grab so typical of war capitalism did not and could not emerge in Britain itself. At the same time, an interventionist state was able to promote land uses deemed helpful to general economic development, for instance by allowing expropriations for the building of turnpikes and canals. Moreover, a highly centralized and bureaucratic state regulated and taxed domestic industry.[42]

Finally, and perhaps most decisive for this early moment in the emergence of industrial capitalism, the mechanisms of war capitalism could be externalized thanks to the state's imperial expansion, in effect reducing capitalists' need to recast the domestic social structure and their dependence on domestic resources, ranging from labor to food to raw materials. Some of the problems in the mobilization of labor, raw materials, territories, and markets had indeed been solved by war capitalism in the Americas, Africa, and Asia. And it was again a strong state (a state fortified by the institutional and financial accumulations of war capitalism) that was the root cause of the ability to externalize some of the labor, land, and resource mobilization. This state could in fact enforce different kinds of institutions in different parts of the world, with slavery and wage labor coexisting, for example.

Manufacturers, merchants, and statesmen constructed a new form of capitalism—a capitalism that would dominate much of the world by the late nineteenth century.

The modern state at its core was sometimes less "visible" than autocratic monarchical rule, and thus seemed "weaker" as its power was increasingly embedded in impersonal rules, laws, and bureaucratic mechanisms. Paradoxically, industrial capitalism made state power less visible as it amplified it. No longer did the personal authority of the king, the lord, or the master, or age-old custom, regulate the market; instead the market was made by explicit rules relentlessly enforced by contracts, laws, and regulations. Weaker states continued to rely on client networks, the subcontracting of authority, and arbitrary rule—characteristics that would not provide fertile ground for industrial capitalism. And as European colonialism spread its tentacles into ever more areas of the world, it further strengthened the state capacity of the colonizers, while at the same time undermining political authority and state capacity among the colonized. Just as state capacity became ever more important, its distribution around the globe became more unequal.

Tellingly, even though Edward Baines argued in 1835 that "this [cotton] trade was not the nursling of government protection," he proceeded to list in chronological order all "interferences of the legislature" that related to the cotton industry, from prohibitions to tariffs—a list that would fill seven pages, a striking reminder of the state's importance to ensuring the "free" market of cotton.[43] In Great Britain and eventually in a few other states, this dependence of capitalists on the state attached them firmly to one another and resulted in a kind of territorialization and "nationalization" of manufacturing capital. Ironically, that link between capitalists and the state would eventually also empower workers, who could deploy the state's dependence on the consent of the governed to mobilize collectively for higher wages and better working conditions.

It was also because of the awe-inspiring capacity of modern states (what Hegel would call the "spirit of history") that war capitalism's way of mobilizing land, labor, and markets would be largely irrelevant within Europe itself. This is in many ways surprising. After all, large-scale and capital-intensive enterprises, the mobilization of vast numbers of workers, and the tight managerial supervision of those workers had all been pioneered to great profit on the plantations of the Americas and seemed to show the way toward the reorganization of production. Yet in Britain itself, war capitalism provided only the foundation, not the nature, of capitalism. To dominate production, workers were neither enslaved nor populations murdered, for capitalists were not fulfilling frontier fantasies beyond the reach of the state. This was revolutionary, but in our world, in which the institutional foundations of industrial capitalism have become commonplace, it is hard to appreciate just how revolutionary it was.

And the relationship between the expansion of manufacturing and the strengthening of the state was mutually reinforcing. Just as the British state undergirded the economic dynamism of the cotton industry, that industry's many progeny became ever more important to the British state. To fuel the wars of the late eighteenth and early nineteenth centuries that established British hegemony in the Atlantic, according to Edward Baines, Britain relied heavily on its commerce, and the most important line of commerce was cotton: "Without the means supplied by her flourishing manufacturers and trade, the country could not have borne up under a conflict as prolonged and exhausting." Cotton goods valued at £150 million were exported between 1773 and 1815, estimated Baines, filling the coffers of manufacturers, merchants—and the state. It was the volume and balance of trade that provided the state the revenues it needed to invest, for example, in expanded naval power in the first place. State revenues indeed increased by a factor of sixteen between the late seventeenth and the early nineteenth centuries, as Britain engaged in these years in a total of fifty-six years of warfare. And fully one-third of tax revenues in 1800 came from customs. As the *Edinburgh Review* remarked in 1835, "How great a degree of our prosperity and power depend on their [manufacturers'] continued improvement and extension." State bureaucrats and rulers understood that manufacturing was a way to produce revenue for the state, as the state itself now rested on the industrial world it had helped create.[44]

The first, lurching stages of this great acceleration, as seen at Quarry Bank Mill, might still have appeared modest. To modern eyes, the new technologies seem quaint, the factories small, and the impact of the cotton industry limited to a few regions in just one small part of the world, while much of the globe, even much of Great Britain, continued as before. The productive capacity of the first factories dotting the English countryside, looked at from a global perspective, was indeed minuscule. After all, Chinese spinners and weavers processed about 420 times as much cotton in 1750 as their counterparts in Britain in 1800, and the numbers for India were similar.[45] In 1800, two decades after Greg's midwifery to the Industrial Revolution, less than one-tenth of 1 percent of global cotton cloth production came from machines invented on the British Isles. Yet once the social and institutional scaffolding of industrial capitalism had been invented in a decades-long conflict between capitalists, aristocrats, the state, workers, and peasants, it could spread to other industries and other parts of the world. The territory for further transformations was huge.

The Industrial Revolution, powered by cotton, was, as historian Eric Hobsbawm has put it, "the most important event in world history." It created a world unlike any that had come before. "This land of long chimneys," as cotton manufacturer Thomas Ashton called it in 1837, was not just different from the centuries-old world of the British countryside, it was also a vast leap from the world of war capitalism that merchants, planters, and state officials had forged over the previous two hundred years. Its spectacle attracted visitors from all over the world, simultaneously awed and horrified by the sheer scale of it all: the endless chimneys, the chaotic cities, the spectacular social transformations. An 1808 English visitor saw in Manchester a town that was "abominably filthy, the Steam Engine is pestiferous, the Dyehouses noisesome and offensive, and the water of the river as black as ink." Alexis de Tocqueville made that same pilgrimage in 1835 and saw a "sort of black smoke [that] covers the city. The sun seen through it is a disk without rays. Under this half daylight 300,000 human beings are ceaselessly at work. A thousand noises disturb this damp, dark labyrinth, but they are not at all the ordinary sounds one hears in great cities." However, Tocqueville added, it was "from this foul drain [that] the greatest stream of human industry flows out to fertilise the whole world. From this filthy sewer pure gold flows. Here humanity attains its most complete development and its most brutish; here civilisation works its miracles, and civilised man is turned back almost into a savage." Observers from the still pastoral United States were terrified by this new Old World; Thomas Jefferson wished that his compatriots would "never . . . twirl a distaff . . . let our workshops remain in Europe."[46]

Within Britain, and within two decades, cotton's evolution was vast. It began as one of the many spoils of imperial expansion, and became the driving commodity behind the Industrial Revolution. From tufted white bolls emerged a new global system: industrial capitalism. There was of course inventiveness and innovation in other industries, but cotton was the only one with a global scope, a strong connection to coercive labor, and a unique level of the state's imperial attention to capture the necessary markets across the world.

Although industrial capitalism would eventually dominate the world, in the immediate aftermath of its birth it helped to expand and sharpen war capitalism elsewhere. That was because England's lopsided lead in the exploitation of industrial capitalism rested in the ability of its merchants to secure ever more inexpensive and predictable supplies of cotton for its factories.[47] And while British cotton manufacturers quite suddenly demanded huge new quantities of cotton, the institutional structures of industrial capitalism were still too immature and provincial to generate the labor and territory needed to produce all this cotton. For a terrible ninety years, from about 1770 to 1860, as we will see, industrial capitalism reinvigorated rather than replaced war capitalism.

In 1858, the president of the Galveston, Houston, and Henderson Railroad Company, Richard B. Kimball, visited Manchester. His observations are startling in their prescience: "As I entered your city, a sort of hum, a prolonged, continuous vibration struck my ear, as if some irresistible and mysterious force was at work. Need I say it was the noise of your spindles and your looms, and of the machinery which drives them? . . . And I said to myself, what connection shall there be between Power in Manchester and Nature in America? What connection shall there be between the cotton fields of Texas, and the Factory, and loom, and spindle of Manchester?"[48] The connection that he felt, but could not name, was the vital cord, still attached, between war capitalism and industrial capitalism.

Chapter Four

Capturing Labor, Conquering Land

Capturing land: Christopher Columbus
arriving on Hispaniola, 1492

*We are far remote from the period when men lived, and died, like
plants, in the spot where destiny had produced them. . . . But of all
the travels originating in curiosity, ambition, or the love of lucre,
not one can be compared in the importance of its results, its extent,
or the influence which it had exerted, to the mere transport of the
produce of a weak shrub,—to the travels which industry has imposed
upon the wool of a cotton-tree, the metamorphoses of which are as
innumerable as our wants and desires.*[1]

—Asiatic Journal, 1826

In 1857, the British economist John T. Danson published his attempt to disentangle the history of the modern cotton textile industry. On the mystery of the "connection between American Slavery and the British Cotton Manufacture," he noted that "there is not, and never has been, any considerable source of supply for cotton, excepting the East-Indies, which is not obviously and exclusively maintained by slave-labour." Efforts to cultivate cotton with free labor had largely failed, he observed, lending support to his conclusion that "as far as yet appears, [cotton] must continue to be grown, chiefly by slave-labour." So ironclad, argued Danson, was the connection between slave labor in the United States and a prospering European cotton industry that "I cannot but deem it superfluous to say one word" about "modifying the existing system."[2]

At first glance, Danson seemed correct. The year his essay was published, a full 68 percent of all cotton arriving in the United Kingdom came from the United States, and slaves grew most of it. Yet the reality that seemed so self-evident to Danson and others was only a recent invention. Indeed, in the five thousand years of the history of the world's cotton industry, slavery had never played an important role. And it was not just slavery that was new. The emerging cotton complex centered in Europe was also unique because it did not draw on the production of nearby peasants for its raw materials. As late as 1791, most of the cotton grown for manufacturing purposes around the world was produced by small farmers in Asia, Africa, and Latin America and consumed locally.[3] When cotton manufacturing exploded in Great Britain, it was unclear where enough cotton would come from to feed its hungry factories. Yet despite these challenges, never before had an industry grown so large so fast. Indeed, it grew as large as it did, as fast as it did, not despite but because of its peculiar spatial arrangements and its ability to draw on slave labor.

In the crucible of the late-eighteenth-century cotton revolution, cotton built its last, but most decisive, link to the newly global, dynamic, and violent form of capitalism, whose signal feature was the coercive expropriation of land and labor. Necessitated by the yawning gap between the imperatives of mechanized manufacturing and the capacities of premodern agriculture, at its core was slavery.[4] Rapidly expanding factories consumed cotton so fast that only the exigencies of war capitalism could secure the necessary reallocation of land and labor. As a result, indigenous people and land-grabbing settlers, slaves and planters, local artisans and factory owners woke to a new century clouded by a constant, if one-sided, state of war. As Danson had understood so well, it was coercion that opened fresh lands and mobilized new labor, becoming the essential ingredient of the emerging empire of cotton—and thus an essential ingredient in forging industrial capitalism. Yet by projecting the world he lived in both backward and forward, Danson missed both the novelty of slavery's essential role and the possibility that it could come to an end.

For millennia, as we have seen, cultivators had grown cotton in Asia, Africa, and the Americas. But while the cotton plant found a favorable environment in large stretches of the world's arable lands, Lancashire, or anywhere else in the British Isles for that matter, was not among them. Outside of the greenhouses at the Royal Gardens at Kew (which to this day showcase the core commodities on which the British Empire rested), Britain and much of Europe was too cold and wet for cotton. Among European leaders, only French revolutionaries, with their fervent belief in inventing the world anew, seriously tried to outwit the local climate and grow cotton—and even they failed.[5]

Indeed, British cotton manufacturing—and later, manufacturing across Europe—seemed a poor bet, for it was the first major industry in human history that lacked locally procured raw materials. In the United Kingdom, woolen and linen manufacturers had relied on Scottish sheep and English flax, the iron industry had used Sheffield iron ore, and the pottery manufacturers had worked up clay found in Staffordshire. Cotton spinning and weaving was different, with British manufacturers entirely dependent upon imports. To flourish, they required not just Asian technologies and African markets, but also raw material from yet another continent. Managing to acquire these materials meant building the first globally integrated manufacturing industry.

Yet in 1780, even as mechanical innovations occurred at a remarkable pace, a key piece of this global integration—the actual supply of cotton—remained undiscovered. The solution that emerged—slaves in the southern United States growing cotton on land expropriated from Native Americans—was far from obvious from the perspective of British cotton manufacturers and merchants. After all, in 1780 no cotton whatsoever arrived from North America. Instead, manufacturers drew on a far-flung network of small-scale suppliers to feed their mills. In the ports of London and Liverpool, bags of the "white gold" arrived from Izmir and Thessaloniki in the Ottoman Empire, from Port-au-Prince and Port

Royal in the Caribbean, from Bombay in India and the Gold Coast in Africa. Raw cotton had traveled comparable routes for many centuries, within Asia, Africa, and the Americas, as well as between Asia and Europe. Syrian cotton had been spun and woven in Egypt, Maharashtra cotton in Bengal, Hainan cotton in Jiangnan, Anatolian cotton in Lucerne, Yucatecan cotton in Teotihuacán, and Macedonian cotton in Venice.[6]

By 1780, the surging production speeds of spinning machines in British factories increasingly strained this traditional nexus. British manufacturers spun about 5.1 million pounds of cotton in 1781, only about two and a half times as much as they had spun eighty-four years earlier. But a mere nine years later in 1790, that figure had multiplied six times. By 1800, the quantity had nearly doubled again to 56 million pounds. In France, growth was slower but nonetheless remarkable: In 1789, 4.3 times more cotton was consumed than in 1750, 11 million pounds. Rapidly falling yarn prices created ever larger groups of consumers, especially in Europe, where cotton, once a luxury product only accessible to the rich, could now be consumed by the many, and in Africa, where it would replace the products of Indian spinners. The increased consumption of raw cotton, as Leeds writer Edward Baines noted in 1835, "has been rapid and steady far beyond all precedents in any other manufacture."[7]

As demand for raw cotton rose, so too did prices. In 1781, prices for cotton in Britain were between two and three times higher than they had been a decade earlier. Manchester manufacturers were "quite convinced that unless some new source of supply could be found the progress of the rising industry would be checked, if not altogether arrested." As a result, "From the 1780s they formed a powerful and influential pressure group in their efforts to acquaint the planters and the British government with their requirements."[8]

This sudden and unprecedented demand for cotton, and the lucrative prices paid for it, according to a contemporary expert, "occasioned a most extraordinary Increase of Culture in every Part, wherever the Climate and Soil could produce it; and, on this Account, every Sinew in the commercial World was strained to supply our Wants." Ottoman growers, who for the past two hundred years had been a major source of raw cotton for Europe, could not satisfy this exploding demand. Indeed, throughout the 1780s, exports from Thessaloniki and Izmir remained nearly level. A severe labor shortage and the tenacity of feudal relations in the Ottoman countryside limited the supply from Anatolia and Macedonia. The labor shortage was such that beginning in the 1770s landowners in western Anatolia brought in thousands of Greek laborers to grow cotton—an expansion that still did not provide the scale necessary for the supply of European industry. The largely precapitalist dependencies that structured the world of rural cultivators, the efforts of peasants to secure their subsistence, the lack of transportation infrastructure, and the continued political independence of the Ottoman state contributed to Europeans' inability to press for the monocultural production of cotton. A rapid reallocation of land and labor for cotton planting proved impossible. Local elites, moreover, remained a powerful counterweight against the increasingly influential presence of Western merchants in port cities such as Izmir and Thessaloniki, hampering the ability of Western capitalists to reform the social structure in the countryside to produce more cotton for world markets. Western merchants were also competing for what cotton there was with domestic spinners, a sizable and relatively prosperous artisan class. As a result, Ottoman cotton soon became marginal to European markets: while between 1786 and 1790 the Ottoman Empire supplied 20 percent of cotton imports to Great Britain, twenty years later it supplied only 1.28 percent and another ten years later a minuscule 0.29 percent. Unable or unwilling to revolutionize their countryside and trade networks, Ottoman cotton farmers and merchants exited the emerging European industrial system.[9]

With this traditional source of cotton production insufficient to meet demand, manufacturers desperately looked elsewhere. Cotton merchant William Rathbone and cotton spinner Richard Arkwright, for example, embarked upon a failed effort to increase the cotton supply from Africa by creating the Sierra Leone Company. Manufacturers also cast an acquisitive eye toward India's bountiful cotton harvests. Given that the East India Company enjoyed significant power on the subcontinent and that India was the ancient home of the world's cotton industry, many expected it to become a major source of fiber. The company, however, reacted warily to Manchester's appeals. The export of raw cotton, they argued, would undermine manufacturing in India and therefore its own profitable export business of cotton cloth. "If the Manufactures of Bengal were to suffer any material Check," warned the East India Company in 1793, "and become considerable decreased, the Revenue of that Country would fall off, and its Population decline beyond the Power of Prevention; for it is not to be expected that even any considerable Encrease in the

Cultivation of raw Materials could become an equivalent for a material Reduction in the Extent and Encouragement of Manufactures."[10] Moreover, such production for export would make peasants unduly dependent on purchasing food grains on the market, "which in an Indifferent Seasin might bring in a scarcity of Grain, nay even a famine, which would bring desolation on the Country, and an annihilation of Revenue."[11] Whatever cotton there was available for export the East India Company shipped to China to finance its purchases of tea, replacing the need to export bullion there. The resistance of the East India Company compounded other difficulties: infrastructure that made moving cotton to the coast often prohibitively expensive, the quality of Indian cotton, especially its short fiber, and a lack of labor in the vast interior of the South Asian subcontinent. In short, Indian cotton exports to Britain proved insufficient to satisfy the growing demand.[12]

More promising than in India, Africa, or Anatolia, it seemed, was the situation in the West Indies and South America. The exploding demand for cotton was no secret to the region's white planters, who had grown small quantities of the fiber since the 1630s. As demand for cotton increased, West Indian and South American merchants increasingly added cotton shipments to their regular trade in sugar and other tropical commodities. They also integrated it with their trade in slaves, as in the case of Liverpool's Tarleton Brothers, whose trade in cotton was at first just a sideline to their trade in human beings.

With fortunes to be made, European merchants in the Caribbean tried to secure more of the white gold. They drew on Caribbean planters who, unlike growers in Africa, Anatolia, and India, had nearly two centuries of experience growing crops for European consumers, most importantly sugar. The planters also controlled two key elements: land suitable for cotton growing and long-standing experience in mobilizing labor to produce for world markets. In the boom years of the 1770s through the 1790s, cotton was especially attractive to two up-and-coming groups of planters. The first consisted of small growers who lacked the capital necessary to start a sugar plantation and wanted a crop that would let them work more marginal lands, with fewer slaves and less investment, and still make fabulous profits. On Saint-Croix, for example, the average cotton plantation drew on the labor of less than a fifth as many slaves as the average sugar plantation. The second group consisted of planters in newly settled territories who planted cotton as a first crop for a few seasons to break the soil and would then use the cotton profits to move into sugar.[13]

Collectively, hundreds of these planters opened up a new "commodity frontier"—a new cotton-producing territory—and with it they began a new chapter in the global history of cotton. As a result of their decisions and the efforts of their slaves, cotton exports from the Caribbean exploded. Between 1781 and 1791, cotton imports quadrupled from the British-controlled islands alone. French planters followed suit, doubling exports of what French manufacturers called "coton des Isles" from Saint-Domingue, the Caribbean's most important cotton island, to France between 1781 and 1791.[14] So rapid was the growth of Caribbean cotton that by 1800 Bahamian planter Nathan Hall reported in awe that the cotton "trade has increased amazingly."[15]

Caribbean cotton came from various sites. Those islands that had been at the forefront of cotton production earlier in the century—Jamaica, Grenada, and Dominica, for example—continued to produce cotton, but their exports remained nearly constant at around two million pounds during the 1770s, and then approximately doubled during the course of the 1780s. The increase in production was (relatively) modest because cotton had found a stable place in the local economy and because sugar cultivation, which required a significant financial investment, was hardly ever given up for cotton.

But on islands with more uncultivated land and fewer sugar plantations, production boomed. On Barbados between 1768 and 1789, cotton exports increased by a factor of eleven, from 240,000 pounds to 2.6 million pounds. First, an ant invasion had decimated Barbados's traditional crop, sugar. Then in 1780 a massive hurricane destroyed much of the island's sugar infrastructure, which could not easily be rebuilt because of limited access to raw materials from revolution-torn North America. Transformed essentially into a huge cotton plantation, Barbados became the most productive cotton island within the British Empire. Similarly, Tobago planters had exported no cotton in 1770 but shipped a full 1.5 million pounds in 1780. And planters in the Bahamas, who had grown virtually no cotton before the 1770s, by 1787 sold nearly half a million pounds to British merchants.[16]

Significant amounts of cotton also found their way to Britain from

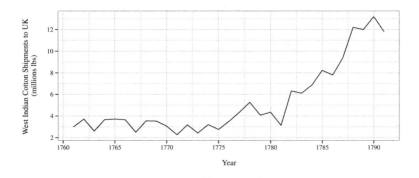

The Caribbean cotton revolution: West Indian cotton shipments to the United Kingdom, 1750–1795, in million of pounds

the French Caribbean islands. There, British merchants profited both from the slower growth of the French cotton industry and the abundant imports of slaves to Saint-Domingue above all. In 1770, for example, the French islands produced an estimated 56 percent of the total Caribbean cotton crop, compared to 35 percent for the British. Saint-Domingue alone shipped 36 percent, or more than all the British islands taken together. Twenty years later the imbalance continued. Of the 14 million pounds of cotton that the French islands produced in 1789, only about 6 million pounds were consumed in France itself, while an estimated 5.7 million pounds were exported from French mainland ports to Great Britain.[17]

As the dependence on cotton produced on the French-controlled islands grew among Europe's cotton manufacturers, Saint-Domingue in particular took on a central role. In 1791, the island, which counted nearly as many cotton as sugar plantations, exported 6.8 million pounds of cotton to France, 58 percent more than eight years earlier, and substantial amounts to Britain. This rapid expansion of cotton production was fueled by the importation of a quarter million African slaves between 1784 and 1791. At the height of the cotton boom, in the 1780s, as cotton prices in France increased by 113 percent over 1770 levels, nearly thirty thousand slaves were shipped to Saint-Domingue annually. That elasticity of the labor supply, a hallmark of war capitalism, was unmatched by any other region of the world. Indeed, as mechanized spinning spread on the European continent, ever more Africans were put in shackles, forced into the holds of ships, sold on the auction block in Port-au-Prince, transported to remote farms, and then forced to clear the land and hoe, sow, prune, and harvest the white gold.[18]

Slavery, in other words, was as essential to the new empire of cotton as proper climate and good soil. It was slavery that allowed these planters to respond rapidly to rising prices and expanding markets. Slavery allowed not only for the mobilization of very large numbers of workers on very short notice, but also for a regime of violent supervision and virtually ceaseless exploitation that matched the needs of a crop that was, in the cold language of economists, "effort intensive."[19] Tellingly, many of the slaves who were doing the backbreaking labor to grow cotton had been and were still being sold for cotton cloth that the European East India companies shipped from various parts of India to western Africa.

Encouraged by their home governments, rising prices, the availability of labor, and, within bounds, land, Caribbean planters became the cutting edge of the cotton revolution. From that moment on, ever newer cotton frontiers replaced one another, motivated by the unrelenting search for land and labor, as well as soils that had yet to escape the ecological exhaustion that so often came with cotton growing. The world's cotton industry relied upon "ceaseless spatial expansion."[20]

Caribbean planters had lengthy experience growing cotton—but so had Ottoman and Indian farmers. The soil and climate of the Caribbean was well suited to cotton—but so was the soil of western Anatolia or central India. Caribbean merchants moved large quantities of cotton easily to European markets—but so did the merchants of Izmir and Surat. Yet Caribbean planters, unlike Ottoman and Indian farmers, faced few constraints on land and labor. With the native population decimated and slaves arriving on an almost daily basis from West Africa, Caribbean planters' ability to respond rapidly to newly emerging markets set them decisively apart from all other cotton growers. While powerful Ottoman and Indian landlords also resorted to coercion to force peasants to work on their cotton estates, plantation slavery, as such, never took root.[21] Moreover, the infusion of capital that enabled the rapid reallocation of resources in the Caribbean was hampered elsewhere by the lack of private ownership of land and the continued political strength of the Ottoman and Indian rulers. Fresh land and new labor, capitalized by virtually unrestrained European merchants, bankers, and planters, precipitated an explosion of cotton growing.

These factors were supplemented by the support, albeit mild, that planters received from their government. Already in 1768 the British Royal Society of the Arts had offered a gold medal "for the best Specimen of West-India cotton," which was claimed ten years later by Andrew Bennet of Tobago, who had spent years studying dozens if not hundreds of varieties of cotton. In 1780, the British government levied a tariff on cotton imported on foreign boats, the "proceeds to be devoted to the encouragement of the growth of cotton in his Majesty's Leeward Islands, and for encouraging the import thereof into Great Britain." Later, the British Board of Trade asked a Polish botanist, Anton Pantaleon Hove, to collect cottonseeds in India and forward them to the Caribbean. And in 1786, Lord Sydney, secretary of state for the colonies, pressured by manufacturers in Manchester, called upon the governors of the West Indian colonies to encourage planters to grow cotton. In response, the governor of Dominica, John Orde, went so far as to promise free land to individuals interested in planting cotton on the island. Such state support would have seemed inconsequential viewed from the vantage point of the late nineteenth century, yet it pointed to a future in which the state's involvement in the global securing of essential raw materials for industrial production would become a widespread concern.[22]

But the true importance of the Caribbean planters was not the cotton that was shipped, though that remained essential, but the institutional innovation that the Caribbean experiment produced: the re-creation of the countryside through bodily coercion, something only possible under war capitalism. Cotton grown by slaves motivated and financed the unprecedented incorporation of newly depopulated territories into the world economy. Slavery and land expropriation on a continental scale created the expansive, and elastic, global cotton supply network necessary for the Industrial Revolution, and with it the mechanisms through which the needs and rhythms of industrial life in Europe could be transferred to the global countryside. In the process, a new kind of slavery (what historians have called "second slavery") emerged that was tightly linked to the intensity and profits of industrial capitalism—a dynamic that soon drew the African continent into its grasp as well, where West African economies increasingly found their focus in supplying sharply rising numbers of workers to the Americas.

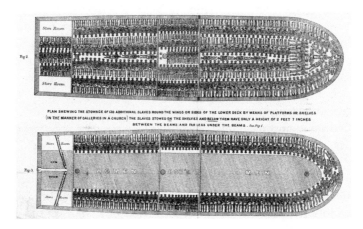

Capturing labor: the decks of a slave ship

Approximately half of all slaves (46 percent, to be precise) sold to the Americas between 1492 and 1888 arrived there in the years after 1780. Slavery's future was now firmly attached to the industrial capitalism that it had enabled.[23]

As the Caribbean cotton explosion shows, war capitalism—exactly because violence was its fundamental characteristic—was portable. Its next stop was South America. With cotton exports from the West Indies rapidly rising but demand spiraling even faster, South American farmers discovered the newly profitable cotton market. In Guyana, between 1789 and 1802 cotton production skyrocketed by a staggering 862 percent, fueled by the concurrent import of about twenty thousand slaves into Surinam and Demerara.[24]

Even more important was Brazil. The first Brazilian cotton arrived in England in 1781, supplementing Caribbean production but soon surpassing it. Cotton was indigenous to many parts of Brazil, and for centuries its planters had exported small quantities. As part of the process of economic modernization of its Brazilian colonies in the latter half of the eighteenth century, Portugal had encouraged the growing of cotton, especially in the northeastern regions of Pernambuco and Maranhão. When early efforts paid off, a surge in the importation of slaves caused one observer to opine that "white cotton turned Maranhão black." Though cotton would eventually become a "poor man's crop," its first explosive expansion in Brazil was fueled by larger slave plantations. As in the West Indies, cotton in Brazil would never challenge sugar and later coffee, but its share of total exports in Brazil grew to a respectable 11 percent in 1800, and 20 percent in the years between 1821 and 1830.[25]

Without any constraints on the availability of land, as in the West Indies, or on labor, as in Anatolia, the volume of Brazilian cotton expanded sharply. Between 1785 and 1792, Brazil overtook the Ottoman Empire in cotton shipments to England. By the end of that period, nearly 8 million pounds of Brazilian cotton had landed in Great Britain, compared to 4.5 million pounds from the Ottoman Empire and 12 million pounds from the West Indies. In Maranhão—then the most important cotton region of Brazil—exports doubled between 1770 and 1780, nearly doubled again by 1790, and nearly tripled once more by 1800. For a few years in the late 1700s, the period when neither West Indian nor Ottoman cotton production had expanded sufficiently and before North American cotton swamped markets, Brazil became a very important supplier to the booming British cotton textile industry. Not only did Brazilian farmers produce significant amounts of cotton, but they were also able to grow a particularly long-staple variety that was better suited to emerging factory technology.[26]

By the 1780s, slaves in the West Indies and South America produced the vast majority of cotton sold on world markets, and this explosive combination of slavery and conquest fueled the Industrial Revolution all the way to 1861. John Tarleton, a successful slave trader and Liverpool cotton merchant, understood that the slave trade, the export of commodities from plantation economies, and the well-being of the British shipping industry were all "mutually blended & connected together." And the combination was stupendously profitable: Cotton and slaves made many merchants rich, with Tarleton calculating, for example, that his "fortune" had tripled between 1770 and 1800.[27]

The risks and costs entailed in the development of its globe-spanning system of supply might have seemed an insurmountable brake on the cotton industry's development. Yet the cotton manufacturers' total dependence on a distant tropical commodity turned out to be their signal breakthrough. Indeed, their factories would likely never have expanded as rapidly without the counterintuitive gamble of relying entirely on faraway land and labor. Already by 1800, Britain alone consumed such fabulous amounts of cotton that 416,081 acres of land were needed to cultivate it. If that cotton had been grown in Britain, it would have taken up 3.7 percent of its arable land, and approximately 90,360 agricultural laborers would have been needed to work these hypothetical cotton fields. In 1860, with the appetite for cotton even greater, more than 1 million workers (or half of all British agricultural workers) would have had to work these fields, which would have taken up 6.3 million acres or 37 percent of all arable land in Great Britain. Alternatively, if we assume that the woolen industry, instead of the cotton industry, had been at the forefront of the Industrial Revolution even more land would have been needed to raise the required number of sheep: 9 million acres in 1815, and 23 million acres in 1830—or more than Britain's entire arable land area. Under both the hypothetical domestic cotton and the wool scenario, land and labor constraints would have made all but impossible the sudden expansion of cloth production. Perhaps even more decisively, such a scenario would have created unimaginable upheaval in the British and European countryside, whose social structure, like that of the Ottoman Empire and India, was not suited for such a massive and quick reallocation of land and labor. The elasticity of supply so essential to the Industrial Revolution thereby rested on reliable access to distant land and foreign labor. The ability of Europe's states and their capitalists to rearrange global economic connections and to violently expropriate land and labor were as important, if not more important, to the ascendency of the West as the traditional explanations of technical inventiveness, cultural proclivities, and the geographical and climatic location of a small group of cotton manufacturers in a remote part of the British Isles.[28]

West Indian and South American cotton thus poured into the markets of Liverpool, London, Le Havre, and Barcelona, in effect allowing for the rapid expansion of mechanized spinning. But there were limits to this expansion. As already mentioned, the West Indian islands themselves had a rather low supply of suitable cotton lands, limiting cotton production and putting it at a long-term disadvantage with sugar. Sugar plantations there as well as in land-rich Brazil also competed with cotton plantations for labor. As a result, beginning in 1790, exports of West Indian cotton declined absolutely: In 1803 only about half as much cotton left the West Indies as in 1790, and its market share in Britain was now reduced to 10 percent. Even preferential treatment at customs, which British-grown cotton was afforded after 1819, could not reverse the tide. By the early nineteenth century, the market share of West Indian cotton was in free fall, "accelerated by the emancipation of the negroes." In Brazil, the lack of a massive redeployment of slaves from sugar into cotton production acted as a brake on the expansion of cotton production. As cotton expert James A. Mann observed, "If Brazil could command the needful labour, there is no question but that she would become a large supplier of our wants."[29]

In 1791, revolution rocked the most important cotton island of all—Saint-Domingue—all but halting production of commodities for world markets, including cotton. In the largest slave revolt in history, Saint-Domingue's enslaved population armed themselves and defeated the French colonial regime, leading to the creation of the state of Haiti and the abolition of slavery on the island. War capitalism had its first major reversal at the hands of its seemingly least powerful actors: Saint-Domingue's hundreds of thousands of slaves. Saint-Domingue cotton production had equaled 24 percent of British cotton imports the year before the revolution, while four years later, in 1795, it was only 4.5 percent. As one British observer put it, "That Island, which has been the grand Source of Supply to us, of the Article of Cotton Wool, is, from these Causes, in a State of Anarchy, Distress, and almost Dissolution." Indeed, he predicted that it was unlikely that "the Soil of the Planters, fertilized by the Thirst and Blood of the Negroes, will always increase the Store of our Coffers, in order to add to the Excess of your Wealth, Extravagance and Voluptuousness." By 1795, cotton exports to France had fallen by 79 percent, and even ten years after the beginning of the revolution, exports had recovered to only one-third of their prerevolutionary level. The French National Assembly compounded British supply anxieties by disallowing the export of raw cotton from French ports. The *Pennsylvania Gazette* in 1792 reported matter-of-factly, "The cotton and indigo . . . must have been deeply injured in 1791, as they were in season during the part of that year when the disturbances were greatest."[30]

The combination of rapidly rising demand for cotton and political upheaval in the Caribbean led to worrisome price spikes for manufacturers dependent on capturing new markets for cotton textiles by competing with Indian production. Throughout 1791 and 1792 John Tarleton reported to his brother that "Cotton is rising daily." By 1795 he found "Cotton up amazingly." In 1790, prices for West Indian cotton peaked at 21 pence per pound, in 1791 at 30 pence, and prices stayed consistently high throughout the 1790s. So traumatic was the experience of revolution for some cotton merchants that as late as 1913 the Rathbone family, one of Liverpool's major cotton traders, remembered that the effect of the upheaval was a doubling of prices for cotton. Once war broke out between France and Britain in 1793, moreover, the import of French West Indian cottons into the British Caribbean ports came to an end.[31]

By the 1790s, therefore, it had become obvious to interested observers that the gap between the demand for and supply of raw cotton in Europe would grow rapidly and continuously for the foreseeable future. As the American writer Tench Coxe put it, "The peculiar fitness of the staple for the conversion into yarn, cloths, &c. by machinery . . . have hitherto made these demands, at home and abroad, very extensive, steady, and increasing."[32] Traditional techniques of procuring cotton had clearly been insufficient. In the West Indies and Brazil, however, building on the experiences of their sugar economies, a new way of producing cotton had been invented that focused clearly on plantations and slavery. And while the production growth in these parts of the world soon reached their limits, or, as in Haiti's case, was curtailed by revolution, there was a nearby region that seemed to meet all conditions for producing an abundant supply of cotton: the newly born United States of America. It was there that cotton production based on slavery would reach unprecedented heights.

Chapter Five

Slavery Takes Command

War capitalism at work: marrying slavery and industry in the *American Cotton Planter* (1853)

As British cotton manufacturing exploded in the 1780s, the pressures on the global countryside to supply the crucial cotton increased at a rapid clip. It was in the middle of that decade, in the winter of 1785, that an American ship sailed into Liverpool harbor. There was nothing remarkable about such a voyage; thousands of ships had brought the bounties of North America to the shores of Britain before, filled to the brim with tobacco, indigo, rice, furs, timber, and other commodities. This ship, however, was different: In its hold, among other goods, were a number of bags of cotton. Such freight seemed suspicious, and Liverpool customs officials immediately impounded the cotton, arguing that it had to be contraband West Indian produce. When the Liverpool merchants Peel, Yates & Co., who had imported the cotton, petitioned the Board of Trade in London a few days later to permit entry, they were told that it "cannot be imported from thence it not being the Produce of the American States."[1]

Indeed, to Europeans in the 1780s, cotton was the product of the

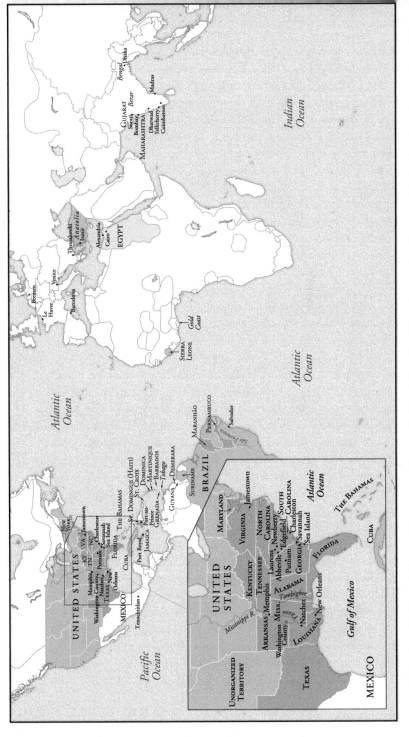

The Revolution of Slavery: European Cotton Industrialization Transforms the Countryside in the Americas, 1780–1865

West Indies, of Brazil, of the Ottoman Empire, and of India—but not of North America. It was all but unimaginable to Liverpool customs officials that cotton could be imported from the United States. That the United States would ever produce significant amounts of cotton seemed even more preposterous. Though cotton was indigenous to the southern parts of the new nation, and though many settlers in South Carolina and Georgia grew small amounts of the fiber for domestic use, it had never been planted primarily for commercial purposes nor exported in significant quantities. As the customs officials undoubtedly knew, American planters used their plentiful land and abundant slave labor to grow tobacco, rice, indigo, and some sugar, but not cotton.[2]

This was, of course, a spectacular misjudgment. The United States was superbly suited for cotton production. The climate and soil of a wide swath of the American South met the conditions under which the cotton plant thrived, with the right amount of rain, the right patterns of rainfall, and the right number of days without frost. Perceptive observers noticed that potential: In a bout of optimism, James Madison had predicted as early as 1786, only a year after the unexpected American cotton sailed into Liverpool harbor, that the United States would turn into a major cotton-growing country, while George Washington believed that "the increase of that new material (cotton) . . . must be of almost infinite consequence to the prosperity of the United States." Philadelphian Tench Coxe, himself a substantial landowner in the South, made a more subtle but nonetheless powerful case for America's cotton-growing potential. In 1794, observing the rapid expansion of cotton manufacturers in Great Britain and rising prices of West Indian cotton in the wake of the uprising in Saint-Domingue, he urged that "this article must be worth the attention of the southern planters." He was encouraged by British industrialists such as Stockport cotton manufacturer John Milne, who embarked in the late 1780s on the long journey across the Atlantic to persuade North Americans to grow cotton.[3]

As predicted by these self-interested observers, cotton production would soon dominate vast swaths of the United States. Indeed, the crop would become so intrinsic to American enterprise that the earlier reality—the dominance of cotton from the Ottoman Empire, the West Indies, and Brazil—has largely been lost. It turned out that Peel, Yates & Co. had anticipated one of the nineteenth century's most consequential dynamics.[4]

. . .

The rapid expansion of cotton in the United States was partly possible because planters used the experience that their colonial ancestors had accumulated in the cultivation of the white gold. As early as 1607, settlers in Jamestown had grown cotton; by the end of the seventeenth century, travelers had introduced cottonseeds from Cyprus and Izmir to American soil. Throughout the eighteenth century, farmers continued to gather knowledge about cotton cultivation from the West Indies and the Mediterranean and planted cottonseeds from these regions, primarily for domestic consumption. During the upheavals of the American struggle for independence, planters grew larger quantities to substitute for the now absent imports of cloth from Britain, and to keep at work slaves whose usual crops—namely tobacco and rice—suddenly lacked a market. South Carolinian planter Ralph Izard, for example, eagerly gave orders in 1775 "for a considerable quantity of cotton to be planted for clothing my negroes."[5]

Quick expansion was made easier because substantial similarities existed between the growing of tobacco and cotton; knowledge accumulated in the cultivation of the former could be used to grow the latter. Moreover, some of the infrastructure that had facilitated the moving of tobacco to world markets could be rededicated to cotton. And during the revolutionary upheavals of the eighteenth century, planters and slaves moved back and forth between the West Indies and North America, bringing with them further knowledge about cotton planting. In 1788, for example, the owners of a slave from Saint Croix advertised him for sale in the United States as "well acquainted with the culture of cotton." The slave-cotton paradigm invented in the West Indies now spread to the North American mainland.[6]

In 1786, American planters also began to notice the rising prices for cotton engendered by the rapid expansion of mechanized cotton textile production in the United Kingdom. That year, planters grew the first long-staple Sea Island cotton, named after the location of their plantations on islands just off the coast of Georgia, with seeds they had brought from the Bahamas. Unlike the local cottons, this cotton had a long, silky fiber, which made it exceedingly well suited for finer yarns and cloths, much in demand by Manchester manufacturers. Though accounts vary, it is possible that a Frank Levett was the first to take this momentous step.

Levett, a native of the great cotton mart of Izmir, had left the rebelling American colonies for the Bahamas, but eventually returned to Georgia, retook possession of his land, and then began a major effort at cotton growing. Others followed his model and the planting of Sea Island cotton spread up and down the coast of South Carolina and Georgia. Exports from South Carolina, for example, ballooned from less than 10,000 pounds in 1790 to 6.4 million pounds in 1800.[7]

Production received a decisive boost in 1791 when rebellion eliminated cotton rival Saint-Domingue, Europe's most important source of cotton, sending prices upward and scattering the entire class of French cotton planters: Some went to Cuba and other islands; many came to the United States. Jean Montalet, for example, one of many of Saint-Domingue's former cotton planters, sought refuge on the mainland, and upon his arrival in South Carolina converted a rice plantation to the growing of cotton. Revolution thus in one stroke both brought needed growing expertise to the United States and increased the financial incentive for American planters to grow cotton. But the slaves' uprising on the plantations of Saint-Domingue also ingrained a sense among manufacturers, planters, and statesmen of the inherent instability of the system of cotton slavery and land expropriations that they were about to expand in North America.[8]

While Sea Island cotton production expanded rapidly, it soon reached its limit, as the variety failed at any substantial distance from the coast. Farther inland, a different strain of cotton thrived, so-called upland cotton, shorter in staple length, with the fiber tightly attached to its seed. It was difficult to remove the seeds with the help of existing gins, but with demand increasing and prices high, planters had their slaves work it up in a slow and tedious process by roller gins modeled after Indian *churkas*.[9]

Yet even with slave labor, the result was not adequate. Planters yearned for a device that would more quickly separate seed from fiber. In 1793, Eli Whitney, only a few months after arriving in Savannah from his college days at Yale, built the first working model of a new kind of cotton gin that was able to rapidly remove the seeds of upland cotton. Overnight, his machine increased ginning productivity by a factor of fifty. News of the innovation spread quickly; farmers everywhere built copies of the gin. Like the jenny and the water frame, Eli's gin overcame yet another bottleneck in the production of cotton textiles. As a result, in what can only be described as a "cotton rush," land on which cotton grew allegedly trebled in price after the invention of the gin, and "the annual income of those who plant it is double to what it was before the introduction of cotton."[10]

Armed with this new technology, cotton production spread rapidly after 1793 into the interior of South Carolina and Georgia. As a result, in 1795 significant amounts of U.S. cotton arrived in Liverpool for the first time; none, as best we know, was seized by customs. As settlers streamed into the region, many of them migrants from the upper South, the countryside was turned upside down—from a thinly inhabited region of native people and farmers who focused on subsistence crops and tobacco to one in the thrall of cotton.[11]

To enable such expanded production, planters brought with them thousands of slaves. In the 1790s, the slave population of the state of Georgia nearly doubled, to sixty thousand. In South Carolina, the number of slaves in the upcountry cotton growing districts grew from twenty-one thousand in 1790 to seventy thousand twenty years later, including fifteen thousand slaves newly brought from Africa. As cotton plantations spread, the proportion of slaves in four typical South Carolina upcountry counties increased from 18.4 percent in 1790 to 39.5 percent in 1820 and to 61.1 percent in 1860. All the way to the Civil War, cotton and slavery would expand in lockstep, as Great Britain and the United States had become the twin hubs of the emerging empire of cotton.[12]

The only substantial problem was the land, as the same patch could not be used for more than a few years without either planting legumes on it or applying expensive guano to it. As one Putnam County, Georgia, planter lamented, "We appear to have but one rule—that is, to make as much cotton as we can, and wear out as much land as we can . . . lands that once produced one thousand pounds of cotton to the acre, will not now bring more than four hundred pounds." Yet even soil exhaustion did not slow the cotton barons; they simply moved farther west and farther south. Newly emptied lands, portable slave labor, and the new ginning technology allowed cotton to be easily transferred to new territories. After 1815, cotton planters moved westward into the rich lands of upland South Carolina and Georgia. Their migration to Alabama and Louisiana, and eventually to Mississippi, Arkansas, and Texas, was choreographed to the movement of cotton prices. While the price of cotton gradually declined over the first half of the nineteenth century, sharp price upswings—such as in the first half of the 1810s, between 1832 and 1837, and again after the mid-1840s—produced expansionist bursts. In

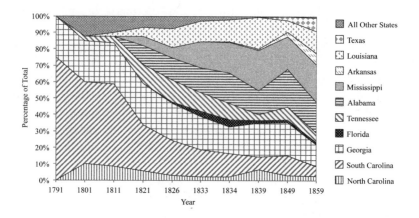

Moving westward: Production of cotton by U.S. states, 1790–1860

1811, one-sixteenth of all cotton grown in the United States came from states and territories west of South Carolina and Georgia, by 1820 that share had reached one-third, and in 1860 three-fourths. New cotton fields sprouted in the sediment-rich lands along the banks of the Mississippi, the upcountry of Alabama, and the black prairie of Arkansas. So rapid was this move westward that by the end of the 1830s, Mississippi already produced more cotton than any other southern state.[13]

The entry of the United States into the empire of cotton was so forceful that cotton cultivation in the American South quickly began to reshape the global cotton market. In 1790, three years before Whitney's invention, the United States had produced 1.5 million pounds of cotton; in 1800 that number grew to 36.5 million pounds, and in 1820 to 167.5 million pounds. Exports to Great Britain increased by a factor of ninety-three between 1791 and 1800, only to multiply another seven times by 1820. By 1802 the United States was already the single most important supplier of cotton to the British market, and by 1857 it would produce about as much cotton as China. American upland cotton, which Whitney's gin worked up so efficiently, was exceedingly well suited to the requirements of British manufacturers: While the gin damaged the fiber, the cotton remained suitable for the production of cheaper, coarser yarns and fabrics in high demand among the lower classes in Europe and elsewhere. But for American supplies, the miracle of the mass production of yarn and cloth, and the ability of new consumers to buy these cheap goods, would have foundered on old realities of the traditional cotton market. The much-vaunted consumer revolution in textiles stemmed from a dramatic transformation in the structure of plantation slavery.[14]

The rise of the United States to dominance in world cotton markets was a radical reversal of fortunes. But why did it happen? As Tench Coxe pointed out in 1817, climate and soil alone did not explain the cotton-producing potential of the United States, because, as he put it, the white gold "can be cultivated in an immense district of the productive zones of the earth."[15] What distinguished the United States from virtually every other cotton-growing area in the world was planters' command of nearly unlimited supplies of land, labor, and capital, and their unparalleled political power. In the Ottoman Empire and India, as we know, powerful indigenous rulers controlled the land, and deeply entrenched social groups struggled over its use. In the West Indies and Brazil, sugar planters competed for land, labor, and power. The United States, and its plentiful land, faced no such encumbrances.

Ever since the first European settlers stepped off their boats, they had pushed inland. The land's native inhabitants had to reckon with what these boats brought—first germs, later steel. In the late eighteenth century, Native Americans still controlled substantial territories only a few hundred miles inland from the coastal provinces, yet they were unable to stop the white settlers' steady encroachment. The settlers eventually won a bloody and centuries-long war, succeeding in turning the land of Native Americans into land that was legally "empty." This was a land whose social structures had been catastrophically weakened or eliminated, a land without most of its people and thus without the entanglements of history. In terms of unencumbered land, the South had no rival in the cotton-growing world.

With the support of southern politicians, the federal government aggressively secured new territories by acquiring land from foreign powers and from forced cessions by Native Americans. In 1803, the Louisiana Purchase nearly doubled the territory of the United States, in 1819 the United States acquired Florida from Spain, and in 1845 it annexed Texas. All of these acquisitions contained lands superbly suited to cotton agriculture. Indeed, by 1850, 67 percent of U.S. cotton grew on land that had

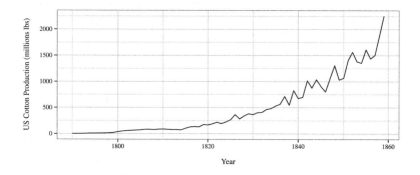

Cotton production in the United States, in millions of pounds, 1790–1859

not been part of the United States half a century earlier. The fledging U.S. government had inaugurated the military-cotton complex.

That territorial expansion, the "great land rush" as geographer John C. Weaver has called this moment more broadly, was tightly linked to the territorial ambitions of planting, manufacturing, and finance capitalists. Cotton planters constantly pushed the boundaries, seeking fresh lands to grow cotton, often moving ahead of the federal government. The frontier space they created was characterized by the near absence of government oversight: The state's monopoly on violence was still a distant dream.[16] But these frontier planters at the rough edges of the empire of cotton had well-dressed and well-spoken company. British banker Thomas Baring, one of the world's greatest cotton merchants, for example, was instrumental in the expansion of the empire of cotton when he financed the purchase of the Louisiana lands, negotiating and selling the bonds that sealed the deal with the French government. Before doing so, Baring asked for approval from the British government for such a vast expansion of the United States, through Henry Addington, the British prime minister. So important was the meeting to Baring that he scribbled in small letters in his notepad:

Sunday, June 19: saw Mr. Addington at Richmond Park, communicated to him the particulars of the business, & answered every question. I asked distinctly if he approved the treaty & our conduct. He said that he thought it would have been wise for this country to pay a million sterling for the transfer of Louisiana from France to America, & that he saw nothing in our conduct but to approve. He appears to consider Louisiana in the hands of America as an additional means for the vent of our manufacturers & Co. in preference to France, besides other motives which we did not discuss, directly of a political nature.[17]

The thrust south and west was far more than just planters searching for fresh land. Expansion served many interests: of a rapidly consolidating state, of western farmers hoping for an outlet to the sea, of manufacturers' need for raw materials, and of British economic and political desires. As industrial capitalism expanded, the zone of war capitalism continued to push outward.

But international treaties alone were not sufficient. To make the land useful to planters, this newly consolidated territory needed to be removed from the control of its native inhabitants. Already in the early 1800s, the Creeks, under duress, had given up claims to land in Georgia that was then converted into cotton farms. A decade later the Creeks suffered further defeats and were forced to sign the Treaty of Fort Jackson, ceding 23 million acres of land in what is today Alabama and Georgia. In the years after 1814, the federal government signed further treaties with the Creeks, Chickasaw, and Choctaws, gaining control over millions of acres of land in the South, including Andrew Jackson's 1818 treaty with the Chickasaw nation that opened western Tennessee to cotton cultivation and the 1819 treaty with the Choctaw nation that gave 5 million acres of land in the Yazoo-Mississippi Delta to the United States in exchange for vastly inferior lands in Oklahoma and Arkansas. Alabama congressman David Hubbard invited the New York and Mississippi Land Company in 1835 to purchase lands from which the Chickasaw had been expelled, which were then turned into cotton lands: "If on my return I should meet with any thing from you in the shape of a distinct proposition to take hold of the public lands in the Chickasaw Nation, I shall then be ready to act immediately, according to the magnitude of your scheme & shall shape my course so as to meet fully the views of your capitalists in my future operation." The company bought approximately twenty-five thousand acres. In 1838, federal troops began removing the Cherokee nation from their ancestral homeland in Georgia, which was to be turned into cotton plantations. Farther south, in Florida, extraordinarily rich cotton lands were expropriated from the Seminoles between 1835 and 1842, the longest war in U.S. history until the Vietnam War. It is no wonder that Mississippi planters, argues one historian, had "an obsessive concern with well-organized and trained militias, adequate weaponry, and a responsive federal army."[18]

Native Americans understood the underlying foundations of the expanding military-cotton complex: Upon removal in 1836, the chief of the Cherokees, John Ross, in a letter to Congress decried that "our property may be plundered before our eyes; violence may be committed on our persons; even our lives may be taken away, and there is none to regard our complaints. We are denationalized; we are disenfranchised. We are deprived of membership in the human family!" The coercion and violence required to mobilize slave labor was matched only by the demands of an expansionist war against indigenous people. Nothing of this kind had even been dreamed of in Anatolia or Gujarat.[19]

If the project of continental consolidation provided access to new cotton lands, it also secured major rivers needed to carry the cotton. America's remarkably cheap transportation costs were not preordained, but the direct result of the expansion of its national territory. Most significant here was the Mississippi, whose surge of cotton freight turned New Orleans, at the river's mouth, into the key American cotton port. But other rivers—the Red River in Louisiana and the Tombigbee and Mobile in Alabama—mattered as well. The first steamboats appeared on the Mississippi in 1817, reducing transport costs, and by the 1830s, railroads connected the new hinterland to river and seaports. The most modern technologies thus made the most brutal exploitation of human labor possible.[20]

The insatiable demand of cotton planters dominated the politics of the new nation, not just because of their reliance on the state to secure and empty new land, but also because of their need for coerced labor. Planters in the United States, unlike elsewhere, enjoyed access to large supplies of cheap labor—what the *American Cotton Planter* would call "the cheapest and most available labor in the world." Cotton, until the advent of mechanized harvesting during the 1940s, was a labor-intensive crop. Even more than the hours required to spin and weave, the shortage of workers to harvest was the most constraining factor in its production. "The true limitation upon the production of cotton," argued the southern journal *De Bow's Review*, "is labor." In the complex agricultural structures of Mughal India and the Ottoman Empire, rural cultivators had to first secure subsistence crops for their own use, thus limiting what they harvested for the market. Indeed, as we have seen, the shortage of labor had been one of the principal constraints on production in western Anatolia and had frustrated efforts to create cotton plantations in India. In Brazil, where slave labor was available, cotton competed poorly with the even greater labor requirements of sugar plantations. And with the British abolition of the slave trade in 1807 it became difficult for West Indian planters to recruit labor.[21]

In the United States, however, nearly any shortage could be fixed, with the right amount of money. The slave markets in New Orleans and elsewhere boomed as cotton did. And as significant, hundreds of thousands of slaves were available to grow cotton because tobacco production in the states of the upper South became less profitable after the American Revolution, encouraging slave owners there to sell their human property. As one British observer remarked perceptively in 1811, "The cultivation of tobacco in Virginia and Maryland, has been less of late an object of attention; and the gangs of negroes formerly engaged in it, have been sent into the southern states, where the American cotton planter, thus reinforced, is enabled to commence his operations with increasing vigour." Indeed, by 1830 fully 1 million people (or one in thirteen Americans) grew cotton in the United States—most of them slaves.[22]

The expansion of cotton production, as a result, reinvigorated slavery and led to an enormous shift of slave labor from the upper to the lower South. In the thirty years after the invention of the gin alone (between 1790 and 1820), a quarter million slaves were forcefully relocated, while between 1783 and the closing of the international slave trade in 1808, traders imported an estimated 170,000 slaves into the United States—or one-third of all slaves imported into North America since 1619. Altogether, the internal slave trade moved up to a million slaves forcefully to the Deep South, most to grow cotton.[23]

To be sure, not all cotton in the United States was grown by slaves on large plantations. Small farmers in the southern upcountry produced cotton as well, and they did so because it provided ready cash and its cultivation, unlike the growing of sugar or rice, did not require significant capital investments. Yet despite their efforts, in aggregate they produced only a small share of the total crop. As we have seen the world over, small farmers focused on securing subsistence crops before growing marketable commodities. Indeed, 85 percent of all cotton picked in the South in 1860 was grown on units larger than a hundred acres; the planters who owned those farms owned 91.2 percent of all slaves. The larger the farm, the better the planter was able to take advantage of the economies of scale inherent in slave-based cotton production. Larger farms could afford the gins to remove seeds and presses to compress loose cotton into tightly pressed bales to lower shipping costs, they could engage in agricultural experiments to wrest more nutrients from cleared soil, and they could buy more slaves to avoid any labor constraints.[24] Cotton demanded quite literally a hunt for labor and a perpetual struggle for its control. Slave traders, slave pens, slave auctions, and the attendant physical and psychological violence of holding millions in bondage were of central importance to the expansion of cotton production in the United States and of the Industrial Revolution in Great Britain.

Better than anyone else, slaves understood the violent foundation of cotton's success. If given an opportunity, they testified in vivid detail to its brutality. John Brown, a fugitive slave, remembered in 1854 how he was "flogged . . . with the cow-hide," and how overseers "hunt[ed] 'stray niggers.' " "When the price [of cotton] rises in the English market," he remembered, "the poor slaves immediately feel the effects, for they are harder driven, and the whip is kept more constantly going." Henry Bibb, another slave, remembered the fearful violence: "At the sound of the overseer's horn, all the slaves came forward and witnessed my punishment. My clothing was stripped off and I was compelled to lie down on the ground with my face to the earth. Four stakes were driven in the ground, to which my hands and feet were tied. Then the overseer stood over me with the lash."[25]

The expansion of cotton manufacturing in Great Britain depended on violence across the Atlantic. Cotton, emptied lands, and slavery indeed became so closely connected to one another that Liverpool cotton merchant William Rathbone VI, on a trip to the United States in 1849, reported to his father that "negroes & everything here fluctuates with Cotton." So crucial was slave labor that the *Liverpool Chronicle and European Times* warned that if slaves ever should be emancipated, cotton cloth prices might double or triple, with devastating consequences for Britain. While brutal coercion weighed like a nightmare upon millions of American slaves, the potential end of such violence was a nightmare to those who gathered the fabulous profits of the empire of cotton.[26]

Slaves picking cotton in a Georgia field

To make such a nightmare less likely, planters in the United States also drew on the third advantage that turned them into the world's leading cotton growers: political power. Southern slaveholders had enshrined the basis of their power into the Constitution with its three-fifths clause. A whole series of slaveholding presidents, Supreme Court judges, and strong representation in both houses of Congress guaranteed seemingly never-ending political support for the institution of slavery. Such power on the national level was enabled and also supplemented by the absence of competing elites in the slaveholding states themselves, and the enormous power slaveholders enjoyed over state governments. These state governments, in the end, also allowed North American cotton planters to amplify their good fortune of navigable rivers near their plantations by building railroads deeper and deeper into the hinterland. In contrast, Brazilian cotton farmers, competing with the interests of the country's powerful sugar growers, were unable to command infrastructure improvements to facilitate cotton exports. Transporting cotton over long distances on mules or horses remained expensive; transporting cotton from the São Francisco River region to the port of Salvador, for example, almost doubled the price of cotton. In India, transportation infrastructure remained similarly poor (it was said that transporting cotton to the port added about 50 percent to its cost in India, but as little as 3 percent in the United States), as cotton merchants and growers in India lacked the capital and power to effect its rapid improvement. The political influence of slaveholders in the American Republic was also decisive because it allowed them to expand the institution of slavery into the newly acquired territories of the South and Southwest, while successfully committing the federal government to a policy of expropriating Native Americans.[27]

In a roundabout way, American independence had turned out to be a blessing for the European, especially the British, cotton industry. Bowing to a century of abolitionist persuasion, Britain in 1834 outlawed slavery within its empire. Some American revolutionaries envisioned a similar extinction of slavery as their own nation evolved, only to see the institution become the engine of the most important cotton-growing region of the world. And independence removed restraints from expropriating Native Americans as well, with the relationship between white settlers and North American Indians now removed from the complex negotiations of European politics. The disjunction of political from economic spaces in fact proved to be crucial for the world's most dynamic industry—with cotton-growing slave owners dominating regional gov-

A cotton carrier, Brazil, 1816

ernments and exerting significant influence on the national government, their interests and the policies of the state could be aligned to a stunning degree, an impossibility for slaveholders within the British Empire.

How these factors came together can be seen, for example, in the Yazoo-Mississippi Delta. Here, in an area of approximately seven thousand square miles, the mighty Mississippi had unloaded its rich sediments for millennia, becoming the seedbed of the world's most productive cotton land. In 1859, as many as sixty thousand Delta slaves produced a staggering 66 million pounds of cotton, nearly ten times as much as was exported from Saint-Domingue to France during the height of its production in the early 1790s.[28]

For the Delta to become the chief grower of the industrial world's most important commodity—a kind of Saudi Arabia of the early nineteenth century—its land had to be taken from its original inhabitants and labor, capital, knowledge, and state power had to be mobilized. Between 1820 and 1832 a series of treaties backed by skirmishes and armed confrontations transferred much of the land from the Choctaws—its native inhabitants—to white settlers. Using wagons, rafts, and flatboats, hopeful cotton planters brought slaves from elsewhere in the South to clear that land of its "jungle-like" vegetation, and later to hoe the soil, sow seeds, prune the young plants, and then harvest the cotton. The news that the Delta was "the most certain cotton planting area in the world" spread through the South; planters who were able to draw on sufficient capital (mostly in the form of labor) and expertise moved in. The plantations they built became substantial businesses: By 1840, Washington County, in the heart of the Delta, counted more than ten slaves for every white inhabitant. By 1850, each and every white family in the county held on average more than eighty slaves. The largest Delta planter, Stephen Duncan, owned 1,036 slaves and the value of his property by the late 1850s was estimated at $1.3 million. While not typical cotton farms, plantations in the Delta were highly capitalized businesses, indeed among the very largest in North America, and the investments necessary would have been beyond the reach of nearly every northern industrialist. Wealth, as viewed from the front porches of the lavish and elegantly furnished mansions in the Delta, appeared to flow out of the soil, the result of a strange alchemy that combined emptied lands, slave labor, and, as we will see, the never-ending flow of European capital.[29]

The growing domination of global cotton markets by planters in fact fed upon itself. As cotton cultivation expanded in the southern United States and as British and eventually continental European consumers became more and more dependent on that supply, institutional links between the South and Europe deepened. European import merchants sent agents to Charleston, Memphis, and New Orleans. They corresponded with business partners across the Atlantic on a regular basis. These merchants built a dense network of shipping connections and integrated the trade in cotton with their other businesses. People engaged in the cotton trade crossed the North Atlantic frequently, forging close business connections, friendships, and even marriages. Such networks, in turn, made transatlantic trade more secure and more predictable, thus lowering costs and giving the United States another decisive advantage over its potential competitors, such as India or Brazil.

At the core of all of these networks was the flow of cotton from the United States to Europe and of capital in the opposite direction. This capital more often than not was secured by mortgages on slaves, giving the owners of these mortgages the right to a particular slave should the debtor default. As historian Bonnie Martin has shown, in Louisiana 88 percent of loans secured by mortgages used slaves as (partial) collateral; in South Carolina it was 82 percent. In total, she estimates that hundreds of millions of dollars of capital was secured by property in humans. Slavery thus allowed not just for the rapid allocation of labor, but also for a swift allocation of capital.[30]

With enormous riches gained from expropriated land and labor, planters invested in agricultural improvements, another illustration of how success begot further success. They experimented, for example, with various cotton hybrids drawing on Indian, Ottoman, Central American, West Indian, and other seeds, creating cotton strains adapted to particular local climates and soils, eventually crafting hundreds upon hundreds of different kinds of cotton. Most significantly, in 1806 a Natchez planter, Walter Burling, brought cottonseeds from Mexico, which had larger bolls that could be more easily picked and, according to experts, "possessed better fiber quality, especially fiber length, and was resistant to 'rot.' " This type of cotton had been cultivated by Native Americans in the central Mexican highlands for centuries, and once brought into the United States it was appropriated by American planters, becoming the "basic germplasm for all subsequent upland cotton cultivars in the United States and around the world." The new cotton could be picked three to four times as fast as the then common Georgia Green Seed cotton. The cruel irony was that Amerindians' ability to develop a strain of cotton well suited for the American environment gave considerable impetus to the expropriation of their lands, and made slave labor on those lands much more productive.[31]

Such innovations in labor control and agriculture were increasingly institutionalized by the construction of dense but distinctly regional networks for the dispersal of knowledge. Books, agricultural institutes, journals such as *De Bow's Review* and the *American Cotton Planter*, along with regional agricultural conventions, all spread information about how to select seeds, how to organize a labor force, how to read the market, how to hoe and plant, and where to invest—in short, how to perfect a "Practical Plantation Economy."[32]

The Industrial Revolution in Europe also actively influenced the evolution of slavery in the American South. Gang labor, by no means new but never so prevalent as on cotton plantations, exemplified the new rhythm of industrial labor, or what one author has called "military agriculture." The systematic mobilization of slave women and children on cotton farms further expanded their output. As a result, cotton production in the United States increased much faster than the number of slaves employed on farms. Some of that increase was related to the embrace of different cotton plants, but there was also a systematic intensification of exploitation. Plantation slavery in the nineteenth-century United States allowed for an organization of labor unlike what was possible in the world's newly emerging industrial heartland. Because plantations were frequently larger than factories and required more substantial capital investments, and because aside from the spike in innovation around the invention of Eli Whitney's gin in the 1790s technological progress in cotton agriculture was limited, productivity gains on plantations could only result from a reorganization of labor. Slave owners secured these productivity gains by taking almost total control of the work process— a direct result of the violent domination of their workers. Nothing of that sort was possible in the world's emerging textile mills, where workers succeeded in maintaining some of the rhythms of the farms, small workshops, and craft guilds from whence they came.[33] The all-encompassing control of workers—a core characteristic of capitalism—experienced its first great success on the cotton plantations of the American South.

Because planters dominated labor in ways radically different from

English merchants' connection to agricultural cultivators in India, or
Ottoman landowners in Anatolia, they could drive their slaves ever harder,
as they came up with increasingly brutal methods of disciplining their
workforce. Indeed, torture, according to historian Edward Baptist, was
at the root of the ability of American planters to produce ever more cotton. Innovative ways of labor accounting further helped planters squeeze
more labor out of their workers. As management scholar Rob Cooke has
argued, "There is no real question nowadays . . . that it [the plantation]
was a site of early development of industrial discipline." And with rising
productivity on cotton plantations, prices fell, allowing British manufacturers to become even more competitive in the markets of the world,
a move that, among many other things, would eventually undermine
manufacturing in India and elsewhere and make the later integration of
that countryside into the global cotton empire much easier.[34]

The rhythm of industrial production also entered the plantation in
other ways. Since the expansion of cotton agriculture depended on the
advance of credit, sometimes secured by mortgages on slaves, most of

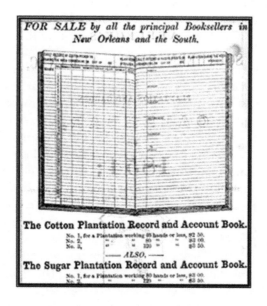

Rationalizing labor control with the whip: Thomas Affleck
markets his cotton plantation account book

which derived from the London money market, its patterns now followed the competitive logic of markets rather than the whimsy of personal aspiration and regional circumstance—capital moved to wherever cotton could be produced in the greatest quantities and at the cheapest cost. To the great lament of southern planters, the factor—a merchant who would sell a planter's cotton, supply him with goods, and provide credit—and with him the London money market, was a decisive source of their wealth and power. But the London money market and the Lancashire manufacturers depended just as much on the local experts in the violent expropriation of land and labor. The old paternalism of East Coast planters, shielded partially by the mercantilist logic of mutually beneficial and protected exchange between motherland and colony of the greater British imperial economy, had given way to a freer, more competitive, and fluid social order mediated by merchant capital. The voracious appetite for accumulation sped the "social metabolism" of cotton production. The logic of war capitalism in fact now emanated from its industrial (wage labor) center in Lancashire. While in the eighteenth century, slavery had enabled industrial takeoff, it now became integral to its continued expansion.[35]

The peculiar combination of expropriated lands, slave labor, and the domination of a state that gave enormous latitude to slave owners over their labor was fabulously profitable for those positioned to embrace it: As early as 1807 a Mississippi cotton plantation was said to return 22.5 percent annually on its investment. Many thousands of planters moved along with the cotton frontier to capture some of these profits. Cotton's

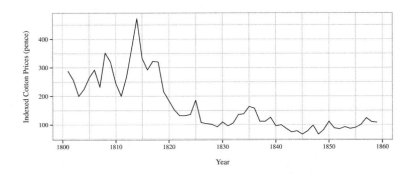

The wages of slavery: indexed cotton prices, American middling, at Liverpool (1860 = 100)

profitability is also revealed by the dramatic increase in the price of slaves: A young adult male slave in New Orleans cost about $500 in 1800, but as much as $1,800 before the Civil War. Consider the story of a young Georgia planter, Joseph Clay. He had bought Royal Vale, a rice plantation in Chatham County, Georgia, in 1782. He grew rice until 1793. That year, hearing of Whitney's gin, he obtained a loan of $32,000, used that money to buy additional slaves, had them convert some of the land to cotton fields, and installed a number of gins. So profitable was the undertaking that a mere seven years later he was able to repay his debt, lavishly redecorate his mansion, and buy additional slaves and gins. When Clay died in 1804, his estate was valued at $276,000.[36]

In similar ways, South Carolina indigo planter Peter Gaillard saw his fortunes revive thanks to the cotton boom. By 1790 Gaillard's indigo business had all but collapsed owing to the disappearance of British markets, and he had resorted to growing food for his family on his plantation. As a friend of his reported, "The disastrous ten years which preceded the introduction of cotton as a market crop involved him, as it did others, in debt and distress." In 1796, however, he began growing cotton—"a brilliant prospect now opened to the eyes of the desponding planters"—a crop so profitable that four years later he had paid back all his debts and in 1803 constructed a new mansion on his property. Coerced labor meant rapid profits; by 1824 he owned five hundred slaves. South Carolinian Wade Hampton I followed suit. His first cotton crop in 1799 allegedly netted a profit of $75,000, and by 1810 he drew $150,000 annually from his cotton plantations. His son would eventually use some of the profits to relocate to the Mississippi Delta in the mid-1840s. Prospective cotton planter Daniel W. Jordan, surveying the opportunities for cotton growing in Mississippi, saw "a field to operate in and here I can make money . . . I can in this State make as much money in 5 years as a man should want."[37]

Fortified by their wealth, confident of their slave-aided ability to squeeze ever more cotton from the land, American cotton planters came to dominate British markets by 1802. By the 1830s they had also captured newly emerging continental European and North American markets. As a result, earlier producers, especially those in the West Indies, suffered: "The Competition, if left perfectly free and unrestricted, cannot be long maintained by the Colonists [in the West Indies]; as the same price that yields a liberal profit to the American Cultivator, is not adequate to defray the charges of cultivation to the Colonist," observed an anonymous letter writer in 1812. Other potential competitors, such as farmers in India, planted cotton on just as much land as North Americans as late as 1850, but their presence on world markets remained marginal.[38]

As this cotton boom violently transformed huge swaths of the North American countryside, it catapulted the United States to a pivotal role in the empire of cotton. In 1791, capital invested in cotton production in Brazil, as estimated by the U.S. Treasury, was still more than ten times greater than in the United States. By 1801, only ten years later, 60 percent more capital was invested in the cotton industry of the United States than that of Brazil. Cotton, even more so than in the Caribbean and Brazil, infused land and slaves alike with unprecedented value, and promised slaveholders spectacular opportunities for profits and power. Already by 1820, cotton constituted 32 percent of all U.S. exports, compared to a minuscule 2.2 percent in 1796. Indeed, more than half of all American exports between 1815 and 1860 consisted of cotton. Cotton so dominated the U.S. economy that cotton production statistics "became an increasingly vital unit in assessing the American economy." It was on the back of cotton, and thus on the backs of slaves, that the U.S. economy ascended in the world.[39]

So important had American cotton become to the Western world that a German economist remarked that "a disappearance of the American North or West would be of less significance to the world, than the elimination of the South." Southern planters, convinced of their central role in the global economy, gleefully announced that they held "THE LEVER THAT WIELDS THE DESTINY OF MODERN CIVILIZATION." As the *American Cotton Planter* put it in 1853, "The slave-labor of the United States, has hitherto conferred and is still conferring inappreciable blessings on mankind. If these blessings continue, slave-labor must also continue, for it is idle to talk of producing Cotton for the world's supply with free labor. It has never yet been successfully grown by voluntary labor."[40]

American cotton farmers had succeeded in turning themselves into the world's most important growers of the industrial age's most important commodity. Their "gigantic plantations," observed a British merchant in Tellicherry, India, "now supply the materials for clothing half the civilized world." And with slave-grown cotton pouring in from the United States, the cost of finished cotton declined, making clothes and sheets affordable for a rapidly expanding market. As the Manchester

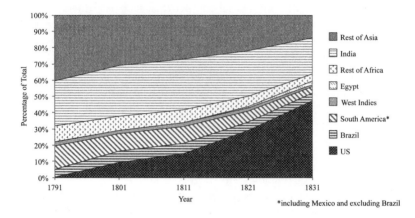

War capitalism recasts the global cotton industry: world's cotton crop, 1791–1831
(rough estimate)

Chamber of Commerce put it in 1825, "We are firmly persuaded that it is in great measure owing to the very low price of the raw material that this manufacture has been of late years so rapidly increased." In 1845, South Carolina's cotton planters agreed: "Nearly one half of the population of Europe . . . have not now the comfort of a cotton shirt," constituting an "untried market . . . opening more and more to our enterprize." The world of cotton, which before 1780 had consisted mostly of scattered regional and local networks, now increasingly became one global matrix with a single nexus. And slavery in the United States was its foundation.[41]

Despite its undeniable success, the dependence of Europe's cotton manufacturers on one country and on one peculiar system of labor disquieted some consumers of raw cotton. As early as the 1810s, British manufacturers in particular began to worry that they had become too dependent on a single supplier for their valuable raw materials. In 1838, the Glasgow Chamber of Commerce and Manufactures shrilly warned of the "alarming fact that Britain is almost entirely dependant on foreign supply for this article, which is now scarcely less necessary than bread." Six years later, "A Cotton Spinner" looked with "great apprehension" at the dependence of the United Kingdom on cotton supplies from the United

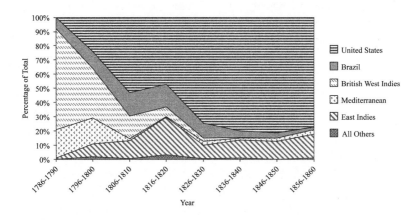

Cotton imports into Great Britain, annual averages, in percent, by country of origin

States. This relationship had become important just as the North American colonies embarked upon their slow and painful move away from the empire, showing that connections across the Atlantic could be severed by political and military action. Cotton manufacturers understood that their prosperity was entirely dependent on the labor of slaves and they "dreaded the severity of the revulsion which must sooner, or later arrive." By 1850, one British observer estimated that 3.5 million people in the United Kingdom were employed by the country's cotton industry—all subject to the whims of American planters and their tenuous hold on their nation's politics.[42]

Cotton manufacturers' concerns about dependence on U.S. cotton focused on three issues. First, they feared that the United States would siphon off ever-increasing amounts of its own cotton in its own factories, which had begun to emerge in significant numbers in the 1810s, making less cotton available to European consumers. Second, British manufacturers in particular were concerned that continental producers would acquire a rising percentage of the world's cotton, competing for American supplies. Third, and most important was "the increasing uncertainty of the continuance of the system of slavery." Drawing on "the blood-stained produce" constituted a "suicidal dependence" on the "crime of American slavery."[43]

In 1835, Thomas Baring carefully observed the United States, expecting that "the further agitation of the Slave question might materially alter the result, acting of course, favourably on prices." How secure, after all, would slave property be in an industrializing America with increasing abolitionist sympathies? Would the political economy of southern planters collide with that of northern economic elites? And could the increasingly expansionist designs of wealthy and powerful slaveholders in the American South and their proto-nationalist project be contained within an industrializing United States? Southern planters, the "lords of the lash," emboldened by their wealth, began to lament their subordinate role within the global economy; their fledgling designs to revolutionize their own position within it were yet another threat to the system as a whole. To the "lords of the loom," raw material producers had to be politically subordinate to the will and direction of industrial capital.[44]

On the plantation itself, another terror was lurking. A visit to the industrial cotton fields of the "black belt" impressed on many observers that slavery was unstable because the war between slaves and their masters could turn at any point. "A Cotton Spinner" warned in 1844 that "the safety of this country depends upon our obtaining an improved supply of Cotton from British India," since in America "on the first opportunity . . . these slave-gangs will naturally disperse, the improvident negroes will cease to grow cotton, and there being no white men to supply their places; Cotton cultivation in America will terminate." He feared an "exterminating war of races—a prospect too horrible to dwell upon." Emancipation, he worried, might shake "our country . . . to [its] very foundations." Talk of runaways, refusals to work, and even outright rebellion kept planters and European cotton manufacturers on their toes. Merchant Francis Carnac Brown warned in 1848 of "a race of discontented slaves, ruled by tyranny, and threatening daily some ruinous outbreak, which it is known must one day come." Americans tried to explain to their European customers that slavery in the United States, unlike in Saint-Domingue, was safe—not least, as Tench Coxe put it, because of the presence of a powerful white militia and because slaves have "no artillery nor arms. Tho they are numerous they are much separated by rivers, Bayos and tracts thickly peopled with whites." But concerns remained.[45]

During these moments of anxiety, European cotton manufacturers looked to other regions of the world for an increased supply of cotton, to places such as Africa and India. French officials eyed Senegal in the 1810s and 1820s as a potential alternative source of cotton, but despite their concerted efforts, little cotton came. In Britain, hopes for non-American cotton focused squarely on India, whose long history of cotton exports seemed to make it superbly suited to supply British factories, not least because manufacturers believed the country had "overflowing supplies of various descriptions of cotton." And India might point toward ways to build a cotton industry not dependent on the inherent instabilities and exigencies of slavery and expropriations. The possibilities of Indian cotton were enumerated and analyzed in literally dozens of books, many with fantastically ambitious titles like *Scinde & The Punjab: The Gems of India in Respect to Their Past and Unparalleled Capabilities of Supplanting the Slave States of America in the Cotton Markets of the World*. Some of these books were not mere pamphlets; John Chapman, a former manufacturer of supplies for the textile industry and railroad promoter in Western India, for example, published in 1851 *The Cotton and Commerce of India, Considered in Relation to the Interests of Great Britain*, with over four hundred pages of detailed accounts of the soil, agricultural practices, land ownership patterns, transportation infrastructure, and trade relations of various parts of India, supported by a vast array of statistical information. Like him, most writers concluded that "the soil and climate" of India was "favourable to the growth of" cotton.[46]

By the 1830s, these individual voices found collective expression. In 1836, the Manchester Chamber of Commerce mentioned Indian cotton for the first time in its *Annual Report*. Four years later, they held a special meeting to pressure the East India Company to do something about cotton production in India, and in 1847 they sent a petition to the House of Commons to similar effect. In 1845 the Manchester Commercial Association, a rival body of local entrepreneurs, even sent a deputation to the directors of the East India Company to urge them to promote cotton growing in India, a subject "of paramount importance to the interests of this district."[47]

Some forward-looking manufacturers began to understand that there might be a deeper, and enduringly profitable, relationship between India as a market for their goods and India as a provider of raw materials. They imagined a world in which Indian peasants would export their cotton and in turn purchase Manchester piece goods: "Nothing can be more natural than that the inhabitants, deprived of a market for their cloths, should be encouraged to cultivate the raw material."[48]

The agitation for Indian cotton reached its height during the 1850s, when prices for U.S. cotton rose once more. To be sure, Manchester cotton interests were still divided on the merits of state intervention to secure Indian cotton, with some believing that things should be left to the market.[49] But by 1857 the "adequate supply of cotton being obtained to sustain the industry of this district" had become a major topic of discussion at the Chamber's annual meetings. Cotton manufacturer, Chamber of Commerce president, and member of Parliament Thomas Bazley believed that "the supply of . . . cotton is altogether inadequate" and demanded that more needed to be done to secure cotton from India, Africa, Australia, and other places, "precisely because the British government does possess that soil." Calling upon spinners to organize to expand cotton production in colonial territories, he was the prime mover behind the creation of the Manchester Cotton Supply Association in 1857 "with a view to having a more abundant and universal supply." Concerned about the increasing volatility of American politics in the wake of the Kansas-Nebraska Act and the Dred Scott decision, the association literally went to the ends of the earth delivering cotton gins, giving advice, and distributing seeds and implements to farmers, while collecting information on various kinds of cotton and various ways of growing it. The association's work was a microcosm of the grand project of cotton capitalists: to transform the global countryside into a cotton-growing complex.[50]

For cotton manufacturers, India beckoned for the obvious reason that it remained one of the world's greatest growers of the white gold. They believed that India produced more cotton than the United States; notoriously imprecise estimates spoke of up to 750 million pounds of cotton consumed annually within India, in addition to its annual exports of 150 million pounds and more. This compared favorably with total U.S. production, in 1839, of 756 million pounds. Traditionally, much of this cotton was used for domestic production, and even cotton that went into long-distance trade usually remained within India. Central Indian cotton had been traded to Madras in the south and Bengal in the east, but with the decline of the Indian cotton cloth export industry, it was increasingly brought to Bombay and from there exported to China and, in limited quantities, to Britain.[51]

The British East India Company had halfheartedly supported efforts to increase such exports since 1788, but the quantities involved were small, not least because of high transport costs. Indeed, until the 1830s, much more cotton was exported to China than to Europe (it paid for the company's purchases of tea), and increases in exports to Europe usually went hand in hand with decreasing exports to China. Thus Indian cotton agriculture did not significantly become more export-oriented.[52]

Yet Manchester manufacturers wanted more. They pressured the British East India Company, the British government, and, later, the British colonial administration to develop a multitude of activities to encourage the growth and export of Indian cotton. Private initiative was insufficient to change India's cotton-growing countryside, as "private companies do not answer" and thus government needed to step in. Infrastructure improvements were first and foremost on their mind, "a bridge [needed to be] built, or a railway made, or canals dug, or cotton cultivated, or machines introduced." In 1810, the company sent out American cotton-seed to be used in India. In 1816, the Board of Directors shipped Whitney gins to Bombay. In 1818, four experimental cotton farms were started. In 1829, further experimental farms were established and land was given to Europeans "to grow the approved kind of cotton." In 1831, the Bombay government created an agency to purchase raw cotton in Southern Mahratta County. In 1839, discussions emerged within the East India Company on more investments in infrastructure, experimental farms, and the shifting of capital out of opium production into cotton. Their cause was aided by legal changes: Starting in 1829, the Bombay government punished with up to seven years in prison people who fraudulently packaged and sold cotton. In 1851, another "Act for the Better Suppression of Frauds" came into effect, with similar goals. Numerous initiatives sought to increase and improve Indian cotton exports. And in 1853, as the British acquired Berar, a territory about 300 miles northeast of Bombay, Lord Dalhousie, governor-general of India, bragged that this "secured the finest cotton tracts which are known to exist in all the continent of India; and thus . . . opened up a great additional channel of supply, through which to make good a felt deficiency in the staple of one great branch of its manufacturing industry."[53]

As important were schemes to collect, appropriate, and disperse knowledge. Efforts to survey the state of Indian cotton agriculture proliferated. In 1830, the administration commissioned detailed reports on cotton cultivation in India. In 1848 the government of India surveyed virtually the entire subcontinent, investigating the potential of each and every region for the increased production of cotton for export. Indeed, as elsewhere, the statistical and informational penetration of territory usually came before the incorporation into the global economy, and at midcentury, Europeans' knowledge about the climate, soil, agricultural diseases, labor supplies, and social structures in many parts of India was still tentative. Simultaneously, exotic seeds, especially of U.S. origin, were introduced into India, new gins delivered, and experimental farms established in Gujarat, in Coimbatore, and elsewhere.[54]

The most significant of these efforts occurred in the 1840s, when the East India Company supported the creation of experimental farms run by U.S.-born cotton planters as a step toward supplanting U.S.-grown cotton with that from India. Several Americans had offered their services "to go to Hindustan." One W. W. Wood, who was "born and bred on Cotton plantations," wrote from New Orleans in June 1842 that he had been "entertaining the Idea for some time of going to India to cultivate the Cotton plant on my own account but would much prefer patronage and support" of the East India Company. He received that support and went, along with nine other planters, to Bombay with seed, gins, and implements brought from the United States. The planters traveled to various parts of India, where they were given land, a house, and a cotton press to grow exotic cotton varieties, mostly from American seed. They hired workers and contracted for the growing of cotton with peasants working on their own account. At first things looked good and the *Asiatic Journal* reported on the "zeal and diligence" of the American planters.[55]

However, despite their best efforts, the farms failed rapidly. Rainfall patterns frustrated plans to use American farming practices. Limitations of infrastructure made transport difficult. There was a growing realization that American practices were too capital-intensive for the conditions in which Indian cotton cultivators found themselves. Indians also opposed the use of so-called waste lands for experimental farms because traditionally "they have been able to feed their cattle without expense upon the wastelands." Moreover, farms failed because peasants paid less attention to the fields on which they worked for hire than their own fields. And then there was outright resistance. One of the American farmers, "Mr. Mercer, a few weeks ago, had his bungalow burnt down, and the estate and works, together with his whole property, destroyed, except the suit of clothes he had on him." At such moments, it certainly did not help that the Americans were "perfect strangers to the habits and Language of the country." As a result, Mercer reported in 1845 that the "the experimental farms were only a useless expense to Government; that the American system of cultivation was not adapted to India, that the Natives of India were, from their knowledge of the climate and capabilities of the soil, able to cultivate better and much more economically than any European, and requested that the farms be abolished . . . "[56]

Indian cultivators, in effect, resisted giving up so-called waste lands, and they did not easily come to be persuaded to work for wages on farms, making a "plantation revolution" along the lines of the one occurring in the Americas unlikely. Indeed, they actively opposed the impositions of colonial officials. The American cotton farmers in India complained that they were "obliged to give way to [their workers'] prejudices." They complained of the "laziness" of Indian cotton pickers, of cotton stolen from their farms, that workers went on strike, forcing them to give in to demands for higher wages, and that capital was lacking, soils were poor, and they "did not succeed in obtaining labor." Eventually they decided that wage labor did not work, with one of the planters stating categorically that "cultivation by paid labor could, under no circumstances, be profitably applied to Cotton in that part of the country."[57]

The experiences in India indeed seemed to confirm cotton's dependence on coercion. Yet slavery, manufacturers began to understand, could not be completely trusted. And since manufacturers' own capital and their own institutions were insufficient to create alternative systems, they turned to the state: They demanded new laws regarding land tenure to secure investments in cotton. They demanded even more investment in experimental farms and the accumulation of agricultural knowledge, more state investment in infrastructure, and a tax on the cultivators that would not discourage cotton growers from investing and improving the quantity and quality of their crops. Cotton capitalists in Britain and India understood that capital had to be infused in the countryside, but they found the conditions there too risky. As the Bombay Chamber of Commerce argued, "An Extension of production, so great as to reach many million of pounds annually, and an improvement in processes so radical as to involve a change in the customs and habits of a whole people, cannot be produced by measures of petty detail, but can only be looked for from the operation of causes and principles of commensurate extent and force."[58]

The British East India Company defended itself vigorously against charges by cotton manufacturers and merchants that it did not sufficiently encourage cotton cultivation in India. By 1836, the East India Company had already published a book in its defense, *Reports and Documents Connected with the Proceedings of the East-India Company in Regard to the Culture and Manufacture of Cotton-Wool, Raw Silk, and Indigo in India*, in which it listed in great detail the myriad of activities it had undertaken. The company accused the merchants instead, demanding from them more vigilance when acquiring cotton in India and a willingness to purchase only clean, well-ginned cotton. As it happened, European cotton merchants and colonial officials would spend the next fifteen years accusing one another of being responsible for the inferior state and insufficient quantities of Indian export cotton.[59]

Yet despite all the bickering and all of these efforts, Indian cotton continued to play only a very minor role on world markets and posed no threat whatsoever to the supremacy of American-grown cotton. To be sure, more Indian cotton came to the United Kingdom, not least because former exports to China were redirected toward Europe. But despite that redirecting of Indian cotton, its market share in the U.K. remained low—ranging from 7.2 percent during the 1830s to 9.9 percent during the 1850s. "The success which has attended the cultivation of this article has not been so great as could be wished," admitted the Revenue Department in 1839. More categorically, for the Bombay Chamber of Commerce, the efforts to improve and expand cotton exports "resulted in signal failure."[60]

As the failed experimental farms had suggested, one important reason was the problematic transportation infrastructure. Cotton was usually brought to market on bullocks and carts, an extremely slow and expensive way to transport the raw material. As late as 1854, there were only thirty-four miles of railroad in India. One expert indeed argued that American cotton was so much more competitive than Indian cotton because of the vastly better system of railroads, and, one should add, a vastly superior system of rivers. There was a disjuncture between the industrial rhythm of Lancashire and the rhythms of economic life in India's cotton-growing countryside. War capitalism had succeeded in bridging this gap by resorting to bodily coercion elsewhere, but not in India.[61]

Perhaps more important than the lack of adequate infrastructure was that the pattern of production of Indian cultivators did not articulate well with the needs of production for export. Indian peasants were still deeply embedded in a cotton economy separate from the cotton upstarts in Europe. They produced cotton for domestic consumption, and more often than not produced their own clothing. What Britain saw as a "failure" is more usefully viewed as evidence for the vast differences in the possibilities and the priorities of cotton production. The monocultural production of cotton, so prevalent in the American South, was unknown. Indian cultivators gave preference to subsistence crops, because they feared they would starve if their market crop did not succeed—one observer described "the cultivators growing Cotton & Grains in their respective fields together, and indiscriminately as their inclinations or interests dictate." Local peasants grew cotton only "as a secondary crop," lamented a British collector.[62]

Moreover, Indians were reluctant to embrace new methods of cultivation and new ways of preparing cotton for market. They resisted the use of exotic seeds. They continued to gin their cotton by footroller or *churka*. This resistance to different ways of growing and processing cotton, so maddening to the British colonialists, was entirely rational from the standpoint of Indian cultivators. After all, the technologies they employed were well adapted to local social and environmental conditions, and so were the indigenous seeds. Moreover, the peasants' biggest customers were indigenous spinners, so they grew cotton that they knew would appeal to the local markets. Under conditions of extreme capital scarcity, it made sense to focus on subsistence crops, proven technology, and established markets. And since capital was not forthcoming, neither from European merchants nor from Indian traders, the revolutionizing of production was difficult if not impossible. Creating a rural proletariat, potentially another strategy to gain control over production, proved just as impossible without clear-cut private property in land, which could be fashioned only with massive expropriations and a powerful presence of the state.[63]

Just as peasants retained control over land, their labor, and the way they produced cotton, indigenous merchants remained powerful in the circuits of exchange, effectively limiting Western encroachment and, with it, the revolutionizing of the countryside. Trade in cotton was until the 1860s still largely dominated by Indian agents, brokers, middlemen, merchants, and even exporters. Despite "strenuous efforts . . . made by British interests to adapt the marketing of cotton to the needs of the export economy," they largely failed. In 1842 the Bombay Chamber of

Commerce took up a perpetual question: "Why is British capital, so powerful everywhere else, and from which so much was expected to be done for India, here so wholly inoperative?" They listed numerous disadvantages to European capitalists: They were few in number, with only forty European merchants in Bombay dealing in cotton. They had to adapt "to a pre-existing state of commerce." They lamented "the opposition and imposition that must inevitably be encountered." And they had to compete with local spinners.[64]

Even when Western merchants operated in the cotton-growing districts, they met opposition at every point: "The cultivators were taught to distrust them, in consequence of their being Europeans, to demand for their Cotton a price far beyond what they accepted from Native dealers. A similar imposition was attempted in every thing—the price of labour, the hire of carts, the rent of warehouses, and the rates of churka men." As a result, the idea of "the maintenance of Establishments in the interior" for European merchants was quite unthinkable and English merchants limited themselves "to the purchase of Cotton when brought here [Bombay] to market." Even though they knew of the need for "Mercantile Agency in the interior of the country" as a precondition for the recasting of cotton production, they were not likely "to risk in a place so remote from their control the large amount of capital requisite to erect the buildings, and furnish the advances to the cultivators, which would be necessary to keep up permanent establishments in Guzerat." In Berar as late as 1848, "the Cotton is usually purchased in small quantities by itinerant Dealers at the Villages where it is produced," with much of the cotton spun by the farmers themselves, and "with no Capitalist in the Country who could make advances to any great extent worth mentioning." Unlike in the United States, they were not yet capable of what a British parliamentary committee in 1847–48 deemed might be necessary: "for European capitalists to place themselves in direct communication with the cultivators of the soil."[65]

In short, Europeans had only very superficially penetrated India's cotton growing. Western merchants had no impact whatsoever on how cotton was produced in the Indian countryside. They had just as little impact on the ways cotton moved from its producers to the traders on the coast. British efforts to grow cotton on large farms with wage labor failed spectacularly, not least because labor could not be mobilized. One superintendent of such a cotton farm wrote that "these people all refuse to come to the Farm when the villagers require their services, and some who have been paid by Government by the month went away saying they were sick and unable to work in the Morning, and in the evening I found them working for the villagers."[66]

Given such troubles, coerced labor seemed an attractive option. Indeed, the example of the great slave-based American system of cotton growing led one commercial resident to ask in 1831 if it might not be better if the company would engage in "a little gentle coercion." Another writer similarly suggested that Europeans should employ "apprentices from the Orphan Schools," while others favored the use of prison and convict labor. All these came to naught—and with them European-run cotton plantations. Instead, the East India Company had to engage constantly with local rulers, local power structures, local property ownership patterns, and local ways of producing things. British difficulties in India clarify the decisive difference from the United States. Though settler conflicts with Native Americans were costly, both in lives and treasure, the result left settlers in full control of the land and its resources. Indigenous ways of doing things were no longer. The local was simply obliterated.[67]

Indian peasants, like their counterparts in Anatolia, western Africa, and elsewhere, had shaped a world in which they could resist the onslaught of European merchant capital. Since Europeans were unable to transfer bodily coercion and all-encompassing expropriation of land to these regions of the world, and since they lacked the power to force some other alternative system of raw material production, much to their lament, their dependence on the United States deepened. As Mr. Dunbar, commissioner of Dhaka, concluded in 1848, "In this ancient and populous Country where land is valuable and rents high, where agricultural Service is almost unknown and the want of skill, energy and enterprise of the agricultural population is proverbial, where the produce is so inferior and the Cost of transportation necessarily so high, competition with America seems a hopeless task."[68]

In contrast to India, Egypt contained the possibility for coercion, expropriation, and even slavery. Cotton as a major export staple came late to Egypt, during the reign of Muhammad Ali Pasha in the 1820s. As part of Ali's effort to create a vibrant domestic cotton industry, in the late 1810s he brought Louis Alexis Jumel, a French textile engineer long since removed to New York City. Jumel chanced across a cotton bush in a Cairo garden with unusually long and strong fiber. With the support of Ali, he developed the strain further, and by 1821 was already harvesting substantial amounts of what came to be called Jumel cotton, finding ready markets in Europe.[69]

Ali understood the potential of this new export crop and ordered it grown throughout the country. Coercion was integral to this project from the beginning. Peasants were forced to cultivate cotton on state-owned lands for their yearly corvée duty, a forced-labor tax. On their own lands they were also forced to plant cotton in specific ways, to sell their crop to the state, and to work without pay. The government set prices for the cotton and controlled all aspects of its transport and sale to foreign merchants in Alexandria, who were explicitly disallowed to directly purchase cotton from Egyptian growers. Workers were also forced to dig canals to water the crop and to build roads that crisscrossed Lower Egypt to move it to market. As *Merchants' Magazine and Commercial Review* observed in New York in 1843, "Cotton is not willingly cultivated by the fellah, and would probably be scarcely produced at all but through the despotic interference of the pasha." In Egypt, unlike the United States where force was exerted by private individuals, violent coercion descended upon rural cultivators from a premodern state.[70]

The Egyptian state also dominated the cotton trade itself. Until the 1850s, in contrast to indebted American planters, Egyptian rulers succeeded in limiting the influence of foreign merchants on the domestic trade in cotton, despite their centrality in organizing the export trade from the Mediteranean port city of Alexandria. The government purchased the cotton at fixed prices, collected it at central warehouses, and then shipped it to Alexandria, where Ali was the only seller of the raw material to foreign merchants. In the 1820s and 1830s, between 10 and 25 percent of the revenues of the Egyptian state derived from this sale of cotton.[71]

Egyptian cotton came to play a significant role in supplying European manufacturers.[72] British factory owners noted in 1825 that such exports had "materially checked the advances which lately occurred in the prices of all other Cottons." But the prime value of Egyptian cotton, they argued, was that it could substitute for American long-staple Sea Island cotton, which they considered important "in the event of any political event depriving us altogether of the Cotton of the United States."[73]

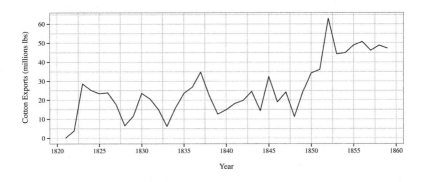

Cotton exports from Egypt, in millions of pounds, 1821–1859

The cataclysmic event did not materialize. Not yet. Instead, cotton flowed ever more cheaply out of the American South. Slavery and the expropriation of native lands, fueled by European capital, combined to feed raw materials relentlessly into Europe's core industry. The massive infusion of European capital transformed the American countryside; land became wealth, and linked across great distances slaves and wage workers, planters and manufacturers, plantations and factories. In the wake of the Industrial Revolution, slavery had become central to the Western world's new political economy. But this capitalism, based on territorial expansion and violent domination of labor, was also inherently unstable: As the *Bremer Handelsblatt* put it in 1853, "the material prosperity of Europe hangs on a thread of cotton. Would slavery suddenly be abolished, cotton production would fall at one stroke by ⅞th, and all cotton industries would be ruined."[74]

Relief for cotton-hungry manufacturers, ironically, came from unexpected quarters, for unexpected reasons: from the slow but steady collapse of competing circuits of cotton manufacturing in Asia. Throughout the first half of the nineteenth century, local cotton craft networks remained a powerful presence in the world. In Africa, Latin America, and throughout Asia, the growing of cotton for household use or local markets remained important; indeed, it is entirely possible that as late as midcentury more cotton entered such limited circulation than entered industrial production. In large parts of Africa, observed Thomas Ellison as late as 1886, "indigenous Cotton has from time immemorial been both grown and manufactured, and the natives are for the most part clothed in fabrics of their own production."[75]

In China as well, using traditional methods of production, spinners and weavers, working mostly in their houses and drawing on the labor of their dependents, continued to serve their very large domestic market. Most of the cotton they consumed came from their own or their neighbors' fields, while others bought cotton from the large cotton merchants of Shanghai and elsewhere. "Early in the fine autumnal mornings," observed a British traveler in 1845, "the roads leading into Shanghae are crowded with bands of coolies from the cotton farms," testifying to a world of cotton distant from the circuits of growing, production, and consumption dominated by Europeans. Japan too had a flourishing domestic trade in locally grown cotton, and produced large amounts of cotton goods in homes and workshops. And Bengal, despite the beginning decline of its export manufacturing industry, still imported huge quantities of raw cotton in the first years of the nineteenth century: In 1802, it was said that Bengal grew a little more than 7 million pounds of cotton, but imported more than 43 million pounds, principally from western India, competing with China and Lancashire for the raw material of its core industry. Despite British designs to the contrary, India continued to be the most prominent example for such alternative circuits of cotton.[76]

Yet while local and regional networks persisted, they would never again flourish. These smaller networks, defined by custom, convenience, and profit, were undermined by the ever-widening veins of European capital and state power. Indeed, the cheapness of cottons enabled by slavery in the United States would help undermine local manufacturing everywhere. Many times over, indeed, the empire of cotton would advance what historian Kären Wigen has called the "making of a periphery." Tench Coxe understood that process already in 1818: The export of British piece goods to India, he perceptively observed, would force Indians "to turn to raising cotton instead of making piece goods they cannot sell." Across the nineteenth century, Europeans gambled on the efficacy of war capitalism again and again; each time they succeeded in planting new fields, in coercing more slaves, in finding additional capital, they enabled the production of more cotton fabrics at cheaper prices, and they pushed their cotton rivals to the periphery. The destruction of each of these alternative circuits of cotton, in turn, would further tip the balance of power in many parts of the world's countryside, making more territory and more labor vulnerable to the encroachment of the global economy. The great irony of this rapacious cycle of war capitalism, as we will see, is that its success laid the foundation for its own demise.[77]

But any hint of demise was distant. In the first half of the nineteenth century, war capitalism seemed a vast and impenetrable machine, a painfully efficient mechanism for profit and power. As Britain's power grew, capitalists in other regions of the world saw the possibilities inherent in the marriage of new technologies and bodily coercion. Certainly, many observers were anxious about the warlike expropriation of native peoples, the violence on the plantation, and the social turmoil in England's industrial cities. Yet wealth and power beckoned to those able to embrace that new world. Throughout France, the German lands, Switzerland, the United States, Lombardy, and elsewhere, capitalists tried to follow the path laid down by Manchester.

Chapter Six

Industrial Capitalism Takes Wing

The Industrial Revolution in Alsace

In 1835, John Masterson Burke, a twenty-three-year-old business manager at the iron foundry of James P. Alair in New York City, set sail for southern Mexico. His destination was the small colonial town of Valladolid. There, Don Pedro Baranda, the onetime governor of Yucatán, and John L. MacGregor, a Scot, had opened Mexico's first steam-powered cotton manufacturing enterprise, a factory that Burke was to direct. They cited the "spontaneous growth of cotton around Valladolid" as the incentive for this venture, but stories of cotton profits from Lancashire to Lowell must have encouraged Baranda and MacGregor as well.[1]

Building a cotton factory in Valladolid, far from shipping facilities and technical expertise, was no small undertaking. Although a New Yorker who passed through in 1842 described the factory as "remarkable for its neat, compact, and business-like appearance," setting up production in Yucatán had been a struggle. To get the Aurora Yucateca started, Burke had brought with him from New York not only the machinery (including the carts required to move these machines from the port to Valladolid) but also four engineers, two of whom promptly died of malaria.

With no architect, the entrepreneurs designed the factory themselves and "twice the arches gave way, and the whole building came down." Nonetheless, Baranda, MacGregor, and Burke eventually got the mill up and running. Drawing on 117 local workers, along with Mayan families who supplied the wood to fire the steam engines and who planted cotton on their maize fields, they churned out 395,000 yards of cloth in the nine years before 1844. Though modest by the standards of Lancashire, this was a spectacular achievement.[2]

That a cotton mill arose in the middle of the tropical wilderness of the Yucatán Peninsula, several days' ride away from the port town of Mérida, and remote from sources of capital, testifies to the powerful attraction that cotton had for entrepreneurs across the globe. After the spread of water-powered spinning machines in Great Britain during the 1780s, mechanized cotton manufacturing spread around the world, at first slowly and then at breakneck speed, from Britain to continental Europe and to the United States, then on to Latin America, to northern Africa, and eventually to India and beyond.

Hundreds, perhaps thousands, of such stories could be told. Take the Wiesental in what is today Germany. Reaching from the highest peaks of the Black Forest in the Duchy of Baden to the Rhine near the Swiss city of Basel, this valley had been a vibrant center for the hand spinning and weaving of cotton since the eighteenth century. Flush with Swiss capital, cheap labor, and a broad network of middlemen, enterprising Basel merchants mobilized thousands of peasants to spin cotton in their homes, workers who came from local farm families unable to find land for their offspring and who were outside the guild restrictions that limited the expansion of production in cities such as Basel. Some of these merchants began to employ very large numbers of these workers, helped by government stipulations that forced children and young adults to spin: In 1795 putting-out merchant Meinrad Montfort from Zell in the Black Forest paid wages to about twenty-five hundred households in which one or more family members spun or wove. Montfort and other such putting-out merchants received the raw cotton from Basel and returned the finished cloth to its merchants, who in turn delivered the goods to the burgeoning cotton printing factories located in Mulhouse, an independent city-state just across the Rhine. So massive was Swiss investment that one historian has called the attendant economic restructuring of the area the "colonialization of the Wiesental."[3]

Already in the eighteenth century, these Swiss entrepreneurs and their

Baden subcontractors had put some spinners and weavers to work in non-mechanized workshops in order to better supervise production. Montfort himself had created as early as 1774 a bleaching workshop in nearby Staufen. Once workers left their homes to labor in workshops, it was only a question of time when mechanical devices for the spinning of cotton, recently invented in England, would come to the Wiesental. Indeed, in 1794—only ten years after Greg's venture in Styal—entrepreneurs erected the first mechanized spinning mill, although government agents forced its closure soon thereafter for fear that mechanization would lead to unemployment, misery, and social upheaval. But this government intervention against industry was a rare exception, and by 1810 modern water frames and mules returned to the valley, invited by a government more favorably inclined to mechanization. Drawing their power from the plentiful streams cascading down the mountainsides of the Black Forest, these mills destroyed hand spinning in short order. The greater availability of yarn, however, resulted in a boom in hand weaving, which for a short period allowed peasants to remain within their farm households. As elsewhere, rising demand and ready capital eventually moved weaving into factories as well. Mulhousian entrepreneur Peter Koechlin, to name but one, created hand-weaving factories in the Wiesental towns of Steinen (in 1816), Schönau (1820), and Zell (1826). With manufacturing moving from their households into factories, peasants in ever greater numbers gave up raising cattle as well as making cheese. By 1860, the Wiesental counted 160,000 mechanized spindles and 8,000 looms, nearly all of them located in factories. Once a remote outpost of subsistence farming, the valley had become yet another dot on the map of the Industrial Revolution. Like the Yucatecan town of Valladolid, it had fallen into the vortex of a globe-spanning capitalist economy linking peasants in the Black Forest and on the Yucatán Peninsula, slaves on the banks of the Mississippi and, as we will see, consumers on the shores of the Río de la Plata.[4]

Hitched behind a well-matched team of entrepreneurs hungry for profits and rulers lusting for power, the mechanized cotton industry successfully colonized the Wiesental, Valladolid, and an ever-larger swath of the world. In 1771, the spinning jenny came to the French city of Rouen, only six years after it had been introduced in the United Kingdom. In 1783, Johann Gottfried Brügelmann, a putting-out merchant in Ratingen near Düsseldorf, did not have enough yarn for his weavers, a problem that would have been impossible to solve just a few years earlier;

now he invested 25,000 reichstaler, gathered about eighty workers, and with the help of a British expert created the first spinning factory in the German-speaking lands. Two years later, the first mechanical spinning machine arrived in Barcelona, a city with such ancient cotton traditions that one of its narrow streets to this day carries the name Carrer del Cotoners. In 1789, Providence merchant Moses Brown hired a skilled British cotton worker, Samuel Slater, and built the first successful spinning factory in America. In 1792, Belgian entrepreneur Lieven Bauwens followed suit and started the first mechanized spinning mill in Twente. A year later, such machines for the first time began twisting yarn in Russia, when the Russian Treasury sponsored Michael Ossovski to start a cotton spinning mill. In 1798, a citizen of the Saxon city of Chemnitz, Christian Friedrich Kreissig, bought twenty-five spinning jennies and started a cotton factory. By 1801, local merchants in St. Gallen in Switzerland had sponsored Marc-Antoine Pellis's creation of the country's first spinning mill, the Spinnerei Aktiengesellschaft. Seven years later, spindles turned in the Lombardian town of Intra on the shores of Lake Maggiore. By 1818, the first mechanized cotton spinning mill began operations in Egypt on orders of Muhammad Ali, and in the mid-1830s, Don Pedro Baranda built the first steam-powered cotton spinning factory in Mexico.[5]

British tinkerers' revolutionary methods for the production of cotton yarn spread rapidly, probably more rapidly than any previous manufacturing technology. It certainly helped that travelers, journals, newspapers, and learned societies trumpeted these wondrous advances. But even more influential must have been the influx of British traders carrying yarn and finished cotton cloth at unbeatable prices. European and North American consumers, introduced to the wonderful properties of cotton through relatively expensive goods made in India, responded swiftly and enthusiastically, as did consumers in regions of the world that had produced their own cotton fabrics for centuries or millennia. As more people bought cheap cottons, entrepreneurs in more countries became convinced that they could produce the same goods. With equal enthusiasm skilled artisans, adventurers, state bureaucrats, and budding entrepreneurs embraced the new machines and techniques. By 1800, as we have seen, the first mechanized spinning mills had sprung up in Britain, France, the German lands, the United States, Russia, Switzerland, the Netherlands, and Belgium. Twenty years later, new mills churned out yarn and cloth in the Habsburg Empire, Denmark, Italy, Egypt, and Spain. And by 1860, mills could be found throughout Europe, North America, India, Mexico, and Brazil. While that year the United Kingdom still controlled 67.4 percent of the world's mechanical spindles, cotton spinning by machines had effectively replaced older ways of doing things in large areas of the world.[6]

The world's mechanized cotton industry was remarkable not only for its rapid global dispersion but also for its feverish rate of growth. Each new spinning mill served as an example to entrepreneurial neighbors that profits awaited those who could master the new world of cotton manufacturing. Belgian industrialization, without precedent in continental Europe in the first decade of the nineteenth century, was an example of this growth: In Ghent alone, its center, there had been only 227 cotton spinners in 1802, but six years later there were already 2,000 such workers, with an additional 1,000 laboring in the surrounding countryside.[7] The number of spindles in the German lands increased from 22,000 in 1800 to 2 million in 1860. Catalonia saw an exponential growth of its cotton industry as well, so much so that it became known as the "little England in the heart of Spain," with nearly 800,000 spindles turning in 1861. By 1828, nine spinning mills had opened in Russia, and by the middle of the nineteenth century Russia had become self-sufficient in cotton textiles. In Mexico, 25,000 spindles and 2,600 looms worked in its fifty-eight mills by 1843. Switzerland counted 1.35 million spindles in 1857. Nearby Alsace housed more than 500,000 mechanical spindles in 1828, and 859,300 in 1846. In the United States, cotton mills opened in Rhode Island (1790), New Jersey (1791), Delaware (1795), New Hampshire (1803), New York (1803), Connecticut (1804), and Maryland (1810). In 1810, according to the U.S. census, there were 269 cotton establishments in the United States with a total of 87,000 spindles. By 1860, there would be 5 million spindles, making cotton textiles the United States' most important manufacturing industry in terms of capital invested, workers employed, and net value of its product.[8]

The rapid spread and exponential growth of mechanized cotton yarn production in so many parts of the world evinces the compelling nature of this new social system. Most obviously, mechanized spinning led to enormous productivity gains; those with sufficient capital to afford the new technology immediately enjoyed a competitive advantage over hand spinners. Once entrepreneurs installed spinning mules in Switzerland,

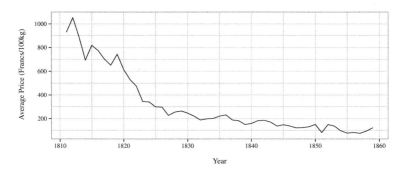

Cotton's dramatic decline in price: average price of
100 kilograms of cotton yarn in Mulhouse, 1811–1860

productivity per worker increased by as much as a factor of a hundred.[9] It
is not surprising that the history of cotton after 1780 had a definite direction: Ever-more productive machines substituted for human labor, turning the world's most important manufacturing industry upside down.

Yet if this new way of spinning cotton yarn was so compelling, should
it not have spread more evenly throughout the globe? Why did it take
ten or more years to travel a few hundred miles to continental Europe,
twenty or more years to cross the Atlantic to the United States, fifty or
more years to reach Mexico and Egypt, and a hundred or more years to
reach India, Japan, China, Argentina, and most of Africa? The spread of
cotton industrialization is puzzling. Clearly it was a vastly more productive way to satisfy a basic human need for cloth. Cotton growing needed
appropriate climates and soil, but cotton manufacturing, as the British
example had shown, needed neither. In fact, the spread of mechanized
cotton manufacturing seemed to follow a universal law of efficiency—yet
with surprisingly particular results.

If we compare mechanized cotton production to the spread of a virus
or an invasive species, then figuring out the underlying causes requires
us to differentiate the vulnerable populations from the resistant ones.
And indeed, even a cursory glance around the edges of these newfangled
machines in the countries and regions that adopted them first reveals
a host of characteristic economic, social, and political relations—the
embryonic features of industrial capitalism. As we have seen in Britain,
this industrial capitalism was a radical departure from the life of centuries

prior. It was one thing for British tinkerers and putting-out merchants to stumble upon a new way of spinning cotton in the last decades of the eighteenth century. But it was an entirely different thing to scale that model by several orders of magnitude and forge it into a new social order. It was the capacity of a newly emerging type of state, as we will see, that was decisive.

To understand the seemingly peculiar patterns of the spread of mechanized cotton manufacturing around the world, and with it industrialization as such, let us chart what the places that followed the British had in common. First and foremost, these early adopters all had a prior history of textile manufacturing. While no guarantee of success, such prior experience was all but required for cotton industrialization. Spinning mills almost always arose in areas that had already sustained vibrant textile industries—no matter if in woolens, flax, or cottons, urban or rural, home-based or in workshops. In the area around Ghent, for example, a long tradition of flax spinning and weaving had trained labor to cotton manufacturing. In the Mexican city of Puebla, mechanical cotton spinning built upon a centuries-long history of cotton spinning and weaving so established that its workers had a cotton producers' guild, and indeed large workshops had emerged even before the advent of mechanization. The situation in the German lands was no different: One economist found that "the modern cotton industry nearly everywhere is building on older home industries." In Russia, the cotton manufacturing industry emerged from eighteenth-century linen and woolen manufacturing; in the United States, New England's textile mills arose in areas in which women especially had a long tradition of spinning yarn and weaving textiles; in Alsace, the history of textile production stretched back to the fifteenth century; and in Switzerland's cotton manufacturing areas, the long and distinguished history of people making cotton fabrics in their homes had resulted in the accumulation of skills and capital. This small-scale work was often the first victim of industry's rise, but it provided the usurpers with skills and labor essential to modern manufacturing.[10]

The focus of the old manufacturing base also shaped the avenues each region followed to industrialization. In some areas of the world, cotton industrialization unfolded from basic spinning, with the weaving and printing of textiles being secondary. In the United States, for

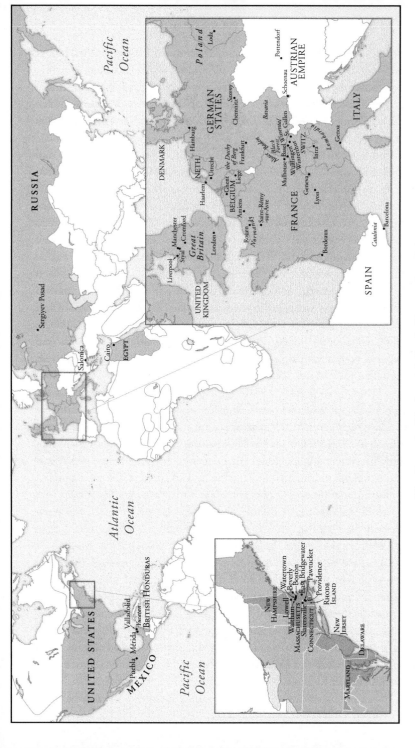

The Spread of Industrial Capitalism, 1780–1860

example, as in England itself, industrialization was led by basic manufacturing, namely spinning, moving next into weaving and, later, printing, the application of colorful designs on cotton cloth imported from elsewhere. In many other parts of the world, among them Belgium, Russia, and Alsace, however, cotton industrialization emerged from a thriving printing industry.[11]

Whether led by spinning or printing, in all of these regions rural people had spun and woven in their cottages, farmhouses, and huts and had done so under the direction of merchants. In Saxony, cotton spinning and weaving extended back to the fifteenth century, with peasants first producing yarn and cloth for their own use. By the eighteenth century, merchants had built a complex putting-out system, advancing raw cotton to farmers to later retrieve finished yarn and cloth from them. Eventually some of these peasants became full-time spinners. By 1799, in and around Chemnitz as many as fifteen thousand people spun cotton in their homes. As workers honed their skills, merchants accumulated capital and marketing expertise.[12]

The Swiss story unfolded similarly. Tens of thousands of people had been busy manufacturing cotton textiles long before machines arrived. Merchants, just like in Saxony, gradually organized this production. When inexpensive British yarn began flooding the Swiss market, many spinners became weavers, continuing to work in their homes. Some of the putting-out merchants, however, saw an opportunity to produce yarn domestically, and they brought workers into factories to work for wages on new English-made machines. At first, industrialization did not eliminate manufacturing in the countryside and in homes, but over time its insatiable hunger for capital and ever greater mechanization shifted power to those merchants most capable of building large factories employing wage workers.[13]

In Italy as well, Lombardian putting-out systems paved the way for the emergence of factory production in the early decades of the nineteenth century. A few hundred miles to the west, in Catalonia, earlier manufacturing in both the countryside as well as in the city of Barcelona had smoothed the path toward factory production, fueled in part by the new accumulation of capital and in part by the creation of a rural group of wage earners who could be moved into factories. Holland's mechanized cotton industry was also built upon and embedded within its putting-out networks, as was Mexico's.[14]

Such a system of home spinning could, at least at first, easily adapt to a more mechanized way of doing things. In the late eighteenth century, for example, some spinners began using jennies in their homes or small workshops, as they had done in Britain a few decades earlier. Eventually, however, merchants nearly everywhere would concentrate production in factories, where it could be better supervised, standardized, and accelerated by the use of water and steam power.[15]

This early manufacturing often, though not always, also provided access to that other ingredient essential for industrial production: capital. Without access to capital, the new ways of producing cotton were impossible: buildings had to be erected, streams diverted, machines built, workers hired, raw materials secured, and expertise recruited, often from long distances and across national boundaries. The merchants' most common strategy was reinvesting capital accumulated in the organization of household production of cotton yarn and cloth into small factories. In Switzerland, for example, former putting-out merchants financed the wave of mechanized spinning mills built after 1806. They began with small factories of a few mules and slowly enlarged them. In Catalonia, by the late eighteenth century, artisan producers had accumulated capital in the nonmechanized and household-based textile industry and then used it to expand and mechanize production. In Alsace, the industry drew its capital and entrepreneurial skills from the older merchant and artisanal elites of the city of Mulhouse. In Russia, the Prokhorov family, cotton manufacturers from Sergiyev Posad, a small city fifty miles from Moscow, followed a similar trajectory. Serfs emancipated by Catherine II, they became small-scale merchants, and then, in 1843, focused on calico printing. Shortly thereafter, they started a small spinning mill and their firm grew rapidly. As the age's most dynamic industry, cotton manufacturing provided ample opportunities for social mobility. Swiss cotton manufacturer Heinrich Kunz started out as a wage worker, but at the time of his death in 1859 he owned eight spinning mills with 150,000 spindles, employing two thousand workers.[16]

Mill owners in the United States also often rose from the ranks of small merchants and skilled artisans. Rhode Island's Samuel Slater had apprenticed himself in England, oversaw other factories, and then migrated to the United States in 1789. Once there, he entered into a partnership with Providence merchant Moses Brown, who was rich from the West Indian provisioning trade and was trying to introduce mechanical spinning in the Browns' Pawtucket factory. Slater proceeded to build British-designed machines from memory, and in December 1790 the factory produced its first yarn. The energetic Slater soon expanded operations, built additional mills, and eventually accumulated sufficient wealth to create his own company in 1799. By 1806 the Rhode Island countryside was graced by the village of Slatersville.[17]

Such successes inspired others: When in 1813 William Holmes, whose "object is to get business for myself," wrote to his brother John that they should build a cotton factory, he reviewed what a nearby factory had cost and concluded from such observations that putting up a factory large enough to eventually accommodate a thousand spindles would cost about $10,000. He was "ready to join & put in 1000 dollars. A spinner who is a workman can be obtained who will put in 500 more & I can get more subscriptions from this quarter if necessary." Once started, these humble investors could "so increase the machinery from the profits of the 200 spindles."[18]

As the example of the Holmes brothers shows, capital requirements in early cotton factories could be quite modest, so modest that even in areas in which the availability of capital was limited, such as Saxony, cotton factories might still flourish in a fashion, despite being small, outdated, and reliant on cheap labor and cheap waterpower. Don Baranda, just as modestly, had invested a total of 40,000 pesos, the equivalent of the annual wages of approximately two hundred skilled workers, in his Valladolid factory in 1835. Even in areas with a greater capital availability, expenditures were measured and conservative. In the French department of Bas-Rhin, part of the cotton complex centered in Mulhouse, a cotton spinning factory only required an average capitalization of 16,216 francs in 1801, allowing the thirty-seven factories that existed to employ an average of eighty-one workers. A weaving factory required more—35,714 francs on average, but this was still a modest amount compared to the 150,000 francs needed for a carriage maker, and the 1.4 million francs that an arms manufacturing establishment required. Later, factories would of course grow: during the first half of the nineteenth century, a mechanized spinning mill might cost between 200,000 and 600,000 francs, an integrated factory with spinning, weaving, and printing operations perhaps as much as 1.5 million francs.[19]

Reinvestments of capital accumulated in the putting-out industry and small artisan workshops combined with tentative investment from large fortunes accumulated in the sometimes fickle world of trade. In some exceptional instances, indeed, huge fortunes were invested in cotton manufacturing as merchant capital attached itself to industrial production. The most dramatic such move was undertaken by a group of Boston merchants looking for new outlets for capital suddenly and ruinously idled due to the American trade embargo against Britain and France from 1807 to 1812. In 1810 Francis Cabot Lowell traveled to the United Kingdom to acquire the blueprints for a cotton mill. Upon his return, he and a group of wealthy Boston merchants had signed the "Articles of Agreement between the Associates of the Boston Manufacturing Company," which created a huge integrated spinning and weaving mill in Waltham near Boston, initially capitalized at $400,000, or a bit more than 2 million francs. The mill focused on inexpensive coarse cotton goods, some of which were sold to clothe slaves, replacing Indian manufactured cloth. (So common did Lowell cloth become among slaves that "Lowell" became the generic term slaves used to describe coarse cottons.) The venture proved hugely profitable, with dividends in most years above 10 percent on the paid-in capital. In 1817, the mills paid peak dividends of 17 percent. By 1823, the Boston Associates expanded further, building more mills in Lowell, about twenty-five miles north of Boston, and creating the largest integrated mills anywhere in the world. This move of American merchant capital into manufacturing marked another tight connection between slavery and industry. Early cotton industrialists such as the Cabot, Brown, and Lowell families all had ties to the slave trade, the West Indian provision trade, and the trade in agricultural commodities grown by slaves. The "lords of the lash" and the "lords of the loom" were, yet again, tightly linked.[20]

The Boston Associates were unusual in the size of their investment, but they were not the only large merchants moving capital into industrial production. Swiss merchants by the early nineteenth century began to invest into the Alsatian cotton industry, and also into the emerging cotton complex of Lombardy. Barcelona merchants followed suit. In Mexico as well, the larger share of the capital invested in cotton manufacturing did not come out of the textile industry itself, but instead from fortunes accumulated in trade. Of the forty-one capitalists who opened cotton factories in Puebla between 1830 and 1849, nineteen had been merchants, five landowners, and only three had previously been involved in textiles.[21]

Wealthy merchants, many of them foreign, also played a central role in the development of the Russian cotton textile industry, none more emblematically than Ludwig Knoop. Born into a middling Bremen merchant family, Knoop had come to Russia in 1839 as an assistant representative of a Manchester merchant firm, de Jersey, importing yarn. He was only eighteen years old but already quite familiar with cotton manufacturing technology and in thrall to its promise. When, four years later, Britain lifted its ban on textile machine exports, a ban that had from 1786 to 1843 outlawed the export of such things as the spinning mule (or blueprints thereof), Knoop began to bring these machines to Russia, along with English engineers and mechanics; he also imported American-grown cotton and secured credits abroad for Russian manufacturers. He built eight spinning mills between 1843 and 1847, eventually selling those factories to Russian entrepreneurs. Riding cotton's meteoric global rise, Knoop became Russia's most prominent industrialist.[22]

Such mobilizations of capital were almost always embedded within kinship networks, the Boston Associates, for example, drew on relatives for investments; so did the Fränkel family of Upper Silesia, who built a large spinning, weaving, and finishing empire in and around Lodz, effectively pooling family capital and management skills. The best example of the importance of family to the emerging cotton industry, however, was Alsace, where a handful of families came to dominate a huge local industry for many generations: the Dollfuses, Koechlins, and Schlumbergers among them. These families intermarried. Pierre Schlumberger, one of Mulhouse's major cotton entrepreneurs, whose spinning mills and printing workshops were valued at 1.3 million francs when he died, had twenty-two children and grandchildren who entered adulthood between 1830 and 1870. Nineteen of them married, fourteen into the Alsatian bourgeoisie, and three into the bourgeoisie of the cotton port of Le Havre. The textile bourgeoisie of Mulhouse thus was extraordinarily cohesive, capable of organizing (in 1826, they founded the Société Industrielle de Mulhouse), and of exerting its power to create a political, social, and economic environment that was conducive to their interests. One descendant, André Koechlin, was aptly dubbed the "Sultan of Mulhouse."[23]

Access to capital and a history in textile production thus were essential to embarking upon the great adventure of manufacturing yarn and cloth

Russia: Ludwig Knoop and his wife

France: André Koechlin

Belgium: Lieven Bauwens

Mexico: Don Pedro Baranda

with machines, but the catalyst that turned these preconditions into full-fledged cotton industrialization was pressure: namely, the competition from British imports. Indeed, throughout the world, the embrace of mechanized cotton manufacturing was motivated by the need to substitute domestic production for foreign—usually British—imports, just as England had fought so hard to replace a reliance on Indian imports with its own domestic products. By 1800, Britain was flooding world markets, exporting huge quantities of cotton yarn and a smaller proportion of cloth: the value of exports to Europe increased by more than twenty times between 1780 and 1805.[24]

At first British manufacturers themselves were important agents in the spread of industrial capitalism. Wright Armitage, for example, a Manchester cotton manufacturer, sent his brother Enoch to the United States to sell his factory's products. In similar ways, McConnel & Kennedy, the Manchester spinners, drew on agents as far away as Hamburg, Switzerland, France, and, in 1825, Leipzig, Belfast, St. Gallen, Thessaloniki, Frankfurt, Calcutta, France, Genoa, and Geneva to sell their yarn. Their business records testify to the ever greater variety of foreign markets they served. While in the 1790s the firm had corresponded nearly exclusively with customers in the United Kingdom, by 1805 it corresponded with business partners in Germany, Portugal, and the United States, and by 1825 with partners in Egypt, France, India, Italy, Poland, and Switzerland. In that year, 30 percent of the firm's letters went to places outside the United Kingdom, testifying to the global scope of their sales. John Rylands, Manchester's first multimillionaire and the builder of an "industrial and commercial empire," started his career as a weaver, turned himself into a manufacturer, and by the 1820s became a wholesale trader, with huge warehouses in Manchester and by 1849 also in London, that supplied the markets of the world.[25]

Eventually, however, mill owners focused on manufacturing only and left the selling to a burgeoning group of merchants. Already in 1815 the city of Manchester had fifteen hundred cotton showrooms that made a panoply of goods available to customers. Foreign-born merchants flocked there. Nathan Rothschild, for example, arrived from Germany in 1798 to acquire textiles for his father's house back in Frankfurt, the first of many German Jews who settled in Manchester. After 1840, a large number of Greeks joined them to serve the needs of the Ottoman Empire and beyond. Merchants located in foreign ports, drawing on the credit of

Capturing the world market: John Rylands,
Manchester, 1869

wealthy British merchants and bankers, became further conduits for the
sale of British textiles. In Buenos Aires, for example, a rapidly growing
group of British merchants sold British yarn and cloth from the earliest years of the nineteenth century, exporting at the same time hides
and other meat products. Hugo (Hugh) Dallas, for example, imported
such yarn and cloth on commission, and sent "information respecting Colours, Assortments, qualities & prices" to British manufacturers
so they could adopt their production to a remote market, where letters
could take six months to arrive.[26]

And Buenos Aires was not the only place in South America where
British merchants traded in cotton. Already by the mid-1820s it has been
estimated that ten British merchant houses were active in Montevideo,
twenty in Lima, fourteen in Mexico City, four in Cartagena, sixty in Rio,
twenty in Bahia, and sixteen in Pernambuco.[27] This tidal wave of exports
flooded the world's nonmechanized cotton industries. Switzerland, one
of Europe's earliest industrializers, witnessed significant imports of British
machine-spun yarn starting in the mid-1790s. As a result, wages in spinning fell dramatically: if a Swiss spinner was able to buy a five-pound loaf

of bread in 1780 with one day's spinning labor, it took between two and two-and-a-half days in 1798. As early as 1802, representatives of British spinning mills traveled to Switzerland to sell their wares in even higher volumes, and by the early 1820s no hand spinners were left in the Swiss countryside. Similar incursions happened in Catalonia, in northwestern Europe, and in the German lands, challenging budding capitalists, rulers, and bureaucrats to embrace mechanized manufacturing. Failure to do so, in effect, meant giving up on cotton, and forgoing what had become a significant source of wealth and, increasingly, a precondition for being "modern." Yet rulers and capitalists in many parts of the world, as we will see, were unable to respond.[28]

British competition was a strong incentive to embark upon something radically new, but no manufacturer could do so without British technology. Though the British government tried to hold on to its monopoly, that technology spread rapidly due to active programs of private and government-directed industrial espionage as well as the unstoppable outflow of skilled British workers and cotton capitalists eager to make their fortunes in new lands. Between the invention of new machines in Britain and their spread elsewhere there was typically only a ten-year lag. In Holland and northwestern Germany, jennies and water frames arrived from England in 1780, while Belgian frames came from France, where jennies had been introduced in 1771. The water frame arrived in Lyon in 1782, after being set up in England in 1769. Samuel Crompton's mule came to Amiens in 1788, just nine years after its invention. Arkwright's machinery, one sociologist remarks, was a "considerable technological breakthrough" but one that nonetheless could "readily diffuse to other regions."[29]

Indeed, in the wake of the Industrial Revolution in Britain, entrepreneurs, rulers, bureaucrats, and scientists from many parts of the world carefully studied the progress of the British cotton industry. They traveled to Britain to acquire blueprints, models, and machines. If machines could not be had openly, entrepreneurs and spies committed the secrets of this new technology to memory, or persuaded skilled British artisans to travel despite the restrictive emigration laws in place up to 1825. Industrial espionage was the order of the day. Between 1798 and 1799, Lieven Bauwens, for example, who brought mechanized cotton spinning to Belgium, traveled to England thirty-two times to study the new ways to spin cotton, sometimes bringing skilled workers along with him. Thomas Somers, who had been sent to Britain by a group of Baltimore manufacturers in 1785, returned with small-scale models of spinning machines. Because knowledge of the early machines remained mostly in the heads of artisans, their movements made this diffusion possible. It has been estimated that more than two thousand British artisans worked in continental Europe, taking with them the beating heart of the English textile industry's know-how.[30]

Everywhere, British entrepreneurs, British expertise, and British artisans played a crucial role. In Normandy, one of the centers of the French cotton industry, brothers Thomas and Frederic Waddington were instrumental in establishing mechanized spinning factories in Saint-Rémy-sur-Avre and Rouen. In 1818, Mulhousian cotton entrepreneur Nicholas Schlumberger hired engineer Job Dixon from England to build spinning machines for him. In 1831, Camille Koechlin traveled to England to investigate cotton techniques there and returned with a number of "Cahier des notes faites en Angleterre," providing a detailed survey of manufacturing techniques, especially as they related to the dyeing of fabrics.[31]

From France, the new machines migrated to adjacent Switzerland. As the Swiss cotton industry suffered mightily from machine-made yarn from Britain, in 1800 the Swiss consul in Bordeaux, Marc Antoine Pellis, approached the government of the Swiss Confederation to import French-made copies of English spinning mules. They were eventually put up in a nationalized monastery in 1801 and their 204 spindles put to work. A year later, some Winterthur merchants brought forty-four of Arkwright's spinning machines to a factory in Wülflingen.[32]

Locations much farther from Lancashire also benefited from the spread of ideas, machines, and people. Mexico drew on British and eventually also American experts, technology, and machines. The U.S. cotton industry itself relied on British technology and on industrial espionage, easily camouflaged by ceaseless trade and immigration. In 1787, Alexander Hamilton (two years before he became secretary of the Treasury) and Tench Coxe sent Andrew Mitchell to Britain to acquire models and drawings of Arkwright's machinery, a project that failed only when Mitchell was caught. Most famously, Francis Cabot Lowell ventured to Britain in 1810, allegedly for "health reasons," and came back with blueprints for his factory at Watertown. The combination of migration and espionage meant knowledge traveled fast: Arkwright's carding engine found its way across the Atlantic in eight short years, Hargreaves's spinning jenny took ten; Arkwright's water frame took twenty-two years, and Crompton's mule only eleven. After 1843, when the export of textile machines from Great Britain was finally made legal, "market seeking by British engineering firms" became an important additional factor in the further spread of textile manufacturing technology.[33]

Once these technologies spread, indigenous machine makers quickly mastered them and adapted them to new purposes and conditions. Saxon entrepreneurs started building simplified versions of British machines as early as 1801, and Swiss artisans followed in 1806. France developed a strong machine-building industry alongside its cotton industry, and that technology in turn was exported all over Europe. German skilled artisans in turn played an important role in the early history of the Russian cotton industry. Barcelona artisans manufactured spinning jennies as early as 1789, Arkwright's water frame in 1793, and Crompton's mule in 1806. Alsatian manufacturers were about fifteen years ahead of their British counterparts in developing dyes and chemicals to fix color to cloth, technology that eventually allowed for the emergence of the huge chemical and pharmaceutical industry around Basel. And in 1831 the American John Thorp invented ring spinning, which proved to be easier to operate and faster, creating more thread per worker. It soon spread to Mexico, Great Britain, and, most significantly, by the end of the century, Japan. The idea of relentless technical innovation, a core characteristic of industrial capitalism, spread beyond the borders of Great Britain—a sign that industrial capitalism had grown wings.[34]

Having access to spinning and weaving technology indeed was just as necessary as access to capital, a prior history of putting-out networks, the pressures of British competition, and a history of some kind with textile manufacturing more generally. Regions such as Papua New Guinea, the Congo Basin, or the interior of the North American continent lacked these conditions, and were thus unlikely to follow the British road. But vast areas of the world saw no industrialization in cottons even though they fulfilled these conditions, Kano in present-day Nigeria, Osaka in Japan, and Ahmedabad in India among them. To be sure, most of Asia's and Africa's cotton industry was still outside the realm of British competition and thus under considerably less pressure to embrace the new manufacturing techniques. Yet some parts of Asia—including India, China, and the Ottoman Empire—did not mechanize despite devastating pressures from British yarn imports. When so many regions did industrialize, what explains their seeming twins that did not? We need to search for an answer elsewhere.

One easy explanation for the uneven development is the salutary effect of war capitalism on European economies. The British case, after all, reveals how important colonial expropriation and slavery and the violent insertion into global networks had been for the radical recasting of the local cotton industry. If industrial capitalism was built on the wages of war capitalism, then perhaps it was the ability to embrace war capitalism that was the fundamental precondition for cotton industrialization. Not only British, but also French, Dutch, and Spanish capitalists could and did draw on colonial raw materials and colonial markets. Still, this is too facile a link. After all, one of war capitalism's most significant contributions to the unfolding of industrial capitalism had been the provision of huge quantities of raw cotton at falling prices. But in many ways that benefit was easily generalized—anyone could travel to Liverpool or, for that matter, New Orleans to purchase cotton and thus benefit from the enormous pressure placed upon the slaves and indigenous peoples of North America. And what about the spread of cotton industrialization in the German lands? Or Switzerland? To be sure, some of their merchants gained riches in the slave trade, and they benefited from the accessibility of slave-grown cotton, but still, these important areas of European industrialization were bereft of colonies.

Moreover, while the prevailing economic model—war capitalism—provided the resources needed, especially raw cotton, for industrialization and many important institutional legacies, the example of Great Britain had shown that war capitalism itself was ill-suited for the next step: the mass production of cotton textiles. Another way of organizing economic activity had to be forged—and transferring that model turned out to be much more challenging than moving machines or mobilizing capital.

What the British example also shows is the importance of the state's capacity to forge conditions conducive to industrialization. Without a powerful state capable of legally, bureaucratically, infrastructurally, and militarily penetrating its own territory, industrialization was all but impossible. Forging markets, protecting domestic industry, creating tools to raise revenues, policing borders, and fostering changes that allowed for the mobilization of wage workers were crucial. Indeed, the capacity of states to foster a domestic cotton industry turns out to be the key division between places that industrialized and those that did not. The map of modern states corresponds almost perfectly to the map of regions that saw early cotton industrialization.

On the most superficial level, states mattered because they made the project of cotton industrialization explicitly their own by engaging in a range of measures to secure the construction of spinning mills. The French revolutionary government, for example, provided loans to Belgian cotton pioneer Bauwens. When Johann Gottfried Brügelmann started the first cotton mill in the German-speaking lands, he received an exclusive privilege and monopoly from the Duchy of Berg. In Saxony, when Karl Friedrich Bernhard and Conrad Wöhler opened the first cotton factories in 1799 with the help of English engineers, they successfully appealed to the local government for direct subsidies and a temporary monopoly. In Russia cotton entrepreneur Michael Ossovski received government loans and a five-year monopoly to start Russia's first mechanized spinning mill in 1798. In Denmark the government heavily subsidized the emerging textile industry and brought skilled workers from abroad. In 1779 it even created the Royal Privileged Cotton Manufacture, known as the "Manchester Factory." Similarly, in the United States, Alexander Hamilton in his "Report on the Subject of Manufactures" in 1791 had strongly advocated a policy of government support for industrial development. And the state proved important, as when in 1786 the Massachusetts legislature sponsored two Scots—Robert and Alexander Barr—to emigrate to East Bridgewater to build a cotton spinning factory. In a similar vein, in 1789 a group of Boston merchants, aided by a $500 grant by the state of Massachusetts, incorporated the Beverly Cotton Manufactory. In Mexico the federal government created the Banco de Avío para Fomento de la Industria Nacional in 1830, to make loans for the building of factories and organized the acquisition of foreign machines and the hiring of foreign technical experts, and in 1826, the government of the state of Puebla supported the travel of mechanics to the United States and Europe to study the techniques of cotton production and to buy machines.[35]

Yet monopolies, subsidies, and the provision of expertise all proved to be fairly minor interventions, sufficient to allow the building of one factory or another, but not enough to embark upon the creation of a significant domestic cotton industry. Indeed, without the novel and powerful state in the heart of industrial capitalism, as we will see later, these efforts could easily fizzle. Much more important was a state's ability to isolate its domestic manufacturing efforts from competition, especially from Britain. But only a few states in the early nineteenth century enjoyed the capacity to police their external borders. Tellingly, the first wave of mechanized cotton spinning came to continental Europe as a direct result of the ability of the expanding French revolutionary republic to keep British manufactured goods from the continent. The blockade of British trade, from November 1806 to April 1814, provided the single most important impetus for continental European cotton industrialization, protecting feeble beginnings so that they could become a full-fledged industry. Just at the moment when the continental cotton industry struggled to emerge, Napoleon's policy isolated it from the devastating competition of English manufacturers; French spinning and weaving operations soon took off. Saxony was similarly affected: In 1806, the cotton industry of Saxony, with Chemnitz at its center, counted 13,200 mechanical spindles, but by 1813, toward the blockade's end, that number had multiplied an extraordinary seventeen times.[36]

The effects of the blockade rippled through other parts of Europe as well. While the first Swiss mechanized cotton mill opened its gates in 1801, the real expansion of the Swiss cotton industry occurred only after 1806, during the continental blockade, when the industry was now able to serve markets formerly served by the British. With the end of the blockade, the Swiss industry experienced a grave crisis, as the continent was again swamped with British wares. The Swiss were compelled to look elsewhere for markets, which they found increasingly in the Americas and the Far East. In Belgium as well, before the continental blockade, many of Ghent's printing workshops still worked with Indian cloths. An 1806 report observed that "in this Department two manufacturers only make the cloths known as calicoes, suitable for printing. Were there an embargo placed on textile imports from India, the Department would soon be able to produce sufficient to satisfy the needs of the numerous printing works of this and other Departments because of the abundance of weavers in the area and because the spinning mills could produce all that is needed." Napoleon unintentionally fulfilled this wish, and huge new opportunities emerged for local manufacturers. Just a year later, Prefect Faipoult was able to report that "no industrial progress has ever taken place more rapidly." In Holland, the Habsburg Empire, and Denmark the stories were quite similar.[37]

A similar impetus was at play in the United States during its periodic conflicts with England. There, the wars of the early nineteenth century proved beneficial to cotton manufacturing enterprises. With Jefferson's Embargo Act of 1807, which blocked the shipment of goods between the United Kingdom, France, and the United States, British textile imports largely disappeared from the market, providing new opportunities to American spinners and weavers: The number of mechanical spindles in the United States increased from 8,000 in 1807 to 130,000 in 1815. There were fifteen cotton mills in 1806, and sixty-two in 1809, with another twenty-five under construction. This astonishing and highly profitable increase encouraged merchants, including Francis Cabot Lowell in Boston, to shift ever more capital into cotton manufacturing.[38]

Napoleon's continental blockade gave a boost to the cotton industry of Europe and the Americas at a crucial moment in its development. By 1815, however, the protective effects of war and revolutionary upheaval in Europe had ended. When peace came to Europe after Napoleon's defeat, British cotton manufacturer Wright Armitage remarked with relief that "a sudden transition from War to Peace has had a great effect on Commerce. . . . I think we are now beginning to feel something of our own superiority over other Nations, in driving them out of the market as Manufacturers."[39]

In some parts of the world, however, the cotton industry had grown so substantially during the years of upheaval that manufacturers had gained sufficient political clout to pressure their governments to protect the emerging industry from being "driven out" and provided states with an interest in and an ability to further develop industries. Wright Armitage was partly wrong. In the United States, a new tariff provided the cotton industry with some protection as early as 1816. Other parts of the world followed suit. In France, "prohibitive tariffs" followed the end of the continental blockade. Prussia and Austria imposed import duties on cotton goods in 1818, Russia in 1820, France in 1822, Italy in 1824, and Bavaria and Württemberg in 1826. France went so far that in 1842 it prohibited the importation of all cotton goods onto its national territory. Protectionism, once seen as a wartime cataclysm, now became a permanent feature of newly industrializing states—who in this respect followed the British example, as Britain had protected its home market from Indian competition just as furiously.[40]

Cotton manufacturers themselves were at the forefront of demanding such protection. Even as late as 1846, far beyond the industry's infancy, Alsatian entrepreneurs created the Comité Mulhousien de l'Association pour la Défense du Travail National, with cotton manufacturers Emile Dollfus and J. A. Schlumberger at the helm, advocating strong protectionist policies. Across the Rhine in Baden, cotton spinners had pressured for tariffs since 1820. Spinners in Saxony also agitated for protective tariffs. When Saxony became part of the Zollverein customs union on January 1, 1834, these spinners gained a much greater domestic market, and additional tariff protection. In negotiating these tariffs among the very states that constituted the Zollverein, Friedrich List, who attended the meetings for Württemberg in 1846, believed, like Alexander Hamilton across the Atlantic, that the "value of manufactures [must] be estimated from a political point of view." Industry, among other things, he argued, mattered for the ability of nations to mobilize for war. This "political point of view," was shared by Catalonian, Habsburg, Russian, Italian, and French rulers who protected their emerging cotton industry by various tariffs and prohibitions, and whose cotton industrialists all clamored for higher import duties.[41]

Even in places farther away from England, domestic cotton industrialization rested on the ability of governments to protect their domestic industries in times of peace as well as war. In the United States, Massachusetts elites, and especially Waltham mill founder Francis Cabot Lowell, influenced the federal government's decision in 1816 to put a protective tariff on low-grade cotton goods, in effect continuing to allow the import of high-quality British textiles, while cornering the market for cheap cottons. Coarse Indian goods, the kind Lowell and his colleagues competed with (and which they indeed had spent much of their previous career importing from India), were effectively subject to duty payments of between 60 and 84 percent of their value until 1846, when the industry had developed to such an extent that it could withstand such competition with lower tariffs.[42]

Mexico's industry, like that of the United States, was a child of protectionism. Since their independence from Spain in 1821, political elites had pursued industrialization. Mexico had had a long-established and thriving nonmechanized textile industry but that industry had come under pressure from cheaply manufactured yarn and cloth imports from Britain and the United States. The newly independent Mexican state tried to address this problem by raising tariffs, or even prohibiting the import of cotton textiles and yarn. Independence meant that Mexico escaped the massive wave of deindustrialization sweeping other parts of the world. The first mechanized cotton mill in Mexico that would last (unlike the Aurora Yucateca) opened in 1835 in Puebla, founded and managed by Esteban de Antuñano, and indeed it was Antuñano himself who most forcefully demanded that the country protect itself from cotton imports. Like Tench Coxe in the United States and Friedrich List in Germany, Antuñano advocated import-substituting industrialization as a path toward wealth and political stability. Responding to pressure from industrialists, as well as to the fear of social unrest, such as the riots in the textile-manufacturing city of Puebla in 1828, the Mexican government passed new tariffs by May 1829 that prohibited the import of coarse cotton clothing, exactly the kind that could be manufactured in Mexico itself. The new tariffs proved successful, and by 1831 new spinning workshops had opened their doors. Antuñano continued to be an eloquent supporter of tariffs, and he warned that lowering tariffs would destroy "in one stroke" all that had been achieved. His own factory, he indeed argued, only existed because of the prohibition to import yarn of grades below Number 21, relatively coarse yarns. Protectionism continued unabated: the new tariff of 1837 again banning the import of cheap cotton yarn and cloth. By 1843, the prohibition of cotton textile imports was written into the Mexican constitution. As a result, the number of cotton mills in Mexico increased from four in 1837 to more than fifty in 1847.[43]

Mexico's independent state, subject to the pressure of deeply entrenched, well-organized, and consciously, programmatically industrialist businessmen who not only could make their interests central to state policies, but in fact often dominated the state, was essential for its move toward industrial capitalism. In Mexico, unlike, for example, Brazil, promoting domestic industry was very much an issue close to the heart of nationalist politicians: As one historian of Mexico observed, "The prosperity of manufacturers depended almost exclusively on the willingness and the capacity of the state to police the marketplace." The independence of Mexico thus mattered a great deal. By 1870, domestic textile producers, most of them in cottons, still supplied 60 percent of the domestic market, compared to just 35–42 percent in India and 11–38 percent in the Ottoman Empire. Mexico's unusually consistent and forceful political commitments to import substitution thus created a position unlike any of its peers in the global South.[44]

The successful forging of industrial capitalism thus rested as much on the capacity of states to create a framework in which manufacturing could thrive as on entrepreneurial initiative. Beyond protectionism, states also played a crucial role in market making by removing internal duties. The Catalonian industry benefited from the removal of internal tariff barriers in the Spanish market, as did the industry in the German lands after the creation of the Zollverein in 1834, which removed the myriad border crossings and tariff payments that had characterized trade in that part of the world. Sometimes the state also became an important customer, as for example in Russia, mostly to equip their militaries. But most important of all was the road building, canal digging, and railway construction that characterized assertive states in the first half of the nineteenth century. These infrastructure projects greatly facilitated the circulation of goods, people, and information, and thus allowed for the emergence of larger and much more integrated markets.[45]

As firsthand witnesses to England's early triumphs, competing states and cotton capitalists also clearly saw a national interest in conquering foreign, often colonial, markets and did what they could to follow suit. Britain itself, of course, relied on imperial expansion to capture markets, in part to sidestep the protectionist policies of continental Europe and the United States. So did the Catalonian industry, which benefited greatly from sales overseas, so much so that the Americas, according to one historian, constituted "the most dynamic market for the producers of the Principality since the late 1770s." And it was a nearly perfect complementarity: Cotton textiles flowed out of Catalonia's cotton industry, while raw cotton, with the encouragement of the Spanish state, came in increasing amounts from the New World to the port of Barcelona.[46] As elsewhere, new forms of integrating colonial territories and industrialization emerged.[47]

As a result, growth rates of the Catalan industry were about equal to those of the British industry—but only until the 1810s, when Spanish holdings in Latin America shrunk drastically. Though Spain had once possessed one of Europe's fastest-growing cotton industries, Spanish producers increasingly found themselves at a disadvantage; without the benefit of colonial markets, merchants could not compete with cheaper British goods, either in former Spanish territories or elsewhere in the Americas. With the declining prospects of the industry, merchant capital divested, showing the importance of the state-sponsored creation of cloth markets.[48]

Mexico: Estéban de Antuñano

Germany: Friedrich List

United States: Tench Coxe

The French and Dutch industries benefited from colonial markets just as much and for much longer. French manufacturers found significant markets within their colonial empire in Africa, Asia, and the Americas. Holland regained Java in 1816, and by 1829, 68 percent of cotton imports to Java originated from the Netherlands. This was not least the result of King William's 1824 Textile Ordinance, a protectionist law that tried to force British manufacturers out of Java. William also created the Nederlandsche Handel-Maatschappij, a semigovernmental firm, with the king as a major investor, buying Dutch cottons and selling them in Java to bring Javanese goods back to Holland. Thus supported, colonial markets were central to Dutch success. Twente's cotton industry in fact became completely dependent on the Javanese market.[49]

When Belgium became part of the Dutch Republic in 1815 as a result of the Congress of Vienna, it profited immediately and tremendously from new access to the Dutch Asian markets. These markets became so important that Belgium's gaining independence in 1830 and losing access to Dutch colonial markets precipitated a severe crisis. Some Belgian firms even packed up and moved to Holland in order to continue to export into the colonies, such as those of Thomas Wilson and Jean Baptiste Theodore Prévinaire, who both moved to Haarlem in 1834.[50]

Even manufacturers in countries without colonies benefited from other states' colonial expansion. Swiss manufacturers, like their British counterparts, responded to the increasing protectionism around them by investing in the Italian and German cotton industry, and by looking for markets farther afield. In the 1850s and 1860s, the production of batiks for Southeast Asia and cotton head shawls for the Islamic world was important to Swiss manufacturers, with the Winterthur merchant house Gebrüder Volkart, for example, selling Swiss cotton goods to India, the eastern Mediterranean, and East Asia.[51]

The ability to shape nearby and distant territories into markets was a capacity that emerged much later, if ever, in much of Africa, Asia, and South America. While skills, markets, capital, and technology were available in many different parts of the world, a state that could protect domestic markets, forge access to remote markets, and create an infrastructure that facilitated manufacturing was the distinctive feature of early industrial leaders. And these increasingly powerful states also forged the institutions necessary to underpin industrial capitalism—from markets for wage labor (enabled by the undermining of precapitalist dependencies in the countryside and alternative means of gaining access to subsistence) to property rights created by laws and administrative infrastructures.

As a result, industrial capitalism, the most revolutionary invention of all, traveled only in very particular ways. The capitalists who managed to follow the British example usually worked within states that embraced the industrialization project and saw national manufacturing as a way to strengthen the state, forging in the process a new relationship between economic activity and national territory. In these states, rulers, bureaucrats, and capitalists could penetrate bounded territories legally, bureaucratically, infrastructurally, and militarily to create conditions that allowed for long-term capital investments, the mobilization of labor, expanding domestic and foreign markets, and protection for national industries from the uncertainties of the global economy. For statesmen in burgeoning nation-states, the calculations about whether to build an industrial society on the British model were straightforward: Industry was a source of wealth, and also of vastly superior tools of warfare. To survive in a competitive state system, prosperity was imperative, and embracing industrial capitalism seemed like a sure way to reach it. For some capitalists, in turn, investing in manufacturing seemed a promising avenue toward wealth—and they pressured their governments to the best of their ability to help forge industrial capitalism, often against the interests and inclinations of competing, often landed elites. Their success was the ultimate key to membership in the cotton industrialization club, and at the center of the "great divergence" in global economic history. And this industrial capitalism, as we will see, would eventually grow strong enough to lessen its dependence on war capitalism during its grand crisis in the 1860s.[52]

Cotton industrialization was thus not only a project of capitalists, as we know, but equally a project of governments. Most miraculously, the emergence of a set of states determined and able to protect domestic cotton manufacturing did not devastate the export-dependent British industry. To the contrary, British cotton manufacturing continued to expand at a rapid clip after 1815. In the first half of the nineteenth century, British production increased by 5 percent annually, and its exports by 6.3 percent. By 1820, British entrepreneurs operated 7 million spindles, and by 1850 21 million. By the 1830s, weaving was also increasingly mechanized, and with the spread of power looms, weavers moved into factories as well. By 1835 there were roughly fifteen hundred cotton manufacturers (some of whom owned multiple mills), and by 1860, four thousand manufacturers owned cotton mills in the British Isles. So important did cotton become to Britain that by 1856 the Manchester Chamber of Commerce accurately described the industry as one "neither surpassed in extent nor in usefulness by any other manufacturing pursuit."[53]

The secrets of British success in the face of protectionism elsewhere were twofold. For one, British manufacturers focused on higher-quality yarn and cloth, since they lacked competition from technologically less advanced manufacturers elsewhere. And Britain increasingly depended on markets in colonial or semicolonial areas of the world. Into the 1850s, more than half of all cottons produced in the United Kingdom were exported. Between 1820 and 1850, Asia and Latin America constituted the most rapidly growing export markets, and Asia's share in particular increased quickly. The British cotton trade avoided the stronger states that could protect their own emerging industries, gravitating instead toward markets that were unable to politically resist the British onslaught.[54]

The tremendous rapacity and unbalanced consequences of war capitalism left in its wake a great diversity: Some states were strengthened, while others were weakened and unable to invest in infrastructure, administrative capacity, and protections of industry. Some states had astounding capacities to manufacture goods on a mass scale; others remained embedded in preindustrial, housebound production. On the one hand, slavery, land expropriations, militarized trade, and colonial expansion had opened up vast new territories and labor pools for cotton growing and created new markets of tremendous vitality. They had helped limit competition in global markets, radically stimulating the international flow of goods, and thus making the project of industrialization the possession of a few privileged parts of the world. They were also at the root of a vast strengthening of states that enabled a few of them to forge the institutions of industrial capitalism. Indeed, the imperial extension of European state power over the globe and its intensification within Europe itself were mutually constitutive for a short but decisive moment.[55] On the other hand, colonial expansion, the slave trade, and slavery itself undermined state capacity in other parts of the world and in so doing limited the likelihood that the newfangled machines, and with them industrial capitalism, would take root there as well.

No place illuminates the double impact of war capitalism on the cotton industry better than Egypt. This North African country, long exceptional in multiple ways, seemed at first to break with its continent and follow the trajectory of Europe. Egypt had within itself many of the preconditions for successful cotton textile industrialization. It had access to raw cotton, grown in ever larger quantities on its own soil. It had a long history of textile production, and cotton was the most important craft industry of its major cities before the Industrial Revolution; in the eighteenth century Egypt was already exporting textiles to France.[56] It had, as we will see, access to British technology. And Egyptians were able to mobilize sufficient amounts of capital. But by 1850 Egypt had not joined the small number of countries experiencing Industrial Revolution.

It all started quite promisingly. Influenced by mercantilist thought, Egypt's ruler, Muhammad Ali, was bent on setting up manufacturing enterprises. Industrialization, he hoped, would strengthen, among other things, Egypt's military power and independence. Ali began an import-substitution project not unlike those of his continental European counterparts. In the early nineteenth century, Egypt had exported significant quantities of grain to Europe, which British merchants paid for with imported textiles that hurt Egyptian textile workshops. In response, Ali put an embargo on these British goods and encouraged Syrian Christians, who historically had dominated the textile trade, to set up factories. In 1815, the first cotton weaving workshop opened with a government-granted monopoly. Three years later, in 1818, the first mechanized cotton spinning mill began operations, rapidly followed by others.[57]

The technology for such industrialization in Egypt, as elsewhere, came directly or indirectly from Britain. At first, Ali imported spinning machines from there and had them set up by British mechanics, but later he brought French engineers to start a domestic machinery industry.[58] So far, cotton industrialization in Egypt followed along the lines of continental Europe, the United States, and Mexico.

The peak of this industrialization effort was reached in the mid-1830s. By 1835 between fifteen thousand and twenty thousand workers labored in thirty cotton factories operating approximately four hundred thousand spindles. Most of the products of these factories served the domestic market, but other fabrics were exported—throughout the Middle East, to places such as Syria and Anatolia, but also into Sudanese and Indian markets. As the German paper *Ausland* remarked in 1831 after reviewing the Egyptian cotton industry, "It is interesting that a barbarian has

Marrying war, capitalism, and
industrialization: Muhammad Ali Pasha

achieved within a few years what Napoleon and the entire continent were
unable to accomplish since the beginning of the century, despite all possible efforts, i.e., to successfully compete with the British in the production of cotton." Such an assessment was only a slight exaggeration: One
expert estimated that by the 1830s Egypt was fifth in the world regarding
cotton spindles per capita, when it counted about 80 mechanized spindles per one thousand population compared to 588 in Great Britain, 265
in Switzerland, 97 in the United States, 90 in France, and 17 in Mexico.[59]

Tellingly, British government officials began to worry about losing
markets to such a "barbarian." Sir John Bowring, a onetime member of
the British Parliament who was later governor of Hong Kong, observed
in 1837 during his travels through Egypt that British cotton textiles, "formerly so much used, are now scarcely at all sent to Egypt since muslins have been woven in the new factories." And such concerns were also
raised in regard to other markets: The Bombay *Asiatic Journal* reported
in 1831 that "an Arab ship . . . from the Red Sea has brought 250 bales of
cotton yarn, the manufacture of Ali Pasha at his spinning mill near Cairo.
It is reported that he has sent 500 bales to Surat, 1,000 to Calcutta, and
that he intends next season to send long cloths, madapollams, etc. What
will the mercantile community say to this new competitor?"[60]

British merchants in India complained. In June 1831 they reported on Egyptian imports into Calcutta, "This twist is of superior quality, even surpassing that imported here from England. . . . Considering these facts, it may be apprehended that the manufactures of Egypt are likely to interfere with similar productions imported into this country from Great Britain." Further examination of Egyptian cotton imports having convinced them that "thread is remarkably strong," they concluded that "considering the advantages the pasha possesses and his vicinity, we conceive the British manufacturer is entitled to greater protection than the above duty, and it is the intention of the agents here to address government on the subject."[61]

What they saw in Egypt impressed other observers as well. When in 1843 French textile manufacturer Jules Poulain studied the cotton mills of Egypt and provided Ali with a detailed report on his observations, he encouraged further efforts at industrialization. According to Poulain, "It is industry that makes the wealth of nations." Poulain, along with Ali, believed that it was "natural [to] manufacture the product of one's agriculture." Indeed, the fact that Egypt grew its own cotton would be a comparative advantage vis-à-vis France and the United Kingdom. If the French succeeded in the Indian town of Pondicherry (where they had just opened a small spinning mill), Poulain believed, the Egyptians could succeed in Egypt as well, not least because an "immense advantage" comes from the fact that labor in Egypt was much cheaper.[62]

And here, at the labor question, Egypt's story began to diverge. Much more than European states, Ali followed the war capitalism model in Egypt itself. Workers were forced to work in the factories. When the first cotton textile workshops opened in the Khurunfish quarter of Cairo sometime between 1816 and 1818, their skilled workers and machines came from Europe, but the one thousand to two thousand rank-and-file workers were Sudanese slaves and Egyptians coerced to work for minimal wages, tightly supervised by the army. These workers were frequently abused. In some ways, this system was not so different from elsewhere—with government inducements for industrialization and orphans being forced to work in factories—but still, coercion was more extreme in Egypt and wage labor remained marginal. In some ways, Egypt's rulers chose the tried-and-true mechanisms of the global plantation complex as its path into the world of the factory. Indeed, Ali demonstrated that war capitalism could, at least in Egypt, and for a short time, give birth to industrialization.[63]

War capitalism may have brought cotton industries to Egypt by herculean determination, but the progeny did not last for long. By the 1850s, Egypt's cotton industry had essentially disappeared, its countryside littered with factory ruins. Egypt was never able to build the institutional framework that would have enabled a full transition to industrial capitalism; even something so basic as wage labor did not take hold. Its reliance on war capitalism, both in the cotton fields and in the cotton factories, ultimately limited the growth of domestic markets. Egypt was, moreover, in the end unable to protect its domestic market. British merchants worked hard to open Egyptian markets for their goods, as Egypt weakened vis-à-vis European powers. The value of British cotton goods exports to Egypt increased by an estimated factor of ten between the second half of the 1820s and the second half of the 1830s. When in 1838 the Anglo-Ottoman Tariff Treaty went into force, setting import duties at only 8 percent ad valorem (that is, a percentage on the value of the product), and in effect forcing free trade upon Egypt, it "destroyed its first mechanized textile industry." Combined with the state's difficulties running cotton mills and the problem of securing sufficient fuel for steam-powered production, a system of "free trade" dominated by Britain made it practically impossible for Egypt to industrialize. Egypt's cotton industry was devastated from two sides: its domestic embrace of war capitalism and its ultimate subjugation to British imperialism. The Egyptian state was powerful domestically, but weak when it came to defining Egypt's position within the global economy, no match for British interests and designs.[64]

The negative impact of war capitalism on industrialization can be seen in one other example: Brazil. At first glance, Brazil was a lot like Egypt. It had a long history of cotton production, and Brazil grew ample quantities of high-quality cotton. An oscillating colonial policy in the eighteenth century had at times encouraged manufacturing in the country's new workshops, yet a 1785 royal decree had disallowed all manufacturing, except for coarse cotton goods, because colonial authorities were concerned that cotton factories competed with the labor requirements of mining. But despite such laws, cotton manufacturing emerged. And when the Portuguese royal family moved to Rio in 1808, these decrees were revoked and a few cotton mills built. These mills remained small and marginal; the São Paulo mill closed in the 1820s because of its lack of access to skilled labor and inability to compete with British textiles.

When in 1844 the Alves Branco tariff raised duties to 30 percent on most foreign manufactures, it encouraged the development of a few new mills, but that tariff, and along with it the industry, were short-lived. As a result, as late as 1865 there were just nine cotton factories in Brazil with just 13,977 spindles—about one-twentieth of those found in Egypt at the height of its cotton industrialization, or one-tenth the number in Mexico.[65]

Brazil, unlike Mexico and, for a while, Egypt, thus failed to develop its own mechanized cotton industry, despite its access to cotton, capital, and technology. Indeed, Brazilian cotton industrialization had to wait until the 1880s.[66] This failure to industrialize was the direct result of the peculiar political economy forged by politically influential slaveholders. These powerful sugar and cotton planters envisioned Brazil's place in the global economy as the provider of agricultural commodities produced by slave labor, a vision that ran counter to a project of domestic industrialization.

In the important sugar-growing state of Bahia, merchants dealing in agricultural commodities, for example, explicitly "opposed industrial development and attempted to thwart it by denying it essential government support"—despite Bahia's access to coal, capital, transportation infrastructure, and raw cotton, all of which made it ripe for industrialization. Instead, the Bahian elite wanted the government to invest in infrastructure to better move goods in and out of the world market and favored allocating labor to agriculture. Most important to them, however, slavery demanded low tariffs to facilitate the flow of sugar and coffee from Brazil into global markets and thus precluded the kind of protectionism that had enabled European, North American, and for a time Egyptian industrialization: The Bahian Commercial Association, a group of merchants, resisted tariffs as vocally and successfully as the planters, as they remained firmly in thrall to the planters' domination.[67]

Brazil's budding cotton entrepreneurs faced other problems as well. As capital was bound up in the production and trade in agricultural commodities produced by slave labor and in the slave trade itself, industrial enterprises often lacked access to credit. Moreover, labor recruitment remained a problem. Because of the prevalence of slavery, little wage labor was available for industrial employment, since Europeans, unwilling to compete with slave labor, preferred to migrate to other parts of the continent, such as Argentina. As a result, mills drew on a mixture of wage and slave labor. But generally, labor was concentrated in agriculture, and merchants saw "industry and transportation . . . as rivals for available labor."[68]

Plantation slavery's imperatives, the case of Brazil shows, could be detrimental to industrialization. Not that slave labor as such was incompatible with manufacturing—to the contrary, slaves could be employed in cotton factories. However, a society dominated by slavery was not conducive to cotton industrialization. Early industrialization depended, globally, on war capitalism, but in regions of the globe in which war capitalism took on its most violent edge cotton industrialization never resulted. Cuba, for example, relied on a massive number of enslaved workers, and yet did not have a single cotton mill during the entire nineteenth century.[69] The state of war between private parties at the heart of war capitalism contradicted the emerging imperatives of industrial capitalism. It was thus not just the capacity of states that explains the spread of cotton manufacturing, but also the distribution of power within them. Slave states were notoriously late and feeble in supporting the political and economic interests of domestic industrializers.

This was also the case in the slave territories within the United States, the only country in the world divided between war and industrial capitalism, a unique characteristic that would eventually spark an unprecedentedly destructive civil war. In the southern United States, one of the world's most dynamic slave economies, there was little cotton industrialization before the 1880s. To be sure, during and after the Revolutionary War some mechanized cotton manufacturing emerged in the southern states, and during the 1830s and thereafter a few textile mills opened their doors. But as late as 1850, southern cotton mills only consumed seventy-eight thousand bales of cotton, or one-sixth of the cotton consumption of New England. Further expansion of manufacturing, just as in Brazil, was hampered by the thriving slave economy that concentrated capital, labor, and entrepreneurial talent on plantations, limited the size of markets, made the region unattractive to European immigrants, and did not force white yeoman farmers into wage work (unlike, say, in New England and the Black Forest).[70]

War capitalism, in different ways, also limited opportunities for industrialization elsewhere. The great premodern cotton power of India did not just fail to leap forward via mechanization, but experienced the world's most rapid and cataclysmic deindustrialization ever. Faced with huge imports of ever cheaper cotton yarns and fabrics from its colonial ruler, and denied the services of its own government, India's cotton industry was decimated—first its production for export, and then its domestic spinning. In the wake of the Industrial Revolution, as we have seen, India lost its once central position in the global cotton industry and, in a great historical irony, eventually became the world's largest market for British cotton exports.

Colonialism, by undermining the state capacity of colonized territories and making them subservient to the interests of the colonizers, was decisive. Huge domestic demand in India, unlike in continental Europe, did not lead to state investment or protection—despite access to cotton, capital, and abundant skill. To be sure, there were some early efforts under French colonial auspices, and indeed, the first mechanized spinning mill on the Indian subcontinent was built in the French colony of Pondicherry in the 1830s, producing guinée cloth for French West African markets. This Indian cotton mill was, as it were, an infertile offspring of European capital, intercolonial trade, and European states. Indian cotton industrialization did not reappear until 1856 when the Parsi merchant Cowasji Nanabhoy Davar opened the first modern cotton mill in Bombay. The true takeoff of India's cotton manufacturing, however, had to wait until the 1870s, when the profits accumulated in the cotton trade during the U.S. Civil War were reinvested into manufacturing.[71]

In the first half of the nineteenth century, many other parts of the world with a vibrant cotton sector did not evolve to mechanized production; all of these cases show that a whole range of factors had to come together to jolt bureaucrats and capitalists into this new world of industrial wealth creation. Even in the Yucatecan city of Valladolid, the promising cotton venture of the Aurora Yucateca came to an end during the late 1840s. Despite Don Pedro Baranda's enormous entrepreneurial energies, his mill eventually faltered. Constant competition from British yarn smuggled in via the weakly guarded border with British Honduras, yarn that was about 40 percent cheaper than the goods produced in his factory, coupled with his inability to access the highly protected Mexican markets thanks to Yucatecan efforts to be independent of Mexico, brought an end to the venture. In 1847, Mayan insurgents captured the city of Valladolid in the War of the Castes, destroying the factory. The local state was too weak to protect its borders, to subdue rebellion, or to create a unified market, showing once again how important the state was to the lasting success of cotton industrialization.[72]

. . .

Colonialism, the embrace of slavery, the expropriation of lands—war capitalism, in short—had enabled the rise of industrial capitalism in some parts of the world, while at the same time making its emergence much less likely everywhere else. Industrial capitalism rested, as we have seen, on a combination of capital and state power—creating markets and mobilizing capital and labor in novel ways. The emergence of industrial capitalism in the first half of the nineteenth century in turn created the conditions for ever greater territorialization—including the greater territorialization of capital, that is, its attachment to particular nation-states.[73]

Crucial to this phase in the history of capitalism was the very diversity of its forms. Capitalism rested on the *coexistence* of war capitalism, with its violent expropriation of land and labor, its peculiar state, and the uncoordinated and unrestrained initiatives of its leading capitalists, with industrial capitalism, with its administratively, infrastructurally, legally and militarily powerful states channeling private initiative. The simultaneity of such different but mutually dependent forms of capitalism might have been the true innovation of the late eighteenth and early nineteenth centuries. It was not global integration by itself but the diversity of forms within that global integration that explained the dramatic but also the wildly different rates of cotton industrialization during these decades.

Capitalism, however, was not static. Enabled by war capitalism, industrial capitalism created powerful new institutions and structures. After the 1780s, a growing number of states built industrial capitalism, eventually allowing for the emergence of new forms of integration of labor, territory, markets, and capital in parts of the world that were, in the mid-nineteenth century, still subject to some of the harshest regimes of war capitalism ever invented. New ways of raising capital, new ways of inserting capital into production, new forms of labor mobilization, new forms of market making, and, last but not least, new forms of the incorporation of land and people into the global capitalist economy would emerge from this fertile yet often violent, even barbaric intersection of war and industrial capitalism. From the 1860s on, capital backed by state power rather than masters backed by expropriation and private physical coercion, would colonize territories and people.

The spread of cotton industrialization in the first half of the nineteenth century, to continental Europe and a few places beyond, showed that slavery and colonial exploitation were not essential to capitalism.[74] Capitalism reinvented itself ongoingly, and the lessons and capabilities of one moment were subsumed in the next. The connections between the global and the local, and among different places, changed constantly. To be sure, the demise of war capitalism stretched out for a century—from the Haitian revolution to the slow decline of slavery in the Americas. But industrial capitalism's institutional innovations facilitated war capitalism's death due to its own contradictions, as strong states, which would spread to more regions of the world, would enable labor mobilization in the global countryside after the end of slavery. The modern world, indeed, has been shaped just as much by war capitalism's death as by its birth.

One of the greatest institutional innovations brought about by capitalists' and statesmen's embrace of industrial capitalism, however, was the invention of new forms of labor mobilization. While capitalism's vast labor in the Americas had been accomplished by enslaved Africans, the huge labor needs of manufacturing industries were met by creating a powerful new system of wage labor. Though wage labor was not free of extralegal coercion, it was a new way to mobilize massive amounts of labor. It put laborers and labor on an entirely different legal, social, and institutional basis—and the ability to do so was the next factor that set some parts of the world apart from others.

Chapter Seven

Mobilizing Industrial Labor

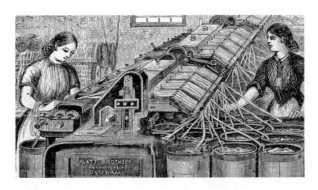

Cotton workers in England

In 1935, while living in Danish exile, a young German writer sat down to consider how the modern world had come into being. Bertolt Brecht channeled his thoughts through the voice of an imaginary "Worker Who Reads." That worker asked many questions, including:

> *Who built Thebes of the seven gates?*
> *In the books you will find the name of kings.*
> *Did the kings haul up the lumps of rock?*
> *And Babylon, many times demolished.*
> *Who raised it up so many times? In what houses*
> *Of gold-glittering Lima did the builders live?*[1]

Brecht might as well have been talking about a very different empire, that of cotton. By his time, the legend of cotton was well documented; history books were filled with the stories of those who harnessed the plant's unique gifts, Richard Arkwright and John Rylands, Francis Cabot Lowell and Eli Whitney. But as with any industry, the empire itself was sustained by millions of unnamed workers, who labored on cotton plantations and farms, and in spinning and weaving mills throughout the world, including in Brecht's hometown of Augsburg. Indeed, it was in Augsburg, as we have seen, that Hans Fugger had accumulated his riches in the nonmechanized production of cottons more than half a millennium earlier.

Like Brecht's haulers and builders, few cotton workers have entered our history books. Most left not even a trace; too often they were illiterate, and almost always their waking hours were occupied with holding body and soul together, leaving little time to write letters or diaries, as their social betters did, and thus few ways for us to piece their lives together. One of the saddest sights to this day is St. Michael's Flags in Manchester, a small park where allegedly forty thousand people, most of them cotton workers, lie buried in unmarked graves, one on top of the other, "an almost industrial process of burying the dead." Ellen Hootton was one of these rare exceptions. Unlike millions of others, she entered the historical record when in June 1833 she was called before His Majesty's Factory Inquiry Commission, which was charged with investigating child labor in British textile mills. Though only ten when she appeared before the committee and frightened, she was already a seasoned worker, a two-year veteran of the cotton mill. Ellen had drawn public attention because a group of middle-class Manchester activists concerned with labor conditions in the factories sprouting in and around their city had sought to use her case to highlight the abuse of children. They asserted that she was a child slave, forced to work not just in metaphorical chains, but in real ones, penalized by a brutal overseer.[2]

The commission, determined to show that the girl was a "notorious liar" who could not be trusted, questioned Ellen, her mother, Mary, and her overseer William Swanton, as well as factory manager John Finch. Yet despite their efforts to whitewash the case, the accusations proved to be essentially true: Ellen was the only child of Mary Hootton, a single mother, who was herself a handloom weaver barely able to make a living. Until she turned seven, Ellen had received some child support from her father, also a weaver, but once that expired her mother brought her down to a nearby factory to add to the family's meager income. After as many as five months of unpaid labor (it was said that she had to learn the trade first), she became one of the many children working at Eccles' Spinning Mill. When asked about her workday, Ellen said it began at five-thirty in the morning and ended at eight in the evening, with two breaks, one for breakfast and one for lunch. The overseer, Mr. Swanton, explained that Ellen worked in a room with twenty-five others, three adults, the rest children. She was, in her own words, a "piecer at throstles"—a tedious job that entailed repairing and reknotting broken threads as they were pulled onto the bobbin of the mule. With constant breakage, often several times a minute, she only had a few seconds to finish her task.

It was all but impossible to keep up with the speed of the machine as it moved back and forth, so she sometimes had "her ends down"—that is, she had not attached the loose and broken ends of the thread fast enough. Such errors were costly. Ellen reported being beaten by Swanton "twice a week" until her "head was sore with his hands." Swanton denied the frequency of the beatings, but admitted using "a strap" to discipline the girl. Her mother, who called her daughter "a naughty, stupid girl," testified that she approved of such corporal punishment, and had even asked Swanton to be more severe to put an end to her habit of running away. Life was hard for Mary Hootton, she desperately needed the girl's wages, and she begged Swanton repeatedly to keep on the girl, despite all the troubles. As Mary said, "I cries many a times."

The beatings, however, were not the worst treatment Ellen experienced at Swanton's hands. One day, when she arrived late to work, Swanton penalized her even more severely: He hung an iron weight around her neck (there was no agreement about whether it weighed sixteen or twenty pounds) and made her walk up and down the factory floor. The other children heckled her, and as a result, "she fell down several times while fighting with the other hands. She fought them with the stick." Even today, nearly two hundred years later, the pain of the girl's life, from the tedium of her work to the violence of her abuse, is hard to fathom.

While the city of Manchester sports a Rylands Library, Harvard University a Lowell student dormitory, and while every grade-school student learns about Richard Arkwright and Eli Whitney, there is of course no library or school named for Ellen Hootton. No one but a handful of historians knows anything about her life. Yet when we think about the world of cotton manufacturing, we should think of Ellen Hootton. Without her labor and that of millions of children, women, and men, the empire of cotton would have never been built. Neither Rylands nor Lowell would have accumulated their riches, and Arkwright's and Eli's inventions would have collected dust in the corner of a barn. Ellen's story highlights the physical violence of punishment, but as important, the more banal violence of economic desperation, which brought ever larger numbers of people into factories, where they spent their lives, quite literally, in the service of the empire of cotton.

Like Ellen Hootton, thousands and, by the 1850s, millions of workers streamed into the world's newly built factories to operate the machines that produced cotton thread and cloth.[3] The ability to mobilize so many women, children, and men to work in factories was awe-inspiring. Many a contemporary was overwhelmed by the sight of hundreds or even thousands of workers walking to and from their places of toil. Every morning before sunrise, thousands of workers walked down narrow paths in the Vosges to the factories in the valley, crawled out of dormitory beds just up the hill from Quarry Bank Mill, left their struggling farms above the Llobregat River, and made their way through crowded Manchester streets to one of the dozens of mills lining its putrid canals. At night they returned to sparse dormitories where they slept several to a bed, or to cold and drafty cottages, or to densely populated and poorly constructed working-class neighborhoods in Barcelona, Chemnitz, or Lowell.

The world had seen extreme poverty and labor exploitation for centuries, but it had never seen a sea of humanity organizing every aspect of their lives around the rhythms of machine production. For at least twelve hours a day, six days a week, women, children, and men fed machines, operated machines, repaired machines, and supervised machines. They opened tightly packed bales of raw cotton, fed piles of cotton into carding machines, they moved the huge carriages of mules back and forth, they tied together broken yarn ends (as did Ellen Hootton), they removed yarn from filled spindles, they supplied necessary roving to the spinning machines, or they simply carried cotton through the factory. Discipline was maintained through petty fines and forced forfeiture of contracts: A list of dismissal cases from one early-nineteenth-century mill had official justifications ranging from banal disciplinary issues, such as "using ill language," to idiosyncratic charges, like "Terrifying S. Pearson with her ugly face." Maintaining a disciplined labor force would prove consistently difficult. In one English mill, of the 780 apprentices recruited in the two decades after 1786, 119 ran away, 65 died, and another 96 had to return to overseers or parents who had originally lent them out. It was, after all, the beginning of the era of William Blake's "dark satanic mill."[4]

Winter or summer, rain or shine, workers ventured into buildings rising several stories high, usually made of brick, and labored in vast rooms, often hot, and almost always humid, dusty, and deafeningly noisy. They worked hard, lived in poverty, and died young. As political economist Leone Levi put it in 1863, "Enter for a moment one of those numerous factories; behold the ranks of thousands of operatives all steadily working; behold how every minute of time, every yard of space, every practiced eye, every dexterous finger, every inventive mind, is at high-pressure service."[5]

It is difficult to overstate the importance and revolutionary nature of this new organization of human labor. Today we take this system for granted: Most of us make a living by selling our labor for a certain number of hours a day; with the result—our paycheck—we purchase the things we need. And we also take for granted that machines set the pace of human activity. Not so in the eighteenth or nineteenth centuries: If we look at the world as a whole, the number of people who would exchange their labor power for wages, especially wages in manufacturing, was tiny. The rhythm of work was determined by many things—by the climate, by custom, by the cycles of nature—but not by machines. People worked because they were compelled to do so as slaves, or because they were the feudal dependents of worldly or ecclesial authorities, or because they produced their own subsistence with tools they owned on land to which they had some rights. The new world of making yarn and cloth, as one of the innumerable cogs in the empire of cotton, was utterly, fundamentally different. Cotton manufacturing rested on the ability to persuade or entice or force people to give up the activities that had organized human life for centuries and join the newly emerging factory proletariat. Though the machines themselves were stunning and world-altering, this shift in the rhythm of work would be even more consequential. They may not have known it, but as Ellen Hootton and untold others streamed into the factory, they were looking at the future, the very industrial capitalism that their labor was building.

The ability to move workers into factories became key to the cotton empire's triumph. As a result, a chasm opened around the world between statesmen and capitalists able to mobilize labor and those who failed. Convincing thousands of people to give up the only way of life they had known was no less complex than installing new machines. Both required, as we have seen, certain legal, social, and political conditions. The transition to the factory was at first concentrated in a few places, and even there encountered tremendous opposition. Success required a lopsided distribution of power that allowed statesmen and capitalists to dominate the lives of individuals and families in ways that still eluded elites in much of Asia and Africa. The power of the state did not just need to be extensive, as it was in many parts of the world, but intensive, focused, and penetrating all realms of life. As a result, in areas of the world in which rulers could not easily subdue alternative means of gaining access to subsistence, it was all but impossible to transition to factory production. Ironically, factory production itself would slowly undermine such alternative ways of organizing economic activity.

To be sure, the Industrial Revolution was mostly about labor-saving technology—as we have seen, productivity in spinning, for example, increased by as much as a hundred times. Still, these labor-saving machines required labor to operate them; as markets for cotton goods expanded explosively in response to falling prices, a rapidly growing cotton industry demanded at first thousands, then tens of thousands, and, in some parts of the world, hundreds of thousands of workers. In Britain, by 1861 there were 446,000 people working in the cotton industry. It has been estimated that in 1800 about 59,700 workers labored in the German cotton industry, a number that increased to 250,300 in 1860. The French industry drew on approximately 200,000 workers, the Swiss cotton industry in 1827 employed 62,400 workers. While the U.S. cotton industry only counted 10,000 wage earners in 1810, that number rose to 122,000 in 1860. Russia in 1814 employed 40,000 cotton workers, and about 150,000 in 1860. Spain in 1867 counted about 105,000 workers in its cotton industry. The global cotton industry rested on proletarianized labor; at the same time it was one of the greatest proletarianizing agents itself.[6]

Before the factory had become a way of life, capital owners had only one model for how to mobilize vast amounts of labor: the plantation economy of the Americas, built on the enslavement of millions of Africans. Many a cotton entrepreneur was intimately familiar with this system; Samuel Greg of Quarry Bank Mill, as we have seen, owned slave plantations on Dominica, and he was far from alone. But such possibilities had been forestalled in Europe because of the new sensibilities about economic man spurred by the Enlightenment and the resulting legal prohibitions against slavery in Europe. Bringing African slaves to

Manchester, Barcelona, or Mulhouse was out of the question; enslaving the local population was also impossible. Moreover, slave labor had significant economic disadvantages—it was difficult to motivate workers under conditions of servitude, and supervision costs were high. Slave labor, moreover, incurred costs year round, sometimes for the life of the worker, and was not easily adjusted to the vexing boom-and-bust cycles of industrial capitalism. The model of the plantation, in other words, did not serve the needs of the factory.

Yet access to labor was crucial to manufacturers the world over. After all, an entrepreneur's significant investment in machines could only be profitable with the promise of a predictable stream of labor to operate those machines. The labor power of women and men, girls and boys, was thus transformed into a commodity.[7] Turning people into factory workers meant turning them into wage workers as well. For most people in Europe and elsewhere, however, wages had not been central to their livelihood. Many who lived off the land or made artisan crafts, not surprisingly, had little incentive to become factory workers. A farmer grew his own sustenance; an artisan created goods he could sell or barter. A factory worker, by contrast, possessed nothing but the power of labor.

Budding capitalists and statesmen thus had to invent new ways to mobilize labor on a massive scale—that "fresh race of beings" that a rural magistrate observed in Lancashire in 1808. If they had envisaged the millions of workers they eventually needed to hire, the problem might have seemed overwhelming—and indeed, sometimes concerns about insufficient labor supply were on their minds. From his home in the West Midlands, a Shrewsbury mill owner complained, for example, in 1803 that the greatest problem in starting his mill was to attract a sufficient number of workers.[8]

These hopeful employers had help, however, especially from the transformation of the countryside that was already decades—and in some places, centuries—in the making. Bonds of mutual obligation between lords and peasants had begun to break down. In Europe, landowners had enclosed huge areas of land, making independent farming less accessible to peasants, and the wave of proto-industrial work had already made manufacturing, and even wage payments, a normal part of many peasants' subsistence.[9]

Moreover, the bureaucratic, military, ideological, and social penetration of a bounded territory by newly consolidating states aided mill owners. Coercion had almost always been a central element in getting people to perform labor for others, a staple for feudal lords and colonial masters alike. Yet one of industrial capitalism's signal features was that coercion would now be increasingly accomplished by the state, its bureaucrats and judges, and not by lords and masters. Many capitalists throughout the world in need of workers feared the decline of personal dependencies such as serfdom, slavery, and apprenticeships, expecting idleness and even anarchy as a result. But in some areas the state had gained sufficient strength to create conditions that secured reliable flows of women, children, and men into factories. Throughout much of Europe, the rights of landowners and capitalists to control labor as personal dependents had been severely curtailed, but at the same time the state had increasingly taken on the role of legally compelling people to work (such as paupers, so-called vagrants, and children). Moreover, by the enclosure of the commons the state had made alternative possibilities of gaining a livelihood increasingly inaccessible, in fact increasing economic pressures on those without property. As legal historian Robert Steinfeld has put it, even "economic coercion is an artifact of the law," that is, of the state.[10]

The state thus created a legal framework for wage labor that made it more fathomable to rising manufacturers. They appreciated that wage labor retained significant nonpecuniary coercive elements—bodily coercion—even in the centers of the new industrial capitalism. Indeed, employers in Britain, the United States, France, Prussia, and Belgium "required and strictly enforced labor agreements in wage labor" and "were using forms of legal compulsion to tie workers to jobs." The 1823 Master and Servant Act, for example, explicitly allowed "English employers to have their workmen sent to the house of correction and held at hard labor for up to three months for breaches of their labor agreements." Between 1857 and 1875, in England and Wales alone, about ten thousand workers annually were prosecuted for "breach of contract," many of them sentenced to prison; cotton workers were frequently among them. In Prussia throughout the nineteenth century, workers could be fined and imprisoned for leaving their job: "Journeymen, helpers, and factory workers, who leave work without permission and without legal justification, or are guilty of shirking or gross disobedience, are to be punished with a fine of twenty Thalers or prison up to fourteen days," determined the Prussian *Gewerbeordnung* of 1845.[11]

Despite powerful state support, recruiting workers remained a huge challenge for budding manufacturers, testifying to the fact that workers themselves, as long as they still had access to other means of subsisting, tried to escape the world of the factory. When apothecary Joan Baptista Sires, for example, opened a cotton factory in the Raval neighborhood of Barcelona in 1770 with twenty-four looms and nineteen printing tables (places for the application of colors on cotton fabrics), one of his most difficult challenges was recruiting the 60 to 150 women and men he needed to keep up production. Turnover was huge, as most workers stayed only for a few months. Sires tried to solve this problem by replicating some elements of the artisan workshop in his factory, providing skilled male workers with the best-paid positions, but also allowing their wives and children to work in the factory, thus increasing the family wage while at the same time saving on their discounted labor. To try to enmesh workers at his factory, Sires allowed some families to live in the buildings, replicating a pattern long typical for artisan workshops throughout Europe.[12]

Fifty years later, in the United States, the problem of labor recruitment had not changed much. The Dover Manufacturing Company in Dover, New Hampshire, had to employ a total of 342 workers in the period from August 1823 to October 1824 just to maintain an average workforce of approximately 140.[13] Workers came and left frequently, as they desperately tried to retain access to a livelihood outside the factory. Entering the factory for a few weeks, they would leave once they had made enough money to hold them over to the selling of their crops or when their labor was needed on the farm.

These patterns of labor recruitment were typical of regions undergo-

The renamed Dover Manufacturing Company mill (date unknown)

ing cotton industrialization. In every case, proto-industrialization and proletarianization intersected. The spread of machine-made yarn, and later cloth, undermined hand spinning and handloom weaving on the farm, creating pressures on textile workers to find income elsewhere. For many, the only other viable solution was the very factory that had undermined their prior source of income. Barcelona entrepreneur Sires, in fact, usually hired workers from the farming areas surrounding the Catalan capital. In Saxony, earlier difficulties in recruiting labor were overcome when cheap yarns pouring out of the first cotton factories outcompeted hand spinners, who were then forced to work in the expanding factories. In Switzerland, the tens of thousands of workers that putting-out merchants kept busy in the vast countryside as far away as the Black Forest provided a huge potential labor reservoir, and indeed many of them eventually moved into factory production. With the rapid expansion of the Alsatian cotton industry and its significant labor needs, entrepreneurs looked to the mountainous areas of the Vosges and the Black Forest for that labor. There, the survival of families still rested on agricultural pursuits and continued to do so even after the onset of factory production: Nearly all workers in the spinning and weaving mills of Wesserling, for example, a small town high above the city of Mulhouse, still owned their own land and supplemented their income by farming as late as 1858. In the search for spinners and weavers, capital moved ever deeper into the countryside, allowing manufacturers to pay extremely low wages because workers could still draw on the unpaid reproductive labor of family members—child rearing and the growing of food among them. Here, as elsewhere, the unfolding of capitalism depended on noncapitalist forms of production and labor.[14]

More often than not, though, workers lost access to land and, faced with the decline of household manufacturing, moved from the countryside into cities. Indeed, cotton industrialization led to huge migrations, often across national borders. In 1815, among the fifteen hundred workers of the Guebwiller firm of Ziegler, Greuter et Cie, 750 were Alsatians, but the rest were migrants from Switzerland and Germany. U.S. textile mills drew on such migrants as well. Thousands of workers moved from the marginal agricultural soils of New England to the newly emerging textile towns, and many workers crossed the Atlantic, such as Irish women and men escaping the potato famine. The Dutch, Belgian, Catalonian, and French cotton industries drew on migrants from the surrounding countryside as well.[15]

These rural workers, abandoning their agricultural pursuits and home-based manufacturing activities, flowed down the mountains and sometimes across the seas into the textile factories of the Black Forest, Switzerland, the Vosges, Catalonia, Saxony, and New England. There they met a population of essentially artisanal workers. Those workers, mostly male, took on the most skilled positions, often with experience from older artisanal workshops, not farm fields. When Neuhaus & Huber created a weaving mill in Biel, Switzerland, in 1830 next to their spinning enterprise, they drew on newly unemployed but highly skilled handloom weavers who had for decades prospered around the town. Skilled workers too migrated over great distances: The cotton cloth factory Schwarz, in the Russian town of Narva, employed in 1822 thirty-five Germans, a French dyer, and a person from Holland. Ludwig Knoop's Kreenholm factory employed in 1857 many British skilled workers. Indeed, French, Mexican, American, and other manufacturers frequently recruited highly skilled workers from abroad.[16]

The vast majority of workers, however, were not skilled and were not recruited; rather, they were driven into factories by changing conditions within the countryside, and especially by the decline of goods made at home that could no longer compete with those made in factories. Perhaps most dramatic was the moment when power looms replaced hand weaving beginning in the 1820s. As a huge wave of misery passed over large parts of Europe, unemployed home-based weavers were ready to move into factories. In response to such conditions, factory employment often became a family strategy to maintain a household's ability to stay on the land, either by sending one member of the family to work at a mill full-time or by sending various members of the family for short stints. That was the case among the workers in Lowell, Massachusetts, where (unmarried) women's factory wages often enabled their families to remain on the land. Migrating into factory labor could give marginal agricultural pursuits another lease on life.[17]

The survival of detailed pay records allows us to take a closer look at one such early cotton mill, the Dover Manufacturing Company, mentioned above: In the sixty-three weeks following August 9, 1823, a total of 305 women, most of them young and unmarried, labored at one point or another in the factory, constituting 89 percent of the workforce. They worked on average for 25.93 weeks, or 41 percent of the total time possible. Indeed, many women entered the factory on a seasonal basis, working for a few months, then returning to other pursuits. To pick just one example, in mid-October forty-three women, or 32 percent of the work-force, took the week off from mill work, to return the following week.

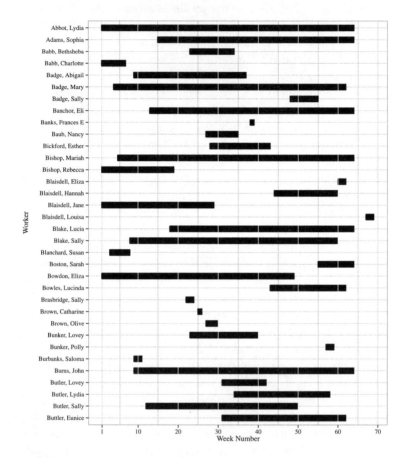

Work patterns at the Dover Manufacturing Company, August 9, 1823–October 16, 1824:
sample of all workers whose surname begins with A or B

The rhythms of agricultural work thus persisted into the factory, and factory work could help families stay on the land. In New Hampshire it was common that one member of the family worked essentially full-time in the mill, while others did so only for a short time, such as the Badge family: While Mary worked full-time, Abigail and Sally only joined her for short stints.

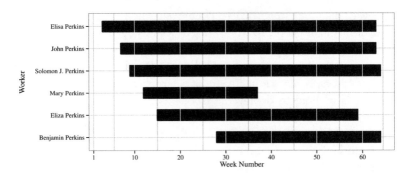

Work patterns of the Perkins family, Dover Manufacturing Company, 1823–1824

But even at the Dover Manufacturing Company in the 1820s, there were already families who were fully proletarianized, whose many members stayed for long periods at the mill. The Perkins family exemplified this pattern; its members, including two men, worked essentially full-time, making it extremely unlikely that they still grew any crops or raised animals. Whatever the precise pattern, it was not the attractiveness of factory labor itself that drew millions of people into the vortex of the cotton mills.[18]

. . .

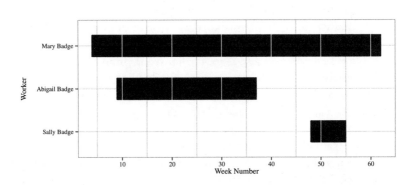

Work patterns of the Badge family, Dover Manufacturing Company, 1823–1824

One way manufacturers tried to circumvent the problem of attracting large numbers of people to work in factories was by recruiting the weakest members of society first, those with the fewest resources to resist. To do so, they built upon long-established relationships of power within households, especially a long history of paternalism that allowed the male head of household to deploy the labor of his wife and children as he saw fit. The emergence of industrial capitalism in fact built upon such older social hierarchies and relations of power and used these as a tool to revolutionize society more broadly. Employers understood that the "cheapness" of their labor rested on the persistence of noncapitalist ways of securing subsistence—a lesson that would eventually also inform the transition to world market production in the cotton-growing countryside in India and elsewhere. The capitalist revolution succeeded because it remained incomplete.

Consequently, children were often the first to enter factory employment, Ellen Hootton among them. Up to half of cotton workers were children, coerced by their parents, who in turn were coerced by the new economic reality. Children were cheap—their wages amounted to between one-third and one-fourth of those paid to adults—relatively obedient, and unlikely to object to extremely repetitive and dull tasks, and if they did, they could be more easily punished than adults. For parents with few resources, children were often the sole source of additional income. McConnel & Kennedy, for example, the Manchester manufacturers we encountered earlier as spinners of fine Sea Island cotton, employed large numbers of children. In 1816, among the 568 workers on their payroll, 257 were sixteen or younger, or 45 percent of the total.[19]

At Quarry Bank Mill, Samuel Greg's pioneering factory near Manchester, many pauper children labored as so-called apprentices. Drawing on parish poorhouses, Greg recruited children as more than half of all his workers between 1784 and 1840. He housed them in dormitories and had them labor for him for seven years. While Greg styled himself as a considerate and paternalist employer, he locked his child worker Esther Price into a specially constructed cell for "disobedience," and made other children work overtime to penalize them for the "crime" of having taken an apple. Again, Greg was far from unusual. Samuel Oldknow, for example, also tapped a thriving market for "apprentices"; in 1796, the parish of Clerkenwell advertised thirty-five boys and thirty-five girls, inviting Oldknow to choose whatever number he would like to take. The *Edin-*

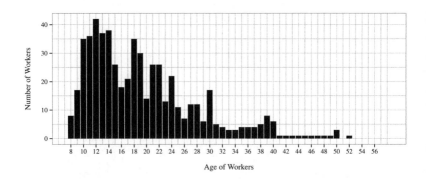

Children make an industrial revolution: McConnel & Kennedy, age of workers, 1816. Total number of workers = 568

burgh Review asserted in 1835 that factories "have been [children's] best and most important academies." Turning them loose on the street would be much worse, they asserted, as spinning mills take "the children out of harm's way."[20]

Amid social acceptance of child labor and urgent need, large numbers of children worked in all aspects of cotton manufacturing. In 1833, 36 percent of all workers in Lancashire cotton factories were younger than sixteen. In 1846 in Belgium, 27 percent of all cotton workers were under sixteen. At a Siegerland spinning factory, of its three hundred workers in 1800, half of them were children between eight and fourteen. And when in 1798 the Russian Treasury allowed Michael Ossovski to build the first mechanical cotton spinning factory, he "received" three hundred children from a Saint Petersburg orphanage. From Saxony to Puebla to the Habsburg Empire, the situation was similar. Catalonian manufacturers located their factories in the foothills of the Pyrenees, home to many struggling farmers, not least because that gave them access to child labor. In Puebla, where most cotton workers were former peasants, debt peons, and textile artisans, children constituted an important part of the workforce, beginning to work at age ten, and sometimes earlier. As late as 1837, a commission of the Société Industrielle de Mulhouse reported that children were engaged in "forced labor" and that they "contributed involuntarily." To improve conditions, the commission recommended that children age eight to ten be limited to ten hours of work per day; twelve

Child workers' dormitory, Quarry Bank Mill

hours for children ten to fourteen; and thirteen hours per day for children fourteen to sixteen years of age. Night shifts should only be permitted for children older than fourteen. Once enforced, they hoped such halfhearted measures would improve children's lives. Yet the Alsatian cotton industry continued to rely to such an extent on child labor that its entrepreneurs vigorously opposed the passage of a law in 1841 limiting such practices. In fact, the invention of childhood that took place among the families of the Mulhousian bourgeoisie, like their counterparts elsewhere in Europe and the United States, rested on the extreme exploitation of child labor in the factories surrounding them. Children from English poorhouses, Danish *Bornehus*, Swedish *Barnhus*, and Russian *priiut dlia sirot* all ended up in textile factories.[21]

Aside from children, women, especially the young and the unmarried, constituted the cotton workforce. Indeed, cotton manufacturing became the most female-dominated manufacturing industry to emerge in the eighteenth and nineteenth centuries. In New Hampshire's Dover mill in the mid-1820s, as mentioned, 89 percent of all workers were women. In Catalonia's cotton industry, up to 70 percent of workers were female. Women dominated the cotton textile workforces throughout Europe and the United States, although male workers dominated in Mexico and Egypt. Such preponderance of women workers resulted all too often in the invisibility of the cotton industry, overshadowed by the male-dominated coal-mining, iron-making, and railroading industries.[22]

Not surprisingly, most of these women came from the countryside. Partly this was the result of families' strategies to retain access to the land by supplementing dwindling agricultural incomes through wage work. Women in much of Europe and North America had been in charge of spinning and weaving for centuries; that trend continued, even as the work itself moved from home to factory, from hand to machine. In 1841, when the young William Rathbone traveled to the United States, he was struck by this prevalence of women workers: At a Paterson, New Jersey, mill, which he found "the most romantically situated mill in the world," he found the "women employed in them are rather sickly looking but very pretty." A few days later, when he looked at the Lowell mills, he observed that the "factory girls are neat and many pretty. They are generally I believe well educated being the daughters of farmers and sometimes even clergymen who go there for a few years without their families to get something as a marriage position." Rathbone, like some of his contemporaries, had a hopelessly romanticized view of women's cotton work.[23]

Thanks to long-standing biases, women's labor was much cheaper. Historians found that "women often earned as little as 45 to 50 percent of males' wages under fixed wage structures." Yet women were not just cheaper workers, they also were less rooted in older work cultures that often regulated the work of male artisan textile workers, work cultures that could and did become the basis of resistance against factory owners. Women's work patterns, along with those of their children, were more easily molded to fit the ceaseless rhythm of machine production.[24]

The availability of women was crucial to the early cotton manufacturers. And it was also what distinguished large parts of Europe (and eventually also Japan) from many other areas of the world. Not that women elsewhere did not work in textile production—they did—but in Europe and North America, unlike in Africa and Asia, women could eventually move out of households and into factories, a critical condition for textile industrialization. In China, for example, the situation was quite different. As historian Kenneth Pomeranz notes, "The Chinese family system did not allow much migration by single women, either to cities or to peripheries, until twentieth-century factories with tightly supervised dormitories made this seem possible within the bounds of respectability." Sociologist Jack Goldstone even argues that the different roles of women explain why Europe industrialized and China did not. In Europe and the United States, women married relatively later and were therefore able to join the factory proletariat before marriage.[25]

Yet favorable legacies of patriarchy and the transformation of the countryside had almost always to be supplemented with more overt forms of coercion. Though the coercion employed by the "lords of the loom" was quite different from that of the "lords of the lash," using force to mobilize labor, to discipline it within factories, and to keep workers from leaving once they had entered factory employment was nearly universal. With their investments in factories at stake, manufacturers embraced coercion and even physical violence, sometimes privately, but more and more often also sanctioned by the state. Orphaned children, as we have seen, frequently had no choice but to work under oppressive conditions in cotton mills. Belgian entrepreneur Lieven Bauwens used "the inmates of the prison of which he was warden" as weavers. In Russia, efforts to staff textile factories with wage workers failed at first, and instead entrepreneurs resorted to coercing people to work, drawing upon "prostitutes, criminals, beggars, and others—some of whom were sentenced to work for life in industry." In the United States, prisoners in Maryland, Louisiana, and Rhode Island spent their days weaving cotton. Even cotton workers who agreed to a wage labor contract often were tied to factories through "some manner of bondage." The management in Knoop's huge Krenholm factory was described by a local Estonian paper as taking "no more care of the people than does a slave-owner of his Negro slaves." The factory not only had its own police force, but also regularly brutalized workers by corporal punishment. In Puebla, Mexico, workers were just as much subject to severe supervision: If they lived in factory compounds, they were sometimes not allowed to have friends or relatives visit, and sometimes even the reading of newspapers was outlawed. And in the Habsburg Empire, cotton mills were akin to military barracks; workers were locked into factories and only allowed to leave on Sundays.[26]

In areas of the world in which slavery prevailed, bodily coercion played an even more important role. In the Americas in particular, the world's center of plantation slavery, significant coerced labor went into cotton manufacturing. In Brazil, native peoples and slaves were forced to work in textile factories. In the southern United States as well, slaves worked in cotton textile production—a system that one historian has aptly termed "coerced proto-industrialization." Thus in the slave zones of the world, slavery fueled industrial production as well.[27]

Compared to cotton growing, the global cotton manufacturing industry as a whole, however, used physical coercion to a much lesser extent in the mobilization of labor. Even in Russia, where before the 1861 emancipation serfs were at times forced to work in textile factories, such coerced workers never constituted more than 3.3 percent of the cotton workforce. New yet sophisticated methods of labor control had emerged instead that did not rest on the enslavement of workers.

Yet lessons learned on large slave plantations still inspired industrialists. Cotton manufacturer Samuel Oldknow, for example, in the mid-1790s tried to gain greater authority over his workers. Unlike the putting-out system that Oldknow knew so well, the factory was unchartered territory to him, and thus he struggled mightily to control his workers. In a first step, he created an attendance book to take systematic note of his workers' presence in the factory. He divided this small book by the rooms in his mill and listed each of the workers in each of the rooms. He divided the day into four quarters and listed during which quarters workers were actually present. In March 1796, for example, the book lists "Mary Lewis 1,2,3,4; Thomas Lewis 1,2,3,4; Peggy Woodale 1; Martha Woodale 1; Samuel Ardern 3,4," and so on. In our perpetually monitored world, such recordkeeping seems quaint, but just like the switch from seasonal work to machine work, so too this notion of keeping track of time was new, and while it was most fully elaborated on slave plantations, it slowly migrated into the world of the factory as well. Mobilizing huge numbers of workers by paying them wages and then supervising their work and assuring that they applied their skills and energy was a work in progress, and new dilemmas continually emerged. Outside the factory—in workers' homes and neighborhoods—employers' authority was even more distant. Instilling discipline proved difficult, with tracking attendance in account books often not sufficient, and so employers frequently also resorted to beating, fining, and firing workers. The rhythm of work and its tight supervision reminded many contemporary observers of the only other large work setting they knew—the slave plantation—even though that made them miss the truly revolutionary nature of what was unfolding in front of their eyes.[28]

Discipline was difficult to enforce and workers difficult to recruit not least because working conditions were often appalling—so much so that slave owners the world over compared the conditions of slave labor in favorable terms to those of industrial workers. In the German cotton industry, for example fourteen- to sixteen-hour workdays, six days a week, were the rule. In Puebla in 1841, hours per day averaged 14.8, including a one-hour lunch break. In France during the Second Empire, workdays averaged twelve hours, though employers could make their workers work as long as they chose to, and until 1873, working hours in textile mills in Barcelona were just as long. Production everywhere was dangerous and the machines deafeningly noisy.[29]

Such conditions had a dramatic impact on workers' health: When the Saxon government sought to recruit soldiers in the 1850s, only 16 percent of spinners and 18 percent of weavers were deemed healthy enough to serve. For many decades, the standard of living of these new cotton factory workers symbolized to contemporaries everything that was wrong with industrialization. "I regret to have to add that the distress of the Laboring poor but most particularly the weaver is great beyond almost description," reported J. Norris to the British secretary of state Robert Peel in 1826. Indeed, a recent analysis of the life expectancy and heights of workers determined that "no increase in food consumption, no increase in longevity or nutritional status, and no improvement in housing" resulted from the Industrial Revolution. The author concluded that "the infant mortality results presented here for the sample parishes in the heartland of the Industrial Revolution provide support for the view that clear evidence of significant improvement in the daily lives of English workers and their families is lacking before the middle of the century" and might have actually had to wait until the 1870s. "I calculate that consumption per capita, adjusted for changes in leisure, remained essentially unchanged between 1760 and 1830." As American labor activist Seth Luther reported in 1833, "The consequence of this excess of toil is, that the growth of the body is checked, and the limbs become weak, and sometimes horribly distorted."[30]

Considering such conditions, it is not surprising that farmers and artisans often resisted being turned into factory workers. With living standards and live expectancy falling, it was entirely rational to fear the factory. Resistance was both individual and collective, and made proletarianization an even more drawn out, often violent process. During the French revolutionary upheavals of the 1780s and 1790s, workers destroyed machines that modernized the cotton manufacturing process, and threatened factory owners associated with the modernization of production. In 1789, for example, hundreds of workers attacked cotton factories in Normandy, the center of the French cotton industry, destroying seven hundred spinning jennies and other machinery. Troops and militias, there and elsewhere, fought such upheavals, but with mixed success. This resistance continued in the 1820s, when French workers opposed the introduction of power looms. So effective was this wave of resistance, and so relatively limited the inexperienced state's ability and willingness to protect its modernizing entrepreneurs, that some capitalists concluded that the path of least resistance was to limit the employment of new machines and instead focus on the production, however labor-intensive, of high-quality goods. The fear of popular uprising became a guiding star in the universe of French entrepreneurs.[31]

Such resistance also characterized the industrialization process in England. Already in the 1740s there had been riots against Kay's flying shuttle, in 1753 there were attacks on "cotton reel" machines; in 1768–69 workers in Lancashire rioted against the introduction of the spinning jenny, and in 1779 Lancashire workers smashed various kinds of machinery. But machine breaking only became truly prevalent in the 1810s, a moment when the state was able and willing to use massive force to repress it. In 1811 and 1812, "steam looms [were] attacked in Stockport and elsewhere," with another wave of machine attacks in 1826.[32]

Workers in other parts of the world also rebelled. In Puebla, weavers' guilds were "extremely hostile" to machine production of cotton yarn. Factory owners adamant about introducing new machines hid innovators and their machines in a "secret place" to be safe from guild hostility. That fear was also prevalent in Veracruz. In Switzerland, weavers revolted in the 1820s, demanding that power looms be outlawed, burning down a factory in Oberuster in 1832. In the Dutch city of Tilburg in 1827, workers objecting to the introduction of steam engines smashed the windows of factory owner Pieter van Dooren.[33]

The expansion of the world's mechanized cotton industry thus not only rested on the deployment of new technologies and access to capital and markets, but also on the ability of capitalists to turn thousands and eventually millions of people into proletarians—and, importantly, to break resistance to the imposition of a radically new way of living and working. As a contemporary observed in England in 1795, "The several modes of accelerating labour have been always stoutly resisted by the labouring class, when the different machinery was first introduced."[34] This was, as one historian has remarked in regard to the Black Forest's Wiesental, a process of "inner colonializations"—the colonialization and domination by capital of ever more territories and social relations. Yet in the face of weakened feudal elites, such a transition was possible—and consolidating states played a key role enabling it.

Indeed, the state became exceedingly important in the repression of working-class collective action, demonstrating once more how decisive state capacity was to industrial capitalism. States passed laws outlawing everything from trade unions, to strikes, to public assemblies, to labor-oriented political parties. States criminalized workers' efforts to improve their working conditions. When machine breaking spread throughout the empire of cotton, as we have seen, states responded. As Luddites in Britain (and also in France) destroyed hundreds of spinning machines in 1811–12, Parliament passed a law in February 1812 that made machine breaking a capital crime. Thirty Luddites were hanged in 1812–13, and nineteen more in 1830. Others were exiled to Australia or imprisoned. And the British state cracked down on workers' collective action in other ways as well: Pitt's Two Acts of 1795 suspended habeas corpus and outlawed gatherings of over fifty people without prior authorization. The Combination Acts of 1799 and 1800 outlawed trade unions—leading, for example, to John Doherty's sentencing to ten years of hard labor in 1818, his crime being membership in the (illegal) Manchester Cotton-Spinners' Society. The British state, not quite trusting the mechanism it had devised to assure social peace, also prepared for battle with workers—between 1792 and 1815 alone, 155 military barracks were built in industrial areas. As one historian concludes, "The magnitude of government repression astonishes." When workers rebelled, mill owners often came to depend on the state to suppress such upheaval, making mill owners' ability to accumulate capital increasingly reliant on the power of nationalizing states—states whose own power rested more and more on successful industrialization.[35]

The struggle to transform workers into proletarians had made industrialists even more dependent on the state, a remarkable testimony to the limits of their power. The territorialization of capital, its growing attachment to and dependence on nation-states, however, also enabled workers to organize collectively to improve their working conditions and wages; eventually it would turn capitalists' dependence on the state into labor's greatest strength. Trade unions and working-class political movements, despite multipronged efforts to repress them, created new pressures on capital across the nineteenth century, pressures that would many decades later radically reshape the world's cotton industry.

Workers not only rebelled against machine production, as we have seen, but also tried to improve their living and working conditions within a system of mechanized production. These efforts were at first feeble, but they eventually gained strength and indeed won higher wages, shorter hours, and better working conditions. In the first half of the nineteenth century, successes were still few and far between, but the struggle abounded. Some working-class associations had already emerged before 1800 among British weavers. In 1792, Stockport and Manchester mule spinners formed unions. In 1807, handloom weavers collected 130,000 signatures to advocate for what they termed a "legal wage." In 1826, riots of cotton workers spread from Manchester, as weavers assembled and threatened to damage power loom factories. A Fred Foster from Manchester reported "with much pleasure" to Secretary of State Robert Peel on April 28, 1826, that once workers assembled in the streets, "the riot act was proclaimed & the principal streets were cleared by detachments of troops." In 1844, weavers famously rebelled in Silesia. In New England, women cotton mill workers walked off their job in Pawtucket, Rhode Island, in 1824, making it the first strike by factory workers in the United States. English mule spinners also brought collective action strategies with them to the United States, especially to New England, and in 1858 the Mule Spinners' Union of Fall River was born. Spanish cotton workers forged a labor movement during the 1840s and 1850s, and the year 1854 saw the first general strike among spinners. In France, textile workers participated in 35 percent of all strikes recorded between 1830 and 1847. Women sometimes took the lead in such collective action: In Lowell, Massachusetts, for example, women workers organized in 1844 the Lowell Female Labor Reform Association, fighting for better working conditions and a shorter workday. Already by midcentury, cotton manufacturers responded to the militancy of their workers by moving their capital elsewhere, with Catalonian entrepreneurs perhaps the vanguard when they increasingly relocated production to isolated factory villages along the Llobregat and the Ter Rivers outside Barcelona to escape their troublesome workers. As in the case of cotton growing, workers' collective action and the spatial arrangements of the world's cotton industry intersected.[36]

Yet these incipient efforts at unionization, strikes, and other forms of collective action directed toward improving wages and the working conditions of cotton workers demonstrate that once the control and mobilization of labor were "nationalized" within powerful states, and indeed became matters of state, workers also gained new opportunities to improve their situation by appealing to the state itself and mobilizing within national political spaces. The nonpecuniary penalties for violation of employment contracts, for example, became increasingly untenable as a result of workers' collective action. When in England large segments of the working class gained the vote in 1867, trade unions pressured the state to limit allowable remedies for workers' breach of contract, and succeeded in 1875. In Germany it took until the revolution of 1918 to end criminal penalties for breach of contract.[37] Indeed, "employment at will"—allowing workers to leave their jobs whenever they decide to do so—was the result of decades of struggle by workers, not a "natural" outgrowth of the emergence of industrial capitalism and even less so the precondition for its emergence. From the factory to the plantation, the expansion of freedom rested on the organization and collective action of workers. The labor market as idealized in modern-day economics textbooks as often as not came about as a result of strikes, unions, and riots.

The empire of cotton from its 1780s beginnings to 1861 in effect rested on two very different forms of labor, and two very different forms of the organization of production. On the western shores of the Atlantic were the vibrant, expanding, and enormously profitable slave plantations, the latest outgrowth of the dynamic war capitalism that Europeans had been building since the sixteenth century. In Europe itself, but also in New England and a few other areas of the world, a much more novel and more dynamic organization of production had emerged: industrial capitalism, with its spectacularly productive spinning and weaving mills based on wage labor. Connected by the mediation of a group of merchants, these two systems grew side by side, the one feeding the power of the other. Capital, personified by merchants, facilitated the rapid expansion of both slave cotton plantations and wage labor cotton factories, connecting the seemingly opposing legacies of the one to the other—until the day one of them collapsed. Once that happened, once slavery within the empire of cotton expired like some distant supernova, its crucial contribution to the construction of industrial capitalism could be written out of our collective memory.

Chapter Eight

Making Cotton Global

The ship *Glad Tidings,* loaded with American cotton,
enters the port of Liverpool, 1865.

Among the most outstanding phenomena of modern times is undoubtedly the annually progressing expansion of this gigantic business sector whose impact on the material and social conditions of both hemispheres emerges so evidently. . . .

While on the far side of the ocean significant and until recently undeveloped tracts of land are transformed into fertile plains, enabling an increasing population and expanding cultivation, they provide our native land an inexhaustible source of national welfare, wages and employment, utilize large capitals, and become the leverage of a magnificent trade whose products will supply the markets of all the zones, combining the most diverse activities transforming raw materials into finished goods.

—Neue Bremer Zeitung, JANUARY 6, 1850[1]

For Walter Benjamin, Paris was the capital of the nineteenth century. For once and future cotton lords, however, the true center of the world was Liverpool. Situated in England's rainy northwest, the city rose from the banks of the river Mersey and the Irish Sea. There, at one of global commerce's most significant crossroads, Liverpool's merchants had accumulated unprecedented wealth and influence by connecting a nascent European manufacturing complex with an ever more martial and expansive cotton hinterland. It was in Liverpool that industrial capitalism and war capitalism met, its merchants applying the logic of the former to the latter, and transforming both in the process. The genius of Liverpool's merchants lay in their ability to combine ingredients often considered antagonistic: wage labor and slavery, industrialization and deindustrialization, free trade and empire, violence and contract.

Liverpool may have been one of the wonders of the world, but not the kind appreciated by tourists. Indeed, "hideousness" was the summation of one early-twentieth-century chronicler. "The chief objects of attraction in Liverpool are, decidedly, the spacious Docks," observed a contemporary dryly. As early as 1832 the docks and harbor walls stretched for two and a half miles, dotted by quays, warehouses, and a "forest of masts." Beyond the Mersey lay the Irish Sea and beyond that the Atlantic Ocean, and it was on that ocean's western shores that most of the world's cotton was grown. Thousands of ships arrived each year, burdened by tightly pressed cotton bales. Thousands of workers, many of them Irish immigrants, unloaded the ships and brought the bales to warehouses. From there most were shipped by canal boats and, after 1830, train to the spinning mills in nearby Lancashire, twenty to fifty miles distant, but some bales also went back on ships to various European ports where first wagons and later trains fed the increasing number of spinning mills dotting the European countryside. No technical marvel, the port was first and foremost a site of perilous, backbreaking labor. Thousands of workers assembled on the rainy streets of Liverpool each morning before dawn, hoping to be hired for a day of handling huge bales of cotton, dangerous work over long hours at low pay.[2]

Liverpool's port was the epicenter of a globe-spanning empire. Its merchants sent ships all over the world, mostly wind-powered, but by the 1850s and 1860s increasingly by steam as well. The captains of those ships navigated perilous seas, rebellious crews, virulent diseases, and economic volatility. Every time James Brown, captain of a Liverpool cotton ship, arrived in the port of New Orleans in the early 1840s, he wasted weeks in the struggle to find bales of cotton to fill his boat. Shipping rates changed constantly, as idle boats in the port meant stiff competition. Market news from Liverpool, as often as not, led to abrupt changes in the price of cotton, delaying his departure. "Parts of the crew have run away," Brown wrote in one of many laments; "hurricanes" and "reports of privateers" further frayed his nerves.[3]

While Liverpool's port was a scene of stupendous muscular labor, the nervous system of the city was its cotton exchange, whose caretakers lived and worked in close proximity to one another. Every morning the city's merchants would meet to trade "on the flags," an outdoor space in the center of town. Cotton broker Samuel Smith remembered that "in all weathers, cold and wet, winter and summer, we stood outside, sometimes sheltering under the arches when the rain and cold were unendurable." Only after 1809, when a handsome exchange building was erected in the center of town did the cotton merchants move inside. The sales room where buyers met sellers in a noisy and seemingly chaotic dance was striking, as "no place in the world affords so elegant and commodious a situation as this is for the purposes of a public exchange," with "sales to a very considerable amount . . . effected in a few minutes."[4]

Thanks to their all-embracing dispositions, the merchants of the city became the ringmasters of a globe-spanning network of cotton growing, crafting, and selling. On Bombay's Apollo wharf, merchants nervously awaited news "from Liverpool." On plantations throughout the American South, "Liverpool prices" were the single most significant piece of news, bordering on obsession for many slave masters.[5] The southern agricultural journal *De Bow's Review* constantly reported on Liverpool prices and how U.S. cotton farmers could pocket a greater share of them. New York's *Merchants' Magazine and Commercial Review* similarly agonized over Liverpool prices. For Ellen Hooton and hundreds of thousands of cotton mill workers like her, Liverpool prices would determine if she would be employed or not. The global preoccupation with Liverpool reflected the tremendous influence the city's merchants enjoyed over large swaths of the earth. When prices rose in Liverpool, planters in Louisiana might decide to purchase fresh cotton lands, and slave traders might find it profitable to move young slaves by the thousands into these new territories. News from Liverpool might on one day help dislodge Native Americans from their land, on another day encourage invest-

The financial pulse of the empire of cotton: "Liverpool prices"
on an Alabama cotton plantation, 1842

ment in Indian railroads, and on another make a family in Switzerland, Gujarat, or Michoacán give up spinning and weaving altogether.[6]

Liverpool, like no other city, concentrated simultaneously on all the core functions of the global cotton trade. Its merchants traded raw cotton, shipped cotton goods, and financed both cotton agriculture and cotton manufacturing. Other cotton cities were more specialized in their activities. Merchants in New Orleans, Alexandria, and Bombay, for example, mastered the export of raw cotton, while Bremen and Le Havre merchants received their shipments. New York and London merchants focused on financing the trade. And widely dispersed merchants in cities from Buenos Aires to Recife, Hamburg to Calcutta received shipments of yarn and cloth and distributed them through their hinterlands.

None of these cities, however, competed seriously with Liverpool. The channels through which cotton flowed were not evenly distributed across the world. They narrowed and widened at certain points, and the volume and velocity of the flow was a direct expression of the distribution of influence; the deeper and faster the network, the greater the power. While Liverpool enjoyed a torrent of trade and information connecting it to many places, hinterland towns in Mississippi or Buenos Aires saw but a lazy, gentle flow to and from very few places. To be at the very beginning or the very end of a "commodity chain" thus was usually a position of relative weakness. The focus of the cotton network on one city, Liverpool, led to new hierarchies of power—an innovative development that replaced older cotton networks and older merchant groups in cities such as Ahmedabad or Surat or Oaxaca. The rise of Liverpool's merchants at the turn to the nineteenth century further moved a multipolar world of cotton into the direction of becoming unipolar.

Seen from the cotton exchange at Liverpool, the world beyond its high windows was essentially a huge cotton production and consumption complex. The voracious appetite for profit demanded ever more lands for the commercial production of cotton, the multiplying of cotton mills, and the opening of cloth markets. This unprecedented and highly leveraged industrial expansion depended for its survival on the permanent transformation of the global countryside to mobilize ever more labor and resources and provide markets. Yet despite the omnipresence of Liverpool capital and its merchants, the nature of these connected transformations looked radically different in the Black Forest, Bombay, or Mississippi.

While Liverpool merchants stood at the heart of this new empire of cotton, in fact constituted it, they were just one of many groups of traders engaged in the global cotton trade. Jointly these traders coordinated the efforts of the hundreds of thousands of slaves, peasants, and planters growing cotton on farms big and small in many different parts of the world. Jointly they connected those raw materials to the thousands of manufacturers who purchased cotton for their factories, manufacturers who in turn sent yarn and cloth to the markets and shops that then sold these cotton goods to millions of consumers. Merchants moved the fiber and cloth from a Mississippi planter or Gujarati farmer to an Oldham or Zwickau spinner, from Manchester manufacturers to the bazaar of

Istanbul, from the factories of Mulhouse to the dry goods merchants of New York. Merchants advanced capital to allow Barbadian planters to grow cotton. They collected cotton from numerous growers and prepared the bales for shipment. They dispatched ships across the world's oceans. They offered cotton to manufacturers and transmitted market information from the bazaar to the factory, from the factory to the port, and from the port to the plantation. And they sold the yarn and fabric that came out of the ever more efficient factories to ever more consumers all over the world. While sometimes owners of plantations and factories, merchants were more often independent intermediaries. They specialized not in growing or making, but in moving. At great headwaters such as Liverpool, they constituted the market; they were its visible hand.

The challenges of forging these ties were as vast as the potential profits. Consider just one chain of links. For a planter in Mississippi to provide cotton to a Manchester manufacturer, a local Mississippi merchant, a so-called factor, had to first provide the planter with credit to acquire slaves, land, and implements. This factor probably drew on London or New York bankers for these resources. Once the cotton had ripened, the factor would offer the cotton for sale to exporting merchants in the port of New Orleans, who would sell it to importing merchants in Liverpool, who would also provide insurance on the bales and organize their shipment to Europe. Once in Liverpool, the importing merchant would ask a selling broker, another type of merchant, to dispose of the cotton. As soon as a buying broker found the cotton to his liking, he would forward it to a manufacturer. The manufacturer would work up the cotton, and then provide it to a merchant who would organize its shipping to a representative in a distant port, for example in Calcutta. Once there, the yarn would be sold to Indian merchants, who would distribute it into the countryside, where it would eventually be bought by an Indian weaver, who would sell it yet again to other traders who would deliver it to the retail merchants in villages and towns. Thus slave-grown Mississippi cotton manufactured into yarn in Lancashire might be woven into a shirt somewhere in the Indian countryside. The empire of cotton consisted of tens of thousands of such ties.

Merchants everywhere constituted these webs, built on credit, trade, information, trust, social connections, and the never-ending search for profit. The scope of the new cotton networks was unprecedented. Never before had any industry connected the activities of so many growers, manufacturers, and consumers across such vast distances. And as a result, never before were merchants so desperately needed. The scale of these networks created unprecedented problems of coordination. Neither peasants nor plantation owners, nor even wealthy manufacturers, could keep the channels upon which their livelihoods rested clear. The ability of merchants to organize the radical spatial rearrangement of the world's most important manufacturing industry was as much of an invention as the more corporal machines and novel labor organization that dotted the globe by the 1850s.[7] Their capital, and the institutional structures of trade they forged, imbued large expanses of the globe—from the newly industrializing villages and cities of Europe to the plantations and farms of Mississippi and Gujarat—with the new rhythms of industrial production. By bridging the seemingly unbridgeable gap between the slave plantation and the factory staffed by wage workers, they created modern capitalism.[8]

These merchants built the trade in cotton and cotton goods into one of the most substantial of the nineteenth century. Between 1800 and 1860, the quantity of raw cotton traded between the United States and Great Britain, by far the most important stream, grew by a factor of 38; the (much smaller) quantity traded between the United States and continental Europe increased during these same years by a factor of 138. Egypt exported 14 times as much cotton in 1860 as it had in 1822. Imports of cotton into France's most important cotton port, Le Havre, grew by nearly 13 times between 1815 and 1860. And along with the growth of the raw cotton trade, the trade in manufactured cottons also exploded: 350,448 pounds of yarn were exported from Britain in 1794; by 1860 that number had increased by a factor of 563. Other commodity trades boomed during these years as well, but not in the same way; coffee exports from Brazil, to cite just one example, increased seven times between 1820 and 1860. But the major economies of the world depended on the cotton trade: France's single most important export product was textiles, most made of cotton. Between 1800 and 1860, cotton goods accounted for about 40 to 50 percent of the value of total British exports. Raw cotton was also by far the most important export good of the United States: In 1820, the value of U.S. cotton exports was some $22 million; leaf tobacco was valued at $8 million, and wheat at less than $500,000. Cotton constituted about 31 percent of U.S. merchandise exports by value. By 1860, the value of tobacco exports had doubled, and wheat exports had increased by a factor of eight—but cotton had mushroomed nearly nine times to $192 million. It now constituted nearly 60 percent of the value of all merchandise exports. As merchants built the world's first truly global economy, cotton took center stage.[9]

Merchants, some of them dealers or brokers, and other agents, import merchants, or factors, accurately judged that there were ample opportunities for profits in this vast new trade. Distinct groups of merchants reaped profits from each of the transactions necessary to bring cotton from the plantation to the consumer.[10] Commissions, interest, and payment for services filled their coffers. Some grew fabulously rich, the Rathbones in Liverpool, the Barings in London, the Rallis in London, Bombay, and elsewhere, the Volkarts in Winterthur, the Siegfrieds in Le Havre, the Wätjens in Bremen, the Forstalls in New Orleans, the Browns in New York, the Cassavettits in Alexandria, and the Jejeebhoys in Bombay prominent among them. Cotton underpinned the vast wealth and power of these families, allowing them to build mansions staffed by large numbers of servants, collect precious artworks, invest in other businesses, and travel the world. But thousands upon thousands of less wealthy cotton merchants, whose names have largely been forgotten, peopled the trade as well. Collectively, they forged new spaces of capital.

For the marriage between slavery and industry to succeed, however, merchants had first to profitably transmit the patterns of machine production and industrial capitalism into the global countryside. The world had no shortage of big dreamers before the nineteenth century, but heretofore no one had been able to realize the potential of the productive hinterlands and vulnerable consumer markets over such great expanses. The process through which these merchants did so was exceedingly complicated—indeed, it rested on a network of actors whose field of vision was often, though not always, quite provincial, and who at times did nothing more than move the logic of industrial capitalism one step closer to rural cotton producers. By merely connecting various places and stages in the process of cotton manufacturing to one another, however, the merchants, often unwittingly, created something quite new. For the first time in history, they drew upon the full diversity of labor regimes, a hallmark of the emerging capitalism—slaves growing cotton, wage workers manufacturing yarn, and slaves as well as wage workers ginning, pressing, loading, and moving cotton bales. In doing so, they helped Europe overcome its resource constraints. Watching these merchants in action, in all their mundane and seemingly inconsequential activities, helps us solve the puzzle of how industrial and war capitalism came to be connected.

Considering their importance in forging the world of modern capitalism, the actual work of merchants seems often almost banal. Most of their time was spent writing letters, talking to suppliers and customers, traveling, and making calculations. Because the empire of cotton they created was so vast, merchants soon specialized in specific aspects of the trade. Some focused on moving cotton from plantations to ports, others on trans-oceanic trade; some concentrated on selling raw cotton to manufacturers, while others speculated in exporting cotton goods, and others distributed imported cotton goods throughout a particular country or region. Usually merchants focused their trade on a particular region, becoming experts on connecting certain parts of the world to one another. Consequently, they had businesses that could look surprisingly different from each other. The global system, in effect, was built not from a central, imperial directive, but rather by myriad actors with local and diverse connections often solving very local problems.

The most urgent problem merchants helped solve was how to supply manufacturers with raw cotton. As the scale and efficiency of the industry increased, and as cotton did not grow anywhere near the factories, manufacturers needed help securing ever greater supplies from the remote reaches of the world. During the 1760s, 1770s, and 1780s, most purchased this cotton from dealers located in the spinning districts themselves, dealers who traded on their own accounts and provided credit to the manufacturers to enable them to purchase it.[11] In 1788, the city of Manchester, for example, counted twenty-two such dealers. The dealers, in turn, bought the cotton from Liverpool merchants who, in the eighteenth and even early nineteenth centuries, were still mostly general merchants for whom cotton was only one of a number of commodities they had on offer.

Yet as the quantity of cotton traded increased dramatically in the first few decades of the nineteenth century, and as manufacturers' demands on the quality and price of the cotton they received changed, cotton manufacturers left this almost quaint world behind. Instead of purchasing cotton from dealers, they began to use brokers. Brokers, in contrast to the dealers, did not take possession of cotton; they instead charged a commission for brokering trades between importing merchants and manufacturers. As a result, mill owners could purchase not just the cotton that their dealers happened to own, but any of the cotton available in the port of Liverpool—getting the quantities and qualities they desired at the cheapest possible price. Brokers provided a more direct connection between manufacturers and cotton-importing merchants, and also organized the market by setting rules and regulations, distributing information, and providing elaborate arbitration services. They "brought to Liverpool the technical knowledge of the industry," argues one scholar, and "they also brought a new kind of administrative skill and efficiency to deal with the problems of what was, virtually, a new trade." As a result, brokers "became central figure[s] in the market." Expert both in the new technical requirements of spinning and in the bewildering Liverpool market, they helped manufacturers to navigate the varieties of cotton available in Liverpool and acquire the cotton qualities they needed for specific manufacturing processes.[12]

By 1790 four such specialized cotton brokers had emerged in Liverpool. Many others followed, and by 1860, 322 brokers walked the streets of that city. They generally operated as small family firms and came from a variety of backgrounds: some were former dealers, others had been spinners, and still others had worked as import merchants. Eventually, brokers specialized even further. Some became buying brokers, purchasing cotton for manufacturers, and others selling brokers, selling cotton for importing merchants.[13]

Thanks to these changes, manufacturers removed themselves from the inspection of cottons in the market. While early in the century manufacturers had personally touched the cottons on sale, they now communicated their needs to brokers who then searched out the cotton they wanted. Ever more specialized in the production of particular qualities of yarns and goods, and demanding ever greater varieties of cotton, manufacturers found going into market to purchase all that cotton impossible. They depended on a constant flow of the crucial raw material into their factories, and brokers guaranteed that supply.

As brokers replaced dealers, they also changed the way cotton was sold. Again, the needs of machine production dictated these changes. Throughout the eighteenth and well into the first half of the nineteenth century, cotton had been traded as a physical commodity. Merchants bought and sold specific sacks of cotton, dealing with a bewildering vari-

ety of different cottons from different parts of the world that had vary-
ing staple lengths, colors, elasticity, and cleanliness. As merchants sold
specific lots in specific sacks, they in effect allowed a purchaser to trace
back each particular parcel of cotton to a particular producer. The 1814
records of cotton broker George Holt show him selling "13 Bags (of cotton) waste Guinam," "6 Bags Barbadoes," "10 Bags Paras, 15 bags Bahis,
25 bags Dyneraras, 10 bags South Island," and unspecified amounts of
further varieties such as "Bengal," "Surat," "Bourbons," "Demarara," and
"Pernam." As Liverpool cotton broker Thomas Ellison observed in 1886,
"Down to the opening of the present century the usual practice was for
the seller to give to the buyer the marks, ship's name, and place of storage
of any lot or lots of cotton which he might have for sale, in order that the
buyer might go to the warehouse and examine the bales for himself." The
enormous natural variety of cotton was thus preserved in the trade, and all
participants in that trade dealt in cotton that they had seen and touched.[14]

When the trade in cotton exploded in the first decades of the nineteenth
century, this system came under strain. Brokers hurried around the port
of Liverpool inspecting hundreds of bags and bales, trying to match specific lots of cotton to the needs of specific manufacturers—manufacturers
who needed particular qualities to produce particular kinds of yarn. Soon
this became all but impossible. Pushed by manufacturers' needs, brokers
sought new institutional solutions. First, they moved from physically
inspecting each sack of cotton to buying by sample.[15] A small batch of
fiber was drawn from each bale and on the basis of that sample a price
was determined and a sale effected. These samples, unlike the bales themselves, could easily be carried around and even mailed. In a second step,
brokers developed clear standards and a precise vocabulary for cotton;
eventually, manufacturers would acquire cotton without even inspecting
samples. They would, in effect, not order a particular bale of cotton from
a particular place, but a particular quality. This was a radical recasting of
the trade.

Cotton shows enormous variability in grade, staple, and character.
As of 1790, no attempt at grading cottons had been made, even though
grades already existed for other commodities, such as sugar and coffee,
for which categories such as "middling" and "good ordinary" were widely
used. In 1796, in Charleston, "Georgia cotton" and upland cotton were
mentioned for the first time as discrete categories, and in 1799 in Philadelphia, note was made of "Georgia Tennessee cotton"—categories that

still reflected place of origin. That year, the *Dictionnaire universel de la géographie commerçante* still listed diverse cottons only by where they were grown. In 1804, however, Charleston merchants listed "common cotton," a category that by 1805 had become "common upland." By 1805, Sea Island cotton was graded into prime, good, fair, middling, and inferior grades. The *Tradesman* spoke in 1809 of "good middling cotton"; in 1815 in the New Orleans market the designation "prime" was used, two years later "first quality" cotton was listed, and another year later "middling cotton" appeared in Charleston, followed in 1822 by "choice prime cotton" in New Orleans and "choice fair" in 1823. The *London Magazine* mentioned these categories by 1820, a decade during which they came into widespread use. These categories were still approximations that could neither be precisely defined nor enforced, but they formed the foundation upon which later enforceable standards would be built. Without such standards, such a high-volume long-distance trade of bulk commodities would have been all but impossible—the vast diversity of nature had to be distilled and classified to make it correspond to the imperatives of machine production.[16]

For standards to work over the long term, purchasers had to be able to verify the quality of the cotton they had purchased. At first these rules and regulations were informal, conventions not written down but personally understood. As trading by sample increased in volume and expanse, traders in far-flung ports and manufacturers demanded rules with "some sense of permanence"—standards protected by institutions. In response, brokers created the Liverpool Cotton Brokers' Association in 1841. One of the first things the Association did was to pass a resolution that all cotton sold by sample was warranted to contain such quality. By 1844, they had defined standards for "fair" and "middling" cotton. In 1846, the American Chamber of Commerce in Liverpool, founded in 1801 by Liverpool merchants trading with the United States, suggested that the brokers "cause samples of the several classes of American Cotton to be taken, to be placed at the disposal of the American Chamber so as to form a standard for reference in all questions as to quality of cotton." Increasingly, the cotton market was no spontaneous interaction of utility-maximizing individuals, but a set of institutions forged outside the market itself.[17]

Once standards were formalized, efforts emerged to apply them internationally. In 1848 the New Orleans Chamber of Commerce wrote to the American Chamber of Commerce in Liverpool about the "great inconveniences which have hitherto frequently attended the operations of the purchasers of Cotton in New Orleans for want of a fixed standard of quality uniform with that of Liverpool and recognized as such by the Trade in both ports." It proposed to create mutual standards for "fair middling & ordinary cotton, both New Orleans and Alabama." These duplicate standards would then be kept in New Orleans and Liverpool, to adjudicate disputes. The American Chamber of Commerce in Liverpool obliged and voted to create such standards. A modern cotton market was now emerging as the result of collectively articulated conventions, with a private association of Liverpool merchants at its core. Capital was changing the way the cotton plant itself was seen—it would soon change the plant itself. In such subtle ways, the unrelenting pressure of capital-intensive factory production moved closer to the growing of cotton itself, forcing the logic of capital upon the logic of nature.[18]

Cotton standards emerged hand in hand with, and indeed enabled, another invention: a trade in cotton that had not yet arrived. For a futures market to work, information and samples had to travel faster than bulk cotton itself, something that seems to have emerged in the 1810s in Liverpool. By 1812, cotton brokers had begun to trade in cotton while it was still on the high seas, exchanging so-called "bills of lading"—documents certifying ownership of certain bales of cotton. Two years later, on August 13, 1814, George Holt sold to George Johnston & Co. one hundred bags of cotton "to arrive" from Amelia Island in ten days. Such trade in the future delivery of cottons increased throughout the first half of the nineteenth century. In 1858, the American Chamber of Commerce in Liverpool explicitly regulated such "to arrive" contracts. This was the moment in which, according to the Baring house in Liverpool, the "hypothecation of shipping documents" began. And not just in Liverpool: Such "to arrive" contracts were also used in the American South by New York merchants before 1860, and in Le Havre, where merchants created *ventes à livrer* contracts as early as 1848. But there and elsewhere, these contracts were still exceptional, and as late as the 1850s cotton broker Samuel Smith observed that "nearly all the business was bona-fide transfers of cotton in warehouse, and it was quite an exception to sell a cargo afloat."[19]

Moreover, during the first half of the nineteenth century selling cotton for future delivery was still based on the eventual delivery of a *particular* parcel of cotton. George Holt had promised in 1814 to deliver particular bags of cotton to Johnston, his customer, not just a certain quality. Yet gradually the connection between a particular contract and a particular batch of cotton began to weaken. Cotton began to be sold that had not yet been shipped, indeed that would only come onto the market in distant months, and might not even have been planted yet.[20] This further abstraction of the trade would blossom during the American Civil War, when true futures dealings came about. The quantifiable, steady, and ongoing demands of mechanized production encouraged an ever greater abstraction of its essential raw material inputs, protecting manufacturers against price fluctuations and enabling them to price their finished goods across global markets.

The chain from factory to plantation, however, had many more links. Liverpool's brokers communicated the needs of manufacturers to another powerful group of cotton traders: the import merchants. In contrast to the brokers, these merchants engaged in transoceanic trade of cotton, handling goods on an incomparably larger scale, with opportunities for profit proportionally greater. In Liverpool and its French competitor, Le Havre, merchants specializing in cotton importation had emerged as early as the late eighteenth century, to be followed in the nineteenth century by merchants in Bremen. They focused on purchasing cotton abroad or, more typically, shipping it for a commission (rather than taking ownership of the cotton) from distant ports to Europe.[21] They, more than any others, directly connected rural producers with the most dynamic manufacturing sector the world had ever known. At first, they helped slavery blossom in Louisiana and Brazil, but later they would enable peasant producers in India to grow cotton for transoceanic markets, and allow Muhammad Ali's domination of Egyptian peasants to turn into profit.

Liverpool's merchants were far and away the world's most important cotton importers. By the mid-1700s they had brought the first cotton to Liverpool; by 1799, a full 50 percent of all British cotton imports arrived there (most of the rest went to London), and by the late 1830s that proportion had grown to 89 percent. Liverpool's merchants cornered the global cotton market in ways few merchants ever have. They succeeded for several reasons. Initially, Liverpool's central position in the Atlantic slave trade set it up well for trade in cotton. Cotton initially arrived, along with sugar, tobacco, and other goods, as return freight from the

West Indies—one of the sides of the triangular trade. Liverpool may have controlled up to 85 percent of the British slave trade, and by its 1807 abolition as much as one-quarter of Liverpool shipping was in slaves; everyone who worked the city's ports, therefore, was experienced with long-distance trade, and also with the cotton-growing regions of the Americas. And, as cotton increasingly came across the Atlantic rather than the Mediterranean, Liverpool was well situated to capitalize. The city also benefited from its location near the spinning districts in and around Manchester, a connection that rapidly improved thanks to the building of canals, improvements on the river Mersey, and eventually, in 1830, the arrival of the world's first railroads. With such connections in place, Liverpool could benefit from the institutional innovations created by its traders.[22]

The most powerful and wealthiest of Liverpool's merchants engaged in the cotton trade. A careful study of the Liverpool cotton import trade has found that in 1820 fully 607 merchants traded cotton. Yet the same study also established that the number of merchants who imported cotton regularly (more than six times a year) was small, 120 in 1820, and 87 in 1839. The import trade was therefore composed of a very large number of merchants who traded small quantities of cotton occasionally, and a few merchants who regularly traded large numbers of bales. Yet as margins fell in the second quarter of the nineteenth century, the merchant community consolidated. In 1820, the leading ten cotton merchants had imported 24 percent of all cotton into Liverpool, and the top thirty cotton importers had imported a total of 37 percent. Nineteen years later, the leading ten traders brought in 36 percent of all cotton and the leading thirty a full 60 percent. That year, 1839, the largest importer of cotton into Liverpool sold more than fifty thousand bales.[23]

While the majority of traders continued importing small quantities of cotton along with other commodities, Liverpool's major cotton traders reaped tremendous rewards by specializing and intensifying their cotton trade. The Rathbone family, one of the city's prime cotton traders, had moved into the cotton trade in the eighteenth century (they supplied Samuel Greg when he opened Quarry Bank Mill), at first adding to and later superseding their older timber, salt, and tobacco trade. Indeed, they were perhaps the first Liverpool firm to receive U.S.-grown cotton. They shipped cotton throughout the first decades of the nineteenth century, and by the 1830s wholly specialized in it. Like many other merchants, they acquired this cotton through agents in southern ports of the United States who had purchased it on the Rathbones' account or who sent it to them on a commission basis. The profits were large: In the years from 1849 to 1853, the Rathbones earned £18,185 from the cotton trade, in the years 1854 to 1858 they made a full £34,983—at a time when a physician might earn £200 a year. The cotton profits of just five years could finance the construction of a huge and fully furnished English country manor; as the nineteenth century wore on, more and more such stately homes dotted Liverpool's countryside.[24]

The Rathbones' trajectory from their earlier trade in other commodities into cotton was typical of the major nineteenth-century transcontinental cotton merchants. But there was another path into the cotton trade. Those whose wealth or skills did not originate in trade itself saw cotton as a promising way to diversify. So spectacularly profitable was the cotton trade that all but a few of the major capitalists of the era sought to gain a footing—bringing with them significant amounts of capital. The Baring family, most notably, made such a move. Along with the Rothschilds, the Barings were Europe's most powerful bankers, and just like the Rothschilds, the Barings forged an important connection to cotton during the first half of the nineteenth century. They also had a long-standing relationship to the United States, not least because they had facilitated that expanding slave power's purchase of Louisiana from the French.

The Barings had begun investing in the cotton business as early as 1812, when they advanced £6,000 to New Orleans merchant Vincent Nolte to start a cotton export house. Thanks to this capital influx, Nolte's "position in the cotton market now became, step by step, more influential," and by the 1820s he traded sixteen thousand to eighteen thousand bales per season. When Francis Baring visited Nolte in the early 1820s to check on his investments, he was, according to Nolte, "evidently gratified when he took his first walk along the so-called Levee . . . and saw it strown [sic], from the upper to the lower suburb, with cotton bales, on which were stamped the marks of my firm." Nolte failed in 1826, however, and the Barings in consequence added an American agent to their operations, Thomas Ward in Boston, to enforce tighter controls over their American investments.[25]

Under Ward's watchful eye, the Barings' London-based cotton business grew rapidly, so much so that by 1832 they had opened an office in Liverpool. Step by step, they built a globe-spanning system of information collecting and trading whose epicenter was Liverpool. It was there that they collected information on the globe's raw cotton supplies, cotton manufacturing, and cotton goods consumption and then translated it into orders to Thomas Ward, who then made arrangements with commission houses in New York, Philadelphia, Charleston, Savannah, Mobile, and New Orleans. The Barings also took shares—that is, they purchased particular lots of cotton forwarded by other commission houses. Funds for both advances and purchases were provided by drafts on Baring Brothers & Company. It was this credit, wielded by merchants like the Barings, that made the brutality of war capitalism more and more efficient, and thus made industrial capitalism more and more profitable.[26]

Riding this wave of activity, in 1833 the Barings became the fifth largest importer of cotton, and between 1839 and 1842 they ascended to the largest, the firm whose "motions are watched" by their competitors. In fiscal year 1839–40 alone, for example, they imported 104,270 bales of cotton—the annual labor product of at least seventy thousand slaves.[27]

The operations of the Barings, like those of the Rathbones, dwarfed those of most of their colleagues—not just in Liverpool, but even more so in Europe's other emerging cotton ports. Still, important cotton merchants emerged elsewhere, catering to the needs of other national cotton industries. On the northern German coast, Bremen rose to prominence during the first half of the nineteenth century as a cotton trading center. The first sacks of cotton landed in 1788; by 1829, Bremen's port counted six merchants trading in cotton, and by 1845 the Bechtel, Vietor, Delius, Meier, Hagendorn, Gildemeister, and Fritze families collectively imported 18,498 bales.[28]

Bremen, unlike Liverpool, did not have a thriving cotton industry in its own hinterland, with most of its cotton imports shipped to manufacturers hundreds of miles away in such places as Saxony and southern Germany. What Bremen had was human ties to the United States. Indeed, Bremen's cotton trade emerged largely as return freight in the holds of ships that had brought European immigrants to the United States. The Bremen cotton merchants of D. H. Wätjen & Co. in January 1852 sent their ship *Albers* from New Orleans to Bremen loaded with cotton, brought immigrants to New Orleans in April, then returned with cotton to Bremen in June. It sailed once more with immigrants to New Orleans in September, before bringing tobacco to London in November. The Bremen cotton trade demonstrated the symbiosis between the export of continental Europe's surplus labor and the import of agricultural commodities. Globalization increasingly fed upon itself.[29]

More significant than the Bremen merchants were their counterparts in Le Havre. Situated on the Norman coast of northwestern France, it was continental Europe's most important cotton port in the first half of the nineteenth century, and supplier to the French, Swiss, and western German industries. In 1830 port workers, as underpaid and overworked as their counterparts in Liverpool, unloaded 153,000 bales, and in 1860, 600,000—accounting for 89 percent of all cotton imports into France. Cotton became as central to Le Havre as it had become to Liverpool. Le Havre's central position in the European cotton trade built, like Liverpool's, on its earlier role in the East India and slave trade, and, like Bremen's, on its role as a major port of embarkation for European migrants to the United States.[30]

As in Liverpool, a growing number of merchants plied the cotton trade in Le Havre; 279 competed for business in 1835. Like their Liverpool counterparts, they operated on a global scale. Jules Siegfried, for example, one of Le Havre's major traders, was born into a family of cotton printers in Mulhouse and learned the business not just in his father's firm in Le Havre, but also via apprenticeships in Manchester and Liverpool. In 1859, his brother Jacques opened a cotton house in New Orleans, eventually turning the firm into the transatlantic Siegfried Frères, with the partners traveling frequently between France and the United States. As in Liverpool, Le Havre cotton merchants infused the trade in raw cotton with the rhythm of machine production.[31]

Jules Lecesne, another French merchant, was even more globetrotting. Trained in England, New York, and Boston, he founded his first cotton-export firm in Mobile, Alabama, in 1840 (a move also made by some Bremen merchants, who settled temporarily in southern towns to get access to cotton and expertise). Ten years later, he created a firm in New Orleans, under the name Jules Lecesne Frères et Cie, in 1851 an agency in Galveston, in 1854 one in New York, in 1857 one in Paris, and in 1858 one in Manchester, all linked to a house in Le Havre. Eventually he had agents working for him in a remarkable range of cities, among them Galveston, New Orleans, Mobile, New York, Havana, Cork, Glasgow, Manchester, Liverpool, Paris—and, of course, Le Havre. He became Le Havre's major cotton importer and supplier of the Alsatian industry, bringing in a full 22 percent of that city's cotton imports in 1860.[32]

As the nineteenth century progressed, European import merchants—

REIMAGINING THE GLOBAL COUNTRYSIDE

Jules Siegfried

Francis Baring

the people who shipped cotton across oceans—faced competition from what would have seemed, early in the century, a most unlikely quarter: the United States of America. In New York, but also in Boston and elsewhere, cotton traders emerged who would come to play an increasingly important role both in the transatlantic cotton trade and in the supply of American cotton mills.

One American firm, Brown Brothers, would eventually join the ranks of the world's most important cotton merchant houses. The Browns were immigrants from Ireland. Alexander Brown founded a modest linen business in 1800 in Baltimore, then branched out into the cotton trade. As part of this diversification, Alexander sent his son William to Liverpool in 1810 to open a house for the importation of American cotton and the export of cotton goods. He sent his other sons to other port cities. Most important of all, in 1825 son James went to New York, with the goal of promoting "the interest of Messrs. William & James Brown & Co., of Liverpool, and of affording greater facility, and the choice of markets, to our southern friends who are disposed to give . . . us their business." By the 1820s, Brown Brothers was among the largest cotton traders between the United States and Liverpool.[33]

From the 1820s to the 1850s, Brown Brothers involved itself in all aspects of the southern cotton trade. The firm offered cotton growers and factors in the South advances on future crops. It arranged shipping to Liverpool; indeed, the Browns themselves owned a number of ships. It provided insurance on cotton in transit. It sold huge quantities of cotton on commission (typically, Brown would advance about two-thirds of the market value of cotton on these consignments), procured from factors, including its own agents in the ports of New Orleans, Mobile, Savannah, and Charleston. Even though the Browns favored the less risky commission business, at times they bought cotton outright and shipped it to Liverpool for sale. In addition, and ever more important, the Browns provided credit and exchange facilities (converting various currencies) to southerners to enable them to trade crops grown by slaves. In the 1830s they advanced $100,000 to New Orleans cotton traders Martin Pleasants & Co., and a $200,000 line of credit to the New Orleans banking house of Yeatman Woods & Co. They also moved capital into a variety of southern banks, among them the Planters' and Merchants' Bank in Mobile, Alabama, and the Merchants' and Traders' Bank of Mississippi. The Browns made themselves central to the global cotton economy and so they became rich. In the flush times of the early 1830s, it has been estimated, Brown Brothers made profits of more than $400,000 per year—enough to buy thirteen one-hundred-foot yachts, or thirteen hundred carriages.[34]

These activities allowed the Brown family to capture a significant share of the global cotton trade, anticipating the rising importance of American merchants in the late-nineteenth-century empire of cotton. William Brown's share of cotton imports into Liverpool amounted to 2.8 percent in 1820, and 7.3 percent in 1839, putting him among the top ten importers of cotton in the world's largest cotton port. In 1838, his brother James in New York handled 178,000 bales of cotton, equaling 15.8 percent of total U.S. cotton exports to the United Kingdom. The Browns would later channel some of their fabulous wealth into railroads, banks, and industrial ventures, and cultural institutions including the Museum of Natural History in New York. Through such diverse investments, the wages of plantation slavery and land expropriation were inscribed within economic and cultural institutions that endured well beyond abolition in 1865.[35]

. . .

Whether in New York or Le Havre, Bremen or Liverpool, the vast majority of the cotton acquired and shipped by these merchants came from territories conquered by force and cultivated by slave labor—first the West Indies and Brazil, eventually the southern United States. Indeed, merchants built particularly dense connections to these apparently remote, rustic, and thinly developed parts of the world. Strikingly, territories dominated by slave labor, in contrast to so many long-settled cotton lands in South Asia and Africa, proved to be uniquely malleable by European capital and capitalists, and particularly adaptable to the patterns of machine production.

Merchants' most significant tool in building these connections was capital in the form of credit. Credit was the magic wand that allowed merchants to recast nature, clear lands, remove native inhabitants, purchase labor, produce crops in definite qualities and quantities, and meet the voracious appetites of manufacturers and their modern cotton machinery. For the time being, these essential steps turned out to be much more difficult, if not impossible, in the absence of slave labor.

The ultimate success of these merchants came not only from their ability to organize complex transactions and transport a bulk commodity over very large distances but from their ability to infuse the rhythms of industrial production into the countryside. As any perusal of a plantation account book reveals, European credit was essential to planters' ability to purchase ever more land and ever more slaves and hold them from one harvest season to the next. Less obviously, but more important, was the way the money market in London insinuated the logic of industrial capitalism among the planters. This is how New Orleans cotton merchant W. Nott described the link: When in 1829 Thomas Baring gave W. Nott & Co. in New Orleans a $10,000 line of credit, Nott in turn was able to advance money to the "Planters of Tennessee against their Drafts on their Factors here in anticipation of the Proceeds of their growing Crops—Drafts which are generally accepted, on the faith of the Planters promise to ship their Crops, when ready, 8, 10 or even 12 months before the Property comes into the acceptors hands." Such a transaction, he continued, was relatively safe because of "the intimate knowledge possessed by J. W. & Co. of every Planter's standing & character, & the constant residence of at least one of the Planters in Nashville . . . in advancing the approximate value of 25 to 30,000 bales of Cotton in a season—as they are supposed to—their reliance is not on the signature of the Factor who is perhaps not good for a fiftieth part of the sum, but on the Planters' punctuality in forwarding his crop to such Factor in time to meet the Draft."[36]

Beyond advancing credit directly to planters, European and New York merchants also invested in southern state bonds and banks that financed a further expansion of cotton planting. In 1829, Baring underwrote Louisiana state bonds issued to finance the Consolidated Association of the Planters of Louisiana Bank. Although the bank was established by planters in 1828, foremost among them Baring's friend Edmond Forstall, when it turned out to be impossible to raise sufficient capital, ultimately the State of Louisiana guaranteed the bonds. Once the bonds were issued, Baring took $1.666 million worth of them. Two years later, by April 1830, the bank had outstanding loans to planters of $1.6 million, secured by property valued at $5 million. In effect, Baring financed a great expansion of the Louisiana plantation complex, enabling the clearing of land and the purchase of slaves, all of which eventually fed into his own huge cotton import business. Few if any places in the world drew such concentrated capital investments as the plantation belt of the United States—and few places were the source of such massive profits.[37]

Much of that European and, increasingly, New York and Boston capital went into the expansion of cotton agriculture via a group of intermediary merchants who connected cotton merchants with American cotton planters—the factors. They completed the chain of traders between factory and plantation. The interaction between the merchants exporting cotton and the factors who connected to the growers was the fulcrum through which European capital pushed the southern countryside toward the rhythms of the machine.

These American middlemen accepted planters' cotton on commission, transported it to ports, and then sold it to merchants such as the Barings and the Browns. This service was of enormous benefit to planters, as it enabled them to sell their products in large coastal markets or even in Europe, giving in effect even the remotest of them access to distant markets. Factors also provided planters with manufactured goods and food supplies. And they were the most significant deliverers of capital into the cotton-growing regions of the U.S. South, channeling credit to planters who used the money to acquire the supplies they needed to tide themselves over until the next cotton harvest and to purchase more land and more slaves to expand the production of cotton.[38]

Interest on these loans—8 percent and more—secured by future cotton harvests, was another source of factors' revenue. Factors drew for capital on European merchants, and thus "the world's money markets, like the world's commodity markets, became available to the cotton planter through his factor." Collecting cotton from slave planters and yeomen farmers and selling it to exporters did not make them the wealthiest traders in the empire of cotton, but it did make them the most numerous. Factors clustered wherever cotton was grown. Embodying coastal capital, they brought the global norms of capital accumulation and the manufacturers' demand for ever cheaper cotton at predictable qualities to the doorsteps of slave plantations.[39]

Cities such as New Orleans, Charleston, and Memphis counted within their confines dozens of factors, who drew huge quantities of cotton to those ports. Indeed, Samuel Smith, a Liverpool cotton broker, reported from New Orleans that "the levee or bank of the great Mississippi river . . . was lined with a double or triple row of cotton steamers extending for miles." So many "cotton bales were piled up on their decks" that "they looked like floating castles." But smaller cities attracted factors, and thus cotton, as well. In the small town of Newport on the St. Marks River in Florida, for example, Daniel Ladd plied his business. Born in Augusta, Maine, in 1817 into a family of merchants, shippers, and textile mill owners, at age sixteen Ladd joined one of his relatives as a clerk in a commission house in Florida, going into business on his own shortly afterward. Newport was a fortunate location for such a business, because the town had emerged by the 1820s as an important port to export cotton grown in northern Florida and southern Georgia. By 1850, Newport and the neighboring town of St. Marks would ship forty-five thousand bales of cotton a year, presenting, according to Ladd's biographer, an opportunity for "his imaginative mind," which "was continually devising ways of turning them into profitable ventures." Ladd provided advances to planters, sold cotton for them on commission, purchased cotton, provided supplies, and offered shipping facilities. Deeply immersed in the slave economy, Ladd himself owned twenty-seven slaves by 1860, and also traded in slaves, advertising in 1847 hats, saddles, and "a field hand and a rough cook." He held many mortgages secured by slaves, for example, "For $100 payable on February 15, 1845, R. H. Crowell pledged a sixteen-year-old Negro girl named Carolyn and 300 bushels of corn." Ladd's business, though local by definition, was connected to the wider world of manufacturing and credit in many different ways. The cotton that Ladd sold was consigned to Boston, Savannah, or especially New York City houses, where most of the capital came from. And agents of Ladd's went yearly to New York to purchase supplies, spending more than $50,000 in 1860.[40]

At bottom, factors like Ladd drew on capital advanced by European merchants and they advanced that capital to planters to enable them to purchase land, slaves, and provisions. Those same European merchants also advanced credit to enable manufacturers to purchase cotton, and provided capital to cloth traders worldwide, enabling them to acquire cotton goods to sell to customers. Without credit, the empire of cotton would have crumbled—indeed, as any foreclosed planter knew only too well, the empire of cotton was at its heart an empire of credit.

Merchants, in turn, gained access to capital from various sources. Partly, they generated capital in the trade itself; many a cotton merchant had begun as a clerk or partner in another merchant's house and then used the accumulated profits to go into trade under his own name. Other merchants, as we have seen, moved their assets from a different line of trade into the cotton business. The Barings did just that, transferring capital from their government loan business and East India engagements into the cotton trade. So did the Browns, who used the capital accumulated in the linen trade to go into cotton; the Rathbones, who used the profits from their diversified trade to specialize in cotton; Nathan Rothschild, who used his father's profits in banking and general trade to invest massively in the textile business; and Bombay merchant Jamsetjee Jejeebhoy, who used profits from the opium trade to get into the cotton export business. Other merchants accumulated riches in the slave trade—Liverpool merchants sometimes shifted into cotton after Britain abolished the slave trade in 1807. And then there were the banks that pooled merchants' resources in cities such as Liverpool, Le Havre, and New York, banks willing to advance credit to traders who in turn could use it to oil the global machinery of cotton production.[41]

Much of this credit was secured by the future delivery of commodities grown by slaves and even by the value of slaves themselves. This link became most obvious when things went wrong—for example, when planters could not repay the advances of their factors and factors could not repay the credit of exporting merchants. In this way, the Browns of New York, who advanced large sums of money to southern planters, came to own at least thirteen cotton plantations in the South, along with hundreds of slaves. In 1842, William and James Brown estimated that the value of these plantations amounted to $348,000, out of a total investment in the South of $1.55 million. James Brown, in fact, sat in his New York office hiring resident managers for slave plantations.[42] The American Chamber of Commerce in Liverpool understood this relationship when it reported at its 1843 meeting that

> it very often happens that in the course of such transactions planters or other persons in Slave holding countries become indebted to British merchants who, with a view to secure themselves from loss, take security from their debtors by means of mortgage of their plantations with the Slaves which form an essential part of the value. In the Commercial transactions between England and the United States of America which a few years since resulted in so heavy a debt owing to this Country, British Merchants either directly or through their Agents were obliged to take securities of this kind to a large amount, many of which are yet unrealized. The debtors in many cases had nothing else to offer.[43]

Not only did individual merchants become slave owners, but more broadly, the flow of credit between Britain and the United States rested to a significant degree on slave property. It was exactly for this reason that in 1843 the American Chamber of Commerce in Liverpool lobbied against the Slave Act, which, they feared, would make "all mortgages [secured by slaves] and other Securities made . . . to accomplish any object or contract in relation to any object" unlawful. People used as collateral, not just as laborers, lubricated the flow of capital, and thus cotton, around the globe with ever greater velocity.[44]

This system of extending credit was vulnerable to disruptions precisely because it was so global in scope. Every one of its parts was related to every other; if people failed in one part of the empire, the crisis could spread rapidly to every other part. Lancashire manufacturers were dependent on foreign markets, and the failure of merchants in these markets to remit payments could create serious problems at home. "As it is about Eleven months since you purchased from us the last parcel of Goods, and our engagements are heavy and will be no doubt pressing this spring, permit us to request from you an early remittance in Cash or produce," exhorted the New York merchants Hamlin and Van Vechten with considerable anxiety. If prices for raw cotton fell rapidly, as sometimes happened, merchants would hold cotton worth less than the advances they had made, making it difficult or impossible for them to pay their debts. The result: the global panics of 1825, 1837, and 1857.[45]

Despite periodic collapses, capital for the most part moved with remarkable ease into the farthest reaches of cotton production in regions of the world dominated by slave labor. It was much harder for European buying brokers, selling brokers, importing merchants, and factors, despite the rapidly growing capital at their command, to penetrate cotton-growing countrysides dominated by peasant labor. The rhythms of peasant production, as we have seen, proved stubborn—much to the voluble frustration of cotton merchants and manufacturers. In fact, the tools of European war capitalism, so effective in North America, did not allow for the full incorporation of land and labor in Asia and Africa into the global cotton nexus. The necessary infrastructure, physical, administrative, military and legal, simply did not exist.

Not that there was no connection between European merchant capital and peasant producers, for example in India. However, the quantities of cotton traded remained limited, and the quality never quite satisfied European manufacturers. The ways cotton was produced in India never meshed well with the particular needs of modern European spinning factories. Indeed, in regions where cotton was grown by peasant labor, European capital did not reach the producers. Instead, local growers retained sufficient control over their land and labor to escape the monocultural production of cotton for global markets, and indigenous merchants retained control over the internal cotton trade—and even exports. As late as 1851, Indian merchants such as Cursetjee Furndoonjee, Cowasji Nanabhoy Davar, and Merwanji Framju Panday exported more cotton bales from India than did European merchants. If anything, European firms were more often subordinate agents for Indian cotton merchants, and borrowers of Indian merchant capital. Indian merchants, of course, also dominated cotton production within India itself, with local capital largely financing cotton growing for export.[46]

The central role of Indian merchants in the trade in raw cotton built upon their earlier role in the cloth trade. In 1788, the Board of Trade in India had reported to the governor-general of the East India Company that the cotton trade "is still very much in the simple inartificial state of the Natives, the business of it greatly depending on them." At first, Indian merchants such as Bombay traders Pestonjee Jemsatjee, Jamsetjee Jejeebhoy, and Sorabje Jevangee were able to translate this expertise in the cloth trade to the trade in raw cotton as well. As a result, throughout the first half of the nineteenth century, the influence of Western merchants in India usually remained limited to coastal cities, and even there they encountered stiff competition from Indian merchants. The Bombay Chamber of Commerce, founded in 1836, counted among its numbers numerous Indian merchants, reflecting their continued importance. As the chamber observed as late as 1847, "Your Committee did not think it proper to hold out any hope that Merchants, as such, could in the present state of European agency and operation in the country, take up any such position, involving as it would do the maintenance of Establishments in the interior: and it was thought proper to add the only support which English Merchants could contemplate affording, must be limited to the purchase of Cotton when brought here to market, and which, it was said, they were quite prepared to do."[47]

In the cotton-growing countryside itself, Indian traders advanced funds to growers, often at exorbitant rates of interest, who in turn sold the raw cotton to brokers, who then advanced the cotton to coastal merchants—a system the British considered "evil," principally because it eluded their control. As Bombay-based merchant John Richards reported in 1832 to the Barings in London, "The Native Merchants exclusively receive the produce from the interior, from along the Coast, the Persian Gulf, the Red Sea, China there are many of them both Hindoos & Parsees that are wealthy, some even possessing large capital. As yet the Business is so completely in their hands that Contracts for Cotton which have been attempted to be entered into with Merchants up the Coast have failed in the attempt." This dominance of non-European capital, along with the continued control over land and labor by local peasants, resulted, among other things, in cotton production geared to the needs of local producers, including local manufacturers, rather than the specifications of distant European mill owners.[48]

The independence of Indian merchants and producers was hardly exceptional in the first half of the nineteenth century; European commercial penetration into the hinterland of cotton-growing areas was still the exception rather than the rule in most of the world. At mid-century, most cotton produced was never traded through the books of European or North American merchants. In China, imported Indian cotton came under the control of Hong merchants who sold it to dealers in the hinterland. In western Anatolia, like India, the trade between its port city, Izmir, and its cotton-producing regions was in the hands of local merchants. In another part of the Ottoman Empire, Egypt, the impact of Western merchants on trade between producers and the port of Alexandria remained just as limited. Until the late 1840s, Muhammad Ali enforced a virtual monopoly of acquiring raw cotton from producers and selling it to coastal merchants, not least by forcing peasants to pay their taxes in cotton. And some newly industrializing areas avoided dependence on imported cotton. In Mexico, for example, the Puebla industrialists either purchased cotton directly from producers or drew on the offers from Veracruz merchants.[49]

Remarkably, throughout the first half of the nineteenth century the penetration of European capital into the global cotton-growing countryside was largely limited to areas in which cotton was grown by slave labor—slavery, not peasant production, was the handmaiden of wage labor at the birth of the Industrial Revolution. Only after slavery became untenable as a mode of labor mobilization and European states had gained vastly increased administrative, judicial, military, and infrastructural capacities thanks to their ability to capture some of the wealth generated by mechanized manufacturing would European capital and state power begin to revolutionize the global countryside in India, Egypt, and, eventually, Central Asia and Africa.

Despite its failure to integrate peasant producers into the empire of cotton, the signal characteristic of the world's first modern manufacturing industry was its global nature. This globalization required globalizers, people who saw the opportunities of the new order and inspired their business communities and their states to collective action to secure it. The principal globalizers were neither the planters nor manufacturers, many intensely local in their mind-set, but instead, as we have seen, the traders who specialized in creating networks that connected cultivators, manufacturers, and consumers.

Forging such global networks took courage and imagination. When Johannes Niederer tendered his services to the Swiss merchant house of Volkart in 1854, he offered to scout market opportunities in Batavia, Australia, Macassar, and Mindanao, Japan, China, Rangoon, Ceylon, and Cape Town. Such globetrotting traders, as one historian has concluded, "ruled the industry." Indeed, manufacturers and growers regularly complained about the power of traders, while many merchants, for their part, looked down upon manufacturers as provincials and gamblers: Robert Creighton, a Pennsylvania cotton trader, warned his sons even in his will against becoming involved in manufacturing, as did Alexander Brown, reminding his son William in 1819 that all members of the firm are "unanimously opposed to any interest being taken in the Cotton Mill."[50]

To become such powerful actors in the empire of cotton and to manage this trade profitably, the Rathbones, Barings, Lecesnes, Wätjens, Rallis, and others constructed dense networks through which information, credit, and goods could flow reliably.[51] Building such networks was extraordinarily difficult. The Rathbones, for example, spent astonishing energy nurturing their links to merchants in New York, Boston, and various southern ports, especially Charleston and New Orleans. They corresponded constantly with business partners, trying to get market updates and gain access to trade opportunities. They also traveled frequently to the United States, and extended stays in North America became a rite of passage for young members of the firm.[52]

Other merchants labored just as hard to create these networks. In 1828, Thomas Baring traveled up the coast of the United States from New Orleans to Boston, researching local business conditions, establishing closer connections to merchants in southern towns to recruit more trade, and granting credit to various southern firms that allowed them to make advances on cotton shipments. Jules Lecesne followed the same path, building branch houses in various cotton ports throughout the Atlantic world, and staffing them with his relatives, who constantly exchanged information on prices and harvests, and who eventually even published a French bulletin on cotton shipments in New Orleans. What was needed above all was reliable information on everything from weather conditions to the temperaments of brokers.[53]

The global cotton trade, as we have seen, rested on credit. Credit rested on trust. Trust, in a global market extended well beyond the kin of any family or tribe, rested on information. Information was accordingly at the core of most merchants' activities. A vast swath of information was potentially relevant to any merchant, but two strands were the most valuable: who paid back their debts, and what would happen to the price of cotton in the coming months. As a result, millions of letters—now housed in dark corners of libraries and archives—exchanged between merchants spoke to these subjects. Expectations about future price movements obviously mattered a great deal, and thus information about factors that could possibly influence prices—the weather in cotton-growing areas, the effects of wars, the state of regional economies—was precious. While institutions such as the Bank of England began gathering such information as well, most of it was still in private hands, collected (and hoarded) for private use only.[54]

Where reliable information was scarce, rumors and gossip filled the void. Reputation made and unmade firms, and the spread of manipulated information could move markets. Being able to provide information, not surprisingly, was a major source of prestige, and a primary way that both an individual merchant and his firm improved their reputation. When the Hamburg merchants of Menge & Niemann offered their services to Phelps, Dodge, a commercial house in New York in 1841, they introduced themselves and their business, then immediately provided information on the development of the Hamburg trade, including a price circular printed under their name, which listed the local prices for a whole range of commodities, including cotton.[55] Doing business with them, they suggested, would give Phelps, Dodge privileged access to useful information.

The need both to have information and to be seen to have it was why at the outset of his career as a Liverpool cotton broker, Samuel Smith immediately launched his own cotton circular, a step that in retrospect he judged "aided not a little in establishing my business." On a grander scale, in his memoir of his life in the cotton industry, Vincent Nolte, the Barings agent in New Orleans, claimed he was the first person to print up a cotton market circular, starting in 1818: "The meteorological weather tables had given me the idea of getting up one similar to them, which should exhibit the course and fluctuations of prices, from week to week, during the shipping period of three successive years, and designate the difference of exchange, each time, by black, red, and blue lines." Such information sharing, he went on to note, had resulted in much new business.[56]

Because production was so dispersed and so global, information was difficult to assemble. In 1845, Frédéric C. Dollfus, a member of one of the oldest cotton manufacturing families in Mulhouse, arrived in the port of Singapore. His goal was to understand what kinds of cotton goods were in demand there, and to inform cotton manufacturers back home what prices they might fetch. After detailed studies of the local markets in Singapore, Dollfus proceeded to Macao, Canton, Hong Kong, Manila, Batavia, and Semarang. Covering some of the most important Asian cotton marts, he shared his hard-won intelligence with an interested audience back home. A year later, Dollfus returned home to Mulhouse.[57]

This trip was just one of many efforts of Mulhouse manufacturers to gain market information. In one of the era's greatest information-gathering ventures, they collected throughout the eighteenth and nineteenth centuries thousands of cloth samples from around the world and took careful notes as to their provenance and local market prices, all in an effort to equip local manufacturers to produce for remote markets. Catalan manufacturers engaged in a very similar though more modest project.[58]

Access to information in turn privileged certain locations within the empire of cotton, as William Rathbone VI realized in 1849, when he predicted that New York would become "more and more the centre of the American trade (guided of course by advices from European markets). . . . Within 10 days sail from England & within an hour of information [by the newly invented telegraph] & communication with New Orleans, St. Louis, Cincinnati, Charleston & a party is in possession of more information of importance than at any other point."[59] Rather than proximity to either cotton-growing or cotton-manufacturing areas, what really counted for the Rathbones and others was access to information. And New York, a city with neither a cotton-growing hinterland nor spinning mills, provided exactly that—although it could not compete with the information, credit, and trade hub that Liverpool had become.

Such was the necessity of knowledge that merchants invented or adopted increasingly more formalized ways of collecting and disseminating information. They created publications dedicated to the task: The *British Packet and Argentine News*, published from August 1826 in Buenos Aires, reported on Latin American and global markets, including cotton yarn and cloth. The *Landbote*, a journal published in Winterthur, disseminated after 1840 regular news about the cotton market of Le Havre. The *Bremer Handelsblatt* reported regularly on cotton harvests, cotton markets, and price developments in that city.[60]

Faster ships meant faster movement of information as well. Already in 1843 the *Asiatic Journal* was able to announce that "English period-icals and newspapers arrive in Bombay almost damp from the press." Bombay, after all, "is very near us now,—a voyage of only five-and-thirty days from London Bridge." When by the 1840s telegraphs began con-necting cotton-growing, -trading, and consumption centers (though not yet across oceans and continents), merchants had even more immediate access to crucial information.[61]

Eventually the desire to formalize access to information became one of the prime reasons for merchants to organize collectively. Liverpool brokers had at first individually assembled information on the state of the cotton trade and dispersed that information to their customers in private circulars. In 1811, however, the brokers agreed to cooperate on the gather-ing of information, though continuing to distribute it privately to cli-ents. Efforts to create a collective price circular for cotton began in 1832, and when in 1841 the Liverpool Cotton Brokers' Association came into being, its ninety members focused principally on collecting and dissemi-nating market information, especially on the "visible supply" of cotton in the market. Such information-gathering bodies emerged everywhere cotton was grown, traded, or made into yarn and cloth. Chambers of commerce were often at the forefront: Manchester merchants gathered in the Society of Merchants beginning in 1794, Le Havre merchants formed a chamber of commerce in 1802, by 1825 there were already twelve such institutions in the United Kingdom alone, in Bombay merchants formed the Bombay Chamber of Commerce in 1836, in the 1830s merchants in Brazil began organizing commercial associations, and by 1858 there were thirty such chambers in the United States. All these bodies gathered mar-ket information, but they were also political lobbies pleading the case for special attention from the burgeoning imperial states.[62]

The dependence of this economic order on reliable information, trust, and credit led merchants to depend on networks created outside the market itself. The fashioning of global trade, just like the emergence of wage labor, rested on social relations that predated the advent of capital-ism. What set merchants apart was not just their ability to accumulate and deploy capital, or even their privileged access to information, but their ability to build and draw upon these networks, networks of trust based on extended family ties, geographical proximity, and shared religious beliefs, ethnic identities, and origin. In a world in which trade was extremely risky and the survival of a firm could depend on the trustworthiness of just one correspondent, reliability was essential. Reliability, however, came more easily when people who had ways of enforcing trust embedded in social connections, creating in effect what one historian has called a "relational capitalism." The importance of these networks was such that Olivier Pétré-Grenouilleau, the leading French historian of merchant communities, concludes that "the characteristics of Atlantic trade did not depend only on the rules of the market." Cotton markets rested more than most on such extra-market social relations.[63]

Physical proximity was one way to establish networks of trust. The global cotton trade concentrated in a relatively small number of trading hubs not least because proximity allowed such networks and supporting institutions to flourish. Nicholas Waterhouse, one of the first cotton brokers in Liverpool, studded his businesses with family members and a network of local "friends." Liverpool merchants more broadly nurtured a code of "strict probity and honour" that regulated their relationships, as Edward Baines observed in 1835.[64]

But these networks needed to stretch halfway across the globe as well. Establishing trust across vast distances was considerably more difficult and required enormous effort. When William Rathbone VI visited New York City in 1841 to energize the cotton business, he wrote to his father of the urgent need to confirm "some valuable friendships." Indeed, the Rathbones' correspondence is full of efforts to create networks of trust and friendship. When Rathbone partner Adam Hodgson scouted the U.S. cotton market in the early 1820s, he reported to Rathbone from New York, "I am so well aware, that our united feeling of mercantile obligation, & personal friendship will render you solicitous to avail yourselves of every opportunity of reciprocating the kindness & confidence which our friends have ever manifested towards us, that I need not remind you in how great a degree I have been experiencing both, ever since I landed in this country." In language reminiscent of a marriage proposal he reported about one merchant house that "they are quite friendly & I think true to us & with the help of an occasional cotton order may be seduced into consignments." Other merchant houses proceeded in similar ways: When the Volkarts wanted to establish themselves in the European cotton trade, they listed a number of Indian, German, English, and Swiss merchant houses as "references" that testified to their respectable character. They appealed to others to "trust" them, and mentioned their "intimate friend[s]." When the Barings wanted to expand trade with India, their Bombay agent identified local traders whom he considered "attentive, intelligent, & very honourable men, in whom you could place confidence with perfect safety."[65]

Family members who did not have to be sought out or specially cultivated were especially crucial to these networks. When in 1805 William Rathbone had problems selling off the cotton he had purchased and urgently needed access to cash, his father and brother each gave him £3,000, helping William to overcome his "considerable anxiety." When the Browns sought to expand their network of agents and correspondents in southern ports, they looked for ties that held. Their Charleston agent, James Adger, originated from northern Ireland, like the Browns, and was an old friend of Alexander's. In Savannah, their agent, John Cumming, was connected by marriage to the Browns, as were representatives in other ports. For the Volkarts, family connections were just as important. Volkart's father-in-law Eduard Forrer established an agency in St. Louis. Theodor Reinhart, after having learned the cotton business in his father's house, in 1876 married Lily Volkart, daughter of the owner of Volkart Brothers, thus uniting two merchant firms, a truly dynastic marriage in the world of cotton.[66]

Consider too one of the most important cotton trading houses of the nineteenth century, the Rallis.[67] Their world-spanning empire had its roots on a small Greek island off the Anatolian coast, as most if not all of the principals of the house of Ralli came from Chios, and indeed, most were members of the Ralli family themselves. John Ralli and Strati Ralli, two brothers, had gone to London to start trading there. In 1822 they brought a third brother, Pandia S. Ralli, to London. In 1825 Strati Ralli opened the office in Manchester to trade in textiles, and in 1827 John Ralli went to Odessa. A fourth brother, living in Istanbul, opened an office in Persia in 1837, and a fifth, Augustus S. Ralli, opened a cotton firm in Marseille. By the 1860s, the house of Ralli had representatives in London (from 1818), Liverpool, Manchester (from 1825), "the Orient" (Constantinople, Odessa), various places within India, including Calcutta (1851), Karachi (1861) and Bombay (1861), and the United States.[68] Ralli thus was able to purchase cotton in the United States, ship it to Liverpool, sell it to manufacturers in Manchester, and then sell the finished goods in Calcutta—all within their own family.

As the example of the Rallis shows, the Greek diaspora, like others—Armenian, Parsis, Jews—played an important role in the global cotton trade. By the last quarter of the eighteenth century, Greeks had become particularly important to networks connecting the Ottoman Empire to the outside world, and were especially prominent in the Egyptian cotton trade. Arriving in Egypt in the first half of the nineteenth century during the first wave of Muhammad Ali's industrialization efforts, they became the largest group of foreign merchants. By 1839, twelve Greek merchant houses, including the Rallis, had captured 33 percent of the Alexandria cotton export market, with the largest Greek house, Tossizza Frères et Cie, exporting 11 percent of Egypt's cotton.[69]

Other diaspora communities played an important role in the global cotton trade. Jews assumed a central position in the global trade of yarn and cotton cloth, partly because earlier discrimination had forced them to work as itinerant traders, often in textiles. The most famous example for this important role are the Rothschilds, who upon entering the textile trade in Manchester mostly found customers among their coreligionists in Frankfurt for the goods they exported to the European continent. Nathan Meyer Rothschild's story can stand in for many others: Born in 1777 into a distinguished Frankfurt banking and merchant family, he went to London for a mercantile apprenticeship in 1798 and a year later moved to Manchester to open his own textile agency, bringing with him plenty of capital. "The nearer I got to England," he remembered in his autobiography, "the cheaper goods were. As soon as I got to Manchester, I laid out all my money, things were so cheap; and I made good profit." He purchased Manchester goods for the Frankfurt and continental European market, and advanced credit to manufacturers. Rothschild's success in Manchester encouraged other Jewish families from Frankfurt to start up businesses in Manchester. As a result, by the early nineteenth century Frankfurt Jewish families played an important role in the continental trade in English cottons.[70]

While it was still exceptional, diaspora networks were sometimes incorporated within firms, gradually lessening the importance of trust networks. The Rallis were such a case, and so, in a more limited way, were the Browns. Perhaps furthest ahead of its time, however, was a Swiss house that incorporated far-flung networks into their firm itself: Volkart Brothers. Founded in 1851 by Salomon Volkart simultaneously in the Swiss town of Winterthur—an important center of the cotton industry—

The revolutionary vanguard: Salomon Volkart, Winterthur,
Switzerland, transforms peasant agriculture.

and in Bombay, the firm began by purchasing raw cotton in India and
exporting manufactured wares to India. As they opened more branch
offices, Volkart Brothers increasingly organized the purchasing of cotton
not only in India but also in other parts of the world, transporting that
cotton to various European ports and then selling it to spinners. By the
late 1850s, Volkart Brothers incorporated a whole range of selling and
buying activities.[71]

Yet at midcentury, Volkart was exceptional; most cotton was still
traded between independent houses mediated by networks of trust. In the
whirl of letters, face-to-face conversations, and travel, as these merchants
developed a familiarity with and connection to people in many different
parts of the world, they became in effect a cosmopolitan community.
Unlike planters or manufacturers, merchants often had closer connections to people far away than to people in their home cities or immediate hinterlands. In a typical midcentury letter, E. Rathbone referred
to business partners or relatives in such diverse places as Cairo, Aden,
Palestine, Alexandria, and France. In Le Havre, as in Alexandria, Liverpool, and Bombay, the merchants came from all over the world—indeed,
only a few of the large merchants were members of ancient families of
Le Havre itself. Rathbone and other merchants inhabited a transnational

community, in which they traveled with ease. People in distant cities and towns engaged in similar lines of business, dressed in similar ways, lived in houses not unlike those at home, read from a similar set of books, had similar views of human nature and political economy, and might have been part of the same family.[72]

Cohesive as a social class and fortified by the institutions they had built, these merchants also developed tremendous political clout from England to France to the United States. They understood early that their trade was deeply embedded within local, national, and global politics; they acted as if they understood instinctively that the state does not intervene in the market, but constitutes it. Their daily experience had taught them that global trade did not arise in a state of nature, but only flourished via careful, conscious regulation. As a result, according to Liverpool cotton broker Samuel Smith, politics was everywhere: "As our business involved much foreign intercourse, and was greatly affected by the course of foreign affairs, especially by wars and the fear of wars, we became as a matter of course keen politicians."[73]

As merchants became "keen politicians" and realized the state's importance for their grand project of integrating cotton cultivators, cotton manufacturers, and cotton consumers, they encountered rulers and bureaucrats who shared many of their inclinations. European states had become increasingly dependent for their very existence on the wealth generated by rapid capital accumulation, including in cottons. Statesmen were thus solicitous toward capitalists, and often submissive when these patrons of the state organized collectively. What set European states apart from other contemporary states such as Japan and China was not just their capacity, but also their responsiveness to the needs of industrial capital.[74]

Though merchants lobbied their governments about anything and everything, among the most important issues was the infrastructure of trade. The construction of docks, storage facilities, railways, and waterways was high on the merchants' agenda, since they directly affected the speed at which goods and information moved through the emerging global economy—and that speed of circulation determined the speed of accumulation.[75]

Though it could seem haphazard and unregulated, subject to the

whims of a few men, trade ultimately also depended on a legal infrastructure devised and enforced by states. Unsurprisingly, merchants spent
much of their political energy on trying to strengthen this legal order and
make it conform to their interests. In the process they increased, both wit-
tingly and unwittingly, the capacity of the state. Conventions, although
agreed upon by merchants themselves, needed enforceable rules, and
merchants understood that no single actor was as efficient in enforcing
these rules as the state. As New York lawyer Daniel Lord explained in
detail in his 1835 "Law of Agency," legal rules had allowed merchants to
have agents and factors in distant places, and to act for them: "It is by this
bringing into aid and subordination, the powers of others . . . that modern commerce touches at once the extremes of longitude, and subdues
alike the Equator and the Poles; She crosses the oceans, tracks the African
deserts, and conquers the plains of Asia."[76]

The "law" became particularly important when it came to the actual
transformation of the global countryside into a supplier of industrial raw
materials and a market for manufactured goods. The more suppliers of
cotton, the more consumers of cotton, the more trade. To make that
transition possible, merchants yearned for a more powerful state presence, especially in the nonslave areas of the world. One of their most
urgent obsessions was to inject the "law" into this global cotton-growing
countryside, though their ability to do so was often frustrated in societies
dominated by peasant production.

The importance of the law was clearest in colonial settings such as
British India. In Bombay, merchants pressured the British government
constantly for new rules and regulations regarding the Indian cotton
trade. "The cotton legislation was not only chronologically the earliest economic legislation of British rule, it was also perhaps the most
advanced legislation in the contemporary economic world," observed
one chronicler of the Indian cotton trade. The rules of the market, and
thus the market itself, emerged at the intersection of merchant collective action and the state. Yet ironically, the more merchants succeeded
in their project of extending the authority of the state, the less trade
depended on the networks of trust that they had forged over prior generations.[77]

As the law increasingly infused the global countryside, and as
state-sponsored infrastructure projects accelerated the movement of
goods, merchants mobilized collectively to use state power to shape

global markets to their benefit in other ways as well. Their industrial policy, in effect, was global. And it was the most global for British merchants and manufacturers. At the center of the empire of cotton, they believed that opening access to foreign markets was a core function of government. In 1821, for example, the Manchester Chamber of Commerce wanted the government to pressure Denmark to reduce its import duties on yarn; in 1822 they demanded freer trade to the East Indies; and later they agitated for the removal of duties between Britain and Ireland and debated "Brazil custom Duties," "Duties on British Goods Imported into Batavia," "duties at Monte Video," trade with Morocco, and "duties at Shanghai." Le Havre merchants pressured for the most unencumbered trade as well.[78]

While most merchants had a clear ideological commitment to free trade, which corresponded perfectly with their interest in market access and cheap labor, they could advocate just as forcefully for creating novel barriers to trade. In fact, their insistence on free trade was remarkably inconsistent. As early as 1794, a number of cotton merchants protested "against the export of cotton twist from England." The export of spun cotton, according to them, threatened British prosperity, as the yarn was woven into fabrics in low-wage Germany, creating unemployment in Britain. In an eerily modern argument, they argued that "Germany's cheaper food enabled them to manufacture by hand cheaper than our workpeople could, they had first deprived our hand loom weavers of employment and now were rapidly progressing with the other departments including spinning." The Manchester Chamber of Commerce similarly opposed the emigration of "English Artizans" and "the free exportation of such Machinery as is employed in our own Manufactories."[79]

Merchants appealed to their national governments to protect access to foreign markets, using both political power and military might. In 1794, the Manchester Society of Merchants talked about the importance of having the Royal Navy protect ships going into the Mediterranean with valuable local manufactures on board. In 1795 they appealed to the government to protect their trade with Germany, and the continent more broadly, by military force. In Manchester, merchants asked the government to protect ships in the Atlantic from pirates, and called for a "large Naval Force."[80]

The merchants' political vision, like their trade, was truly global, stretching from "sound dues payable upon cotton twist exported to the

Baltic" to colonial debt laws bent on opening India as a market. In Britain, India soon emerged as the "chief question." For cotton mill owner Henry Ashworth, the Indian market would provide unlimited opportunities, if opened by the proper governmental interventions: "Now, although I am as great a stickler perhaps as most here for adhesion to sound free-trade principles, it does not always follow that in dealing with people who are not as advanced political economists as ourselves, that we should delay our movements until they have become converted. ('Hear')." As a dabbling economist, Ashworth understood intuitively that economic thinking helps "format the economy"—makes possible the formerly impossible—which is exactly what it would do a few decades later in India.[81]

Calling for the state to convert Indian peasants into producers of cotton for world markets formed one part of merchants' much larger project of bringing the state into the global cotton-growing countryside. They understood that unlike in the slave-dominated cotton-growing areas of the world, in India and elsewhere they needed the capacity of the imperial state to effect the transformations they hoped for. What they did not anticipate was that the more they furthered the state-building project, the more they were diminishing their own importance to the empire of cotton.

Henry Ashworth understood more explicitly than many others the way the world of trade rested on powerful states structuring global markets, and he unabashedly celebrated the involvement of the British state in the interests of its merchants and manufacturers. Industrializing states depended on a flourishing manufacturing economy for their strength and social stability. Even statesmen of no great vision could grasp the importance of securing a reliable supply of raw materials for domestic industry and of creating a market for its products. So fast was their rate of growth, and so fierce their competition, that European states sought to transform the global countryside simultaneously into a supplier of materials for their industrial enterprises and into consumers for the resulting products. Having transformed their own countrysides in the search for labor, they sought to deploy that experience to the rest of the world, making the particular form of that integration into nothing less than a "law of nature."

This new, conveniently and divinely ordained mission unintentionally but no less surely lessened the dependence of industrial capitalism on some of the earlier mechanisms of war capitalism—especially the wholesale expropriation of native peoples and the mobilization of labor through slavery. With a greater capacity to lay down market-directed infrastructure, and a legal apparatus geared toward infusing European capital into the global countryside and mobilizing workers, merchants redoubled their efforts to reorient peasant agriculture toward the production of cotton for world markets. As states grew stronger, merchants were able to infuse unprecedented flows of capital, and with it the logic of industrial production, into heretofore independent hinterlands. The British merchant house of Baring by the 1840s diversified the sources of its cotton supply by importing from Bombay. European capitalists also entered the trade with the Egyptian cotton-producing fellaheen. In the late 1840s and early 1850s, with the weakening of the governmental monopoly on the internal cotton trade, merchants, especially of Greek heritage, penetrated the interior and began to purchase cotton from peasants directly. But perhaps most forward-looking was the model developed by Volkart Brothers. Their Indian cotton traders, riding on the coattails of an expanding imperial government, moved ever closer to local producers themselves, so that by 1875 the Volkarts and their European colleagues exported more than twice as much cotton as their once dominant Indian counterparts.[82]

Before European capital could find its partners in the imperial states of the late 1800s, however, the cotton empire would be shocked by the region of the world where slavery and industrial capitalism seemed most powerfully and profitably conjoined: the United States. Everywhere else, slavery and industrial capitalism seemed to coexist perfectly well. But everywhere else, as we know, these two engines of profit were separated by national boundaries. Not so in North America. For the United States, unlike any other part of the world, brought war capitalism and industrial capitalism within the same national territory. No political union could contain forever the contrary political forces of both systems.

As the United States found its economic footing, slave owners and industrial capitalists made increasingly different demands on the state. American manufacturers and a few of its merchants, like their counterparts in Britain and elsewhere, gained confidence that the mechanisms of industrial capitalism could be moved into the global cotton-growing countryside and could indeed secure sufficient supplies of the raw material. Boston cotton manufacturer Edward Atkinson became a fervent believer in wage labor, as he observed his ability to mobilize and discipline large numbers of workers in his mill. As elsewhere in the world, American industrialists like Atkinson hitched their political interests to a strengthening national government.[83] Cotton-growing slave owners, on the other hand, favored the political economy of Atlantic trade, and depended on the state's willingness to secure more lands for plantation agriculture and to enforce and support the institution of slavery. They feared that any strengthening of the federal government might interfere with their mastery over labor. Slavery, after all, required constant violence against potentially rebellious slaves, and that violence rested on the state's willingness to condone it. Slave owners therefore felt an overpowering need to secure control over the state, or, at the very least, to keep the opponents of slavery out of the national halls of power.

Yet that control was increasingly elusive. A small but growing group of Americans who sought to construct a political economy of domestic industrialization emerged from the dynamic industrial economy of the northern states. Their political needs, like those of the planters, required control of state institutions. But unlike southerners, northern industrial capitalists drew increasing political strength from a relatively stable political coalition with commercial farmers and even segments of a rapidly expanding working class. These capitalists drew encouragement from the fact that a small but growing number of merchants, so long the planters' most significant northern allies, were increasingly embracing the project of domestic industrialization as well—even though they hesitated to challenge the slave regime in the South directly. Tellingly, the United States' most important cotton traders, the Browns, slowly began to specialize in the foreign exchange business and to invest in industrial enterprises—railroads, for example, but also the Novelty Iron Works in New York.[84]

Such moves made sense because their former commodity trade, with its low entry costs, was always open to new competitors who were willing to take on greater risks and operate on narrower margins. Low entry barriers created a cotton market that included a very large number of smaller operators, eventually pushing wealthier traders into emerging, even more profitable lines of business, that had greater capital requirements. Joining the Browns, foreign capitalists like the Barings also increasingly diversified, especially into railroads, coal mining, and manufacturing. They understood better than others that with the state's capacity expanding, the role of merchant capital was diminishing, and that a future beckoned in which industrialists, in conjunction with the state, would be able to burrow even further into the global countryside to find still more land and labor for the production and consumption of cotton. The most forward-looking manufacturers and merchants discerned that such new forms of domination would decisively weaken the power of commodity producers, and thus eliminate one of the most threatening sources of instability in the empire of cotton, and with it, global capitalism.[85]

This shifting balance of social power among different business groups proved momentous. The United States was unique in that the schism between economic elites was so great that, in a moment of great crisis, even merchant capitalists aligned with slave owners dropped their old allies. This was radically different from other slave-owning societies, such as Brazil, where planters and export merchants formed a unified political bloc, with agreement that domestic industrialization constituted a threat to their economic interests and that slave labor was indispensable.[86]

The realignment of the economic elites of the United States, along with the promise of tapping nonslave hinterlands as the Volkarts had done in India, threw the rising costs and diminishing benefits of combining slavery and industrial capitalism into high relief. In 1861, the mix exploded, and the ensuing American Civil War became a turning point not just for that young republic, but also for the history of global capitalism.

Chapter Nine

A War Reverberates Around the World

Viewed from abroad, cotton was central to the American struggle:
Punch comments on the American Civil War.

A crisis illuminates best the foundations of the global empire of cotton. The American Civil War was such a crisis. By the time shots were fired on Fort Sumter in April 1861, cotton was the core ingredient of the world's most important manufacturing industry. The manufacture of cotton yarn and cloth had grown into "the greatest industry that ever had or could by possibility have ever existed in any age or country," according to the self-congratulatory but essentially accurate account of British cotton merchant John Benjamin Smith. By multiple measures—the sheer numbers employed, the value of output, profitability—the cotton empire had no parallel. One author boldly estimated that in 1862, fully 20 million people worldwide—one out of every sixty-five people alive—were involved in the cultivation of cotton or the production of cotton cloth. In England alone, which still counted two-thirds of the world's mechanical spindles in its factories, the livelihood of between one-fifth and one-fourth of the population was based on the industry; one-tenth of all British capital was invested in it, and close to one-half of all exports consisted of cotton yarn and cloth. Whole regions of Europe and the United States had come to depend on a predictable supply of cheap cotton. Except for wheat, no "raw product," so the *Journal of the Statistical Society* of London declared, had "so complete a hold upon the wants of the race."[1]

The industry that brought great wealth to European manufacturers and merchants, and bleak employment to hundreds of thousands of mill workers, had also catapulted the United States onto center stage of the world economy, building "the most successful agricultural industry in the States of America which has been ever contemplated or realized." Cotton exports alone put the United States on the world economic map. On the eve of the Civil War, raw cotton constituted 61 percent of the value of all U.S. products shipped abroad. Before the beginnings of the cotton boom in the 1780s, North America had been a promising but marginal player in the global economy. Now, in 1861, the flagship of global capitalism, Great Britain, found itself dangerously dependent on the white gold shipped out of New York, New Orleans, Charleston, and other American ports. By the late 1850s, cotton grown in the United States accounted for 77 percent of the 800 million pounds of cotton consumed in Britain. It also accounted for 90 percent of the 192 million pounds used in France, 60 percent of the 115 million pounds spun in the Zollverein, and 92 percent of the 102 million pounds manufactured in Russia.[2]

The reason for America's quick ascent to market dominance was simple. The United States more than any other country had elastic supplies of the three crucial ingredients that went into the production of raw cotton: labor, land, and credit. As *The Economist* put it in 1861, the United States had become so successful in the world's cotton markets because the planters' "soil is marvelously fertile and costs him nothing; his labour has hitherto been abundant, unremitting and on the increase; the arrangements and mercantile organizations for cleaning and forwarding the cotton are all there."[3] By midcentury, cotton had become central to the prosperity of the Atlantic world. Poet John Greenleaf Whittier called it the "Haschish of the West," a drug that was creating powerful hallucinatory dreams of territorial expansion, of judges who decide that "right is wrong," of heaven as "a snug plantation" with "angel negro overseers."[4]

Slavery stood at the center of the most dynamic and far-reaching production complex in human history. Herman Merivale, British colonial bureaucrat, noted that Manchester's and Liverpool's "opulence is as really owing to the toil and suffering of the negro, as if his hands had excavated their docks and fabricated their steam-engines." Capital accumulation in peripheral commodity production, according to Merivale, was necessary for metropolitan economic expansion, and access to labor, if necessary by coercion, was a precondition for turning abundant lands into productive suppliers of raw materials.[5]

Whether celebrating the material advances generated from slavery or calling for slavery's abolition, many contemporaries agreed by the 1850s that global economic development required physical coercion. Karl Marx sharpened the arguments made all around him by concluding in 1853 that "bourgeois civilization" and "barbarity" were joined at the hip. But such an argument was simply common sense in elite circles. French geographer Élisée Reclus, writing in the *Revue des Deux Mondes*, for example, came to essentially the same conclusion: "The industrial prosperity of England appears to be intimately tied to the progress of slavery." Southern planters agreed passionately: Cotton, and thus slavery, were indispensable to the modern world, the very foundation of the United States' and Europe's astonishing material advances. As South Carolina senator and cotton planter James Henry Hammond put it famously on the floor of the Senate, "England would topple headlong and carry the whole civilized world with her" if the system of slave-powered cotton growing would be threatened. "No power on earth dares to make war upon it. Cotton *is* king."[6]

Slavery enabled the stunning advances of industry, and the accompanying profit. Contemporaries, however, worried that this vast and sparkling machine was merely a façade, amplifying the long-standing European worries about the political stability of the United States that we have encountered earlier. As "an industry tributary to foreign countries," observed British political economist Leone Levi, the European cotton industry was potentially vulnerable, even though its well-being, according to a French observer, had "become a question of life or death for tens of thousands of workers, a question of prosperity or misery for all the developed industrial countries."[7]

Most important, slavery itself seemed potentially hazardous to stability—

a "treacherous foundation," as the Manchester Cotton Supply Association put it—not just because of the sectional tensions it generated in the United States, but also because slaves could resist and even rebel: "The system of slave labour was not to be safely trusted," the association declared in 1861. "The dread of slave insurrection and civil discord," the *Cotton Supply Reporter* complained, was ever present. Even the London money market reflected these concerns, as bonds for southern railroads carried higher interest than those for northern roads. "This mistrust arises," reported the *Westminster Review* in 1850 "from a shrewd calculation of the dangers, in both a moral and physical sense, which hang over a state of society whose foundations are laid in injustice and violence."[8]

American slavery had begun to threaten the very prosperity it produced, as the distinctive political economy of the cotton South collided with the incipient political economy of free labor and domestic industrialization of the North. In addition, the violent expansion of both these economies westward brought crisis after crisis to their nascent national institutions.[9] Ample supplies of fertile land and bonded labor had made the South into Lancashire's plantation, but by 1860 large numbers of Americans, especially in the northern states, protested such semicolonial dependence. They, in time, sparked a second American revolution. Fearing for the security of their human property, southern slave owners struck out on their own, gambling that their European partners would intervene to preserve the world economy and with it their own exceptionally profitable role. Southern planters understood that their cotton kingdom rested not only on plentiful land and labor, but also upon their political ability to preserve the institution of slavery and to project it into the new cotton lands of the American West. Continued territorial expansion of slavery was vital to secure both its economic, and even more so its political viability, which was threatened as never before by an alarmingly sectional Republican Party. Slave owners understood the challenge to their power over human chattel represented by the new party's project of strengthening the claims of power between the national state and its citizens—an equally necessary condition for its free labor and free soil ideology.

Yet from a global perspective, the outbreak of war between the Confederacy and the Union in April 1861 was a struggle not only over American territorial integrity and the future of its "peculiar institution," but also over global capitalism's dependence on slave labor across the world. The Civil War in the United States was an acid test for the entire industrial order: Could it adapt to the even temporary loss of its providential partner—the expansive, slave-powered antebellum United States—before social chaos and economic collapse brought their empire to ruins? As John Marshman, editor of the Baptist missionary newspaper *Friend of India*, observed in March 1863, "It may be said that the prosperity of the South has been based on the gigantic crime of holding three or four millions of human beings in a state of slavery, and it is difficult to divest the mind of the conviction that the day of reckoning from the throne of the Eternal has come."[10]

The day of reckoning arrived on April 12, 1861. On that spring day, Confederate troops fired on the federal garrison at Fort Sumter, South Carolina. It was a quintessentially local event, a small crack in the world's core production and trade system, but the resulting crisis illuminated brilliantly the underlying foundations of the global cotton industry and with it of capitalism. Columbia University political scientist Francis Lieber predicted "neither cotton nor slavery will come forth from this war as they went into it." With its shocking duration and destructiveness, the American struggle marked the world's first truly global raw materials crisis, and proved midwife to the emergence of new global networks of labor, capital, and state power. Thus one of the most important chapters in the history of global capital and labor unfolded on the battlefields of provincial North America.[11]

The outbreak of the Civil War severed in one stroke the relationships that had underpinned the worldwide web of cotton production and global capitalism since the 1780s. In an effort to force British diplomatic recognition, the Confederate government banned all cotton exports. By the time the Confederacy realized this policy was doomed, a northern blockade effectively kept most cotton from leaving the South. Though smuggling persisted, and most smugglers' runs succeeded, the blockade's deterrent effects removed most cotton-carrying ships from the southern trade. Consequently, exports to Europe fell from 3.8 million bales in 1860 to virtually nothing in 1862. The effects of the resulting "cotton famine," as it came to be known, quickly rippled outward, reshaping industry—and the larger society—in places ranging from Manchester to Alexandria. With only slight hyperbole, the Chamber of Commerce in the Saxon cotton manufacturing city of Chemnitz reported in 1865 that "never in the history of trade have there been such grand and consequential movements as in the past four years."[12]

A mad scramble ensued. The effort was all the more desperate as no one could predict when the war would end and when, if ever, cotton production would revive in the American South. "What are we to do," asked the editors of the *Liverpool Mercury* in January 1861, if "this most precarious source of supply should suddenly fail us?" Once it did fail, this question was foremost on the minds of policy makers, merchants, manufacturers, workers, and peasants around the globe.[13]

At first, the panic of European cotton manufacturers was allayed by the fact that cotton imports in the previous few years had been extremely high, leaving sufficient stocks in major ports and factories for the coming months or even a year. Yarn and cloth markets from Buenos Aires to Calcutta, moreover, were glutted. With initial expectations that the war would be short, cuts in cotton exports from the American South meant rising prices for the stock at hand, which holders of cotton and cotton goods welcomed. Looking back at the early months of the war, *Moskva*, the voice of Moscow's industrialists, reported that the conflict at first helped "rid us of our own crisis in the cotton industry, which was about to erupt" due to overproduction.[14]

Eventually, however, dwindling supplies and rising prices began to paralyze production. In the late summer of 1861, Charles Francis Adams, the U.S. ambassador to England, wrote to his son Henry that "this cotton question is beginning to pinch." By early 1862, as total imports of cotton into Britain fell by a little over 50 percent compared to the previous year, and imports from the United States by 96 percent, mills began shutting down for a few days each week, or entirely. Cotton prices had quadrupled from their prewar levels and, consequently, manufacturers closed shops and tens of thousands of operatives found themselves out of work. As early as November 1861, Lancashire manufacturers had shut 6 percent of their factories and introduced shorter shifts in two-thirds of them. By early 1863, a quarter of the inhabitants of Lancashire—more than half a million individuals—were out of work, receiving some form of public or private assistance. Weaver John O'Neil, who lived in Low Moor Mill in Lancashire, described his plight in his diary: "Sad and weary . . . and can hardly keep myself living." In response to such misery "Unemployed Operatives" sent memorials to the Home Office, demanding relief.[15]

By 1863, unemployed workers rioted in the streets of several British cotton towns, underscoring the explosive social consequences of the cotton famine. The home secretary received requests from town authorities for information on "how the military are to be obtained if required in any future Emergency." Troops were soon stationed. Even cotton merchant William Rathbone reported to his son in the spring of 1862 that "the distress among the Poor here and in the Manufacturing districts is great, and I fear on the increase." So serious was the crisis that thousands of miles from Europe the merchants of the Bombay Chamber of Commerce collected funds "in aid of the distressed mill hands of Lancashire." "Anxiety" and "apprehension" began to spread.[16]

Similar crises unfolded on the European continent. In France, manufacturers closed mills because they could not afford high cotton prices as imports of U.S. cotton fell from more than 600,000 bales in 1860 to 4,169 in 1863. The effect was especially severe on manufacturers of coarse cottons, such as the ones in Normandy, for whom the price of cotton determined much of the total price of production. By 1863, three-fifths of the looms in Normandy were idle, while in the districts of Colmar and Belfort, where higher-quality cottons were produced, 35 percent of all spindles and 41 percent of all looms remained unused. That same year, a French national relief committee estimated that a quarter million textile workers were unemployed. In the textile towns of Alsace posters went up proclaiming, "Du pain ou la mort" (Bread or death).[17]

Lesser cotton centers also experienced severe distress: In the German lands of the Zollverein, imports of raw cotton fell by about 50 percent between 1861 and 1864 and hundreds of factory owners sent their workers home. Of the approximately three hundred thousand people engaged in the cotton industry in Saxony alone, one-third had lost their jobs by the fall of 1863, while the rest worked much shorter hours. In the northern part of the United States, removed from battle itself but not its consequences, tens of thousands of cotton workers lost employment, but the social effects were less severe because many found employment in the booming woolen mills that produced clothing for the Union army, or enlisted. In Moscow, however, 75 percent of all cotton spinning operations had shut down by 1863. Workers and manufacturers would have agreed with the U.S. consul in the German city of Stettin that "this war and its consequences stand before the whole civilized world as an interposing fate, which no nation, however insignificant its direct relations to the field of contest may be, is enabled entirely to avoid."[18]

While manufacturers closed mills and spinners and weavers suffered, cotton merchants lived—for a brief time—through a golden age. Rising prices for cotton led to a frenzy with "doctors, parsons, lawyers, wives and widows, and tradesmen speculating in it." Cotton shipments changed hands many times between speculators before being delivered to factories; with each exchange a small profit could be made. Baring Brothers, confirmed in the summer of 1863 that the "amount of money made and still making in this article is almost fabulous; for three years or more not a bale has arrived from India but has paid profit and mostly a large one." Liverpool cotton brokers gained as well from the presence of many speculators in the market (resulting in many transactions), and also rising prices (their commissions were a percentage of the value). In 1861, the total value of cotton imports had been £39.7 million and in 1864 it had reached £84 million, despite a much-reduced volume.[19]

As price volatility and speculation spread, so too did traders' efforts to institutionalize speculative market transactions, especially forward selling. By 1863, the Liverpool Cotton Brokers' Association had created a standard form that could be used by merchants making contracts about the future delivery of cotton, and Liverpool newspapers began reporting forward prices of Indian cotton. That year, "time bargains" had even begun to be established in Bombay, providing new opportunities for "men afflicted with a passion for gambling." The war, in fact, resulted "in a revolutionary modernization of trade" in which the establishment of a formal futures market was perhaps the most important element.[20]

While merchants and speculators benefited from the global scramble for cotton, manufacturers loudly and frantically demanded the opening of new sources of the fiber. In France, factory owners from different cotton manufacturing regions continuously pressured the imperial government. "It is therefore urgently necessary to develop . . . new fields of production," wrote the Chamber of Commerce of the city of Rouen. In 1862 a group of cotton manufacturers from Senones in the Vosges appealed to Napoleon III to bring Chinese workers to Algeria to grow cotton there. That year, cotton manufacturer Jacques Siegfried presented a "memoir" to the Société Industrielle de Mulhouse to advocate cotton growing in Algeria, supported by the Chamber of Commerce in Mulhouse: "No colonization for cotton, cotton for colonization." When Antoine Herzog, a wealthy Alsatian cotton manufacturer, sat down in 1864 to pen a book on *L'Algérie et la crise cotonnière*, he hoped that France would recognize that it was "at the mercy of the political vicissitudes of a single people," and therefore needed to "develop . . . by all possible means the cotton culture of countries that are capable of producing [it], and, in a special way, in our colonies." Herzog personally pleaded with Napoleon for an audience to have him support colonial cotton-growing efforts and even traveled to Algeria to investigate the opportunities for cotton production there.[21]

Pressured by manufacturers and concerned about the suffering and mobilization of cotton workers, government bureaucrats expressed concerns as well. Cotton, after all, was central to their national economies and ultimately to the maintenance of social peace. Some European officials advocated recognition of the Confederacy and breaking the Union blockade to secure that urgently needed cotton. Others hoped for new sources of cotton from places outside the United States—especially the two European powers that had both substantial cotton industries and large colonial holdings, Britain and France. Even before the outbreak of the war, British foreign secretary Lord John Russell had hastened to assure the cotton manufacturers of Manchester that his government would do all in its power to secure cotton from sources outside the United States. Yet in July 1862 the American consul to the Egyptian city of Alexandria, William Thayer, reported that "statesmen are almost paralyzed with terror at the hopelessness of relief for the evils in prospect." The Prussian minister to Washington, Freiherr von Gerolt, along with his British and French counterparts, repeated many times in his meetings with U.S. secretary of state William Seward how important cotton was to their countries' economic well-being. On numerous occasions, the House of Commons, the House of Lords, and the French Senate debated the "cotton question."[22]

This intense public concern with securing access to cheaply priced raw materials essential to national industries was a clear departure from the past. Since the 1780s, raw cotton markets had been decisively dominated by merchants, but now cotton had become a matter of state, a state empowered not least by decades of merchant political mobilization. Heavy investments in industrial production, a novelty in human history, demanded a constant supply of land, labor, and money. As political leaders grappled with the cotton famine, they saw that the emergence of industrial capitalism had made them just as dependent on a predictable supply of cheap raw materials as the manufacturers themselves. Lord Palmerston warned in October 1861 that England must have cotton because "we cannot allow millions of our People to perish." The French

Ministry of Colonies commissioned reports on cotton growing prospects in such diverse places as Guyana, Siam, Algeria, Egypt, and Senegal. The outlines of a new kind of imperialism began to emerge.[23]

Responding to the urgent demand for cotton, forty-six hundred miles to the east of Liverpool and ninety-two hundred miles from Antietam, Indian merchants and cultivators, British colonial bureaucrats, and Manchester manufacturers embarked on a frantic race to grow cotton for world markets. As we have seen, Britain had tried to cultivate India as a reliable source of cotton since the 1820s, yet the effort had been, according to the Bombay Chamber of Commerce, "a signal failure." Indeed, as *The Economist* noted before the outbreak of the Civil War, "As long as there were negroes in the Southern States, and those negroes could be kept to work, it would have been venturesome, not enterprising" to grow cotton for world markets in India.[24]

The bombardment of Fort Sumter, however, announced that India's hour had come. For cotton merchants, manufacturers, and statesmen, no place seemed more promising a source of cotton than India. Indeed, it was "the only remedy for the misery that appeared to be hanging over us," according to Edmund Potter of the Manchester Chamber of Commerce. During the American Civil War, British cotton capitalists and colonial bureaucrats worked feverishly to increase India's cotton output and move it to market. "Cotton," as one observer wrote from Nagpore in July 1861, "appears to me to be the leading topic of the day," and the English-language press of India was filled with hundreds if not thousands of stories about cotton. Manchester manufacturers shipped cottonseed to Bombay to be distributed to growers; they moved cotton gins and cotton presses into the countryside; and they talked about investing in railroads to remove cotton to the coast. They ran afoul, however, of India's well-known obstacles. In 1862, when the Manchester Cotton Supply Association sent cotton gins and presses to India, they planned to unload them in the newly constructed port of Sedashegur, close to areas in which cotton was grown. Yet when the ships arrived, they found that the port had not been finished. Eventually they moved the gins and presses to another port, which did have facilities for unloading, but the road linking this port to the cotton-growing areas was not complete and the machinery could not be moved.[25]

Confronted with such problems, British cotton manufacturers, especially through the channels of two organizations they dominated, the Manchester Chamber of Commerce and the Manchester Cotton Supply Association, redoubled their efforts to transform the Indian countryside. After all, asked Manchester Chamber of Commerce member Henry Ashworth, "what is the value of our possessions if we do not use them?" Ashworth and others pressed a newly receptive British government for massive infrastructure investments, changes in criminal codes to make the adulteration of cotton a crime, and new property laws to create clearly defined and easily marketable property in land.[26]

Such pressures by manufacturers and merchants to bring the state in did not fall on deaf ears. Already in September 1861, the finance minister of India, Samuel Laing, met with representatives of cotton interests in Manchester to discuss ways to improve Indian cotton production, meetings that would continue in Manchester, London, and Bombay throughout the war. Charles Wood, the British foreign secretary for India, saw the urgency as well, recommending "to get as much as possible from India." British colonial officials wrote dozens of reports to investigate the cotton-growing potential of this or that area of India.[27]

The British government and manufacturers agreed that the administrative, legal, and infrastructural capacity of the imperial state needed to be pushed into the Indian countryside. Perhaps most important was manufacturers' pressure to create a new kind of legal environment in order to facilitate European investment in and domination of cotton production. Cotton capitalists wanted to change Indian contract law to make "penal the breach of contract where advances have been made," giving "the advancer an absolute lien upon the crop he advances upon to the extent of his advances," allowing for penalties including prison at hard labor. If merchants could secure such an absolute claim on cotton grown with the support of their capital, investment would be encouraged, and it would help overcome "the difficulty of enforcing the observance of legal Contracts with the agricultural Population of India." Such a system would permit cultivators to devote their efforts entirely to cash crops, since advances would allow them to purchase food grains before their own cotton crop ripened. Eventually this pressure succeeded; new contract laws were imposed. In 1863, moreover, criminal laws were enacted that made the adulteration of cotton a crime punishable by imprisonment at hard labor.[28]

Such market making went hand in hand with physical infrastructure projects serving both the interests of the "Manchester people" and the colonial state, especially the construction of railroads, which, as Charles Wood remarked, would not only move cotton to ports but also allow for the quick movement of troops to subdue rebellions. During the first year of the war alone, government expenditures on infrastructure projects in India nearly doubled. When in 1864 the British government for India allocated £7 million to "Public Works," the *Times of India* commented that the "budget . . . may be considered as devoted to the express object of opening up readier access from the field to the market." Wood himself, concerned about the pressures from Manchester, wrote in March 1863 to Sir Charles Trevelyan, India's finance minister, to urge him to spend more aggressively on infrastructure improvements, as not to do so would be a "suicidal act." "These roads," warned Wood, "we must make." Moreover, the colonial government reduced the cotton-goods import duty from 10 to 5 percent, a reduction that British manufacturers strongly favored since they believed the duties gave "a fictitious encouragement to . . . mechanically produced manufactures," thereby "diverting the capital and labour of India from the cultivation of the varied productions which the soil would yield in great abundance." India's future, they agreed, was not in manufacturing, but in the provision of raw cotton to European industry.[29]

Yet despite such far-reaching interventions, manufacturers remained dissatisfied with the British government. Their decades-old calls for more state intervention now took on nearly hysterical tones, hastening the emergence of an even tighter relationship between merchants, manufacturers, and the imperial state, a relationship that became the hallmark of the empire of cotton during the last third of the nineteenth century and beyond.

The Manchester Chamber of Commerce consistently complained about the government's lack of commitment to cotton. Frustrated manufacturers tried to increase pressure by taking their cause to Parliament. In June 1862 members of Parliament from cotton-consuming districts demanded greater government commitment to infrastructure improvements in India to facilitate the movement of cotton to world markets. "The supply of cotton," argued Stockport MP John Benjamin Smith on the occasion of this debate, "is not a mere Lancashire question—it is a question of great national importance." These sentiments became so strong that Lancashire manufacturers eventually complained publicly about Charles Wood, and members of the Cotton Supply Association demanded nothing less than "the impeachment of the incompetent Minister." The British government replied in kind, with Wood regularly expressing his annoyance with "the Manchester people." The manufacturers' and the government's interests never entirely converged, because Charles Wood and other British government officials were acutely aware of the dangers of upsetting India's fragile social order in the wake of the Rebellion of 1857, which had severely challenged British rule in India. They understood, unlike many manufacturers, that the transformation of the Indian countryside was a gigantic project that entailed great risks.[30]

Yet like no other crisis before it, the cotton famine opened new vistas on colonial raw material production. Even *The Economist*, the world's leading publicist for the benefits of laissez-faire capitalism, eventually endorsed state involvement in securing cotton, especially from India. It was hard to justify these steps in terms of the "laws of supply and demand," but eventually *The Economist*—and with it many others—found a way: "The answer, at least a great part of the answer is, that there appears to exist in many important parts of Indian society very peculiar difficulties, which to some extent impede and counteract the action of the primary motives upon which political economy depends for its efficacy." In India, it continued, "The primitive prerequisites of common political economy . . . are not satisfied. You have a good-demanding Englishman, but, in plain English, not a good-supplying Indian." For that reason, "There is no relaxation of the rules of political economy in the interference of Government in a state of facts like this. Government does not interfere to prevent the effect and operation of 'supply and demand,' but to create that operation to ensure that effect. . . . There is no greater anomaly in recommending an unusual policy for a State destitute of the ordinary economical capacities, than in recommending an unusual method of education for a child both blind and deaf."[31]

Unlikely champions joined in this clamor for state intervention in the global cotton-growing countryside. Cotton manufacturer, member of Parliament, and free trade advocate Richard Cobden, for example, agreed that Adam Smith's ideas were not applicable when it came to India. Along the same lines, the Manchester Chamber of Commerce called a special meeting in July 1862 regarding the supply of cotton from India, demanding "that public aid be given for this object by forwarding such public works as will facilitate the production and transport of cotton to the port of shipment, such as works of irrigation, roads, or railways, and by amending and perfecting the Laws of Contract and Land Tenure." Manufacturers and colonial bureaucrats, faced with the cotton famine, became increasingly impatient with the workings of the market. As the superintendent of the Cotton Gin Factory in the Dharwar Collectorate reported in May 1862, while "we are strongly impressed with the belief, that, as a general rule, it is not judicious to interfere by legislative enactments in matters connected with trade, but looking to the circumstances of the present case, . . . to the immense importance of the questions at the present time affecting not only local, but national, interests, and to the apparent inefficiency of the present law, we are forced to the conviction that exceptional and more stringent legislation is necessary." Wood, too, had come to believe that the operation of the "laws of supply and demand" would not suffice to bring more cotton from India to Britain, despite his fractious relations with the louder elements of the cotton interests. Indian cultivators, so he believed, preferred leisure to accumulation, resulting in lower production when prices were high. India needed state reform and coercion if it hoped to replace the American South in the cotton economy. The crisis of slavery forced the imperial states to insert themselves in new ways into the global cotton-growing countryside.[32]

The effectiveness of government interventions was furthered by rapidly rising prices that lubricated the often balky transition to world market production. The value of Indian cotton more than quadrupled during the first two years of the war. As a result, Indian cultivators began planting cotton on newly cleared land as well as on land once devoted to food crops. This unprecedented dedication to export agriculture, according to the U.S. consul in Calcutta, created "supplies of unanticipated magnitude." It paid handsomely during the war years and helped European cotton manufacturers secure some of the raw material they needed to keep their factories running. Whereas India had only contributed 16 percent of Britain's supply of raw cotton in 1860, and 1.1 percent of France's in 1857, it contributed 75 percent in 1862 in Britain and as much as 70 percent in France. Some of this cotton had been diverted from domestic use and competing foreign markets (especially China), while the rest was the result of a 50 percent increase in production.[33]

Rural producers in western India in general and the province of Berar—which the British had only acquired in 1853—in particular were most responsible for this increase in output. The explosive growth of

Bombay can indeed be traced to the Civil War years, as Indian cotton left its old channels of trade into Bengal and moved toward the great European entrepôt. By 1863, ships burdened with cotton even sailed out of Bombay harbor to New York. European merchants and manufacturers complained about the poor quality of Indian cotton—it was less clean, of shorter staple, and required the adjustment of machines—but Indian cotton prevented the total collapse of the European cotton industries. "The American slaveholders have done more to promote the development of the resources of India by British capital," observed the *Cotton Supply Reporter*, "than British capitalists would ever have done without their interference." The crisis of American slavery in effect forced and enabled the reconfiguration of the cotton-growing countryside elsewhere.[34]

The wave of activity that transformed parts of India also rippled through Egypt's lower Nile Delta. In response to the desperate search by cotton manufacturers for new sources of raw cotton, the Ottoman viceroy Muhammad Sa'id Pasha quickly set about converting his own large landholdings into vast cotton farms. According to Massachusetts cotton manufacturer Edward Atkinson, Muhammad Sa'id became at a stroke "the largest and best cultivator of cotton in the world," but unbeknownst to Atkinson, he did so in the context of an enormous wave of coercion and violence descending on the Egyptian countryside, including the importation of additional slaves from the Sudan.[35]

From the viceroy's vantage point, his long-term project of modernizing Egypt through the sale of cotton on world markets, a project, as we have seen, begun about four decades earlier under Pasha Muhammad Ali, now seemed closer than ever to fruition. New railroads, new canals, new cotton gins, and new cotton presses were built. By 1864, 40 percent of all fertile land in Lower Egypt had been converted to cotton farms. Egyptian rural cultivators, the fellaheen, quintupled their cotton production between 1860 and 1865 from 50.1 million to 250.7 million pounds, marking a permanent economic change of such significance that historians of Egypt rank the American Civil War among the most crucial events in that country's nineteenth-century history. The fourteenfold increase in the value of cotton exports was "an economic revolution." And it was not surprising that when the viceroy traveled to Manchester in 1862 in the midst of the American Civil War, he was given a hero's welcome.[36]

The effects of the Civil War also reached the northeastern coast of Brazil. Decades earlier, subsistence farmers had occupied land belonging

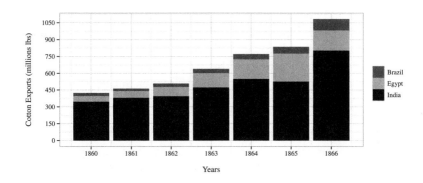

Cotton exports, 1860–66, in million pounds

to large estate owners in and around Pernambuco. Over time these peasants began to cultivate small amounts of cotton to obtain cash for necessities and taxes. When prices for cotton surged during the war and British credit flooded the countryside, farmers abandoned their subsistence crops to plant cotton for the world market. Collectively, these cultivators more than doubled Brazilian cotton exports between 1860 and 1865.[37]

Rural cultivators in other regions of the world also responded to the cotton famine. Western Anatolia, for example, saw its exports more than triple to 31.5 million pounds by 1863, thanks to a coordinated effort by private British cotton capitalists and the Imperial Command in Istanbul, which created special privileges for cotton growers, distributed American cottonseed, and extended railroads into the hinterland to facilitate the transport of cotton to the coast. French colonial officials in Algeria labored to increase cotton production during the Civil War, pressured by manufacturers and the Société Industrielle de Mulhouse, and supported by a number of private companies that raised capital and set up operations there. In Argentina "the experiments to spread the cultivation of cotton were started several times, especially during the period of 1862–1865 . . .when the export of cotton from the United States declined as a result of the Civil War." In Mexico, a future cotton power, cotton planting increased to serve the Union market, and the value of cotton exports skyrocketed by a factor of eight between 1861 and 1865. The Peruvian cotton industry's exports quadrupled. Similarly, one of the world's largest crops, Chinese cotton, broke over the steep banks of its broad domestic market and poured into world markets. Transcaucasian and Central Asian cotton made its presence felt in Moscow and Saint Petersburg. West African cotton, thanks to the joint efforts of African merchants and French colonialists, found eager buyers in Alsace and Normandy. And along the Atlantic coast of Africa, in the future German colony of Togo, African merchants employed their slaves in the production of cotton for shipment to Liverpool.[38]

The cotton rush indeed sparked even more fanciful scenarios among political economists, manufacturers, and merchants who hoped that this or that region of the world would fill the gap left by the war, testifying to the chaotic and experimental nature of this response to the Civil War. The *Manchester Guardian* repeatedly trumpeted the cotton prospects of various parts of Africa, India, Australia, and the Middle East. "L'Afrique est le vrai pays du coton," pronounced one French observer optimistically in 1864. "Queensland," argued the Australian *Queensland Guardian* in 1861, "must be cottonized." To the chagrin of cotton manufacturers and gullible investors, not all such plans worked out during the war years. The quantity of African, Argentinean, and Central Asian cotton sold on the world market remained small and the obstacles in those regions remained too great for private capital, even in concert with desperate European governments, to overcome.[39]

Nonetheless, during the American Civil War, merchants, manufacturers, and statesmen glimpsed the future shape of the empire of cotton. They engaged, as Samuel B. Ruggles explained to the New York Chamber of Commerce, in a "great effort for the commercial emancipation of the civilized nations of the earth."[40] Because of them, Indian, Egyptian, and Brazilian cotton became a major presence on Western markets. Their experience during the cotton famine, moreover, had opened bold new vistas of colonial adventure and state involvement in commodity markets. While private investment and lobbying of the state had characterized the antebellum efforts of cotton merchants and manufacturers, the cotton famine sharply raised the dependence of these cotton capitalists on the state and on their own political sophistication. Colonialism had become a matter of urgent self-interest, as capitalists grasped how vulnerable their global networks and huge capital investments were to local disruption and how unstable slavery had become.

.   .   .

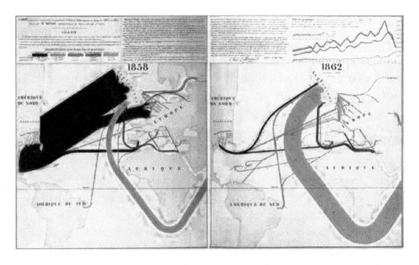

"The biggest commercial catastrophe in the world." French engineer Charles Joseph Minard maps the impact of the Civil War on the global cotton industry.

Yet the question of the future role of American cotton in the global economy remained. Would it return to market? And if so, would slaves still be growing it?

Some cotton manufacturers and merchants in Europe went as far as to hope for a permanent separation of the Union to enable the continued growing of cotton by slaves in an internationally recognized Confederacy. They believed that the cotton empire depended for the foreseeable future on slavery. In France, the *procureur général* reported widespread sentiments among mill owners in the textile region of Alsace that "from a commercial point of view, the separation would be a boon for us due to the ease that the South was willing to give the European Trade." The *procureur général* of Colmar observed in 1862 that public opinion more and more favors the "prompt recognition of the Confederacy." Le Havre merchants were nearly as vocal in their support for the cause of the Confederacy, the *Courier du Havre* being at the forefront of such sentiments. Many of the propertied in Great Britain similarly opposed the northern cause, motivated by antidemocratic attitudes and a preference for a divided and weakened power in North America, yet concerns about cotton certainly came into their calculations as well: When John Arthur Roebuck advocated in the House of Commons for the recognition of the

Confederacy, he did not tire of mentioning the fate of Lancashire textile workers and their need for cotton. Tellingly, Liverpool, the world's largest cotton port, was the most pro-Confederate place in the world outside the Confederacy itself. Liverpool merchants helped bring out cotton from ports blockaded by the Union navy, built warships for the Confederacy, and supplied the South with military equipment and credit. The Liverpool Southern Club, as well as the Central Association for the Recognition of the Confederate States, agitated for permanent separation. Even the Liverpool Chamber of Commerce entertained the benefits of an independent Confederacy. Liverpool's mercantile community believed, as the Browns' Liverpool partner Francis Alexander Hamilton wrote in August 1861, that "no earthly power could reunite the two sections," and that a Union victory was "an utter impossibility."[41]

Liverpool was not alone. In Manchester, the Southern Club and the Manchester Southern Independence Association agitated for the South. In 1862, thousands of participants, some of them workers, staged rallies in British cotton towns, demanding government recognition of the

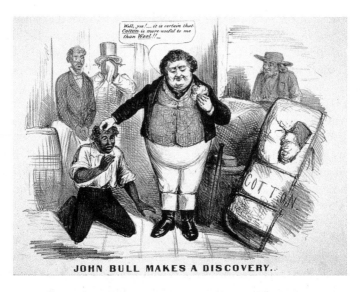

JOHN BULL MAKES A DISCOVERY.

"Well, yes! it is certain that 'Cotton' is more useful to me than 'Wool!!' "
Northerners fear that Britain will abandon its neutrality
to secure cotton, 1862 or 1863.

Confederacy. Even though many workers supported the Union as its struggle became increasingly identified with the struggle for free labor, elite sentiment tended to favor the Confederacy with the president of the Manchester Chamber of Commerce expressing his expectation that "permanent secession of the Southern States was inevitable."[42]

Such sentiments, while not universal among cotton manufacturers and merchants, had the potential to influence the position of governments, especially of Britain and France, toward the American war. The Union, which had an overwhelming interest in maintaining the neutrality of European governments, took the threat seriously. The Confederacy, for its part, saw gaining international recognition as its single most important foreign policy goal. Of course there were good reasons not to intervene: Britain had to consider the fate of its Canadian provinces, and its growing dependence on wheat and corn imports from the northern United States, while continental powers such as France, Russia, and Prussia had an interest in maintaining a strong United States to balance British economic and military power. But European mediation of the conflict and even European recognition of the Confederacy always remained a possibility, its advocates almost invariably touting the advantages of an independent Confederacy as a source of cotton.[43]

Social upheaval, including demonstrations, riots, and strikes (more than fifty in France alone) in the cotton manufacturing regions increased the anxiety of state bureaucrats and capitalists. Before becoming prime minister of Great Britain, William Gladstone, among others, cited this fear of social upheaval in Lancashire as a reason for European intervention in the American conflict. In 1862, in a public speech, Gladstone drew a dire picture of the social and financial impact of the cotton famine, though lauding the patience of England's workers, comparing the importance of the cotton famine to the other two calamities that had befallen the British Empire, the Irish famine and the Indian mutiny.[44]

Cotton interests constantly pressured the Lincoln administration to keep the needs of European cotton consumers in mind. The diplomatic correspondence between the British Foreign Office and the British embassy in Washington, D.C., suggests that Foreign Minister Earl Russell along with the French government exerted considerable pressure on the Union administration. "I went to the State department on the 25th [of July 1863] and spoke to Mr. Seward about the cotton," reported the British ambassador to Washington, Lord Lyons, to London. "I told him

that we had waited with the greatest patience while the military operations were going on upon the Mississippi, but that now the River was
open, and the time has come at which we had been promised an ample
supply. What was he prepared to do to redeem his promises?" Lincoln
was well aware of the importance of cotton in the conflict. In his first
annual message on December 3, 1861, he argued that "the principal lever
relied on by the insurgents for exciting foreign nations to hostility against
us . . . is the embarrassment of commerce." And by mid-1862, as the cabinet discussed Lincoln's plan for emancipation of slaves in rebel states,
Seward argued successfully against such "immediate promulgation" and
"strongly in favor of cotton and foreign governments." Seward feared
that announcement of emancipation would lead to European recognition of the Confederacy. His ears close to the ground, he recognized the
potentially revolutionary implications of the American struggle to global
capitalism and urged caution.[45]

American diplomats too were frequently reminded of Europe's urgent
need for cotton. When William Thayer, the American consul to Alexandria, Egypt, traveled to London in the summer of 1862, he reported to
Seward that recognition was very much on the mind of British policy

Securing raw materials globally, reminding Lincoln of the need for cotton:
Lord Lyons, as photographed by Mathew Brady

elites. That same year, the American minister to Brussels, Henry Sanford, was confronted by the French secretary of state, who cautioned
that "We are nearly out of cotton, and cotton we must have." When in
the spring of 1862 Louis Napoleon conversed with William L. Dayton,
the U.S. minister in Paris, he hoped "that something will be done by
your government to relieve the difficulties here, growing out of the want
of cotton." Pressured by widespread demands among cotton industrialists, the French government engaged in diplomatic efforts to end the
American conflict, so that, as Mulhouse cotton manufacturer Gustave
Imbert-Koechlin pronounced, "peace may reign between the two American states." Confederate diplomats in Europe, encouraged by such complaints, knew that Europe's need for southern cotton was the strongest
arrow in their diplomatic arsenal and launched it with increasing desperation as the tide of war turned against the South.[46]

Union diplomats desperately tried to counteract such sentiments
by making concerted efforts to communicate to the European public
directly. Charles Francis Adams advised his son in 1861 that it would be
useful if he would author a pamphlet about the cotton question. "Two
things are necessary to the production of cotton—an abundance of
labor and a cotton soil," he wrote. "Look into the question of soil first,"
he advised, arguing that a whole range of places around the globe had
the necessary environmental conditions to grow cotton. In some parts
of the world, he added, labor was abundant as well, such as in India and
Egypt, while in other parts of the world "there is no labor and here the
cooly question rises." Adams saw an opportunity in the war to allow
other cotton producers to emerge, and to undo permanently the South's
near monopoly. "The importance of this struggle [for the blockade and
for new sources of cotton] cannot be overestimated." On "the consequent
cotton pressure throughout the world hangs the destruction of American
slavery."[47]

Indeed, the best way to make the war against the Confederacy pal-
atable to powerful cotton interests in Europe was to demonstrate that
inexpensive cotton could be secured elsewhere. And the U.S. government
indeed did its best to encourage production in other parts of the world,
for example by moving vast quantities of cottonseed abroad. Washington, wrote Seward in April 1862, had "an obvious duty . . . to examine the
capacities of other countries for cotton culture and stimulate it as much
as possible, and thus to counteract the destructive designs of the factious

monopolists at home." Egypt, with its long-staple crop, was of particular importance in these calculations since it could replace American exports with a high-quality substitute, unlike Indian cotton. Throughout the war years, Thayer met regularly with the viceroy to discuss cotton production and eventually hired a confidant of the viceroy, Ayoub Bey Trabulsi, to examine "the cottons of Egypt." Thanks to such contacts, Thayer was able to report by November 1862 that "the Vice Roy has exerted his influence to aid in the increased cultivation . . . he has . . . advised all the large proprietors hereafter to sow one fourth of their land with cotton. As the advice of His Highness is practically equivalent to a command, the proprietors have commenced . . . to expedite the great agricultural revolution now in progress."[48]

Seward projected confidence that such efforts would succeed and especially emphasized the unforeseen effects of global cotton production on the South's bid for independence. "The insurrectionary cotton States will be blind to their own welfare if they do not see how their prosperity and all their hopes are passing away, when they find Egypt, Asia Minor and India supplying the world with cotton, and California furnishing the gold for its purchase."[49]

And indeed, these overtures of American policy makers did help to defuse tensions between Washington and European capitals. In the spring of 1862, Baring Brothers Liverpool expressed the view that war between the United States and Great Britain was less likely "provided we get a large import from India." Charles Wood argued in August 1862 that "our only domestic trouble, . . . the distress in Lancashire, . . . may be much mitigated, if any reasonable quantity worth speaking of can come from India beyond what she sent last year." By 1863, widespread cotton imports from India had alleviated the cotton crisis in France. Indeed by early 1864 the *procureurs généraux* of various cotton manufacturing districts could report that cotton imports from India and Egypt had relieved pressure on manufacturers, as factories started slowly to produce again and, as a result, "the struggle . . . lost a great deal of interest in our *département*."[50] As Seward put it a few years after the war, in 1872, when he came to the Indian city of Agra—the site of the Taj Mahal—to visit a cotton gin there, "From the tomb of the Mogul monarch Of India, Akbar, we passed to the tomb of the pretended monarch of America, King Cotton."[51]

Once significant amounts of cotton arrived from sources other than the United States, the political pressure on European governments from cotton interests declined. Edward Atkinson, the Boston cotton manufacturer, was relieved that the "supposed dependence of Europe upon the Cotton States has proved to be an utter fallacy," and thought it possible that soon "Europe will become absolutely independent of this country for her supply." By 1863, even those whose livelihood depended on cotton, and who had once been advocates of the cause of the southern states, began to envision a diverse supply network of raw cotton without reliance on slaves.[52]

Some even began to see the obstinacy of the South, in its demands for independence and its attachment to slavery, as the real cause of disruption to the world economy. After all, cotton merchants and manufacturers, unlike southern planters and their government, were not invested in a particular source of cotton—the American South—nor in a particular system of labor to produce it—slavery. All they required was a secure and predictable supply of inexpensive cotton in the qualities they desired.

Yet it was one thing to respond to short-term supply disruptions resulting from a blockade, and another to imagine an empire of cotton without slavery. Based on their readings of the history of the cotton empire during the previous eighty years, many merchants and manufacturers feared that the potential disruption of the "deep relationship between slavery and cotton production" might, as the *Bremer Handelsblatt* put it, "destroy one of the essential conditions of the mass production" of cotton textiles.[53]

As early as 1861, when Union general John C. Frémont emancipated slaves in Missouri, *The Economist* worried that such a "fearful measure" might spread to other slaveholding states, "inflict[ing] utter ruin and universal desolation on those fertile territories." The *Cotton Supply Reporter* went as far as to evoke "the horrors of a second St. Domingue," should the war become a war for emancipation, and predicted that in such a case the United States' "marvelous cotton-producing industry must suddenly collapse." It was not surprising that people with such beliefs would come to see the fall of Richmond as of such consequence, according to the hyperventilating *Bremer Handelsblatt*, that even the "richest imagination was too poor to envisage its implications."[54]

Considering these fears, it was the more remarkable that 4 million slaves in the United States—among them the world's most important cotton growers—gained their freedom during or immediately after the

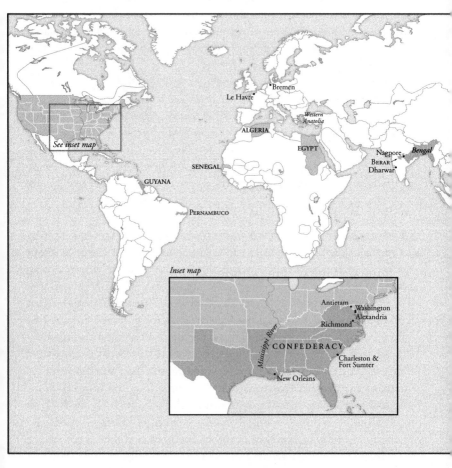

The Impact of the American Civil War on the
Global Cotton Industry, 1861–1865

war. Encouraged by their perception of their masters' weakness in the face of a national government bent on subduing the rebels, slaves embarked upon an agrarian insurrection. By deserting plantations, withdrawing their labor power, giving intelligence to federal troops, and eventually taking up arms as Union soldiers, American slaves pressed to make a sectional war into a war of emancipation. And they succeeded. Never before and never thereafter did cotton growers revolt with similar success, their strength fortuitously amplified by a deep and irreconcilable split within the nation's elite.[55]

With slavery unlikely to be resurrected in face of such unprecedented revolt, cotton capitalists searched for new ways to mobilize cotton-growing labor. They could not find much reassurance in past cotton-growing experiences in other regions of the world. At prevailing antebellum world market prices, few cultivators in India, Brazil, or Africa, had produced much cotton for European markets, despite the best efforts of some manufacturers. Peasants had tenaciously clung to subsistence farming, and the fraction who did cultivate cotton for markets sold it to nearby spinners, not to Liverpool or Le Havre merchants. Even in the United States itself, as slaves gained their freedom during the war, many of them quickly abandoned the industrial rhythm of the plantation and instead tried to focus on subsistence agriculture.[56]

Moreover, the experience of earlier emancipations in the Caribbean, in Saint-Domingue above all, had deflated the hopes of merchants and manufacturers about cash-crop production by former slaves. As early as 1841, Herman Merivale had observed that it was difficult to compel "the negroes to perform hired labour while they have their own provision grounds, and other resources, at their disposal." The (British) Select Committee investigating "the existing relations between Employers and Labourers" in the West Indies had similarly noted in 1842 that the production of agricultural commodities had diminished in the wake of emancipation because "the labourers are enabled to live in comfort and to acquire wealth without, for the most part, labouring on the estates of the Planters for more than three or four days in a week." As *The Economist* put it, "in the tropics Nature has given man the benefit, or the curse, of a perpetual poor law, a prodigality of food which of itself established a minimum of wages."[57]

For British colonial official W. H. Holmes the dilemma was clear: "When the slave became a free man . . . his first desire was also to become independent; to be completely his own master." In Guyana, which he studied carefully, "a trifling amount of labour procures the few luxuries, which a most fertile soil fails to place within reach," making it unlikely that farmers would grow export crops for wages. Vegetables, fish, and fruit were available for the asking, a situation that, "in my opinion, [has] been fraught with evil consequences." French colonial bureaucrats had come to essentially the same conclusion: Once "free . . . the Black . . . returns to the hut of the savage." Freedpeople's retreat into subsistence agriculture, envisioned by so many former slaves as a true foundation for their new freedom, was the worst nightmare of cotton merchants and manufacturers the world over.[58] European observers' concerns about freedpeople were further amplified by developments in the Caribbean, such as the 1865 Morant Bay Rebellion in Jamaica, when a group of black Jamaicans revolted against the harsh punishment the colonial administration had inflicted on a group of squatters, a rebellion that was suppressed by an orgy of violence by British troops.

Landowners, manufacturers, merchants, and statesmen concluded from this reading of past experiences that emancipation was potentially threatening to the well-being of the world's mechanized cotton industry. Consequently, they worked zealously to find ways to reconstruct durably the worldwide web of cotton production, to transform the global countryside without resorting to slavery. Already during the war itself, in articles and books, speeches and letters, they belabored the question of if and where cotton could be grown by nonslave labor. Edward Atkinson, for example, contributed to this debate as early as 1861 with his *Cheap Cotton by Free Labor*, and one year later, William Holmes's *Free Cotton: How and Where to Grow It* extended the discussion. An anonymous French author added his voice the same year with *Les blancs et les noirs en Amérique et le coton dans les deux mondes*.[59]

Soon such treatises were informed by lessons drawn from the Civil War experiences. The sudden turn to nonslave cotton during the Civil War years in Egypt, Brazil, and India as well as in Union-controlled zones of the American South represented, after all, a global experiment: What would a world with cotton but without slaves look like?

These rehearsals—for a new postwar, postslavery cotton empire—nurtured two somewhat contradictory faiths. Few observers reckoned that enough cotton could be procured to permit cotton manufacturing to continue its dramatic expansion even without slavery. This was, for example, the judgment of the English Ladies' Free Grown Cotton movement, a loose association of women who committed themselves to purchasing only cloth produced with free labor cotton. And, perhaps most optimistically, it was embraced by Republicans in the United States such as Edward Atkinson, who believed that cotton production in the American South could be expanded dramatically through the use of "free labor"—that is, as long as freedpeople did not remain content with subsistence agriculture. Atkinson, impressed by his own successes in staffing his cotton mills with wage workers, fervently believed that the future of the United States'—and the world's—cotton supply depended on the ability of southern landowners and the southern states to motivate freed slaves to produce cotton.[60]

Yet the Civil War experience also had shown that nonslave cotton had entered world markets only under conditions of unsustainably high prices; after all, the price of Indian cotton had more than quadrupled and earlier efforts to bring Indian cotton to market at lower prices had largely failed. Moreover, from the perspective of 1864 and 1865, emancipation was accompanied by considerable social turmoil in the American South. Cotton capitalists' widespread belief that freedom would bring a permanent reduction in the supplies of raw cotton was thus reasonable and was expressed most directly in the fact that postbellum cotton prices remained well above their prewar level. Breathless reports came into Liverpool, such as the one received by the Rathbones which predicted that "negro labour could not be depended on for next year." The Barings, in turn, asserted that "few appear to think that labour can be sufficiently reorganized in the South to plant and pick a crop next season exceeding 1½ million bales." (In 1860, the cotton crop had been 5.4 million bales.)[61]

As fears of permanently reduced cotton harvests spread through cotton circles, pressure for a reconstruction of plantation agriculture in the American South after the defeat of the Confederacy mounted, especially the orderly return of cotton cultivators to the fields. The *Bremer Handelsblatt* called for a policy of forgiveness toward the defeated planter elite. In the spring of 1865, the British minister to Washington, Sir Frederick William Adolphus Bruce, reported back to London on the status of Reconstruction, severely critiquing the "ultra-Republicans," and reminding President Andrew Johnson to take into account the urgent need to revive cotton production. The question of if and how freedpeople would work occupied him; he feared that "the emancipation of the Negroes will be a great blow to the material prosperity of the cotton and sugar growing States." Concerned about upheavals in the South and critical of efforts to extend suffrage rights to freedpeople, he approvingly reported in May 1865 that "everywhere measures are being taken to force the Negroes to work, and to teach them that freedom means working for wages instead of masters."[62]

Yet cotton capitalists and government bureaucrats also had learned much broader lessons during the war. Most important, they understood that labor, not land, constrained the production of cotton. Members of the Manchester Cotton Supply Association, the world's leading experts on such matters, understood that land and climate of a "quality equal and in many cases superior to that" of America was available in many different parts of the globe. But these experts on global cotton found that "the very first requisite, which was labor" was more difficult to find. As the British finance minister for India, Samuel Laing, remarked, "The question of the abolition of slavery over the world, depends probably upon the question whether cotton produced by free labor in India can undersell cotton the produce of slavery in America."[63]

But where should this labor come from? During the Civil War, as we have seen, the efforts of cotton interests focused squarely on accessing labor in regions that formerly had not grown significant amounts of cotton for European markets. The president of the Cotton Supply Association summarized this strategy succinctly: "We are now opening up the interior." This strategy had a long history; the Civil War, however, had focused the energies of capitalists and statesmen in unprecedented ways.[64]

This rapid geographic expansion of the global web of cotton production was deeply entangled with efforts to find new ways to motivate rural cultivators to grow the white gold and move it to market. How could rulers make peasants grow crops that, as political scientist Timothy Mitchell put it so well, "they could not eat, or process to serve local needs"? Or how could, as the French observer M. J. Mathieu asked far less delicately in 1861, "black workers be disciplined and stimulated"?[65]

Throughout the empire of cotton, bureaucrats and capitalists agonized over the question of whether "the negroe will from now on be a industrious worker."[66] In an unusually long article, *The Economist* took the occasion of the end of the Civil War to engage in an extended deliberation on the issue, arguing:

There is probably no one point of politics which involves economic results so wide or so permanent as the relation between the white and the dark races of the world. . . . It is probably the destiny, it is even now the function, it is certainly the interest of the European, and more particularly of the English family of mankind, to guide and urge and control the industrial enterprises of all Asia, of all Africa, and of those portions of America settled by African, Asiatic, or hybrid races. Those enterprises are very large indeed. . . . The one necessity essential to the development of these new sources of prosperity is the arrangement of some industrial system under which very large bodies of dark labourers will work willingly under a very few European supervisors. It is not only individual labour which is required, but organized labour, labour so scientifically arranged that the maximum of result shall be obtained at a minimum of cost, that immense sudden efforts, such as are required in tunnel cutting, cotton picking and many other operations, shall be possible without strikes or quarrels, and that, above all, there shall be no unnatural addition to the price of labour in the shape of bribes to the workmen to obey orders naturally repulsive to their prejudices.

To be sure, *The Economist* argued, "All these ends were secured, it must freely be acknowledged, by slavery. For the mere execution of great works cheaply no organization could be equal to that which placed the skilled European at the top, and made him despotic master of the half-skilled black or copper-coloured labourer below. . . ." But slavery had also "moral and social consequences which are not beneficial." And for that reason, "A new organization therefore must be commenced, and the only one as yet found to work effectively is . . . one based upon perfect freedom and mutual self-interest. . . . If, however, complete freedom is to be the principle adopted, it is clear that the dark races must in some way or other be induced to obey white men willingly."[67]

But how would "the dark races . . . be induced to obey white men willingly"? The Civil War had unintentionally transformed the possibilities for where and how cotton might be grown, overturning in one stroke the balance between coerced and free labor in the global web of cotton production. The determined efforts of slaves themselves and the advance of the Union army bolstered by newly freed men and women had destroyed the system of chattel slavery that for 250 years had fueled both war capitalism and the Industrial Revolution. But the newly emerging order in the world's cotton fields was still up for grabs.[68]

The outlines of what this reconstruction would look like were only glimpsed here and there during the Civil War itself. Yet by century's end, the world of cotton would look dramatically different. The speed and flexibility with which merchants, manufacturers, and agricultural producers responded to the crisis revealed their adaptability and, not least, their capacity for marshaling new, indirect, but far-reaching forms of state power to secure labor in place of direct ownership of human beings. "The emancipation of the enslaved races and the regeneration of the people of the East," observed the *Revue de Deux Mondes* perceptively, "were intimately connected."[69]

When the guns fell silent on the North American continent in April 1865, the greatest turmoil in the eighty-five-year history of a European-dominated cotton industry came to an end. New systems for the mobilization of labor had been tested around the world—from coolie workers to sharecropping to wage labor—and while it was still uncertain if cotton production would return to antebellum levels, belief in the possibility of "free labor" cotton had become nearly universal. As former slaves throughout the United States celebrated their freedom, manufacturers and workers looked forward to factories running again at capacity, fueled by newly plentiful cotton supplies.

Merchants, however, had little to celebrate. "The peace rumor caused almost a panic," reported Baring Brothers Liverpool to their counterparts in London in February 1865. When the *Indian Daily News*, in an "extraordinary" issue, reported in early March of the capture of Charleston by Union forces, it observed, "Panic in Liverpool. Cotton down to one shilling," a panic that rapidly spread to Bombay itself. Boston ice merchant Calvin W. Smith reported from Bombay that "I am sorry to say such long faces I never saw on any set of mortals as the English & Parsees put on here. Our success at home is their ruination. Let that war end in one year, and there will be more failures in this town, than in any one place anywhere. Such wild speculation as has been going on here for the last four years, never was heard of before." In Liverpool panic prevailed as well. Liverpool cotton merchant Samuel Smith remembered, "It was pitiable to see men who had bought fine mansions and costly picture galleries, hanging about 'the flags,' watching the chance of borrowing a guinea from an old friend."[70]

This global panic illuminated to peasants, workers, manufacturers, and merchants how closely intertwined developments all over the world had become. Battles fought in rural Virginia reverberated in small villages in Berar and Lower Egypt, a farmer's crop choice in Brazil rested on his reading of the Liverpool market, and real estate prices collapsed in Bombay as soon as news of the Union's destruction of Richmond reached India's shores. A British observer was amazed at these new global links that the Civil War had brought to the fore. "We have seen how potent and how quick," he wrote, "the effect of 'price' was in the most distant parts of our globe."[71]

The world indeed had become smaller, and the way cotton held parts of it together had changed significantly. If the Civil War was a moment of crisis for the empire of cotton, it was also a rehearsal for its reconstruction. Cotton capitalists were confident from their triumphs in recasting industrial production at home. As they surveyed the ashes of the South, they saw promising new levers that might move the mountain of free labor into cotton cultivation with new lands, new labor relations, and new connections between them. But perhaps most important, cotton capitalists had learned that the lucrative global trade networks they had spun could only be protected and maintained by unprecedented state activism. Meanwhile, statesmen understood that these networks had become essential to the social order of their nations and hence a crucial bulwark of political legitimacy, resources, and power. Thus the French observer was correct when he predicted in 1863, "The empire of cotton is ensured; King Cotton is not dethroned."[72]

Chapter Ten

Global Reconstruction

Indian cultivators delivering cotton to an upcountry Volkart Brothers agency. Probably Khamgaon, 1870s.

In the fall of 1865, Captain William Hickens of the British Royal Engineers traveled through the states of the defeated Confederacy. Dispatched by the Foreign Office to evaluate the prospects of cotton growing, Hickens met with planters, brokers, "and other individuals connected with cotton." In his report to the British secretary of state, the Earl of Clarendon, he expressed great pessimism about the possibility of the American South again producing large quantities of cotton at prices comparable to those of the antebellum years. For 1866, he expected at most 1 million bales of cotton to come from southern plantations and farms, one-quarter of the last prewar harvest. The reason for his dismal assessment was straightforward: There was not enough labor in the South to plow, seed, prune, and harvest all that cotton. "So completely has the system of labour been disorganized by the emancipation of the slaves," he lamented, that cotton harvests for the foreseeable future would be vastly reduced. Planters in Louisiana had told Hickens that "there is the greatest difficulty in getting a fair day's work out of the negroes," as the freedpeople have "no idea of the sanctity of a contract, and will . . . evade the performance of [their] part of it." The solution, Hickens concluded, was the growing of cotton by white settlers, who would eventually be able to grow a crop "as large each year as before the war," but never again as cheaply as "in the old days."[1]

In April 1865, the question that was first and foremost on the minds of cotton capitalists and statesmen was if and when the cotton planters of the American South would resume their position within the empire of cotton. This question, virtually all observers agreed with Hickens, boiled down to just one issue: labor. Manchester cotton manufacturer Edmund Ashworth was all but certain that "the blacks who had once worked by the whip would be slow to work for wages." Liverpool cotton broker Maurice Williams put the issue succinctly: "Now as the *power* to *force* this labor is for ever taken away and that it was mainly owing to this power that the Southern States were enabled to raise such enormous Crops of Cotton as previously to supply four fifths the Consumption of the world it may naturally be expected that free laborers toiling mainly for themselves cannot for years until their number be materially increased be expected to produce any large quantity compared with former crops."[2]

Just as slaves had revolutionized the cotton empire, emancipation forced cotton capitalists toward their own revolution—a frantic search for new ways to organize the cotton-growing labor of the world. Reconciling the emancipation of America's cotton growers with the need for ever more raw cotton was not easily accomplished. Yet cotton manufacturers' insatiable demand for inexpensive cotton made sure that the "cotton question" remained high on the agenda. Raw cotton imports were so voluminous that they were generally the most costly item in the trade of the industrialized nations of Europe, and cotton exports were at the very top of the list of goods brought from there to foreign markets. With hundreds of thousands of workers finding employment in textile mills, these supplies and outlets were crucial to securing the social stability of European and North American societies. To maintain an industry so important required a global reconstruction of the empire of cotton; a search for innovative combinations of land, labor, capital, and state power.[3]

The continued rapid growth of the industry over the next half century

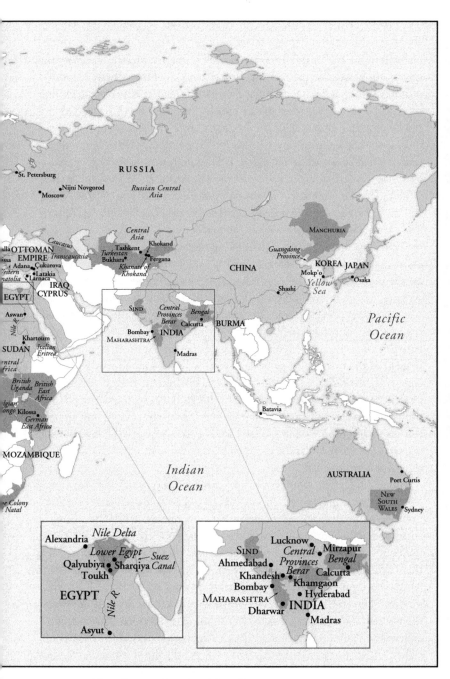

The Cotton Empire After Slavery, 1865–1920

amplified this need: Global cotton consumption doubled from 1860 to 1890, and then by 1920 doubled once more. "Among the larger industrial changes of the last thirty years few exceed, in importance and interest, the marvelous growth of the manufacture of cotton by machinery," reported economist Elijah Helm in 1903. British spinners remained the world's most important consumers of raw cotton, but their needs expanded at a slower rate than before 1860. In the 1840s, their cotton consumption had increased by 4.8 percent annually, but by the 1870s and 1880s that rate of increase had dropped to 1.4 percent. Britain's spinning slowdown, however, was more than made up by the demand from spinners in the rapidly growing cotton industries of western and eastern Europe, North America, and, by the early twentieth century, Brazil, Mexico, India, China, and Japan. In the years between 1860 and 1920 mechanical spindles in the world's cotton industry tripled, as entrepreneurs and workers set another 100 million spindles in motion—half of them in the forty years before 1900, and the other half in the first two decades of the twentieth century. The spread of power looms was dramatic as well. In 1860 there were 650,000 power looms; the number reached 3.2 million by 1929. Continental Europe slowly increased its share of global cotton spindles between 1860 and 1900 rising from a quarter of the total in 1860 to 30 percent at the turn of the century. America also increased its share at the expense of Britain, rising from a 10 percent share in 1860 to around 20 percent in 1900.[4] The primary effect of this shift was to give a much larger number of states and capitalists an interest in cheap cotton, and thus in the transformation of the global countryside, hoping to draw an ever wider swath of the world's hinterland into the circuits of metropolitan capital accumulation.[5]

That the demand for raw cotton exploded just when the traditional way of organizing its production—slavery—had collapsed gave increased urgency to capitalists' and government bureaucrats' efforts to mobilize cotton-growing workers. As we have seen, most cultivators had a strong preference for producing for their families and communities, not for the world market. While small growers from India to Alabama to West Africa were not averse to participating in markets, even long-distance markets, and did take advantage of opportunities for profit that availed themselves, their strategies were almost always embedded within a world of family subsistence, ties of mutual obligation, political arrangements, rights, and customary practices that made production for the market sec-

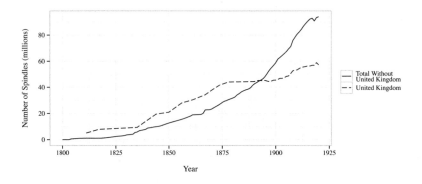

Number of factory spindles, United Kingdom and
world without United Kingdom, 1800–1920

ondary. They were reluctant to give up household-focused production, and, in certain regions, collectively strong enough to resist the encroachments of European and North American capitalists and imperial administrators. Moreover, agricultural wages were too low and too insecure to entice rural cultivators to give up subsistence production, as much greater risks were not balanced by the possibility of higher rewards.[6]

The reconstruction of the empire of cotton, at its core, required the diligent effort of cotton industrialists, merchants, landowners, and state bureaucrats to undermine such preferences, drawing, in the process, on the powers of newly consolidating nation-states, and sanctioning legal—and often illegal—coercion to make rural farmers into the cultivators and eventually consumers of commodities. They sought to revolutionize the countryside by spreading capitalist social relations, including credit, private ownership in land, and contract law. They sought—and eventually found—what French colonial officials aptly called "a new mode of exploitation."[7] The transformation of the countryside they furthered was most intimately linked to the globalized nature of industrial production. Earlier forms of global trade had been based on the exchange of goods produced in all kinds of distinctly noncapitalist ways—by serfs and within households, for example. Now the wealth and coercive might of globalizing entrepreneurs and imperial statesmen was transforming the production regimes of people around the globe by commodifying both their labor and their land—as they had done in previous centuries in the Americas, albeit in different forms. In Asia and Africa the "great transformation" reached, for the first time, into areas remote from port cities. The logic of industrial capitalism in effect brought about a new form of global economic integration. The rising power of manufacturers, and the particular form of capital they controlled, created a new relationship between capital and territory as well as the people who dwelled on it, and allowed for new ways to mobilize their labor.

New forms of labor—including new forms of coercion, violence, and expropriation—spread over ever larger areas of the cotton-growing parts of the globe. Domination now rested not so much on the authority of the master but on the purportedly impersonal but far from impartial social mechanisms of the market, the law, and the state. The new systems of labor that emerged from these sometimes violent but almost always asymmetrical struggles between industrialists, merchants, agricultural producers, workers, rulers, and bureaucrats became the mainspring of the production of cotton until the advent of commercially viable mechanical harvesting in the United States during the 1940s, and of a new global political economy.[8]

Even though contemporaries were uncertain if and when American growers would return to dominating world market production of cotton, no one doubted that the labor of formerly enslaved cotton growers would be the foundation of any possible resurgence of American cotton exports, and with it the revival and continued expansion of the world's cotton industry. In 1865, merchants, journalists, and diplomats, many from Europe, pored over maps and tables and sent scouts to the southern countryside to discover information on what labor system might replace slavery.[9] The core question, they quickly learned, was whether or not freedpeople would return to the cotton fields. Many wondered if former slaves could be kept working on the land that they had tilled for more than half a century, and if they could be made to continue growing cotton now that outright bodily coercion had become illegal. Certainly some optimistic voices could be heard: Boston cotton manufacturer Edward Atkinson upheld his fervent belief in the superior productivity of free labor, including in the production of cotton. Others believed that the "pinchings of want" would "correct" the "prevailing indolence of the colored people," forcing them back to the cotton fields.[10]

Yet most were considerably more pessimistic: "The cultivation of the hitherto great Southern staples, will of necessity be abandoned," predicted the *Southern Cultivator*. Cotton merchant J. R. Busk, William Rathbone's U.S. agent, while hoping that "the pacification of the South will not be indefinitely postponed by radical measures," advised that "negro labour could not be depended on for next year." George McHenry from London went even further and argued in his *The Cotton Supply of the United States of America*, that only reenslavement would bring forth cotton: "Cotton can only be cultivated extensively in the Southern States by negro labour, and negro labour can only be controlled under the semi-patriarchal system called slavery." Cotton experts in India concurred, with some self-interest, as the Bombay cotton commissioner G. F. Forbes predicted that former slaves would spend their time "sleeping under the nearest tree."[11]

Throughout Europe and the United States, economic and political elites agreed that former slaves must continue to grow cotton. And they also agreed that the question of cotton boiled down to labor. As lawyer and Union general Francis C. Barlow put it to his friend Henry Lee Higginson, a wealthy Bostonian who hoped in 1865 to purchase a cotton plantation in the South, "Making money there is a simple question of being able to make the darkies work." The question of "negro labor" agitated the minds of landowners, bureaucrats, former slaves, and self-appointed experts on such matters from around the globe. As the *Southern Cultivator* summarized that discussion, "The all absorbing subject, [is] what kind of labor is best for us." And indeed, the question of how "to manage negro labor successfully" filled the pages of the journal. Many "experts" feared that freedpeople, as they had in the West Indies a generation earlier, would engage in subsistence agriculture. To prevent such "evil consequences," some advocated the payment of monetary wages, others a system of sharecropping, while again others preferred an effort to maintain gang labor. A subscriber from South Carolina remarked that "the negro [is] the proper, legitimate and divinely ordained laborer of the South . . . [who] has become wild in the exuberance of his freedom . . . and will be trained to work as a free man. He cannot be permitted to become what he is in St. Domingo." The *Macon Telegraph* of Georgia put it more succinctly in the spring of 1865: "the great question now before our people is how to appropriate all the African labor of the country."[12]

Some of the answers to the question of "how to appropriate all the

African labor of the country" had already been found during the war, when Union generals and northern investors tried to resurrect cotton production in areas of the South captured by Union troops. Most prominent were the efforts on the Sea Islands off the coast of South Carolina and Georgia—an important cotton-growing area for many decades—where northerners such as Edward Atkinson bought cotton plantations and tried to implement their vision of "free labor." They foresaw a world in which freedpeople would continue to grow export crops for wages, a project they embraced with infectious enthusiasm. Because freedpeople often had a different idea as to what freedom entailed—namely, land ownership and control over their labor—there, as elsewhere, the Union army obliged freed slaves to work for wages on plantations. Such measures did not bode well for the freed slaves' hopes and aspirations.[13]

It took a multiyear struggle on plantations, in local courthouses, in state capitols, and in Washington to determine the outlines of a new system of labor in the cotton-growing regions of the United States. That struggle began the moment the fighting ended, when plantation owners, devastated by the economic and political effects of defeat in war, sought to restore a plantation world as close to slavery as possible. To be sure, contracts now had to be made and wages paid—the *Macon Telegraph* advised its readers in May 1865 with some regret that "remuneration for labor will hereafter be necessary"—but beyond that, life was to go on as before. Former slaves, living in the hovels they had inhabited before emancipation, were to hoe, plant, weed, and harvest under the supervision of overseers. Money or, more typically, a share of the crop, would compensate them for their efforts.[14]

An early 1866 contract of cotton planter Alonzo T. Mial of Wake County, North Carolina, with twenty-seven freedpeople stipulated work from sunrise to sunset, with some additional activities after sunset, and a commitment to "attend to the plantation on Sundays." There was no pay for sick time or leaves. The workers received in return ten dollars a month, and an additional fifteen pounds of bacon and one bushel of meal. Similarly, in the southwestern corner of Georgia, a prime cotton-growing area, upon emancipation planters hired their former slaves as wage workers, unilaterally imposing restrictive conditions and minimal pay—so little that it amounted to no more than "life's necessities" plus one-tenth of the corn crop (and none of the cotton). The situation was nearly the same in the Yazoo-Mississippi Delta, perhaps the world's most important cotton-growing region, where landlords paid wages, but also tried to limit freedpeople's mobility and to force them to remain on plantations and plant cotton. Since most freedmen and -women possessed hardly anything, landlords imposed these conditions unilaterally, forcing yearlong contracts on their workers, binding them to the plantation until after harvest time.[15]

Left to their own devices, planters imagined a reconstruction of the empire of cotton based on some form of wage labor, leaving the structure of land ownership, the rhythm of work, and the pattern of plantation life largely unchanged. They had powerful allies among the economic and political elites of Europe whose single-minded focus was on getting more cotton from the United States.

Planters, however, were not left to their own devices. They encountered freedpeople determined to create a world radically different from slavery—indeed, a world in which the production of commodities for international markets would no longer be their prime concern. Freedpeople believed, for good reasons, that only access to land would secure their newfound freedom, and they argued that their support for the Union war effort and their unpaid labor under slavery had given them the right to such lands. Many believed that upon Union victory, forty acres and a mule would await them. A group of freedmen in Virginia, for example, had a very clear and completely accurate idea as to why "we have a divine right to the land." They recalled that "our wives, our children, our husbands, has been sold over and over again to purchase the lands we now locates upon. . . . And den didn't we clear the land, and raise the crops of corn, ob tobacco, ob rice, ob sugar, ob ebery ting. And den didn't dem large cities in de North grow up on de cotton and de sugars and de rice dat we made?" Slavery amounted to the theft of the just rewards of their labor—a theft now to be compensated by the redistribution of land.[16]

Yet freedpeople's hope of turning themselves into landowning subsistence peasants was short-lived. Much of the land confiscated during the war was returned to its original owners as early as the fall of 1865. Without access to land, it was difficult for freedpeople to exert much control over their labor. With President Andrew Johnson's lenient Reconstruction policy, moreover, former slave owners regained much of their political influence, and they used their restored local and regional political power to deploy the machinery of the state to limit the claims of freedpeople to economic resources and power. One of the first things these "reconstructed" state governments did was to try to enforce labor discipline and keep workers on plantations. So-called black codes, passed as early as November 1865 in Mississippi, required freedpeople to sign labor contracts that defined mobility as "vagrancy." And although the federal government, via the Freedmen's Bureau, corrected some of the most flagrant violations of "free labor," many in the U.S. government also believed that the coercive power of the state was needed to transform freedpeople into wage workers. An assistant commissioner of the Freedmen's Bureau for Louisiana argued in July 1865, for example, that it was necessary "that freedmen everywhere be enjoined to work, and in doing so, they will, in all cases, enter into free and voluntary contracts." The irony of being freely enjoined escaped this commissioner, and many others. Indeed, freedpeople not employed were threatened with compulsory labor.[17] Northerners legitimized these "compulsory contracts," as historian Amy Dru Stanley has called them, as a measure to help guide freedpeople into freedom. At the same time, alternative ways of gaining access to subsistence, such as allowing animals to graze on public lands, hunting, fishing, and gathering fruits and nuts were increasingly restricted.[18]

Cotton capitalists generally welcomed such measures, with the *Commercial and Financial Chronicle*, speaking for New York's business community, expressing its hope that freedpeople's mobility "cannot be deemed anything more than a temporary state of affairs, to be corrected by the joint influence of the vagrancy laws and the necessity of the vagrants." In the face of such powerful opposition, many freedpeople felt that they "shall be forever made hewers of wood and drawers of water"— and, we might add, cultivators of cotton. Divorced from access to alternative means of subsistence—a situation radically different from rural cultivators in India or Africa—freedpeople seemed comparatively easy to convert into agricultural proletarians.[19]

Yet the defeat of freedpeople's aspirations was not the end of the story. So blatant was the attempt by white southern elites to reimpose a system of labor akin to slavery, and so flagrant was their effort to ignore their defeat in war, that northerners began to mobilize against the Reconstruction policies of President Johnson. Thanks to the efforts of former slaves and their northern allies, freedpeople in 1866 gained citizenship rights, and in 1867 the right to vote, which allowed them to use their growing political power to improve their situation on plantations. By

1867, Congress had reestablished military authority over southern states. Northern support and the political mobilization of freedpeople in turn made black workers more able to articulate their demands on plantations themselves, and by 1867 "freedpeople walked out of the fields and off their jobs." They were helped by a shortage of labor, the result of men working fewer hours than they had under slavery and many women and children retreating from field labor altogether. Consequently, slaves managed to negotiate somewhat better contracts. Contracts in the Delta, for example, paid higher wages and offered better conditions than those of the previous year. Moreover, freedwomen, who had an increasingly difficult time finding a place for themselves and their children in a plantation world that favored physically strong men, struggled and mobilized for their own inclusion into the world of labor contracts. Such were the "weapons of the weak."[20]

Even more important, freedpeople demanded to work independently, in family units, and with access to subsistence crops. Planters were now unable to unilaterally dominate work arrangements. Freedpeople, in turn, were still unable to own land. By 1867, neither was able to impose their will entirely on the other. Consequently, a social compromise emerged, in which African-American families worked particular plots of land without day-to-day supervision, received supplies from landlords, and would then be paid with a share of the crop they had grown. Such sharecropping arrangements spread like wildfire through the cotton-growing regions of the United States, with gang labor, the prevalent system during slavery, nearly disappearing. As the *Southern Cultivator* observed in November 1867, the "first change that must occur . . . is the subdivision of landed estates." By 1868, even the Yazoo-Mississippi Delta saw widespread sharecropping, and by 1900 more than three-quarters of all black farmers in Arkansas, South Carolina, Mississippi, Louisiana, Alabama, and Georgia were sharecroppers, retaining a share of the crop, or renters, who paid a fixed sum to the landowner but retained the crop.[21]

Alonzo T. Mial now discarded signed wage contracts with his liberated former slaves and subdivided his plantation into plots for sharecropping. As elsewhere in the South, the precise character of these arrangements varied—sometimes Mial agreed to a division of the crop, sometimes he rented land for fixed quantities of certain crops or even for outright money payments. In a typical sharecropping contract, Mial gave access to thirty to thirty-five acres of land to a sharecropper, along with farming implements. In turn, he received half of the harvest. Mial's tenants were contractually obliged to build fences, repair bridges, clean stables, dig ditches—all of which was "to be done to my satisfaction, and must be done over until I am satisfied that it is done as it should be." In short, he concluded, "All must work under my direction." For Mial, sharecropping reduced supervision costs, while still giving him the power to direct tenants and to decide which crops to grow.[22]

The spread of sharecropping as the dominant system of labor in the cotton-growing regions of the United States testified to the collective strength of freedpeople, allowing them to escape a far worse system of gang labor for wages on plantations. Sharecropping gave freedmen and -women a modicum of control over their own labor, allowed them to evade day-to-day supervision so reminiscent of slavery, and permitted families—instead of individuals—to contract with landowners and to decide on the allocation of the labor of men, women, and children.

Yet in many ways, theirs was a hollow victory. The emerging patterns of land ownership, systems of labor, and the mechanism of credit supply made all but certain that farmers in the American South would have to grow cotton, and that growing cotton would create poverty. When planters and merchants provided croppers with the supplies they needed, they charged exorbitant interest. Consequently, the crop was barely sufficient to pay creditors at the end of the harvest season. On the Runnymede Plantation in Leflore County in the Mississippi Delta, for example, croppers paid 25 percent interest to purchase food and 35 percent to purchase clothing. High debts to merchants and landlords in turn forced sharecroppers to grow ever more cotton, the only crop that could always be made into money, even though its proceeds per bale diminished. Operating in an environment of expensive credit, a marginal position in the nation's political economy, and falling prices, rural cultivators watched their incomes deteriorate, a fate they shared with most farmers across the globe who now produced for world markets.[23]

The measure of their defeat became especially clear after 1873, as the economic and political environment shifted drastically. That year marked the onset of the greatest international economic crisis of the nineteenth century to date. The rate of growth of demand for cotton plunged below its antebellum averages, just when many new producers turned out ever more cotton. With world market prices for cotton declining, profits for growers diminished. At the same time, the structure of tenancy, debt, and the marketing of the crop in the postbellum South continued to create enormous pressure on farmers to produce ever more cotton, despite—or even because of—falling prices. While it was perfectly rational for each farmer to embrace cotton, such a concentration was self-defeating for the region as a whole.[24]

As the economic situation of cotton growers deteriorated, and as northern willingness to intervene on behalf of the freedpeople waned, their political strength diminished as well. Landowners violently repressed black collective action, increasingly reasserting their own political power. They captured control of state legislatures, and these newly constituted "redeemer" legislatures proceeded to disenfranchise black cotton growers, ensured that their children would be crippled by poor-quality schooling, and refused them access to legal protection. Landowners backed up their return to political dominance over the governmental institutions of the South with an unprecedented campaign of violence expressly designed to curtail cotton growers' political activities: Lynchings in the Mississippi Delta alone numbered a hundred between 1888 and 1930. For cotton merchants in Europe the planters' return to political power was welcome news, Baring Brothers London receiving a telegram on September 16, 1874, from the New Orleans firm Forstall and Sons, "State government overturned by people conservative officers in power."

As landowners secured more political power, they moved quickly to control African-American labor. When post-Reconstruction redeemer legislatures altered lien laws to give landlords a primary claim on the cotton crop, indebted freedpeople sank to a state of dependency without even the little bargaining power their sharehold had once provided. Another blow came when legislators modified "criminal law to make plantation workers susceptible to arrest, conviction, and prison sentence [for indebtedness], stripping sharecroppers of rights to growing crops, thereby reducing them to the legal equivalent of wage workers, and curtailing customary rights to the bounty of nature." In 1872, the Georgia state supreme court went so far as "den[ying] croppers decision-making prerogatives and legal rights to their growing crops." Indeed, increasingly the courts defined sharecroppers not so much as tenants but as wage workers. Simultaneously, landowners used the machinery of the state to limit the mobility of labor. In 1904, for example, the Mississippi state legislature enacted a new vagrancy law aimed at driving "negro loafers to the field." The relationship between landlords and rural cultivators might

Sharecroppers in a cotton field, Louisiana, 1920

have been fundamentally different from what it had been during slavery, but by the turn of the century, cotton growers still lived in grinding poverty with few rights and no political voice.[25]

Ironically, at the same time that landlords consolidated their regional power, they themselves experienced what historian Steven Hahn describes as a "rather dramatic and irreversible decline in power" within the national economy. Bound to worsening cotton prices, faced with protectionist tariffs for products they consumed, and plagued by the scarcity and high cost of capital, they became junior partners in the political economy of domestic industrialization that had emerged during the Civil War. Globally, this group of cotton growers was never as powerful as the merchants, but prior to the Civil War they had enjoyed regional political control and very significant national political influence. But now power decisively moved away from raw material providers such as them. Though they did not know it at the time, the Civil War had disempowered the world's last politically powerful group of cotton growers. From the vantage point of cotton manufacturers, this marginalization stabilized the empire of cotton, making the recurrence of the kind of upheaval that had emerged in defense of slavery quite unlikely.[26]

If slaves-turned-sharecroppers produced ever more cotton for world markets, so did the white yeoman farmers of the upcountry South. During slavery, little cotton had been produced by white yeoman farmers, who typically grew subsistence crops. Yet after the war the situation changed: In areas where cotton production had once been marginal, and in which households relied on subsistence crops and household manufacturing for their livelihood, growing cotton became the order of the day. In the majority white farms of the Georgia upcountry, for example, the amount of cotton produced per thousand bushels of corn—a subsistence crop—tripled between 1860 and 1880.[27]

What explains this expansion of cotton production by yeoman farmers? In the wake of the war, transportation, communications, and selling facilities spread rapidly into formerly isolated areas of the South. Railroad mileage in Georgia had, for instance, tripled during the 1870s. The infrastructural penetration of new cotton-growing territories transformed the countryside. With the railroads came stores and merchants, as well as ginning and pressing facilities. Yeoman farmers, devastated by the war, now raised cotton to gain access to cash. As merchants moved into even

Cotton production by white farmers increased dramatically: "Six-year-old Warren Frakes. Mother said he picked 41 pounds yesterday 'An I don't make him pick; he picked some last year.' Has about 20 pounds in his bag. Comanche County, Oklahoma."

the smallest hinterland towns, yeoman farmers could easily sell that cotton, while at the same time enjoying broader access to manufactured goods, fertilizers, and, importantly, credit. "Such credit was important to recover from the effects of the war," observed a German social scientist in 1906, "but once enmeshed in the credit system, farmers were also forced to grow ever more cotton, because merchants would only place liens against a crop that could be easily sold." Many white farmers lost their farms as a result, and by 1880 one-third of them rented the land they worked on. In effect, the capitalist transformation of yeoman farmers made them more like their black sharecropping brethren: Increasingly these whites lost control of the only things they owned—their land and their subsistence crops. Yet their shift in crops was exceedingly important to the global cotton economy. White yeoman farmers had produced at most 17 percent of all U.S. cotton before the Civil War; by 1880 their share had increased to 44 percent.[28]

While white yeoman farmers and former slaves grew the vast majority of southern cotton, they were not alone. A scattered group of planters appealed "to see German and Chinese Immigrants" brought to the South and in the early twentieth century, efforts were made to bring Italian immigrants to the Mississippi Delta. A few immigrant workers did end up working for wages on Louisiana cotton plantations, but they never became a major part of the workforce, as much more lucrative opportunities beckoned immigrants in other parts of the Americas. More important as a source of labor were leased convicts. James Monroe Smith's twenty-thousand-acre plantation in Oglethorpe County, Georgia, for example, which produced annually three thousand bales of cotton by 1904, counted many convicts among its more than one thousand workers. Previously, Smith's constant problem had been labor recruitment and in 1879 he had found a solution by investing in the Penitentiary Company Three, set up to rent convicts throughout the state. As a one-quarter owner of that company, Smith had access to one-quarter of its convicts. In addition, Smith employed convicts from local jails. These workers were treated with great violence, shot dead if they tried to escape. So harsh was the treatment that Smith was eventually the subject of a state inquiry and an 1886 letter writer to the *Cartersville Courant* accused him of severely whipping convicts, noting that some prisoners received as many as 225 lashes—a charge he denied.[29]

As Smith's example shows, the mobilization of labor for cotton grow-

Controlling labor: prisoners on Parchman Farm, Mississippi, c. 1930

ing in the United States went hand in hand with coercion. The degree of violence was in some ways surprising, considering that freedpeople's transition to proletarian agricultural labor was much easier to effect than that of Indian or African rural cultivators, who enjoyed a greater degree of control over land and their labor. Yet the violence descending upon the countryside of the U.S. South testified in an indirect way to the enormously powerful desire of freedpeople for a different way of life and was as much a sign of the weakness of landowners as their strength. It took the determined initiative of landowners in alliance with the state to guarantee that rural cultivators' efforts at building subsistence-oriented economies were undermined and their labor deployed for the production of agricultural commodities for world markets. Few observers in 1865 had expected such a spectacularly successful transition away from slavery and toward new systems of labor—a transition that filled with hope the hearts of imperial statesmen and metropolitan cotton manufacturers the world over.[30]

As struggles on plantations, in statehouses, and in the halls of power in Washington, D.C., determined labor regimes in the cotton-growing regions of the South, Reconstruction resulted in a rapid, vast, and permanent increase in the production of cotton for world markets in the United States. American rural cultivators recovered, despite all predictions to the contrary, their position as the world's leading producers of raw cotton. By 1870 their total production had surpassed their previous high, set in 1860. By 1877 they had regained their prewar market share in Great Britain. By 1880 they exported more cotton than they had in 1860. And by 1891 sharecroppers, family farmers, and plantation owners in the United States grew twice as much cotton as in 1861 and supplied 81 percent of the British, 66 percent of the French, and 61 percent of the German market. So successful was the reconstruction of cotton growing in the United States that it came to be seen by imperial bureaucrats and capitalists everywhere as a model. Imperialists of all stripes and colors, from Great Britain to Germany to Japan, studied the United States to draw lessons for their own cotton-growing projects, and American cotton growers became sought-after experts, advising colonial governments on the transition to commercial cotton production.[31]

The emergence of new forms of cotton-growing labor in the United States was, in the wake of the emancipation of the world's preeminent cotton growers, the single most important change within the empire of cotton. Yet in other parts of the world, partly encouraged by the crisis of cotton production in the United States, manufacturers, merchants, and bureaucrats accelerated the transformation of the countryside that had already begun during the Civil War, though by varied methods and with divergent results. Thanks to their activities, between 1865 and 1920 several million sharecroppers, wage workers, and peasant operators in Asia, Africa, and the Americas began to grow the white gold for the spinning mills of Europe and North America, and by the turn of the century, for factories in Japan, India, Brazil, and China as well.

In the last decades of the nineteenth century it was India that experienced the most dramatic expansion of cotton production for world markets. Indeed, at the end of the Civil War in the United States, the Bombay Chamber of Commerce had already observed that the "emancipation of American slaves [was] a matter of paramount importance" for the future of India's cotton industry, signifying a permanent change in the social structure of a large swath of the Indian countryside and in the trade of India. While Indian rural producers were not able to hold on to their dominant position in world cotton markets after the war (especially after 1876), their production for export still rose rapidly, expanding from 260 million pounds in 1858 to nearly 1.2 billion pounds in 1914. Export merchants, however, no longer sold most of this much larger crop to manufacturers in India's two traditional markets—Great Britain and China—but instead found buyers in continental Europe and, after the turn of the century, among Japanese spinners. By 1910, only 6 percent of Indian cotton exports went to Great Britain, while Japan consumed 38 percent, and continental Europe 50 percent. Continental and Japanese manufacturers, in contrast to their British counterparts, had adjusted their machines to work up the shorter Indian staple, successfully mixing Indian with American cotton, producing coarser cloth. As a result, in the thirty years after 1860, continental European consumption of Indian cotton increased sixty-two-fold, "a substantial help," as the Bremen Chamber of Commerce put it in 1913. To supply these needs, cotton acreage in India expanded, and by the late 1880s in some areas of India (such as Berar) one-third of all land was under cotton. This expansion of export occurred simultaneously with an explosion in the number of mechanized spindles in India itself. Indeed, by 1894, less than 50 percent of the Indian cotton harvest was exported, as Indian cotton mills consumed about 518 million pounds of cotton and an additional 224 to 336 million pounds were used in hand spinning.[32]

While Indian cotton played an important role in the coarse goods market, Brazilian cotton matched the quality of the U.S. crop much better. As a result, in Brazil cotton exports expanded in the last third of the nineteenth century. During the 1850s they had averaged 32.4 million pounds per year. During the following three decades, Brazil exported an average of 66.7 million pounds of cotton annually—despite the simultaneous growth of domestic cotton manufacturing by a factor of fifty-three. In 1920, Brazil produced 220 million pounds of cotton, of which it exported one-quarter.[33]

Meanwhile in Egypt, fellaheen had quintupled their cotton production between 1860 and 1865 from 50.1 million to 250.7 million pounds. To be sure, Egyptian cotton was of much higher quality than much of the U.S. crop; it was, as Roger Seyrig, a French cotton manufacturer observed, "an article of luxury." After the U.S. Civil War, its production at first fell significantly to about 125 million pounds, but by 1872 merchants shipped again more than 200 million pounds from the port of Alexandria to European destinations. Even during the post–Civil War trough of cotton production, Egypt's output was still two and a half times as large as it had been before the Civil War. And by 1920, it produced 598 million pounds of cotton, or twelve times as much as in 1860. A full 40 percent of all land in Lower Egypt was planted in cotton. To some, Egypt now seemed like a giant cotton plantation.[34]

By the last third of the nineteenth century, Egyptian, Brazilian, and Indian cotton had become a significant new presence on world markets. In 1883, cotton from these regions had captured a full 31 percent of the (now much larger) continental European market, or a little more than twice as much as in 1860.[35]

The expansion of cotton growing on multiple continents was all the more remarkable because it happened without slavery. The problem that had vexed cotton capitalists since the 1820s, namely how to make non-enslaved rural cultivators into growers of cotton for world markets, moved toward a resolution that seemed to please the interests of European and North American cotton manufacturers and statesmen. Yet, as in the American South, which in many ways came to serve as a model of how such a transition could be effected, the precise ways in which rural cultivators became growers of cotton for world markets varied widely and were the outcome of drawn-out conflicts among labor, landowners, providers of capital, and imperial bureaucrats.

What all these struggles to recast the global countryside had in common was that states now played an important role. New forms of coercion, instituted and carried out by the state, replaced the outright physical violence of masters that had been so important to slave labor. This does not mean that physical violence was absent, but it was secondary compared to the pressures that came from contracts, the law, and taxation. As states developed new sovereignty over territory they also extended their sovereignty over labor, testifying to the new institutional strength of industrial capitalism.

Khamgaon was a small city, a town really, in Berar, the center of the large western Indian district that had long been renowned for the quality of its cottons. Decades before the arrival of the British, some of this cotton had been exported on bullock carts to Mirzapore on the Ganges and then shipped to Calcutta, but farmers never specialized exclusively in the fiber and grew many other things as well, while also engaging in spinning and weaving. Indeed, the trade in "raw thread" spun locally had dwarfed the trade in raw cotton. Things began to change by 1825 with the rise of an export market in raw cotton, when the Parsi merchants Messrs. Pestanji and Company brought the first cotton on "pack oxen" to Bombay. Dissatisfied with the slow expansion of that trade, Britain assumed political control over Berar in 1853—a position that served Lancashire manufacturers well when during the American Civil War Berar became "one of the very finest cotton fields in India."[36]

As the British colonial administration and Lancashire manufacturers saw the potential of Berar as a major cotton-growing area, and upon the urgings of British manufacturers, the colonial state completed in 1870 a railroad to Khamgaon (paid for by Berar's "surplus revenue"), which now had an estimated nine thousand inhabitants. "The last obstacle has been removed, and for the future direct communication by steam exists between this the largest emporium of cotton in Western India and the ports of Europe, which will take every bale that can be brought into its market," celebrated Mr. C. B. Saunders, the British resident at Hyderabad. When the railroad arrived in Khamgaon, none other than the viceroy himself spoke at the opening celebration, a day on which "the Court House, the Factories, the Cotton Market, and every prominent point were gaily decked with flags." He reminded his listeners, many of whom were cotton merchants, that "we all know that the cotton famine in America had a great deal to do in stimulating the development and production of cotton in this country." Such new production for world markets, he argued, not only benefited the development of India itself, but was also "conferring vast benefits on a class which at a very recent period, in a time of great suffering and distress, displayed almost heroic qualities"—the operatives in the cotton manufacturing districts of Lancashire. Symbolizing the centrality of cotton to the colonial project in Berar, the viceroy eventually "drove to the cotton market, in which a monster triumphal arch, composed chiefly of cotton bales, had been erected" in his and the new railroad's honor.[37]

With the railroad came the telegraph. Now a Liverpool merchant could wire an order for cotton to Berar and receive it on the docks of the Mersey just six weeks later, the journey on a steamer from Bombay to Liverpool accomplished in twenty-one days thanks to the newly opened Suez Canal.[38] The impact of such infrastructure projects was staggering, with Berar cotton commissioner Harry Rivett-Carnac expecting that soon

the cotton grown around Khamgaon, purchased at the market there, and pressed at the adjoining factories, may not have to

leave the rails, from the time that it is rolled from the press-house
into the wagon, until its arrival on the wharf at Bombay; and
it will not be difficult to calculate the time that will be necessary, with the assistance of the telegraph which joins Khamgaon
and Liverpool, the complete railway communication between
the market and the port of shipment, and with, perhaps, the
Suez Canal to assist still further in the transport of our cotton,
to execute an order sent from Liverpool and to land the required
number of Khamgaon bales in Lancashire.[39]

British India might indeed be considered the archetype for the flexible pragmatism by which states helped capitalists gain access to cotton-
growing labor, and how capitalists then found ways to mobilize that
labor. Pushed by Lancashire manufacturers and cotton merchants from
Liverpool to Bombay, the British colonial government in India continued its project, which had accelerated significantly during the U.S. Civil
War, of promoting the transformation of the cotton-growing countryside. The impact was swift: As late as 1853, Berar had remained largely
removed from world markets, with a village-oriented economy with a
substantial household manufacturing sector. By the 1870s, however,
much of Berar's economic activity focused on the production of raw cotton for world markets. A British colonial official observed by the middle
of that decade that in Berar, "Cotton is grown almost entirely for export.
The manufacture of home cloth has been undermined by the importation of English Piece Goods, and many of the weaver class have become
ordinary labourers." This reorientation of the local economy also pushed
people into agricultural labor, as for example the *banjaras* (traditional
owners of carts who had transported cotton), and weavers as well as spinners, found themselves out of employment and increasingly dependent
on agricultural pursuits. Indeed, forty years later a gazetteer could report
that Berar's once thriving cotton manufacturing industry had all but disappeared "since the advent of the railway."[40] As Rivett-Carnac explained
in 1869,

Now it is not too much to hope, that, with a branch railway
to this tract, European piece goods might be imported so as to
undersell the native cloth. And the effect would be, that, not
only would a larger supply of the raw material be obtained,—for
what is now worked up into yarn would be exported,—but the

large population now employed in spinning and weaving would be made available for agricultural labour, and thus the jungle land might be broken up and the cultivation extended.

For Secretary of State for India Charles Wood, such changes to the Indian social structure produced a sense of déjà vu: "The conclusions drawn from the Cotton papers are on the whole satisfactory. The Native weavers are exactly the class of people whom I remember in my early days on the Moor Edges in the West Riding. Every small farmer had 20 to 50 acres of land, and two or three looms in his house. The factories and mills destroyed all weaving of this kind, and now they are exclusively agriculturalists. Your Indian hybrids [that is, people who combined farming with household manufacturing] will end in the same way." Contemporaries like Wood understood that they were part of a grand move to transform the world's countryside into the producer of raw materials and consumer of manufactured goods (as well as, eventually, a supplier of labor to factories), and they took pride in their role.[41]

Altogether, Berar became one of the world's most significant laboratories for the reconstruction of the empire of cotton. Its diversified agricultural economy was turned into ever greater specialization on cotton crops. As *The Asiatic* reflected in 1872, "A pressure unknown before was put upon the people to grow cotton." While in 1861 cotton was harvested on 629,000 acres of land in Berar, that acreage had nearly doubled by 1865, and then doubled once more by the 1880s. By the early twentieth century, Berar alone produced one-quarter of the Indian cotton harvest—a harvest larger than that of all of Egypt. As one observer put it, Berar had "become a perfect garden of cotton."[42]

In Egypt, as in India and the United States, the expansion of cotton agriculture was a direct result of the powerful interventions of the state. A redefinition of property rights in the last third of the nineteenth century made possible a massive redistribution of land away from villages and nomadic peoples to the well-connected owners of huge estates. Before that transformation, property in Egypt provided the right to shares of the revenue of the land, which meant that ownership claims to particular pieces of land were usually shared among various individuals, communities, religious authorities, and the state.[43] Such multifaceted claims effectively hindered the purchase and sale of land; by the later decades of the nineteenth century such property rights stood in the way of a further commercialization of agriculture.

As a result, the Egyptian government, motivated by its desire to extract more taxes to pay for the expansion of the nation's infrastructure and the mushrooming service on its enormous debt, as well as its desire to better control its people, moved toward conferring property rights in very large estates to well-placed individuals. At first these estates were merely "tax responsibilities" of their owners, but by the 1870s they became their outright private property, much of which consisted of land taken, usually forcibly, from villages. Now that the cotton-growing estates increasingly were held as the outright property of large landowners, the villagers who once had controlled some of the revenue of the land, and some rights of settlement, fell entirely on the mercy of these landowners. These new estate owners could force peasants to live in special "private villages" that controlled most aspects of their lives. Those cultivators who did not do what was asked of them were expelled, joining the ever-growing ranks of the landless agricultural proletariat.[44]

The rights of the new owners were far-reaching, including their ability to "imprison, expel, starve, exploit, and exercise many other forms of arbitrary, exceptional, and, if necessary, violent powers." As a result, these estates represented a "system of supervision and coercion that succeeded for the first time in fixing cultivators permanently on the land." To make land into the exclusive possession of single individuals had required what political scientist Timothy Mitchell has described as the "violence of property making." These new property rights spread rapidly: In 1863, estate owners controlled one-seventh of the cultivated land area of Egypt, by 1875 almost twice as much, and by 1901 a full 50 percent.[45] In 1895, just 11,788 individuals held nearly half of all lands in Egypt, while the other half was held by 727,047 proprietors. Some of these estates were huge; Ibrahim Mourad, for example, controlled thirteen thousand acres in Toukh, worked by twenty thousand cultivators, dwarfed only by the mammoth estates that Egypt's ruler, Isma'il Pasha, had personally seized.[46]

As elsewhere, the transformation of the Egyptian cotton-growing countryside rested on a vast pyramid of credit. At the bottom, workers on cotton estates were almost always in debt to moneylenders and landowners, constantly threatened by debt bondage. Landowners, in turn, received credit from local merchants, many of them foreigners. The largest landowner of all, Isma'il, accumulated such debts that in 1878, in the wake of falling cotton prices, he signed over his estates to his creditors, the Rothschilds. At the same time, the Egyptian state took out massive loans to finance the digging of irrigation canals (largely by resorting to forced labor), the building of railroads, and the import of steam pumps. So staggering were the amounts borrowed that the state eventually went bankrupt, despite ever greater pressure on the Egyptian people to produce for export markets. That debt brought Egypt as a whole into the arms of the British: With diminishing proceeds from cotton, Egypt could not service its debt, lost sovereign control, and was eventually taken over by the British government in 1882.[47]

As the examples of Egypt and India show, by the last third of the nineteenth century, rulers and bureaucrats played a critical role in the effort to further cotton growing for world markets. They did so partly because their own power rested on access to resources and was made more stable by the relative social peace that came from humming mills. But they also acted at the behest of powerful capitalists—either because rulers and capitalists were largely the same group of elites, as in the case of Egypt, or because statesmen were subject to concerted lobbying and political pressure, such as in the case of Britain and France and, as we will see, Germany.

States' desire to mobilize cotton-growing labor now led to unprecedented claims upon their subjects, as states increasingly defined and enforced the rules of the market. From Berar to the Nile Delta to Minas Gerais, governments and courts undermined older collective claims to resources such as grazing and hunting rights, forcing peasants to dedicate themselves single-mindedly to the production of cotton. Berar's natural landscape, for example, was turned upside down by a vast British effort to survey the land, followed by the encouragement of the British to turn so called "waste lands" into cotton farms. "Waste lands" once had been open to the collective use of farmers, but now increasingly were turned into private property. In the process, extensive forests that traditionally had been the source of firewood and wild foods were logged, and grasslands put under the plow that had in earlier times served as communal grazing lands. Logging further reduced the forests to feed the steam presses of Western merchants in the major Berar cotton towns. In some parts of the world, such deforestation led to significantly altered patterns of rainfall, undermining the very colonial cotton craze that had incited deforestation in the first place.[48]

Court-enforced lien laws, moreover, gave creditors another means to undermine peasants' claims to the land and enmesh them further in a quagmire of debt, which forced them to grow ever more cotton. The systems of mutual dependence and personal domination that had characterized the countryside of Berar, the American South, and elsewhere before the U.S. Civil War gave way to a world in which creditors backed by the state turned rural cultivators into producers and consumers of commodities. As an anonymous British writer on Indian cotton explained, "Where there is no intelligent population to lead the way, a Government must do what in more civilized countries can safely be left to private enterprise."⁴⁹

The creation of private property in land became yet another state-led project, in India and elsewhere. British cotton manufactures, demanding that the colonial government "set its colonial house in order," called for new forms of land tenure, as they perceived the old system of communal ownership as "obstructive to the rights of individual ownership, and to its effective cultivation." They saw private property in land as a precondition for increasing production of cotton. Individuals were to gain clear title in land that then could be bought, sold, rented, or mortgaged. These new property rights were quite a departure: In precolonial Berar, for example, relations between various social groups had been characterized by a "master-servant relationship of social status in the caste hierarchy" in which "the produce of the soil . . . was divided according to social ranking." Individuals did not control particular pieces of land, but instead enjoyed rights to a share of the harvest. A British colonial official perceptively compared that "system, if system it may be called," to "medieval Europe." Once the British arrived on the scene, however, the land was surveyed, boundaries between various landowners clearly demarcated, and taxes on each parcel set. A class of *khatedars* was created who controlled the land, and in turn were made responsible for tax payments. By 1870, a British colonial official was able to report that the revolution was succeeding. In Berar "the occupant of land is its absolute proprietor." Because the *khatedars* owned land, but no capital, they were dependent on moneylenders, to whom they now were able to mortgage the land they controlled. To work the land, these *khatedars* brought in sharecroppers, who in turn received their working capital from moneylenders. There and elsewhere in India, it was the large landowners, and moneylenders, who drew significant profit from the extension of cotton culture for export, unlike the vast majority of small landholders or land-less peasants, who entered a morass of debt and poverty.[50]

With private property in land spreading throughout the global coun-tryside, landowners could now also be made responsible for the payment of taxes, to be paid in cash, which in turn encouraged the production of cash crops. In the Indian province of Maharashtra, as in Berar, British efforts to increase revenue and encourage peasants to produce for distant markets led to the weakening of the collective nature of villages. Individ-ual peasants, instead of villages as a whole, were now responsible for taxes. Moneylenders thereby gained new power over peasants' land and labor, as rural cultivators became dependent on advances to pay their taxes. In similar ways, in the Çukurova, the Ottoman state increasingly taxed local populations, and as a result, people had to engage in wage labor, or were forced to work on infrastructure projects. Cotton production benefited from their need for cash—just like in the United States—because "cotton is the one article," observed the Cotton Department in Bombay in 1877, "that always commands the readiest and best sales."[51]

While Indian cotton growers usually held on to their land, unlike freedpeople in the United States, they had to draw on advances not just for tax payments, but also to purchase implements, cottonseeds, and even grains to hold them over until harvest time. New contract laws allowed these same moneylenders to enjoy a modest security when mak-ing advances to peasants. New property rights in fact favored the com-mercialization of agriculture not just because they made for easier land transactions, but also because they allowed for the infusion of capital, for which the land itself could now serve as collateral. Cultivators paid exorbitant rates of interest on these loans (30 percent annually was not unusual), and in turn they signed over their cotton crop to moneylend-ers, usually many months before the harvest—creating what one histo-rian has called "debt bondage."[52]

Moneylenders—*sowkars*—had been deeply rooted in villages and had advanced credit to peasants for a long time before the arrival of the Brit-ish. However, they had been embedded within a moral economy that had forced them to support peasants in years of poor harvests, a lifeline that increasingly disappeared in the more commercialized economy that Brit-ish colonialism was building. While moneylenders could acquire modest wealth, and large landowners could benefit from the availability of capital (allowing them to focus on a cash crop with hired labor), small landholders, sharecroppers, and especially landless agricultural wage workers were most at risk. As prices for cotton continued to fall for nearly thirty years after the Civil War, this mass of "modernizing" farmers were thrust into more and more desperate circumstances; many of them would eventually perish in famines that swept the cotton-growing districts of India during the 1890s.[53]

New infrastructures, new laws, and new property rights invaded the global countryside on the trails of strengthening and expanding states, making the kind of transformations possible that still had been unimaginable a few decades earlier. State involvement in cotton was furthered in many other ways. Perhaps the most comprehensive endeavor was the systematic effort to collect and disseminate information about all aspects of cotton agriculture. Huge compilations about climate and soil conditions, production trends, patterns of land ownership, seed qualities, and labor systems increasingly filled governmental office files, much of the same information that in previous decades merchants had laboriously gathered and transmitted via letters or circulars. In part this was a straightforward effort to systematize and appropriate indigenous knowledge. Observing Indian peasants' efforts to grow cotton could yield useful information about best practices under specific environmental conditions, which could then be transferred to Africa or elsewhere. Similarly, specific strains of cotton could be collected and then sent to other parts of the world—indeed, governments enabled a vastly accelerated circulation of biological matter throughout the world. But more important than either of these two tasks was a very simple effort to take stock—to observe what was there in the social and natural world, to translate that information into numbers, force it into tables, compile it, and then send it out throughout the empire of cotton. These numbers clarified the "potential" of certain places and suggested certain policies to actualize that potential.[54]

Throughout the cotton-growing world, governments embarked on such efforts. In 1866, the colonial government of India created the "Cotton Commissioner for the Central Provinces and the Berars," a colonial bureaucrat who collected scrupulously detailed information on cotton-growing regions. Harry Rivett-Carnac, an intrepid agent of the cotton empire's expansion, came to fill this position, traveling up and down Berar, living in a railroad carriage with an attached "horse-box, so that I could, whenever necessary, ride off to some important point in the district where my presence was required," all to "extend and improve the cultivation in order to increase the supply; then to undertake all necessary measures to assist the trade in getting these supplies to the coast in good order and without delay." The revolutionary transformation of the world's countryside rested on the shoulders of such government bureaucrats. By 1873, the Indian government expanded these activities and centralized them by creating a Fibres and Silk Branch that studied the production of cotton, among other fibers, throughout India in exacting detail.[55]

Other countries followed suit. The United States in 1862 established a Department of Agriculture, which soon began to work on cotton. The department first collected statistical information, but soon broadened its activities by studying diseases affecting the cotton plant, trying to identify cotton strains particularly suited for particular environmental conditions, and breeding improved cotton strains. The department also applied itself to the pressing question of how cotton could be grown in western states such as Arizona. In 1897, Russia created an Administration of Agriculture and State Domains in its newly acquired Central Asian possessions, whose focus was cotton. In Egypt, the government provided detailed information about agricultural best practices to cotton farmers and by 1919 created a ministry of agriculture to expand on these efforts—a model later studied and appropriated by the Belgian colonial authorities in the Congo.[56]

The collection of information went hand in hand with governmental efforts to recast cotton agriculture directly: British colonial officials distributed American cottonseeds to Indian peasants, worked on changing Indian cotton strains, and encouraged peasants to use new agricultural methods. The Egyptian Société Royale d'Agriculture experimented with model farms. Local peasants often resisted such projects, for not only was the planting of new cotton strains more labor-intensive, but it was also riskier because they had not been proven in the local climate. Few projects provided increased remuneration to offset these burdens, and it took powerful pressures to make them succeed.[57]

Despite working in concert, powerful governments and capital-rich merchants and landowners did not always accomplish their grand projects. Government records are replete with efforts of rural cultivators to delay, or even halt, the reordering of their economies. In Dhawar in western India, for example, peasants retained a strong preference for growing indigenous varieties of cotton, and also for privileging food crops, despite sustained efforts by British colonial officials to introduce American varieties. Local varieties were much better adapted to the local climate, commanded a ready local market, and fit better into the household economies because they could be ginned locally.[58] Sudanese peasants, as the Austrian consul general reported from Khartoum in 1877, refused to grow increasing amounts of cotton because "the native searches and finds his means of subsistence in much easier ways and in less taxing occupations than the difficult and relatively unprofitable cultivation of the soil." In Iraq, a German observer remarked in 1919 that "the awakening of a greater willingness to labor is prevented by the presence of cultures in the country which provide the laborer effortlessly everything he needs for nourishment and for all other necessities"—an argument made by colonial officials the world over. In Burma, a British bureaucrat regretfully observed "the indifference shown to cotton-growing as a paying industry by the Burmese peasantry themselves, who look upon it as of very secondary importance and are not likely to take much interest in cotton while they can make, with much less trouble, handsome profits in their paddy crops."[59]

The significance of these struggles can perhaps best be seen in an area where production failed, despite decisive efforts: Australia. Starting in the early twentieth century, the British colonial administration made efforts to grow cotton in a continent with virtually unlimited supplies of land perfectly suited for cotton agriculture. Despite these efforts, cotton production expanded only slowly. The *Adelaide Advertiser* understood the reasons well: While abundant land was suitable for the growing of cotton, what was missing was cheap labor to plant, hoe, and harvest the crop. The chief difficulty facing any sort of expansion, reported the Advisory Committee of Science and Industry, "is the high cost of picking by hand." Because of the shortage of cheap labor, and because white settlers had options far better than cotton, the committee observed in 1918 that "cotton growing in Australia is now practically extinct." Theo Price, president of the New York Price-Campbell Cotton Picker Corporation, advising the government of Australia on such matters in 1917, understood the reasons perfectly: "Cotton culture is largely a matter of labor. Unless you can be assured of an abundant supply of labor, it is going to be difficult to cultivate cotton on anything like a large scale. I do not know what your immigration laws in Australia are but if you can bring the Chinese in . . . I think [it may] be practicable to develop cotton growing rapidly."

"Labor conditions," concluded the *Sydney Evening News* in 1920, "are not conducive to the establishment of the cotton industry on an economic basis." Without access to abundant cheap labor, the cotton market could not be satiated.[60]

Yet despite such setbacks, cotton capitalists sought labor, and ever more of it. In the cotton-growing regions of India, Brazil, and Egypt, as in the United States, the empire of cotton expanded as landowners, colonial bureaucrats, merchants, and local political elites such as the landlords of the American South were able to turn rural cultivators into producers and consumers of commodities.[61] The precise arrangements found to mobilize their labor differed from place to place because they depended on the relative local, regional, or colonial distribution of social power.[62] Industrial capitalism's great strength derived exactly from its continued ability to connect to different systems of labor, and especially to draw on the extraordinary cheapness of production made possible by the incomplete transformation of the world of rural cultivators, a world in which family labor often remained uncompensated and subsistence was to some extent still produced within households. Local and regional circumstances encrusted in traditions and the distribution of social power shaped the emerging labor arrangements. It mattered, for example, that cotton growers in the United States enjoyed access to the franchise for a little more than two decades (limiting the political power of landowners), just as it mattered that economies in Africa remained vibrant and largely independent of European capital. As a result, some rural cultivators turned into sharecroppers, others into renters, and again others into wage workers. Even as their power and traditional way of life was steadily stripped away, they still maintained some influence—indeed, they still had more sway over their daily lives than the millions of unskilled workers laboring in spinning and weaving mills.[63]

Rural cultivators, landowners, merchants, and bureaucrats struggled over the shape of the new empire of cotton and the forms of labor within it, constrained by the startling imbalances of power in particular locales and the unequal relationship between various parts of the world. By the end of the nineteenth century, sharecropping and tenant farming had become the dominant mode of mobilizing labor for similar reasons that they dominated in the United States: Rural cultivators preferred the autonomy of working without day-to-day supervision, and they generally resisted being turned into wage workers. In Berar, sharecropping tenants worked the land of *khatedar* landowners, receiving their working capital from moneylenders. In Egypt, most of the crop was grown not by "hired labor," but instead by "small occupiers themselves," some sharecroppers, some owners, all of whom were able to draw upon the labor of their families; indeed, most cotton in Egypt was picked by children. In Brazil, sharecropping, along with small family farms, spread. On large estates tenant families "paid" for their land rent by giving a share of the crop to the owners. In Peru, landowners rented their land to cultivators in response to the closing of the trade in Chinese indentured workers in 1874 and their inability to attract peasants to work for wages. In the Çukurova, which had been largely unsettled before the advent of cotton agriculture toward the end of the nineteenth century, large-scale landholdings were in need of labor, and most of that labor was recruited through sharecropping arrangements along with some migrant wage laborers.[64]

Wherever sharecropping prevailed, tenant farmers as well as small owner-operators became dependent on outside capital. In Sind, India, for example, peasants sold the crop to moneylenders as soon as they had sown it, to pay for loans they had received to enable them to focus on cotton in the first place, "in part being hard cash, part grain, and cotton seed, cloth, bajri, flour & c. for the family and workmen." Moneylending merchants, there and elsewhere, often determined the farming decisions of peasants, since they were the ones who advanced seeds and implements. Interest rates between 12 and 24 percent were typical, but could skyrocket to as much as 150 percent annually. In the Çukurova sharecroppers drew on credit from landowners and merchants, who charged interest rates of 15 to 20 percent, and as a result, "Merchant capital, despite the limitations of labor scarcity, gained control over the land and the production process."[65]

Thus by the end of the nineteenth century most of the world's cotton would be grown by cultivators who worked their own or rented land with family labor, but instead of subsistence or local production, these cultivators would be drawn into the global cotton market by a novel infusion of metropolitan capital. Sharecropping, crop liens, and powerful local merchants in control of capital would quickly become the new normal, shaping a countryside of laborers who were not enslaved, but not quite free either. These cotton farmers, the world over, would be deeply enmeshed in debt, vulnerable to world market fluctuations, generally poor, and subject to newly created vagrancy statutes and labor contracts designed to keep them on the land. They would be politically marginalized. And they would often be subject to extraeconomic coercion. Such a system was not without precedent. But now, supercharged with private capital and the state's legal, administrative, and infrastructure advances, it began to structure the global cotton-growing countryside to an unprecedented extent.[66]

A small but growing number of rural cultivators, however, turned into poorly paid wage workers in the world's cotton fields. They were the least powerful. Often their descent into wage work had been the result of their worsening situation as highly indebted sharecroppers, tenants, or owners of small farms. Becoming a wage worker was a measure of their defeat. In Egypt, by 1907, nearly 40 percent of all agriculturalists had become landless laborers. In India as well, the number of wage workers on cotton lands tended to increase across the nineteenth century: In Khandesh, the greater orientation toward cotton agriculture and the attendant legal and social changes resulted in an ever-increasing percentage of land devoted to the white gold and a wave of proletarianization, so that by 1872 one in four adult men worked for wages.[67]

In northern Mexico too, proletarianization swept the cotton fields. After 1884, landowners in La Laguna made use of new railroads and a new irrigation infrastructure to build a huge cotton-growing complex, "making it Mexico's most important commercial agricultural area." Tens of thousands of workers populated the fields, some residing on plantations and others hired by the week or month, as the rural population, many of them migrants from elsewhere in Mexico, increased from twenty thousand to two hundred thousand between 1880 and 1910, with an additional forty thousand migrant workers arriving during harvest time. As a result, the cotton farms expanded at breakneck speed, increasing production by a factor of five in the ten years before 1890, and then doubling in the next decade. Some of these haciendas were extremely large. The Luján family, for example, owned forty-five thousand hectares. These industrial outposts were often highly mechanized, sporting presses, gins, and cotton oil mills.[68]

La Laguna cotton workers were as completely proletarianized as any in the world. Some plantations maintained a force of semiskilled workers, organized into gangs of eight to twelve, led by a foreman who took responsibility for cultivating specific lots. Some large haciendas had recruited several thousand such workers, who worked twelve hours a day six days a week. These workers joined the agricultural proletariat because they had lost their erstwhile communal access to the resources of the land due to the concentration of landownership. Many of these workers eventually arrived in La Laguna on private rail lines, packed like cattle in boxcars. Since there was no land available for these migrants, there was no possibility of engaging in subsistence agriculture.[69]

Instead, "The landlord's rule was law," observes one historian, as haciendas enforced labor discipline with the help of uniformed private police forces, jails, and the "physical punishment" of workers. Some plantations even built a *cepo de campaña*—a specially made "cage . . . to punish troublesome workers." Migrant workers were often supervised by armed guards stationed in the fields. The state helped to enforce labor discipline, with towns enacting "strict vagrancy laws to keep [those workers] outside the central area when they were not working." This resort to physical coercion was widespread in the world's cotton-growing areas and was important in the United States, Peru, Egypt, and elsewhere. Capitalism's awe-inspiring advances continued to rest not just on a great variety of labor regimes, but on a staggering degree of violence.[70]

Controlling labor: Armed guards secure cotton-picking labor in La Laguna, Mexico.

. . .

Within that reconstructed empire of cotton, the newly empowered states of Europe and North America were everywhere. After all, the capitalists' project of accumulation by securing labor and the bureaucrats' project of state formation by controlling populations evolved hand in hand.[71] In their struggles at home, in the heartlands of industrial capitalism, cotton capitalists had learned that to transform the countryside, to transform society, they must reinforce their wealth with state power. Enabled by the new bureaucratic, legal, military, and infrastructural capacity of states, a capacity that had directly grown from the wages of war capitalism, manufacturers and merchants incorporated ever more people and ever more areas of the world into the global economy in general, and in the production of cotton for world markets in particular.

By the late nineteenth century, the dynamics of industrial capitalism had accelerated to such an extent that capitalists and statesmen made a concerted effort to speed up the collapse of noncapitalist social formations, or at the very least to connect them to the capitalist world market. To break the reluctance of people to embrace these new and revolutionary arrangements of work and social relations, they at times embraced coercion. They were unwilling to wait, as cotton manufacturer Henry Ashworth had put it so well in front of the Manchester Chamber of Commerce in 1863, "until price has done it." For labor to be turned into a commodity, workers had to be "liberated" from the matrix of mutual obligations that had historically sustained them. They believed, at the same time, that land had to be "liberated" from noneconomic ties and made into a freely marketable commodity. This "liberation" rested ideologically on the naturalizing of certain historically specific ways of organizing production, and was thus enabled by economic, social, cultural, and even racial hierarchies it had helped to produce. Capitalists were the age's true revolutionaries.[72]

Rulers and bureaucrats supported this project because securing access to raw materials, including extracting cotton, became increasingly a touchstone of national politics. As they consolidated their states, the rearrangement of global economic connections in fact became a project they deliberately embarked upon—indeed, the late-nineteenth-century acceleration of global economic integration went hand in hand with a strengthening and consolidation of nation-states themselves. Powerful states, rulers, and bureaucrats depended on strong national industries, which in turn depended on raw materials and markets—for such industries produced wealth that could be taxed, and provided employment for millions, all of which in turn increased social stability and further strengthened the state.[73]

The construction of markets, including global markets, was thus a political process. As more and more states competed for access to raw materials, labor, and markets, this political process was ever more framed by nation-states. National economies, empires, and national capitalists became increasingly the basic building blocks of the new global political economy. As the colonial world became an important supplier of raw materials and a significant market for some industries (up to 60 percent of British cotton goods exports, for example, went to India and the Far East), industrial capitalism took on a new cast, with states securing political control over territories that provided raw materials and markets. One-quarter of the globe "was distributed or redistributed as colonies" between 1876 and 1915, testifying to the rapidly growing importance of bounded territory. Statesmen and capitalists in effect fused their respective goals of power and accumulation, and in the process forged an entirely new form of capitalist globalization. The methods of industrial capitalism, developed in the world of factory production in England and elsewhere, now went global, increasingly replacing the true-and-tried methods of war capitalism.[74]

Ironically, the project to strengthen newly consolidating nation-states and "national" economies increasingly also became an international project, best symbolized by the international cotton congresses that met regularly starting after 1905, bringing together merchants, manufacturers, planters, and bureaucrats in places such as Manchester, Vienna, Paris, Brussels, Milan, London, Stockholm, and Alexandria. By 1927, seventeen countries participated. They discussed cotton-growing conditions in various parts of the world, and tried to identify best practices. They also reviewed exemplary efforts to increase cotton production, discussing, for example, in great detail the German experiences with cotton agriculture in colonial Togo. The congresses were part and parcel of a global discourse among capitalists and bureaucrats on how to reconcile the needs of metropolitan economies for cheap and plentiful agricultural commodities from the periphery with new forms of labor. In Paris, the experts at the Ministry of Colonies constituted a commission aptly named the

"Commission du Régime du Travail aux Colonies," in Berlin and Chicago budding social scientists explored the possibilities of "free labor" regimes in securing access to agricultural commodities, and the Spanish ambassador to Paris asked the French minister of the colonies to report on the French experience with emancipation and its effect on labor supply. The British colonial authorities in Bombay inquired into the mobilization of labor in Russian Central Asia. And in the 1910s, the Japanese Ministry of Agriculture and Commerce, set on expanding cotton production in colonial Korea, investigated the efforts of European nations to use "free labor" for the growing of cotton in their colonial possession. Postcolonial and postcapitalist regimes, as we will see, were just as eager to learn from these experiences, and often implemented these lessons with an eager radicalism that overshadowed even their teachers' revolutionary designs. As competitive nation-states strengthened in a few regions of the world, they shared a burning wish to reconstruct the global countryside, and embedded their policies in strategies transcending any particular nation-state. Again, state formation and globalization unfolded hand in glove.[75]

And while the dilemmas of "free labor" would remain central to global conversations, by the 1870s, from the perspective of cotton capitalists, the crisis of the empire of cotton that had emerged from the emancipation of cotton growing workers had been resolved. The newfound ability of capitalists and states to transform the global cotton-growing countryside with the tools of industrial capitalism allowed for ever more cotton to arrive at ever cheaper prices in the ports of Liverpool, Bremen, Le Havre, Osaka, and Boston. So successful was the recombination of labor, land, capital, and state power that cotton prices in Liverpool not only returned to pre–Civil War levels, but fell further. In 1870, a pound of cotton in the United States had cost 24 cents; in 1894, that price had fallen to just 7 cents—below its cost before the Civil War (when it was about 11 cents.) In response, the Manchester Cotton Supply Association, which had been at the forefront of much of the push to make peasants the world over into cotton growers for export, disbanded in 1872. The defeat of the economic and political aspirations of freedpeople in the American South and the successful inventions of new systems of labor there and elsewhere had inspired confidence that the revolutionary activities of capital would continue to succeed in recasting the global countryside.[76]

Chapter Eleven

Destructions

Cotton merchants in India.

The rapid expansion of industrial capitalism after 1865, as we have seen, transformed even more of the global countryside. Manufacturers in the industrial heartlands of cotton's empire demanded raw material, labor, and markets, and their voracity was felt by the majority of humanity who lived far from the urban centers of Europe and North America. With the abolition of slavery in the United States, cultivators in India, Egypt, the American South, Brazil, and, a few decades later, West Africa and Central Asia found themselves drawn into new systems of labor, producing vast and increasing quantities of cotton. Thanks to their backbreaking and ill-remunerated labor, well into the twentieth century trade in cotton and cotton goods "was still by far the largest single trade" in both the Atlantic world and Asia. Even as late as the 1930s, the Japanese cotton traders of

Toyo Menka Kaisha asserted that "cotton is indisputably the prime commodity in the international trade of the world."[1]

In more general terms, the emergence of new systems of labor and the stunning increase in raw cotton output pointed to one of the most revolutionary projects of industrial capitalism, the creation of a new relationship between manufacturing centers and the countryside. By the 1870s, as we have seen, capitalists had done what a few decades earlier seemed impossible: fully integrated an ever larger swath of the global countryside into serving the needs of industrial production without drawing on the institution of slavery. The reason for this success was clear: Powerful imperial states—which had come about not least thanks to merchants' and manufacturers' persistent agitation—now possessed the means to reach deeply into once remote parts of the world. The agents of industrial capitalism rode railways that penetrated Berar, sent cotton prices over telegraph cables that crossed the Atlantic, and followed behind military expeditions that "pacified" Tashkent and Tanganyika.

These cotton kings riding on the coattails of a strengthened state furthered a double process of creative destruction. They pushed metropolitan capital closer to cotton producers outside the world's slave areas, in the process often destroying older merchant networks that had moved cotton from field to factory prior to the 1860s. And they undermined hand spinning and handloom weaving, effecting the world's most significant wave of deindustrialization ever. Millions of people, especially women, gave up their spinning and weaving, work that had structured their societies for centuries or even millennia.

In the last third of the nineteenth century, metropolitan capital and manufactured goods moved into ever greater areas of the world's countryside. The success of European merchants was most remarkable in a huge area in which they had traditionally been the weakest: Asia. It was there that they managed to move closer to the actual producers and consumers of cotton. By the 1870s, for example, Berar's central market town, Khamgaon, hosted merchants from Britain, Germany, France, Italy, Switzerland, and the Habsburg Empire, all focused on acquiring raw cotton. These merchants sent Indian agents into the nearby growing areas to purchase the material raw, then they had it cleaned and pressed before shipping it to the port of Bombay. They had now truly gained control of the cotton trade, replacing a world they had inherited from previous generations in which "the trade was entirely in the hands of the local dealers."[2]

It had been the terminal crisis of slave labor that pushed European and later also Japanese merchants inland beyond the port cities of India, Egypt, western Africa, and elsewhere. Already upon the first sign of disintegration of slavery in 1861, manufacturers in the Manchester Cotton Supply Association had hoped that Europeans could be "induce[d] . . . to take up their position in the interior of India and superintend the trade among Natives." A year later, the India Office in London had conveyed to the governor in council in Bombay that it supported the "establishment of Agencies in these districts, for the purpose of purchasing cotton direct from the cultivating classes, instead of through middlemen." Doing this in India was not so easy, however, because Indian cotton dealers were deeply rooted in both the local cotton trade and the social structure of cotton-producing villages—in fact, without revolutionizing the Indian social structure it was hard to imagine that European capitalists would ever be able to replace their Indian counterparts. But they did, not least thanks to the support they received from an increasingly powerful imperial state, and by 1878 a British colonial administrator observed that "the [cotton] trade [of Berar] . . . has fallen almost entirely into the hands of European merchants."[3]

Among the European capitalists who came to dominate cotton production in a remote hinterland of industrial capitalism such as Berar's Khamgaon was the firm of Volkart Brothers. Headquartered in the quaint town of Winterthur near the shores of Lake Constance, these Swiss merchants had been active in the Indian cotton trade since 1851, relying on the services of Indian brokers to purchase cotton for European markets. In the last third of the nineteenth century, however, they had moved their capital ever closer to the actual cotton growers, creating purchasing agencies in cotton-growing regions of India, including Khamgaon, and erecting cotton gins and presses. Agents in the employ of Volkart would purchase cotton from local dealers, have it processed in the firm's own gins, then press it at "Volkart's Press" and send it by rail to Bombay, where it was branded by Volkart agents to be shipped to Liverpool, Le Havre, or Bremen to be sold to mill owners who put great trust in the "VB" stamped on the bales. While the old system had relied on many intermediary merchants, Volkart now single-handedly connected cotton growers to cotton manufacturers.[4]

European capital moves into the Indian countryside:
Volkart Brothers cotton press in Berar.

By 1883, sixteen Volkart presses dotted the Berar countryside and by 1920 Volkart would be the largest shipper of Indian-grown cotton, selling more than 180,000 bales, or one-quarter of the total exports. And the Volkarts were not alone. They worked side by side the agencies, gins, and presses of other European merchants, including the Rallis, Knoops, and Siegfrieds. In the early twentieth century, Japanese cotton trading firms joined in: Toyo Menka Kaisha alone counted 156 Indian subagencies by 1926, and most of the firm's profits derived from such hinterland trading activities.[5]

As European and Japanese exporters moved into once remote cotton-producing towns, rural cultivators were able to sell their products to global markets. To be sure, smaller dealers and moneylenders who connected the growers to European and Japanese merchants persisted, providing Indian peasants with the capital they needed to acquire seeds, pay their taxes, and tide them over to the next harvest, almost always at ruinous rates of interest. These *sowkars* were deeply rooted in the villages and European dealers depended on them—just as the locals needed the access to the markets and capital provided by European traders.[6]

Despite the persistence of *sowkars,* however, long-dominant Indian cotton merchants who, as late as the 1850s, had played a major role in the export of cotton, were pushed to the margins of the trade. Despite the riches that they had accumulated during the American Civil War, many went under during the rapid fall in cotton prices in its aftermath. Moreover, the changes in transportation infrastructure and the advent of the telegraphic connection to Liverpool and with it the trade in futures on Indian cotton squeezed the speculative profits of merchants who sold on consignment. Major European merchants responded by vertically integrating their businesses—connecting growers and manufacturers—as the Volkarts had done with spectacular success, a move that Indian merchants, who lacked the ability to establish a presence close to European manufacturers, could not replicate. As a result, Indian merchants were increasingly under pressure, especially in the overseas trade. In 1861, they still exported 67 percent of all cotton from Bombay, but by 1875 their share had fallen to just 28 percent, and it kept declining. Unable to compete in the overseas cotton trade, some of these merchants would invest their capital in fledgling Indian cotton mills.[7]

Elsewhere in the world, the infusion of capital into cotton production evolved in similar ways. In Egypt, for one, "merchants sent agents out into the villages to buy small lots," either from local traders or from the cultivators directly, replacing the once total monopoly of the Egyptian viceroy. Many of these merchants were Greeks who had come to Egypt in the wake of the cotton boom of the Civil War, and almost all were part of family or place-of-origin networks that stretched not just into Greece but also to Trieste, Marseille, London, and Manchester.[8]

In the Çukurova in western Anatolia, things followed a similar pattern with Greek and Christian Arab merchants taking on that role, at first in interaction with Armenian traders who connected their transmediterranean networks to the rural cultivators themselves. By the 1880s, however, foreign banks and trading companies had moved in, muscling aside local capitalists. In 1906, the German Cotton Society of the Levant began its operations, in 1909 the Deutsche Orient Bank opened a branch in Mersin, and a year later Deutsche Bank began investing heavily in irrigation schemes. In exceptional cases, the capitalization of the countryside went even one step further, with foreign investors owning entire cotton plantations. In La Laguna, Mexico, British investors operated the huge cotton-growing hacienda Compañía Agricola, Industrial y Colonizadora del Tlahualilo; in

VOLKART BROTHERS' BUYING AND SELLING ORGANISATION

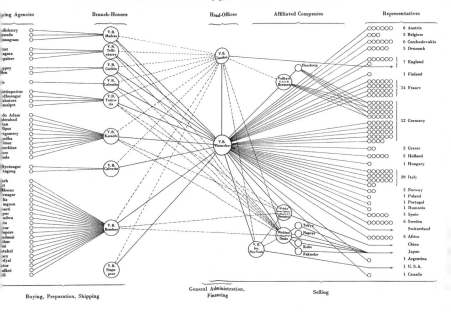

Volkart Brothers, Swiss cotton merchants,
connecting cotton growers and manufacturers, 1925: purchasing and sales organization

Mississippi, the British Spinners Ltd. owned the Delta and Pine Land Company with its thirty-seven thousand acres of cotton lands.[9]

Even in the cotton states of North America, long subject to vast infusions of European capital, the relationship between merchants and cotton growers increasingly evolved toward the imperial model pioneered in India and Egypt, which worked to marginalize cotton growers. Before the Civil War, the United States had been exceptional as the only major cotton-growing area in the world dependent on and receptive to European capital. But in the United States, unlike, for instance, India, merchants had played a relatively subordinate role vis-à-vis the powerful growers of cotton—the planters. That changed in the late nineteenth century, as merchants gained new powers and capital entered the southern countryside in new ways.[10]

The slow disappearance of factors was at the core of the recasting of the cotton trade in the United States. Where factors had typically

Jean D. Zerbini: Greek cotton merchant in Egypt

advanced capital to planters, sold their crops, and provided them with supplies, now they were displaced by merchants who settled in interior towns. As transportation and communication access to the southern hinterland improved dramatically in the wake of the Civil War, and as the empire of cotton moved farther into the West, growers sold their cotton directly to merchants or mill agents, or even to foreign buyers, instead of entrusting it for sale to a factor in a distant port. As a result, interior Texas cities such as Dallas, far away from the ocean, became important cotton-trading places in their own right. As early as 1880, Dallas counted thirty-three such cotton buyers, many of them agents of giant European and American firms, such as Alexander Sprunt of Wilmington, North Carolina, or Frank and Monroe Anderson, who, along with Will Clayton, organized Anderson, Clayton & Co. to become the largest cotton dealers in the world.[11]

With the purchasing of cotton moving into American hinterland towns, cotton presses and gins were built there as well, and experts, such as cotton classifiers, moved in, paralleling developments in India, Egypt, and elsewhere. Local merchants began purchasing the crop, as the telegraph communicated Liverpool and New York prices rapidly to the remotest southern towns, just as it did to Khamgaon. At the same time, the railroads increasingly brought a panoply of goods to small rural stores, further undermining the former role of the factor as supplier of plantations. And these merchants increasingly provided credit to grow-ers, usurping yet another function of antebellum factors. The old factors responded to this new situation by becoming interior buyers themselves, another blow to the old system of factorage. As a result, "cotton market-ing moved inland," and by the early 1870s representatives of Manchester spinners purchased cotton directly in towns such as Memphis. Alexander Sprunt and Son, for example, ran purchasing agencies all over the south-ern states and selling agencies in Bremen, Liverpool, New England, and Japan, paralleling in many ways Volkart's operations in India.[12]

In India, Egypt, the United States, and elsewhere metropolitan capital gained new powers over cotton growers, marginalizing both local con-trol over the trade as well as the formerly powerful cotton planters of the American South now defeated in war. Yet ironically, under manufacturers' pressure to deliver the cheapest possible cotton, the commission-intensive business of importers, brokers, and factors were increasingly squeezed as well, and eventually replaced by a much simpler—and much less expensive—system of trade. In fact, so successful had merchants become in connect-ing distant growers and manufacturers to one another that their own labor had become less and less important.

Pressured by manufacturers who sought to cut transaction costs, the myriad intermediaries who had moved cotton from the plantation to the factory before the 1860s consolidated, to be replaced by a few vertically integrated cotton dealers. New characters now strode onto the cotton empire's stage, people who would connect growers directly to manufac-turers. The old-style importers and brokers declined. Some, such as the Browns, in a savvy move, had already mostly exited the cotton business before the Civil War. Others, such as the Rathbones, accumulated huge losses after the war, and then retreated from the trade. Lower transaction costs meant lower profits for people invested in the cotton trade, giving a premium to those able to secure a vastly increased quantity of goods. One of the nineteenth century's greatest authorities on the global cotton trade, Thomas Ellison, estimated that between 1870 and 1886 transaction costs, as a percentage of the value of the traded cotton, fell by 2.5 percent.[13]

The role of merchants also changed because, as the result of the state-driven transformation of the countryside, connecting growers and producers of raw cotton had become much simpler. As we have seen, states projected themselves into the world's countryside, using contract law, new forms of property rights in land, railroads, and the imperial control of territory, giving manufacturers a more direct and immediate access to the world's countryside and its increasingly marginalized cotton growers.

The importance of old-fashioned importers, brokers, and factors within the empire of cotton declined even more as the global cotton trade was increasingly dominated by a small number of cotton exchanges. Trades on these exchanges no longer rested on trust networks forged by religious, kin, or place-of-origin solidarities. Instead, these institutions were impersonal marketplaces in which anyone at any time could trade in any quantity and quality of cotton for immediate or future delivery, or could speculate on the future price movements of cotton that had not been shipped, or perhaps not even grown. Such cotton exchanges spread rapidly across the globe: In 1869, the New York Cotton Exchange opened, followed by the New Orleans Cotton Exchange in 1871, and further exchanges in Le Havre, Bremen, Osaka, Shanghai, São Paulo, Bombay, and Alexandria. These exchanges specialized in the trading of contracts on the future delivery of cotton. Such "to arrive" trading, as we have seen, had already emerged in a sporadic way before the 1860s, but now "futures" took off to become the dominant mode of the global cotton trade, made possible by the accelerated speed at which information traveled around the globe, facilitated, most crucially, by the laying of the first transatlantic telegraph cable in 1866.[14]

These emerging commodity markets were sophisticated institutions. They would have been unrecognizable to the Holts and Drinkwaters, and their counterparts, who hurried around the port of Liverpool in the 1810s inspecting sacks of cotton arriving from the Americas. Now trade was highly abstracted from the actual physical cotton and highly standardized, the great variety of nature molded through conventions and contracts into categories that corresponded to the abstractions capital required to make it commensurable.

Most important was the standardization of cotton itself. The huge natural variety of cotton, for the purposes of trades in futures, was impossible to handle and thus was fictitiously reduced to just one—"middling upland"—and contracts were standardized to specific lot sizes of this quality. These standards, as we have seen, had been defined in the years before the American Civil War by the Liverpool Cotton Brokers' Association. In the 1870s its successor organization, the Liverpool Cotton Association, took over this definition of quality and the implementation

A dockworker weighing cotton in the Port of Liverpool

of standards—a direct consequence of the city's central position in the global cotton empire. Detailed rules for the classification of cottons, and mechanisms for the arbitration of disputes between sellers and buyers, made both the knowledge and the trust networks of previous generations of merchants much less central. As historian Kenneth Lipartito notes, the "speculation in futures helped to impose worldwide supply and demand conditions on local markets, thus moving the entire cotton trade towards the ideal of a single market with a single, internationally determined price for each grade of cotton."[15]

As a result of this restructuring of the global cotton market, business grew rapidly. While the New York Cotton Exchange traded contracts for the future delivery of 5 million bales in 1871–72 (slightly more than the actual harvest), it traded contracts on 32 million bales ten years later—an amount seven and a half times the actual cotton harvest. The global cotton trade now took place not in securing actual cotton, but in speculating on future price movements of the commodity. That speculation was made possible by the exchanges' ability to create one "world price" for cotton, a price available at any minute of the day in all cotton-growing

The New York Cotton Exchange, 1923

and -manufacturing centers.[16] No longer was the trade in cotton shaped by the leisurely pace of importers, factors, and brokers walking the streets of port towns throughout the empire of cotton—now the rhythms of industrial capital and, increasingly, of finance dominated the cotton trade.

The role of merchants diminished not least because many of their core functions were usurped by states. Even the all-important standards on which contracts increasingly rested, based as we have seen on private contractual arrangements of merchants and enforced by the Liverpool Cotton Association, were after the turn of the century increasingly defined and enforced by state classifiers in the United States. The shift of the all-important power of definition from private associations such as the Liverpool Cotton Association to the state, from England to the

United States, was the result of the growing U.S. influence on the global economy, and also the political pressure of cotton producers in the United States, who felt disadvantaged by Liverpool's rules. In 1914, the "Official Cotton Standards of the United States" were created, their use required for all futures transactions. In 1923, the Cotton Standards Act made it illegal to use any other standards for American cotton in interstate or foreign commerce, and as a result these standards also guided transactions on European cotton exchanges. With government classifiers in government classing rooms housed in cotton exchanges, the state had entrenched itself in the very heart of the global cotton trade.[17]

Moreover, the state also became an important supplier of statistics that made the market more legible, rendering much less central the sophisticated networks of information gathering and exchange that merchants had forged through huge investments in time and treasure. Beginning in July 1863, the U.S. Department of Agriculture issued monthly reports on cotton production. In 1894 it launched the annual *Agricultural Yearbook*, a huge compendium of statistics, and by 1900 it was issuing crop reports collected by "41 full-time, paid statistic agents and their 7,500 assistants. 2,400 volunteer county correspondents and their 6,800 assistants and 40,000 volunteer township or district correspondents." Two years later, the Census Bureau was charged by Congress to collect annually "the statistics of the cotton production of the country as returned by ginners." By 1905, there was even an International Institute of Agriculture with its own statistics bureau, created by none other than the king of Italy. The state, centrally concerned with the reliable flow of inexpensive raw materials into the vortex of manufacturing enterprises, now quite literally made the market.[18]

Not content with marginalizing both cotton growers and older merchant networks, imperial statesmen, manufacturers, and new kinds of commodity dealers also worked diligently on their long-term project of destroying the older worlds of cotton that still persisted in many regions. They drove a complex dynamic of deindustrialization in the now global countryside. Each spinner and weaver who gave up her or his handicraft created a potential new market for European and North American manufacturers, who, as we have seen, had already ousted Indian textiles from world markets earlier in the century. But now, in the last third of the nineteenth century, statesmen, manufacturers, and dealers broke through local barriers to foreign cotton consumption in the former heartlands of the worlds of cotton. Rural cultivators and former spinners and weavers in many parts of the world became first-time buyers of European, North American, and eventually Japanese yarn and cloth.

No market was more important than the ancient home of the world's cotton industry. Asia's cotton markets were vast, and winning them was the grand prize that British, French, Dutch, Spanish, and American imperialism bestowed, not just on Lancashire manufacturers, but on some continental European, North American, and Japanese manufacturers as well.[19] India in particular became a huge market—already in 1843 it was for British manufacturers their most important customer, and it remained central for about a century thereafter. By 1900, 78 percent of the total production of the British cotton industry was exported, much of it to India.[20]

European manufacturers' success was the more remarkable in light of their earlier failures. In the early decades of the nineteenth century, high transportation costs had made inland markets in Asia as well as Africa largely inaccessible, and even in markets open to European merchants, selling European cotton goods was difficult. A typical story of these early years suggests the reasons why: British merchant Richard Kay, who traded cotton with India and China, went to Calcutta to sell yarn. There he was overwhelmed by the difficulties he encountered, annoyed by the "tribe of native merchants." He suffered from the heat, and became sick on his travels to outlying villages. When he went to Allahabad, he complained about being "pestered with all sorts of dealers, viz cloth merchants." In the vast Indian subcontinent, the *Asiatic Journal* reported, "Nearly the whole inland trade in European goods is in [local merchants'] hands, and they furnish at present the principal medium for procuring an extended circulation for our broadcloths, cotton, copper, iron, & c." As a result, "British manufactured goods have as yet displaced, but to a very limited extent, the Native cotton cloth manufactures of Western India, and it is impossible for them to do so until improved means of transit and communication enable the respective manufacturers to compete on more equal terms."[21]

Yet already by the 1830s, in a great reversal of one of the world's oldest trade patterns, larger quantities of British-manufactured cottons began to flow into places where for centuries and even millennia hand

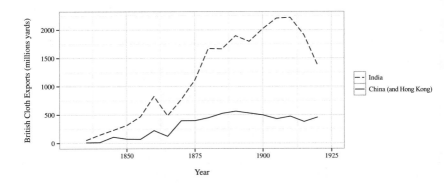

Capturing the Asian market: British cloth exports to India and China,
in millions of yards, 1820–1920

spinning and weaving had flourished, to be followed by French, Swiss, and other products. When "free trade" was imposed upon the Ottoman Empire in 1838 and British cloth "flooded the market in Izmir," local cotton workers lost their ability to maintain their old production regime. In coastal southeastern Africa, cotton yarn and cloth imports also began to devastate the local cotton textile industry. In Mexico, European cotton imports had a serious impact on local manufacturing—before tariffs enabled Mexican industrialization, Guadalajara's industry had been, as one historian found, "virtually eliminated." In Oaxaca, 450 out of 500 looms ceased operating. In China, the 1842 Treaty of Nanking forced the opening of markets, and the subsequent influx of European and North American yarn and cloth had a "devastating" effect, especially on China's hand spinners.[22]

India was the grandest market of them all. By 1832, the great house of Baring, never one to miss a chance for profit, partnered with a local merchant house in Calcutta, Gisborne and Company, to export British yarn. It also financed the yarn and cloth trade to China and Egypt. Thanks to the efforts of merchants like Gisborne, increasing quantities of British cottons flowed into the Indian market, "to an extent that might have been previously considered impossible," according to the Bombay Chamber of Commerce in 1853. Tellingly, Manchester manufacturers McConnel & Kennedy, who had earlier in the century found most of their yarn cus-

tomers in continental Europe, by the 1860s were corresponding mostly
with customers in Calcutta, Alexandria, and similarly distant parts of
the world, while Fielden Brothers expanded production so rapidly that
they began to think about sending cloth for the "mass of poor people" to
Calcutta. Machine production demanded ever more markets to remain
profitable.[23] Yet despite these efforts, in the first half of the nineteenth
century the older centers of the world of cotton still retained significant
handicraft production. By 1850, Britain's market share in India, it has
been estimated, was only 11.5 percent.[24]

Capturing these ancient markets took many decades, the final breakthrough only occurring on the backs of imperial states. Indeed, creating markets for metropolitan manufacturers was a conscious project of
colonial administrations. The global South was to be a market for metropolitan industry, not a competitor, and a supplier of raw materials and
labor, and both required the destruction of indigenous manufacturing.
Colonial governments created systems of tariffs and excise duties that
discriminated against indigenous producers. They also prioritized the
construction of new infrastructures tailored not to local needs but to
global market access. They also devoted significant time and money to

Agents of deindustrialization: K. Astardjan, cotton merchants
of Armenian heritage, with branch offices in Constantinople,
Manchester, and elsewhere, presenting samples of Manchester
cloth to customers in Haskovo (in modern-day Bulgaria), 1886

the study of foreign cloth markets to help their manufacturers compete in distant places. The Bombay Chamber of Commerce had urged in 1853 "to ascertain, if possible, what are the principal seats of consumption for each particular description of goods, and what the route by which such goods arrive at their respective ultimate destination. . . . It is a matter of great interest, both to the Merchants of Bombay and to Manufacturers at home, to know more definitely to what extent and in what direction the import trade of Western Indies is being extended." Twenty years later, in 1873, J. Forbes Watson's *Collection of Specimens and Illustrations of the Textile Manufacturers of India (Second Series)*, a beautiful four-volume set of books, contained hundreds of samples of Indian cloth, including detailed descriptions, with length, width, weight, and place of origin. Some samples even list their price per yard—all to enable European manufacturers to compete in Indian markets by copying these fabrics. And in 1906 "the secretary of state deputed an India office official to examine the products of the handlooms of India with a view to ascertaining whether any of the

Selling cotton yarn to India: Volkart Brothers
markets to local tastes.

Indian-made goods could not be profitably supplied by the power-loom industry of Great Britain."[25]

China's markets were just as tempting. In 1887, a British bureaucrat stationed in Ning-po issued a "Report on the Native Cotton Manufacturers of the District of Ning-Po" to the Manchester Chamber of Commerce in which he "furnish[ed] samples of the cotton cloths . . . in common wear here." The British consul in China years earlier had already forwarded two boxes of "ordinary clothing worn by the labouring population of several districts of China, to the Manchester Chamber of Commerce, including accounts of the costs of these." It was exhibited in Manchester at the Chamber of Commerce for two days and "received many visitors." And the efforts of manufacturers and imperial governments were successful. Britain's market share in India increased to about 60 percent in 1880. Bengali merchants protested against the wave of British imports, but to no avail.[26]

As cotton yarn and cloth from the heartlands of the world's cotton industry flowed into the world's cotton-growing areas newly constituted as backwaters, they brought with them a tsunami of deindustrialization. "The importation of cheap machine-made piece goods has in many parts driven the native spinners and weavers altogether out of the market, and many have had to take to working on the roads, or have been engaged as farm-labourers," observed Berar cotton commissioner Harry Rivett-Carnac in 1869.

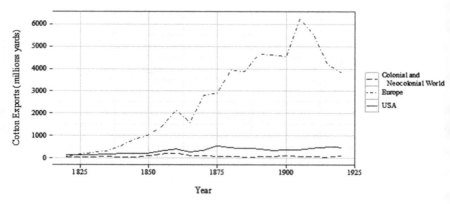

Clothing the colonial and neocolonial world: cotton cloth exports from the UK, 1820–1920, by destination

In the middle of the nineteenth century, millions of people still spun and wove by hand, as they had done for centuries. Competition from industrially produced yarn and cloth had begun to undermine that production in the first half of the century, especially in Europe and North America, and it had effectively destroyed cloth production for export in India. In the centers of the old worlds of cotton, however, where people produced yarn and cloth within households for local consumption, these changes still seemed remote. But now in the last third of the nineteenth century this was about to change. Usually these changes unfolded slowly and were at first hardly noticeable—a new railroad line opened bringing in yarns from faraway factories, for example—but sometimes they could also occur quite suddenly. In India the American Civil War was such an event. During that war, many spinners found themselves unable to compete with the market price for their crucial raw material. The Madras Chamber of Commerce in its 1863 report observed that "the enhanced price of Cotton has rendered the position of the Cotton Weavers of this Presidency one of great difficulty." As a result, the number of weavers decreased by as much as 50 percent during the American war, with former weavers moving into agricultural labor. Thus in a large swath of India, integration into the world market went hand in hand with widespread "peasantization," not, as one might expect, proletarianization.[27]

As former craft workers were drawn into cotton cultivation, deindustrialization swept over their world in the following decades. In Berar, "The manufacture of home made cloth has been undermined by the importation of English Piece Goods, and many of the weaver class have become ordinary labourers," remarked the assistant commissioner in charge of cotton of the government of India in 1874. With less cloth manufactured at home, reported Berar's cotton commissioner, "The home-made cloths affect not at all the supply of raw materials which England confidently expects from the Berars."[28]

For European cotton manufacturers this was reason to celebrate. When Edmund Potter spoke at the Manchester Chamber of Commerce he was cheered by "hear, hear" calls from the otherwise staid audience:

> The great expenditure in our military operations; the great outlay in making public works . . . and the increasing consumption by this country . . . of the agricultural products of India; all these things have circulated money among and raised in some degree

"Dacca" calicoes, now manufactured in Britain:
Gidlow Mills in Wigan, as seen in 1908

the social condition of the ryots [cultivators] of that country, so that their consumption of manufactured goods has increased. One letter informs me that in some districts the weavers are leaving their ill-paid operations in that handicraft, and are resuming the occupation we wish them to follow, namely, agricultural operations—("Hear, hear")—because there is no question the real interest of India would be best promoted by developing the agricultural products of its fertile soil. ("Hear")[29]

For British cotton merchants and manufacturers, news of the deindustrialization of India was so welcome that it allowed for a slight relaxation of decorum.

By the end of the century, that decline had brought with it social catastrophe. In Bengal "from every district it is reported that owing to the widespread use of European piece-goods, which are cheaper and finer, though not always more durable, Indian manufactured goods have gradually disappeared." One district, Parganas, testified that "weavers have been largely driven from their hereditary calling to agriculture." When famine struck the Bombay Presidency in 1896–97 the final report of the Revenue Department stated that weavers suffered "not only from the failure of crops and high prices but from the absence of demand for their products." Such stories can be told about many regions of the world.[30]

Yet despite these pessimistic reports, domestic production did not disappear. In the Ottoman Empire weavers took advantage of access to cheaper (imported) yarn, and catered successfully to highly differentiated local markets, doing fairly well throughout the nineteenth century. Historians of China have observed that while hand spinning diminished rapidly (by 1913 only 25 percent of all yarn used in China was spun at home), weaving remained, and during the 1930s 70 percent of cloth was still produced in homes, indeed well into the socialist period home manufacturing survived. In Latin America, the home-based production of cottons persisted as well, especially among indigenous communities. Historians of African manufacturing also observe that "contemporary statements as to the complete hegemony of import cottons have no validity outside fairly restricted zones"—basically places near European settlements. Even in India, as the British colonial Department of Commerce and Industry reported in 1906, "The weaving of cloth by hand is not, however, by any means extinct, after agriculture it is still the most important occupation of the native of India, and is pursued, in some parts, as an independent means of livelihood or in order to supplement the earnings derived from agriculture, and in others, as a purely domestic occupation."[31]

As the world shifted under their feet, and without the power to respond politically to these shifts, local cotton producers adapted as well as they could. At first, faced with the loss of their export markets, they retooled to supply domestic consumers, by producing coarser goods. They also focused, often successfully, on market niches not supplied by European manufacturers, and on producing more durable cloth. The Commerce and Industries Department reported with some regret of "the difficulty of penetrating too many of the up-country markets, the effects of custom, of caste, of religious beliefs, of the barter system, and so on, has prevented the process from proceeding with the rapidity which it would otherwise have attained." As late as 1920, there were still about 2.5 million handloom weavers remaining in India. Even Mahatma Gandhi, who made the devastating impact of colonialism on domestic industry a key aspect of his political campaigns, admitted in 1930 that "next to agriculture, hand-weaving is still the largest and most widespread industry throughout the whole of India"—not least because despite all the rapid advances, the capitalist reorganization of the countryside remained far from complete in the early twentieth century.[32]

If these adjustments did not suffice, weavers tried to reduce the costs of their product by moving production farther into the countryside and giving female household members a more prominent role in production. In the Ottoman Empire, cotton textile production increasingly moved away from male, guild-based labor toward female and child labor, often in the countryside. Deindustrialization, as often as not, shaped gender inequalities as it undermined household economies. Indeed, the ability of local manufacturing to survive was often rooted in the gendered social structure of the countryside, where workers, often women, were idle during parts of the year, and families perceived the "cost" of continuing to produce textiles for family consumption or even sale as extremely low. "In Assam and Burma," tellingly reported the Department of Industry and Commerce, "weaving forms part of a girl's education and woman's ordinary household duties. The family . . . is supplied in this manner, and the articles turned out are seldom offered for sale; when the surplus production is disposed of in the local market, the cost of the labour spent in the domestic occupation practiced during leisure hours is not taken into consideration in calculating the price." The incomplete transition to capitalism, in fact, enabled the super-exploitation of members of households who could labor for less than the cost of their subsistence.[33]

Spinners and weavers also tried collectively to resist the destruction of their ancient industries—from the Black Forest to China to India—but their movements confronted the ever more concentrated power of imperial states allied closely with manufacturers. In the early nineteenth century, spinners in the Black Forest had set machinery ablaze. In 1860, spinners rioted in Guangzhou in response to waves of European imports.[34] But states did not take kindly to such rebellions. A group of Indian weavers reported on tax collectors resorting to torture to force them to pay their taxes

> by Binding up with chords and wood cut out for the purpose, the most delicate and private places, by placing stone on their head and backs; By making them to stand in the sun, by pinch-

ing the thighs and the ears, by pulling the whiskers, by tying the locks of one man to that of one another, by sealing the doors of Houses, by selling at Auction the Property of others which they obtained by force of arms, by the confinement of some of us, without allowing them to go to their means; by abusing and striking some, and abusing others and making use of violent and coercive means.[35]

Unrestrained violence did not just characterize the world of the slave plantation. Weavers understood the logic of this new political economy well, though they lacked the power to alter it: "Those who come to India from Europe . . . after having collected large fortunes, take the same to Europe, all which is obtained from our Labour, but we ourselves are left without means of support."[36]

Despite individual resistance and collective protest, the overall trend was unwavering and ultimately devastating: around the globe millions of household cotton spinners and weavers lost their ability to spin and weave. In India alone, historian Tirthankar Roy concluded, "There is undeniable empirical evidence that the community of hand-spinners gave up spinning on a large scale, and this factor alone may account for a loss of industrial employment to the extent of 4–5 million persons." Other historians have suggested that the loss of manufacturing between 1830 and 1860 amounted to between 2 and 6 million full-time jobs in India alone. The vast expansion of cotton manufacturing in Europe and the increasing orientation of large swaths of the global countryside toward the growing of cotton for export destabilized and even destroyed ancient cotton manufacturing—with devastating consequences for spinners, weavers, and rural cultivators alike.[37]

Life in much of the world's cotton-growing countryside had always been difficult at best. A focus on growing cotton for export could, both theoretically and in fact, be beneficial to rural cultivators. Many peasants, as we have seen, profited from rising cotton prices during the American Civil War. Yet the radical recasting of ever larger swaths of the world's countryside also had less positive consequences. Most crucially, it undermined food security. During the American Civil War, British officials in Ahmedabad, Haira, and Surat had reported that "the increasing area of land devoted to cultivation of Articles of Export, such as Cotton . . . [has led to a] proportionate decrease in cultivation of articles of food." As a result, food prices rose between 1861 and 1865 by more than 325 percent, and even Sir Charles Trevelyan had to admit that "at the present high prices of food, the body of the people, in several parts of India, are barely able to subsist." In Egypt, the situation was quite similar. Once a grain-exporting country, it became dependent on imports of food crops as the result of its greater dedication to cotton during the American Civil War. When in the summer of 1863 disease killed nearly all of Egypt's cattle, a food crisis emerged in which tens of thousands of *felaheen* perished.[38]

The increasing world market orientation of cotton cultivators also had significant effects on social structures. Throughout western India's Maharashtra, for example, British efforts to increase revenue and encourage peasants to participate in distant markets led to the undermining of the collective nature of villages, making individual peasants instead of villages as a whole responsible for taxes, and handing judicial power to distant courts instead of village-based and peasant-dominated tribunals. The market now increasingly subsumed all aspects of society, not just in Lancashire or Alsace, but in Berar and Lower Egypt as well. In Anatolia, "a large-scale transition to a cash-crop economy" took place in response to the cotton boom, with cotton replacing food crops, the abolition of feudal social relations in the countryside, and the financing of the crop by local merchants who charged peasants interest rates between 33 and 50 percent. In Egypt as well, the booming cotton export industry, according to historian Alan Richards, "destroyed the old quasi-communal forms of land tenure, broke up the protective web of village social relations, replaced them with private property in land and individual tax responsibility, and helped create four classes: large landowners . . . , rich peasants . . . , small peasant landowners, and a landless class." As early as the 1840s, the government had begun compelling peasants to grow specific crops, including cotton, and to "deliver them to government warehouses." Peasants had responded to this pressure by leaving the land in droves, which the government took as a reason to deny any claims to the land by those who had "deserted" it. By 1862, anyone who left the land for more than two months lost his claim to the property. In 1863, when Isma'il, Egypt's new ruler, took power, he focused his efforts on creating large estates, giving land to relatives and officials in his government, and forcing peasants to work on infrastructure projects and on his own plantations. Resistance to such measures was violently repressed.[39]

The most serious impact on cotton farmers, however, emerged after the American Civil War. Once world market prices declined after the onset of the global depression of 1873, Indian, Egyptian, Brazilian, and American rural cultivators had a hard time making up for lost income, as falling prices made it ever more difficult to repay loans and make tax payments. The price for Surat cotton delivered in Liverpool between 1873 and 1876 fell by 38 percent. Cotton growers in Brazil, Egypt, India, the United States, and elsewhere, often highly indebted to local moneylenders, now faced plummeting returns on their cash crops. In India and Brazil, the problems were compounded by severe droughts that led to a rapid increase in food prices. Though historians disagree as to how much the fall in world market prices affected cotton growers, at the very least world market integration increased the economic uncertainty faced by people in remote corners of the world. Their incomes, and quite literally their survival, were now linked to global price fluctuations over which they had no control. All too often, the only response open to farmers with little control over the land was to grow more cotton to make up for lost income due to falling prices—which resulted in a glut of cotton that depressed prices even further.

What wage workers, tenants, and sharecroppers had in common was that they had lost access to subsistence agriculture—basic production and consumption now depended on global markets. While "cotton [was once] a subordinate product" and "the ryot [did] not neglect the raising of food for the sake of cotton, however high its price may be, for in doing so he runs the risk of starvation," by the late nineteenth century millions of rural cultivators became primarily dependent on cotton. Moreover, as world market integration usually went along with social differentiation, a growing group of landless tenants and agricultural laborers periodically faced life-threatening difficulty in accessing food crops. In Africa, one author found that "cotton and food insecurity went hand in hand." In La Laguna, Mexico, an unprecedented percentage of children suffered from malnutrition. In Argentina, misery characterized small cotton-growing farms.[40]

Between 1864 and 1873 the amount of cotton that a tenant or farmer had to produce to buy a given quantity of Berar's most important food grain, jowar, doubled, and then it doubled again by 1878. Perhaps even more significant, the relative price of grains to cotton changed dramatically from year to year (changes of 20 percent or even 40 percent were not exceptional), introducing a new level of uncertainty into cotton growers' precarious lives. As one historian of India has remarked, "Successful participation in markets requires economic autonomy and the capacity to take risks and sustain losses. Poor and indebted peasants had neither." Contemporaries believed that this crisis was at least partly the result of the diversion of land and labor away from food crops and toward cotton. As the colonial government of India observed in 1874, "The more the area's food stocks is diminished in favor of fibres, the greater the danger from any failure of the monsoon becomes, & the greater appears to be the necessity of some security against the consequences of such failure." Indeed, cotton production for export typically produced a quagmire of poverty, debt, and underdevelopment well into the twentieth century. As H. E. Neguib Shakour Pasha, the director of the Gharbieh Land Company in Cairo, reminded his audience during a speech to the Congress of the International Federation of Master Cotton Spinners' and Manufacturers' Associations, "You have only to go to the villages and see the dwellings our people live in, their very small interest in life, their hard work from morning till evening without distractions would give you an idea as to how the Egyptian peasant lives his gloomy and uninteresting existence."[41]

The causes of the uncertainties they faced often remained mysterious to rural cultivators themselves. The cotton commissioner for Berar, Harry Rivett-Carnac, reported in 1868 that "the great rise and then the sudden fall in the price of cotton, and the constant fluctuations in the market, by which the cultivator, in even the most remote of the cotton-growing villages is affected, has led some of the less intelligent to regard cotton not only with distrust, but with a certain degree of awe." Traveling into the "more distant parts of the cotton-growing tracts of the Provinces," he found people who were mystified as to why the price of cotton changed rapidly, as they "find some difficulty in realizing the present state of the trade, and the fact that, by means of the Electric Telegraph, the throbbings of the pulse of the Home markets communicate themselves instantly to Hingunghat and other trade centres throughout the country." These cotton growers told Rivett-Carnac that they attributed such volatility to "luck," "a war," the "kindness of a paternal Government," or that the "the Queen had given every one in England new clothes" on the occasion of the crown prince's wedding.[42] These cultivators understood perfectly well that remote events over which they had no control now determined the most basic conditions of their existence.

This uncertainty could be life-threatening on a massive scale. In 1877

Famine victims, probably 1899, India

and again in the late 1890s, Berar, as well as northeastern Brazil, witnessed the starvation of millions of cultivators as cotton prices fell while food grain prices rose, putting food out of reach of many cotton producers. Specializing in cotton could result in disaster, as in the 1870s famine, which was not caused by a lack of food (indeed, food grains continued to be exported from Berar), but by the inability of the poorest agricultural laborers to buy urgently needed food grains. In India alone, between 6 and 10 million people died in the famines of the late 1870s. Observed one gazetteer, "Had Berar been an isolated tract dependent on its own resources, it is possible that in the plain taluks [British administrative units] there would have been no famine." High prices had made food unavailable to many peasants and agricultural laborers, and during the 1900 famine, another 8.5 percent of the population of Berar died, with the greatest numbers of deaths occurring in districts most specialized in cotton production. Landless agricultural workers and former weavers in particular suffered, "for not only did they have to pay more for their food, but their wages are reduced from the competition" of workers from other regions. The British medical journal *The Lancet* estimated that famine death during the 1890s totaled 19 million, with fatalities concentrated in the tracts of India that had recently been recast to produce cotton for export. In the town of Risod, a contemporary observed that people "died like flies."[43]

. . .

Experiencing a new kind of uncertainty thanks to world market integration, and squeezed by moneylenders, cotton growers in India, Brazil, Mexico, and the southern United States took a desperate and dangerous step: They rebelled. In Egypt, agricultural workers led by Ahmed al-Shaqi had revolted as early as 1865. In India, the Deccan Riots of May and June 1875 targeted moneylenders and merchants—figures who symbolized the recasting of the countryside. During the 1873–74 Quebra Quilos revolt, Brazilian peasants, many of whom had just a few years earlier switched to cotton production, destroyed land records and refused to pay taxes they could no longer afford in the wake of the global fall of cotton prices. In 1899, widespread grain riots occurred again, often drawing in hundreds of people even in small villages. At the same time, cotton farmers in the southern United States also organized. They formed the Farmers Alliance and launched a political movement, Populism, demanding that the state relieve them of some of the economic pressures that had wreaked havoc in their lives, a movement that reared its head again during the first decade of the twentieth century when several hundred thousand farmers joined the Southern Cotton Association and the National Farmers' Union. Cotton populism spread as far as Egypt, where Wady E. Medawar in 1900 formulated a program of agrarian reform much like the one advanced by cotton farmers in the United States, including cooperative societies, agricultural improvement associations, mechanisms to provide cheap credit to farmers, and an organization of rural cultivators that would interweave private and public initiative. Around the same time, Mexican cotton workers in La Laguna deployed "insubordination, theft, banditry" and other forms of collective action to improve their situation. Food shortages led to grain riots, brutally repressed by private armies backed by federal troops. Strategies of resistance varied according to political regime, ranging from creating cooperatives and running for political office in Texas to murdering moneylenders in India.[44]

The rebellion of cotton cultivators at times had a significant impact on national politics, as in the United States, where Populists influenced the critical presidential election of 1896 and forced a greater presence of the state in the cotton trade, but also in Mexico, where they played an important role in the Mexican Revolution of the 1910s. But the integration of many areas of the world into the global cotton empire also made "cotton nationalism" a major theme in twentieth-century anticolonial struggles. Most prominently, Indian nationalists invoked their country's recast role in the global cotton economy as one of the most damaging effects of colonialism, and envisaged a postcolonial economy in which India would become again a major cotton power.[45]

In future decades, these movements would revolutionize the empire of cotton once again. But before this happened, the powerful new combination of manufacturers and imperial statesmen who had emerged after the American Civil War furthered the integration of the global cotton-producing countryside in ever more parts of the world, including Korea, Central Asia, and Africa. The tentacles of the empire of cotton spread ever farther. And that imperial expansion, in often surprising ways, would also come to influence the postcolonial and even postcapitalist cotton industry, and with it twentieth-century global capitalism.

Chapter Twelve

The New Cotton Imperialism

New frontiers: Cotton expedition to Togo. Members of the expedition
that introduced American cotton-growing methods into Togo,
including technical experts from Tuskegee Institute, celebrate their first
harvest by posing with three bales of cotton, 1901. From left to right
are the chief of Gyeasekang; unidentified; Akpanya von Boem, a chief;
John Robinson (from Tuskegee); Lieutenant Smend; Waldermeer Horn,
the vice governor of Togo; unidentified; James N. Calloway (from
Tuskegee); and Allen Burks (from Tuskegee).

In 1902, Sako Tsuneaki, the director of agricultural affairs in the Japanese Ministry of Agriculture, whiled away the time on a steamer journey
from China to Korea with Wakamatsu Tosaburo, a Japanese government official newly transferred from Shashi, China, to Mokpo, Korea.
As they traveled across the Yellow Sea, the two discussed the prospects of
expanding cotton agriculture in eastern Asia in order to feed the factories
mushrooming around Osaka and elsewhere. In 1893, Japan had imported
about 125 million pounds of raw cotton. By 1902 imports, mostly from

India and the United States, had increased to 446 million pounds; by 1920, they would rise to more than 1 billion pounds. Perhaps, agricultural bureaucrat Sako suggested, Korean rural cultivators could be made to produce more cotton for Japanese factories. Wakamatsu concurred, observing that in Shashi, where he had just spent some years, a vibrant cotton-growing industry had emerged. Upon landing in Korea the two resolved to investigate local cotton-growing practices and to find ways to increase production.[1]

Informed by his earlier observations in China, Wakamatsu began to experiment with various cotton strains on small model farms. Two years later, in 1904, members of the Japanese Imperial Diet (the parliament) and the House of Peers, as well as cotton manufacturers, created the Association for the Cultivation of Cotton in Korea, "following the example of the British Cotton Growing Association," which had been created just two years earlier. The association systematized and expanded Wakamatsu's efforts, focusing especially on the introduction of American cotton strains, building a cotton gin, and eventually presenting a report to the government of Korea with recommendations to increase cotton production. By 1906, Japanese spinners had established the Korean Cotton Corporation in Osaka with a branch office in Mokpo, providing loans to Korean rural cultivators who mortgaged their cotton crops to the company. Expanding their activities rapidly, the Japanese spinners gained "control over much of the raw cotton produced in the peninsula's southern cotton belt." They were aided in this project by the many agents sent into the Korean countryside by Japanese cotton merchants to purchase the white gold.[2]

When Japan began its occupation of Korea in 1910, the new colonial government took steps to further expand cotton production. In March 1912, "the Governor-General issued . . . an instruction to the Provincial Governments of the southern part . . . concerning encouragement of the plantation of upland cotton." Both Japanese cotton capitalists and imperial administrators worried that Japan's dependence on cotton imports might endanger the growth of its manufacturing industry. They especially hoped to disentangle themselves from the British Empire, given that by 1909, 62 percent of Japanese cotton imports arrived from India.[3]

Cotton from colonial Korea, and from Japan's other colonial possessions, Manchuria and Taiwan, was one potential solution. Korean farmers had traditionally produced cotton alongside other crops such as beans and vegetables on their smallholdings, often in the same fields. Most of the fiber was consumed in the domestic manufacture of cloth. Japanese colonialists hoped to recast this indigenous cotton industry just like their British peers had done in India: by cultivating new lands, persuading farmers to convert more of their existing fields to cotton growing, conducting agricultural experiments to improve yields and quality, and providing state supervision of the selling of the crop. They drew upon the experiences of rival cotton powers: The Japanese Ministry of Agriculture and Commerce had indeed investigated the cotton-growing efforts of the Germans in Togo, the French in French Soudan (modern-day Mali), and the British in the Sudan. Both the Association for the Cultivation of Cotton in Korea, founded in 1904, and the Cotton Cultivation Expansion Plan of 1912 borrowed significant elements from these foreign models.[4]

These efforts bore fruit. Korean cotton exports to Japan increased from an annual average of 37 million pounds between 1904 and 1908 to 165 million pounds between 1916 and 1920. Cotton exports from Japanese-controlled Kwantung province in China provided another 4.1 million pounds. The production of cotton from American seeds increased at a particularly rapid rate. By 1915, 263,069 Korean cultivators grew 37 million pounds. Thanks to the efforts of the colonial state, the Japa-

Japanese colonial officials with Korean cotton growers in a field, c. 1912

nese cotton industry had domesticated a small but growing colonial cotton complex.[5]

Stories like this could be told about many parts of the world. As states took on an ever more important role in constituting the new systems of labor that came to characterize the cotton-growing countryside after 1865, they also secured vast new territories on which cotton could be grown, dominating them militarily, politically, and bureaucratically. Sovereignty over labor, they all understood, became linked to territorial control. By the late nineteenth century contemporary observers treated as commonplace that the transition to cotton production for world markets rested most fundamentally on that domination of territory by newly empowered imperial states. Having lived through the grand defeat of slavery in the American South and experiencing often insurmountable hurdles to transform the global countryside, cotton manufacturers in particular, concerned with continuous access to inexpensive cotton and markets, pressured their governments to exert more control over ever more extensive cotton-growing lands.

The consolidation of states in the United States, Egypt, the Ottoman Empire, and elsewhere, as well as the expansion of imperial control over colonial territories in Korea, western Africa, and Central Asia, significantly extended the reach of the cotton empire in the decades after the American Civil War. Conquest and control, however, did not by itself produce cotton. Expansion demanded incorporation strategies, and state bureaucrats and capitalists systematically applied lessons learned from the mobilization of cotton-growing workers in the United States after emancipation. In some cases, they removed native populations to make land available for cotton-growing settlers, as in eastern Africa. But more typically in the period after the American Civil War, they folded their new subjects into the global cotton-growing complex by constructing infrastructure, creating new labor regimes, and recasting local social structures. This happened in western Anatolia, Central Asia, and western as well as central Africa. This metamorphosis frequently rested on coercion and violence, but not on enslavement. And its particular pace and extent varied with the particular ways these societies had been organized before incorporation and with the relative capacity of colonizing states. Indeed, integration into the global economy sometimes failed or bogged down when imperial subjects successfully retained control of their land and their labor.[6]

These exceptions, however, test the rule: In most cases, emancipation and the emergence of a new imperialism went hand in hand. Slavery became free labor, local sovereignties gave way to nation-states and empires, mule and camel trails to railroads, and war capitalism to scientific agricultural reform, carried out by eager colonial agents drawing on the lessons learned from industrial capitalism. States brought military domination and pacification, infrastructure and property rights in land. And as these states constituted new far-reaching global networks, global networks in turn fostered the strengthening of states.

In the wake of the nineteenth century's great struggles for emancipation, European cotton-consuming countries, the United States, and Japan moved decisively to control and exploit territories where cotton could be grown. This "cotton rush" of sorts reached its zenith at the turn of the century, when new imperial powers embraced it with as much zeal as the older colonial states had done during the Civil War. The reasons were straightforward: While the ability of cotton capitalists to return African-American workers to the growing of cotton for world markets by the 1870s had taken some pressure off the world's countryside, long-established concerns among cotton manufacturers and statesmen about secure and inexpensive cotton supplies were amplified by the late nineteenth century.

As cotton prices rose for the first time in a quarter century—between 1898 and 1913 by 121 percent—European and Japanese manufacturers expressed concerns that the United States would consume increasing percentages of the cotton harvested on its fields in its own factories, leading to shortages and even higher prices. These concerns were further amplified by the temporarily successful efforts by some speculators to "corner" the market and force higher prices by manipulating future and spot transactions on the newly established cotton exchanges. Once these corners failed, a wave of "cotton populism" swept the southern countryside of the United States, with cotton growers determined to collectively enable higher prices for their crops. The boll weevil, an agricultural pest that had begun to spread on American cotton farms in 1892, also seemed to threaten cotton production, and there were pressures on demand as well with cotton factories spreading to new areas of the world. British manufacturers, for example, observed that continental Europeans now consumed one-third of the entire U.S. cotton harvest, which was more than British factories. "One shudders," warned British author Edmund D.

Morel, "to contemplate the consequences which would ensue if anything should again prevent Lancashire from obtaining her share of the cotton crop of America." Rising prices, reported an association of German industrialists, meant a huge sacrifice for the hundreds of thousands of workers employed in German cotton factories. So great was the concern for world cotton supplies at the turn of the century that some modern-day scholars have called this moment a "second cotton famine."[7]

At the same time, the general notion of "raw material independence" became an increasingly important political goal for policy makers and capitalists in Europe and Japan. The idea of securing cotton on lands controlled by imperial states gained traction. As a result, the global cotton "commodity frontier" was pushed into even more numerous areas of the world, intensifying what one historian has so aptly termed "the great land rush."[8]

The expansion of the empire of cotton, as we know, was hardly a new development. Yet the effort at its more "national" organization was a true departure, considering how deeply the cotton industry had been embedded within global trade networks that crossed national and imperial boundaries, and that rested on the connections crafted by merchants. As industrial capital, not merchant capital, became ever more important to states, and as these states became ever more important to national capitalists, the old merchant-dominated order became less relevant, and statesmen and manufacturers increasingly perceived it as potentially threatening to their power, their wealth, and their ability to maintain social stability.

Perhaps most remarkable for its audacity was Russia's attempt to secure "domestic" supplies of the white gold. Since the early 1800s, farsighted government bureaucrats, along with a group of merchants and manufacturers, had imagined Transcaucasia and Central Asia as a source of raw cotton to "prevent all those negative consequences that might arise due to long factory stoppages," as manufacturer Aleksandr Shipov argued. The Russian commander in chief in the Caucasus, Baron G. V. Rosen, had envisaged as early as 1833 that the cotton growers there "would be our Negroes." Yet as late as 1857, such efforts reaped few rewards—Central Asian cotton supplied only 6.5 percent of the needs of the Russian industry.[9]

During the 1860s, however, efforts to promote Central Asian cotton exploded, as a small group of cotton mill owners, united in the Central Asian Trading Association, met in Moscow to find ways to grow more

cotton for Russian factories. Encouraged by a tripling of prices during
the U.S. Civil War, cotton exports from Central Asia to Russia increased
nearly fivefold to 24 million pounds between 1861 and 1864. In a key
moment in 1865, Russia captured Tashkent and the Central Asian khan-
ate of Khokand, which were to become important cotton-growing areas
in the future. Manufacturers began to pressure the Russian government
to further its acquisition of Central Asian territories. In 1869 the Russian Industrial Society, which brought together a wide variety of entrepreneurs, published numerous petitions agitating for deepening Russia's
intervention in Central Asia in order to create a market for Russian goods
and a source for cotton fibers. The government responded favorably, in
part because of its geostrategic desire to counter British moves in Central
Asia, but also because the import of cotton weighed heavily on its balance of trade. By 1890, raw cotton constituted 20 percent of the value of
all Russian imports. The capture of Central Asian territories only whet-
ted the appetite of Russian entrepreneurs. In 1904, Russian industrialists,
among them textile manufacturer Baron Andrei L'vovich Knoop, the son
of Ludwig Knoop, whom we encountered earlier as a Bremen merchant
moving to Russia, created the Commission to Develop Russian Cotton
Growing to investigate further possibilities for the expansion of cotton
agriculture in Central Asia.[10]

Central Asian cotton, as a result, was launched on a path of rapid
state-backed expansion, similar to what happened simultaneously in
India. After the consolidation of Russian rule over Central Asia in the
1860s and 1870s, the imperial government, at the urging of Russian cotton capitalists, systematically worked to increase cotton production. In
1871, Russian colonial bureaucrat Shtaba L. Kostenko commanded that
"the aim of all of our efforts has to be the striving to remove from our
inner markets the American cotton and to replace it with our own, Central Asian one." To make this possible, the colonial administration undertook large-scale infrastructure projects, such as the building of railroads.
In remote areas it had taken up to six months to transport cotton by
camel to the nearest railroad station; now the same journey took two
days. The government sponsored seed plantations and sent agronomists
to help farmers improve agricultural techniques. In addition, the government began planning large-scale irrigation projects and sent bureaucrats
to the United States to study American cotton growing. They eventually
procured American cottonseeds and distributed them to local peasants;

by the late 1880s more than half of the Central Asian cotton crop derived from these seeds. At the same time, large Russian cotton manufacturers erected cotton gins in Turkestan and sent out agents who advanced credit to local growers on the security of their future crop.[11]

As time went on, the colonial state and Russian capitalists increasingly involved themselves in the production process itself, something they had previously avoided. Despite persistent conflicts between the state, which was bent on integrating the territory, and capitalists, who were set on maximizing profits, such efforts resulted in a dramatic increase in the area of cotton sown. In Turkestan, for example, the size of cotton land increased by approximately forty-eight times in the five decades after 1870. As early as the 1880s, growers in Turkestan produced a quarter of all cotton used in Russian cotton factories, and more than half by 1909, enough for one historian to call the province "the cotton colony of Russian capitalism." The state protected its colonial cotton production by levying duties on raw cotton imports, which by 1905 had risen to about 43 percent of the value of cotton. In 1902, a British traveler observed that "the growing of cotton . . . has now become the main occupation of the inhabitants of all the Central Asian Khanates." And by the early 1920s, the Central Asian city of Khokand, a center of the cotton trade, came to be called "cottonopolis." Russia had turned itself into one of the most important cotton-growing countries in the world, ranking fifth behind the United States, India, China, and Egypt.[12]

The radical changes that the Russian state and Russian and Central Asian capitalists were able to effect led others to look with envy at their success. In 1902, German economist August Etienne remarked with genuine admiration that Russia "approaches with rapid steps inexorably its objective to make the Russian cotton industry independent from America." Russia deserved praise, since "with its Asiatic cotton culture it has shown the rest of Europe, what energetic will and well planned cooperation between national and private forces can do to solve the cotton question." A new cotton imperialism had begun to take shape.[13]

Other imperial powers soon embarked upon their own ventures. They had concluded, with Etienne, that "in the overseas program of the European peoples, the encouragement of cotton culture must take a leading role, with the explicit goal to emancipate oneself from America."[14] Invoking memories of the U.S. Civil War, Etienne employed arguments for the state's support of national capitalists that were spreading like wild-

fire through European capitals. States, after all, could speed up the commercialization of potential cotton-growing areas of the world in ways
beyond the reach of individual merchants and masters.[15]

As a result, cotton and colonial expansion went hand in hand, not
only for Russia and Japan, which desperately tried to catch up in the
grand game of securing raw materials for domestic industries, but also for
expansionist stalwarts like Great Britain, France, and the United States,
as well as marginal imperial powers such as Portugal, Germany, Belgium,
and Italy.[16]

Everywhere, European manufacturers, at times supported by textile
workers and their unions, were the driving force behind this recasting,
pressuring their governments to draw more cotton out of various colonial
possessions in Asia and Africa. In Britain, such imperial cotton projects
had the longest history—recall the enormous range of activities that the
Manchester Cotton Supply Association had embarked upon. After the
U.S. Civil War, imperial cotton projects continued, although at a lower
level, having become less essential as American cotton rushed back onto
global markets. But the desire for colonial cotton reached again fever
pitch around the turn of the century as manufacturing volume and prices
rose and new competitors emerged. In 1901, the Oldham Textile Employers' Association observed that "the importance . . . [of] the Growth of
Cotton within the limits of the Empire . . . cannot be over-estimated."
A year later, British cotton manufacturers founded the British Cotton
Growing Association in the cotton metropolis of Manchester, funded by
both manufacturers and textile workers' unions. The association believed
that "all the cotton Lancashire requires can be grown within the limits of
the Empire." The Oldham Master Cotton Spinners' Association agreed:
"an important commercial nation like our own ought not to be dependent on other countries for the supply of cotton which might possibly
be grown within the limits of the empire." By 1916, the Empire Cotton
Growing Association joined in the struggle for colonial cotton—though,
unlike the British Cotton Growing Association, under the auspices of the
government itself. This government institution devoted itself to raising
cotton in the colonies, as "it is essential for the future prosperity of the
country and for the welfare of the Colonies, that cotton growing should
be developed as rapidly as possible in all suitable parts of the Empire."
As late as 1924, the parliamentary secretary of the British and Foreign
Anti-Slavery and Aborigines Protection Society, John Harris, reported

that a British government commission was investigating "to see what steps can be taken to encourage the negroes of the British Empire to grow cotton in such a volume as to gradually free us from the danger of short supply."[17]

In France, cotton manufacturers led the charge for colonial cotton as well. These efforts, as elsewhere, had begun during the American Civil War years, and survived into the postwar decades. In 1867, Mulhouse cotton manufacturer Frédéric Engel-Dollfus agitated for colonial cotton, and in 1889 Louis Faidherbe, a French colonial official with extensive experience in Guadeloupe, Algeria, and Senegal, sounded the same note that "the culture of cotton is the most powerful element in the success of colonization." By the turn of the century, French colonial cotton projects took on increasing urgency: In 1903 French textile entrepreneurs founded the Association Cotonnière Coloniale so as to encourage colonial cotton production and promote "the independence of our national cotton industry."[18]

Cotton manufacturers in other parts of Europe followed suit. Belgian manufacturers in 1901 created the Association Cotonnière de Belgique, which by 1903 had begun to push for cotton growing in the Belgian Congo, including shortly thereafter bringing American cotton planters from Texas to Central Africa. In 1904, Portuguese bureaucrats and manu-

Louis Faidherbe, French colonial
official

facturers founded a colonial cotton-growing association along the lines
of the British Cotton Growing Association. Italian colonialists, upon the
urging of manufacturers organized in the Italian Colonial Cotton Association, focused on expanding cotton production in Italian-controlled
Eritrea.

Despite the United States' domination of cotton export markets,
even there cotton manufacturers pressured for a territorial expansion of
cotton production. Such agitation had a long history, and the connection
between territorial expansion and cotton growing had been an important
strand of discussions among northern economic elites in the antebellum decades. Massachusetts cotton manufacturer Edward Atkinson, an
enthusiastic believer in what he called "free labor cotton," had pointed
out during the 1860s the great potential for expanded cotton production in Texas, called upon the government to remove native peoples from
areas that could be used for cotton agriculture, and pushed for the construction of railroads to transport cotton to the coast. These sentiments
became ever more prominent after the Civil War. In 1868, New England
manufacturers, including Atkinson, in cooperation with southern cotton
planters, created the National Association of Cotton Manufacturers and
Planters, which sought to promote the expansion of cotton agriculture,
primarily in Mississippi and Texas, a project strikingly similar to those of
Europe's imperial elites. In the early twentieth century, the New England
Cotton Manufacturers' Association continued to press for territorial
expansion of cotton agriculture.[19] To make such expansion feasible, they
sought the twin elements of state-sponsored infrastructure projects, such
as the building of levees on the Mississippi, and "the introduction of a
working population into the Cotton States."[20]

The first wave of this incorporation focused on the territorial expansion of
cotton growing in parts of the world that already supplied the white gold
to global markets. As we have seen, after the Civil War, Britain steadily
strengthened its colonial control in India. Tellingly, when the nizam of
Hyderabad requested in 1876 that Berar be returned to his control, the
British refused, even though the nizam's government communicated
clearly to Manchester interests that it was "keenly aware of the importance of developing the cultivation of cotton in these dominions, and in
the future I shall gladly give my attention to fostering the increase of this

production." Egypt, deeply enmeshed in the global cotton economy, by 1882 was transformed into a British colony, alleviating concerns among manufacturers about the "most damaging effect" created by the "unfortunate embroglio in Egypt"—that state's default on its international debt. Territorial control in Egypt went hand in hand with the expansion of cotton agriculture. In 1861, cotton was grown on 259,513 acres, fifty years later on 1,767,678 acres. The land for this expansion came partly from the rededication of wheat fields, but also from irrigating formerly unproductive lands now made accessible to commercial agriculture by the construction of roads and railways. By 1899 the Egyptian Delta Railways Company transported 245 million pounds of cotton, 40 percent of the entire annual harvest. And by 1902 the dams at Aswan and Asyut enabled a year-round supply of water in the cotton-growing areas.[21]

But by the early twentieth century, new cotton-growing areas of the world also saw an enormous growth of their output. There was an extension of cotton agriculture in the Ottoman Empire's Çukurova, for example, where land once used by nomadic tribes for the herding of animals was increasingly turned into cotton farms. By 1908, a quarter of its cultivatable land was used for cotton. In Brazil, cotton cultivation had expanded during the cotton boom of the 1860s into Ceará, where subsistence farmers now became ever more involved in production for world markets. By 1921–22, 1.4 million acres of land were under cotton cultivation, and by the 1930s Brazil had become the world's fourth most important cotton grower, thanks to state support in the form of infrastructure construction and institution building, such as the creation of the Instituto Agronômico de Campinas.[22]

In other older cotton-growing areas, commercial production expanded as well. In Peru, ever more land was rededicated to cotton agriculture, and as a result cotton exports increased dramatically, from an annual average of 0.71 million pounds in the years between 1861 and 1865 to an annual average of 59 million pounds between 1916 and 1920. A few thousand miles to the South, in Argentina, the government made great efforts to enable the industrializing nation to become self-sufficient in raw cotton, part of a larger program of import-substitution growth.[23]

Of the greatest magnitude, however, in terms of additional output of cotton was the further extension of the U.S. cotton complex. Its expansion had been in some ways comparable to that of Russia—state agents and military units had captured contiguous territory and sponsored the construction of new infrastructures to make it accessible. As in Russia, the state would later drain wastelands, contain waterways, and build irrigation infrastructures. Yet while Russia mobilized Central Asian cultivators and forcefully settled nomads to grow cotton (as had also been the case in the Ottoman Empire's Çukurova), the United States removed most indigenous inhabitants from cotton-growing soils as it encouraged citizens from farther east to move in, combining, as historian John C. Weaver has put it, "defiant private initiative" with "the ordered, state-backed certainties of property rights."[24]

Capturing and incorporating new territories as a strategy to increase cotton production for world markets was thus not just significant in the context of European colonial expansion. The U.S. cotton empire expanded at a rapid clip and entered entirely new territories. Before the Civil War, in 1860, 5,386,897 bales of cotton had been produced in the United States, but in 1920 production had increased two and a half times, to 13,429,000 bales, and the territory used for cotton grew rapidly. Twenty-two million acres of additional land was plowed under, or a little more than the total area of the state of South Carolina, or that of the nation of Portugal.[25]

In the United States, the expansion of land under cotton occurred in two distinct ways. Cotton production expanded into the remoter hinterlands of older American cotton states such as Georgia and the Carolinas, now made accessible by railroads, where white upcountry farmers began growing much larger quantities. In the South Atlantic states, annual production, for example, increased by a factor of 3.1 between 1860 and 1920. In Tennessee, Alabama, and Mississippi, by contrast, annual cotton production stayed level until the end of the century, and declined by about 25 percent in 1920, due to the exhaustion of cotton soils and the emergence of more productive cotton-growing areas farther west. Yet even despite the tired soil, cotton production dramatically expanded in some areas, such as in the Yazoo-Mississippi Delta, where large numbers of African Americans cultivated cotton, enabled by new railroads, canals, and levees. As a result, by 1900, "one of the most highly specialized cotton producing areas in the world" emerged. The most dramatic expansion of cotton agriculture, however, occurred farther to the west. In Arkansas, Louisiana, Oklahoma, and Texas, the production of cotton exploded from

1,576,594 bales in 1860 to 7,283,000 bales in 1920—a factor of 4.6 in the half century after the U.S. Civil War. By far the most important expansion took place in Texas, a state whose farmers had only produced 431,463 bales of cotton in 1860, but produced ten times as many, 4,345,000 bales, in 1920. Indeed, the cotton growth of 1920 in Texas alone equaled about 80 percent of that of the entire South in 1860. And by the late 1910s and early 1920s, vast investments in irrigation infrastructure by the federal government enabled a further extension of cotton agriculture into the arid lands of Arizona and California.[26]

Territorial expansion—"the great land rush"—was thus crucial to the position of the United States within the empire of cotton, paralleling developments in other parts of the world. Most of these new cotton-growing territories had been captured from Mexico in 1848, and without their acquisition, Mexico, not the United States, might have been the world's premier cotton producer by the early twentieth century.

The incorporation of these territories relied as much on infrastructure advances as it did on land grabs. As with India and Africa, cotton bloomed alongside the railroad. There were no railroads in Oklahoma before the mid-1880s, but by 1919, 6,534 miles of railroad crisscrossed the state. In Texas, there were 711 miles of railroad in 1870, but 16,113 miles in 1919, including into the fertile lands of the blackland prairie, which the Houston and Texas Central had connected to Dallas in 1872. Once it had done so, cotton production exploded: Dallas County cultivators grew 3,834 bales of cotton in 1870 but 21,649 bales in 1880—an increase of 465 percent in only one decade.[27]

The arrival of cotton growers in most cases displaced the indigenous inhabitants. In the antebellum decades, native peoples who had inhabited the cotton-growing territories of Georgia, Alabama, and Mississippi had been pushed farther west. Now pressure resumed. In October 1865, the Kiowa and Comanche were forced to give up land in central Texas, west Kansas, and eastern New Mexico—land that was turned, among other things, into cotton plantations. Shortly thereafter, many of the Texas plains Indians were pushed into reservations in Oklahoma, and so were the last southwestern Indians during the Red River War of 1874 and 1875, thereby freeing up further land for cotton growing.[28]

Yet Oklahoma ultimately provided little protection for these Native Americans. By the 1880s, the old Oklahoma and Indian territories came under pressure from white settlers who hoped to displace the native population from the most fertile lands. In 1889 the U.S. government gave in and paid the Creeks and Seminoles to surrender claims to land in the center of Oklahoma. Over the next few years, further "land runs" in various parts of Oklahoma put ever more pressure on native people. Many white settlers began to grow cotton, as Oklahoma's fertile soil and its infrastructural opening to the world market, thanks to railroad construction, made such expansion a profitable proposition. By 1907, when Oklahoma became a state, cotton was grown on more than 2 million acres and production had reached 862,000 bales, compared to 425 bales grown on 1,109 acres in 1890. Cleveland County, to cite just one example, produced thirty-nine bales of cotton in 1890, but 11,554 bales in 1909, on land that was once the home of the Quapaw. Creek and Seminole Indians later lived there, tribes that had been forced to leave the southeastern parts of the United States during the late 1820s and 1830s where their lands once before had been turned into cotton plantations. Cotton planters chased America's native peoples from their land, though eventually they hired some of them to work on cotton plantations. In Oklahoma, as elsewhere, the dispossession of America's native people and the expansion of cotton-growing territories went hand in hand—state coercion, indeed, was central to the further expansion of the empire of cotton.[29]

The territorial expansion of the empire of cotton in the United States, Central Asia, Egypt, and Korea, among other places, was vast. Yet statesmen and capitalists pushed the cotton frontier ever further, and Africa, in particular, became the focus of European efforts. These European efforts in fact were directly related to the United States' and Russia's successful expansion of their respective cotton empires, and focused on the goal of emancipating themselves from the United States' cotton supply. Africa, in other words, was to be the "South" and "West" of Europe—a supplier of raw materials, labor, and agricultural commodities that were deemed necessary to confront the global challenge of a rising United States with its seemingly limitless supplies of industrial raw materials, and also of a Russia whose very territorial extent embodied a rising "threat."[30] Imperial efforts at cotton growing in Africa were the cutting edge of the cotton empire's new "national" constitution.

Take Germany, for example. In the last decade of the nineteenth century this latecomer to colonialism engaged in frantic efforts to secure cotton from its African possessions. This was not surprising considering that by 1900 the German cotton industry was the most significant on the European continent and, indeed, the third largest in the world. Despite significant productivity increases, the number of workers directly engaged in cotton spinning and weaving had increased to nearly four hundred thousand, with an estimated one in eight German industrial workers so employed by 1913, making the "healthy development of our cotton industry a vital question for our national economy." The value of their output was the most considerable of all domestic industries and constituted the nation's most important export product. In 1897, the German cotton industry produced goods valued at 1 billion marks, or about 36 percent more than those of the next largest industry, coal, and 45 percent more than the industry that symbolized Germany's economic miracle and all too often overshadows our historical imagination, the male-dominated iron and steel industry. And no other German industry was so reliant on other countries for its crucial raw material. Because all raw cotton came from abroad, it amounted to Germany's costliest import. A full 1 billion pounds of cotton were imported into Germany in 1902. "King Cotton has become the most powerful ruler," observed cotton manufacturer Karl E. Supf, "he has deeply affected the social conditions, yes, even entirely rearranged them."[31]

Considering the size of the industry, German cotton industrialists understandably expressed a desire to secure an ample, regular, and inexpensive supply of raw cotton. From the beginnings of a German mechanized cotton industry that supply had largely come from the United States. However, the cotton shortages of the 1860s had indelibly etched in the minds of cotton industrialists and statesmen the danger of depending on the United States for raw cotton. Indian and Egyptian cotton did gain market share during the crisis, but by the 1880s and 1890s the United States again supplied—depending on the years—between 50 and 90 percent of cotton to the German industry.[32] Such overwhelming market dominance worried cotton interests. By late century, these concerns sharpened as German cotton importers realized that new, competing low-cost manufacturers were emerging in places such as Japan, the southern United States, and Mexico.

German manufacturers and statesmen could do little to alter this situation before their creation of a colonial empire in the 1880s. Once Germany acquired colonies in Africa and the South Seas, however, new ways of solving the "cotton question" emerged. Interest in African cotton reached fever pitch at the turn of the century, when cotton industrialists spoke of a global *"Baumwollkulturkampf"*—a "cotton-growing struggle." Following these concerns, in 1896 these manufacturers created the Colonial Economic Committee (Kolonial-Wirtschaftliches Komitee), an organization devoted to utilizing colonies as a source of raw materials for home industries. More than four hundred German cotton industrialists contributed funds to its operation.[33]

Four factors spurred cotton industrialists' interest in raw cotton production in German colonies. They were deeply concerned about the rise in cotton prices at century's end, which more than doubled between 1898 and 1904. German industrialists argued that the ever greater use of cotton by the two major growing countries, the United States and India, was the root cause of such increases, which they saw as permanent. Most dramatically, the United States had used only about 20 percent of its home-grown cotton in its own factories before the Civil War, yet by the 1870s that proportion had grown to around 33 percent and to nearly 50 percent after 1900. Moreover, like many American industrialists and landowners, German manufacturers feared that the United States lacked sufficient cheap labor to plant, prune, and harvest all the additional cotton now required on global markets. Labor shortages, they argued, would eventually limit the expansion of American cotton agriculture. The cotton market remained volatile, and these price fluctuations made it difficult to plan profitable production. Colonial cotton, in contrast, promised to ensure stable and low prices, and as an added benefit could prevent a repeat of the market disruption they had experienced during the cotton famine of the 1860s.[34]

With that scarcity in mind, manufacturers feared that demand for U.S. cotton by newly emerging manufacturing nations, especially Japan, would further diminish their supplies. And in a strategic move meant to secure broad political support for their agenda, cotton manufacturers argued that a prosperous cotton industry was essential to combatting working-class upheaval. Karl Supf invoked the terrible social effects of the American Civil War, and concluded that "it [was] obvious that a crisis . . . in the cotton industry would include a social danger whose results are unpredictable." Even the generally anticolonial Social Democrats expressed their hope that colonial cotton would break the "cotton monopoly" of the United States. The fantastic plan of these cotton industrialists was to grow cotton for German manufacturers on German-controlled soil under German supervision—in fact, to become more like their American and Russian competitors.[35]

With these arguments, cotton industrialists moved boldly into Germany's public arena. Their interests intersected with those of powerful statesmen and bureaucrats who argued that securing colonial cotton was of great geostrategic importance. As the scholar, engineer, and Africa expert Ernst K. Henrici observed in 1899, "In the great economic competition among peoples, mass production and mass consumption are becoming central. Our colonies, if they should be of real benefit to the mother country, need to aspire towards delivering great quantities of raw materials, so that they can in turn purchase great quantities of the industrial products of the motherland." Only colonial cotton production, argued economist Karl Helfferich, could break the "economic rule of America over the European cotton industry." Colonial cotton, in short, was the only way to resist "American rape."[36]

Colonial cotton symbolized the new symbiosis of a powerful nation-state with powerful national industries. This symbiosis in fact characterized a new form of global capitalism centered on the strengthening of national capital in rival capitalist nations.[37]

Cotton growing was important to European expansion in Africa from its very beginning, just as Africa had provided much of the labor that had enabled cotton industrialization since the 1780s. For example, in 1888—only four years after its African explorations had begun—Germany embarked upon its first systematic trials of growing cotton for world markets on the African continent. In May 1890, a Samoan cotton planter, Ferdinand Goldberg, arrived in the German colony of Togo to investigate the possibilities of cotton growing there. While his experiment failed, in 1900, as we will see, the German imperial government made another effort, recruiting cotton farmers from Alabama to go to Togo and expand its cotton agriculture. At the same time, colonial bureaucrats and cotton manufacturers built huge cotton plantations in German East Africa. In 1907, German textile industrialists Heinrich and Fritz Otto opened a cotton farm in Kilossa; three years later, about a thousand workers cultivated cotton on a full 37,065 acres. Soon the Ottos were joined by the Leipziger Baumwollspinnerei and by manufacturer Hermann Schubert from Zittau in Saxony.[38]

French cotton manufacturers and colonial bureaucrats made similar efforts. In the French Soudan, in Côte d'Ivoire, and in French Equatorial Africa, colonial penetration went hand in hand with an effort to secure cotton—the French minister of colonies studied the prospects for colonial cotton in great detail. African cotton exports to France at first only supplied a very small percentage of the cotton used by the French industry, but they increased rapidly. Côte d'Ivoire, for example, supplied next to no cotton in 1912, but more than 4.4 million pounds in 1925. In other colonies, similar developments occurred. Portuguese colonialists in Mozambique began their first cotton-growing experiments in 1901, an effort that produced 6 million pounds by 1928. The Belgians had begun their first tentative cotton-growing efforts in the Congo territory in 1890, yet production only exploded in the 1920s, and at a cost of tremendous violence. In 1920, rural cultivators produced 3.4 million pounds of cotton in the Belgian Congo, 98.8 million pounds in 1931, and 312 million pounds in 1941. This was a respectable amount, equaling about 15 percent of the production of the United States before the Civil War, when King Cotton reigned supreme.[39]

The British, however, undertook the most significant effort to grow cotton in Africa. By 1913, 74 percent of all cotton exported from Africa to Europe came out of British colonies. In the eyes of the British Cotton Growing Association, no other part of the world had "larger latent possibilities than our West African possessions," with plenty of land and labor available. As Africa's people could no longer be sold to the Americas, Europeans concluded that they might profitably be encouraged or compelled to grow agricultural commodities for world markets at home. Altogether, Africa exported more than 2.315 billion pounds of cotton in 1930, a little more than the United States in the year before the Civil War.[40]

Taken together, between 1860 and 1920, 55 million acres of land in Africa, Asia, and the Americas, at the very least, were newly planted with cotton for world markets—an area larger than that of Massachusetts, Vermont, Rhode Island, Connecticut, New Hampshire, and New York combined. Approximately 80 percent of all that new cotton-growing land was situated in territories that had not grown cotton in 1860, the vast majority of which had come under the effective control of colonial powers only during those years. Indeed, by 1905, cotton experts estimated, a full 15 million people, or about 1 percent of the world's population, were engaged in the growing of cotton. Imperial expansion and the production of ever more cotton for world markets were inextricably linked.[41]

. . .

With the territorial scope of the cotton empire spreading on the wings of powerful imperial states, the struggles over labor mobilization spread as well. Territory alone never sufficed. Indeed, the core question that continued to face these states was the same as it had been in 1865, upon the emancipation of cotton workers in the United States: how to motivate rural cultivators to grow cotton for world markets—that is, how to effect the transformation of the countryside. As the French Association Cotonnière Coloniale put it, it was easy to secure land, but that land "needs arms, labor."[42]

No colonial ruler followed the example of the United States, which had made cotton-growing territories available by removing the native peoples who had dwelled on those lands for centuries. Native peoples in places such as the Çukurova, Central Asia, Egypt, and East Africa were certainly also forced to abandon their use of the land to make space for cotton—a wave of expropriation that accompanied the geographic spread of cotton agriculture in particular, and capitalism in general. Yet colonial governments and strengthening nation-states usually tried to integrate these rural cultivators into the cotton-growing complex. Instead of displacing them, colonizers drew upon their labor in three distinct ways. In some settings, such as India, Central Asia, and western Africa, cotton continued to be produced by indigenous farmers and sold to Western merchants. In other parts of the world, labor was mobilized by settling formerly nomadic people. This was the case, as we will see, in Central Asia, and in the Çukurova, where nomadic groups who for centuries had herded their animals on these plains were settled so as to make space for Anatolia's most significant cotton-growing complex. In yet other areas, settlers from elsewhere came to organize cotton growing by indigenous people on plantations, such as in Algeria and German East Africa, but also in parts of Mexico and Argentina.[43]

No matter which strategy colonial bureaucrats and capitalists employed, eventually the push toward commercial cotton agriculture, as we have seen elsewhere in the cotton countryside, permanently recast social structures. Russian Central Asia provides one example for such a shift. Before Russian occupation, Central Asians grew cotton, spun yarn, and wove cloth, using some for their own needs and exporting the rest to distant markets. Indeed, throughout Central Asia, cotton and cotton products were the most significant industry. Caravans of up to five thousand camels traversed the steppes between the Central Asian khanates and Russia carrying cotton cloth and yarn. The raw cotton for this thriving industry was harvested on small family farms as one crop among many, often sharing the same field with rows of wheat. Most of the cotton grown by family labor was used for the production of textiles within the household, while local merchants bought small quantities to be worked up for trade in more distant markets.[44]

Central Asia was thus a source of manufactured cotton textiles for Russia. In the last decades of the nineteenth century, however, after Russia captured these territories, it became, as we have seen, a supplier of raw cotton for the factories in Moscow and Saint Petersburg, and a market for Russian cotton cloth. To effect that transition, Russian entrepreneurs and colonial bureaucrats rapidly and radically reshaped the cotton-growing countryside. At first, as elsewhere in the empire of cotton, metropolitan merchants and agents of Russian textile firms arrived, purchasing cotton from small farmers and providing them with credit, enabling them to specialize in a nonedible crop. Once cotton exports expanded, these firms increasingly specialized in exporting the crop to metropolitan Russia, and an indigenous capitalist class emerged to deal with the myriad peasant producers, a development roughly parallel to what was unfolding in the southern United States and in India. They provided essential working capital to small farmers, typically charging interest of between 40 and 60 percent annually, though rates of more than 100 percent were not unknown. Such exorbitant interest rates, combined with one or two poor harvests or a price downturn, usually sufficed to make peasants entirely dependent on these advancing merchants even when they did not lose outright control over the land.[45]

By the 1880s, Russian entrepreneurs set out to create large cotton plantations to supplement the cotton grown by small farmers. These plantations, however, quickly failed due to labor shortages. As elsewhere, rural cultivators were reluctant to work for wages and instead preferred to work their own or rented land. As one German observer remarked, "There are only a few propertyless, who can be considered for this kind of work. Landless natives prefer to cultivate on their own account small rented fields. For these reasons, the sowing of cotton on large plantations occurs too late in the season. . . . Entrepreneurs, who own large plantations, find themselves forced to rent them in small units to the natives, under the condition that all cotton grown is to be delivered to the landlord."[46]

As a result of both the inability to mobilize sufficient numbers of workers for large cotton plantations and the tenuous situation of owner-occupiers, a system of sharecropping increasingly emerged, akin to the one prevailing in the U.S. South. The German consul in Saint Petersburg remarked on these changing social relations in 1909, noting that "more and more of the land of long-settled planters is being absorbed by capital-rich merchants; the former owners of the soil in many cases continue to work their former properties as renters of the purchasers of the land." As a result of the crisis of owner-occupiers, middlemen acquired large tracts of land, while the refusal of these landless rural cultivators to work for wages on plantations forced landowners to employ them as sharecroppers. The class structure of this portion of the cotton zone, as elsewhere, changed significantly in the course of a few decades, with the emergence of a large group of indebted farmers and landless agricultural workers.[47]

Sharecropping, however, was often just a way station on a path toward wage labor. An ever larger number of cultivators eventually became hired laborers, despite their preferences, as a result of a large wave of expropria-

"The second hilling of cotton with native hoes":
Central Asian cotton growers, 1913

tion that swept the cotton-growing countryside. Small farmers, highly indebted, lost access to the land and thus were left with few options but to sell their labor. In the cotton district of Fergana, there were approximately two hundred thousand landless workers by 1910. By 1914, 25 to 30 percent of the Fergana population was landless, as the Central Asian countryside, thanks to the determined actions of the Russian state and its cotton capitalists, came to resemble that of the American South. In addition, many of the nomads of Turkestan, losing land and access to fodder crops for their animals, were now forced to settle and make themselves available as agricultural laborers. Globalization once more fixed people to particular places, particularly those places that were not their own, while divorcing them from control over agricultural resources.[48]

This drastic recasting of Central Asian economies opened up new markets for Russian cotton manufacturers, and by 1889 a British traveler observed that "money . . . is being taken from the pockets of Bombay and Manchester, and transferred to the pockets of Nijni Novgorod and Moscow." This escalating focus on cotton growing, as elsewhere, had a grave impact on food security. Like other cotton-growing areas of the world, Central Asia now became dependent on food imports, while at the same time peasants' income became "highly vulnerable to fluctuations in" the cotton market. By World War I, the recast class structure, along with a huge deficit in food crops thanks to the reorientation of local agriculture toward cash crops, produced terrible famines, resulting in significant depopulation. In Turkestan, for example, the population fell by 1.3 million people, or 18.5 percent, between 1914 and 1921.[49]

As states' efforts to control territories by administrative, infrastructural, legal, and military means sharpened along with their capabilities and resources, the question of how precisely to mobilize cotton-growing labor remained prominent. Expertise was in high demand. The surprising, even unlikely story, of how a small group of African Americans, the descendants of slaves, came to play an important role in the efforts by German colonists to recast cotton agriculture in Togo illustrates both the efforts to access colonial sources of cotton for national industries and the ongoing struggle to find cotton-growing labor.

It was a stormy November morning in 1900 when the *Graf Waldersee* steamed out of the port of New York for its journey across the Atlantic to the German city of Hamburg. Among the more than two thousand travelers who glanced one last time at the receding steeples of Trinity Church, the towering Manhattan Life Insurance Building, and the Statue of Liberty, four passengers stood out: James N. Calloway, John Robinson, Allen Burks, and Shepard Harris. All were the sons of slaves, from Alabama, and connected to Booker T. Washington's Tuskegee Industrial and Normal Institute. Calloway was a teacher, and Robinson, Burks, and Harris were students or recent graduates. Perhaps even more remarkable was their mission: They had boarded the *Graf Waldersee* that morning as part of a journey that was to bring them to new jobs in a faraway land—the German colony of Togo, a sliver of West Africa that the Germans had acquired in 1884. In the ancient homeland of the Ewe, these African Americans were to instruct the German colonialists and their subjects on how to grow cotton for export, "to determine the possibility of a rational cotton culture as a native culture, and . . . to show the marketability of the product for German industry.[50]

For the next eight years, these Tuskegee experts advised German colonialists on how to extract more cotton for export from African rural cultivators. They built experimental cotton farms, introduced new strains of cotton, opened a "cotton school," expanded the local infrastructure, and used increasingly coercive measures to force local cultivators to grow cotton for world markets. And indeed, between 1900 and 1913, cotton exports from Togo increased by a factor of thirty-five.[51]

Bereft of experience in cotton growing, German colonial bureaucrats and textile industrialists had looked to the United States for expertise in such matters and immediately had settled on the possibilities of recruiting African Americans to their colonial cotton venue, assuming, like most of their imperial counterparts, that "cotton culture since time immemorial [is] the Negro's favorite culture." To do so, in the summer of 1900 a German aristocrat and agricultural attaché at the German embassy in Washington, D.C., Beno von Herman auf Wain, traveled to Roslindale, Massachusetts, to meet African-American activist and Tuskegee leader Booker T. Washington, asking him for help in recruiting cotton planters and a mechanic "to teach the Negroes there [in Togo] how to plant and harvest cotton in a rational and scientific way." By late September, Washington was able to confirm that he had selected four men who were ready to go. James Calloway, forty, director of the cotton section of Tuskegee, was to direct the mission and supervise its younger members. He had been in charge of Tuskegee's eight-hundred-acre farm and spoke some German. He was to be joined by John Winfrey Robinson, an 1897 Tuskegee graduate; Allen Burks, a 1900 Tuskegee graduate; and Shepard Harris, who had entered Tuskegee in 1886 and had learned the carpentry trade there. They were all the sons of slaves, and according to Washington, the ancestors of two of these experts "came from this part of Africa." Washington insisted to von Herman that "I should very much hope that your Company will not make the same mistake that has been made in the South among our people, that is, teach them to raise nothing but cotton. I find that they make much better progress financially and otherwise where they are taught to raise something to eat at the same time they are raising cotton."[52]

Once Calloway, Robinson, Burks, and Harris arrived in Togo, their operations unfolded in grand style. On land once controlled by the king of Tove, they ventured to build a cotton farm much like the ones they had left behind in the United States. With the help of two hundred local men they cleared the high grass and trees, while local women and children collected the remaining roots to burn them. As a result of such and other exertions, by May they had planted about twenty-five of these acres in cotton and by July about one hundred acres. Starting systematically and virtually ignoring the accumulated experience of the people of Tove, Calloway and his colleagues planted fields with different kinds of cotton at various times to investigate what cotton would grow best and when it should be sown. By April, Calloway reported proudly to Booker T. Washington that "our work looks quite promising . . . and we believe that we will make cotton."[53]

Despite these energetic beginnings the Tuskegee experts soon encountered numerous difficulties. For the African-American planters, for example, it was unimaginable to run a successful cotton farm without draft animals, but the rural cultivators around Tove, reported John Robinson in astonishment, "were as afraid of a horse or cow as a common American youth is of a 'mad dog.'" Not only were they unfamiliar with using draft animals, but the animals themselves did not survive long in the local disease environment. Unanticipated patterns of rainfall also created problems. When the rains started in July, the cotton that the Tuskegee experts had planted right after their arrival rotted. They could have learned as much from local cultivators, but their firm belief in the superiority of their own methods and their inability to communicate in the local language precluded such lessons. The Tuskegee experts also faced nearly insurmountable problems relating to the lack of infrastructure. In order to get their ginning equipment from the beach near Lomé, where they had left it upon arrival a few months earlier, to Tove, they first had to widen the road to make it passable for their wagons. They then needed to hire thirty people to draw the carts, and they still took more than two weeks to return with the equipment. Such reliance on human muscle power also hindered the ginning process.[54]

Despite these frustrations, Calloway, Robinson, Burks, and Harris harvested one bale of Egyptian cotton and four bales of American cotton on their experimental farm in the early summer and five more bales of American cotton in November and December. Considering the enormous input of labor, land, and expertise, this was a meager harvest, but both Calloway and the Colonial Economic Committee considered it a success. The committee concluded that the local climate was indeed, as expected, favorable for the growing of high-quality cotton, that the indigenous population was willing to embrace the crop, and that plenty of land was available to grow cotton, perhaps as much as in Egypt. Calloway concurred, suggesting that production could be expanded further by creating markets where indigenous people could bring their cotton for sale, and by educating rural producers in agricultural techniques, especially the use of plows and draft animals. If these reforms were embraced, Calloway expected that "in a few years we shall be able to export many thousands bales of cotton from this colony. This will not have an effect on the market of the world; it will nevertheless be of great advantage to Germany and especially to the 2½ millions of natives of this colony."[55]

The amount of cotton grown by the Tuskegee experts during their first year in Togo may have been exceedingly small, but the goal of the Colonial Economic Committee had never been to make Calloway and his colleagues into major cotton growers. What German industrialists instead had hoped for was to learn from these experienced cotton farmers and to then transfer that knowledge to local growers. Their goal from the beginning was to make cotton production in Togo a "*Volkskultur*," a people's culture, and not, as elsewhere in the German colonial empire, a "*Plantagenkultur*," a plantation culture.[56]

This choice was partly based on the tremendous problems German cotton interests had encountered with the mobilization of labor for their plantations in German East Africa. These plantations, many of them run by German textile industrialists, had had trouble securing a sufficient number of African laborers, who by and large were not willing to work there. Though local German planters had tried to persuade the colonial administration to raise taxes in order to force rural producers to work for wages, the government had been reluctant to do so, fearing open rebellion.[57]

Such German experiences paralleled those of other colonial powers. In British East Africa it was clearly understood by experts that "the dearth of labour is the most serious difficulty. . . . Coolies must be brought from a distance, as the inhabitants, who get four crops a year off the land without putting themselves to any inconvenience whatever, cannot be got to see that there is any reason why they should work for hire." Wage labor, in fact, was extremely difficult to institutionalize. In British Uganda as well, growing cotton had "consistently been opposed by the peasant growers who are its principal intended beneficiaries." As a result, British colonialists came to believe that "the native will do better work when farming on his own account than when working for wages on a plantation owned by Europeans."[58]

German cotton policy, like that of other colonial powers, was influenced by its encounter with the region's inhabitants, the Ewe, and their old and thriving indigenous cotton industry. For centuries, rural cultivators had interspersed their fields with cotton plants, which local women spun into yarn and men wove into cloth. Throughout the nineteenth century, some of this cotton had also been traded across substantial distances. During the American Civil War, some had even entered world markets, as local rulers had created cotton plantations that they worked with slave laborers, allegedly exporting twenty to forty bales of cotton a month to Liverpool. As late as 1908, the German colonial government reported that manufactured European textiles had not yet destroyed the indigenous spinning and weaving industry. Such a thriving cotton textile industry indeed could be found throughout most of Africa, despite European imports of cloth.[59]

It was this thriving domestic industry that the German colonialists hoped to recast when they expanded their influence into the Togolese hinterland during the 1890s. They hoped that they would be able to change its internal orientation to an external one, just like the British had been able to do in India, and the Russians in Central Asia. Thanks to the exposure to "scientific" agriculture, infrastructure improvements, and incentives provided by "free" markets, indigenous farmers were to grow more cotton of a uniform quality and then sell it to German merchants—just like former slaves had done in the United States. This *"Eingeborenenkultur"*—native culture—was another attempt, after share-cropping, to solve the vexing question of labor that had been at the core of the world cotton industry since the emancipation of slaves in the United States thirty-five years earlier.[60]

Unable to mobilize labor for colonial cotton growing on plantations, and inspired by the expansion of "free labor" cotton in the United States as well as the seemingly successful transmission of these experiences to Togo by the Tuskegee experts, German cotton interests hoped to set up a small number of model farms that would serve as examples to the Ewe. Moreover, the German colonial administration, along with the Tuskegee experts, developed a number of policies to promote their common goals: to encourage Ewe cotton growers to produce more well-ginned and -packed cotton and move it speedily to market. First, to improve the quality of cotton, the Colonial Economic Committee, along with private German investors such as the Deutsche Togogesellschaft, set up gins throughout the cotton-growing areas of Togo. Growers thus did not need to gin the cotton themselves nor to transport the much heavier raw cotton over long distances. Purchasers, in turn, gained control of the cotton much earlier in the production process. Second, the colonial government tried to make the cotton more uniform in appearance by distributing seeds to growers. Here, the studies of the Tuskegee experts mattered a great deal, as they had experimented with Egyptian, American, Peruvian, and Brazilian seeds and had also cataloged existing seeds in Togo. After 1911, an American variety, mixed with Togo strains, was marketed under the name "Togo Sea-Island" and was the only strain distributed by the German authorities. Third, to encourage rural cultivators to grow more cotton, the colonial government set minimum prices for the purchase of cotton, presumably making it less risky for growers to plant cotton. Fourth, to export this cotton, Tuskegee experts, colonial authorities, and the committee concentrated on gaining control of the cotton market, at the beginning mainly by sending members of the cotton expedition, including Calloway and Robinson, to remote areas to purchase cotton from growers. Indeed, by 1902, the Tuskegeans had fanned out over a large area of Togo, running various experimental farms and purchasing cotton whenever there was an opportunity to do so. They had also participated in the building and supervising of cotton collecting stations in various towns.[61]

Price guarantees, ginning facilities, seed selection, and control over markets were critical measures to make more cotton available to German merchants, but even more crucial was the rapid development of an infrastructure to move cotton to the coast. When Calloway and his colleagues first arrived in Togo, it took fifteen days to go to Lomé and return, in wagons pulled by local workers. By 1907, when a railroad connected the most important cotton areas to the coast, transportation time had been cut to a few hours.[62]

In all of these measures, the colonial state played a central role. Indeed, prices, markets, and infrastructure were creations of the colonial administration. And the colonial state's role went further: By taxing rural cultivators and making these taxes payable in labor, the state coerced them to, among other things, carry cotton from Tove to the coast, to build railroads, and even to clear land for cotton.[63] By recasting the context in which rural cultivators came to make their decisions, they hoped to bend their inclinations toward embracing world market production of cotton.

Taken together, the efforts of the Tuskegee experts and the colonial government were spectacularly effective. Cotton exports from Togo rose from 31,863 pounds in 1902 to 238,472 pounds in 1904, and 1,125,993 pounds in 1909. This was only a minuscule part of German cotton imports (indeed, Germany never got more than half a percent of its cotton supply from its colonies), but the rate of expansion (increasing by a factor of thirty-five in seven years) suggested that colonial cotton would have a bright future.[64]

Yet despite such a promising beginning, after 1909, further increases in cotton exports eluded the Tuskegee experts, the Colonial Economic Committee, and the German colonial administration. In 1913, the last full year of German colonial rule in Togo, cotton exports were slightly lower than they had been in 1909. The limits to such an expansion were largely rooted in the ways cotton fitted into the agricultural schemes of local producers. Ewe cultivators, after all, had their own ideas about commodity production, ideas that did not necessarily correspond with those of the Tuskegee experts or the German colonialists.

As elsewhere in the global countryside, cultivators desired to maintain economic and social patterns that gave them control over their work, subsistence, and lives. Traditionally, women had interspersed their corn and yam fields with cotton plants. This provided them with an additional

Removing cotton from the hinterland: a train loaded with cotton bales
in the German colony of Togo, 1905

crop that did not require much additional labor, as the land had to be
hoed and weeded in any case. At first the production and eventual export
of cotton was not necessarily disruptive of these agricultural patterns.
The fact that cotton occupied such a definite place within traditional
work patterns and a long-standing gendered division of labor, however,
placed severe limits on how much this culture could be extended. To the
chagrin of German colonial authorities, it meant, among other things,
that Togolese peasants refused to engage in the monocultural production of cotton, which according to a German report was much disliked
because it was much more labor-intensive and not necessarily more profitable. Corn and yams, moreover, provided cultivators with food, no
matter what the price of cotton. The prices German colonial administrators and merchants offered for raw cotton were too low to persuade peasants to risk abandoning their subsistence crops and to engage only in the
backbreaking work of cotton monoculture. Indeed, even colonial cotton
enthusiast August Etienne recognized dryly that an exclusive focus on the
growing of cotton "entails some risk for peasant economies."[65]

Moreover, cotton exports were limited by keen competition from
indigenous spinners for the white gold. Hans Gruner, the head of the Ger-

Cotton spinning in Togo

man administrative post Misahöhe Station, reported in December 1901, "As in other things the native artisans spoil the price of the raw material, as they receive for the products of their skill unusually high prices." These spinners and weavers, said Gruner, though few in numbers, were willing to pay 50 pfennige for a pound of clean cotton—significantly more than the 25 to 30 pfennigs the German colonialists offered.[66]

Such price discrepancies show that a market in cotton never developed; indeed German merchants who wanted to purchase cotton in Togo had to formally guarantee that they would not pay more than the price stipulated by the colonial administration. Throughout Africa, colonial authorities created such highly regulated and supervised markets, which became increasingly coercive to break peasants' preference to sell cotton to the thriving and more profitable local cotton industry.[67]

European colonialists competed with African purchasers of raw cotton and the continued strength of the domestic cotton industry. They understood clearly, as British economist William Allan McPhee argued in 1926, that "part of the problem, then, is to divert the supply of cotton from the Nigerian hand-looms to the power-looms of Lancashire." The goal was to replace indigenous cloth with imported cloth, to set people free to grow cotton to export it to Europe, a lesson that European cotton kings had learned in India first. Frederick John D. Lugard, a British colonial official in Nigeria, hoped for the decline of cotton manufacturing in the old weaving city of Kano ("Africa's Manchester") to facilitate greater exports, since "the cotton of Zaria will then cease to come to the looms of Kano." To destroy that industry, a "better class of English cloth than that now imported is required, which will supersede the native, and so bring the raw cotton on to the market." Best of all, "The industries of spinning thread, weaving and dyeing afford . . . occupation to many thousands who may possibly become additional producers of raw cotton." Deindustrialization, in his eyes, was the prerequisite for incorporating this African territory and its people into the orbit of Manchester.[68]

Last but not least, the very fact that most African cultivators remained far removed from world markets and experienced little if any commercialization of their lives meant that they felt little economic pressure to produce cash crops, unlike, for example, upcountry farmers in the United States. Thus the Ewe could back up their preference for mixed farming with their ability to maintain it. In precolonial Togo, the Ewe had bought and sold some goods on markets and engaged in long-distance trade. But even after the arrival of the Germans, capitalist social relations had only very marginally penetrated Togo; rural cultivators resisted the logic of long-distance markets in favor of long-established local exchanges and safeguarding their own subsistence production. German colonial officials bemoaned that "unlike America, the peasant here is not dependent on cotton growing for his subsistence. The latter always has access to other crops, and his needs are so low, that he can live without any cash income for extended periods of time." The "dread of starving" that British abolitionists had hoped would replace the "dread of being flogged" as a motivation for colonial people to produce crops for world markets failed in Togo in the face of plentiful alternatives. Such resistance to the global marketplace, moreover, had astonishing staying power, because the Germans were unable to institute systems of exploitive credit relations.[69]

Even before Togo's cotton cultivation stagnated, German colonial authorities understood these forces well. They began to look to experiences elsewhere so as to learn how rural producers could be pressured to increase their production of cotton. Colonial Economic Committee member Karl Supf, aware of the tensions between subsistence and world market production, suggested that the goal of colonial policy should be "to bring the Natives into economic dependence upon us." One way to do so, he suggested, was to increase local taxes and make them payable in cotton. Alternatively, the governor of Togo suggested in December 1903 that small sums of money, secured by future cotton harvests, be advanced to peasants to enable them to focus on cotton, as "an emphatic influence of the governmental agencies on the natives at least for a number of years is essential." He thought the government should explicitly look for ways to "pressure those natives, who took on responsibilities by voluntarily accepting seeds, credit or advances or other support for cotton growing." Yet despite their willingness to force cultivators, the Germans found old habits difficult to break, especially because the relatively weak presence of the German colonial state left the resilient social structure of rural producers, predicated on the continued access to plentiful land, largely untouched. Railroads, markets, and price guarantees were not sufficient to persuade growers to abandon subsistence agriculture.[70]

With efforts to involve rural cultivators in debt schemes faltering, and outright expropriation of land beyond the power of the colonial administration, other forms of coercion became more appealing. While cotton manufacturer Karl Supf recommended "slight pressure," local colonial administrator Georg A. Schmidt suggested the need for "strong pressure" as the best way to increase cotton production. Colonialists systematically undermined markets by setting fixed prices that were completely detached from the world market price, compelling cultivators to bring their cotton to market in ways exactly prescribed by the colonial administration, eliminating middlemen, forcing certain cotton strains on producers, and, last but not least, extracting labor from peasants by force. Not only were roads, railways, and cotton gins built by forced labor, but colonial authorities also asserted ever tighter control over cotton production and the trade of raw cotton. Local government officials supervised the planting of cotton, tried to make sure that fields were regularly weeded, and secured a timely harvest. By 1911, for example, the German administration had created forty-seven authorized buying stations throughout the cotton-growing areas to make sure the sale of cotton occurred only under the watchful eyes of the government; at times, soldiers took on the task of purchasing cotton. A year later, in January 1912, the administration further ordered that every ginning or mercantile company send only government-licensed purchasers to markets. They also stipulated that sellers had to separate good- and poor-quality cotton at all times. By 1914, rules as to how cotton had to be treated were honed further and now included corporal punishment for indigenous growers who violated them. As time went by, force, violence, and coercion became ever more central to German policy.[71]

Such emphasis on coercion increasingly brought conflicts between the Tuskegee teachers and the German colonists. Most pointedly, Robinson believed in the importance of growing subsistence crops along with cotton. He advocated the joint development of cotton and food crops in "harmonious ways," and his teachings reflected Washington's concern that rural African Americans focused too much on the growing of cotton and too little on providing their own subsistence. In fact Robinson brought with him the memory of the defeated struggles of freedpeople in the United States. In an exceptionally wide-ranging letter, Robinson opined that "the source and life of all governments are its people, and the first duty of the government is to maintain this life and source. Consequently, the people are its first and Chief Concern. For that same reason we wish to teach the people cotton culture, because it is good for them, they will gain wealth thereby and the Colony grow richer." "But," Robinson continued, "the people cannot live by Cotton alone. Therefore we should begin now to teach them. Where they grow only maize we will teach them to grow more maize and better maize, and also Cotton. Where they grow now Yams and Cotton they must be shown how to grow larger Yams and finer Cotton." To effect such a slow transition, Robinson believed, it was important not to coerce peasants and instead to involve them with "as little excitement and inconvenience" as possible. Robinson and his colleagues from Alabama, however, were increasingly ignored by the German colonial administration.[72]

Throughout Africa, indeed, coercion became an ever more powerful means of extracting cotton. In Côte d'Ivoire, peasants were forced to grow cotton in specially designated fields under the supervision of local colonial officials. In the Belgian Congo, by 1917 cotton production was made a "culture obligatoire" in which peasants were forced to grow certain amounts and to sell them at below market prices. Those who did not produce sufficient quantities were penalized. If work was not done according to expectations, severe punishments were meted out, including whippings. In the French Soudan, peasants were similarly forced to grow cotton. Peasants in Mozambique faced "sexual degradation and beatings . . . by which the government agent compelled people to produce cotton." The regime of violence was so terrifying that as late as the 1970s, the word "cotton" still evoked, according to two historians, "an almost automatic response: suffering."[73]

Yet in Togo, all these efforts yielded minimal results. After the peak year of 1909, Togo never produced more cotton while under German rule. The experiences of other colonial powers in many other parts of Africa were similar. Meanwhile, the German colonial authorities watched with envy the great expansion of cotton production in Central Asia and western India, where Russian and British colonialists had virtually recast local social structures to make them conducive to cash-crop production. To reorient an economy toward the world market in the absence of clear-cut economic incentives, social relations in the countryside had to be drastically recast—a process that usually took either several decades, as in India, or severe violence, as in the slavery-dominated societies of the American South, the West Indies, and Brazil. To be sure, Africans adapted rapidly to a new set of incentives, as (in a very different context) the pioneering efforts of Gold Coast peasants in the 1890s and 1900s to produce cocoa for world markets demonstrate. But in the absence of such incentives, the Germans in Togo could not wait long enough, nor did they have the administrative, economic, or military capacity to shorten the process. It was only during the 1920s, when France got to govern much of the territory of Togo, that world market production of cotton expanded significantly—three times between 1913 and 1938. But, tellingly, cotton production only truly took off after independence, and

Forced cotton cultivation by peasants in the Belgian Congo, c. 1920

today Togo exports 84 million pounds of cotton, or seventy-five times as much as under German rule. Togo is still one of the world's poorest countries.[74]

The venture of a small group of Tuskegee cotton experts in Togo speaks to a story much larger than itself. The encounter between African Americans one generation removed from slavery, German colonial authorities, and Togolese rural cultivators illuminates a vast recasting of the empire of cotton—and with it global capitalism—in the early twentieth century. Imperial states had taken on unprecedented importance in structuring global raw cotton markets: They secured huge swaths of territory on which cotton could be grown and they used their accumulated bureaucratic, infrastructural, and military might to mobilize cotton-growing labor. And such commitments were only one facet of policies that also included import duties, imperial preferences, and powerful national industrial policies. Within the empire of cotton, global networks had spread their geographic reach and intensified significantly. States shaped these networks, demonstrating how state formation and globalization were part and parcel of the same processes. States captured territories, facilitated their infrastructural incorporation, and mobilized workers to labor on this new land. Wherever we look—in the colonial world, in Russia, in the United States—the control of the cotton-growing countryside depended ever more on powerful nation-states and empires.

To be sure, imperial powers competed with one another over the control of territory, but in their search for ways to make potential cotton-growing lands serve the interests of metropolitan industries, people from all over the empire of cotton also tried to learn from each other's experiences. French, Japanese, and British cotton interests, for example, observed the German activities in Togo closely; they sent delegates to meet with John Robinson. J. Arthur Hutton, the chairman of the British Cotton Growing Association, even saw German efforts in Togo as a model for African cotton growing. The French government now monitored cotton harvests globally and its consulate in Saint Petersburg reported in great detail on developments in Central Asian cotton, as did the German consulate. Though all these efforts were fundamentally about isolating national industries from the vagaries of the world market, they themselves formed part of a new global conversation on cotton. Cotton manufacturers' shared interests in the transformation of the global countryside transcended national boundaries, resulting in the formation of an incipient transnational bourgeoisie during the period before World War I as manufacturers from a wide variety of countries met not just to discuss how to make rural cultivators in Egypt, India, or elsewhere grow more cotton, but also to take pleasure rides on the Nile or dance in the concert halls of Vienna.[75]

The lessons learned from the imperial recasting of the global cotton-growing countryside eventually spread, during the twentieth century, to the most unlikely places: the Soviet Union, independent India, and then to the People's Republic of China. It was the Indian Central Cotton Committee, largely under Indian control, that finally succeeded in recasting Indian cotton agriculture to better suit the needs of its mills in the 1920s and beyond. Just as tellingly, in 1923 the cotton experts of the German Colonial Economic Committee, with the support of some of Germany's major banks and cotton industrialists, became involved in

The revolutionary vanguard II:
Azerbaijan, Soviet cotton
production, 1937

Soviet Central Asia's cotton industry. After having lost the German colonial empire, the object of their work, in World War I they hoped to find yet another source of cotton for German industry, while their Soviet partners eagerly read the publications that the Germans had produced before the war on colonial cotton and hoped to make use of German expertise. The orders that the Soviet cotton committee received in 1923 from the Council of Work and Defense in Moscow were almost identical to the many documents that colonial cotton bureaucrats had produced in Africa, Asia, and elsewhere.[76]

One of the effects of this new political economy of strengthened imperial nation-states was the marginalization of areas once central to regional or even global networks of exchange and power.[77] Nation-states everywhere now focused on their industrial cores and their attendant political economies, leaving little if any space for the political demands of the producers of agricultural commodities such as the planters in the American South had enjoyed before 1865. After the American Civil War, in fact, cotton growers throughout the world had become politically and economically marginalized—a new global periphery had emerged in which millions of farmers, sharecroppers, peasants, and agricultural laborers toiled to keep up industrial capitalism's awe-inspiring advances, while themselves not sharing in them. The particular ways in which regions, countries, and even entire continents were integrated into this new industrial capitalism drastically sharpened global inequalities and cemented them through much of the twentieth century.

Yet despite the enormously more important role of nation-states and empires—a direct result of the overcoming of war capitalism—the cotton empire remained as global as ever. By 1910, for example, it included Indian merchants selling Ugandan cotton to Japan. Former American slaves advised German colonialists in Togo. An Indian from Madras, who had apprenticed in a German textile mill, now directed a cotton plantation in German East Africa. Texas farmers walked the Congolese countryside along with Egyptian agricultural experts to advise their Belgian hosts how to expand cotton production. Russian agricultural experts scouted the Indian, Egyptian, and U.S. countryside to study irrigation schemes. And Japanese agricultural bureaucrats carefully observed cotton agriculture in German West Africa. By 1913, E. R. Bartley Denniss, member of Parliament for the British cotton manufacturing town of Oldham, had concluded, quite perceptively, that the question of cotton supply had become "a world question. The cotton industry of the world is one which makes nations dependent upon one another more than any other industry that exists."[78]

This new geography of global capitalism, so decisively constructed by European and North American states and capitalists, ironically would also bring to an end the more than one-hundred-year dominance of Europe and North America, the twin hubs of the empire of cotton. As the vast expansion of cotton agriculture fed the factories spreading throughout the world, the number of spindles that dotted the global countryside exploded. In 1865, 57 million spindles turned worldwide. By 1920 that number had increased to 155 million.[79] Yet increasingly, these spindles and looms did not twist yarn and weave fabrics in the cities and countryside of western Europe and the northern United States, but in those of the global South.

Chapter Thirteen

The Return of the Global South

The rise of the South: cotton mill near Petropolis, Brazil, c. 1922

Sprawling along the shores of the river Sabarmati near India's western coast, Ahmedabad today is a bustling metropolis of 6 million people. It is Gujarat's most important city. But just a century and a half ago, it was still essentially a medieval town with "its old institutions . . . flourishing; the sarafs and mahajans . . . dominat[ing] trade and industry; the ancient crafts . . . the basis of its prosperity; and its imports and exports mov[ing] on pack animals along the narrow unpaved lanes, flanked by high, unpainted wooden houses, and through the guarded gates in its walls." All that changed, however, with the unprecedented profits and productivity of a new wave of Indian cotton manufacturing. On May 30,

1861, Ranchhodlal Chhotalal ordered steam-powered spinning machines into motion for the first time in the city's history. A few years earlier, the youthful Chhotalal had floated the idea of creating a spinning mill while working as a clerk in a government office. Inspired by the opening of cotton mills in Bombay, he understood that the new technology might radically recast India's industry. Not discouraged by a general lack of enthusiasm among Ahmedabad's commercial classes, he eventually found some merchants and bankers to back his venture. The novel machinery was ordered from Great Britain, complete with a team of British mechanics; after several months Chhotalal's spinning machines arrived in a lurching processional of bullock carts.[1]

In May 1861, sixty-five Shapur Mill workers set twenty-five hundred spindles in motion. While this was but a hobby shop in size, even by contemporary Bombay standards, one fact made it a lighthouse of future investment: The factory was profitable right from the beginning. By early 1865 Chhotalal had hired an additional 235 workers and expanded the mill to ten thousand spindles, and also added one hundred power looms.[2]

Ahmedabad's spectacular rise as one of the world's prime cotton manufacturing locales was only partly due to these cutting-edge British machines. The new enterprises drew deeply from Ahmedabad's long history in cottons. Local merchants, organized in guilds, had for many centuries engaged in the long-distance trade in cottons. Some had accumulated significant amounts of capital in the process, and when the British took over the city from the Marathas in 1818, those merchants continued to play a prominent role in local and long-distance trade. Even after British cotton yarns began to arrive in large quantities by the 1830s, displacing local handicraft manufacturers, many of these merchants incorporated foreign-made yarn into their operations, continuing to finance the domestic weaving sector.[3]

Despite Chhotalal's early success and the region's cotton history, most of the merchants and traditional business classes of Ahmedabad remained reluctant to invest in further mills, content for the time being with high rates of return on moneylending. The transformative wave of cotton mill construction hit those shores only in the 1870s. By then, the deepening crisis in the export-dependent countryside made moneylending less certain, and capital-rich Ahmedadians turned to cotton manufacturing. The Jain merchants Masukhbhai and Jamnabhai Bhagubhai were the first members of Ahmedabad's merchant class to take the plunge. In 1877, they opened the Gujarat Spinning and Weaving Company with

11,561 spindles and 209 looms. In quick order, other merchant families, increasingly shut out of transoceanic trade, followed suit. As in Europe a few decades earlier, old commercial capital was now reinvested in textile manufacturing, soon accounting for the vast majority of investments. And as in the Alsatian city of Mulhouse and elsewhere, these investors were tightly linked to one another. Vaishnav Vanias and Jains dominated the industry. Members of these castes institutionalized their social connections through organizations such as the Jain Conference and the Gujarat Vaishya Sabha, among whose leaders were the city's mill owners.[4] Thanks to the entrepreneurial capital of Ahmedabad's merchants, by 1918, fifty-one cotton mills dotted the banks of the Sabarmati and thirty-five thousand laborers streamed each morning through their gates and toiled relentlessly to turn these investments into profits.

Soon the world was full of such Manchesters, as the growth of the cotton empire went along with its continued movement. The spatial arrangements of the global cotton industry—and with it, of capitalism—were in constant flux. Not only was cotton being grown in new parts of the world, but increasingly it was being spun, woven, and finished in new parts of the world as well. The days of a cotton empire led by the North Atlantic countries were numbered.

Most precipitous was the declining importance of cotton manufacturing in the United Kingdom. In 1860, 61 percent of the world's mechanical spindles had turned there, but by 1900 that percentage had declined to 43 percent and by 1930 to 34 percent. Thanks to workers' struggles for better working conditions, British machines also operated for fewer hours than machines elsewhere. They were also generally older, and thus their share of global output was even smaller, just 11 percent by 1932. The interwar years in particular were an "almost unmitigated disaster" for the British industry, once the workshop of the world, with cotton textiles its leading export. Shipments to Asia, Britain's most important market, collapsed after World War I, with exports to India declining by 46 percent from prewar years, to the Dutch East Indies by 55 percent, and to China by 59 percent. As a result, the British industry began its painful dissolution not simply in relative terms in a growing world economy, but eventually in real losses: 43 percent of all British looms disappeared between 1919 and 1939, along with 41 percent of its mule spindles between 1926 and 1938, and the number of cotton workers fell by 45 percent between 1920 and 1939.[5]

As Britain's industry began to lose its global predominance, continental Europe and the United States retained until 1930 their global share of cotton spindles, at 30 and 20 percent respectively. Yet the reign of these North Atlantic countries in the cotton empire would eventually be cut short by the slower but inexorable rise of the mechanized cotton industry in the vast global South. Indeed, by the 1920s the cotton factories of New England "experienced a collapse . . . even more thorough-going" then the ones of old England. Among the usurpers, Japan was by far the most impressive. In 1880 the country had a mere eight thousand cotton spindles. By 1930, Japan put 7 million spindles in motion, at which point its share of spindles globally was 4.3 percent, just behind Germany (6.7 percent), France (6.2 percent), and Russia (4.6 percent). Japan by 1920 counted only 6.7 percent as many spindles as Great Britain, but by 1937 that number had skyrocketed to 32 percent. It was also the largest investor in cotton production in China, where the industry expanded rapidly from just under a million spindles in 1908 to nearly 4 million in 1930. India was in a similar position, although it started from a slightly stronger base: from 1.6 million spindles in 1877, rising to nearly 9 million in 1930. By the twentieth century, the Asian cotton industry had turned into the world's fastest-growing, as the world's cotton industry returned to where it had largely originated.[6]

Cotton, while becoming clearly less important to the global economy in an age of vast steel mills, chemical plants, and electrical machinery industries, went through a significant geographic shift, foreshadowing, as it had a century before, the next phase of global capitalism. While many mid-nineteenth-century Europeans had persuaded themselves that the wonders of modern industry were reserved to them because of such unchangeable factors as the local climate and geography, their superior religious beliefs and "culture," or even their "racial" characteristics, the geographic shifts of the world's first modern industry showed anyone willing to see that essentializing the particular global geography of a particular moment in the history of capitalism was nothing but a self-serving justification for global inequality. The history of the empire of cotton, in fact, proved them wrong.

This rise of cotton manufacturers in the global South resulted from a shift in the balance of social power in both the heartland of industrial capitalism and its periphery. Industrial capitalism had altered class structures not only in Europe and North America, but also in the global South, which witnessed the rise of new inequalities in state strength and

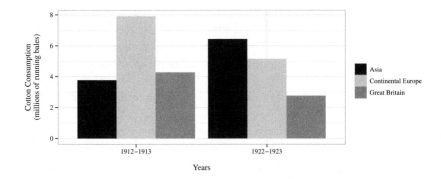

Factory consumption of all kinds of cotton, in millions of running bales

wealth. Two groups played a decisive role in this century-long story: workers in Europe and the northeastern United States, and aspiring cotton capitalists in the global South. They contributed independently to a pair of mutually reinforcing processes: nationalizing social conflicts and strengthening states. As workers organized across the United States and Europe, their collective action increased labor costs. This made low-wage producers elsewhere competitive on global markets, even though those operations were often less efficient. At the same time, capitalists in the global South supported state policies conducive to their own project of domestic industrialization. They could also draw on a pool of low-wage workers, many of whom had been displaced by the rapid transformation of the countryside. This combination of huge wage differentials and the construction of activist states shifted the geography of global cotton manufacturing more rapidly than most observers thought possible. In short, assertive northern workers and politically sophisticated southern capitalists changed the shape of the empire of cotton, foreshadowing the new global division of labor so familiar today.[7]

As collective action of cotton workers in Europe and New England began to affect the global geography of cotton manufacturing, their efforts mirrored an equally profound shift of the nineteenth century: the individual and collective action of slaves and freedpeople, whose struggles had shifted the geography of cotton growing. Of course, cotton manufacturing work-ers had acted collectively before the 1860s. But in the late nineteenth century and thereafter, strikes, unions, and working-class political parties mushroomed under the increasingly warm light of the nation-state, and succeeded in creating much-improved conditions for workers.

The Massachusetts city of Fall River, one of the United States' most important cotton manufacturing centers, is but one of many examples. Early in the nineteenth century, easy access to waterpower had attracted the attention of entrepreneurs to the region. In 1813, Dexter Wheeler and his cousin David Anthony opened the "Fall River Manufactory," followed by numerous similar ventures. By 1837, the city boasted ten cotton mills feeding on a workforce of sons and daughters from the local countryside. Helped by easy shipping access to New York markets, Fall River soon rose to become the nation's leading producer of printed cotton cloth. From 1865 to 1880, the number of factories in Fall River increased fivefold; at the industry's peak, around 1920, the city counted 111 mills, one-eighth of the United States' total spinning capacity, and a textile workforce of some thirty thousand people, nearly as many as in Ahmedabad.[8]

Workers in Fall River consistently organized to improve their wages and working conditions. Thirteen major strikes occurred between 1848 and 1904. Some, like the 1865 mule spinners' strike, involved only one craft's struggle for higher wages; others, like the 1904 strike, shut down almost every mill in the city for months. In fact, Fall River workers' mounting militancy eventually impelled the Massachusetts Bureau of Statistics of Labor to launch a formal investigation into the question posed by an 1881 letter from a Massachusetts state representative: "Why is it that the working people of Fall River are in constant turmoil?"[9]

Workers' militancy was in part driven by the conditions in which they worked and lived. Cotton mills, just as in Ellen Hootton's time a century earlier, remained noisy, polluted, and dangerous places. Factories, now often powered by steam instead of water, had increased in size and often combined spinning and weaving operations. The movements of bobbins and shuttles, power transmission belts, and metal parts assaulted the ears of children, women, and men, cotton dust filled the air and their lungs, and all too often pieces of clothing, hair, or limbs got stuck in machines, grotesquely injuring workers. The workday was harshly regimented and seemingly unending, providing spinners and weavers with little time off. The effects of such work regimes continued to be profound: Among the textile workers of the German city of Aachen, for example, an estimated half of all children died before celebrating their first birthday, an unusually high rate of child mortality. Even during relatively prosperous times, workers suffered subsistence wages and wretched, congested housing. An 1875 Massachusetts Bureau of Statistics of Labor investigation, for example, found one unskilled laborer in Fall River with a family of seven living on a yearly salary of $395.20—below subsistence levels—supplemented by the wages of his twelve-year-old daughter who worked beside him in the mill. His family lived in an "out of repair" five-room tenement "in the worst part of the city." They were in debt, and the only ray of hope was that the next summer would see another child coming of age to send into the mills alongside father and daughter.[10]

In response, Fall River's cotton workers organized. Bolstered by the transplanted cultures of working-class solidarity and militancy brought across the Atlantic by British workers, their often militant strikes allowed them to score a number of pathbreaking victories. In 1866, the mule spinners' union led a successful citywide drive for a ten-hour workday. In 1886, that same union secured a wide-ranging agreement to set the wages of New Bedford, Fall River, and Lawrence spinners on a "sliding scale" based on the price of cotton measured against the selling price of print cloth. In the fallout of the citywide 1904 strike, Fall River mills also accepted the demands of weavers' unions for a sliding scale wage agreement. As early as the 1890s, the city's skilled textile workers began taking an interest in national union organization, and over the next half a century Fall River workers joined or created various regional labor organizations.[11]

Moreover, Fall River's cotton workers along with their New England counterparts succeeded in improving their wages and working conditions, at least in part because as citizens of the United States they enjoyed political influence. Most important, they translated their right to vote into improvements in the workplace. In Fall River and elsewhere, unions and strikes became factors in politics, as it was all but impossible for the government to ignore the demands of enfranchised and mobilized workers.

And Fall River's story was far from exceptional. In France during the early twentieth century, the number of strikes among its approximately 165,000 cotton workers increased rapidly. In 1909, for example, a particularly strike-prone year, there were 198 such strikes

Textile strike, 1934: Firestone Mill, Fall River

with more than thirty thousand participants. Unions also became a growing force in French politics.[12]

In the German industry cotton workers as early as the 1840s had organized collectively. By the early twentieth century, about 25 percent of them were unionized, and in some areas, such as Saxony, the percentage was even higher. These workers were unusually political—in Saxony's cotton industry, for example, "the socialists rule almost unchallenged." One of German social democracy's greatest figures, August Bebel, was elected to the Reichstag with the votes of the weavers of Glauchau-Meerane, and the 1869 founding of the Sozialdemokratische Arbeiterpartei (SPD) had strong support in the textile areas of Saxony and Thuringia.[13]

In Russia, nearly half a million cotton textile workers came to play a key political role as well, especially during the revolutionary upheavals of 1905 and 1918–19, building on many decades of union activities and strikes. The first major strike occurred in the Russian cotton industry in May 1870 at the Nevsky spinning mill in Saint Petersburg, when eight hundred workers left their machines. Two years later, five thousand workers walked out of the Kreenholm cotton mill. Between 1870 and 1894, a total of eighty-five strikes occurred in the cotton textile industry, with 53,341 workers participating; between 1895 and 1900, 139,154 workers participated in 188 such strikes. During the huge 1905 strike wave, workers took part in 1,008 walkouts, succeeding in improving working conditions, shortening the workday, and gaining higher wages. Further waves of cotton workers' strikes hit the Russian industry in 1912 with 135,000 cotton workers, in 1913 with 180,000 workers, and 1914 with 233,000 workers participating, with some of these strikes taking on overtly political tones. When cotton workers' strikes broke out again in 1917, they became a central part of the revolutionary turmoil of that year.[14]

In Switzerland, cotton workers mobilized, albeit less dramatically than in Russia, in the late nineteenth century. In 1908 they created the national Schweizerische Textilarbeiterverband (STAV), the Swiss union of textile workers, which fought for improved working conditions and higher wages and embraced socialist ideas. In Catalonia, socialists and anarchists dominated many mills, with the cotton industry rocked by frequent confrontations between owners and well-organized workers, with massive strikes in 1890 for shorter hours, with bombings of mill owners' houses, and, in 1909, during the *Setmana Tràgica,* with violent insurrection in Barcelona. In the Dutch industry, many strikes occurred around the turn of the century, and in its center, Twente, 60 percent of cotton workers had organized in unions by 1929.[15]

Lancashire, the heartland of the global cotton industry, witnessed the influence and national scope of unions earlier than anywhere else, and served as an inspiration and a source of organizers for cotton workers in other parts of the world, including Fall River. Unions had created national organizations in spinning by 1870 (the Amalgamated Spinners Association), and in 1884, in weaving (the Amalgamated Weavers Association). The Trade Union Congress, bringing British unions together in all sectors of the economy, had been created two years earlier. The spinners' union, which organized the most highly skilled workers in spinning mills, had by the 1880s organized almost 90 percent of all workers, making it perhaps "the most powerful union in the world." They succeeded in raising wages, improving working conditions, and managing technological development. The Spinners were among the "best organized and best-financed workers' organizations in Britain," and they extracted premium wages and captured a large portion of the increasing productivity of the industry from the 1880s to the 1920s. The Cardroom Workers and Weavers, larger, more diffuse, and less committed to exclusive craft practices, also won significant gains for workers. According to a study of data from 1890, the union wage premium for skilled, semiskilled, and unskilled workers in cotton textiles was around 12 percent, a significant margin, providing material rewards for the unionized workers of the cotton districts. The working conditions were still hot and humid and the hours long and hard, but militant, massive, and disciplined collective action from the cotton workers managed to force employers into sharing the profits from increasing industrial productivity.[16]

The mobilization of cotton workers did not in all cases succeed in improving local working and living conditions, but collectively, workers of these North Atlantic nations reduced their hours of work, improved working conditions, increased their wages, and won political influence—often with the tacit support of strengthening states that were above all concerned with social stability and under pressure from politically mobilized and at times enfranchised workers. This trend was magnified by the tendency of wages to roughly converge within national economies, which allowed even less well organized cotton workers to benefit from the collective mobilizations of other groups of workers.[17]

As a result, workers in western and northern Europe and the northeastern parts of the United States spent less and less time at work. Cotton workers in the Saxon town of Crimmitschau demanded in 1903, "One more hour for us! One more hour for our families! One more hour for living!" And even if all too often their demands were unsuccessful, over the years they managed to decrease their working hours from an annual average of 3,190 hours in 1865 to 2,475 hours in 1913. In France, labor legislation in 1892 restricted women to the eleven-hour workday, to be reduced further in subsequent years. In January 1919 the Spanish government gave cotton workers the eight-hour day.[18]

As hours declined, wages increased. In Germany, spinners in 1865 had been paid an average of 390 marks per year. In 1913 they made 860 marks annually, or, in real terms, 53 percent more. In Alsace, there was also a "remarkable" increase of wages between 1870 and 1913. Mulhousian mule spinners had made between 40 and 48 francs every two weeks in 1870, but took home 65 to 75 francs in 1910, which in real terms equaled a doubling of their wages. In Rhode Island, hourly wages of male weavers climbed from 13.5 cents an hour in 1890 to 59.8 cents by 1920; for loom-fixers, wages rose from 18.4 cents an hour in 1890 to 79.1 in 1920.

Even doffers, unskilled laborers generally excluded from formal labor organization, saw their wages rise. In 1890, the average male doffer might expect a daily wage of 135 cents; by 1920, their wages had shot up to 484 cents, an inflation-adjusted 50 percent rise, while the more skilled loom-fixers saw a near doubling of their real wages.[19]

Workers not only improved their wages and working conditions through collective action at the workplace, but they also succeeded in getting newly strengthened nation-states to pass legislation that improved their welfare. Germany enacted a whole slew of worker-friendly legislation: When compulsory schooling came about after 1871, children under twelve years could no longer work in factories, and the effective work time of children under fourteen was thereby limited. Laws in 1910 stipulated that women could not work more than ten hours on weekdays and eight hours on Saturdays, while children under thirteen were now not allowed to work at all. Massachusetts passed its first labor laws in 1836, factory safety rules in 1877, and by 1898 outlawed night work for women and minors, in effect closing factories at night. In Switzerland, as elsewhere, labor laws increased labor costs, as already in 1877 the maximum number of hours for textile workers was limited to eleven, night work for women was outlawed, and child labor for workers under fourteen was declared illegal.[20]

After World War I taxes on employers also surged, demonstrating that the administrative, judicial, and military capacity of the state, so vital for industrial capitalism, came at a rising cost. Indeed, the tensions that led to war in the first place had emerged from the tightening connections between national capital, nation-states, and national territories. The competition between increasingly powerful states rested on the mobilization of their citizens into mass armies and the marshaling of taxes to fund those armies and produce war materials. Under such pressures to extract money and people, states were forced to legitimize themselves democratically.

For European and North American capitalists, this dependence on powerful states—the principal source of their strength—was now also their single greatest weakness, because these states in effect enabled working-class power on the shop floor and in politics. From the perspective of capitalists, indeed, the state was Janus-faced. It enabled the emergence of industrial capitalism, including the mobilization of labor in the global countryside, but it also "trapped" capitalists, as workers would use access to national politics to better their working conditions and wages. As a result, social conflicts that had once been primarily global (as when the mobilization of slaves in Saint-Domingue affected the interests of cotton manufacturers in Britain), or local (as when Indian peasants refused to labor on British cotton plantations), now increasingly became national.

Rising production costs in the core areas of the Industrial Revolution in Britain, continental Europe, and North America, along with unrelenting price competition, in turn dimmed the once blazing profitability of cotton manufacturing. From 1890, northern manufacturers in the United States complained about falling profits. One author reports that dividend payments in German cotton spinning corporations hovered between just 4 and 6 percent between 1900 and 1911, a far cry from the profits that British entrepreneurs had depended on a century earlier. In the Oldham and Rochdale spinning industry, the very heart of Lancashire, average return on capital was low: 3.85 percent from 1886 to 1892, 3.92 percent from 1893 to 1903, rising to 7.89 percent from 1904 to 1910. British cotton capitalists, spoiled by decades of enormous profits, experienced during the 1920s a "rapid fall in spinning company profits."[21]

In some parts of the world, manufacturers responded to rising wages by investing in improved production techniques. New spinning machines and looms allowed for greater output per worker, and in Germany, for example, productivity in spinning more than tripled between 1865 and 1913, and in weaving increased by a factor of six. Such productivity advances meant that wages formed a diminishing portion of total production costs. In German spinning, the share of wages fell from 78 percent of total costs in 1800 to 39 percent in 1913, and in weaving, less dramatically, from 77 to 57 percent.

But in the face of manufacturers' inability to manipulate the price of other inputs, especially raw cotton, wage costs continued to remain important, and thus had a significant impact on profitability. After all, as of 1910, Chinese wages were just 10.8 percent of those in Great Britain and 6.1 percent of those prevalent in the United States, while Chinese workers also labored nearly twice as many hours as their New England counterparts—5,302 hours versus 3,000 hours. Such low-wage competition was found in even more places and it mattered. By the 1920s, for example, competition from Czech and Russian producers proved to be a threat to the German cotton industry. In the long run, cotton manufacturing became a "race to the bottom."[22]

Manufacturers tried to respond to such pressures by using their access to ever more powerful governments to insulate their respective national industries from global competition. Germany's cotton industry depended on an intricate tariff regime catering to the very specific needs of very specific sectors of its cotton industry. As manufacturers organized (in 1870, for example, the Verein Süddeutscher Baumwollindustrieller was founded), they successfully lobbied the state to support their interests, with the *Deutsche Volkswirthschaftliche Correspondenz* arguing that tariff protections were the only means by which the German industry could survive the pressures of imports—a benefit not available to Indian, Chinese, or Egyptian manufacturers. Such tariff protections were important elsewhere too. Italy effectively protected its home market with tariffs on cotton goods passed in 1878 and 1888. In France, at the behest of its cotton manufacturers, increasingly protectionist tariffs had fueled cotton industry profits since the 1880s, especially since 1892 with the passing of the Méline Tariff.[23] The United States also saw the strengthening of its protectionist regime in the last half of the nineteenth century. In 1861, the Morrill Tariff increased duties on imported cotton goods, and while the Tariff Act of 1883 lowered tariffs on cheaper cottons (qualities that American manufacturers could easily produce), it increased them on higher qualities, a trend that continued with the Tariff Act of 1890.

Imperial markets also became ever more important as the new imperialism that had arisen out of the ashes of the nineteenth-century "second slavery" now paid dividends—for some. It paid, for a while, for Catalan manufacturers, who gained in the 1880s more protected access to the remaining Spanish colonies, including a monopoly in the Cuban market. It supported the interests of Russian cotton industrialists in gaining access to the Central Asian territories. It protected British manufacturers from Indian competition. Even in the United States, following the demands of cotton manufacturers such as Edward Atkinson, the government aggressively helped manufacturers gain access to markets abroad, especially in Latin America, the destination of half of U.S. cotton exports.[24]

Despite the frantic efforts of European and New England cotton manufacturers to secure their exalted position within the global empire of cotton, rising labor costs were a powerful countervailing force. The result of the opportunities and constraints created by the nationalization of both labor and capital, rising labor costs opened up new possibilities for manufacturing in those parts of the world in which labor was cheaper and less constrained by state regulations.

As a result, the global South welcomed back home the world's cotton industry in the twentieth century, reversing a century-long departure. At first that move was hardly perceptible, and as late as 1900 was not much more than a flicker on the horizon, but by the 1920s it was the object of widespread debate—a debate, especially in Great Britain and New England, with alarmist undertones.[25] To take but one example, the *Times* of London reported in 1927 on

> the worst spell of bad trade [Lancashire's industry] has encountered since the appalling cotton famine of the sixties, which was caused by the American Civil War. . . . The chief factor in this alarming decline has been the falling off of the great markets of the Far East—India, China, &c. . . . Whereas in 1913 the Far East absorbed 61.6 per cent of our total exports of piece goods, the percentage had fallen in 1925 to 41.8. . . . Both in India and in China there has been a very large increase in home production, and in both countries the rapidly expanding Japanese industry—which has so far been working on the two-shift basis with a 120-hour week, as opposed to Lancashire's maximum of 48—has tended to displace imports from Great Britain.[26]

At about the same time, the governor of Massachusetts, James Michael Curley, forecasted accurately the complete destruction of the New England cotton industry in the absence of massive federal intervention. As local industry representatives concocted in 1935 a "Buy American-Made Goods" campaign to undercut the threat of Japanese imports, Curley met with cotton manufacturers presenting plans to slash wages in Massachusetts in an effort to narrow the gaping wage differential between the American North and South. Despite such protests, the North Atlantic moment in cottons was over, its vaunted productivity and state sponsors no match for the precipitous wage differentials and the burgeoning nation-states of the global South.[27]

The move of cotton manufacturing into the global South began, as had so many of the industry's disruptions, in the United States. Unlike Europe, its working class was never nationalized to the same degree. Labor markets in the United States were highly segmented, with huge differences in

The empire strikes back: Mahatma Gandhi visits Lancashire, chatting with British cotton workers, 1931.

wages in its own national territory. As a result of the peculiar settlement between the expropriated slave owners and industrial capitalism after the Civil War, the United States had a global South within its own territory. And the United States also had its own class of global South capitalists who had, just like their Indian counterparts, accumulated wealth in the trade of raw cotton, ready to move some of it into manufacturing enterprises. The exceptional combination of extensive territory and limited political, economic, and social integration between North and South was the envy of European capitalists—and the first harbinger of the global fate of European cotton manufactures as well.[28]

By 1910, the cotton manufacturing industry of the U.S. South was the world's third largest, after that of Great Britain and the northern states of the Union. This was an amazing departure. At the end of the Civil War there had been hardly any significant cotton manufacturing in the states of the former Confederacy, and as late as 1879 there were seventeen times as many spindles in the North than in the South. Then, however, growth rates in the South skyrocketed—during the 1880s, to an annual 17.6 percent, during the 1890s to 19.1 percent, and to 14.3 percent during the 1900s. To be sure, the cotton industry in the northern states of the Union continued to grow as well, but it did so at a distinctly slower rate of around 4 percent per year. By the 1920s, the northern industry, for the first time, actually shrunk, and by 1925 the U.S. South had more spindles than the North. By 1965, the ratio was 24 to 1, a radical reversal of fortunes.[29]

The massive relocation into the southern United States had begun, decades earlier, at the Atlanta International Cotton Exposition of 1881. There, cotton machinery was sold to the "Exposition Cotton Mills," which became in fact a functioning mill. Endowed with huge supplies of cheap labor and supportive local and regional governments, budding local manufacturers opened additional mills in short order. Lax labor laws, low taxes, low wages, and the absence of trade unions made the South alluring to cotton manufacturers, a region of the United States, according to an industry publication, "where the labor agitator is not such a power, and where the manufacturers are not constantly harassed by new and nagging restrictions." As a result, the period from 1922 to 1933 saw the closing of some ninety-three Massachusetts cotton mills; in the six years after 1922 alone, Massachusetts would come to shed some 40 percent of its total textile workforce. In Fall River, in the decade after 1920, half of the city's mills disappeared.[30]

It was not the proximity to cotton fields that explains this sudden expansion of cotton manufacturing in the U.S. South. Indeed, the slightly lower costs in accessing cotton were offset by the cost of shipping finished goods to northern markets. The secret of success was plentiful and cheap labor. The destruction of slavery and the attendant transformation of the countryside had created a large and malleable pool of low-wage workers for the cotton factories, at first mostly white rural workers, who had once been tenant farmers, and later African American workers, most of them former sharecroppers. As one contemporary observed, southern cotton growers left the farms "like rats leaving a sinking ship." As a result, a 1922 study by the Massachusetts Department of Labor and Industries revealed that whereas the average hourly wage of a Massachusetts mill worker was 41 cents, the going rate was 29 cents in North Carolina, 24 cents in Georgia, 23 cents in South Carolina, and a mere 21 cents in Alabama.[31]

The low wages paid to these workers were even lower because cotton mills could draw on a large number of very young and very cheap workers—a direct result of the low level of national integration of the American working class. In 1905, 23 percent of all workers in southern cotton mills were younger than sixteen, compared to only 6 percent in the northern states. Thanks to the absence of national standards, people also worked longer hours in the South—sixty-four hours per week, even seventy-five hours, was not uncommon. In fact, cotton industrialists' influence over southern state governments—and the disenfranchisement of large segments of the local working class that began during the 1880s—allowed for much laxer labor laws than in other states of the Union, a defining characteristic of emerging cotton industries throughout the global South. Cotton industrialization, moreover, had strong backing from state governments, whose legislators and governors were vulnerable to the enormous influence and power of organized industrialists.[32]

Aware of their own rising costs and declining profits, cotton capitalists in Europe also sought to relocate to places with lower wage costs. But none were able to follow directly the U.S. model, because no other industrial country contained within itself such uneven regional conditions or the legacy of slavery. Still, there were some tentative British investments, such as in India. Other British firms invested in manufacturing in the Ottoman Empire, especially around Izmir and Istanbul, and in Portugal and Russia. In China, foreign-owned mills became important, especially Japanese investments, but also a few operated by English and German investors. In Egypt, British entrepreneurs created in 1894 the Egyptian Cotton Manufacturing Company, followed in 1899 by the Alexandria Anglo-Egyptian Spinning and Weaving Company and then, a year later, the Cairo Egyptian Cotton Mills Limited. French investments became important in the Mexican cotton industry. In Brazil during the first decades of the twentieth century, British, Belgian, and Dutch entrepreneurs opened mills. German textile manufacturers as well invested in low-wage regions. One of the major outlets for German cotton capital was Poland, especially the area around Lodz that the chamber of commerce of the Saxon city of Leipzig called an "offshoot of our German, especially Saxon, textile industry." This "Manchester of the East" experienced a huge boom between 1870 and 1914, seeing the emergence of gigantic factories, such as Carl Scheibler's mill, with seventy-five hundred workers on its payroll.[33]

· · ·

The global South, North Carolina, early twentieth century: "One of the spinners in Whitnel Cotton Mill. She was 51 inches high. Has been in the mill one year. Sometimes works at night. . . . When asked how old she was, she hesitated, then said, 'I don't remember.' "

Cotton industrialists in the former core manufacturing areas of Europe and North America staggered, and then fell, under the combined weight of the twin pressures of mobilized workers and democratic states. They also, as capitalists, felt the pull of new investment opportunities in new industries. Owners of capital in the global South, conversely, awoke to the profit potential of industrial capitalism, and realized the opportunity in their own backyards, their low-cost labor. These entrepreneurs often found themselves surrounded by workers experienced in textile production, had access to modern textile technology, and were master manipulators of their home markets, having often sold imported cotton wares for decades. Like the entrepreneurs of Ahmedabad, they understood that to be profitable, industrial capitalism needed strong states to build infrastructures, protect markets, enforce property rights, and maintain an advantageous labor market. They encountered in their state-building projects more and more activists who, with the rise of national indepen-

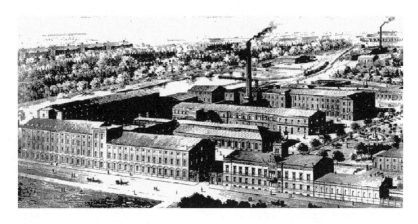

Searching for cheap labor: German industrialist Carl Scheibler invests in the Lodz cotton industry, late nineteenth century.

dence movements, appreciated the power latent in a vibrant industrial economy. The model of industrial capitalism so successfully forged in Europe and North America during the first decades of the nineteenth century now took wing in the global South—tantalizing the imagination of capitalists and state builders, and reshaping the geography of the global economy.[34]

Ideas about industrial capitalism, inspired by the British example, had reached the far corners of the world already by the early nineteenth century. During the cotton revolutions of Germany, Egypt, the United States, and Mexico, forethinking statesmen and capitalists in each country, including Friedrich List, Muhammad Ali, Tench Coxe, and Esteban de Antuñano, had engaged in these discussions and drawn political conclusions from them. By the late nineteenth century, others beyond Europe took note as well. Faced by the pressures from imported cotton wares on domestic handicraft industries and desiring to build an industrial economy, Brazilian, Japanese, Chinese, and other statesmen and capitalists searched for ways to replace imports with domestic production, this time mixing a unique blend of state-building and capital accumulation efforts.

The debate on how to withstand European imperialism and how to take advantage of the new ways toward profit by building manufacturing capacity spread around the world. As early as 1862, Chenk Kuan-ying, a Chinese merchant, had published *Sheng-shih wei-yen* (*Warnings to a Seemingly Prosperous Age*), advocating industrialization. Thirty-five years later, entrepreneur Zhang Jian followed in his footsteps. Concerned with huge imports of cotton yarn and cloth, and especially with the stipulations of the 1895 Treaty of Shimonoseki that allowed for the establishment of foreign-owned cotton mills, he advocated domestic industrialization, and, following words with deeds, built a spinning factory in his native district of Nantong. "People," he argued, "all say that foreign nations maintain themselves through commerce. This is a superficial view. They do not know that the foreign nations' riches and strength is industry. . . . Therefore we must concentrate with single purpose to promote industry. . . . Factories should be set up to produce items of foreign goods which have the greatest sale in China."[35]

Zhang was part of a school of thinkers throughout the global South, among them also Ch'en Chih and Hsueh Fu-ch'eng in China, who tried to reenvision their nations' roles in the global economy. They focused on regaining domestic markets, undoing the process of deindustrialization, introducing Western technology, and, like List, Ali, Coxe, and Antuñano, coaxing the state into supporting industrialization. Arguing that industrial progress equaled national progress, they wanted local industries protected against imports. "The local production of coarse cottons," observed the Brazilian Associação Industrial in 1881, "is being warred upon by foreign competitors and if legislative measures do not come to the industry's aid, all the effort and capital employed to date will be wasted." Referring explicitly to the protectionism of Germany and the United States, they called upon the state to support manufacturing in "young lands." Cotton mills were no less than a "patriotic undertaking."[36] Similarly, Inoue Shozo of Japan's Industrial Development Bureau concluded from a study trip to Germany in 1870 that

I want to make our country equal of Europe and America. . . . After having read something of world history and geography in my search for the source of wealth, the military power, the civilization, and the enlightenment of present-day Western nations, I realized that the source must lie in technology, industry, commerce, and foreign trade. In order to apply these precepts and make the nation rich and strong, we must first of all instruct the people about industry. Then we can manufacture a variety of

Zhang Jian, advocate of
Chinese industrialization

goods and export them, import those articles we lack, and accumulate wealth from abroad.[37]

Such ideas became a mainstay of anti-imperialist conversations, from
Japan to India, from West Africa to Southeast Asia. Strong nation-states,
these thinkers hoped, might one day protect domestic manufacturers,
build infrastructure, mobilize labor, and help manufacturers capture
export markets. There was no little irony in the fact that anticolonial
nationalism as often as not drew on the lessons of colonialism itself.[38]

Yet putting such ideas into practice remained difficult. First, budding
industrialists had to gain control of the levers of state power, overcoming
competing elites. In the U.S. South, for example, cotton manufacturers
could dominate state governments only because of the loss of power of
slaveholding elites. In Brazil, Japan, and elsewhere, the struggle against
rival agrarian elites was far more protracted.

Brazil's cotton industry, for example, unlike the region's poster child,
Mexico, was weak until the 1890s, despite a significant market for cotton
goods, significant local capital accumulation, and large foreign imports.
In 1866, Brazil counted as few as nine spinning mills, with a negligible
15,000 spindles as most textiles were either imported or produced on
plantations. The number of mills increased very slowly in the following
decades, but then it virtually exploded. By 1921, the industry had 242 cotton mills with 1,521,300 spindles and 57,208 looms, employing 108,960

workers. The industry continued to grow, and by 1927, on the eve of the Depression, it consisted of 354 mills.[39]

The three decades after 1892 have been called the golden age of Brazilian cotton manufacturing. It was in the wake of the abolition of slavery in 1888 that manufacturing elites gained greater influence over the government and managed to create policies conducive to their interests, especially tariffs. In 1860, the tariff on cotton had been at a low 30 percent of the value of imports, by 1880 it had doubled to around 60 percent, and after drawn-out battles it increased to as much as 100 percent in 1885. It rose further in 1886, 1889, and 1900. The protectionist 1900 tariffs then remained in effect for three decades, creating a protected market hugely profitable to manufacturers. As a result, by 1920, 75 to 85 percent of all cotton goods used in Brazil were spun and woven domestically. As an Englishman put it in 1921 with some regret, "Twenty-five years ago Brazil was an excellent market for Manchester. . . . First the grays dropped out, and now all these goods are being manufactured in the country and only the very finest qualities remain to be imported."[40]

By the 1890s, Brazilian manufacturers had helped shape the state in ways congenial to their interests. At the same time, unlike their European and New England competitors, they retained access to extremely cheap labor. The vast majority of workers came "from local orphanages, foundling homes, and poorhouses, and from the unemployed urban classes of the cities." Children as young as ten, along with women, populated the shop floors. As late as 1920, when the minimum legal age for employ-

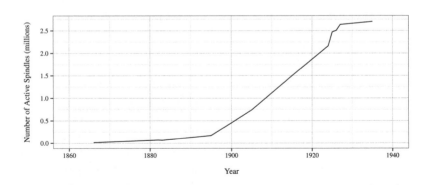

After emancipation, Brazil's cotton industry takes off: number of spindles, 1866–1934.

ment in mills had been raised to fourteen, children much younger were found laboring in the mills and in some instances women and children would work fourteen or even seventeen hours per day. As a cynical contemporary observer saw it, Brazilian children gave a "few years of their labor, at an age when character is forming and regular habits of industry can be acquired."[41]

Cheap labor and tariffs combined with more dynamic markets. Slavery had suppressed internal markets, as many plantations engaged in production of rough textiles, and free-labor immigration had stagnated because of competition from slave labor. Now huge numbers of immigrants came into Brazil, and they, along with newly emancipated agricultural workers, began to purchase textiles in domestic markets. As a result, Brazil finally joined the region's leading cotton producer, Mexico (whose industry continued to expand in no small part due to a national policy of protectionism), on the road to cotton industrialization. From Brazil, the model spread to neighboring Argentina, which saw the opening of its first cotton mill in 1906. There too, the promotion of cotton industrialization became a deliberate project of the state.[42]

Japan experienced an even greater boom in cotton manufacturing. Indeed, it was of such magnitude that Japan became in the course of just a few decades the world's dominant cotton manufacturing power.[43] Japan's history shares some features with Brazil in the late nineteenth century: Neither of these countries was subject to direct colonial rule, but they were vulnerable to significant influences from abroad. They faced huge cotton textile imports. Their economic elites were rooted in a political economy radically different from that of domestic industrialization, but those elites saw new elements emerging that altered the sources of their income and the policy predilections of their class. At the turn of the twentieth century, they were poised for a revolutionary transformation of the state, made no less revolutionary by sharp differences in outcomes.

Japan's history of mechanical cotton production came later than Brazil's, but with equally inauspicious beginnings. In 1867, in Kagoshima City in Kyushu, local rulers of the domain of Satsuma imported six thousand spindles from England. Two other small factories opened around the same time, one in Sakai and the other near Tokyo. Confronted by a flood of imported yarn thanks to the forced opening of the Japanese market by the Treaty of Amity and Commerce of 1858, none of these pioneering projects succeeded commercially.[44]

Faced with these failures and an ever-rising tide of imported cotton goods that had captured a third of the Japanese market, the government began to take a more active role in promoting cotton industrialization. The 1868 Meiji Restoration had brought a more centralized and modernizing regime to power, concentrating the once dispersed powers from the feudal domains of the Tokugawa samurai, whose system of vandalage had dominated Japan for 270 years. From the 1870s, the new nation-state began to pursue a more active policy to promote industry—and cottons were foremost on the new rulers' minds. A member of the Diet, the Japanese parliament, explained: "Because Japanese are clever and can work for cheap wages, they must buy simple goods from abroad, add manual labor, and ship them abroad"—a project for which cotton was superbly suited. The pressure of Western imperialism, as elsewhere, had inspired manufacturing as a nationalist project.[45]

From 1879 to the mid-1880s, the minister of home affairs, Ito Hirobumi, expanded domestic spinning capacity by organizing ten spinning mills with two thousand spindles each, importing them from Great Britain, and giving them on favorable terms to local entrepreneurs. These mills failed as commercial enterprises because their scale of production was too small to make them profitable. But unlike their predecessors they introduced new policies that turned into the key factors for the success of Japan's industrialization: a switch to much cheaper Chinese cotton (in lieu of domestically grown cotton); experimental labor systems that would structure Japanese textile industrialization long into the future (such as the day and night shift system, which gave cost advantages over Indian competitors); and encouragement of government managers to become entrepreneurs themselves. These mills, moreover, created the "ideological roots" of low-wage, harsh-labor regimes, drawing on women whose pay was below subsistence levels, combined with a powerful rhetorical commitment to paternal care, and a transfer of power from samurai and merchants to managers and factory owners.[46]

Easing the shock of such rapid industrialization was Japan's long history in cotton textiles. For centuries, Japanese farmers had grown, spun, and woven cotton in their households for domestic consumption and local markets. By the nineteenth century a thriving putting-out industry had emerged in the countryside, an industry that at first received an enormous boost from the importation of cheap yarns in the wake of the forced opening of Japan's ports.[47]

By 1880, with the possibilities of mechanized cotton spinning demonstrated by government-organized mills, merchants created more—and much more substantial—factories, supported by a state committed to domestic industrialization. That year, the head of the (private) First National Bank, Shibusawa Eiichi, backed the Osaka Spinning Co., which would start operations in 1883 with 10,500 spindles. It was profitable from the beginning. Encouraged, others followed suit, opening several mills of similar size. Using English-trained Japanese engineers, these mills were all incorporated and tapped capital from nobles and wealthy merchants. These new factories were able to outperform British imports in price and even quality. Indeed, as early as 1890, Japan's mill owners were able to dominate their home market, and by 1895 hand spinning had almost completely disappeared. Such successful spinning industrialization, in turn, allowed for the further expansion of weaving in the countryside.[48]

This industrial capitalism forged in Japan, however, was not solely the offspring of nationalist politicians: Emerging industrial interests had applied tremendous pressures on the state and had organized early on for political coordination. The Japanese Spinners' Association had formed itself as a leading lobby in 1882, pressuring the government for policies favorable to cotton industrialization, most importantly the discontinuation of the import tax on raw cotton (which was meant to protect Japanese cotton farmers) and an end to export fees on yarn. The Greater Japan Cotton Spinners' Association followed suit in 1888. In fact, industrialists helped build the very state that supported their interests. Capitalists and rulers were able to implement these lessons because they defeated the visions of rival elites but faced no significant democratic mass movements to contest their control over the state.[49]

A strong state dedicated to the political economy of domestic industrialization mattered tremendously to Japan, but in ways quite different from Brazil. Tariffs at first played no role in Japan's industrialization because the international treaties that had been forced on the nation by Western powers precluded protectionism, and there was indeed no tariff protection before 1911. The state, however, played a key role in importing the new technology, and, perhaps more importantly, helped Japanese capitalists gain access to foreign markets that could be served competitively because of Japan's extremely low labor costs. Prefectural author-

Building a Japanese cotton
industry: Shibusawa Eiichi
(1840–1931)

ities set up "industrial laboratories" that investigated the special needs
of foreign markets and provided weaving companies with blueprints as
to what kind of cloth would sell where—just as the French and British governments had done in the eighteenth century. The Japanese state
also collected market information, which included consular commercial
reports, industrial exhibitions, trade missions, "the dispatch of specific
students to foreign countries in order to conduct research on specific
industries, and commodity exhibition centres abroad . . . , export cartels
from 1906, trade commissioners from 1910, and world tours and business
missions undertaken by exporters." The government, moreover, stood as
the ultimate guarantor for all kinds of debts that were essential for the
success of the industry.[50]

The Japanese government acquired the ability to support local cotton
industrialists in part because of the spoils of war. Indeed, the Japanese
story once more demonstrates the tight link between colonial expansion
and industrial capitalism—the one, in effect, enabling the other. Repa-
rations gained from the 1894–95 Sino-Japanese War—essentially a land
grab—were used to subsidize the nation's shipping industry, thus helping
cotton exports, and fueled the government's ability to provide credit to
the country's trading firms and forgo the revenue generated by duties on
raw cotton imports, which were removed in 1896, cheapening the industry's essential raw material.[51]

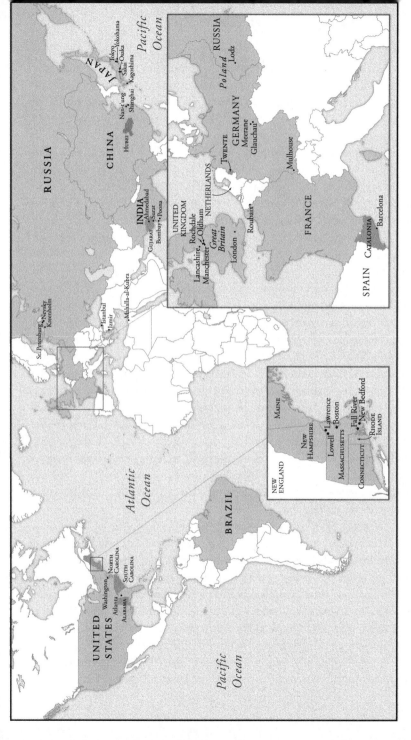

The Rise of the Global South in the Empire of Cotton, 1880–1940

In one of its most decisive effects, the war also provided new markets, which would soon become supremely important to Japan's industrialization. China turned into Japan's most important buyer of yarn and cloth, until 1929, when it gained itself the ability to impose tariffs. By 1894 China consumed 92 percent of all Japanese exports, and by 1897–98, exports of cotton yarn, especially to China, constituted 28 percent of total Japanese spinning output. During World War I, with British manufacturers sidelined, Japan made its deepest penetration to date of the Chinese market. When exports of yarn declined, those of cotton cloth expanded. Between 1903 and 1929, indeed, more than half of all Japanese cotton cloth exports went to China.[52]

During the 1920s, the percentage share of cotton cloth exports to India increased as well, from about 12 percent in 1926 to about 50 percent in 1932. And, again, a state committed to industrialization mattered greatly: The Japanese government exerted political pressure on the British colonial government in India to facilitate their entry into that market. As India's cotton growers became dependent on the Japanese export market, the Japanese government was able to negotiate low tariff barriers for the import of manufactured cottons into India, despite objections from Lancashire manufacturers. When in 1930 the Indian government began discriminating against such imports from Japan in response to pressures from Lancashire, Japanese cotton manufacturers decided to boycott raw cotton from India. That created a problem for India, because remittances to London were paid from these exports. In the Indo-Japanese trade negotiations of 1933 these differences were reconciled, allowing for a freer flow of goods to India from Japan and vice versa. In 1913–14, Japan had exported 7 million yards of cotton piece goods to India; in 1933 it exported 579 million yards.[53]

Low-cost labor was as important as state support to Japan's success. Japanese cotton manufacturers, like manufacturers elsewhere, spent much time thinking about the "problem of labor." Labor costs in Japanese mills were even lower than in India and about one-eighth of those in Lancashire. Initially, mills recruited their workers from their immediate surroundings, but as time went on they increasingly relied on labor recruiters who brought workers from more distant locations, literally scouring the countryside in search of poor farming families.[54]

Women especially were pushed out of the countryside and into factories. In 1897, 79 percent of workers in Japanese cotton factories were female. Most of these women were very young, between fifteen and twenty-five years old, and 15 percent were below age fourteen. Typically they would start working at age thirteen and retire at age twenty, upon marriage. For women workers themselves, employment in factories was a particular moment in their life cycle, related to their preindustrial spinning and weaving within the household, and often motivated by an effort to accumulate savings for a dowry. This massive wave of very young women moving into factories was facilitated by Japanese manufacturers' early embrace of ring spinning, which required mostly unskilled labor.[55]

These young women were subject to extreme exploitation. Away from the protection that their families might have provided, most lived in dormitories next to the mills—company boarding houses that were places of surveillance and disciplinary action. (In this way conditions were quite similar to those in Lowell, Massachusetts, nearly a century earlier.) One 1911 study found that workers often shared beds, and had as little as twenty-seven square feet of space. To stem high rates of labor turnover, companies embraced a rhetoric of paternalism, and at times also more substantive paternalist policies. For the companies, short commutes and total control over the workforce allowed them to exploit their labor to the utmost, operating under a two-shift system, each lasting twelve hours, making perfect use of capital expenses by continuously running the machines.[56]

The state had made possible such low-wage competitiveness by resisting any protective legislation for factory workers in the cotton industry. The Factory Act of 1911 was only extended to cover women and children in the textile industry in 1920. The collective action of Japanese mill owners had postponed the passage of protective labor legislation for forty years—undoubtedly helped by a franchise restricted to propertied men.[57]

Women's principal strategy of resistance to such conditions was absconding, the same tactic Ellen Hootton had employed a century earlier at Eccles' Mill in Lancashire. Turnover, indeed, was tremendous—in 1897, 40 percent of all workers left the factories within six months of taking up employment. In 1900, fewer than half of all spinning workers in Kwansai had worked for their employer for more than a year. Employers responded by locking boarding houses at night, forbidding women to leave them during their free time, and retaining part of their wages until they had served out their employment contracts.[58]

Thanks to this availability of extraordinarily cheap and disenfranchised labor, Japan's cotton industry continued its rapid expansion.[59] By 1902, domestic production had largely replaced imports. By 1909, Japanese spinning factories were the fifth largest consumers of raw cotton in the world. With spinning concentrated in large factories, weaving, including handloom weaving, continued to thrive in the countryside, with multiple small entrepreneurs organizing labor, and eventually, by the 1910s and 1920s, the introduction of power looms in their often very small shops. The value of the cotton industry's output continued to increase thereafter from 19 million yen in 1903 to 405 million yen in 1919. The years between 1920 and 1937 were a golden age for the Japanese cotton industry. In 1933, Japan for the first time exported more cotton cloth than Great Britain, France, and Germany, and was the world's third cotton power after the United Kingdom and the United States. By 1937, Japan had captured 37 percent of the globally traded cotton cloth market, compared to just 27 percent for England. Thanks to this explosion of cotton manufacturing in Japan, Asia as a whole had become again a net exporter of cottons, after a hiatus of about a century and a half.[60]

In the U.S. South, Brazil, and Japan, budding manufacturers overcame competing elites and won the support of the state for domestic industrialization only with considerable difficulty. Yet their difficulties paled in comparison to those in the global South who confronted powerful colonial overlords. Those capitalists fought not just competing elites domestically, or other social groups, but also powerful imperial states

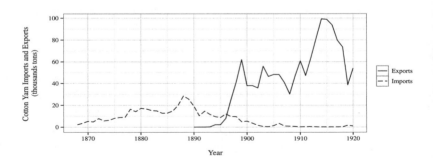

Asian industrialists turn the tables: cotton yarn imports and exports,
Japan (in thousands of tons), 1868–1918

and their economic elites, who were determined to preserve their access to colonial markets and who opposed alternative projects of industrialization. To sustain that struggle, they were forced far beyond the other cotton upstarts to cultivate a mass ideology of nationalism, and to work in concert with other social groups. For them, colonial dependency on the global scene translated into often devastating weakness domestically.

Take Egypt, for example. One of the world's premier cotton-growing countries and one of the earliest cotton industrializers, it failed in its efforts to build a thriving cottage industry until the 1930s. The failure was not for lack of trying. In 1895 a number of capitalists formed the Société Anonyme Egyptienne pour la Filature et le Tissage du Cotton in Cairo, and four years later two additional mills opened their doors. Never very profitable, these mills expired under the weight of an 8 percent tax on the value of their yarn and cloth production and competition from textile imports, especially after Egypt became essentially a free-trade appendage of the British Empire. One-quarter to one-third of all imports into Egypt between 1880 and 1914 consisted of cotton textiles—profitably spun and woven in Britain. There and elsewhere, the colonial state subordinated the project of local industrialization to its efforts to secure export markets for European manufacturers.[61]

Things began to change slowly during World War I, and the newly created Filature Nationale d'Egypte blossomed for a short while. It expanded further in anticipation of tariff reforms in 1930, promoted by an increasingly strident nationalist movement. That tariff reform increased import duties substantially, and soon made domestic industrialization possible, especially in cottons. Most prominently, the ardently nationalist economist and entrepreneur Tal'at Harb, who had created Bank Misr in 1920, drawing on the capital of wealthy landowners, created the Misr Spinning and Weaving Company in the early 1930s, which was well capitalized and expanded rapidly. By 1945, 25,000 of the 117,272 Egyptian textile workers spun and wove cottons in this mill. Tariffs, in effect, had been a gift of the state to its "nascent bourgeoisie."[62]

Stories like Egypt's indicated to capital owners throughout the global South that they needed to create a state supportive of their project of domestic industrialization, and that under conditions of colonialism such a state could not be forged. India, more than any other country, exemplifies this history. On the face of it, India enjoyed all the preconditions for successful cotton industrialization—markets, access to technol-

Anticolonialism reshapes global capitalism:
Tal'at Harb, nationalist economist
and builder of one of the world's largest
cotton mills in Mahalla al-Kubra, Egypt

ogy, skilled labor, low wages, and capital-rich merchants. There was even
a powerful state lording over India. Overcoming competing elites also
proved not to be overwhelmingly difficult. Still, dominated by a foreign
colonial power, Indian industrialists faced insurmountable hurdles to
molding the kind of state they so urgently wanted—hurdles that eventually would draw them into an anticolonial struggle that, while successful,
would also weaken their dominance over workers and peasants.

India's cotton industry emerged, as we have seen, principally in the
cities of Bombay and Ahmedabad in the wake of the American Civil
War. To be sure, the Bombay Spinning and Weaving Company had commenced production as early as 1854, and by 1861 there were 12 spinning
mills in India. Yet the true expansion occurred only after 1865, drawing
on the profits Indian merchants had accumulated during the years of
very high raw cotton prices. Indian capitalists, increasingly pushed out of
the raw cotton trade by European dealers such as the Volkarts, redirected
their capital into cotton mills. By 1875, they had opened 27 mills. In
1897, there were 102 mills in the Bombay Presidency alone. The number
of spindles exploded, from 1.5 million in 1879 to nearly 9 million in 1929.
Cotton manufacturing would come to dominate the Indian manufacturing economy.[63]

India's dynamic entrepreneurial class drew to the best of their ability upon the British colonial state. Export markets within the colonial empire, for example, became highly prized, with much of the industry's markets to be found within the British sphere of influence—by the 1890s, 80 percent of the yarn exported from Bombay went to China.[64] This state also created infrastructures, laws, regulations, and rules within which economic life was increasingly embedded. As the state pushed for a massive commercialization of the countryside, more dynamic markets for manufactured goods emerged, which benefited Indian cotton manufacturers.

Indian cotton industrialists initially also drew on the colonial state for the mobilization of labor—after all, changes within the countryside drove huge numbers of workers into cities and into cotton mills. During 1896, an estimated 146,000 workers labored in Indian cotton mills, and 625,000 in 1940, a significant figure for a country that hardly saw any other factory production. As elsewhere, the first generation of mill workers remained in touch with the villages from which they hailed. For many families, sending one member into the city to work in a factory was a strategy to retain access to land. But unlike elsewhere in the empire of cotton, most of these workers were men. The roots of India's proletariat, like its bourgeoisie, were to be found in cottons. Indeed, "cheap labor" was widely seen as India's most distinctive competitive advantage—a proletariat created by, among other factors, the decisive actions of a powerful colonial state.[65]

But while no doubt crucial to many aspects of cotton industrialization, the colonial state in India was peculiar and often destructive of local industrial dreams—it was, after all, subject to the pressures of statesmen and capitalists in England, not in India. This peculiarity showed with regard to labor. As elsewhere, working conditions in the Indian cotton textile mills were terrible. Days lasted thirteen to fourteen hours during summer, and ten to twelve hours in winter. Temperatures in mills often exceeded 90 degrees. Mill owners justified these conditions, in the words of the Bombay Millowners' Association in 1910, by arguing that their workers were "mere machines of blind industrialism, having no initiative of their own and with no great consideration for the future," words that would have sounded strangely familiar to European manufacturers a century earlier. Yet unlike in Japan, and in a sign that Indian capitalists enjoyed significantly less sway over the state than their Japanese counterparts, working conditions improved and labor costs increased thanks to government intervention. The Indian Factory Act of 1891, passed at the behest of Lancashire cotton manufacturers concerned with Indian competition, limited the number of hours children were allowed to work in mills. Labor legislation in 1891 and 1911 further regulated child labor, women's work, and hours. While working conditions and wages remained abysmal, Indian mill owners still opposed these acts, complaining about the low productivity of their workers and arguing that "any restrictive legislation sought to be imposed on us at the insistence of our friends of Lancashire will have to be resisted in a strenuous manner." Yet confronted with British textile workers' self-serving protests against "the excessive working hours in the Bombay mills and the employment of children" and with Lancashire mill owners fearing for their export markets, they failed. Subduing labor under conditions of colonialism proved difficult.[66]

Most striking, however, was the exceptional character of the colonial state in India when it came to the question of market access. Its greatest success, in many ways, was to facilitate the vast influx of British cotton goods, making India into Lancashire's most important market, and severely damaging its handicraft industry.[67] Industrialization and deindustrialization thus intersected on the Indian subcontinent—and it was the Janus-faced nature of the Indian state, strong but beholden to foreign interests, that delayed and stunted Indian cotton industrialization. Indian capitalists had to share the spoils of the British-initiated transformation of the subcontinent with a powerful group of foreign capitalists and statesmen.[68]

Capital-rich elites in the global South from Ahmedabad to Rowan County, North Carolina, from Petropolis to Osaka, from Mahalla-al-Kubra to Veracruz tried to jump on the cotton industrialization bandwagon, and in doing so they learned about the importance of strong states to industrialization. If they were unusually perceptive, they recognized the emerging weaknesses of European and North American cotton capital rooted in that same tight link to the nation-state. Their experiences were quite different. While in Brazil, the southern United States, and Japan they succeeded by gaining power over competing elites and then by forging a state responsive to their needs, in Egypt and India the project of domestic industrialization encountered a powerful hurdle—the colonial state itself. But wherever global South capitalists succeeded in carving out a niche for themselves in the global cotton industry, they did so because two processes emerged simultaneously: the nationalization of social conflict in the core countries of the first Industrial Revolution, which increased labor costs, and the construction of states favoring a project of domestic industrialization and keeping down labor costs in the global South. It was in China that these stories came together.

Cotton industrialization came to China later than to the U.S. South, Japan, India, or Brazil. This was not for lack of experience in cotton manufacturing, difficulty obtaining raw cotton, the absence of markets or capital, or lack of access to modern manufacturing technology. As we know, China had one of the world's oldest and largest cotton manufacturing complexes, and indeed until the mid-nineteenth century Chinese peasants were the single most significant growers of cotton globally, nearly all of which was manufactured into yarn and cloth domestically. In turn, the spinning and weaving of cotton were China's most important manufacturing activities.[69]

Despite such ideal preconditions for cotton industrialization, mechanization only began at the end of the nineteenth century. To some extent the very vibrancy of Chinese traditional cotton manufacturing made industrialization more difficult. As with much of the cotton belt prior to the nineteenth century, millions of peasants in China's countryside produced cottons for their own use or for nearby markets, with little pressure to do otherwise. As late as midcentury, 45 percent of peasant households may have produced cloth. Moreover, Western imperialists began to put pressure on China's port cities, deluging the country in the second half of the nineteenth century with yarn and cloth. European merchants and European governments (along with those from the United States) pressured the Chinese state for market access, with the 1877 Chefoo convention, for example, stipulating further access to deep-sea as well as Yangtze ports, and the abolition of internal duties. "The foreign merchant has waited long and patiently for the attainment of these objects," argued one such Western merchant in 1877. "In his opinion they are essential [. . .] for the successful development of his trade with China." Indeed, market penetration was a clearly articulated political goal of all imperial powers. As a result, the import of cotton goods into China increased tremendously, yarn by a factor of twenty-four, while cloth imports doubled between the 1880s and 1910s. By 1916 the U.S. Department of Commerce called China "the largest market for cotton yarns in the world," including for U.S. manufacturers. At first, the vast majority of cotton yarn and cloth imports into China originated from the United Kingdom and the United States. After 1900, imports came mostly from Japanese manufacturers.[70]

Such market opening rested on the uses of imperial power, that is, strong North Atlantic states committed to providing market access to their own industrialists. In 1882, for example, the United States sent a gunboat to Shanghai to support its cotton interests. Four years earlier, Peng Ruzong had founded a cotton company—the Shanghai Cotton Cloth Mill—which received a ten-year monopoly in 1882. When William S. Wetmore, head of the American merchant firm Frazer and Co., began acquiring Chinese investors for a competing mill, the Shanghai Cotton Cloth Mill immediately entreated the Chinese government to defend its interests. Trumped-up arrest warrants were issued for the American firm's two principal Chinese investors, forcing both into hiding. The newly appointed U.S. minister to China decided it was time "to impress upon the Chinese the fact that we were a government, with power to maintain our rights under the treaties." The U.S. corvette *Ashuelot* was promptly stationed in Shanghai for the winter, on orders approved by President Chester A. Arthur himself.[71]

Faced with a flood of imports, the tantalizing prospects of profiting from mechanized cotton production, and the desire to strengthen the Chinese state vis-à-vis Western imperial powers, modernizing elites, both within the state bureaucracy and among capitalists, began to favor a project of domestic industrialization. As unlikely allies in that project, they teamed up with foreign entrepreneurs, especially from Japan, who in their search for ever cheaper labor invested heavily in the Chinese cotton industry. Together they created one of the most rapidly growing cotton industries in the world.

The first modern Chinese cotton mill, the Shanghai Cotton Cloth Mill, as we have seen, began operations in the early 1880s. At first the industry grew slowly. By 1896 there were only 12 mills with 412,000 spindles. Two decades later, the number had risen to 31 mills with somewhat more than 1 million spindles. Then came World War I, which played a similar role for Chinese cotton industrialization, and Asia's more generally, as the Napoleonic Wars had done for continental Europe 125 years earlier. Its protectionist effects created a mill building boom, and by 1925 there were 118 mills with more than 3 million spindles, employing 252,031 workers, half of them in Shanghai alone. The growth of cotton manufacturing in China after 1914 was indeed the fastest in the world. Globally, the number of spindles increased by 14 percent between 1913 and 1931—but in China it skyrocketed by 297 percent, or twenty times as fast. Taking 1913 as the base year, by 1931 the number of China's spindles increased to 397, Japan's to 313, India's to 150, the United States' to 106, while Russia's declined to 99, Great Britain's to 99, and Germany's to 97. The same was the case with mechanical looms: The number of such looms more than tripled in China between 1913 and 1925, nearly tripled in Japan, but slightly declined in Great Britain.[72]

By the early 1920s, Chinese cotton yarn manufacturing had gained a dominant position in the domestic market, and by 1925 China was able to export more cotton manufactures than it imported. By 1937, it was once again self-sufficient in cotton yarn and goods: As recently as 1875, 98.1 percent of all yarn in China had still been spun by hand, but by 1931 only 16.3 percent of all yarn was so manufactured, while nearly all the rest came out of domestic factories. Cotton had become China's most important factory industry; according to writer Chong Su, "Shanghai is fast becoming the Manchester of the Far East."[73]

This industry drew, as elsewhere, on cheap labor; indeed, labor in China was cheaper than anywhere else in the world, including Japan. When the U.S. Department of Commerce reported in 1916 on the situation in Chinese cotton mills, it found tens of thousands of workers laboring day and night on twelve-hour shifts, with the only break for twelve hours on Sundays. Their pay amounted to about 10 U.S. cents a day. With working hours "longer than in any other country in the world" and no child labor laws on the books, China was the world's lowest-cost producer. Even owners of cotton mills in Bombay feared Chinese competition, not least because, unlike them, China's industry "enjoys perfect immunity from restrictive factory legislation."[74]

Even in a context of low-cost labor, Chinese manufacturers showed a clear preference for the very cheapest workers—children and women. By 1897, 79 percent of workers in these spinning factories were female, and 15 percent boys and girls younger than fourteen years old. If earlier in the nineteenth century women could not be moved into factories, as mentioned, by the 1890s changes within the countryside, not least occasioned by low-cost imports of cotton yarn, had made women's labor available. Female or male, rural migrants became the core of the workforce, often

416 EMPIRE OF COTTON

hired directly in the countryside under conditions involving significant coercion. Privileged male workers within the factories, so called "Number Ones," engaged them in return for "gifts." Workers, especially women, were often traded, as very poor families sold their daughters into mill labor, with their wages controlled at least in part by others, a status that closely resembled bonded labor and was very difficult to escape.[75]

Another decisive factor in the rise of the Chinese cotton industry was government support. State bureaucrats believed that China needed cotton mills to withstand foreign pressures and they used their albeit limited state capacity to provide strategic support to these enterprises. Just like in Japan and elsewhere, they did so partly under pressure from ever better organized and mobilized urban economic elites. The Chinese state helped keep labor costs down by repressing workers' collective action with a strong police or even army presence in cotton mills. During the 1920s, Shanghai mill owners, with the support of Kuomintang leader Chiang Kai-shek, went along with the murder of thousands of left-leaning labor leaders. But the state mattered in other ways as well. At times it granted monopoly rights to certain enterprises to attract capital, and on occasion the state provided what one author has called "bureaucratic capital" to enable the start up of a mill. Provincial governments promised low taxes and other supports, along with loans and even machines. But the financial means, and indeed the power, of the government was quite limited, especially after the defeat in the 1895 war against Japan, which saddled China with indemnity payments. It was only in the 1920s and 1930s, when Chinese nationalists called for a boycott of Japanese goods, and after 1929, when China regained the capacity to create tariff barriers, an ability that it had lost in 1842, that Chinese industrialists could begin to compete effectively.[76]

Unlike the situation in Japan, or, for that matter, other parts of the world, Chinese investments in cotton mills were rapidly combined with, and eventually superseded by, international investments. The reason for this unusual deep penetration by foreign capital was the very weakness of the Chinese state: The 1895 Treaty of Shimonoseki that ended the Sino-Japanese War, as mentioned, explicitly allowed for the establishment of foreign-owned mills in China. Two years later, the first foreign-owned mill opened, and by 1898 there were already four such mills in Shanghai. Many followed. Some of these mills drew on British and German capital and expertise, but the vast majority were of Japanese origin.

Ultimately, the Japanese cotton industry created its own low-wage production complex across the East China Sea, just as the Germans would do in Poland and the manufacturers of New England in the states of the U.S. South. The first Japanese-owned mill opened in 1902 in Shanghai, drawn by labor costs only half of what they had been in Japan. Chinese workers lacked any of the paternalist welfare benefits increasingly enjoyed by Japanese workers. Such investments made Japanese-owned mills the fastest-growing segment of the Chinese cotton industry, and by 1925 nearly half of Chinese spinning capacity was foreign-owned, overwhelmingly by the Japanese.[77]

Considering the importance of states to industrial capitalism's political economy, and the onslaught of an ever larger number of imperial powers such as the United States and Germany, it is not surprising that economic elites throughout the global South aspired to forge such states as well. European and North American statesmen and capitalists resisted them in this project, however, and in turn became even more dependent on their respective states, states strengthened by the colonial project and whose tasks now included containing ever more vibrant anticolonial movements. The ensuing struggle was fierce and violent, creating for budding manufacturers in the global South conditions fundamentally different from the ones their counterparts had faced a hundred years earlier in western Europe and the United States. Because their opponents—mighty North

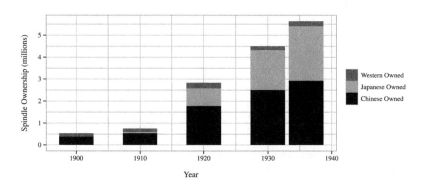

Ownership of spindles in Chinese cotton production, 1900–1936

Atlantic states tightly linked to wealthy capitalists—were so powerful, the new entrepreneurs were forced to build coalitions with increasingly mobilized and nationalized groups of workers and peasants within their own societies. As they were unable to fight on both foreign and popular fronts, their dependence on subordinate social groups in the process of state making distinguished their trajectory toward industrialization from Europe's or North America's. The legacy of colonialism would remain a powerful influence long after independence even while decolonialization became perhaps the single most significant event in the history of twentieth-century capitalism.

As capital-rich merchants and bankers along with their rulers in the global South worked to create conditions conducive to cotton industrialization, and industrialization more broadly, they developed a devastating critique of colonialism. Entrepreneurs in Shanghai, Mahalla al-Kubra, Ahmedabad, and elsewhere saw the urgent need for a state responsive to their interests—a goal that brought them into open opposition to foreign powers.[78] Indian cotton capitalists were among the most eloquent, as they vocally accused the colonial state of being beholden to the interests of Lancashire. British colonialism, they argued, had failed to allow Indian capitalists the benefit of protected markets, as the tariff policy of the colonial government was guided by the principle of allowing for the massive importation of English yarn and cloth.

In response to such discrimination, Indian capitalists mobilized politically. In Bombay, they formed the Millowners' Association to articulate their demands. Ahmedabad's Gujarati counterparts followed suit and organized the Gujarat Industrial Association, advocating for protectionism. One of their first struggles began in the 1890s against the excise tax that they were forced to pay on their products to make up for modest import duties, a tax they found to be "not fair on any principle"—"an altogether unnecessary and indefensible sop to Lancashire." This struggle carried into the new century, with mill owner and activist Ambalal Sakarlal Desai complaining at the Indian National Congress meeting in Ahmedabad in 1902 that the "heavy duties imposed on the textile industry are unjustly borne by every householder of Ahmedabad."[79]

In this conflict, the mill owners encountered Indian nationalists, who focused a significant share of their agitation on the ill effects of British colonialism on Indian cotton industrialization. *The Mahratta,* published in Poona by militant nationalist Bal Gangadhar Tilak, consistently

Narottam Morarjee, cotton manufacturer and chairman
of the Bombay Millowners' Association, 1894

expressed opposition to colonial tariff policies. It favored mass protests against the cotton duties bill and accused the colonial government of "sacrificing" India for Lancashire through the "cotton duties crime." A year later, the colonial government sent Tilak to jail for sedition. Even Gopal Krishna Gokhale, founder of the Servants of India Society and a leader of the Indian National Congress, who could not agree on much with Tilak, was opposed to the tariff policies of the British in regard to cotton. When the Imperial Legislative Council was enlarged in India in 1911, mill owner Ratanji Dadabhoy Tata demanded abolition of the excise duties, supported by fifteen of the sixteen Indian members. For freedom fighter Mahatma Gandhi, these duties were "an instance of fiscal injustice . . . unparalleled in any civilized country of modern times." Indeed, the struggle over the excise duty on cotton goods was one of the first great flare-ups of the anticolonial struggle, as the political interests of cotton manufacturers became important to Indian anticolonialism more broadly.[80]

Cotton capitalists not only sought relief from excise taxes and protection; they also wanted the state to be more supportive in their efforts to capture export markets. Indian mill owners, like their British counterparts, recognized the promise of distant markets—in Africa, for example—and went so far as to produce cloth specifically designed for the tastes of East Africans. But they bemoaned that "there really exists no official organization for the supply to Indian merchants and manufacturers of the trade intelligence so indispensable to their enterprise which the Foreign Office and the Board of Trade purvey to the British trader." Such market information, gathered by governments, had become increasingly important to manufacturers. To access foreign markets they needed the support of the state, support that the colonial government, unlike, for example, the contemporary Japanese government, was not likely to provide.[81]

One of the strategies that Indian nationalists increasingly advocated in opposition to the British presence in India was to encourage consumption of domestically manufactured textiles. The first Indian Industrial Conference meeting in 1905, bringing together industrialists from all over India, decided to "foster and extend the use of such manufactures in India in preference to foreign goods." That demand intersected with the emerging Swadeshi movement, which advocated Indian self-sufficiency, especially in cottons, and symbolized the confluence of cotton entrepreneurs and the emerging nationalist political elites. Tilak was "glad to find that associations and leagues have been formed in various places to advocate the necessity of using native cloth and thus ousting Lancashire and Manchester from the Indian market," and the increasingly influential Indian National Congress, founded in 1885, supported the Swadeshi movement. Indian entrepreneurs agreed: Ahmedabad textile pioneer Ranchhodlal Chhotalal, along with others, created the Swadeshi Udhyam Vardhak Mandli (Organization for the Promotion of Indigenous Industry); Jamshetji Nusserwanji Tata named one of his mills the Swadeshi Mill; and Ambalal Sakarlal Desai, of the Ahmedabad Merchants Spinning Company, strongly supported Swadeshi. As the Chairman of the Bombay Millowners' Association, Vithaldas Damodar Thackersey remarked at the annual meeting in 1907, he was "glad to see . . . the increased interest which the public take in indigenous industries under the impulse of the Swadeshi movement." Hopes ran high that domestic industrialization would restore India's former importance to the global economy. Symbolizing the great significance of cotton to nationalism and anticolonialism, a few years later Gandhi not only wrote a history of cotton in India, but also publicly spun cotton on a spinning wheel, the same mechanism that the Indian National Congress chose in 1930 as the centerpiece for its flag.[82]

Gandhi was nostalgic about homespun cotton, but Indian industrialists had a realpolitik appreciation of decolonialization. They agreed with Gandhi that the radical spatial recasting of the global cotton industry in the nineteenth century was one of the most damaging effects of colonialism—but they also had a significant interest in furthering the colonial project of turning rural cotton spinners and weavers into the producers and consumers of commodities, with Sir Purshotamdas Thakurdas, mill owner and president of the East India Cotton Association, urging in 1919 that "measures must be taken to protect the quality of Indian cotton." Indian mill owners fought just as strenuously for recasting the Indian countryside as their British counterparts had done. Tata himself suggested that longer-staple cotton be grown in India in order to enable domestic manufacturers. When a group of Surat cotton merchants met in April 1919 they discussed measures to maintain the quality of local cottons. And Purshotamdas Thakurdas saw an urgent need to improve Indian cotton, as otherwise it would "militate considerably against the Weaving Industry of India." Indian capitalists now became deeply immersed in questions of cotton supply: Vithaldas Damodar Thackersey of the Bombay Millowners' Association demanded government support for the cultivation of long-staple cottons to "revolutionize the whole industry." By 1910, the association went so far as to laud the efforts of the British Cotton Growing Association to improve cotton growing in India: "We cannot but deplore the absence of legislation against the adulteration of cotton in this country."[83] Eventually, cotton nationalism did not lead to a return

Protest in the empire of cotton: flag of the Indian National Congress and Gandhi spinning at home

to the preindustrial world of cotton symbolized by Gandhi's spinning wheel, but instead to a massive wave of state-sponsored industrialization that radically recast the empire of cotton once more, drawing millions of displaced rural cultivators into cotton factories, to work for wages only a fraction of the ones paid in Lancashire, in Lowell, or in the valleys of the Black Forest.[84]

More so than perhaps anywhere else in the world, cotton and nationalism became intertwined in India. Textile industrialists became supporters of the independence movement, and its leaders in turn made domestic cotton industrialization a prime goal. As Gandhi, who enjoyed close connections to Ahmedabad's mill owners, put it in 1930, "The cotton textile industry is a valuable national asset giving employment to a large number of people, effecting the prosperity of the people of India, and its safety and progress must continue to receive attention of her capitalists, labour leaders, politicians and economists." For many Indian nationalists, independence would, among other things, make possible the development of a home market and import-substitution industrialization—the "reconstruction of her entire political and eco-

Postcolonial state building: Prime Minister Pandit Jawaharlal Nehru being received by cotton mill owner Purshotamdas Thakurdas (with cane), industrialist Naval Tata, Maharashtra governor Sri Prakasa (second right), and Maharashtra chief minister Y. B. Chavan at the office of the Indian Merchants Chamber in Bombay on February 3, 1958

nomic life," according to a 1934 book by scholar and engineer Mokshagundam Visvesvaraya. Creating a state conducive to domestic industrialization threw Indian cotton industrialists, like their Egyptian, Chinese, and eventually African and Southeast Asian counterparts, into skirmishes with the colonial state, as a global social conflict came to focus increasingly on the control of the state.[85]

Despite unprecedented differences in wealth as well as state strength, and despite a thick bulwark of racism that pinned much of humanity to subordinate roles, the struggle to break out of the imperial system succeeded, across the globe, by the second half of the twentieth century. Sometimes small victories came even before the great wave of decolonialization, such as in India, when tariffs began to protect the Indian industry against Japanese competition, and when the hated excise duty was repealed in 1926.[86] Such victories—and even more so decolonialization itself—came not as a result of the political strength of global South capitalists alone, but because nationalist movements were able to draw on large numbers of newly mobilized peasants and workers. Indeed, decolonialization almost always rested on mass mobilization, and thus the construction of nation-states in the formerly colonial world looked drastically different from their constitution in Europe and North America a century and a half earlier.

Capitalists' dependence on workers and peasants in their struggle to create a state conducive to the interests of national capital, however, weakened those same capitalists in the long run. Not surprisingly, global South cotton capitalists remained quite ambivalent about popular anticolonial mobilizations. Indeed, at times fear drove them into the arms of the colonizing power. In Korea, the Japanese colonialists observed in 1919 that "wealthy Koreans have recently grown extremely fearful of the radicalization of popular sentiment." Indian industrialists were generally on the moderate side of agitation as well, not least because they feared the militancy of their workers; "the truculence of the mill-hands needs to be checkmated in time," said the Bombay Millowners' Association, reporting after a round of rioting in 1909 that they "have lost their hold over them." Industrialist Ratanji Tata supported the Servants of India Society for similar reasons, embracing the nationalist call for a program of "industrial development of the country," but also hoping that the society would

retain its moderate positions. Manufacturer Purshotamdas Thakurdas
pushed strongly against Gandhi and the non-cooperation movement,
and tried to draw on the support of Indian capitalists for his position.
The need to forge a state dedicated to the interests of national capital, in
a colonial setting such as India, in effect brought national capitalists into
an uneasy alliance with politically mobilizing workers and peasants. In
the wake of the depression of 1929, Indian industrialists saw little alternative but to hitch their political fortunes to a Congress Party whose
mass base increasingly was to be found among India's peasants. When
they started planning for a postindependence economy, they acknowledged in the 1944 Bombay Plan the centrality of government planning,
with a "supreme economic council" coordinating most sectors of the
economy—laying the groundwork for India's first five-year plan in 1950.
Five-year plans of the kind that spread from Russia to China to India
had decisively not been on the minds of Lancashire, Alsatian, or New
England manufacturers a century earlier.[87]

Throughout the global South, indeed, cotton workers played key
roles in the struggles for national independence, in addition to joining unions and engaging in vast strike movements. Social and national
struggles merged more often than not. Some of the twenty-five thousand workers at Egypt's huge Misr Spinning and Weaving Company
in Mahalla al-Kubra, for example, played a key role in the struggle for
Egyptian independence. There and elsewhere, tens of thousands of cotton workers went on strike in 1946 and 1947 to demand better conditions
of employment—and the removal of British troops from Egypt.[88]

Chinese textile workers mobilized just as much, and—eventually—
would come to play an important role in the struggle against Western
powers, and in the 1949 revolution. They struck frequently, 209 times
between 1918 and 1929. When workers walked out of the Japanese-owned
Naigai Wata Kaisha mill in May 1925, they provoked "the famous May 30
incident," a day of rallies culminating in the killing of thirteen Chinese
protesters by the police. This incident fueled a wave of popular discon-
tent and the growth of Chinese trade unionism. Cotton workers at times
also joined the Communist Party and took on an important role in the
revolutionary struggle between 1946 and 1949.[89]

In India as well, the struggle for higher wages and better working
conditions merged with the anticolonial struggle. Indian cotton workers
had mobilized collectively since the late nineteenth century; indeed, the

first strike had occurred in 1874, followed by many more during the 1880s. In 1895 workers rioted for better working conditions, and in 1918 Gandhi himself played a leading but conciliatory role in an Ahmedabad textile workers' strike. Narayan Malhar Joshi's Bombay Textile Labor Union was founded in 1925, in the context of a general strike against the mill owners' effort to cut wages by 10 percent. By 1927 that union had approximately one hundred thousand members, and four hundred thousand by 1938, a powerful group of workers in conflicts with their employers, yet also an important pillar in the struggle for national independence.[90]

As cotton workers assumed an important role in anticolonial struggles, they would eventually translate their role into further social and economic gains. In China, just a few years after the revolution, the cotton industry was nationalized and set on an enormous trajectory of expansion (albeit one that brought little benefit to China's rural masses). In India, protectionism and state investments channeled by five-year plans led to the growth of the cotton industry, while postindependence labor activism led to significant wage gains. Wages for Indian cotton workers increased by 65 percent between 1950 and 1963, even as the price of output only rose 18 percent. In Egypt, independence at first brought significant new protective labor legislation and, especially, an important

Indian cotton workers organize: textile unionists in Bombay, early 1920s

role for the state in the mediation of labor conflict. Eventually, independence brought significant changes to the Egyptian economy, as raw cotton exports—the staple export of the Egyptian economy for more than a hundred years—stagnated as more and more cotton was used in domestic manufacturing. "Arab socialism" brought improvements to workers, but also the repression of independent trade union activities. During the 1960s, under Gamal Abdel Nasser, the cotton industry was nationalized. The strength and political importance of the working class had in effect resulted in the expropriation of local cotton capitalists, coupled with the belief that industrialization was necessary for the defense of the state itself. Capitalists' dependence on workers (and peasants) in the struggle against the colonial state had now translated into diminished powers.[91]

Not only was the balance of social power between workers and capitalists different in these postcolonial societies; the state's relationship to society was different as well. As these latecomers to cotton industrialization faced a world unlike that confronted by the first wave of industrializers in England, continental Europe, and North America, they believed that they needed to make the transition to industrial capitalism more swiftly, including the mobilization of labor, territory, markets, and raw materials. As industrial capitalism rested on the state, such "Great Leaps Forward" led as often as not to extreme statist outcomes in the postcolonial world—with postcolonial or even postcapitalist regimes now deploying the tools of the colonial integration of territory, resources, and especially labor with much greater radicalism.[92] Industrial capitalism had become central to the survival of the state itself, a state that often now prioritized the *industrial* in industrial capitalism. In fact, capitalism at times seemed to stand in the way of industrialization.

Yet even though Soviet Russia, Communist China, and independent India and Egypt represented variations of the most radical merger of the state and capital, of industrialization and political consolidation, capital by the 1950s had been hedged in by nation-states more generally. It was only after the 1970s, as we shall see, that industrialists began to emancipate themselves from their age-old dependence on particular states. Capitalists, so long dependent on strong states to pursue their project of industrial capitalism, now began overcoming their greatest weakness—the territorialization of capital. It was at this point that the empire of cotton took on the shape of today.

Chapter 14

The Weave and the Weft: An Epilogue

The empire of cotton I: Walmart, 2013

The empire of cotton II: Bangladesh, April 2013

Europe's reign over the cotton empire ended with a whimper. It was the year 1963, the year Liverpool's most renowned band, the Beatles, was first heard in the United States, the year the Reverend Martin Luther King Jr. had "a dream that one day even the state of Mississippi . . . will be transformed into an oasis of freedom and justice," and the year when the huge Bhakra Dam opened in India, providing water to 2.8 million acres of land, much of it cotton fields. On a rainy and cold December morning, a group of Liverpudlians met at the Cotton Exchange Building on Old Hall Street. They were there not to rule over their empire, but to dismantle it. The day's task was to auction off the "valuable club furnishings" that for the previous century had graced the offices of the Liverpool Cotton Association. Attendees purchased close to a hundred items, including a "trader's Desk in Mahogany," "Mahogany Quotation Board frames," a "Weather Map of the United States in Mahogany Frame," and S. A. Hobby's painting *Cotton Plant*. The Cotton Exchange Building itself had been sold a year earlier for lack of business.[1]

Founded in 1841, for more than a century the association had played a central role in regulating the global cotton trade. As the buyers of chairs, desks, lamps, shelves, sofas, and paintings carted their loot through the streets of this increasingly sad city, it would have been difficult, if not impossible, for them to imagine that a mere hundred years earlier, Liverpool was one of the world's wealthiest cities, a vital linchpin connecting cotton growers in the Americas, Africa, and Asia with European manufacturers and customers all across the globe.

But by 1963, Europe's domination of the empire of cotton was over. By the late 1960s, the United Kingdom could only claim 2.8 percent of global cotton cloth exports, a market it had so decisively dominated for a century and a half. Of the more than six hundred thousand workers who had once labored in British mills, only thirty thousand remained. Cotton towns crumbled as workers whose families had labored on mules and looms for generations found themselves unemployed. The symbolic evidence of the continent's fall had come in 1958, when the Manchester Chamber of Commerce, long an adamant champion of free trade, reversed course and declared that the British cotton industry needed protection—an unintended but obvious expression of defeat. Yet while Europe, and increasingly the United States, had become marginal to this marvelously productive and frighteningly violent system of production, the empire itself persisted. Indeed, while today's cotton industry would be nearly unrecognizable to the nineteenth-century members of the Liverpool Cotton Association or the Manchester Chamber of Commerce, the world today creates and consumes more cotton than ever before.[2]

Chances are the shirt or pants or socks you are wearing as you read this are made out of cotton. Those pieces have found their way to you, just as cotton has clothed your parents and grandparents and great-grandparents, thanks to the efforts of growers, spinners, weavers, tailors, and merchants in distant parts of the globe, each inhabiting a world quite different from one another. Yet while a century ago your shirt would have likely been sewn in a shop in New York or Chicago, using fabric spun and woven in New England, from bolls grown in the American South, today it is probably made of cotton grown in China, India, Uzbekistan, or Senegal, spun and woven in China, Turkey, or Pakistan, and then manufactured in a place like Bangladesh or Vietnam. If any part of the cotton empire, whose rise this book has charted, was involved in your shirt at all, that unlikely, vestigial element would be American-grown cotton. Twenty-five thousand highly capitalized cotton farmers remain in the United States, mostly in Arizona and Texas. The cotton they grow is so uncompetitive on the world market that they receive enormous federal subsidies to continue to farm it, subsidies that in some years equal the GDP of the country of Benin (coincidentally, another important cotton grower).[3]

While a small group of American cotton farmers hangs on, the cotton mills that were once so important to the economies of Europe and North America alike are nearly gone. If those hulking buildings have not been torn down, they have been turned into shopping malls, artist studios, industrial-chic condos, or museums. Indeed, the downfall of the cotton industry in the global North has created a boom in textile museums. You can visit the Boots Cotton Mills Museum in Lowell, Massachusetts, Quarry Bank Mill near Manchester, the former Wesserling mill turned museum just outside Mulhouse, the Memphis Cotton Museum housed in the former Memphis Cotton Exchange, the textile museum of Wiesenthal in the Black Forest, James Henry Hammond's Redcliffe Plantation in South Carolina, the twenty-mile-long hiking trail of the Ruta de les Colònies along the Llobregat River in Spain's Catalonia with its eighteen abandoned cotton mills, and dozens, perhaps hundreds of other sites as well. The empire of cotton, which for a century and a half shaped and reshaped global capitalism in its image, is now the object of family outings. Parents and their kids wander the quaint-looking factories in their often idyllic surroundings; they watch the spinners and weavers in period costume who demonstrate the workings of the antiquated machines, holding their ears to block the noise of power looms and staring at photographs of children—prematurely aged, as if from a different planet—who not too long ago worked sixty-hour weeks on those same machines. Cotton plantations, too, have been reshaped for tourists. Here, though, the horrors of slave labor are downplayed or hidden—often intentionally overpowered by the sights of magnificent mansions, beautiful vistas, and well-tended gardens. But none of these historic curiosities can display the greatest invention of the empire of cotton: the globe-spanning network that connected growers, manufacturers, and consumers, a network, that, though radically altered and far from these museums, persists to this day.

As European and North American tourists gaze at the remnants of the empire of cotton, and communities and workers from Fall River to Oldham struggle with the aftereffects of postindustrial devastation, millions of workers stream into textile mills in China, India, Pakistan, and elsewhere, while further millions of farmers tend to cotton crops in Africa, Asia, and the Americas. Thanks to their often ill-paid efforts, about 98 percent of all garments sold in the United States today are made abroad. China alone supplies the United States with about 40 percent of all apparel, followed by Vietnam, Bangladesh, Indonesia, Honduras, Cambodia, Mexico, India, El Salvador, and Pakistan. Fabric and yarn no

The ruins of the empire of cotton: Cal Rosal, Spain, 2013

longer come primarily from the United Kingdom or even the American South: China, India, Pakistan, and Turkey spin and weave the most cotton globally. Today, China's factories contain nearly half of the world's spindles and looms, working up 43 percent of the world's raw cotton (Asia's total is 82.2 percent), while North America uses 4.2 percent and western Europe 0.7 percent of the global cotton harvest. After more than two hundred years, most global cotton use is once again concentrated in the pre-1780 heartlands of the cotton industry. As a managing director of the New York textile firm Olah Inc. put it, "China's industry is such a large portion of the global market that, plainly put, the global industry goes the way of China." Moreover, it is less and less likely that the shirt on your back is made of cotton at all: Beginning in the mid-1990s, production of synthetic fiber began to outpace cotton textile manufacturing. Today, about 52 million metric tons of petroleum-based synthetic fiber is produced annually to make, for instance, the fleece jacket you might be wearing, almost twice the worldwide figure for cotton.[4]

The centers of growing have shifted in parallel with the shift in manufacturing. While in 1860 the United States had a near monopoly on cotton growing for export, today only 14 percent of cotton worldwide is grown in North America. Instead, China and India lead the way, producing 34 million and 26 million bales of cotton yearly, compared to the United States' 17 million bales. Global production has increased by a factor of seven since 1920, with cotton growing becoming immensely important to the economies of many countries, particularly in Asia and West Africa. It has been estimated that 10 million farmers in Central and West Africa alone depend on cotton. Worldwide, estimates of the number of people involved in the growing and manufacturing of cotton range from approximately 110 million households involved in the growing of cotton, 90 million in its transportation, ginning, and warehousing, and another 60 million workers operating spinning and weaving machines and stitching together clothing, to a total for all branches of that industry of 350 million people. This number, never before reached in one industry, represents between 3 and 4 percent of the world's population. More than 35 million hectares of land are dedicated to the growing of cotton, the equivalent of the surface area of Germany.[5]

Some nations, just like European colonial powers in Africa a century earlier, have policies in place to force farmers to produce cotton, despite its often devastating environmental and financial consequences. Uzbeki-

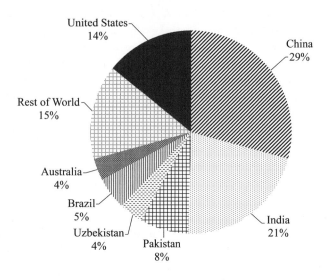

Asia as the world center for cotton growing:
the global cotton crop, 2012

stan, for instance, one of the globe's top ten cotton exporters, continues
to force its farming population to grow cotton despite the fact that the
need to irrigate its dry lands has essentially drained the Aral Sea and
turned much of the country into virtual salt flats. As one Uzbek cotton
farmer told a journalist, "We are destroying ourselves. . . . Why are we
planting cotton, and what are we getting from it?" Moreover, the emergence of new, genetically modified cotton plants has doubly amplified the
burdens of many farmers. The seeds for these plants are more expensive
to buy and maintain, but they are also far more productive, thus pushing costs up at the same time that they push cotton prices down. Many
Tajik cotton farmers, for instance, are locked in a cycle of debt and forced
cotton production just like their counterparts a century ago in India and
the American South. Indeed, cotton growers have remained relatively
powerless. In India in 2005, after a season of weak rains and crop failures, hundreds of heavily indebted farmers of genetically modified cotton
committed suicide by drinking their own pesticides, a trend that persists
to this day. Cotton production continues to be an often brutal ordeal. For
most farmers and workers, cotton is far from the cuddly "fabric of our
lives" touted by marketers for the American cotton industry.[6]

One of the few geographic consistencies between the beginning of the twenty-first century and the world before the Industrial Revolution of the 1780s is the reemergence of Asia in the world of cotton. Both the growing of cotton and the manufacturing of yarn and cloth continue on their remigration to Asia, a process that began in the 1920s. We have seen how budding Asian capitalists and state-building nationalists studied Europeans' penetration of territory and mastery over labor and applied those techniques to their own postcolonial and, eventually, even postcapitalist hinterlands. These states found novel ways to wed the methods of industrial capitalism to nationalist development projects; bureaucrats and statesmen of all stripes dreamed of "great leaps" forward. In a century, these states redrew the geographic boundaries of the empire of cotton; the combination of low wages and powerful states enabled cotton growing and manufacturing to flourish once again in the corner of the world where cotton was first grown, five thousand years earlier. So powerful has the rise of Asia been that Asian states, China first among them, are increasingly eager to set the rules of the global cotton trade, a privilege once enjoyed by Liverpool merchants and, later, the American government.[7]

In the course of that return to Asia, the balance of power between growers, manufacturers, merchants, and statesmen shifted again, starting after the 1970s. Consider that today it is commonplace for cotton grown in Uzbekistan, Togo, or India to make its way through a Hong Kong textile mill, then to a Vietnamese sewing shop, and finally onto a clothing rack in Kansas City. It is not the distances that are new; rather, it is the way the elaborate networks that move the fiber through its various iterations are held together. Instead of manufacturers, or cotton or cloth merchants, it is massive retailers like Walmart, Metro, and Carrefour that have come to dominate the commodity chains linking contractors, subcontractors, farmers, mills, and sweatshops. Manufacturers no longer "push" their products upon consumers; instead, products are "pulled" across oceans by retailers, allowing them to pit manufacturers, contractors, and workers against one another to ensure the quickest speed and lowest cost.[8]

This reemergence of merchants, particularly from the 1990s on, in the form of retailers and branded apparel sellers as key actors comes as a surprise. In some ways, of course, their power is reminiscent of the importance of merchants in the first half of the nineteenth century. Yet since the 1860s, as we have seen, the central actors in the empire of cotton had been states in conjunction with manufacturers. States moved to the forefront in the grand project of transforming the global cotton-growing countryside, and in the process created a central role for national manufacturers and, within careful limits, for organized textile workers as well. These trends further accelerated in the twentieth century. In the United Kingdom, to cite the most prominent example, the British government, in response to wartime conditions, took over the entire cotton market in 1941, including the purchase and distribution of raw cotton. After the war, government control continued, and to the great lament of the Liverpool Cotton Association, the government's Raw Cotton Commission remained the sole purchaser and distributor of cotton in Britain. Merchants who had built a globe-spanning network were reduced to begging the government for some consideration of their interests. As the *New York Times* put it in 1946, "It would be difficult to imagine a more direct blow to the whole system of free world markets." Yet the *Times* editors also registered, accurately, that "this action with regard to cotton seems to illustrate a world-wide bureaucratic distrust of the free market . . . combined with a boundless faith in the magic of government 'planning.'" It was only when a Conservative government came to power and in 1953 passed the Cotton Bill that the Liverpool market reopened, but even then it continued to be structured by "subsidies, duties and currency imbalances." And it was in response to "the contraction of the merchant element in the market" that the Liverpool Cotton Association would eventually reorganize itself in 1963—and sell its furniture.[9]

Across the Atlantic, the government also came to play an ever more important role in the cotton industry. In response to the devastating agricultural crisis of the 1920s and the subsequent Great Depression, the New Deal created the Agricultural Adjustment Administration, which regulated production to match demand and provided subsidies to cotton farmers—roles that continue to this day with ever increasing controversy. Cotton growers and manufacturers themselves, cognizant of the increasing importance of government, founded the National Cotton Council in 1939 to lobby Washington and promote market and scientific research on cotton. The Foreign Agricultural Service, an agency within the U.S. Department of Agriculture, was founded in 1953 to open markets for American cotton all over the world. Its mission continues unabated today. Throughout this period, tariffs and other protectionist measures tried to keep America's increasingly besieged cotton spinning and weaving industry afloat. Yet in 1965, even in the cotton center of Fall River, the last cotton mill closed its doors.[10] By the 1970s, America's cotton complex, as well as the remnants of its British counterpart, was completely dependent on government policies.

Though cotton merchants had facilitated the rise of the cotton empire in the nineteenth century, by the middle of the twentieth they could do little more than watch the state's ascendancy. On the most extreme edge, Spain's Francisco Franco and Argentina's Juan Perón, among others, pushed for domestic cotton growing to insulate the nation from the world market. Yet the power of government projected itself nowhere more than in postcolonial and postcapitalist states, best exemplified by China's "leap forward" and India's five-year plans. In Communist China and independent India, state planners envisioned vast expansions in growth and manufacturing; production skyrocketed. In China, low prices for seeds, fertilizers, and farm supplies and generous farm credits, along with the encouragement of the use of fertilizers and insecticides on consolidated, state-owned land, and the preferential treatment of high-yield cotton strains, resulted in startling increases in cotton output. Cotton manufacturing took off as well: In 1952, the People's Republic of China produced 656,000 tons of cotton thread, a remarkable increase from previous decades but still well behind the world's leaders. By 1957 China had turned itself into the world's third largest manufacturer of cotton yarns, its output two and a half times that of the United Kingdom. And in 1983 3.27 million tons poured out of its huge state-owned cotton mills.[11] The growth of India's industry followed suit.[12]

The dominance of China, a self-proclaimed peasants' and workers' state, would have seemed like a hallucination to the cotton kings of the early nineteenth century—to the Hammonds of South Carolina, the Rylandses of Manchester, the Dollfuses of Mulhouse, the Barings of Liverpool, and the Volkarts of Winterthur. They could not have imagined that by 2008 a semimilitary unit of the People's Republic of China, the Xinjiang Production and Construction Corps, would grow 1.3 million tons of cotton, or 5 percent of the world's total. Yet the coupling of state building and industrialization was the norm. That marriage would succeed in other parts of the world as well, such as the Soviet Union, which further recast cotton agriculture in Central Asia to facilitate a truly spectacular increase in the output of raw cotton. In 1980 the Soviet Union produced nearly 6 billion pounds of cotton, making it the world's largest producer after

Chinese propaganda poster: We sell dry, clean,
neat, and selected cotton to the state,
Wu Shaoyun, 1958

China. These stratospheric gains—production increased by about 70 percent between 1950 and 1966 alone—were only possible because of massive state investments in irrigation, fertilizers, and machinery.[13]

Such recourse to the state in postcolonial and postcapitalist societies was not a return to the war capitalism of the eighteenth and early nineteenth centuries, but a sharpening of the tools and an enhancing of the methods of industrial capitalism. Even though force continued to play an important role in mobilizing labor, outright physical coercion now represented industrial capitalism's most extreme edge. While differences between the global South and Europe and North America were significant, from a long-term perspective what is most remarkable is the way that over the course of the twentieth century the trajectory of the empire of cotton converged more and more with the goals of state-led development.[14] State-directed economic planning, which had claimed its first great victories in Europe's scattered imperial possessions, was by the 1950s the globe's efficient and seemingly inevitable norm.

Yet the particular form of the state's reign in the twentieth century would be as brief as the merchant's reign in the nineteenth century. As mentioned, by the 1970s, with the decline of cotton manufacturing in Europe and the United States, and with the slow dissolution of the alliance between manufacturers and the state, the empire of cotton saw the emergence of a new breed of merchant—not the well-connected individual walking the streets of Liverpool inspecting cotton bales, but immense corporations that source their branded goods globally to sell them to consumers worldwide. The growth of this new group was aided immeasurably by two broader shifts that they had nothing to do with. As manufacturing, particularly of cotton textiles, became much less important to European and North American economies, the ability of north Atlantic states to shape the cotton industry shrank accordingly. But these merchants also grew more powerful as an unintended result of one of the state's great successes. By the mid-twentieth century, governments had transformed the global countryside; the capitalization of everyday life had reached an unprecedented level. Most of the world's people were now inextricably tied to both commodity production and consumption. As a result, capitalists no longer needed the state to turn rural cultivators into cotton growers, a reservoir of factory labor, and consumers of those textiles. That process was already far advanced, meaning that these new merchants can now profit from a larger market of consumers and a larger labor reservoir than has ever existed in human history.

But their successes were also due to their ability to organize production globally, and to create branded goods and the sales channels to offer them for purchase all over the world. Unlike in the nineteenth century, these modern merchants focus not on the trade in raw cotton, yarn, and cloth, but on the apparel business. They source cotton, yarn, cloth, and clothing from the cheapest suppliers they can locate, without engaging in manufacturing themselves. They then focus their energies on developing channels to sell those goods, with branding, as in the case of the American company Gap ("Get together"), Chinese Meters/bonwe ("Be different"), and German Adidas ("Adidas is all in"), but also with the development of new forms of retailing, as in the case of Walmart (United States), Lojas Americanas S.A. (Brazil), and Carrefour (France). To dominate this global cotton supply chain, these merchants still depend on state power, but their reliance on any one specific state has lessened considerably. As a result, they foster competition not just between manufacturers and growers, but among states. In today's empire of cotton, merchants have finally managed to emancipate themselves from their previous dependence on particular states. As a result, the protections that strong nation-states offered, to at least some of their workers, for at least part of the twentieth century, have been gradually eroded. Workers today are increasingly at the mercy of corporations that can easily shift all forms of production around the globe. Globalization is nothing new in the empire of cotton, but the ability of capitalists to utilize a number of states and thus remain free of the demands of all of them, is new. The state, the very institution that facilitated capitalists' rise to wealth and power in the first place, is now increasingly desperate for their investments.

Yet the prominence of today's apparel giants and retailers should not blind us to ongoing patterns; these cotton capitalists continue to rely on the state—in many subtle ways, and some not so subtle ways. In the United States, as mentioned, huge subsidies keep cotton farmers in business: In 2001, the U.S. government paid a record $4 billion in subsidies to cotton growers, a cost that exceeded the market value of the crop by 30 percent. To put it another way, these subsidies amounted to triple that year's USAID payments to all of Africa, a part of the world where production costs for cotton were only about a third of what they were in the United States. In fact, in 2002, Brazil lodged a lawsuit against the United States through the World Trade Organization, alleging that the government's cotton subsidies violated its own previous trade commitments. As part of the settlement, the U.S. government now also supports the Brazilian cotton economy, at a rate of $147.3 million a year. The European Union, in similar ways, produces its own small cotton harvest, in Spain and Greece, thanks to subsidies ranging from 160 to 189 percent of the world price for cotton. Highly subsidized cotton then is dumped onto world markets, depressing prices for the much more competitive cotton growers in Africa and elsewhere.[15]

Elsewhere, states continue their active role in labor mobilization, making more cotton available for retailers to fashion into ever cheaper clothes. In Uzbekistan, the government forces children to help out in the cotton harvest (it has been estimated that up to 2 million children younger than fifteen are sent to the cotton fields), a "system [that] is only

Children harvesting cotton in Uzbekistan

sustainable under conditions of political repression," reports the International Crisis Group.[16] In China the repression of independent trade union activity keeps wages low. The emancipation of capitalists from the state is thus not complete—the state still matters greatly—but because cotton capital itself has become fluid and not tied to particular territories, specific nation-states matter much less. Not only has the geographic shape of the empire of cotton shifted once more, but also the balance of power between growers, merchants, manufacturers, and the state. Capitalism's endless revolution continues.

Today's empire of cotton, just as it has for the last 250 years, connects growers, traders, spinners, weavers, manufacturers, and consumers over huge geographic distances in ever-changing spatial arrangements. This fundamental innovation—the connection across space—was first forged by connecting slavery and wage labor in the vicious cauldron of war capitalism, and has remained at the core of the empire of cotton ever since. Yet the geography of these connections has changed radically. Nodes once central within the empire of cotton—Lancashire, for example—have been marginalized, while formerly unimportant nodes, especially China, have become its very core.

The geographical rearrangement of economic relations is not just a noteworthy element of capitalism or an interesting aspect of its history; rather the constant shifting recombination of various systems of labor, and various compositions of capital and polities is the very essence of capitalism. As capitalists search for ever cheaper labor, better infrastructure, and greater markets, they combine and recombine the world's workers and consumers, and the world's lands and its raw materials, in ever new ways.[17] In that process, the collective action (or lack thereof) of workers matters a great deal, as do the policies (or lack thereof) of states. We have seen that the history of capital and cotton can only be understood if we consider the history of many different places and groups of people. Looking at just one part of the empire leads to vast misunderstandings, for example the characterization of the past fifty years as a world of deindustrialization (as some European and North American social scientists have described it), when exactly the opposite is true, as the greatest wave of industrialization ever has overtaken the globe.

Capitalists, from the Barings of the eighteenth century to the titans of today's global retailers, forged many of the connections that created the world we recognize today. Exploration of this history, however, reveals that capitalists and states arose hand in hand, each facilitating the ascendancy of the other. It is easy to assume, in our relentlessly branded world, that today's vast corporations exist entirely on their own. Yet such a simplification misses the reality that, historically, capitalists' greatest source of strength was their ability to rely on unusually powerful states—and simultaneously, for much of capitalism's history, the greatest weakness of these same capitalists was that dependence on the state. It was this dependence that gave workers an opening to improve the conditions of their labor. We now know that the increasing emancipation of capital from particular nation-states has dramatic consequences for the world's workers. Workers' successes in improving their conditions almost always lead to the reallocation of capital. For the last several decades, Walmart and other retail giants have continually moved their production from one poor country to a slightly poorer one, lured by the promise of workers even more eager and even more inexpensive. Even Chinese production is now threatened by lower-wage producers.[18] The empire of cotton has continued to facilitate a giant race to the bottom, limited only by the spatial constraints of the planet.

The constant reshuffling of the empire of cotton, ranging from its geography to its systems of labor, points toward an essential element of capitalism: its ability to constantly adapt. Again and again, a seemingly insurmountable crisis in one part of the empire generated a response elsewhere; capitalism both demands and creates a state of permanent revolution.

This permanent revolution is only possible because of the existence of places and people whose lives can be turned upside down. These frontiers of capitalism are often to be found in the world's countryside, and the journey through the empire of cotton reveals that the global countryside should be at the center of our thinking about the origins of the modern world. Although our historical imaginations are usually dominated by cities, factories, and industrial workers, we have seen that much of the emergence of the modern world occurred in the countryside—by the often violent turning of rural people into the creators and consumers of commodities made or used elsewhere.

This emphasis on the countryside allows for an equally important emphasis—the importance of coercion and violence to the history of capitalism. Slavery, colonialism, and forced labor, among other forms of violence, were not aberrations in the history of capitalism, but were at its very core. The violence of market making—forcing people to labor in certain locations and in certain ways—has been a constant throughout the history of the empire of cotton.

This emphasis calls into question some of the most ingrained insights into the history of the modern world—for example, conceptualizing the nineteenth century, as is so often done, as an age of "bourgeois civilization," in contrast with the twentieth century, which historian Eric Hobsbawm has termed the "age of catastrophe."[19] An assessment such as this can only be derived from a vision of the world that focuses its moral judgments on Europe. Looked at from the perspective of much of Asia, Africa, and the Americas, one can argue just the opposite—that the nineteenth century was an age of barbarity and catastrophe, as slavery and imperialism devastated first one pocket of the globe and then another. It is the twentieth century, by contrast, that saw the weakening of imperial powers and thus allowed more of the world's people to determine their own futures and shake off the shackles of colonial domination. Without its Eurocentric distortions, decolonialization would be at the very center of the narrative we tell about the twentieth century—and this retelling would allow us to see that global capitalism today is most fundamentally shaped by the struggles for independence. Either way, our journey through the empire of cotton has shown that civilization and barbarity are linked at the hip, both in the evolution of the world's first global industry and in the many other industries that have modeled themselves after it.

Violence and coercion, in turn, are as adaptive as the capitalism they enable, and they continue to play an important role in the empire of cotton to this day. Cotton growers are still forced to grow the crop; workers are still held as virtual prisoners in factories. Moreover, the fruits of their activities continue to be distributed in radically unequal ways—with cotton growers in Benin, for example, making a dollar a day or less, while the owners of cotton growing businesses in the United States have collectively received government subsidies of more than $35 billion between 1995 and 2010.[20] Workers in Bangladesh stitch together clothing under absurdly dangerous conditions for very low wages, while consumers in the United States and Europe can purchase those pieces with abandon, at prices that often seem impossibly low.

Within this larger story of domination and exploitation, however, sits a parallel story of liberation and creativity. The unfolding of global capitalism, and its awesome adaptations during the past 250 years, has resulted in enormous advances in productivity. As late as the 1950s, it took sixty days of hard spinning and weaving labor to produce enough clothing to fulfill the most minimal subsistence needs of a family of five in northern China. Today, the average American family (albeit at 2.5 persons also smaller than the Chinese family of the 1950s) spends only 3.4 percent of its household income on much more ample clothing—that is, the equivalent of approximately eight days of labor. Agriculture and industry have virtually exploded, as capitalist social relations have enabled a growth in the churning out of goods that has never been matched by any other system of production. Tellingly, today there are expectations that cotton production will triple or quadruple again by 2050. The human capacity to organize our efforts in ever more productive ways should give us hope, the hope that our unprecedented domination over nature will allow us also the wisdom, the power, and the strength to create a society that serves the needs of all the world's people—an empire of cotton that is not only productive, but also just. Considering the perpetual clashes of power at the center of cotton's story, a just world might seem like an idle dream. Yet, as we have witnessed in the preceding pages, the least powerful members of cotton's empire have consistently tried to create such a world and at times also have succeeded in effecting dramatic changes: A world that seems stable and permanent in one moment can be radically transformed in the next. The capitalist revolution, after all, perpetually re-creates our world, just as the world's looms perpetually manufacture new materials.[21]

Acknowledgments

Researching and writing this book in many ways parallels its subject, involving, as it did, people and documents from all over the world. The journey was a great adventure. I will never forget the days during the depths of the Argentine financial crisis when I was sitting in the basement archives of the Banco de la Provincia de Buenos Aires and heard the heavy metal gates of the bank's front door go noisily up and down in a predictable rhythm, to protect the building from demonstrators who passed the bank. I will never forget the reception room of the National Archives of Cairo, where I spent many hours sipping tea with its director as he tried to get me access to early nineteenth-century records that the state deemed too sensitive to be perused by a historian. I will never forget the moment a librarian at the Musée de l'Impression sur Etoffes in the French city of Mulhouse opened the door to a room filled to the ceiling with eighteenth- and nineteenth-century cotton textile samples. And I will never forget sitting in the courtyard of the bar of the Colònia Vidal in the Llobregat valley of Catalonia in Spain imagining the lives that generations of workers spent in this company town, serving the needs of a voracious cotton mill.

This book has been researched on every continent and I am grateful to the librarians and archivists who, under often difficult circumstances, have protected the materials on which this book is based and made them accessible to me. I specifically thank those who helped me at the archives of the Japanese Spinners Association in Osaka, the National Archives of Australia, the National Archives and Library of Egypt, the rare books collection at the American University of Cairo, the National Archives of India, the Nehru Memorial Museum and Library in New Delhi, the Maharashtra State Archives in Mumbai, the Bombay Chamber of Commerce, the Bombay Millowners' Association, the (Bombay) Asia Library, the Archives nationales d'outre mer in Aix-en-Provence, the Archives Nationales and the Archives diplomatiques—Quai d'Orsay in Paris, the Société Industri-elle and the Musée de l'Impression sur Etoffes in Mulhouse, the Volkart Archives in Winterthur, the Chamber of Commerce in Barcelona, the Bundesarchiv Berlin, the Handelskammer Hamburg, the Handelskam-mer Bremen, the Bremer Baumwollbörse, the Staatsarchiv Bremen, the ING Baring Archives, the National Archives of the United Kingdom in Kew, the Guildhall Library, the British Library, and the Bank of England Archive in London, the Manchester Archives and Local Studies, the John R. Rylands Library, the Greater Manchester County Record Office, the Liverpool Record Office, the library of the University of Liverpool, the Merseyside Maritime Museum, the Historical Collections at Harvard Business School, Widener Library, the Massachusetts Historical Soci-ety, the New-York Historical Society, the New York Public Library, the Archivo General de la Nación in Mexico, the Biblioteca Pedro Sainz de Baranda of Valladolid, the Banco de Provincia de Buenos Aires, and the Biblioteca Tornquist in Buenos Aires.

Along the way, many research assistants helped me master the mate-rials. In Canberra, Australia, Lawrence Niewójt assisted me, as did Nat-suko Kitani in Osaka. Amit Mishra supported my work in Delhi, Dr. Abdel-Wahid in Cairo, Amilcar Challu in Buenos Aires, and Pauline Per-etz in Paris. Over the years, many research assistants also helped me work through what became a very complicated history, among them, in Cam-bridge, Rudi Batzell, Par Cassel, Lui Chang, Jane Chen, Marlee Chong, Eli Cook, Rui Dong, Balraj Gill, Heather Souvaine Horn, Louis Hyman, Diana Kimball, Noam Maggor, Maximillian Mason, Paul Mathis, Shaun Nichols, Nathan Pearl-Rosenthal, Arjun Ramamurti, Leonid Sidorov, Liat Spiro, Luise Tremel, Niki Usher, Ann Wilson, Julie Yen, and Jenny Zhang, and, in Freiburg, Lukas Bowinkelmann, Ralf Meindl, Lukas Nemela, and Carsten Vogelpohl. Thank you to all of you—I could not have done it without your help. And also thanks to my students at Har-vard University, whose never-ending curiosity helped propel my own.

I also want to thank the people and audiences who engaged with my work in Sydney, Tokyo, Osaka, Seoul, Hong Kong, New Delhi, Kolkata, Tel Aviv, Dakar, Leipzig, Jena, Frankfurt, Munich, Linz, Amsterdam, Basel, Zurich, Geneva, Nottingham, London, Manchester, Brighton, São Paulo, and Buenos Aires, as well as at universities all over the United States.

Thank you also to Jane Garrett of Alfred A. Knopf for her early en-couragement of this project; to William Kirby at Harvard for his belief in me; to Shigeru Akita and Takeshi Abe for helping me navigate the resources available in Osaka; to Jun Furuya for always making me feel welcome in Tokyo (and helping me navigate the worst earthquake in Japan's history); to Babacar Fall and Omar Gueye for their hospitality in Dakar; to Rafael Marquese for debating the subjects of this book over a delicious meal of Maranhão cuisine in São Paulo; to Charles Forcey, the world's foremost magician of words; to John Killick at Leeds for providing me with some of his unpublished work; to Gavin Wright for his feedback at an early stage; to Peter Knight for pointing me to some important sources; to Cyrus Veeser for his sharp insights; to Julia Seibert in Cairo for helping me understand the impact of colonialism on African labor regimes; to Mauro and all the Palas in Alghero for allowing me to write in their good company in a beautiful part of the world; to my extended family in Liverpool—John, Heather, Ian, and Andrew McFadzean—who introduced me to the city that like no other has been synonymous with the history of cotton when they allowed me to spend summers as a high school student working in their small corner store selling newspapers and sweets; to Dieter Plehwe in Berlin for our endless conversation about capitalism, and his friendship; to Christine Desan at Harvard Law School for having helped make capitalism studies respectable; to Gilles Palsky in Paris, who helped me get access to some extraordinary maps about the global cotton trade; to Uta Beckert for her leads on Mesopotamian cotton; to Neus Santamaria of the Consorci del Parc Fluvial del Llobregat for helping me understand the extraordinary story of Catalonian industrialization; to Aditya and Mridula Mukerjee, Prabhu Mohapatra, and all my friends in New Delhi for including me in their never-ending conversations on the great inequalities that characterize the world and India; and to Irfan Habib in New Delhi, Sakae Tsunoya in Sakai, Eric Foner in New York, Jürgen Osterhammel in Konstanz, and Ibrahima Thioub in Dakar for engaging with my ideas and for being such inspiring historians. Last but not least, a special thank-you to my colleague and friend Charles Maier, whose early encouragement made all the difference.

A book such as this needs significant resources to be written and I am grateful for the good luck of having had access to such resources, a privilege that very few historians in the world enjoy. A grant from the Kittredge Fund made the early stages of the research possible. Later, at Harvard, the David Rockefeller Center for Latin American Studies, the Milton Fund, the Asia Center, the Reischauer Institute for Japanese

Studies, and, especially, the Weatherhead Center for International Affairs provided urgently needed resources. I started conceptualizing the book when I spent a year at the Center for Scholars and Writers at the New York Public Library, and its director, Peter Gay, created a most inspiring setting for thinking about a new project and for thinking big. Later the Humboldt Foundation awarded me a prize that allowed me to dedicate a year to the research of this book, and still later the Freiburg Institute for Advanced Studies, the American Council of Learned Societies, and the Weatherhead Center for International Affairs at Harvard University provided me with time away from teaching to draft the manuscript. At a moment when support for the humanities and social sciences is rapidly shrinking I cannot thank these institutions enough for their belief that understanding how our world turned out the way it did continues to matter.

When the manuscript was nearly done, a group of friends read some or all of it and provided valuable feedback, and I thank Elizabeth Blackmar, Sugata Bose, Vincent Brown, Franz-Josef Brüggemeier, Stanley Engermann, Eric Foner, Andrew Gordon, Steven Hahn, Noam Maggor, Terry Martin, Amit Mishra, Roger Owen, Michael Ralph, Seth Rockman, Dan Smail, Marcel van der Linden, Cyrus Veeser, and John Womack. Their wisdom and insights made a significant difference, even though I have ignored, at my peril, some of their advice.

Many people have helped put this manuscript into shape. David Lobenstine and Martha Schulmann made a heroic effort to help me edit, and Victoria Wilson and Audrey Silverman shepherded it expertly through production.

Most important, however, I want to thank my family. Lisa McGirr was there from the very beginning, read numerous drafts of every chapter, and helped me along when things got difficult. The dedication is a very small thank-you for all her support. My children, Noah and Pascal, grew up alongside this book. Only recently did they tell me that discussions on cotton were such a prominent feature in our house that for many years they had believed that I was a "professor of cotton." They will be relieved to see me move on to something else.

Notes

INTRODUCTION

1. *The Thirty-Ninth Annual Report of the Board of Directors of the Manchester Chamber of Commerce for the Year 1859* (Manchester: Cave & Sever, 1860), 18, 19, 22, 23, 33, 34, 38, 39, 45.

2. "Liverpool. By Order of the Liverpool Cotton Association Ltd., Catalogue of the Valuable Club Furnishings etc. to be Sold by Auction by Marsh Lyons & Co., Tuesday, 17th December 1963," Greater Manchester County Record Office, Manchester, UK.

3. "Monthly Economic Letter: U.S. and Global Market Fundamentals," *Cotton Incorporated*, accessed January 23, 2013, http://www.cottoninc.com/corporate/Market -Data/MonthlyEconomicLetter/; "The Fabric of Our Lives," accessed July 1, 2012, http://www.thefabricofourlives.com/.

4. The average weight of a sheep fleece in the United States is 7.3 pounds according to "Fast Facts . . . About American Wool," American Sheep Industry Association, accessed March 10, 2013, www.sheepusa.org/get_file/file_id/5ab52656e6d6e32821aa9f177bf05876. The total weight of the world's cotton crop was divided by this number to find how many sheep it would take to produce the same amount of wool by weight. Government of South Australia, "Grazing livestock—a sustainable and productive approach," Adelaide & Mt Lofty Ranges Natural Resource Management Board, accessed March 10, 2013, www.amlrnrm.sa.gov.au/Portals/2/landholders_info/grazing _web.pdf; "European Union," CIA—The World Factbook, accessed March 16, 2013, https://www.cia.gov/library/publications/the-world-factbook/geos/ee.html. According to the first source, it was assumed that one hectare of land can support ten dry sheep, if available for grazing twelve months of the year. This was used to calculate the area of land required to sustain 7 billion sheep and then that was compared to the size of the EU, which is 4,324,782 km^2 according to the CIA World Factbook.

5. Edward Baines, *History of the Cotton Manufacture in Great Britain* (London: H. Fisher, R. Fisher, and P. Jackson, 1835), 5–6; see Kenneth Pomeranz, *The Great Divergence: China, Europe, and the Making of the Modern World Economy* (Princeton, NJ: Princeton University Press, 2000).

6. Jared Diamond, *Guns, Germs, and Steel: The Fates of Human Societies* (New York: Norton, 1998); David Landes, *The Wealth and Poverty of Nations: Why Some Are So Rich and Some So Poor* (New York: Norton, 1998); Niall Ferguson, *The West and the Rest* (New York: Allen Lane, 2011); Robert Brenner, "Agrarian Class Structure and

Economic Development in Pre-industrial Europe," *Past and Present* no. 70 (February 1976): 30–75; Robert Brenner, "The Agrarian Roots of European Capitalism," *Past and Present*, no. 97 (November 1982): 16–113; E. P. Thompson, *The Making of the English Working Class* (New York: Pantheon, 1963).

7. There is a vibrant literature on slavery and capitalism, including Eric Williams, *Capitalism and Slavery* (New York: Russell & Russell, 1961); Rafael de Bivar Marquese, "As desventuras de um conceito: Capitalismo histórico e a historiografia sobre escravidão brasileira," *Revista de Historia* 169 (July/December 2013), 223–53; Philip McMichael, "Slavery in the Regime of Wage Labor: Beyond Paternalism in the U.S. Cotton Culture," *Social Concept* 6 (1991): 10–28; Barbara L. Solow and Stanley L. Engerman, *British Capitalism and Caribbean Slavery: The Legacy of Eric Williams* (New York: Cambridge University Press, 1987); Gavin Wright, *The Political Economy of the Cotton South: Households, Markets, and Wealth in the Nineteenth Century* (New York: Norton, 1978); Joseph E. Inikori, *Africans and the Industrial Revolution in England: A Study in International Trade and Development* (New York: Cambridge University Press, 2002); Dale Tomich, "The Second Slavery: Mass Slavery, World-Economy, and Comparative Microhistories," *Review: A Journal of the Fernand Braudel Center* 31, no. 3 (2008); Robin Blackburn, *The American Crucible: Slavery, Emancipation and Human Rights* (London: Verso, 2011).

8. *Cotton Supply Reporter*, no. 37 (March 1, 1860): 33.

9. Andrew Ure, *The Cotton Manufacture of Great Britain Systematically Investigated, and Illustrated by 150 Original Figures*, vol. 1 (London: Charles Knight, 1836), 67–68.

10. Bruno Biedermann, "Die Versorgung der russischen Baumwollindustrie mit Baumwolle eigener Produktion" (PhD dissertation, University of Heidelberg, 1907), 4; Edward Atkinson, *Cotton: Articles from the New York Herald* (Boston: Albert J. Wright, 1877), 4.

11. E. J. Donnell, *Chronological and Statistical History of Cotton* (New York: James Sutton & Co., 1872), v.

12. There exists a vast literature on this topic, including Immanuel Wallerstein, *The Modern World-System*, vol. 3, *The Second Great Expansion of the Capitalist World-Economy, 1730–1840s* (San Diego: Academic Press, 1989); Dale W. Tomich, *Slavery in the Circuit of Sugar: Martinique and the World Economy, 1830–1848* (Baltimore: Johns Hopkins University Press, 1990); Andre Gunder Frank, *ReOrient: Global Economy in the Asian Age* (Berkeley: University of California Press, 1998); Abdoulaye Ly, *La théorisation de la connexion capitaliste des continents* (Dakar: IFAAN, 1994); John Gallagher and Ronald Robinson, "The Imperialism of Free Trade," *Economic History Review*, Second Series, 51 (1953): 1–15; Patrick Wolfe, "History and Imperialism: A Century of Theory," *American Historical Review* 102 (April 1997): 388–420.

13. Baines, *History of the Cotton Manufacture*, 530–31.

14. See, for example, Gene Dattel, *Cotton and Race in the Making of America: The Human Costs of Economic Power* (Chicago: Ivan Dee, 2009); Morris de Camp Crawford, *The Heritage of Cotton: The Fibre of Two Worlds and Many Ages* (New York: G. P. Putnam's Sons, 1924).

15. The global history literature is burgeoning. It is hardly a new invention, however. Just recall early contributions such as Abdoulaye Ly, *La Compagnie du Sénégal* (Paris:

Présence Africaine, 1958); Marc Bloch, "Toward a Comparative History of European Societies," in Frederic Chapin Lane and Jelle C. Riemersma, eds., *Enterprise and Secular Change: Readings in Economic History* (Homewood, IL: R. D. Irwin, 1953); Williams, *Capitalism and Slavery*; C. L. R. James, *The Black Jacobins* (London: Secker & Warburg, 1938). See also C. A. Bayly, *The Birth of the Modern World, 1780–1914: Global Connections and Comparisons* (Malden, MA: Blackwell, 2004); Jürgen Oster-hammel, *The Transformation of the World: A Global History of the Nineteenth Century* (Princeton, NJ: Princeton University Press, 2014). For overviews of the literature see Sebastian Conrad, *Globalgeschichte: Eine Einführung* (Munich: Beck, 2013); Dominic Sachsenmaier, *Global Perspectives in Global History: Theories and Approaches in a Connected World* (New York: Cambridge University Press, 2011); Sven Beckert and Dominic Sachsenmaier, *Global History Globally* (forthcoming); Bruce Mazlich and Ralph Buultjens, *Conceptualizing Global History* (Boulder, CO: Westview Press, 1993); Jerry Bentley, "The Task of World History" (unpublished paper, in author's possession). See also Robert C. Allen, *The British Industrial Revolution in Global Perspective* (Cambridge: Cambridge University Press, 2009); Jan Luiten van Zanden, *The Long Road to Industrial Revolution: The European Economy in a Global Perspective, 1000–1800* (Amsterdam: Brill, 2009) and the excellent work of Patrick O'Brien, for example, "European Economic Development: The Contribution of the Periphery," *Economic History Review*, Second Series, 35 (February 1982): 1–18.

16. Studies on commodities have been many in recent years. See especially Sydney Mintz, *Sweetness and Power: The Place of Sugar in Modern History* (New York: Viking, 1985); Mark Kurlansky, *Salt: A World History* (New York: Walker and Co., 2002); Barbara Freese, *Coal: A Human History* (Cambridge, MA: Perseus, 2003); Pietra Rivoli, *The Travels of a T-shirt in the Global Economy: An Economist Examines the Markets, Power and Politics of World Trade* (Hoboken, NJ: John Wiley & Sons, 2005); Larry Zuckerman, *The Potato: How the Humble Spud Rescued the Western World* (Boston: Faber & Faber, 1998); Wolfgang Mönninghoff, *King Cotton: Kulturgeschichte der Baumwolle* (Düsseldorf: Artemis & Winkler, 2006); Mark Kurlansky, *Cod: A Biography of the Fish That Changed the World* (New York: Walker & Co., 1997); Allan Macfarlane and Gerry Martin, *Glass: A World History* (Chicago: University of Chicago Press, 2002); Stephen Yaffa, *Big Cotton: How a Humble Fiber Created Fortunes, Wrecked Civilizations, and Put America on the Map* (New York: Penguin, 2005); Erik Orsenna, *Voyage aux pays du coton: Petit précis de mondialisation* (Paris: Fayard, 2006); Iain Gateley, *Tobacco: A Cultural History of How an Exotic Plant Seduced Civilization* (New York: Grove, 2001); Heinrich Eduard Jacob, *Kaffee: Die Biographie eines weltwirtschaftlichen Stoffes* (Munich: Oekom Verlag, 2006). A beautiful discussion of the "biography of things" can be found in the 1929 discussion of Sergej Tretjakow, "Die Biographie des Dings," in Heiner Boehnke, ed., *Die Arbeit des Schriftstellers* (Reinbeck: Rowolt, 1972), 81–86; more generally on commodities, see Jens Soentgen, "Geschichten über Stoffe," *Arbeitsblätter für die Sachbuchforschung* (October 2005): 1–25; Jennifer Bair, "Global Capitalism and Commodity Chains: Looking Back, Going Forward," *Competition and Change* 9 (June 2005): 153–80; Immanuel Wallerstein, *Commodity Chains in the World-Economy, 1590–1790* (Binghamton, NY: Fernand Braudel Center, 2000). A good example for a successfully recast economic history is William Cronon,

Nature's Metropolis: Chicago and the Great West (New York: Norton, 1991). Good discussions on the rich historiography on the Industrial Revolution can be found in Inikori, *Africans and the Industrial Revolution in England,* chapter 2; William J. Ashworth, "The Ghost of Rostow: Science, Culture and the British Industrial Revolution," *Historical Science* 46 (2008): 249–74. For an emphasis on the importance of the spatial aspects of capitalism see David Harvey, *Spaces of Capital: Towards a Critical Geography* (New York: Routledge, 2001).

CHAPTER ONE: THE RISE OF A GLOBAL COMMODITY

1. The cotton grown in these towns was most probably *G. hirsutum Palmeri*, a kind of cotton known to have grown in what is today the Mexican states of Oaxaca and Guerrero. The description of the plant is from C. Wayne Smith and J. Tom Cothren, eds., *Cotton: Origin, History, Technology, and Production* (New York: John Wiley & Sons, 1999), 11; Angus Maddison, *The World Economy: A Millennial Perspective* (Paris: Development Centre of the Organisation for Economic Co-operation and Development, 2001), 263; Frances F. Berdan, "Cotton in Aztec Mexico: Production, Distribution and Uses," *Mexican Studies* 3 (1987): 241ff.; Joseph B. Mountjoy, "Prehispanic Cultural Development Along the Southern Coast of West Mexico," in Shirley Goren-stein, ed., *Greater Mesoamerica: The Archeology of West and Northwest Mexico* (Salt Lake City: University of Utah Press, 2000), 106; Donald D. Brandt, "The Primitive and Modern Economy of the Middle Rio Balsas, Guerrero and Michoacan," Eighth American Scientific Congress, Section 8, History and Geography (Washington, DC, 1940), Abstract; for the weight of a bale of cotton in sixteenth-century Mexico see José Rodríguez Vallejo, *Ixcatl, el algodón mexicano* (Mexico: Fondo de Cultura Económica, 1976), 64.

2. K. D. Hake and T. A. Kerby, "Cotton and the Environment," *Cotton Production Manual* (UCANR Publications, 1996), 324–27; Frederick Wilkinson, *The Story of the Cotton Plant* (New York: D. Appleton & Company, 1899), 39.

3. There is some (slight) disagreement between Gavin Wright, *The Political Economy of the Cotton South: Households, Markets, and Wealth in the Nineteenth Century* (New York: Norton, 1978), 14–15, and Jason Clay, *World Agriculture and the Environment: A Commodity-by-Commodity Guide to Impacts and Practices* (Washington, DC: Island Press, 2004), 284–87.

4. Ralf Kittler, Manfred Kaysar, and Mark Stoneking, "Molecular Evolution of *Pediculus humanus* and the Origin of Clothing," *Current Biology* 13 (August 19, 2003): 1414–15; for a much earlier dating of spinning and weaving see Eliso Kvabadze et al., "30,000 Year-Old Wild Flax Fibres," *Science* 11 (September 2009): 1359.

5. Almut Bohnsack, *Spinnen und Weben: Entwicklung von Technik und Arbeit im Textilgewerbe* (Reinbek: Rowohlt, 1981), 31–32; "Kleidung," in Johannes Hoops, *Reallexikon der Germanischen Altertumskunde,* vol. 16 (Berlin: Walter de Gruyter, 2000), 603–25; Mary Schoeser, *World Textiles: A Concise History* (New York: Thames & Hudson World of Art, 2003), 20; "Kleidung," in Max Ebert, ed., *Reallexikon der Vorgeschichte,* vol. 6 (Berlin: Walter de Gruyter, 1926), 380–94; Harry Bates Brown, *Cotton: History, Species, Varieties, Morphology, Breeding, Culture, Diseases, Marketing, and Uses* (New York: McGraw-Hill, 1938), 1.

6. See for example T. W. Rhys Davids, trans., *Vinaya Texts* (Oxford: Clarendon Press, 1885), 168; Georg Buehler, trans., *The Sacred Laws of the Âryas* (Oxford: Clarendon Press, 1882), 165, 169, 170; Vijaya Ramaswamy, *Textiles and Weavers in South India* (New York: Oxford University Press, 2006), 1, 57; Doran Ross, ed., *Wrapped in Pride: Ghanaian Kente and African American Identity* (Los Angeles: UCLA Fowler Museum of Cultural History, 1998), 77; Frank Goldtooth, as recorded by Stanley A. Fishler, *In the Beginning: A Navajo Creation Myth* (Salt Lake City: University of Utah Press, 1953), 16; Aileen O'Bryan, *The Dîné: Origin Myths of the Navajo Indians*, Smithsonian Institution, Bureau of American Ethnology, Bulletin 163 (Washington, DC: Government Printing Office, 1956), 38; Francesca Bray, "Textile Production and Gender Roles in China, 1000–1700," *Chinese Science* 12 (1995): 116; Anthony Winterbourne, *When the Norns Have Spoken: Fate in Germanic Paganism* (Madison, NJ: Fairleigh Dickinson University Press, 2004), 96.

7. C. L. Brubaker et al., "The Origin and Domestication of Cotton," in C. Wayne Smith and J. Tom Cothren, eds., *Cotton: Origin, History, Technology, and Production* (New York: John Wiley & Sons, 1999), 4, 5–6, 12, 17, 22; Wafaa M. Amer and Osama A. Momtaz, "Historic Background of Egyptian Cotton (2600 BC–AD 1910)," *Archives of Natural History* 26 (1999): 219.

8. Thomas Robson Hay and Hal R. Taylor, "Cotton," in William Darrach Halsey and Emanuel Friedman, eds., *Collier's Encyclopedia, with Bibliography and Index* (New York: Macmillan Educational Co., 1981), 387; A. Lucas, *Ancient Egyptian Materials and Industries*, 4th ed., revised by J. R. Harris (London: Edward Arnold, 1962), 147; Richard H. Meadow, "The Origins and Spread of Agriculture and Pastoralism in Northwestern South Asia," in David R. Harris, ed., *The Origins and Spread of Agriculture and Pastoralism in Eurasia* (London: UCL Press, 1996), 396; for a traditional Indian account of these classics, see S. V. Puntambekar and N. S. Varadachari, *Hand-Spinning and Hand-Weaving: An Essay* (Ahmedabad: All India Spinners' Association, 1926), 1–9; James Mann, *The Cotton Trade of Great Britain* (London: Simpkin, Marshall & Co., 1860), 1, 2–3; Brown, *Cotton*, 2; see Herodotus, *The Histories*, ed. A. R. Burn, trans. Aubrey de Sélincourt, rev. ed., Penguin Classics (Harmondsworth, UK: Penguin, 1972), 245; Arno S. Pearse, *The Cotton Industry of India, Being the Report of the Journey to India* (Manchester: Taylor, Garnett, Evans, 1930), 15; J. Forbes Royle, *On the Culture and Commerce of Cotton in India and Elsewhere: With an Account of the Experiments Made by the Hon. East India Company up to the Present Time* (London: Smith, Elder & Co., 1851), 116ff.

9. Brown, *Cotton*, 5; Edward Baines, *History of the Cotton Manufacture in Great Britain* (London: H. Fisher, R. Fisher, and P. Jackson, 1835), 65–70; Prasannan Parthasarathi, "Cotton Textiles in the Indian Subcontinent, 1200–1800," in Giorgio Riello and Prasannan Parthasarathi, eds., *The Spinning World: A Global History of Cotton Textiles, 1200–1850* (New York: Oxford University Press, 2009), 23–25.

10. H. Wescher, "Die Baumwolle im Altertum," in *Ciba-Rundschau* 45 (June 1940): 1635; Alwin Oppel, *Die Baumwolle* (Leipzig: Duncker & Humblot, 1902), 206–7; Clinton G. Gilroy, *The History of Silk, Cotton, Linen, Wool, and Other Fibrous Substances* (New York: Harper & Brothers, 1845), 334; Marco Polo, *Travels of Marco Polo* (Westminster, MD: Modern Library, 2001), 174; Baines, *History of the Cotton Manufacture*, 56, 58.

11. A. G. Hopkins, *An Economic History of West Africa* (New York: Columbia University Press, 1973), 48; M. D. C. Crawford, *The Heritage of Cotton: The Fibre of Two Worlds and Many Ages* (New York: G. P. Putnam's Sons, 1924), 46; Amer and Momtaz, "Historic Background," 212; Oppel, *Die Baumwolle*, 209; William H. Prescott, *History of the Conquest of Peru* (Westminster, MD: Modern Library, 2000), 51, 108, 300.

12. Gilroy, *History of Silk*, 331–32; Smith and Hirth, "Development of Prehispanic Cotton-Spinning," 353; Barbara L. Stark, Lynette Heller, and Michael A. Ohnersorgen, "People with Cloth: Mesoamerican Economic Change from the Perspective of Cotton in South-Central Veracruz," *Latin American Antiquity* 9 (March 1978): 9, 25, 27; Crawford, *Heritage*, 32, 35; Smith and Hirth, "Development of Prehispanic Cotton-Spinning," 355; Barbara Ann Hall, "Spindle Whorls and Cotton Production at Middle Classic Matacapan and in the Gulf Lowlands," in Barbara L. Stark and Philip J. Arnold III, eds., *Olmec to Aztec: Settlement Patterns in the Ancient Gulf Lowlands* (Tucson: University of Arizona Press, 1997), 117, 133, 134.

13. Juan de Villagutierre Soto-Mayor, *History of the Conquest of the Province of the Itza*, 1st English edition, translated from the 2nd Spanish edition by Robert D. Wood (Culver City, CA: Labyrinthos, 1983), 197; Berdan, "Cotton in Aztec Mexico," 235–38, 239; Smith and Hirth, "Development of Prehispanic Cotton-Spinning," 356; R. B. Handy, "History and General Statistics of Cotton," in *The Cotton Plant: Its History, Botany, Chemistry, Culture, Enemies, and Uses*, prepared under the supervision of A. C. True, United States Department of Agriculture, Office of Experiment Stations, Bulletin 33 (Washington, DC: Government Printing Office, 1896), 63; United States, *Historical Statistics of the United States, Colonial Times to 1970*, vol. 1 (Washington, DC: U.S. Dept. of Commerce, Bureau of the Census, 1975), Series K-550–563, "Hay, Cotton, Cottonseed, Shorn Wool, and Tobacco—Acreage, Production, and Price: 1790 to 1970," 518; Hall, "Spindle Whorls," 118; Stark, Heller, and Ohnersorgen, "People with Cloth," 14, 29.

14. Brown, *Cotton*, 14; Kate Peck Kent, *Prehistoric Textiles of the Southwest* (Santa Fe, NM: School of American Research Press, 1983), 9, 27, 28, 29; the quote about blankets is from Ward Alan Minge, "Effectos del Pais: A History of Weaving Along the Rio Grande," in Nora Fisher, ed., *Rio Grande Textiles* (Santa Fe: Museum of New Mexico Press, 1994), 6; Kate Peck Kent, *Pueblo Indian Textiles: A Living Tradition* (Santa Fe, NM: School of American Research Press, 1983), 26; Crawford, *Heritage*, 37; David Watts, *The West Indies: Patterns of Development, Culture and Environmental Change Since 1492* (Cambridge: Cambridge University Press, 1990), 65, 89, 174; Mann, *Cotton Trade*, 4; Christopher Columbus, *The Diario of Christopher Columbus's first voyage to America: 1492–1493*, abstracted by Fray Bartolomé de las Casas, transcribed and translated into English, with notes and a concordance of the Spanish, by Oliver Dunn and James E. Kelley Jr. (Norman: University of Oklahoma Press, 1989), 131–35; see entries of October 16, November 3, and November 5, 1492, 85–91, 131, 135.

15. Pliny the Elder, *The Natural History of Pliny*, vol. 4, trans. John Bostock and H. T. Riley (London: Henry G. Bohn, 1856), 134–35; Mann, *Cotton Trade*, 3; Christopher Ehret, *The Civilizations of Africa: A History to 1800* (Charlottesville: University Press of Virginia, 2002), 67–68; Ross, *Wrapped in Pride*, 75; Lars Sundström, *The Trade of Guinea* (Lund: Hakan Ohlssons Boktryckeri, 1965), 148; F. L. Griffith and

G. M. Crowfoot, "On the Early Use of Cotton in the Nile Valley," *Journal of Egyptian Archeology* 20 (1934): 7; Amer and Momtaz, "Historic Background," 212, 214, 215, 217.

16. M. Kouame Aka, "Production et circulation des cotonnades en Afrique de l'Ouest du XIème siècle a la fin de la conquette coloniale (1921)" (PhD dissertation, Université de Cocody-Abidjan, 2013), 18, 41; Marion Johnson, "Technology, Competition, and African Crafts," in Clive Dewey and A. G. Hopkins, eds., *The Imperial Impact: Studies in the Economic History of Africa and India* (London: Athlone Press, 1978), 176, 195, 201; Venice Lamb and Judy Holmes, *Nigerian Weaving* (Roxford: H. A. & V. M. Lamb, 1980), 15, 16; Marion Johnson, "Cloth Strips and History," *West African Journal of Archaeology* 7 (1977): 169; Philip D. Curtin, *Economic Change in Precolonial Africa: Senegambia in the Era of the Slave Trade* (Madison: University of Wisconsin Press, 1975), 48; Marion Johnson, "Cloth as Money: The Cloth Strip Currencies of Africa," in Dale Idiens and K. G. Pointing, *Textiles of Africa* (Bath: Pasold Research Fund, 1980), 201. Patricia Davison and Patrick Harries, "Cotton Weaving in South-east Africa: Its History and Technology," in Idiens and Pointing, *Textiles of Africa*, 177, 179, 180; Marie Philiponeau, *Le coton et l'Islam: Fil d'une histoire africaine* (Algiers: Casbah Editions, 2009), 15, 17; Ross, *Wrapped in Pride*, 75; Rita Bolland, *Tellem Textiles: Archaeological Finds from Burial Caves in Mali's Bandiagara Cliff* (Leiden: Rijksmuseum voor Volkenkunde, 1991); Leo Africanus, *The History and Description of Africa and of the Notable Things Therein Contained, Done in the English in the Year 1600 by John Pory*, vol. 3 (London: Hakluyt Society, 1896), 823, 824.

17. For the notion of the multiple origins of cotton and its domestication see Meadow, "Origins," 397.

18. Brown, *Cotton*, 8; Maureen Fennell Mazzaoui, *The Italian Cotton Industry in the Later Middle Ages, 1100–1600* (Cambridge: Cambridge University Press, 1981), 11, 15, 17–18; Lucas, *Ancient Egyptian Materials*, 148; Hartmut Schmoekel, *Ur, Assur und Babylon: Drei Jahrtausende im Zweistromland* (Stuttgart: Gustav Klipper Verlag, 1958), 131; Baines, *History of the Cotton Manufacture*, 27; Richard W. Bulliet, *Cotton, Climate, and Camels in Early Islamic Iran: A Moment in World History* (New York: Columbia University Press, 2009), 1, 8, 46; Marco Polo, *Travels*, 22, 26, 36, 54, 58, 59, 60, 174, 247, 253, 255.

19. Chao Kuo-Chun, *Agrarian Policy of the Chinese Communist Party, 1921–1959* (Westport, CT: Greenwood Press, 1977), 5, 8ff.

20. Craig Dietrich, "Cotton Culture and Manufacture in Early Ch'ing China," in W. E. Willmott, ed., *Economic Organization in Chinese Society* (Stanford, CA: Stanford University Press, 1972), 111ff.; Mi Chü Wiens, "Cotton Textile Production and Rural Social Transformation in Early Modern China," *Journal of the Institute of Chinese Studies of the Chinese University of Hong Kong* 7 (December 1974): 516–19; Frederick W. Mote and Denis Twitchett, eds., *The Cambridge History of China*, vol. 7, *The Ming Dynasty, 1368–1644*, part 1 (New York: Cambridge University Press, 1998), 256, 507; Kenneth Pomeranz, "Beyond the East-West Binary: Resituating Development Paths in the Eighteenth-Century World," *Journal of Asian Studies* 61 (May 2002): 569; United States, *Historical Statistics*, 518.

21. Anthony Reid, *Southeast Asia in the Age of Commerce, 1450–1680*, vol. 1, *The Lands Below the Winds* (New Haven, CT: Yale University Press, 1988), 90; Crawford, *Heri-*

tage, 7; William B. Hauser, *Economic Institutional Change in Tokugawa Japan: Osaka and the Kinai Cotton Trade* (Cambridge: Cambridge University Press, 1974), 117–20; Mikio Sumiya and Koji Taira, eds., *An Outline of Japanese Economic History, 1603– 1940: Major Works and Research Findings* (Tokyo: University of Tokyo Press, 1979), 99–100.

22. Stark, Heller, and Ohnersorgen, "People with Cloth," 10, 29; Howard F. Cline, "The Spirit of Enterprise in Yucatan," in Lewis Hanke, ed., *History of Latin American Civilization*, vol. 2 (London: Methuen, 1969), 137; Johnson, "Technology," 259; Thomas J. Bassett, *The Peasant Cotton Revolution in West Africa: Côte d'Ivoire, 1880–1995* (New York: Cambridge University Press, 2001), 33; James Forbes, *Oriental Memoirs: A Narrative of Seventeen Years Residence in India*, vol. 2 (London: Richard Bentley, 1834), 34; Moritz Schanz, "Die Baumwolle in Russisch-Asien," *Beihefte zum Tropenpflanzer* 15 (1914): 2; on Korea see Tozaburo Tsukida, *Kankoku ni okeru mensaku chosa* (Tokyo: No-shomu sho noji shikenjyo, 1905), 1–3, 76–83.

23. Oppel, *Die Baumwolle*, 201; Berdan, "Cotton in Aztec Mexico," 241; Hall, "Spindle Whorls," 120; Sundström, *Trade of Guinea*, 147; Curtin, *Economic Change*, 50, 212; Brown, *Cotton*, 8; Reid, *Southeast Asia*, 93; Gilroy, *History of Silk*, 339; Carla M. Sinopoli, *The Political Economy of Craft Production: Crafting Empire in South India, c. 1350–1650* (Cambridge: Cambridge University Press, 2003), 185; A. Campbell, "Notes on the State of the Arts of Cotton Spinning, Weaving, Printing and Dyeing in Nepal," *Journal of the Asiatic Society of Bengal* (Calcutta) 5 (January to December 1836): 222.

24. Hall, "Spindle Whorls," 115, 116, 120, 122, 124; Davison and Harries, "Cotton Weaving," 182; Oppel, *Die Baumwolle*, 209; Prescott, *Conquest of Peru*, 51; Gilroy, *History of Silk*, 339, 343; Curtin, *Economic Change*, 213; Kent, *Prehistoric Textiles*, 35; Kent, *Pueblo Indian*, 28; Reid, *Southeast Asia*, 93; Sundström, *Trade of Guinea*, 148–49; Lamb and Holmes, *Nigerian Weaving*, 10–11; Johnson, "Technology," 261.

25. Reid, *Southeast Asia*, 94.

26. Berdan, "Cotton in Aztec Mexico," 242, 259; Mote and Twitchett, *Ming Dynasty*, 507, 690ff.; K. N. Chaudhuri, "The Organisation and Structure of Textile Production in India," in Tirthankar Roy, ed., *Cloth and Commerce: Textiles in Colonial India* (Waltnut Creek, CA: AltaMira Press, 1996), 71; Wiens, "Cotton Textile," 520; Sinopoli, *Political Economy*, 177.

27. Berdan, "Cotton in Aztec Mexico," 242; Bray, "Textile Production," 119; Sundström, *Trade of Guinea*, 162; Curtin, *Economic Change*, 212; Davison and Harries, "Cotton Weaving," 187; Johnson, "Cloth as Money," 193–202; Reid, *Southeast Asia*, 90; Sundström, *Trade of Guinea*, 164; Stark, Heller, and Ohnersorgen, "People with Cloth," 9.

28. Smith and Hirth, "Development of Prehispanic Cotton-Spinning," 356; Bulliet, *Cotton, Climate, and Camels*, 46, 59; Philiponeau, *Coton et l'Islam*, 25; Pedro Machado, "Awash in a Sea of Cloth: Gujarat, Africa and the Western Indian Ocean Trade, 1300–1800," in Riello and Parthasarathi, eds., *The Spinning World*, 161–79; the importance of traders' distance from the polities they originated from is also emphasized by Gil J. Stein, *Rethinking World-Systems: Diasporas, Colonies, and Interaction in Uruk Mesopotamia* (Tucson: University of Arizona Press, 1999), 173.

29. See Hall, "Spindle Whorls," 115; Stark, Heller, and Ohnersorgen, "People with Cloth," 9; Berdan, "Cotton in Aztec Mexico," 247ff., 258; Kent, *Prehistoric Textiles*, 28; Volney H. Jones, "A Summary of Data on Aboriginal Cotton of the Southwest," *University of New Mexico Bulletin, Symposium on Prehistoric Agriculture*, vol. 296 (October 15, 1936), 60; Reid, *Southeast Asia,* 91; Sundström, *Trade of Guinea*, 147; Bassett, *Peasant Cotton*, 34; Curtin, *Economic Change*, 212–13; Halil Inalcik, "The Ottoman State: Economy and Society, 1300–1600," in Halil Inalcik and Donald Quataert, eds., *An Economic and Social History of the Ottoman Empire, 1300–1914* (Cambridge: Cambridge University Press, 1994), 296; Hauser, *Economic Institutional Change*, 59.

30. Sundström, *Trade of Guinea*, 156, 157; Ramaswamy, *Textiles*, 25, 70–72; Chaudhuri, "Organisation," 55; Inalcik, "Ottoman State," 352; Mann, *Cotton Trade*, 2–3, 23; Smith and Cothren, *Cotton*, 68–69; Baines, *History of the Cotton Manufacture*, 24, 76; Wescher, "Die Baumwolle," 1639; Gilroy, *History of Silk*, 321; John Peter Wild and Felicity Wild, "Rome and India: Early Indian Cotton Textiles from Berenike, Red Sea Coast of Egypt," in Ruth Barnes, ed., *Textiles in Indian Ocean Societies* (New York: Routledge, 2005), 11–16; Surendra Gopal, *Commerce and Crafts in Gujarat, 16th and 17th Centuries: A Study in the Impact of European Expansion on Precapitalist Economy* (New Delhi: People's Publishing House, 1975), 3; the quote on the Indo-Levant trade is in Inalcik, "Ottoman State," 355, see also 350, 354, 355; Eliyahu Ashtor, "The Venetian Cotton Trade in Syria in the Later Middle Ages," *Studi Medievali*, ser. 3, vol. 17 (1976): 690; Suraiya Faroqhi, "Crisis and Change, 1590–1699," in Inalcik and Quataert, eds., *An Economic and Social History of the Ottoman Empire,* 524; Eugen Wirt, "Aleppo im 19. Jahrhundert," in Hans Geord Majer, ed., *Osmanische Studien zur Wirtschafts- und Sozialgeschichte* (Wiesbaden: Otto Harrassowitz, 1986), 186–205; Sinopoli, *Political Economy*, 179.

31. Crawford, *Heritage*, 6, 69; Reid, *Southeast Asia*, 90, 95; in Sinnappah Arasaratnam and Aniruddha Ray, *Masulipatnam and Cambay: A History of Two Port-Towns, 1500–1800* (New Delhi: Munshiram Manoharlal Publishers, 1994), 121; for some informative maps on Gujarat's overseas trade as well as its domestic trade during this period, see Gopal, *Commerce and Crafts*, 16, 80, 160; Mazzaoui, *Italian Cotton*, 9–11; Beverly Lemire, "Revising the Historical Narrative: India, Europe, and the Cotton Trade, c. 1300–1800," in Riello and Parthasarathi, eds., *The Spinning World*, 226.

32. B. C. Allen, *Eastern Bengal District Gazetteers: Dacca* (Allahabad: Pioneer Press, 1912), 106; Sinopoli, *Political Economy*, 186; Baines, *History of the Cotton Manufacture*, 75; Ramaswamy, *Textiles*, 44, 53, 55; Wiens, "Cotton Textile," 522, 528; Yueksel Duman, "Notables, Textiles and Copper in Ottoman Tokat, 1750–1840" (PhD dissertation, State University of New York at Binghamton, 1998); Mazzaoui, *Italian Cotton*, 22; Max Freiherr von Oppenheim, *Der Tell Halaf: Eine neue Kultur im ältesten Mesopotamien* (Leipzig: Brockhaus, 1931), 70; Sundström, *Trade of Guinea*, 147; Lamb and Holmes, *Nigerian Weaving*, 10; Curtin, *Economic Change*, 48; Aka, *Production*, 69; Youssoupha Mbargane Guissé, "Ecrire l'histoire économique des artisans et createurs de l'Afrique de l'Ouest" (presentation, Université Cheikh Anta Diop, Dakar, Senegal, December 2011); Hauser, *Economic Institutional Change*, 20–30.

33. Chaudhuri, "Organisation," 49, 51, 53; Hameeda Hossain, "The Alienation of Weavers: Impact of the Conflict Between the Revenue and Commercial Interests of the East India Company, 1750–1800," in Roy, ed., *Cloth and Commerce*, 117; Suraiya Faroqhi, "Notes on the Production of Cotton and Cotton Cloth in Sixteenth- and Seventeenth-Century Anatolia," in Huri Islamoglu-Inan, ed., *The Ottoman Empire and the World-Economy* (New York: Cambridge University Press, 1987), 267, 268; Inalcik, "Ottoman State"; Huri Islamoglu-Inan, *State and Peasant in the Ottoman Empire: Agrarian Power Relations and Regional Economic Development in Ottoman Anatolia During the Sixteenth Century* (Leiden: E. J. Brill, 1994), 223, 235; Socrates D. Petmezas, "Patterns of Protoindustrialization in the Ottoman Empire: The Case of Eastern Thessaly, ca. 1750–1860," *Journal of European Economic History* (1991): 589; Prasannan Parthasarathi, "Merchants and the Rise of Colonialism," in Burton Stein and Sanjay Subrahmanyam, eds., *Institutions and Economic Change in South Asia* (Delhi: Oxford University Press, 1996), 96, 98; S. Arasaratnam, "Weavers, Merchants and Company: The Handloom Industry in Southeastern India, 1750–90," in Roy, ed., *Cloth and Commerce*, 87; Bray, "Textile Production," 127.

34. Smith and Hirth, "Development of Prehispanic Cotton-Spinning," 349; Angela Lakwete, *Inventing the Cotton Gin: Machine and Myth in Antebellum America* (Baltimore: John Hopkins University Press, 2005), 11–12; Mazzaoui, *Italian Cotton*, 74–82, 89; Smith and Hirth, "Development of Prehispanic Cotton-Spinning," 354–55; John H. A. Munro, *Textiles, Towns and Trade: Essays in the Economic History of Late-Medieval England and the Low Countries* (Brookfield, VT: Variorum, 1994), 8, 15; Maureen Fennell Mazzaoui, "The Cotton Industry of Northern Italy in the Late Middle Ages, 1150–1450," *Journal of Economic History* 32 (1972): 274.

35. Alan L. Olmstead and Paul W. Rhode, *Creating Abundance: Biological Innovation and American Agricultural Development* (New York: Cambridge University Press, 2008), 108–9; John Hebron Moore, "Cotton Breeding in the Old South," *Agricultural History* 30, no. 3 (July 1956): 95–104; John Hebron Moore, *Agriculture in Ante-Bellum Mississippi* (New York: Bookman Associates, 1958), 13–36, 97; Lewis Cecil Gray, *History of Agriculture in the Southern United States to 1860*, vol. 2 (Washington, DC: Carnegie Institution of Washington, 1933), 689–90; James Lawrence Watkins, *King Cotton: A Historical and Statistical Review, 1790 to 1908* (New York: J. L. Watkins, 1908), 13; Bassett, *Peasant Cotton*, 33; Mazzaoui, *Italian Cotton*, 20–21; Bulliet, *Cotton, Climate, and Camels*, 40; Chaudhuri, "Organisation," 75.

36. Mahatma Gandhi, *The Indian Cotton Textile Industry: Its Past, Present and Future* (Calcutta: G. N. Mitra, 1930), 6.

37. As quoted in Henry Lee, *The Vegetable Lamb of Tartary: A Curious Fable of the Cotton Plant* (London: Sampson Low, Marston, Searle, & Rivington, 1887), 5.

38. Mann, *Cotton Trade*, 5; Oppel, *Die Baumwolle*, 39; see also exhibits at Museu Tèxtil i d'Indumentària, Barcelona, Spain.

39. That the Crusades were crucial to the introduction of the cotton textile industry into Europe is confirmed by "Baumwolle," entry in *Lexikon des Mittelalters*, vol. 1 (Munich: Artemis Verlag, 1980), 1670.

40. Alfred P. Wadsworth and Julia De Lacy Mann, *The Cotton Trade and Industrial Lan-*

cashire, 1600–1780 (Manchester: Manchester University Press, 1931), 15; Mazzaoui, "Cotton Industry," 263; Ashtor, "Venetian Cotton," 677.

41. During the twelfth century, cotton manufacturing arose in places such as southern France, Catalonia, and, most significantly, northern Italy. See Mazzaoui, "Cotton Industry," 268; Wescher, "Die Baumwolle," 1643, 1644; Mazzaoui, *Italian Cotton*, 114.

42. Mazzaoui, *Italian Cotton*, 64, 66, 69; Mazzaoui, "Cotton Industry," 271, 273, 276; Wescher, "Die Baumwolle," 1643.

43. Mazzaoui, *Italian Cotton*, 7, 29, 63; Mazzaoui, "Cotton Industry," 265.

44. Mazzaoui, *Italian Cotton*, 53; Ashtor, "Venetian Cotton," 675, 676, 697; Mazzaoui, *Italian Cotton*, 35.

45. Mazzaoui, *Italian Cotton*, 65–66, 74–82, 89; Lakwete, *Inventing the Cotton Gin*, 11–12; Mazzaoui, "Cotton Industry," 274, 275; Bohnsack, *Spinnen und Weben*, 65–66, 37, 63, 67, 114, 115; Karl-Heinz Ludwig, "Spinnen im Mittelalter unter besonderer Berücksichtigung der Arbeiten, cum rota," *Technikgeschichte* 57 (1990): 78; Eric Broudy, *The Book of Looms: A History of the Handloom from Ancient Times to the Present* (Hanover, NH: Brown University Press, 1979), 102; Munro, *Textiles*, 8, 15.

46. Mazzaoui, *Italian Cotton*, xi, 29.

47. Mazzaoui, *Italian Cotton*, 139, 144, 150, 152; Mazzaoui, "Cotton Industry," 282, 284; Wolfgang von Stromer, *Die Gründung der Baumwollindustrie in Mitteleuropa* (Stuttgart: Hiersemann, 1978), 84–86; Eugen Nübling, *Ulms Baumwollweberei im Mittelalter* (Leipzig: Duncker & Humblot, 1890), 146.

48. Von Stromer, *Die Gründung*, 32; Götz Freiherr von Poelnitz, *Die Fugger* (Tübingen: J. C. B. Mohr, 1981); Richard Ehrenberg, *Capital and Finance in the Age of the Renaissance: A Study of the Fuggers and Their Connections*, trans. H. M. Lucas (New York: Harcourt, 1928).

49. Von Stromer, *Die Gründung*, 1, 2, 8, 21, 128, 139, 148; Nübling, *Ulms Baumwollweberei*, 141; Bohnsack, *Spinnen und Weben*, 152.

50. Mazzaoui, *Italian Cotton*, 141; Von Stromer, *Die Gründung*, 88.

51. Mazzaoui, *Italian Cotton*, 55, 54, 154; Wadsworth and Mann, *Cotton Trade*, 23; Inalcik, "Ottoman State," 365; Daniel Goffman, "Izmir: From Village to Colonial Port City," in Edhem Eldem, Daniel Goffman, and Bruce Masters, eds., *The Ottoman City Between East and West: Aleppo, Izmir, and Istanbul* (Cambridge: Cambridge University Press, 1999), 79–134.

52. Nübling, *Ulms Baumwollweberei*, 166.

CHAPTER TWO: BUILDING WAR CAPITALISM

1. I am using the term "network" here instead of "system" or "world system" because I want to emphasize the continued importance of local distributions of social, economic, and political power to shaping the nature of the connections between various parts of the world. In this I am inspired by Gil J. Stein, *Rethinking World-Systems: Diasporas, Colonies, and Interaction in Uruk Mesopotamia* (Tucson: University of Arizona Press, 1999), especially 171.

2. Om Prakash, *The New Cambridge History of India,* vol. 2, *European Commercial*

Enterprise in Pre-Colonial India (Cambridge: Cambridge University Press, 1998), 23; Surendra Gopal, *Commerce and Crafts in Gujarat, 16th and 17th Centuries: A Study in the Impact of European Expansion on Precapitalist Economy* (New Delhi: People's Publishing House, 1975), 10–11, 18, 26, 28, 58.

3. Céline Cousquer, *Nantes: Une capitale française des Indiennes au XVIIIe siècle* (Nantes: Coiffard Editions, 2002), 17.

4. Sinnappah Arasaratnam, "Weavers, Merchants and Company: The Handloom Industry in Southeastern India, 1750–90," in Tirthankar Roy, ed., *Cloth and Commerce: Textiles in Colonial India* (Walnut Creek, CA: AltaMira Press, 1996), 90; James Mann, *The Cotton Trade of Great Britain* (London: Simpkin, Marshall & Co., 1860), 2; Walter R. Cassels, *Cotton: An Account of Its Culture in the Bombay Presidency* (Bombay: Bombay Education Society's Press, 1862), 77; Beverly Lemire, *Fashion's Favourite: The Cotton Trade and the Consumer in Britain, 1660–1800* (Oxford: Pasold Research Fund, 1991), 15; Hameeda Hossain, *The Company Weavers of Bengal: The East India Company and the Organization of Textile Production in Bengal, 1750–1813* (Delhi: Oxford University Press, 1988), 65; Proceeding, Bombay Castle, November 10, 1776, in Bombay Commercial Proceedings, P/414, 47, Oriental and India Office Collections, British Library, London; Stephen Broadberry and Bishnupriya Gupta, "Cotton Textiles and the Great Divergence: Lancashire, India and Shifting Competitive Advantage, 1600–1850," CEPR Discussion Paper No. 5183, London, Centre for Economic Policy Research, August 2005, Table 3, p. 32; Daniel Defoe and John McVeagh, *A Review of the State of the British Nation*, vol. 4, *1707–08* (London: Pickering & Chatto, 2006), 606.

5. See for example Factory Records, Dacca, 1779, Record Group G 15, col. 21 (1779), in Oriental and India Office Collections, British Library, London; John Irwin and P. R. Schwartz, *Studies in Indo-European Textile History* (Ahmedabad: Calico Museum of Textiles, 1966).

6. K. N. Chaudhuri, "European Trade with India," in *The Cambridge Economic History of India*, vol. 1, *c. 1200–c. 1750* (Cambridge: Cambridge University Press, 1982), 405–6; Arasaratnam, "Weavers, Merchants and Company," 92, 94; Copy of the Petition of Dadabo Monackjee, Contractor for the Investment anno 1779, in Factory Records, G 36 (Surat), 58, Oriental and India Office Collections, British Library, London; Cousquer, *Nantes*, 31.

7. Hameeda Hossain, "The Alienation of Weavers: Impact of the Conflict Between the Revenue and Commercial Interests of the East India Company, 1750–1800," in Roy, ed., *Cloth and Commerce*, 119, 117; Atul Chandra Pradhan, "British Trade in Cotton Goods and the Decline of the Cotton Industry in Orissa," in Nihar Ranjan Patnaik, ed., *Economic History of Orissa* (New Delhi: Indus Publishing Co., 1997), 244; Arasaratnam, "Weavers, Merchants and Company," 90; Shantha Hariharan, *Cotton Textiles and Corporate Buyers in Cottonopolis: A Study of Purchases and Prices in Gujarat, 1600–1800* (Delhi: Manak Publications, 2002), 49.

8. Memorandum of the Method of Providing Cloth at Dacca, 1676, in Factory Records, Miscellaneous, vol. 26, Oriental and India Office Collections, British Library, London.

9. Minutes of the Commercial Proceedings at Bombay Castle, April 15, 1800, in Min-

utes of Commercial Proceedings at Bombay Castle from April 15, 1800, to December 31, 1800, in Bombay Commercial Proceedings, P/414, Box 66, Oriental and India Office Collections, British Library, London; Copy of the Petition of Dadabo Monackjee, 1779, Factory Records Surat, 1780, Box 58, record G 36 (Surat), Oriental and India Office Collections, British Library; Report of John Taylor on the Cotton Textiles of Dacca, Home Miscellaneous Series, 456, p. 91, Oriental and India Office Collections, British Library; Lakshmi Subramanian, *Indigenous Capital and Imperial Expansion: Bombay, Surat and the West Coast* (Delhi: Oxford University Press, 1996), 15.

10. John Styles, "What Were Cottons for in the Early Industrial Revolution?" in Giorgio Riello and Prasannan Parthasarathi, eds., *The Spinning World: A Global History of Cotton Textiles, 1200–1850* (New York: Oxford University Press, 2009), 307–26; Halil Inalcik, "The Ottoman State: Economy and Society, 1300–1600," in Halil Inalcik and Donald Quataert, eds., *An Economic and Social History of the Ottoman Empire, 1300–1914* (Cambridge: Cambridge University Press, 1994), 354; Pedro Machado, "Awash in a Sea of Cloth: Gujarat, Africa and the Western Indian Ocean Trade, 1300–1800," in Riello and Parthasarasi, *The Spinning World*, 169; Subramanian, *Indigenous Capital*, 4.

11. Maureen Fennell Mazzaoui, *The Italian Cotton Industry in the Later Middle Ages, 1100–1600* (Cambridge: Cambridge University Press, 1981), 157.

12. "Assessing the Slave Trade," The Trans-Atlantic Slave Trade Database, accessed April 5, 2013, http://www.slavevoyages.org/tast/assessment/estimates.faces.

13. David Richardson, "West African Consumption Patterns and Their Influence on the Eighteenth-Century English Slave Trade," in Henry A. Gemery and Jan S. Hogendorn, eds., *The Uncommon Market: Essays in the Economic History of the Atlantic Slave Trade* (New York: Academic Press, 1979), 304; Joseph C. Miller, "Imports at Luanda, Angola 1785–1823," in G. Liesegang, H. Pasch, and A. Jones, eds., *Figuring African Trade: Proceedings of the Symposium on the Quantification and Structure of the Import and Export and Long-Distance Trade in Africa 1800–1913* (Berlin: Reimer, 1986), 164, 192; George Metcalf, "A Microcosm of Why Africans Sold Slaves: Akan Consumption Patterns in the 1770s," *Journal of African History* 28, no. 3 (January 1, 1987): 378–80.

14. Harry Hamilton Johnston, *The Kilima-Njaro Expedition: A Record of Scientific Exploration in Eastern Equatorial Africa* (London: Kegan, Paul, Trench & Co., 1886), 45; the European traveler is quoted in Jeremy Prestholdt, "On the Global Repercussions of East African Consumerism," *American Historical Review* 109, no. 3 (June 1, 2004): 761, 765; Robert Harms, *The Diligent: A Voyage Through the Worlds of the Slave Trade* (New York: Basic Books, 2002), 81; Miles to Shoolbred, 25 July 1779, T70/1483, National Archives of the UK, Kew, as quoted in Metcalf, "A Microcosm of Why Africans Sold Slaves," 388.

15. See also Carl Wennerlind, *Casualties of Credit: The English Financial Revolution, 1620–1720* (Cambridge, MA: Harvard University Press, 2011); Adam Smith, *An Inquiry into the Nature and Causes of the Wealth of Nations*, bk. IV, ch. VII, pt. II, vol. II, Edwin Cannan, ed. (Chicago: University of Chicago Press, 1976), 75.

16. Mazzaoui, *Italian Cotton*, 162; Alfred P. Wadsworth and Julia De Lacy Mann, *The Cotton Trade and Industrial Lancashire, 1600–1780* (Manchester: Manchester Uni-

versity Press, 1931), 116; Mann, *The Cotton Trade of Great Britain*, 5; Wolfgang von Stromer, *Die Gründung der Baumwollindustrie in Mitteleuropa* (Stuttgart: Hiersemann, 1978), 28; H. Wescher, "Die Baumwolle im Altertum," in *Ciba-Rundschau* 45 (June 1940): 1644–45.

17. Wadsworth and Mann, *The Cotton Trade*, 11, 15, 19, 21, 72.

18. Ibid., 4, 5, 27, 29, 42, 55, 73. Wool manufacturing had pioneered this move into the European countryside. See Herman van der Wee, "The Western European Woolen Industries, 1500–1750," in David Jenkins, *The Cambridge History of Western Textiles* (Cambridge: Cambridge University Press, 2003), 399.

19. Wadsworth and Mann, *The Cotton Trade*, 36.

20. Mann, *The Cotton Trade of Great Britain*, 6; Edward Baines, *History of the Cotton Manufacture in Great Britain* (London: Fisher, Fisher and Jackson, 1835), 109; Bernard Lepetit, "Frankreich, 1750–1850," in Wolfram Fischer et al., eds, *Handbuch der Europäischen Wirtschafts- und Sozialgeschichte*, vol. 4 (Stuttgart: Klett-Verlag für Wissen und Bildung, 1993), 487.

21. Wadsworth and Mann, *The Cotton Trade*, 187.

22. For an overview of that trade see Elena Frangakis-Syrett, "Trade Between the Ottoman Empire and Western Europe: The Case of Izmir in the Eighteenth Century," *New Perspectives on Turkey* 2 (1988): 1–18; Baines, *History of the Cotton Manufacture*, 304; Mann, *The Cotton Trade of Great Britain*, 23. Ellison wrongly asserts that "down to about twenty years before the close of the last century the cotton imported into Great Britain came almost entirely from the Mediterranean, chiefly from Smyrna"; see Thomas Ellison, *The Cotton Trade of Great Britain: Including a History of the Liverpool Cotton Market* (London and Liverpool: Effingham Wilson, 1886), 81. On Thessaloniki see Nicolas Svoronos, *Le commerce de Salonique au XVIIIe siècle* (Paris: Presses Universitaires de France, 1956); Manchester Cotton Supply Association, *Cotton Culture in New or Partially Developed Sources of Supply: Report of Proceedings* (Manchester: Cotton Supply Association, 1862), 30, as quoted in Oran Kurmus, "The Cotton Famine and Its Effects on the Ottoman Empire," in Huri Islamoglu-Inan, ed., *The Ottoman Empire and the World-Economy* (Cambridge: Cambridge University Press, 1987), 161; Resat Kasaba, *The Ottoman Empire and the World Economy: The Nineteenth Century* (Albany: State University of New York Press, 1988), 21. For general background see also Bruce McGowan, *Economic Life in Ottoman Europe: Taxation, Trade and the Struggle for Land, 1600–1800* (Cambridge: Cambridge University Press, 1981).

23. Wadsworth and Mann, *The Cotton Trade*, 183; "Allotment of goods to be sold by the Royal African Company of England," Treasury Department, T 70/1515, National Archives of the UK, Kew.

24. Wadsworth and Mann, *The Cotton Trade*, 186; Lowell Joseph Ragatz, *Statistics for the Study of British Caribbean Economic History, 1763–1833* (London: Bryan Edwards Press, 1927), 22; Lowell Joseph Ragatz, *The Fall of the Planter Class in the British Caribbean* (New York: Century Co., 1928), 39.

25. This is also explicitly argued in regard to the Ottoman Empire by Elena Frangakis-Syrett, *The Commerce of Smyrna in the Eighteenth Century (1700–1820)* (Athens: Centre for Asia Minor Studies, 1992), 14; Svoronos, *Le commerce de Salonique au XVIIIe siècle*, 246.

26. Joseph E. Inikori, *Africans and the Industrial Revolution in England: A Study in International Trade and Economic Development* (New York: Cambridge University Press, 2002), 429–31.

27. Arasaratnam, "Weavers, Merchants and Company," 100; K. N. Chaudhuri, *The Trading World of Asia and the English East India Company, 1660–1760* (Cambridge: Cambridge University Press, 1978), 259; Debendra Bijoy Mitra, *The Cotton Weavers of Bengal, 1757–1833* (Calcutta: Firma KLM Private Limited, 1978), 5; Prasannan Parthasarathi, "Merchants and the Rise of Colonialism," in Burton Stein and Sanjay Subrahmanyam, eds., *Institutions and Economic Change in South Asia* (Delhi: Oxford University Press, 1996), 89.

28. Arasaratnam, "Weavers, Merchants and Company," 85; Diary, Consultation, 18 January 1796, in Surat Factory Diary No. 53, part 1, 1795–1796, Maharashtra State Archives, Mumbai; the importance of economic and political power is also emphasized by Mitra, *The Cotton Weavers of Bengal*, 4; B. C. Allen, *Eastern Bengal District Gazetteers: Dacca* (Allahabad: Pioneer Press, 1912), 38–39; Subramanian, *Indigenous Capital*, 202–3, 332.

29. K. N. Chaudhuri, "The Organisation and Structure of Textile Production in India," in Roy, *Cloth and Commerce*, 59.

30. Commercial Board Minute laid before the Board, Surat, September 12, 1795, in Surat Factory Diary No. 53, part 1, 1795–1796, Maharashtra State Archives, Mumbai.

31. Copy of Letter from Gamut Farmer, President, Surat, to Mr. John Griffith, Esq., Governor in Council Bombay, December 12, 1795, in Surat Factory Diary No. 53, part 1, 1795–1796, Maharashtra State Archives, Mumbai; Arasaratnam, "Weavers, Merchants and Company," 86; Board of Trade, Report of Commercial Occurrences, September 12, 1787, in Reports to the Governor General from the Board of Trade, RG 172, Box 393, Home Miscellaneous, Oriental and India Office Collections, British Library, London; Letter from John Griffith, Bombay Castle to William [illegible], Esq., Chief President, October 27, 1795, in Surat Factory Diary No. 53, part 1, 1795–1796, Maharashtra State Archives; Hossain, "The Alienation of Weavers," 121, 125; Mitra, *The Cotton Weavers of Bengal*, 9; Dispatch, London, May 29, 1799, in Bombay Dispatches, E/4, 1014, Oriental and India Office Collections, British Library, London.

32. Parthasarathi, "Merchants and the Rise of Colonialism," 99–100; Arasaratnam, "Weavers, Merchants and Company," 107, 109; Chaudhuri, "The Organisation and Structure of Textile Production in India," 58–59; Chaudhuri, *The Trading World of Asia and the English East India Company*, 261.

33. Arasaratnam, "Weavers, Merchants and Company," 102, 107; Mitra, *The Cotton Weavers of Bengal*, 48; Hossain, "The Alienation of Weavers," 124–25.

34. Bowanny Sankar Mukherjee as quoted in Hossain, "The Alienation of Weavers," 129; Om Prakah, "Textile Manufacturing and Trade Without and with Coercion: The Indian Experience in the Eighteenth Century" (unpublished paper, Global Economic History Network Conference Osaka, December 2004), 26, accessed July 3, 2013, http://www.lse.ac.uk/economicHistory/Research/GEHN/GEHNPDF/Prakash-GEHN5.pdf; Hossain, *The Company Weavers of Bengal*, 52; Vijaya Ramaswamy, *Textiles and Weavers in South India* (New York: Oxford University Press, 2006), xiii, 170; Copy of Letter from Board of Directors, London, April 20, 1795, to our President in

Council at Bombay, in Surat Factory Diary No. 53, part 1, 1795–1796, in Maharashtra State Archives, Mumbai.

35. The importance of resistance is also stressed by Mitra, *The Cotton Weavers of Bengal*, 7; the importance of mobility is stressed by Chaudhuri, *The Trading World of Asia and the English East India Company*, 252; Arasaratnam, "Weavers, Merchants and Company," 103; see also Details Regarding Weaving in Bengal, Home Miscellaneous Series, 795, pp. 18–22, Oriental and India Office Collections, British Library, London.

36. Commercial Board Minute laid before the Board, Surat, September 12, 1795, in Surat Factory Diary No. 53, part 1, 1795–1796, Maharashtra State Archives, Mumbai; Homes Miscellaneous Series, 795, pp. 18–22, Oriental and India Office Collections, British Library, London. See also Parthasarathi, "Merchants and the Rise of Colonialism," 94.

37. Amalendu Guha, "The Decline of India's Cotton Handicrafts, 1800–1905: A Quantitative Macro-study," *Calcutta Historical Journal* 17 (1989): 41–42; Chaudhuri, "The Organisation and Structure of Textile Production in India," 60; in 1786–87 it was estimated that 16,403 weavers were active in and around Dhaka. Homes Miscellaneous Series, 795, pp. 18–22, Oriental and India Office Collections, British Library, London; Diary, Consultation, January 18, 1796, in Surat Factory Diary No. 53, part 1, 1795–1796, Maharashtra State Archives, Mumbai.

38. Dispatch from East India Company, London to Bombay, March 22, 1765, in Dispatches to Bombay, E/4, 997, Oriental and India Office Collections, British Library, London, p. 611.

39. Report of the Select Committee of the Court of Directors of the East India Company, Upon the Subject of the Cotton Manufacture of this Country, 1793, Home Miscellaneous Series, 401, p. 1, Oriental and India Office Collections, British Library, London.

40. Inikori, *Africans and the Industrial Revolution in England*, 430; Inalcik, "The Ottoman State," 355.

41. M. D. C. Crawford, *The Heritage of Cotton: The Fibre of Two Worlds and Many Ages* (New York: G. P. Putnam's Sons, 1924), xvii; the parliamentary debate is quoted in Cassels, *Cotton*, 1; the pamphlet is quoted in Baines, *History of the Cotton Manufacture*, 75; Defoe and McVeagh, *A Review of the State of the British Nation*, vol. 4, 605–6; Copy of Memorial of the Callicoe Printers to the Lords of the Treasury, Received, May 4, 1779, Treasury Department, T 1, 552, National Archives of the UK, Kew. See, along very similar lines, "The Memorial of the Several Persons whose Names are herunto subscribed on behalf of themselves and other Callico Printers of Great Britain," received July 1, 1780, at the Lords Commissioners of His Majesty's Treasury, Treasury Department, T1, 563/72–78, National Archives of the UK, Kew.

42. As quoted in S. V. Puntambekar and N. S. Varadachari, *Hand-Spinning and Hand-Weaving: An Essay* (Ahmedabad: All India Spinners' Association, 1926), 49, 51ff., 58; Inikori, *Africans and the Industrial Revolution in England*, 431–32; Crawford, *The Heritage of Cotton*, xvii; Baines, *History of the Cotton Manufacture*, 79; Wadsworth and Mann, *The Cotton Trade*, 132; Crawford, *The Heritage of Cotton*, xvii; Lemire, *Fashion's Favourite*, 42; Petition to the Treasury by Robert Gardiner, in Treasury Department, T1, 517/ 100–101, National Archives of the UK, Kew; Wadsworth and Mann, *The Cotton Trade*, 128; Letter of Vincent Mathias to the Treasury, July 24, 1767, Treasury Department, T 1, 457, National Archives of the UK, Kew.

43. Cousquer, *Nantes*, 12, 23, 43; *Arrêt du conseil d'état du roi, 10 juillet 1785* (Paris: L'Imprimerie Royale, 1785); André Zysberg, *Les Galériens: Vies et destiny de 60,000 porçats sur les galeres de France, 1680–1748* (Paris: Sevid, 1987); Marc Vigié, *Les Galériens du Roi, 1661–1715* (Paris: Fayard, 1985).

44. Wadsworth and Mann, *The Cotton Trade*, 118–19; *Examen des effets que doivent produire dans le commerce de France, l'usage et la fabrication des toiles peintes* (Paris: Chez la Veuve Delaguette, 1759); Friedrich Wilhelm, King of Prussia, *Edict dass von Dato an zu rechnen nach Ablauf acht Monathen in der Chur-Marck Magdeburgischen, Halberstadtschem und Pommern niemand einigen gedruckten oder gemahlten Zitz oder Cattun weiter tragen soll* (Berlin: G. Schlechtiger, 1721); Yuksel Duman, "Notables, Textiles and Copper in Ottoman Tokat, 1750–1840" (PhD dissertation, State University of New York at Binghamton, 1998), 144–45.

45. François-Xavier Legoux de Flaix, *Essai historique, géographique et politique sur l'Indoustan, avec le tableau de son commerce*, vol. 2 (Paris: Pougin, 1807), 326; Lemire, *Fashion's Favourite*, 3–42.

46. See also George Bryan Souza, "Convergence Before Divergence: Global Maritime Economic History and Material Culture," *International Journal of Maritime History* 17, no. 1 (2005): 17–27; Georges Roques, "La manière de négocier dans les Indes Orientales," Fonds Français 14614, Bibliothèque National, Paris; Paul R. Schwartz, "L'impression sur coton à Ahmedabad (Inde) en 1678," *Bulletin de la Société Industrielle de Mulhouse*, no. 1 (1967): 9–25; Cousquer, *Nantes*, 18–20; Jean Ryhiner, *Traité sur la fabrication et le commerce des toiles peintes, commencés en 1766*, Archive du Musée de l'Impression sur Étoffes, Mulhouse, France. See also the 1758 *Réflexions sur les avantages de la libre fabrication et de l'usage des toiles peintes en France* (Geneva: n.p., 1758), Archive du Musée de l'Impression sur Etoffes, Mulhouse, France; M. Delormois, *L'art de faire l'indienne à l'instar d'Angleterre, et de composer toutes les couleurs, bon teint, propres à l'indienne* (Paris: Charles-Antoine Jambert, 1770); Legoux de Flaix, *Essai historique*, vol. 2, 165, 331, as quoted in Florence d'Souza, "Legoux de Flaix's Observations on Indian Technologies Unknown in Europe," in K. S. Mathew, ed., *French in India and Indian Nationalism*, vol. 1 (Delhi: B.R. Publishing Corporation, 1999), 323–24.

47. Dorte Raaschou, "Un document Danois sur la fabrication des toiles Peintes à Tranquebar, aux Indes, à la fin du XVIII siècle," in *Bulletin de la Société Industrielle de Mulhouse*, no. 4 (1967): 9–21; Wadsworth and Mann, *The Cotton Trade*, 119; Inikori, *Africans and the Industrial Revolution in England*, 432; *Philosophical Magazine* 30 (1808): 259; *Philosophical Magazine* 1 (1798): 4. See also S. D. Chapman, *The Cotton Industry in the Industrial Revolution* (London: Macmillan, 1972), 12; *Philosophical Magazine* 1 (1798): 126.

48. Cotton Goods Manufacturers, Petition to the Lords Commissioner of His Majesty's Treasury, Treasury Department, T 1, 676/30, National Archives of the UK, Kew; Dispatch, November 21, 1787, Bombay Dispatches, E/4, 1004, Oriental and India Office Collections, British Library, London.

49. Chapman, *The Cotton Industry in the Industrial Revolution*, 16.

50. Marion Johnson, "Technology, Competition, and African Crafts," in Clive Dewey and A. G. Hopkins, eds., *The Imperial Impact: Studies in the Economic History of Africa and India* (London: Athlone Press, 1978), 262; Irwin and Schwartz, *Studies in Indo-*

European Textile History, 12. We know that throughout the eighteenth century, slaves were by far the most important "export" from Africa, amounting to between 80 and 90 percent of total trade. J. S. Hogendorn and H. A. Gemery, "The 'Hidden Half' of the Anglo-African Trade in the Eighteenth Century: The Significance of Marion Johnson's Statistical Research," in David Henige and T. C. McCaskie, eds., *West African Economic and Social History: Studies in Memory of Marion Johnson* (Madison: African Studies Program, University of Wisconsin Press, 1990), 90; Extract Letter, East India Company, Commercial Department, London, to Bombay, May 4, 1791, in Home Miss. 374, Oriental and India Office Collections, British Library, London; Cousquer, *Nantes*, 32; de Flaix is quoted in Richard Roberts, "West Africa and the Pondicherry Textile Industry," in Roy, ed., *Cloth and Commerce*, 142.

51. Wadsworth and Mann, *The Cotton Trade*, 116, 127, 147; Inikori, *Africans and the Industrial Revolution in England*, 434–35, 448; Smith, *An Inquiry into the Nature and Causes of the Wealth of Nations*, bk. IV, ch. I, vol. I, 470.

52. Wadsworth and Mann, *The Cotton Trade*, 122, 131, 151, 154; Extract Letter to Bombay, Commercial Department, May 4, 1791, in Home Miscellaneous 374, Oriental and India Office Collections, British Library, London.

53. Maurice Dobb, *Studies in the Development of Capitalism* (New York: International Publishers, 1947), 277; George Unwin, in introduction to George W. Daniels, *The Early English Cotton Industry* (Manchester: Manchester University Press, 1920), xxx. This is brilliantly shown by Daron Acemoglu, Simon Johnson, and James Robinson, "The Rise of Europe: Atlantic Trade, Institutional Change and Economic Growth," National Bureau of Economic Research Working Paper No. 9378, December 2002. What is missing in their account, however, is the continued importance of war capitalist institutions in other parts of the world, outside the European core.

54. See here the important work of Wennerlind, *Casualties of Credit*, esp. 223–25; Inikori, *Africans and the Industrial Revolution in England*, 478–79; P. K. O'Brien and S. L. Engerman, "Exports and the Growth of the British Economy from the Glorious Revolution to the Peace of Amiens," in Barbara Solow, ed., *Slavery and the Rise of the Atlantic System* (New York: Cambridge University Press, 1991), 191.

55. Cited in Peter Spencer, *Samuel Greg, 1758–1834* (Styal, Cheshire, UK: Quarry Bank Mill, 1989).

56. See for example Kevin H. O'Rourke and Jeffrey G. Williamson, "After Columbus: Explaining Europe's Overseas Trade Boom, 1500–1800," *Journal of Economic History* 62 (2002): 417–56; Dennis O. Flynn and Arturo Giraldez, "Path Dependence, Time Lags and the Birth of Globalization: A Critique of O'Rourke and Williamson," *European Review of Economic History* 8 (2004): 81–108; Janet Abu-Lughod, *The World System in the Thirteenth Century: Dead-End or Precursor?* (Washington, DC: American Historical Association, 1993); Andre Gunder Frank, *ReOrient: Global Economy in the Asian Age* (Berkeley: University of California Press, 1988). I am agreeing with Joseph E. Inikori, who has argued for the importance of "integrated commodity-production processes across the globe" to the history of globalization. See Joseph E. Inikori, "Africa and the Globalization Process: Western Africa, 1450–1850," *Journal of Global History* (2007): 63–86.

57. Mann, *The Cotton Trade of Great Britain*, 20.

CHAPTER THREE: THE WAGES OF WAR CAPITALISM

1. Anthony Howe, *The Cotton Masters, 1830–1860* (Oxford: Clarendon Press, 1984), 41; Michael James, *From Smuggling to Cotton Kings: The Greg Story* (Cirencester, UK: Memoirs, 2010), 4, 8–9, 37–40; Mary B. Rose, *The Gregs of Quarry Bank Mill: The Rise and Decline of a Family Firm, 1750–1914* (Cambridge: Cambridge University Press, 1986), 5.

2. Caitlin C. Rosenthal, "Slavery's Scientific Management: Accounting for Mastery," in Sven Beckert and Seth Rockman, eds., *Slavery's Capitalism: A New History of American Economic Development* (Philadelphia: University of Pennsylvania Press, forthcoming, 2015). A good discussion of the importance of slavery to industrialization can also be found in Robin Blackburn, *The American Crucible: Slavery, Emancipation and Human Rights* (London: Verso, 2011), 104–7.

3. The importance of the Atlantic trade in the great divergence is also emphasized by Daron Acemoglu, Simon Johnson, and James Robinson, "The Rise of Europe: Atlantic Trade, Institutional Change and Economic Growth," National Bureau of Economic Research Working Paper No. 9378, December 2002, esp. 4; The depth of British society's involvement with slavery, and the significant material benefits that it drew from it, are demonstrated by Nicholas Draper, *The Price of Emancipation: Slave-Ownership, Compensation and British Society at the End of Slavery* (Cambridge: Cambridge University Press, 2010).

4. Rose, *The Gregs of Quarry Bank Mill*, 15–16, 20. He was, in fact, as his biographer Mary B. Rose argued, "responding to the growing demand for cloth"—a demand that he knew of firsthand. See Mary B. Rose, "The Role of the Family in Providing Capital and Managerial Talent in Samuel Greg and Company, 1784–1840," *Business History* 19, no. 1 (1977): 37–53.

5. James, *From Smuggling to Cotton Kings*, 21. For the conversion: Eric Nye, "Pounds Sterling to Dollars: Historical Conversion of Currency," University of Wyoming, accessed January 9, 2013, http://uwacadweb.uwyo.edu/numimage/currency.htm. Indeed, between 1801 and 1804, 59 percent of Greg's production went to the United States; see Rose, *The Gregs of Quarry Bank Mill*, 24, 28, 30 33. For interest rates on bonds see David Stasavage, *Public Debt and the Birth of the Democratic State: France and Great Britain, 1688–1789* (Cambridge: Cambridge University Press, 2003), 96.

6. See David Landes, *The Unbound Prometheus: Technical Change and Industrial Development in Western Europe from 1750 to the Present*, 2nd ed. (New York: Cambridge University Press, 2003); David Landes, *The Wealth and Poverty of Nations: Why Some Are So Rich and Some So Poor* (New York: Norton, 1998); Niall Ferguson, *Civilization: The West and the Rest* (New York: Penguin, 2011); Jared Diamond, *Guns, Germs, and Steel: The Fates of Human Societies* (New York: Norton, 1998). For an overview see also Joseph E. Inikori, *Africans and the Industrial Revolution in England: A Study in International Trade and Economic Development* (New York: Cambridge University Press, 2002), chapter 2.

7. M. D. C. Crawford, *The Heritage of Cotton: The Fibre of Two Worlds and Many Ages* (New York: G. P. Putnam's Sons, 1924), v; Angus Maddison, *The World Economy: A Millennial Perspective* (Paris: Development Centre of the Organisation for Economic

Co-operation and Development, 2001), 27. Even someone who emphasizes the slow-
ness of the acceleration of economic growth in the Industrial Revolution like Nicholas Crafts still sees it as a watershed to "faster TFP growth." See Nicholas Crafts,
"The First Industrial Revolution: Resolving the Slow Growth/Rapid Industrialization Paradox," *Journal of the European Economic Association* 3, no. 2/3 (May 2005):
525–39, here 533. But see Peter Temin, "Two Views of the Industrial Revolution,"
Journal of Economic History 57 (March 1997): 63–82, for a restatement of the impact
of the Industrial Revolution on the British economy as a whole. There are nearly as
many explanations for the Industrial Revolution as there are books on it. For a good
overview see Inikori, *Africans and the Industrial Revolution in England*, chapter 2. But
long-term and slow cultural or institutional change cannot explain the rather rapid
divergence of Britain from other parts of the world.

8. Peter Spencer, *Samuel Greg, 1758–1834* (Styal: Quarry Bank Mill, 1989), 6.

9. Maurice Dobb, *Studies in the Development of Capitalism* (New York: International
Publishers, 1964), 294; Eric Hobsbawm, *The Age of Revolution, 1789–1848* (London:
Abacus, 1977), 49; Rose, *The Gregs of Quarry Bank Mill*, 7; Stephen Broadberry and
Bishnupriya Gupta, "Cotton Textiles and the Great Divergence: Lancashire, India
and Shifting Competitive Advantage, 1600–1850," CEPR Discussion Paper No. 5183,
London, Centre for Economic Policy Research, August 2005, 7.

10. Broadberry and Gupta, "Cotton Textiles and the Great Divergence," 27. Robert C.
Allen rightly emphasizes the importance of the demand for more efficient machinery
as a core driver for the Industrial Revolution. However, that demand for machines
ultimately derived from the existence of vast markets for cotton goods and the ability of
British capitalists to serve them. See Robert C. Allen, *The British Industrial Revolution
in Global Perspective* (New York: Cambridge University Press, 2009), for example p. 137.

11. The best exposition of this argument is to be found in Allen, *The British Industrial
Revolution*; See also Broadberry and Gupta, "Cotton Textiles and the Great Diver-
gence"; K. N. Chaudhuri, "The Organisation and Structure of Textile Production in
India," in Tirthankar Roy, ed., *Cloth and Commerce: Textiles in Colonial India* (Wal-
nut Creek, CA: AltaMira Press, 1996), 74; Friedrich Hassler, *Vom Spinnen und Weben*
(Munich: R. Oldenbourg, 1952), 7.

12. Almut Bohnsack, *Spinnen und Weben: Entwicklung von Technik und Arbeit im Textilgewerbe* (Reinbeck: Rowohlt, 1981), 25, 201.

13. Mike Williams and D. A. Farnie, *Cotton Mills in Greater Manchester* (Preston, UK:
Carnegie, 1992), 9.

14. S. & W. Salte to Samuel Oldknow, November 5, 1787, Record Group SO/1,265,
Oldknow Papers, John Rylands Library, Manchester.

15. S. D. Chapman, *The Cotton Industry in the Industrial Revolution* (London: Macmillan,
1972), 20; Broadberry and Gupta, "Cotton Textiles and the Great Divergence," 23.

16. Edward Baines, *History of the Cotton Manufacture in Great Britain* (London;
H. Fisher, R. Fisher, and P. Jackson, 1835) 353; Price of Mule Yarn from 1796 to
1843 sold by McConnel & Kennedy, Manchester, in McConnel & Kennedy Papers,
record group MCK, file 3/3/8, John Rylands Library, Manchester; C. Knick Harley,
"Cotton Textile Prices and the Industrial Revolution," *Economic History Review*, New
Series, 51, no. 1 (February 1998): 59.

17. These numbers are just approximations. See Broadberry and Gupta, "Cotton Textiles and the Great Divergence," 8, 26; Chapman, *The Cotton Industry in the Industrial Revolution*, 22, 29; Howe, *The Cotton Masters*, 6.

18. Hobsbawm, *The Age of Revolution*, 46; Allen, *The British Industrial Revolution*, 191; Dobb, *Studies in the Development of Capitalism*, 269; Salvin Brothers of Castle Eden Co., Durham, to McConnel & Kennedy, Castle Eden, July 22, 1795, Letters, 1795, record group MCK, box 2/1/1, in McConnel & Kennedy Papers, John Rylands Library, Manchester.

19. Patrick O'Brien, "The Geopolitics of a Global Industry: Eurasian Divergence and the Mechanization of Cotton Textile Production in England," in Giorgio Riello and Prasannan Parthasarathi, eds., *The Spinning World: A Global History of Cotton Textiles, 1200–1850* (New York: Oxford University Press, 2009), 360. See also, Dobb, *Studies in the Development of Capitalism*, 258.

20. For instance, the first "large purpose-built cotton-spinning mill" in the greater Manchester area was the Shudehill Mill, built around 1782. It was two hundred feet in length, thirty feet wide, and five stories high. See Williams and Farnie, *Cotton Mills in Greater Manchester*, 50; Stanley D. Chapman, *The Early Factory Masters: The Transition to the Factory System in the Midlands Textile Industry* (Newton Abbot, Devon, UK: David & Charles, 1967), 65.

21. Williams and Farnie, *Cotton Mills in Greater Manchester*, 4–9; Harold Catling, *The Spinning Mule* (Newton Abbot, Devon, UK: David & Charles, 1970), 150.

22. Charles Tilly, "Social Change in Modern Europe: The Big Picture," in Lenard R. Berlanstein, ed., *The Industrial Revolution and Work in Nineteenth-Century Europe* (London and New York: Routledge, 1992), 53.

23. M. Elvin, "The High-Level Equilibrium Trap: The Causes of the Decline of Invention in the Traditional Chinese Textile Industries," in W. E. Willmott, ed., *Economic Organization in Chinese Society* (Stanford, CA: Stanford University Press, 1972), 137ff. See also Sucheta Mazumdar, *Sugar and Society in China: Peasants, Technology and the World Market* (Cambridge, MA: Harvard University Press, 1998), 183; Philip C. C. Huang, *The Peasant Family and Rural Development in the Yangzi Delta, 1350–1988* (Stanford, CA: Stanford University Press, 1990), 44.

24. For this argument see Roy Bin Wong, *China Transformed: Historical Change and the Limits of European Experience* (Ithaca, NY: Cornell University Press, 1997); Chaudhuri, "The Organisation and Structure of Textile Production in India," 57.

25. Rose, *The Gregs of Quarry Bank Mill*, 39–40; Chapman, *The Cotton Industry in the Industrial Revolution*, 29; William Emerson to McConnel & Kennedy, Belfast, December 8, 1795, in John Rylands Library, Manchester.

26. Chapman, *The Cotton Industry in the Industrial Revolution*, 29, 32; Howe, *The Cotton Masters*, 9, 11–12.

27. A. C. Howe, "Oldknow, Samuel (1756–1828)," in H. C. G. Matthew and Brian Harrison, eds., *Oxford Dictionary of National Biography* (Oxford: Oxford University Press, 2004); George Unwin, *Samuel Oldknow and the Arkwrights: The Industrial Revolution at Stockport and Marple* (New York: A. M. Kelley, 1968), 2, 6, 45, 107, 123, 127, 135, 140.

28. Chapman, *The Cotton Industry in the Industrial Revolution*, 31, 37–41; Howe, *The*

Cotton Masters, 24, 27; M. J. Daunton, *Progress and Poverty: An Economic and Social History of Britain, 1700–1850* (New York: Oxford University Press, 1995), 199; Dobb, *Studies in the Development of Capitalism*, 268.

29. Partnership Agreement Between Benjamin Sanford, William Sanford, John Kennedy, and James McConnel, 1791: 1/2; Personal Ledger, 1795–1801: 3/1/1, Papers of McConnel & Kennedy, John Rylands Library, Manchester.

30. N. F. R. Crafts, *British Economic Growth During the Industrial Revolution* (New York: Oxford University Press, 1985), 22; Bohnsack, *Spinnen und Weben*, 26; Allen, *The British Industrial Revolution*, 182; Howe, *The Cotton Masters*, 1, 51.

31. Fernand Braudel, *Afterthoughts on Material Civilization and Capitalism* (Baltimore: Johns Hopkins University Press, 1977), 109.

32. Beverly Lemire, *Fashion's Favourite: The Cotton Trade and the Consumer in Britain, 1660–1800* (Oxford: Oxford University Press, 1991).

33. Baines, *History of the Cotton Manufacture in Great Britain*, 335; R. C. Allen and J. L. Weisdorf, "Was There an 'Industrious Revolution' Before the Industrial Revolution? An Empirical Exercise for England, c. 1300–1830," *Economic History Review* 64, no. 3 (2011): 715–29; P. K. O'Brien and S. L. Engerman, "Exports and the Growth of the British Economy from the Glorious Revolution to the Peace of Amiens," in Barbara Solow, ed., *Slavery and the Rise of the Atlantic System* (New York: Cambridge University Press, 1991), 184, 188, 200; Broadberry and Gupta, "Cotton Textiles and the Great Divergence," 5; Baines, *History of the Cotton Manufacture in Great Britain*, 349–50; For the general point see Inikori, *Africans and the Industrial Revolution in England*, 436, 450; Hobsbawm, *The Age of Revolution*, 49. The table on page 74 is based on figures in Tables X and XI in Elizabeth Boody Schumpeter and T. S. Ashton, *English Overseas Trade Statistics, 1697–1808* (Oxford: Clarendon Press, 1960), 29–34. Table X provides values of the principal English exports of textile goods, excluding woolens, for the years 1697 to 1771, 1775, and 1780 in pounds sterling. Table XI provides quantities and values of the principal British exports of textile goods, excluding woolens, for 1772–1807 in pounds sterling, with the years 1772–91 including England and Wales and 1792–1807 including all of Great Britain.

34. O'Brien and Engerman, "Exports and the Growth of the British Economy," 185; Baines, *History of the Cotton Manufacture in Great Britain*, 349.

35. Debendra Bijoy Mitra, *The Cotton Weavers of Bengal, 1757–1833* (Calcutta: Firm KLM Private Ltd., 1978), 25; John Taylor, *Account of the District of Dacca by the Commercial Resident Mr. John Taylor in a Letter to the Board of Trade at Calcutta dated 30th November 1800 with P.S. 2 November 1801 and Inclosures, In Reply to a Letter from the Board dated 6th February 1798 transmitting Copy of the 115th Paragraph of the General Letter from the Court of Directors dated 9th May 1797 Inviting the Collection of Materials for the use of the Company's Historiographer*, Home Miscellaneous Series, 456, Box F, pp. 111–12, Oriental and India Office Collections, British Library, London; *The Principal Heads of the History and Statistics of the Dacca Division* (Calcutta: E. M. Lewis, 1868), 129; Shantha Harihara, *Cotton Textiles and Corporate Buyers in Cottonopolis: A Study of Purchases and Prices in Gujarat, 1600–1800* (Delhi: Manak, 2002), 75; "Extracts from the Reports of the Reporter of External Commerce in Bengal; from the year 1795 to the latest Period for which the same can be made up," in *House of Commons*

Papers, vol. 8 (1812–13), 23. See also Konrad Specker, "Madras Handlooms in the Nineteenth Century," in Roy, ed., *Cloth and Commerce*, 179; G. A. Prinsep, *Remarks on the External Commerce and Exchanges of Bengal* (London: Kingsbury, Parbury, and Allen, 1823), 28; "The East-India and China Trade," *Asiatic Journal and Monthly Register for British India and Its Dependencies* 28, no. 164 (August 1829): 150.

36. O'Brien and Engerman, "Exports and the Growth of the British Economy," 177–209; Inikori, *Africans and the Industrial Revolution in England*, 445, 447–48; Kenneth Pomeranz, *The Great Divergence: China, Europe, and the Making of the Modern World Economy* (Princeton, NJ: Princeton University Press, 2000), 266; Marion Johnson, "Technology, Competition, and African Crafts," in Clive Dewey and A. G. Hopkins, eds., *The Imperial Impact: Studies in the Economic History of Africa and India* (London: Athlone Press, 1978), 263.

37. To amplify: Institutions, as many observers have remarked, matter a great deal. The problem, however, is to define these institutions and root their emergence in a particular historical process. Institutions are not a question of the "will" of historical actors; they are instead the result of the confluence of a number of factors, and, most important of all, of particular balances of social power. As we will see in later chapters, the social and political configurations of many parts of the world did not lend themselves to such an embrace of industrial capitalism, or the institutions that usually go with it. The report of the French commission is cited in Henry Brooke Parnell, *On Financial Reform*, 3rd ed. (London: John Murray, 1832), 84; William J. Ashworth, "The Ghost of Rostow: Science, Culture and the British Industrial Revolution," *History of Science* 156 (2008): 261.

38. On the Royal Navy, see O'Brien and Engerman, "Exports and the Growth of the British Economy," 189–90. I agree here with the more recent literature that emphasizes the crucial importance of institutions. The argument has been made most persuasively by Daron Acemoglu and James A. Robinson, *Why Nations Fail: The Origins of Power, Prosperity, and Poverty* (New York: Crown Business, 2012). However, in Acemoglu and Robinson's account, these institutions remain somewhat amorphous and their own histories (and with it their roots in war capitalism) remain unspecified. For an insistence on the importance of institutions see also Niall Ferguson, *Civilization: The Six Killer Apps of Western Power* (London: Penguin, 2012).

39. See here also the intriguing argument by Acemoglu et al., "The Rise of Europe."

40. Howe, *The Cotton Masters*, 90, 94.

41. Petition of manufacturers of calicoes, muslins and other cotton goods in Glasgow asking for extension of exemption for Auction Duty Act, July 1, 1789 (received), Treasury Department, record group T 1, 676/30, National Archives of the UK, Kew.

42. See Allen, *The British Industrial Revolution*, 5.

43. Baines, *History of the Cotton Manufacture in Great Britain*, 321–29.

44. Ibid., 503–4; William J. Ashworth, *Customs and Excise Trade, Production, and Consumption in England, 1640–1845* (Oxford: Oxford University Press, 2003), 4, 8; O'Brien and Engerman, "Exports and the Growth of the British Economy," 206; *Edinburgh Review, or Critical Journal* 61 (July 1835): 455.

45. Making use of the numbers provided by Kenneth Pomeranz, which can only be considered rough estimates, the precise factor is 417. Pomeranz, *The Great Divergence*,

139, 337; Kenneth Pomeranz, "Beyond the East-West Binary: Resituating Development Paths in the Eighteenth-Century World," *Journal of Asian Studies* 61, no. 2 (May 1, 2002): 569; Baines, *History of the Cotton Manufacture in Great Britain*, 215.

46. Hobsbawm, *The Age of Revolution*, 44; Thomas Ashton to William Rathbone VI, Flowery Fields, January 17, 1837, Record Group RP.IX.1.48–63, Rathbone Papers, University of Liverpool, Special Collections and Archives, Liverpool; the English visitor is quoted in Asa Briggs, *Victorian Cities* (Berkeley and Los Angeles: University of California Press, 1970), 89; Alexis de Tocqueville, *Journeys to England and Ireland*, trans. George Lawrence and K. P. Mayer, ed. K. P. Mayer (London: Transaction Publishers, 2003), 107–8; Thomas Jefferson, *Notes on the State of Virginia*, Query XIX.

47. Dale Tomich and Michael Zeuske, "The Second Slavery: Mass Slavery, World-Economy, and Comparative Microhistories," *Review: A Journal of the Fernand Braudel Center* 31, no. 3 (2008), 91–100; Michael Zeuske, "The Second Slavery: Modernity, Mobility, and Identity of Captives in Nineteenth-Century Cuba and the Atlantic World," in Javier Lavina and Michael Zeuske, eds., *The Second Slavery: Mass Slaveries and Modernity in the Americas and in the Atlantic Basin* (Berlin, Münster, and New York: LIT Verlag, 2013); Dale Tomich, Rafael Marquese, and Ricardo Salles, eds., *Frontiers of Slavery* (Binghamton: State University of New York Press, forthcoming).

48. J. De Cordova, *The Cultivation of Cotton in Texas: The Advantages of Free Labour, A Lecture Delivered at the Town Hall, Manchester, on Tuesday, the 28th day of September, 1858, before the Cotton Supply Association* (London: J. King & Co., 1858), 70–71.

CHAPTER FOUR: CAPTURING LABOR, CONQUERING LAND

1. A. Moreau de Jonnes, "Travels of a Pound of Cotton," *Asiatic Journal and Monthly Register for British India and Its Dependencies* 21 (January–June 1826) (London: Kingsbury, Parbury & Allen, 1826), 23.

2. J. T. Danson, "On the Existing Connection Between American Slavery and the British Cotton Manufacture," *Journal of the Statistical Society of London* 20 (March 1857): 7, 19. For a similar argument see also Elisée Reclus, "Le coton et la crise Améri-caine," *Revue des Deux Mondes* 37 (1862): 176, 187. Arguments about the connection between capitalism and slavery can also be found in Philip McMichael, "Slavery in Capitalism: The Rise and Demise of the U.S. Ante-Bellum Cotton Culture," *Theory and Society* 20 (June 1991): 321–49; Joseph E. Inikori, *Africans and the Industrial Revolution in England: A Study in International Trade and Economic Development* (New York: Cambridge University Press, 2003); and Eric Williams, *Capitalism and Slavery* (Chapel Hill: University of North Carolina Press, 1994).

3. "Cotton, Raw, Quantity Consumed and Manufactured," in Levi Woodbury, United States Deptartment of the Treasury, *Letter from the Secretary of the Treasury transmitting Tables and Notes on the Cultivation, Manufacture, and Foreign Trade of Cotton* (1836), 40.

4. For the concept of "second slavery" see Dale Tomich, "The Second Slavery: Mass Slavery, World-Economy, and Comparative Histories," *Review: A Journal of the Fernand Braudel Center* 31, no. 3 (2008). For the commodity frontier see Jason W. Moore, "Sugar and the Expansion of the Early Modern World-Economy: Commod-

ity Frontiers, Ecological Transformation, and Industrialization," *Review: A Journal of the Fernand Braudel Center* 23, no. 3 (2000): 409–33. See also Robin Blackburn, *The American Crucible: Slavery, Emancipation and Human Rights* (London: Verso, 2011), 22.

5. On cotton growing in France see C. P. De Lasteyrie, *Du cotonnier et de sa culture* (Paris: Bertrand, 1808); *Notice sur le coton, sa culture, et sur la posibilité de le cultiver dans le département de la Gironde*, 3rd ed. (Bordeaux: L'Imprimerie de Brossier, 1823); on this effort see also Morris R. Chew, *History of the Kingdom of Cotton and Cotton Statistics of the World* (New Orleans: W. B. Stansbury & Co., 1884), 48. On efforts to grow cotton in Lancashire see John Holt, *General View of the Agriculture of the County of Lancaster* (London: G. Nicol, 1795), 207.

6. N. G. Svoronos, *Le commerce de Salonique au XVIIIe siècle* (Paris: Presses Universitaires de France, 1956), 67; Bombay Dispatches, IO/E/4, 996, pp. 351, 657; British Library, Oriental and India Office Collections, British Library, London; Eliyahu Ashtor, "The Venetian Cotton Trade in Syria in the Later Middle Ages," *Studi Medievali*, ser. 3, vol. 17 (1976): 676, 682, 686.

7. In 1790, the cotton consumption of Great Britain amounted to 30.6 million pounds. Edward Baines, *History of the Cotton Manufacture in Great Britain* (London: H. Fisher, R. Fisher, and P. Jackson, 1835), 215, 347, 348; Thomas Ellison, *The Cotton Trade of Great Britain* (London: Effingham Wilson, Royal Exchange, 1886), 49; Joel Mokyr, *The Lever of Riches: Technological Creativity and Economic Progress* (New York: Oxford University Press, 1990), 99; Bernard Lepetit, "Frankreich, 1750–1850," in Wolfram Fischer et al., eds, *Handbuch der Europäischen Wirtschafts- und Sozialgeschichte*, vol. 4 (Stuttgart: Klett-Cotta, 1993), 487; *Bremer Handelsblatt* 2 (1851): 4.

8. Ellison, *The Cotton Trade*, 82–83; Michael M. Edwards, *The Growth of the British Cotton Trade, 1780–1815* (Manchester: Manchester University Press, 1967), 75.

9. William Edensor, *An Address to the Spinners and Manufacturers of Cotton Wool, Upon the Present Situation of the Market* (London: The Author, 1792), 15. There was always a shortage of labor, which meant that production on plantations was unimaginable. Huri Islamoglu-Inan, "State and Peasants in the Ottoman Empire: A Study of Peasant Economy in North-Central Anatolia During the Sixteenth Century," in Huri Islamoglu-Inan, ed., *The Ottoman Empire and the World Economy* (New York: Cambridge University Press, 1987), 126; Elena Frangakis-Syrett, *The Commerce of Smyrna in the Eighteenth Century (1700–1820)* (Athens: Centre for Asia Minor Studies, 1992), 11, 236; Resat Kasaba, *The Ottoman Empire and the World Economy: The Nineteenth Century* (Albany: State University of New York Press, 1988), 25–27. On the capital shortage see Donald Quataert, "The Commercialization of Agriculture in Ottoman Turkey, 1800–1914," *International Journal of Turkish Studies* 1 (1980): 44–45. On the importance of political independence see Sevket Pamuk, *The Ottoman Empire and European Capitalism, 1820–1913* (Cambridge: Cambridge University Press, 1987), 53; Ellison, *The Cotton Trade*, 82–83; Edwards, *The Growth of the British Cotton Trade*, 86.

10. Report of the Select Committee of the Court of Directors of the East India Company, Upon the Subject of the Cotton Manufacture of this Country, 1793, Home Miscellaneous Series, 401, Oriental and India Office Collections, British Library, London.

11. "Objections to the Annexed Plan," November 10, 1790, Home Miscellaneous Series, 434, Oriental and India Office Collections, British Library, London.

12. See for example Edwards, *The Growth of the British Cotton Trade*, 75, 82–83; Ellison, *The Cotton Trade*, 28, 84; East-India Company, Reports and Documents Connected with the Proceedings of the East-India Company in Regard to the Culture and Manufacture of Cotton-Wool, Raw Silk, and Indigo in India (London: East-India Company, 1836); Copy of letter by George Smith to Charles Earl Cornwallis, Calcutta, October 26, 1789, in Home Miscellaneous Series, 434, Oriental and India Office Collections, British Library, London; Various Copies of Letters Copied into a Book relating to Cotton, 729–54, in Home Miscellaneous Series, 374, Oriental and India Office Collections, British Library.

13. On the long history of cotton in the Caribbean see David Watts, *The West Indies: Patterns of Development, Culture and Environmental Change Since 1492* (Cambridge: Cambridge University Press, 1987), 158–59, 183, 194, 296; Charles Mackenzie, *Facts, Relative to the Present State of the British Cotton Colonies and to the Connection of their Interests* (Edinburgh: James Clarke, 1811); Daniel McKinnen, *A Tour Through the British West Indies, in the Years 1802 and 1803: Giving a Particular Account of the Bahama Islands* (London: White, 1804); George F. Tyson Jr., "On the Periphery of the Peripheries: The Cotton Plantations of St. Croix, Danish West Indies, 1735–1815," *Journal of Caribbean History* 26, no. 1 (1992): 3, 6–8; "Tableau de Commerce, &c. de St. Domingue," in Bryan Edwards, *An Historical Survey of the Island of Saint Domingo* (London: Printed for John Stockdale, 1801), 230–31.

14. "Report from the Select Committee on the Commercial State of the West India Colonies," in Great Britain, House of Commons, Sessional Papers, 1807, III (65), pp. 73–78, as quoted in Ragatz, *Statistics*, 22; Edwards, *The Growth of the British Cotton Trade*, 250; Selwyn H. H. Carrington, *The British West Indies During the American Revolution* (Dordrecht: Foris, 1988), 31; "An Account of all Cotton Wool of the Growth of the British Empire Imported annually into that part of Great Britain Called England," National Archives of the UK, Kew, Treasury Department, T 64/275, in the chart on page 90. The numbers (totals, and details for 1786) in the chart on page 90 are from Baines, *History of the Cotton Manufacture*, 347.

15. "Report from the Select Committee on the Commercial State of the West India Colonies," in Great Britain, House of Commons, Sessional Papers, 1807, III (65), pp. 73–78, as quoted in Lowell J. Ragatz, *Statistics for the Study of British Caribbean Economic History, 1763–1833* (London: Bryan Edwards Press, 1928), 22; Lowell J. Ragatz, *The Fall of the Planter Class in the British Caribbean, 1763–1833: A Study in Social and Economic History* (New York: Century Co., 1928), 38; M. Placide-Justin, *Histoire politique et statistique de l'île d'Hayti, Saint-Domingue; écrite sur des documents officiels et des notes communiquées par Sir James Barskett, agent du gouvernement britannique dans les Antilles* (Paris: Brière, 1826), 501. On "coton des isles" see Robert Lévy, *Histoire économique de l'industrie cotonnière en Alsace* (Paris: F. Alcan, 1912), 56; Nathan Hall to John King, Nassau, May 27, 1800, Box 15, CO 23, National Archives of the UK, Kew.

16. Robert H. Schomburgk, *The History of Barbados: Comprising a Geographical and Statistical Description of the Island; a Sketch of the Historical Events Since the Settle-*

ment; and an Account of Its Geology and Natural Productions (London: Longman, Brown, Green and Longmans, 1848), 640; Edwards, *The Growth of the British Cotton Trade*, 79; Selwyn Carrington, "The American Revolution and the British West Indies Economy," *Journal of Interdisciplinary History* 17 (1987): 841–42; Edward N. Rappaport and José Fernandez-Partagas, "The Deadliest Atlantic Tropical Cyclones, 1492–1996," National Hurricane Center, National Weather Service, May 28, 1995, accessed August 6, 2010, http://www.nhc.noaa.gov/pastdeadly.shtml; Ragatz, *Statistics*, 15; S. G. Stephens, "Cotton Growing in the West Indies During the Eighteenth and Nineteenth Centuries," *Tropical Agriculture* 21 (February 1944): 23–29; Wallace Brown, *The Good Americans: The Loyalists in the American Revolution* (New York: Morrow, 1969), 2; Gail Saunders, *Bahamian Loyalists and Their Slaves* (London: Macmillan Caribbean, 1983), 37.

17. David Eltis, "The Slave Economies of the Caribbean: Structure, Performance, Evolution and Significance," in Franklin W. Knight, ed., *General History of the Caribbean*, vol. 3, *The Slave Societies of the Caribbean* (London: Unesco Publishing, 1997), 113, Table 3:1. On production see Edwards, *The Growth of the British Cotton Trade*, 79. On French demand and reexports from European French ports see Jean Tarrade, *Le commerce colonial de la France à la fin de l'Ancien Régime* (Paris: Presses Universitaires de France, 1972), 748–49, 753. I assumed that most of the colonial cotton reexported from France went to Great Britain.

18. In 1790, there were 705 cotton plantations on the island, compared to 792 sugar plantations. Edwards, *An Historical Survey*, 163–65, 230, 231. On Saint-Domingue cotton production see also Schomburgk, *The History of Barbados*, 150; Ragatz, *The Fall of the Planter Class*, 39, 125; David Eltis et al., *The Trans-Atlantic Slave Trade: A Database on CD-Rom* (Cambridge: Cambridge University Press, 1999); Tarrade, *Le commerce colonial*, 759.

19. Stefano Fenoaltea, "Slavery and Supervision in Comparative Perspective: A Model," *Journal of Economic History* 44 (September 1984): 635–68.

20. Moore, "Sugar," 412, 428.

21. Resat Kasaba, "Incorporation of the Ottoman Empire," *Review* 10, Supplement (Summer/Fall 1987): 827.

22. *Transactions of the Society Instituted at London for the Encouragement of Arts, Manufactures, and Commerce* 1 (London: Dodsley, 1783), 254; Ellison, *The Cotton Trade*, 28; Edwards, *The Growth of the British Cotton Trade*, 77; Governor Orde to Lord Sydney, Roseau, Dominica, June 13, 1786, in Colonial Office, 71/10, National Archives of the UK; President Lucas to Lord Sydney, Granada, June 9, 1786, Dispatches Granada, Colonial Office, 101/26; Governor D. Parry to Lord Sydney, Barbados, May 31, 1786, Dispatches Barbados, Colonial Office, 28/60, National Archives of the UK; President Brown to Sydney, New Providence, 23 February 1786, in Dispatches Bahamas, Colonial Office 23/15, National Archives of the UK. On the pressure by manufacturers see also Edwards, *The Growth of the British Cotton Trade*, 75–76; Governor Orde to Lord Sydney, Rouseau, Dominica, March 30, 1788, National Archives of the UK.

23. The role of slavery in the history of capitalism has been the subject of many debates, and is ably summarized by Robin Blackburn, *The Making of New World Slavery: From*

the Baroque to the Modern, 1492–1800 (New York: Verso, 1997), 509–80. See also the important article by Ronald Bailey, "The Other Side of Slavery: Black Labor, Cotton, and Textile Industrialization in Great Britain and the United States," *Agricultural History* 68 (Spring 1994): 35–50; Seymour Drescher, *Capitalism and Antislavery: British Mobilization in Comparative Perspective* (New York: Oxford University Press, 1987), 9. The notion of "second slavery" is from Dale Tomich and Michael Zeuske, "The Second Slavery: Mass Slavery, World-Economy, and Comparative Microhistories," *Review: A Journal of the Fernand Braudel Center* 31, no. 3 (2008). Catherine Coquery-Vidrovitch argues that this expansion of slavery in the Americas also led to a "second slavery" in Africa. See Catherine Coquery-Vidrovitch, "African Slaves and Atlantic Metissage: A Periodization 1400–1880," paper presented at "2nd Slaveries and the Atlantization of the Americas" colloquium, University of Cologne, July 2012; Voyages: The Trans-Atlantic Slave Trade Database, http://www.slavevoyages.org, accessed January 31, 2013.

24. Alan H. Adamson, *Sugar Without Slaves: The Political Economy of British Guiana, 1838–1904* (New Haven: Yale University Press, 1972), 24; Johannes Postma, *The Dutch in the Atlantic Slave Trade, 1600–1815* (Cambridge: Cambridge University Press, 1990), 288.

25. See for example, Roger Hunt, *Observations Upon Brazilian Cotton Wool, for the Information of the Planter and With a View to Its Improvement* (London: Steel, 1808), 3; Morris R. Chew, *History of the Kingdom of Cotton and Cotton Statistics of the World* (New Orleans: W. B. Stansbury & Co., 1889), 28; John C. Branner, *Cotton in the Empire of Brazil: The Antiquity, Methods and Extent of Its Cultivation; Together with Statistics of Exportation and Home Consumption* (Washington, DC: Government Printing Office, 1885), 9, 46; Celso Furtado, *The Economic Growth of Brazil: A Survey from Colonial to Modern Times* (Berkeley and Los Angeles: University of California Press, 1965), 97; Caio Prado, *The Colonial Background of Modern Brazil* (Berkeley and Los Angeles: University of California Press, 1969), 171–73, cited on 458; Luiz Cordelio Barbosa, "Cotton in 19th Century Brazil: Dependency and Development" (PhD dissertation, University of Washington, 1989), 31; Francisco de Assis Leal Mesquita, "Vida e morte da economia algodoeira do Maranhão, uma análise das relações de produção na cultura do algodão, 1850–1890" (PhD dissertation, Universidade Federal do Maranhão, 1987), 50.

26. Beshara Doumani, *Rediscovering Palestine: Merchants and Peasants in Jabal Nablus, 1700–1900* (Berkeley and Los Angeles: University of California Press, 1995), 99; William Milburn, *Oriental Commerce: Containing a Geographical Description of the Principal Places in the East Indies, China, and Japan, With Their Produce, Manufactures, and Trade* (London: Black, Parry & Co., 1813), 281; Mesquita, "Vida e morte," 63; Edwards, *The Growth of the British Cotton Trade*, 83.

27. John Tarleton to Clayton Tarleton, St. James's Hotel, February 5, 1788, 920 TAR, Box 4, Letter 5, Tarleton Papers, Liverpool Records Office, Liverpool. For cotton merchants owning a plantation see Sandbach, Tinne & Co. Papers, Merseyside Maritime Museum, Liverpool. For cotton merchants trading in slaves see John Tarleton to Clayton Tarleton, April 29, 1790, letter 8, 4, 920 TAR, Tarleton Papers, Liverpool Records Office; Annual Profit and Loss Accounts of John Tarleton, 920 TAR, Box 2 and Box 5, Liverpool Records Office.

28. In 1820, 873,312 acres of land were needed to cultivate the cotton consumed by British industry, which would have taken up 7.8 percent of Britain's arable land and employed 198,738 agricultural laborers. The amount of cotton consumed in 1840 required 3,273,414 acres of land, which would have taken up 29 percent of British arable land and 544,066 agricultural laborers. Cotton consumption in 1820 (152,829,633 pounds according to Mann, *The Cotton Trade of Great Britain*, 93–4) divided by 1820 yield per acre (175 pounds according to Whartenby, "Land and Labor Productivity," 54); 1820 required cotton acreage (873,312 acres) as a share of 1827 arable land (11,143,370 acres). Figure for arable land taken from Rowland E. Prothero, *English Farming Past and Present* (New York: Benjamin Blom, Inc., 1972 [1st ed. London, 1917]), [("Table 2.–1827") and Select Committee on Emigration, 1827. Evidence of Mr. W. Couling. *Sessional Papers*, 1827, vol. v., p. 361]. 1840 cotton consumption (592,488,010 pounds according to Mann, *The Cotton Trade of Great Britain*, 94) divided by 1840 yield per acre (181 pounds according to Whartenby, "Land and Labor Productivity," 54). Cotton consumption in 1860 (1,140,599,712 pounds) divided by 1840 yield of cotton per acre in the United States (181 pounds). And 1860 cotton consumption divided by 1840 yield per worker (1,089 pounds) in the United States. See also Kenneth Pomeranz, *The Great Divergence: China, Europe, and the Making of the Modern World Economy* (Princeton, NJ: Princeton University Press, 2000), 276, 315. Edwards, *The Growth of the British Cotton Trade*, 75. The resistance to change in the European agricultural system is also emphasized by Philip McMichael, "Slavery in Capitalism: The Rise and Demise of the U.S. Ante-Bellum Cotton Culture," *Theory and Society* 20 (June 1991): 326. For discussion of the great divergence see also David Landes, *The Unbound Prometheus: Technical Change and Industrial Development in Western Europe from 1750 to the Present*, 2nd ed. (New York: Cambridge University Press, 2003); David Landes, *The Wealth and Poverty of Nations: Why Some Are So Rich and Some So Poor* (New York: Norton, 1998); Niall Ferguson, *Civilization: The West and the Rest* (New York: Penguin, 2011); Jared Diamond, *Guns, Germs, and Steel: The Fates of Human Societies* (New York: Norton, 1998). For an overview see also Inikori, *Africans and the Industrial Revolution in England,* chapter 2.

29. This is also argued for the West Indies by Ragatz, *Statistics*, 10, 370. On the importance of sugar as a competitor to cotton see Imperial Department of Agriculture for the West Indies, *Information Relating to Cotton Cultivation in the West Indies* (Barbados: Commissioner of Agriculture for the West Indies, 1903). Edwards, *The Growth of the British Cotton Trade*, 79, 250. Luiz Cordelio Barbosa, "Cotton in 19th Century Brazil: Dependency and Development" (PhD dissertation, University of Washington, 1989), 170; James Mann, *The Cotton Trade of Great Britain* (London: Simpkin, Marshall & Co., 1860), 79, 80, 86; DB 176, Sandbach, Tinne & Co. Papers, Merseyside Maritime Museum, Liverpool.

30. Edensor, *An Address to the Spinners and Manufacturers of Cotton Wool*, 14, 21–3; Franklin, *The Present State of Hayti (St. Domingo), with Remarks on Its Agriculture, Commerce, Laws, Religion, Finances, and Population, etc.* (London: J. Murray, 1828), 123; *Pennsylvania Gazette,* June 13, 1792.

31. John Tarleton to Clayton Tarleton, September 27, 1792, letter 33, February 4, 1795, letter 75, 920 TAR, Tarleton Papers, Liverpool Records Office, Liverpool. See also

Orhan Kurmus, "The Cotton Famine and Its Effects on the Ottoman Empire," Huri Islamoglu-Inan, ed., *The Ottoman Empire and the World Economy* (New York: Cambridge University Press, 1987), 16; Brian R. Mitchell, *Abstract of British Historical Statistics* (Cambridge: Cambridge University Press, 1962), 490. On rising prices see also Stanley Dumbell, "Early Liverpool Cotton Imports and the Organisation of the Cotton Market in the Eighteenth Century," *Economic Journal* 33 (September 1923): 370; Emily A. Rathbone, ed., *Records of the Rathbone Family* (Edinburgh: R. & R. Clark, 1913), 47; Edwards, *The Growth of the British Cotton Trade*, 88.

32. Tench Coxe, *A Memoir of February, 1817, Upon the Subject of the Cotton Wool Cultivation, the Cotton Trade and the Cotton Manufactories of the United States of America* (Philadelphia: Philadelphia Society for the Promotion of American Manufactures, 1817), 3.

CHAPTER FIVE: SLAVERY TAKES COMMAND

1. Petition, To the Right Honorable the Lords of His Majesty's Privy Council for Trade and Foreign Plantations, December 8, 1785, in Board of Trade, National Archives of the UK, Kew. Other sources speak of a similar incident in 1784. See for example Morris R. Chew, *History of the Kingdom of Cotton and Cotton Statistics of the World* (New Orleans: W. B. Stansbury & Co., 1884), 37.

2. See, for example, Ernst von Halle, *Baumwollproduktion und Pflanzungswirtschaft in den Nordamerikanischen Südstaaten, part 1, Die Sklavenzeit* (Leipzig: Verlag von Duncker & Humblot, 1897), 16–17; Jay Treaty, Article XII; Thomas Ellison, *The Cotton Trade of Great Britain* (London: Effingham Wilson, Royal Exchange, 1886), 85; Chew, *History of the Kingdom of Cotton*, 45.

3. Gavin Wright, *The Political Economy of the Cotton South: Households, Markets, and Wealth in the Nineteenth Century* (New York: Norton, 1978), 14; Chew, *History of the Kingdom of Cotton*, 39; George Washington to Thomas Jefferson, February 13, 1789, reprinted in Jared Sparks, *The Writings of George Washington*, vol. 9 (Boston: Russell, Odiorne, and Metcalf & Hilliard, Gray, and Co., 1835), 470; Tench Coxe, *A Memoir of February 1817, Upon the Subject of the Cotton Wool Cultivation, the Cotton Trade, and the Cotton Manufactories of the United States of America* (Philadelphia: Philadelphia Society for the Promotion of American Manufactures, 1817), 2; on Coxe in general see James A. B. Scherer, *Cotton as a World Power: A Study in the Economic Interpretation of History* (New York: F. A. Stokes Co., 1916), 122–23; Tench Coxe, *View of the United States of America* (Philadelphia: William Hall, 1794), 20; Michael M. Edwards, *The Growth of the British Cotton Trade, 1780–1815* (Manchester: Manchester University Press, 1967), 87; Tench Coxe to Robert Livingston, June 10, 1802, in Papers of Tench Coxe, Correspondence and General Papers, June 1802, Film A 201, reel 74, Historical Society of Pennsylvania.

4. "Cotton. Cultivation, manufacture, and foreign trade of. Letter from the Secretary of the Treasury," March 4, 1836 (Washington, DC: Blair & Rives, 1836), 8, accessed July 29, 2013, http://catalog.hathitrust.org/Record/011159609.

5. Joyce Chaplin, "Creating a Cotton South in Georgia and South Carolina, 1760–

1815," *Journal of Southern History* 57 (May 1991): 178; Lewis Cecil Gray, *History of Agriculture in the Southern United States to 1860*, vol. 2 (Washington, DC: Carnegie Institution of Washington, 1933), 673; Chew, *History of the Kingdom of Cotton*, 36, 41; on the household production of cotton and cotton cloth see also Scherer, *Cotton as a World Power*, 124–25; Ralph Izard to Henry Laurens, Bath, December 20, 1775, as reprinted in *Correspondence of Mr. Ralph Izard of South Carolina, From the Year 1774 to 1804; With a Short Memoir* (New York: Charles S. Francis & Co., 1844), 174, see also 16, 82, 246, 296, 300, 370, 386, 390.

6. John Hebron Moore, *The Emergence of the Cotton Kingdom in the Old Southwest: Mississippi, 1770–1860* (Baton Rouge: Louisiana State University Press, 1988), 77; Chaplin, "Creating a Cotton South," 177, 188, 193.

7. Edwards, *The Growth of the British Cotton Trade*, 80, 85; Chew, *History of the Kingdom of Cotton*, 40. However, there was and continues to be substantial controversy as to who planted the first cotton. See Nichol Turnbull, "The Beginning of Cotton Cultivation in Georgia," *Georgia Historical Quarterly* 2, no. 1 (March 1917): 39–45; Gray, *History of Agriculture*, 675–79; S. G. Stephen, "The Origins of Sea Island Cotton," *Agricultural History* 50 (1976): 391–99; Trapman, Schmidt & Co. to McConnel & Kennedy, Charleston, January 3, 1824, record group MCK, Box 2/1/30, Letters Received by McConnel & Kennedy, Papers of McConnel & Kennedy, John Rylands Library, Manchester.

8. "La Rapida Transformacion del Paisaje Viorgen de Guantanamo por los immigrantes Franceses (1802–1809)," in Levi Marrero, *Cuba: Economía y sociedad*, vol. 11, *Azúcar, ilustración y conciencia, 1763–1868* (Madrid: Editorial Playor, 1983), 148; Moore, *The Emergence of the Cotton Kingdom*, 4; Edwards, *The Growth of the British Cotton Trade*, 92; Brian Schoen, *The Fragile Fabric of Union: Cotton, Federal Politics, and the Global Origins of the Civil War* (Baltimore: Johns Hopkins University Press, 2009), 12.

9. Wright, *The Political Economy of the Cotton South*, 13; Gray, *History of Agriculture*, 735.

10. Wright, *The Political Economy of the Cotton South*, 13; on Whitney see Scherer, *Cotton as a World Power*, 155–67; Stuart W. Bruchey, *Cotton and the Growth of the American Economy, 1790–1860: Sources and Readings* (New York: Harcourt, Brace & World, 1967), 45; Angela Lakwete, *Inventing the Cotton Gin: Machine and Myth in Antebellum America* (Baltimore: Johns Hopkins University Press, 2003) disagrees, in my eyes unpersuasively, with this account; David Ramsay, *Ramsay's History of South Carolina, From Its First Settlement in 1670 to the Year 1808*, vol. 2 (Newberry, SC: W. J. Duffie, 1858), 214.

11. Stanley Dumbell, "Early Liverpool Cotton Imports and the Organisation of the Cotton Market in the Eighteenth Century," *Economic Journal* 33 (September 1923): 370; Chaplin, "Creating a Cotton South," 187; here she summarizes one such story; Gray, *History of Agriculture*, 685; Lacy K. Ford, "Self-Sufficiency, Cotton, and Economic Development in the South Carolina Upcountry, 1800–1860," *Journal of Economic History* 45 (June 1985): 261–67.

12. The numbers are from Adam Rothman, "The Expansion of Slavery in the Deep South, 1790–1820" (PhD dissertation, Columbia University, 2000), 20; Allan Kulikoff, "Uprooted People: Black Migrants in the Age of the American Revolution, 1790–1820," in Ira Berlin and Ronald Hoffman, eds., *Slavery and Freedom in the Age*

of the American Revolution (Charlottesville: University Press of Virginia, 1983), 149; Peter A. Coclanis and Lacy K. Ford, "The South Carolina Economy Reconstructed and Reconsidered: Structure, Output, and Performance, 1670–1985," in Winfred B. Moore Jr. et al., *Developing Dixie: Modernization in a Traditional Society* (New York: Greenwood Press, 1988), 97; Allan Kulikoff, "Uprooted People," 149; Gray, *History of Agriculture*, 685.

13. *Farmer's Register*, vol. 1, 490, as quoted in William Chandler Bagley, *Soil Exhaustion and the Civil War* (Washington, DC: American Council on Public Affairs, 1942), 18–19; Bruchey, *Cotton and the Growth of the American Economy*, 80–81.

14. United States, Department of Commerce and Bureau of the Census, *Historical Statistics of the United States, Colonial Times to 1970*, Part 1 (Washington, DC: Government Printing Office, 1975), 518; Edward Baines, *History of the Cotton Manufacture in Great Britain* (London: H. Fisher, R. Fisher, and P. Jackson, 1835), 302; Edwards, *The Growth of the British Cotton Trade*, 89, 95; Ramsay, *Ramsay's History of South Carolina*, 121.

15. Coxe, *A Memoir of February 1817*, 3.

16. For a most interesting discussion on frontier spaces see John C. Weaver, *The Great Land Rush and the Making of the Modern World, 1650–1900* (Montreal: McGill–Queen's University Press, 2003), 72–76.

17. Note by Thomas Baring, Sunday, June 19, in NP 1. A. 4. 13, Northbrook Papers, Baring Brothers, ING Baring Archive, London.

18. Gray, *History of Agriculture*, 686, 901; the story is summarized in Rothman, "The Expansion of Slavery in the Deep South," 155–69; see also Daniel H. Usner Jr., *American Indians in the Lower Mississippi Valley: Social and Economic Histories* (Lincoln: University of Nebraska Press, 1998), 83–89; James C. Cobb, *The Most Southern Place on Earth: The Mississippi Delta and the Roots of Regional Identity* (New York: Oxford University Press, 1992), 7; Lawrence G. Gundersen Jr., "West Tennessee and the Cotton Frontier, 1818–1840," *West Tennessee Historical Society Papers* 52 (1998): 25–43; David Hubbard to J. D. Beers, March 7, 1835, in New York and Mississippi Land Company Records, 1835–1889, State Historical Society of Wisconsin, Madison. Thanks to Richard Rabinowitz for bringing this source to my attention.

19. Dewi Ioan Ball and Joy Porter, eds., *Competing Voices from Native America* (Santa Barbara, CA: Greenwood Press, 2009), 85–87.

20. This story is related in fascinating detail in Rothman, "The Expansion of Slavery in the Deep South," 20ff.; Gray, *History of Agriculture*, 709; Moore, *The Emergence of the Cotton Kingdom*, 6; John F. Stover, *The Routledge Historical Atlas of the American Railroads* (New York: Routledge, 1999), 15.

21. *American Cotton Planter* 1 (1853): 152; *De Bow's Review* 11 (September 1851): 308; see also James Mann, *The Cotton Trade of Great Britain* (London: Simpkin, Marshall & Co., 1860), 53; Elena Frangakis-Syrett, *The Commerce of Smyrna in the Eighteenth Century (1700–1820)* (Athens: Centre for Asia Minor Studies, 1992), 237.

22. Charles Mackenzie, *Facts, Relative to the Present State of the British Cotton Colonies and to the Connection of Their Interests* (Edinburgh: James Clarke, 1811), 35; "Cotton. Cultivation, manufacture, and foreign trade of. Letter from the Secretary of the Treasury," March 4, 1836 (Washington, DC: Blair & Rives, 1836), 16, accessed July 29, 2013, http://catalog.hathitrust.org/Record/011159609.

23. Allan Kulikoff, "Uprooted People," 143–52; James McMillan, "The Final Victims: The Demography, Atlantic Origins, Merchants, and Nature of the Post-Revolutionary Foreign Slave Trade to North America, 1783–1810" (PhD dissertation, Duke University, 1999), 40–98; Walter Johnson, "Introduction," in Walter Johnson, ed., *The Chattel Principle: Internal Slave Trades in the Americas* (New Haven, CT: Yale University Press, 2004), 6; Walter Johnson, *Soul by Soul: Life Inside the Antebellum Slave Market* (Cambridge, MA: Harvard University Press, 2001); Rothman, "The Expansion of Slavery in the Deep South," 59, 84, 314; Scherer, *Cotton as a World Power*, 151; Michael Tadman, *Speculators and Slaves: Masters, Traders, and Slaves in the Old South* (Madison: University of Wisconsin Press, 1989), 12.

24. See John H. Moore, "Two Cotton Kingdoms," *Agricultural History* 60, no. 4 (Fall 1986): 1–16; numbers are from Wright, *The Political Economy of the Cotton South*, 27–28; Ronald Bailey, "The Other Side of Slavery: Black Labor, Cotton, and Textile Industrialization in Great Britain and the United States," *Agricultural History* 68 (Spring 1994): 38.

25. John Brown, *Slave Life in Georgia: A Narrative of the Life, Sufferings, and Escape of John Brown, a Fugitive Slave, Now in England: Electronic Edition*, ed. Louis Alexis Chamerovzow (Chapel Hill: University of North Carolina, 2001), 11, 27, 171–72, http://doc south.unc.edu/neh/jbrown/jbrown.html, originally published in 1854; Henry Bibb, *Narrative of the Life and Adventures of Henry Bibb, an American Slave, Written by Himself: Electronic Edition* (Chapel Hill: University of North Carolina, 2000), 132, http:// docsouth.unc.edu/neh/bibb/bibb.html, originally published in 1815.

26. William Rathbone VI to Rathbone Brothers, February 2, 1849, RP/ XXIV.2.4, File of Correspondence, Letters from William Rathbone VI while in America, Rathbone Papers, Special Collections and Archives, University of Liverpool, Liverpool; *The Liverpool Chronicle* is quoted in *Bremer Handelsblatt* 93 (1853): 6.

27. This whole story is developed in John Casper Branner, *Cotton in the Empire of Brazil: The Antiquity, Methods and Extent of Its Cultivation, Together with Statistics of Exportation and Home Consumption* (Washington, DC: Goverment Printing Office, 1885), 25–27, and Luiz Cordelio Barbosa, "Cotton in 19th Century Brazil: Dependency and Development" (PhD dissertation, University of Washington, 1989), 7, 9, 65; Eugene W. Ridings Jr., "The Merchant Elite and the Development of Brazil: The Case of Bahia During the Empire," *Journal of Interamerican Studies and World Affairs* 15, no. 3 (August 1973): 343; Gray, *History of Agriculture*, 694; see also Rothman, "The Expansion of Slavery in the Deep South," 55; Chaplin, "Creating a Cotton South," 193.

28. At 400 pounds to the bale. The numbers are from Moore, *The Emergence of the Cotton Kingdom*, 129.

29. Cobb, *The Most Southern Place on Earth*, 7–10.

30. Bonnie Martin, "Slavery's Invisible Engine: Mortgaging Human Property," *Journal of Southern History* 76, no. 4 (November 2010): 840–41.

31. C. Wayne Smith and J. Tom Cothren, eds., *Cotton: Origin, History, Technology, and Production* (New York: John Wiley & Sons, 1999), 103, 122; on the various origins of American cotton see also Whitemarsh B. Seabrook, *A Memoir of the Origin, Cultivation and Uses of Cotton* (Charleston, SC: Miller & Browne, 1844), 15; John H. Moore, "Cotton Breeding in the Old South," *Agricultural History* 30 (1956): 97; Moore, *The Emergence of the Cotton Kingdom*, 35; Gray, *History of Agriculture*, 691.

32. *American Cotton Planter* 2 (May 1854): 160.

33. W. E. B. DuBois, *The Suppression of the African Slave-Trade to the United States of America* (New York: General Books LLC, 2009), 140; Edgar T. Thompson, *Plantation Societies, Race Relations, and the South: The Regimentation of Population: Selected Papers of Edgar T. Thompson* (Durham, NC: Duke University Press, 1975), 217; Alan L. Olmstead and Paul W. Rhode, "Slave Productivity on Cotton Production by Gender, Age, Season, and Scale," accessed June 11, 2012, www.iga.ucdavis.edu/Research/all-uc/conferences/spring-2010; Bailey, "The Other Side of Slavery," 36.

34. Caitlin C. Rosenthal, "Slavery's Scientific Management: Accounting for Mastery," in Sven Beckert and Seth Rockman, eds., *Slavery's Capitalism: A New History of American Economic Development* (Philadelphia: University of Pennsylvania Press, forthcoming, 2015); Frederick Law Olmstead, *A Journey in the Back Country* (Williamstown, MA: Corner House, 1972), 153–54, originally published in 1860; Bill Cooke, "The Denial of Slavery in Management Studies," *Journal of Management Studies* 40 (December 2003): 1913. The importance of "biological innovation" has been shown most recently by Alan L. Olmstead and Paul W. Rhode, "Biological Innovation and Productivity Growth in the Antebellum Cotton Economy," National Bureau of Economic Research Working Paper No. 14142, June 2008; Alan L. Olmstead and Paul W. Rhode, *Biological Innovation and American Agricultural Development* (New York: Cambridge University Press, 2008). It has also been effectively critiqued by Edward Baptist, "The Whipping-Machine" (unpublished paper, Conference on Slavery and Capitalism, Brown and Harvard Universities, March 10, 2011, in author's possession). For the importance of falling prices to gaining dominance in markets, see Stephen Broadberry and Bishnupriya Gupta, "Cotton Textiles and the Great Divergence: Lancashire, India and Shifting Competitive Advantage, 1600–1850," Center for Economic Policy Research (April 12, 2005), accessed December 12, 2012, www.cepr.org/meets/wkcn/1/1626/papers/Broadberry.pdf.

35. See for this argument Philip McMichael, "Slavery in Capitalism: The Rise and Demise of the U.S. Ante-Bellum Cotton Culture," *Theory and Society* 20 (June 1991): 335; for the concept of social metabolism see the work of Juan Martinez Alier, for example Juan Martinez Alier and Inge Ropke, eds., *Recent Developments in Ecological Economics* (Northampton, MA: Edward Elgar Publishing, 2008); see also Dale W. Tomich, *Through the Prism of Slavery* (Lanham, MD: Rowman & Littlefield, 2004), 61.

36. Gray, *History of Agriculture,* 688; Eugene Genovese, "Cotton, Slavery and Soil Exhaustion in the Old South," *Cotton History Review* 2 (1961): 3–17; on the prices of slaves see Adam Rothman, "The Domestic Slave Trade in America: The Lifeblood of the Southern Slave System," in Johnson, ed., *The Chattel Principle,* 95; on Clay see Savannah Unit Georgia Writers' Project, Work Projects Administration in Georgia, "The Plantation of the Royal Vale," *Georgia Historical Quarterly* 27 (March 1943): 97–99. For an analysis of slavery see Robert Fogel and Stanley Engerman, *Time on the Cross: The Economics of American Negro Slavery* (Boston: Little, Brown & Co., 1974).

37. Samuel Dubose and Frederick A. Porcher, *A Contribution to the History of the Huguenots of South Carolina* (New York: Knickerbocker Press, 1887), 19, 21; Edwards, *The Growth of the British Cotton Trade,* 91; Coclanis and Ford, "The South Carolina Economy Reconstructed and Reconsidered," 97; Cobb, *The Most Southern Place on*

Earth, 10; Daniel W. Jordan to Emily Jordan, Plymouth, August 3, 1833, in Daniel W. Jordan Papers, Special Collections Department, Perkins Library, Duke University.

38. Philo-Colonus, *A Letter to S. Perceval on the Expediency of Imposing a Duty on Cotton Wool of Foreign Growth, Imported into Great Britain* (London: J. Cawthorn, 1812), 9; Lowell Joseph Ragatz, *Statistics for the Study of British Caribbean Economic History, 1763–1833* (London: Bryan Edwards Press, 1927), 16; Planters' and Merchants' Resolution Concerning Import of Cotton Wool from the United States, 1813, in Official Papers of First Earl of Liverpool, Add. Mss. 38252, f. 78, Liverpool Papers, Manuscript Collections, British Library; John Gladstone, *Letters Addressed to the Right Honourable The Earl of Clancarty, President of the Board of Trade, on the Inexpediency of Permitting the Importation of Cotton Wool from the United States During the Present War* (London: J. M. Richardson, 1813), 7. In western India alone, 4 million acres of land were cultivated with cotton in 1850, with significantly more land under cotton in other parts of India. In the United States in 1850, around 7 million acres were under cotton. Amalendu Guha, "Raw Cotton of Western India: 1750–1850," *Indian Economic and Social History Review* 9 (January 1972): 25.

39. U.S. Treasury Department Report, 1836, p. 16, as quoted in Barbosa, "Cotton in 19th Century Brazil," 150; see also Rothman, "The Expansion of Slavery in the Deep South," 15. For the importance of the Industrial Revolution to slavery's dynamic in the United States, see also Barbara Jeanne Fields, "The Advent of Capitalist Agriculture: The New South in a Bourgeois World," in Thavolia Glymph, ed., *Essays on the Postbellum Southern Economy* (Arlington: Texas A&M University Press, 1985), 77; Wright, *The Political Economy of the Cotton South*, 13; Scherer, *Cotton as a World Power*, 150; *The Proceedings of the Agricultural Convention of the State Agricultural Society of South Carolina: From 1839 to 1845—Inclusive* (Columbia, SC: Summer & Carroll, 1846), 322; Rohit T. Aggarwala, "Domestic Networks as a Basis for New York City's Rise to Pre-eminence, 1780–1812" (unpublished paper presented at the Business History Conference, Le Creusot, France, June 19, 2004), 21; Michael Hovland, "The Cotton Ginnings Reports Program at the Bureau of the Census," *Agricultural History* 68 (Spring 1994): 147; Bruchey, *Cotton and the Growth of the American Economy*, 2.

40. Halle, *Baumwollproduktion und Pflanzungswirtschaft*, viii; *Organization of the Cotton Power: Communication of the President* (Macon, GA: Lewis B. Andrews Book and Job Printer, 1858), 7; *American Cotton Planter* 1 (January 1853): 11.

41. The importance of locating the southern plantation economy within the global economy is often lost among historians of the American South. See Immanuel Wallerstein, "American Slavery and the Capitalist World-Economy," *American Journal of Sociology* 81 (March 1976): 1208; Francis Carnac Brown, *Free Trade and the Cotton Question with Reference to India* (London: Effingham Wilson, 1848), 43; Copy of a Memorial Respecting the Levant Trade to the Right Honourable the Board of Privy Council for Trade and Foreign Plantations, as copied in Proceedings of the Manchester Chamber of Commerce, meeting of February 9, 1825, in M8/2/1, Proceedings of the Manchester Chamber of Commerce, 1821–27, Archives of the Manchester Chamber of Commerce, Manchester Archives and Local Studies, Manchester; *The Proceedings of the Agricultural Convention of the State Agricultural Society of South Carolina*, 323.

42. Letter by [illegible] to "My Dear Sir" (a former president of the Board of Trade), Liverpool, June 16, 1828, in Document f255, Huskisson Papers, Manuscript Collections,

British Library, London; "Memorial of the Directors of the Chamber of Commerce and Manufactures Established by Royal Charter in the City of Glasgow, 15 December 1838," in *Official Papers Connected with the Improved Cultivation of Cotton* (Calcutta: G. H. Huttmann, 1839), 6, 8; A Cotton Spinner, *India Our Hope; Or, Remarks Upon our Supply of Cotton* (Manchester: J. Clarke, 1844), 13; Mann, *The Cotton Trade of Great Britain*, 56; Mac Culloch, as quoted in *Bremer Handelsblatt* 1 (1851): 5.

43. A Cotton Spinner, *India Our Hope*, 5; J. G. Collins, *An Essay in Favour of the Colonialization of the North and North-West Provinces of India, with Regard to the Question of Increased Cotton Supply and Its Bearing on the Slave Trade* (London: W. H. Allen & Co., n.d., c. 1859), 35; John Gunn Collins, *Scinde & The Punjab: The Gems of India in Respect to Their Past and Unparalleled Capabilities of Supplanting the Slave States of America in the Cotton Markets of the World, or, An Appeal to the English Nation on Behalf of Its Great Cotton Interest, Threatened with Inadequate Supplies of the Raw Material* (Manchester: A. Ireland, 1858), 10; these arguments are also summarized in *Bremer Handelsblatt*, August 8, 1857, 281.

44. Baring Brothers Liverpool to Baring Brothers London, Liverpool, October 22, 1835, in HC3.35,2, House Correspondence, ING Baring Archive, London; for that issue see also Schoen, *The Fragile Fabric of Union*, 1–10.

45. A Cotton Spinner, *The Safety of Britain and the Suppression of Slavery: A Letter to the Right Hon. Sir Robert Peel on the Importance of an Improved Supply of Cotton from India* (London: Simpkin, Marshall, 1845), 3, 4; A Cotton Spinner, *India Our Hope*, 6; Brown, *Free Trade and the Cotton Question*, 44; Collins, *Scinde & The Punjab*, 5; Anonymous, *The Cotton Trade of India: Quaere: Can India Not Supply England with Cotton?* (London: Spottiswoode, 1839); Committee of Commerce and Agriculture of the Royal Asiatic Society, *On the Cultivation of Cotton in India* (London: Harrison & Co., 1840); John Forbes Royle, *Essay on the Productive Resources of India* (London: Wm. H. Allen, 1840); Tench Coxe to Robert Livingston, June 10, 1802, in Papers of Tench Coxe, Correspondence and General Papers, June 1802, Film A 201, reel 74, Historical Society of Pennsylvania.

46. See, for example, Ministère de la Marine et des Colonies to the Secrétaire d'État de l'Intérieur, Paris, January 27, 1819; Société d'Encouragement pour l'Industrie Nationale to Secrétaire d'État de l'Intérieur, Paris, October 17, 1821, in F12–2196, "Machine à égrainer le coton," Archives Nationales, Paris; A Cotton Spinner, *India Our Hope*, 15; An Indian Civil Servant, *Usurers and Ryots, Being an Answer to the Question "Why Does Not India Produce More Cotton?"* (London: Smith, Elder & Co, 1856); Collins, *Scinde & The Punjab*, 5; Anonymous, *The Cotton Trade of India*; Committee of Commerce and Agriculture of the Royal Asiatic Society, *On the Cultivation of Cotton in India*; Royle, *Essay on the Productive Resources of India*, 314; J. Chapman, *The Cotton and Commerce of India* (London: John Chapman, 1851).

47. See, for example, *Report from the Select Committee on the Growth of Cotton in India*, House of Commons, Parliamentary Papers, 1847–48, vol. IX; *The Sixteenth Annual Report of the Board of Directors of the Chamber of Commerce and Manufactures at Manchester for the Year 1836* (Manchester: Henry Smith, 1837), 13; *The Thirty-Sixth Annual Report of the Board of Directors of the Chamber of Commerce and Manufactures at Manchester for the Year 1856* (Manchester: James Collins, 1857), 34; *The Seventeenth Annual*

Report of the Board of Directors of the Chamber of Commerce and Manufactures at Manchester for the Year 1836 (Manchester: Henry Smith, 1838), 17; Resolution Passed at the Meeting of the Board of Directors, Manchester Commercial Association, November 13, 1845, M8, 7/1, Manchester Commercial Association Papers, Manchester Archives and Local Studies, Manchester. For further pressure see Copy of Letter of John Peel, Manchester Commercial Association, to the Chairman of the Court of Directors of the Honourable East India Company, Manchester, March 1, 1848, in Home Department, Revenue Branch, October 28, 1849, Nos. 3/4, in National Archives of India, New Delhi; Thomas Bazley to Thomas Baring, Manchester, September 9, 1857, in House Correspondence, NP 6.3.1., Thomas Bazley, ING Baring Archive, London.

48. Arthur W. Silver, *Manchester Men and Indian Cotton, 1847–1872* (Manchester: Manchester University Press, 1966), 58; "Memorial of the Manchester Chamber of Commerce, dated December 1838," and "Memorial of the Directors of the Chamber of Commerce and Manufactures Established by Royal Charter in the City of Glasgow, 15 December 1838," in *Official Papers Connected with the Improved Cultivation of Cotton*, 6, 8, 10; Mann, *The Cotton Trade of Great Britain*, 62; Karl Marx, *Karl Marx on Colonialism and Modernization* (Garden City, NJ: Doubleday, 1968), 100–101.

49. Silver, *Manchester Men and Indian Cotton*, 61.

50. *The Thirty-Sixth Annual Report of the Board of Directors*, 13, 31–45; *The Thirty-Eighth Annual Report of the Board of Directors of the Chamber of Commerce and Manufactures at Manchester for the Year 1858* (Manchester: James Collins, 1859), 14–43; *The Thirty-Seventh Annual Report of the Board of Directors of the Chamber of Commerce and Manufactures at Manchester for the Year 1857* (Manchester: James Collins, 1858), 11–12. For the Manchester Cotton Supply Association see Cotton Supply Association, *Report of an Important Meeting Held at Manchester May 21, 1857* (Manchester: Galt, Kerruish, & Kirby, 1857), 2.

51. See for example *Report from the Select Committee on the Growth of Cotton in India*, House of Commons, iii; *Asiatic Journal and Monthly Register*, New Series, 30 (September–December 1839): 304; Mann, *The Cotton Trade of Great Britain*, 65; Committee of Commerce and Agriculture of the Royal Asiatic Society, *On the Cultivation of Cotton in India*, 17; Guha, "Raw Cotton of Western India," 2.

52. Silver, *Manchester Men and Indian Cotton*, 31, 34; Guha, "Raw Cotton of Western India," 5, 33; Frederic Wakeman Jr., "The Canton Trade and the Opium War," in John K. Fairbank, ed., *The Cambridge History of China*, vol. 10, part 1 (Cambridge: Cambridge University Press, 1978), 171. In the mid-1840s exports from Bombay to China amounted to about 40 million pounds; *De Bow's Review* 1 (April 1846), pp. 295–96. See also Sucheta Mazumdar, *Sugar and Society in China: Peasants, Technology and the World Market* (Cambridge, MA: Harvard University Press, 1998), 105–6.

53. See the assessment of the *Calcutta Review*: "Bombay Cottons and Indian Railways," *Calcutta Review* 26 (June 1850): 331; M. L. Dantwala, *A Hundred Years of Indian Cotton* (Bombay: East India Cotton Association, 1947), 45–46; see also K. L. Tuteja, "Agricultural Technology in Gujarat: A Study of Exotic Seed and Saw Gins, 1800–50," *Indian Historical Review* 17, nos. 1–3 (1990–91): 136–51; J. G. Medicott, *Cotton Hand-Book for Bengal* (Calcutta: Savielle & Cranenburgh, 1862), 296; "Cot-

ton in Southern Mahratta Country, Agency for the Purchase of Cotton Established," Compilations Vol. 27/355, 1831, Compilation No. 395, Revenue Department, Maharashtra State Archives, Mumbai; Minute by the Vice President, Metcalfe, March 3, 1831, in Revenue Department, Revenue Branch, "A," July 1831, No. 69/74, Part B, in National Archives of India, New Delhi; Home Department, Revenue Branch, G.G., August 1839, No. 1/4, in National Archives of India; Silver, *Manchester Men and Indian Cotton*, 74; on various other measures taken by the company to improve and increase Indian cotton exports see J. Forbes Royle, *On the Culture and Commerce of Cotton in India and Elsewhere: With an Account of the Experiments Made by the Hon. East India Company Up to the Present Time* (London: Smith, Elder, & Co., 1851), 86–90.

54. See for example Territorial Department, Revenue—Cotton to Thomas Williamson, Secretary to Government, June 21, 1830, in 43/324/1830, Compilations, Revenue Department, Maharashtra State Archives, Mumbai; "Abstract of the Replies of Local Authorities to the Board's Circular of 21st February 1848 Calling for Certain Information Relative to the Cultivation of Cotton in India and Required by the Honourable Court of Directors," in Home Department, Revenue Branch, December 2, 1848, Nos. 10–18, in National Archives of India, New Delhi; see also "Prospects of Cotton Cultivation in the Saugor and Narbadda Territories in the Nizam's Dominions," August 12, 1848, No. 3–11, National Archives of India; "Capabilities of the Bombay Presidency for Supplying Cotton in the Event of an Increased Demand from Europe," March 1, 1850, Revenue Branch, Home Department, National Archives of India; Revenue Department, Compilations Vol. 6/413, 1832, Compilation No. 62, Cotton Experimental Farm, Guzerat, Maharashtra State Archives; Compilations Vol. 10/478, 1833, Compilation No. 5, Cotton Experimental Farm, Guzerat, Revenue Department, Maharashtra State Archives; *Asiatic Journal and Monthly Register,* New Series, 21 (September–December 1836): 220, 22 (January–April 1837): 234, and 38 (1842): 371; Tuteja, "Agricultural Technology in Gujarat": 137; Committee of Commerce and Agriculture of the Royal Asiatic Society, *On the Cultivation of Cotton in India*, 15.

55. See for example "Cotton Cultivation Under the Superintendence of the American Cotton Planters in N.W. Provinces, Bombay and Madras," January 17, 1842, No. 13–17, Revenue Department, Home Department, National Archives of India, New Delhi; John MacFarquhar to East India Company, New Orleans, January 13, 1842, W. W. Wood to East India Company, New Orleans, June 10, 1842, Two Letters dated 13 January and 10 June to the Directors of the East India Company, MSS EUR C157, in Oriental and India Office Collections, British Library, London; Home Department, Revenue Branch, G.G., August 1839, No. 1/4, in National Archives of India; see also Resolution dated September 21, 1841, by the Revenue Branch of the Government of India, Revenue Department, Revenue Branch, 21st September 1840, No. 1/3, National Archives of India; Letter by [illegible] to T. H. Maddok, Territorial Department Revenue, Bombay, 10 February 1842, in Revenue and Agriculture Department, Revenue Branch, February 28, 1842, Nos. 2–5, National Archives of India; Medicott, *Cotton Hand-Book for Bengal*, 305; *Asiatic Journal and Monthly Register,* New Series, 36 (September–December 1841): 343.

56. Silver, *Manchester Men and Indian Cotton*, 37–39; *Asiatic Journal and Monthly Register*, New Series, 35 (May–August 1841): 502; copy of letter from C. W. Martin, Superintendent Cotton Farm in Gujerat, Broach, November 1830 to William Stubbs, Esq., Principal Collector, Surat, in Compilations Vol. 22/350, 1831, Revenue Department, Maharashtra State Archives, Mumbai; Gibbs, Broach, October 5, 1831, to Thomas Williamson, Esq., secretary of Government, in Compilations Vol. 22/350, 1831, Revenue Department, Maharashtra State Archives; *Asiatic Journal and Monthly Register*, New Series, 39 (1842): 106; letter by [illegible] to T. H. Maddok, Territorial Department Revenue, Bombay, 10 February 1842, in Revenue and Agriculture Department, Revenue Branch, February 28, 1842, Nos. 2–5, National Archives of India, New Delhi; *Report of the Bombay Chamber of Commerce for the Year 1846–47* (Bombay: American Mission Press, 1847), 5.

57. Medicott, *Cotton Hand-Book for Bengal*, 320, 322, 323, 331, 340, 352, 366.

58. *Annual Report of the Transactions of the Bombay Chamber of Commerce for the Official Year 1840–41* (Bombay: Bombay Times and Journal of Commerce Press, 1841), 112–19; copy of a letter of John Peel, Manchester Commercial Association, to the Chairman of the Court of Directors of the Honourable East India Company, London, March 1, 1848, in Manchester Commercial Association, October 18, 1848, No. 3–4, Revenue Branch, Home Department, National Archives of India, New Delhi; Committee of Commerce and Agriculture of the Royal Asiatic Society, *On the Cultivation of Cotton in India*, 4.

59. East-India Company, *Reports and Documents Connected with the Proceedings of the East-India Company in Regard to the Culture and Manufacture of Cotton-Wool, Raw Silk, and Indigo in India* (London: East-India Company, 1836); reprinted letter of W. W. Bell, Collector's Office, Dharwar, 10 January 1850 to H. E. Goldsmid, Secretary of Government, Bombay, reprinted in *Report of the Bombay Chamber of Commerce for the Year 1849–50* (Bombay: American Mission Press, 1850), 26; Bombay Chamber of Commerce, *Annual Report of the Bombay Chamber of Commerce for the Official Year 1840–41*, 104.

60. Ellison, *The Cotton Trade*, 99; Revenue Department No. 4 of 1839, Reprinted in *Official Papers Connected with the Improved Cultivation of Cotton*, 1, consulted in Asiatic Society of Bombay Library, Mumbai; *Annual Report of the Bombay Chamber of Commerce for the Year 1859/60* (Bombay: Bombay Gazette Press, 1860), xxviii.

61. Mann, *The Cotton Trade of Great Britain*, 70; C. W. Grant, *Bombay Cotton and Indian Railways* (London: Longman, Brown, Green and Longman, 1850), 9.

62. Tuteja, "Agricultural Technology in Gujarat"; "Replies to the Queries Proposed by the Government of India, given by [illegible] Viccajee, Regarding the Cotton Trade in the Nizam's Country," Home Department, Revenue Branch, August 12, 1848, No. 3–11, p. 167, in National Archives of India, New Delhi; Report from Kaira Collector to Revenue Department, Neriad, March 22, 1823, Compilations Vol. 8/60, 1823, in Revenue Department, Maharashtra State Archives, Mumbai.

63. Tuteja, "Agricultural Technology in Gujarat," 147, 151; Letter of Chartles Lurh (?), in charge of experimental cotton farm in Dharwar, February 21, 1831, to Thomas Williamson, Esq., Secretary to Government, Bombay, Compilations Vol. 22/350, 1831, in Revenue Department, Maharashtra State Archives, Mumbai; *Report from the*

Select Committee on the Growth of Cotton in India, House of Commons, 5; Tuteja, "Agricultural Technology in Gujarat"; Letter by J. P. Simson, Secretary to Government, The Warehousekeeper and Commercial Account, Bombay Castle, 18 May 1820, Compilations Vol. 4, 1821, Commercial Department, in Maharashtra State Archives, Mumbai.

64. For a detailed account of how indigenous merchants moved cotton from the growers to the market see Cotton Trade in Bombay, 1811, in Despatches to Bombay, E4/1027, pp. 135–47, Oriental and India Office Collections, British Library, London. See also Marika Vicziany, "Bombay Merchants and Structural Changes in the Export Community, 1850 to 1880," in *Economy and Society: Essays in Indian Economic and Social History* (Delhi: Oxford University Press, 1979), 63–196; Marika Vicziany, *The Cotton Trade and the Commercial Development of Bombay, 1855–75* (London: University of London Press, 1975), especially 170–71; Dantwala, *A Hundred Years of Indian Cotton*, 37; Bombay Chamber of Commerce, *Annual Report of the Bombay Chamber of Commerce for the Official Year 1840–41*, III; Letter from [illegible], Commercial Resident Office, Broach, January 6, 1825, to Gilbert More, Acting Secretary of Government, Bombay, in Compilations Vol. 26, 1825, "Consultation Cotton Investment," Commercial Department, in Maharashtra State Archives, Mumbai; Report from Kaira Collector to Revenue Department, Neriad, March 22, 1823, in Compilations Vol. 8/60, 1823, Revenue Department, Maharashtra State Archives.

65. *Annual Report of the Bombay Chamber of Commerce for the Year 1846–47* (Bombay: American Mission Press, 1847), 7; Committee of Commerce and Agriculture of the Royal Asiatic Society, *On the Cultivation of Cotton in India*, 4; *Annual Report of the Bombay Chamber of Commerce for the Year 1849–50* (Bombay: American Mission Press, 1850), 7; Bombay Chamber of Commerce, *Annual Report of the Bombay Chamber of Commerce for the Official Year 1840–41*, 110–11; Captain M. Taylor to Colonel Low, Reports on District of Sharapoor, Sharapoor, June 23, 1848, in "Prospects of Cotton Cultivation in the Saugor and Narbadda Territories in the Nizam's Dominions," August 12, 1848, No. 3–11, Revenue Branch, Home Department, National Archives of India, New Delhi; *Report from the Select Committee on the Growth of Cotton in India*, House of Commons, v.

66. Bombay Chamber of Commerce, *Annual Report of the Bombay Chamber of Commerce for the Official Year 1840–41*, 104, 107; Copy of letter from C. W. Martin, Superintendent Cotton Farm in Gujerat, Broach, November 1830 to William Stubbs, Esq., Principal Collector, Surat, Compilations Vol. 22/350, 1831, Revenue Department, in Maharahstra State Archives, Mumbai. See also Martin to Stubbs, 1st October 1831, Compilations Vol. 22/350, 1831, Revenue Department, in Maharashtra State Archives, Mumbai.

67. Peely, Acting Commercial Resident, Northern Factories, July 21, 1831, to Charles Norris, Esq., Civil Secretary to Government, Bombay, Compilations Vol. 22/350, 1831, Revenue Department, in Maharashtra State Archives, Mumbai; Committee of Commerce and Agriculture of the Royal Asiatic Society, *On the Cultivation of Cotton in India*, 13; Letter by H. A. Harrison, 1st Assistant Collector, Ootacmund, October 14, 1832, to L. R. Reid, Esq., Secretary to Government, Bombay, Compilations Vol. 7/412, 1832, in Maharashtra State Archives, Mumbai; "Cotton Farms,

Proceedings respecting the formation of _____ in the Vicinity of Jails," Compilation No. 118, in Maharashtra State Archives, Mumbai; copy of letter of T. H. Balier (?), Collector, Dharwar, 19th August 1825 to William Chaplin, Esq., Commissioner, Poona, in Compilations Vol. 26, 1835, "Consultation Cotton Investment," in Commercial Department, Maharashtra State Archives, Mumbai; long discussions on slavery in India can be found in *Asiatic Journal and Monthly Register*, New Series, 15 (September–December 1834): 81–90. See also Factory Records, Dacca, G 15, 21 (1779), Oriental and India Office Collections, British Library, London.

68. Copy of letter from J. Dunbar, Commissioner of Dacca, to Sudder, Board of Revenue, September 27, 1848, in Home Department, Revenue Branch, December 2, 1848, Nos. 10–18, in National Archives of India, New Delhi.

69. E. R. J. Owen, *Cotton and the Egyptian Economy, 1820–1914: A Study in Trade and Development* (Oxford: Clarendon Press, 1969), 12; George R. Gliddon, *A Memoir on the Cotton of Egypt* (London: James Madden & Co., 1841), 11.

70. Owen, *Cotton and the Egyptian Economy*, 28–29, 32, 47; Gliddon, *A Memoir on the Cotton of Egypt*; "Commerce of Egypt," in *Hunt's Merchants' Magazine and Commercial Review* 8 (January 1843): 22; John Bowring, "Report on Egypt and Candia," in Great Britain, Parliamentary Papers, 1840, vol. XXI, 19; Christos Hadziiossifm, "La Colonie Grecque en Egypte, 1833–1836" (PhD dissertation, Sorbonne, 1980), 111; John Bowring, "Report on Egypt and Candia (1840)," cited in Owen, *Cotton and the Egyptian Economy*, 318.

71. Owen, *Cotton and the Egyptian Economy*, 36–37, 40.

72. The graph on page 133 is based on information from "Commerce of Egypt," 22; Owen, *Cotton and the Egyptian Economy*, 34; Table 1, "Volume, Value, and Price of Egyptian Cotton Exports, 1821–1837," 45; Table 5, "Volume, Value, and Price of Egyptian Cotton Exports, 1838–1859," 73.

73. From about 1823 to 1840. Robert Lévy, *Histoire économique de l'industrie cotonnière en Alsace: Étude de sociologie descriptive* (Paris: F. Alcan, 1912), 58; copy of a Memorial Respecting the Levant Trade to the Right Honourable The Board of Privy Council for Trade and Foreign Plantations, as copied in Proceedings of the Manchester Chamber of Commerce, meeting of February 9, 1825, in M8/2/1, Proceedings of the Manchester Chamber of Commerce, 1821–27, Archives of the Manchester Chamber of Commerce, Manchester Archives and Local Studies, Manchester.

74. *Bremer Handelsblatt* (1853), as quoted in Ludwig Beutin, *Von 3 Ballen zum Weltmarkt: Kleine Bremer Baumwollchronik, 1788–1872* (Bremen: Verlag Franz Leuwer, 1934), 25; Philip McMichael, "Slavery in Capitalism," 327.

75. Thomas Ellison, *A Hand-Book of the Cotton Trade, or, A Glance at the Past History, Present Condition, and the Future Prospects of the Cotton Commerce of the World* (London: Longman, Brown, Green, Longmans, and Roberts, 1858), 96.

76. Albert Feuerwerker, "Handicraft and Manufactured Cotton Textiles in China, 1871–1910," *Journal of Economic History* 30 (June 1970): 340; Kang Chao, *The Development of Cotton Textile Production in China* (Cambridge, MA: Harvard University Press, 1977), 4–13; Robert Fortune, *Three Years' Wanderings in the Northern Provinces of China, Including a Visit to the Tea, Silk, and Cotton Countries, With an Account of the Agriculture and Horticulture of the Chinese, New Plants, etc.* (London: John Murray,

1847), 275; Koh Sung Jae, *Stages of Industrial Development in Asia: A Comparative History of the Cotton Industry in Japan, India, China and Korea* (Philadelphia: University of Pennsylvania Press, 1966), 28, 38, 45; William B. Hauser, *Economic Institutional Change in Tokugawa Japan: Osaka and the Kinai Cotton Trade* (Cambridge: Cambridge University Press, 1974), 59, 117–20; Hameeda Hossain, *The Company of Weavers of Bengal: The East India Company and the Organization of Textile Production in Bengal, 1750–1813* (Delhi: Oxford University Press, 1988), 28.

77. Kären Wigen, *The Making of a Japanese Periphery, 1750–1920* (Berkeley: University of California Press, 1995); Tench Coxe, *An Addition, of December 1818, to the Memoir, of February and August 1817, on the Subject of the Cotton Culture, the Cotton Commerce, and the Cotton Manufacture of the United States, etc.* (Philadelphia: n.p., 1818), 3; "Extracts and Abstract of a letter from W. Dunbar, Officiating Commissioner of Revenue in the Dacca Division, to Lord B. of [illegible], dated Dacca, May 2, 1844," in MSS EUR F 78, 44, Wood Papers, Oriental and India Office Collections, British Library, London.

CHAPTER SIX: INDUSTRIAL CAPITALISM TAKES WING

1. For biographical information on Burke see *National Cyclopaedia of American Biography*, vol. 20 (New York: James T. White, 1929), 79. For Baranda see "Pedro Sainz de Baranda," in *Enciclopedia Yucatanense*, vol. 7 (Ciudad de Mexico, D.F.: Edición oficial del Gobierno de Yucatan, 1977), 51–67; John L. Stephens, *Incidents of Travel in Yucatan*, vol. 2 (New York: Harper & Brothers, 1843), 329.

2. Stephens, *Incidents*, 330; Howard F. Cline, "The 'Aurora Yucateca' and the Spirit of Enterprise in Yucatan, 1821–1847," *Hispanic American Historical Review* 27, no. 1 (February 1947): 39–44; *Enciclopedia Yucatanense*, vol. 7, 61–62. See also Othón Baños Ramírez, *Sociedad, estructura agraria, estado en Yucatán* (Mérida: Universidad Autónoma de Yucatán, 1990), 24.

3. Gisela Müller, "Die Entstehung und Entwicklung der Wiesentäler Textilindustrie bis zum Jahre 1945" (PhD dissertation, University of Basel, 1965), 35, 36; Richard Dietsche, "Die industrielle Entwicklung des Wiesentales bis zum Jahre 1870" (PhD dissertation, University of Basel, 1937), 16, 18, 30, 34, 37; Walter Bodmer, *Die Entwicklung der schweizerischen Textilwirtschaft im Rahmen der übrigen Industrien und Wirtschaftszweige* (Zürich: Verlag Berichthaus, 1960), 226.

4. Dietsche, "Die industrielle Entwicklung," 18, 20, 21, 34, 47, 48, 61, 76; Friedrich Deher, *Staufen und der obere Breisgau: Chronik einer Landschaft* (Karlsruhe: Verlag G. Braun, 1967), 191–92; Eberhard Gothein, *Wirtschaftsgeschichte des Schwarzwaldes und der angrenzenden Landschaften* (Strassburg: Karl J. Truebner, 1892), 754; Müller, "Die Entstehung und Entwicklung," 33, 47; Hugo Ott, "Der Schwarzwald: Die wirtschaftliche Entwicklung seit dem ausgehenden 18. Jahrhundert," in Franz Quarthal, ed., *Zwischen Schwarzwald und Schwäbischer Alb: Das Land am oberen Neckar* (Sigmaringen: Thorbecke, 1984), 399.

5. Arthur L. Dunham, "The Development of the Cotton Industry in France and the Anglo-French Treaty of Commerce of 1860," *Economic History Review* 1, no. 2 (Janu-

ary 1928): 282; Gerhard Adelmann, *Die Baumwollgewerbe Nordwestdeutschlands und der westlichen Nachbarländer beim Übergang von der vorindustriellen zur frühindustriellen Zeit, 1750–1815* (Stuttgart: Franz Steiner Verlag, 2001), 76; R. M. R. Dehn, *The German Cotton Industry* (Manchester: Manchester University Press, 1913), 3; J. K. J. Thomson, *A Distinctive Industrialization: Cotton in Barcelona, 1728–1832* (Cambridge: Cambridge University Press, 1992), 248; J. Dhondt, "The Cotton Industry at Ghent During the French Regime," in F. Crouzet, W. H. Chaloner, and W. M. Stern, eds., *Essays in European Economic History, 1789–1914* (London: Edward Arnold, 1969), 18; Georg Meerwein, "Die Entwicklung der Chemnitzer bezw. sächsischen Baumwollspinnerei von 1789–1879" (PhD dissertation, University of Heidelberg, 1914), 19; Rudolf Forberger, *Die industrielle Revolution in Sachsen 1800–1861, Bd. 1, zweiter Halbband: Die Revolution der Produktivkräfte in Sachsen 1800–1830. Übersichten zur Fabrikentwicklung* (Berlin: Akademie-Verlag, 1982), 14; Albert Tanner, "The Cotton Industry of Eastern Switzerland, 1750–1914: From Proto-industry to Factory and Cottage Industry," *Textile History* 23, no. 2 (1992): 139; Wolfgang Müller, "Die Textilindustrie des Raumes Puebla (Mexiko) im 19. Jahrhundert" (PhD dissertation, University of Bonn, 1977), 144; E. R. J. Owen, *Cotton and the Egyptian Economy, 1820–1914: A Study in Trade and Development* (Oxford: Clarendon Press, 1969), 23–24.

6. On concerns among British manufacturers about this spread, see *The Sixteenth Annual Report of the Board of Directors of the Chamber of Commerce and Manufactures at Manchester for the Year 1836 Made to the Annual General Meeting of the Members, held February 13th 1837* (Manchester: Henry Smith, 1837), 13.

7. Sydney Pollard emphasizes correctly that industrialization was at this point (before railroads) not a national development, but a regional one; there were industrializing regions in Europe (e.g., Catalonia). Sydney Pollard, *Peaceful Conquest: The Industrialization of Europe, 1760–1970* (New York: Oxford University Press, 1981); see also Joel Mokyr, *Industrialization in the Low Countries, 1795–1850* (New Haven, CT: Yale University Press, 1976), 26, 28.

8. Günter Kirchhain, "Das Wachstum der deutschen Baumwollindustrie im 19. Jahrhundert: Eine historische Modellstudie zur empirischen Wachstumsforschung" (PhD dissertation, University of Münster, 1973), 30, 41; Francisco Mariano Nipho, *Estafeta de Londres* (Madrid: n.p., 1770), 44, as quoted in Pierre Vilar, *La Catalogne dans l'Espagne moderne: Recherches sur le fondements économiques des structures nationales*, vol. 2 (Paris: S.E.V.P.E.N., 1962), 10; Pavel A. Khromov, *Ékonomika Rossii Perioda Promyshlennogo Kapitalizma* (Moscow: 1963), 80; Howard F. Cline, "Spirit of Enterprise in Yucatan," in Lewis Hanke, ed., *History of Latin American Civilization*, vol. 2 (London: Methuen, 1969), 133; Adelmann, *Die Baumwollgewerbe Nordwestdeutschlands*, 153; Dunham, "The Development of the Cotton Industry," 288; B. M. Biucchi, "Switzerland, 1700–1914," in Carlo M. Cipolla, ed., *The Fontana Economic History of Europe*, vol. 4, part 2 (Glasgow: Collins, 1977), 634; Robert Lévy, *Histoire économique de l'industrie cotonnière en Alsace* (Paris: Felix Alcan, 1912), 87, 89; United States Census Bureau, *Manufactures of the United States in 1860; Compiled from the Original Returns of the Eighth Census under the Direction of the Secretary of the Interior* (Washington, DC: Government Printing Office, 1865), xvii; Ronald Bailey, "The

Slave(ry) Trade and the Development of Capitalism in the United States: The Textile Industry in New England," in Joseph E. Inikori and Stanley L. Engerman, eds., *The Atlantic Slave Trade: Effects on Economies, Societies, and Peoples in Africa, the Americas, and Europe* (Durham, NC: Duke University Press, 1992), 221.

9. Bodmer, *Die Entwicklung der schweizerischen Textilwirtschaft*, 281.

10. Dhondt, "The Cotton Industry at Ghent," 15; Müller, "Die Textilindustrie des Raumes," 33; Max Hamburger, "Standortgeschichte der deutschen Baumwoll-Industrie" (PhD dissertation, University of Heidelberg, 1911), 19; Wallace Daniel, "Entrepreneurship and the Russian Textile Industry: From Peter the Great to Catherine the Great," *Russian Review* 54, no. 1 (January 1995): 1–25; Lévy, *Histoire économique*, 1ff.; Bodmer, *Die Entwicklung der schweizerischen Textilwirtschaft*, 181–203.

11. Adelmann, *Die Baumwollgewerbe Nordwestdeutschlands*, 16, 54; Maurice Lévy Leboyer, *Les banques européennes et l'industrialisation internationale dans la première moitié du XIXe siècle* (Paris: [Faculté des Lettres et Sciences Humaines de Paris], 1964); Dhondt, "The Cotton Industry at Ghent," 16; William L. Blackwell, *The Beginnings of Russian Industrialization, 1800–1860* (Princeton, NJ: Princeton University Press, 1968), 44; M. V. Konotopov et al. *Istoriia otechestvennoĭ tekstil' noi promyshlennosti* (Moscow, 1992), 94, 96. This process is also detailed for Alsace in Raymond Oberlé, "La siècle des lumières et les débuts de l'industrialisation," in George Livet and Raymond Oberlé, eds., *Histoire de Mulhouse des origines à nos jours* (Strasbourg: Istra, 1977), 127; Paul Leuilliot, "L'essor économique du XIXe siècle et les transformations de la cité," in Livet and Oberlé, eds., *Histoire de Mulhouse*, 182.

12. For the concept of proto-industrialization see P. Kriedte, H. Medick, and J. Schlumbohm, *Industrialization Before Industrialization: Rural Industry in the Genesis of Capitalism* (New York: Cambridge University Press, 1981); Meerwein, "Die Entwicklung der Chemnitzer," 17–18; Thomson, *A Distinctive Industrialization*, 13.

13. Albert Tanner, *Spulen, Weben, Sticken: Die Industrialisierung in Appenzell Ausserrhoden* (Zürich: Juris Druck, 1982), 8, 19; Bodmer, *Die Entwicklung der schweizerischen Textilwirtschaft*, 231; John Bowring, *Bericht an das Englische Parlament über den Handel, die Fabriken und Gewerbe der Schweiz* (Zürich: Orell, Fuessli und Compagnie, 1837), 37.

14. Shepard B. Clough, *The Economic History of Modern Italy* (New York: Columbia University Press, 1964), 62; Thomson, *A Distinctive Industrialization*, 12; Adelmann, *Die Baumwollgewerbe Nordwestdeutschlands*, 49. On the *obrajes* see the important work by Richard J. Salvucci, *Textiles and Capitalism in Mexico: An Economic History of the Obrajes, 1539–1840* (Princeton, NJ: Princeton University Press, 1987); Müller, "Die Textilindustrie des Raumes Puebla," 34.

15. Meerwein, "Die Entwicklung der Chemnitzer," 18.

16. Bodmer, *Die Entwicklung der schweizerischen Textilwirtschaft*, 279, 339; Thomson, *A Distinctive Industrialization*, 208; Lévy, *Histoire économique*, 1ff., 14–52; Roger Portal, "Muscovite Industrialists: The Cotton Sector, 1861–1914," in Blackwell, ed., *Russian Economic Development*, 174.

17. Barbara M. Tucker, *Samuel Slater and the Origins of the American Textile Industry, 1790–1860* (Ithaca, NY: Cornell University Press, 1984), 52, 97.

18. William Holmes to James Holmes, Kingston, March 10, 1813, in Folder 49, John Holmes Papers, Manuscripts and Archives Division, New York Public Library, New York.

19. Meerwein, "Die Entwicklung der Chemnitzer," 32; *Enciclopedia Yucatanense*, vol. 7, 62. On the annual wages of skilled workers see Michael P. Costeloe, *The Central Republic in Mexico, 1835–1846: Hombres de Bien in the Age of Santa Anna* (New York: Cambridge University Press, 1993), 108. Hau, *L'industrialisation de l'Alsace*, 328, 330, 340.

20. Robert F. Dalzell, *Enterprising Elite: The Boston Associates and the World They Made* (Cambridge, MA: Harvard University Press, 1987), 27. The exchange rate is taken from Patrick Kelly, *The Universal Cambist and Commercial Instructor: Being a General Treatise on Exchange, Including Monies, Coins, Weights and Measures of All Trading Nations and Their Colonies*, vol. 1 (London: Lackington, Allen, and Co. [et al.], 1811), 12; Thomas Dublin, "Rural Putting-Out Work in Early Nineteenth-Century New England: Women and the Transition to Capitalism in the Countryside," *New England Quarterly* 64, no. 4 (December 1, 1991): 536–37. See the analysis of ex-slaves' narratives at "Ex-Slave Narratives: Lowell Cloth," accessed August 12, 2013, http://library.uml.edu/clh/All/Lowcl.htm; Pierre Gervais, "The Cotton 'Factory' in a Pre-industrial Economy: An Exploration of the Boston Manufacturing Company, 1815–1820" (unpublished paper, in author's possession, 2003), 3; Peter Temin, "Product Quality and Vertical Integration in the Early Cotton Textile Industry," *Journal of Economic History* 48, no. 4 (December 1988): 897; Ronald Bailey, "The Other Side of Slavery: Black Labor, Cotton, and Textile Industrialization in Great Britain and the United States," *Agricultural History* 68, no. 2 (Spring 1994): 45, 49.

21. Hau, *L'industrialisation de l'Alsace*, 335–38; Heinrich Herkner, *Die oberelsässische Baumwollindustrie und ihre Arbeiter* (Strassburg: K. J. Trübner, 1887), 92; Pierre-Alain Wavre, "Swiss Investments in Italy from the XVIIIth to the XXth Century," *Journal of European Economic History* 17, no. 1 (Spring 1988), 86–87; Thomson, *A Distinctive Industrialization*, 7, 117 ; Müller, "Die Textilindustrie des Raumes Puebla," 225, 244.

22. M. L. Gavlin, *Iz istorii rossiĭskogo predprinimatel'stva: dinastiia Knopov: nauchno-analiticheskiĭ obzor* (Moscow: INION AN SSSR, 1995), 12, 14, 16, 19, 21, 29ff., 36; Blackwell, *The Beginnings*, 241.

23. Hau, *L'industrialisation de l'Alsace*, 388; Paulette Teissonniere-Jestin, "Itinéraire social d'une grande famille mulhousienne: Les Schlumberger de 1830 à 1930" (PhD dissertation, University of Limoges, 1982), 129, 149; *Bulletin de la Société Industrielle de Mulhouse* 1 (1828); *Bulletin de la Société Industrielle de Mulhouse* 2 (1829); *Bulletin de la Société Industrielle de Mulhouse* 22 (1832): 113–36 ; David Allen Harvey, *Constructing Class and Nationality in Alsace, 1830–1945* (Dekalb: Northern Illinois University Press, 2001), 49.

24. Adelmann, *Die Baumwollgewerbe Nordwestdeutschlands*, 67.

25. Wright Armitage to Enoch Armitage, Dukinfield, April 16, 1817, in Armitage Papers, Manuscripts and Archives Division, New York Public Library, New York; see also the letters in the Papers of McConnel & Kennedy, record group MCK, box 2/1/1; Letterbook, 1805–1810, box 2/2/3; Letterbook, May 1814 to September 1816, box 2/2/5; Consignments Book, 1809–1829, box 3/3/11; Buchanan, Mann & Co. to McConnel

& Kennedy, Calcutta, November 3, 1824, box 2/1/30, all in Papers of McConnel & Kennedy, John Rylands Library, Manchester; William Radcliffe, *Origin of the New System of Manufacture Commonly Called "Power-loom Weaving" and the Purposes for which this System was Invented and Brought into Use* (Stockport: J. Lomax, 1828), 131. Analysis of all correspondence of McConnel & Kennedy for the year 1825 in McConnel & Kennedy Papers, Record Group MCK/2, John Rylands Library, Manchester; D. A. Farnie, *John Rylands of Manchester* (Manchester: John Rylands University Library of Manchester, 1993), 5, 10, 13. See also Memorial Book for John Rylands, 1888, Manchester, Record Group JRL/2/2, Archive of Rylands & Sons Ltd, John Rylands Library, Manchester.

26. Yarn Delivery Book, 1836–38, record group MCK, box 3/3/12, Papers of McConnel & Kennedy, John Rylands Library, Manchester; Stanley Chapman, *Merchant Enterprise in Britain: From the Industrial Revolution to World War I* (Cambridge: Cambridge University Press, 1992), 62, 69ff., 92, 109, 113, 133, 136, 139, 164, 168, 173, 176; Bill Williams, *The Making of Manchester Jewry, 1740–1875* (Manchester: Manchester University Press, 1976), 81. Farnie, *John Rylands*, 4; *British Packet and Argentine News*, February 9, 1850, August 3, 1850; Vera Blinn Reber, *British Mercantile Houses in Buenos Aires, 1810–1880* (Cambridge, MA: Harvard University Press, 1979), 58, 59; Carlos Newland, "Exports and Terms of Trade in Argentina, 1811–1870," *Bulletin of Latin American Research* 17, no. 3 (1998): 409–16; D. C. M. Platt, *Latin America and British Trade, 1806–1914* (London: Adam & Charles Black, 1972), 15, 39; H. S. Ferns, "Investment and Trade Between Britain and Argentina in the Nineteenth Century," *Economic History Review*, New Series, 3, no. 2 (1950): 207, 210; Blankenhagen & Gethen to Hugh Dallas, London, November 18, 1818, file 003/1–1/24, Dallas Papers, in Banco de la Provincia de Buenos Aires, Archivo y Museo Históricos, Buenos Aires. See also R. F. Alexander to Hugh Dallas, Glasgow, March 19, 1819, in ibid. Some merchants also wrote to Dallas and asked him if he would accept consignments from them; see for example Baggott y Par to Hugh Dallas, Liverpool, April 2, 1821, in ibid., file 003/1–1/13; King & Morrison to Hugh Dallas, Glasgow, April 25, 1819, in Blankenhagen & Gethen to Hugh Dallas, London, November 18, 1818, in ibid.

27. D. C. M. Platt, *Latin America and British Trade*, 39, 42, 51; Eugene W. Ridings, "Business Associationalism, the Legitimation of Enterprise, and the Emergence of a Business Elite in Nineteenth-Century Brazil," *Business History Review* 63, no. 4 (Winter 1989): 758; Stanley J. Stein, *The Brazilian Cotton Manufacture: Textile Enterprise in an Underdeveloped Area, 1850–1950* (Cambridge, MA: Harvard University Press, 1957), 8–9, 14.

28. Bodmer, *Die Entwicklung der schweizerischen Textilwirtschaft*, 231, 276, 281; Adelmann, *Die Baumwollgewerbe Nordwestdeutschlands*, 58; Dehn, *The German Cotton Industry*, 3.

29. See Warren C. Scoville, "Spread of Techniques: Minority Migrations and the Diffusion of Technology," *Journal of Economic History* 11, no. 4 (1951): 347–60; Adelmann, *Die Baumwollgewerbe Nordwestdeutschlands*, 72; Dunham, "The Development of the Cotton Industry," 283; Jack A. Goldstone, "Gender, Work, and Culture: Why the Industrial Revolution Came Early to England but Late to China," *Sociological Perspectives* 39, no. 1 (Spring 1996): 2.

30. W. O. Henderson, *Britain and Industrial Europe, 1750–1870: Studies in British Influ-*

ence on the Industrial Revolution in Western Europe (Liverpool: Liverpool University Press, 1954), 4, 7, 102, 267; Kristine Bruland, *British Technology and European Industrialization: The Norwegian Textile Industry in the Mid-Nineteenth Century* (New York: Cambridge University Press, 1989), 3, 14; David J. Jeremy, *Damming the Flood: British Government Efforts to Check the Outflow of Technicians and Machinery, 1780–1843* (Boston: Harvard Business School Press, 1977), 32–33; Jan Dhont and Marinette Bruwier, "The Low Countries, 1700–1914," in Cipolla, ed., *The Fontana Economic History of Europe*, vol. 4, part 1, 348; Adelmann, *Die Baumwollgewerbe Nordwestdeutschlands*, 77, 127; David J. Jeremy, *Transatlantic Industrial Revolution: The Diffusion of Textile Technology Between Britain and America, 1790–1830* (North Andover and Cambridge, MA: Merrimack Valley Textile Museum/MIT Press, 1981), 17; David Landes, *The Unbound Prometheus: Technological Change and Industrial Development in Western Europe from 1750 to the Present* (Cambridge: Cambridge University Press, 1969), 148; Rondo Cameron, "The Diffusion of Technology as a Problem in Economic History," *Economic Geography* 51, no. 3 (July 1975): 221; John Macgregor, *The Commercial and Financial Legislation of Europe and North America* (London: Henry Hooper, 1841), 290.

31. Dominique Barjot, "Les entrepreneurs de Normandie, du Maine et de l'Anjou à l'époque du Second Empire," *Annales de Normandie* 38, no. 2–3 (May–July 1988): 99–103; Henderson, *Britain and Industrial Europe*, 12, 28; Paul Leuilliot, "L'essor économique du XIXe siècle et les transformations de la cité," in Livet and Oberlé, eds., *Histoire de Mulhouse*, 184. See Camille Koechlin, Cahier des notes faites en Angleterre 1831, 667 Ko 22 I, Collection Koechlin, Bibliothèque, Musée de l'Impression sur Etoffes, Mulhouse, France.

32. Bodmer, *Die Entwicklung der schweizerischen Textilwirtschaft*, 276–77; Thomson, *A Distinctive Industrialization*, 249; Henderson, *Britain and Industrial Europe*, 142, 194–95; Andrea Komlosy, "Austria and Czechoslovakia: The Habsburg Monarchy and Its Successor States," in Lex Heerma van Voss, Els Hiemstra-Kuperus, and Elise van Nederveen Meerkerk, eds., *The Ashgate Companion to the History of Textile Workers, 1650–2000* (Burlington, VT: Ashgate, 2010), 53.

33. Müller, "Die Textilindustrie des Raumes Puebla," 108, 109, 237; Jeremy, *Transatlantic Industrial Revolution*, 5, 6, 77, 78; Dalzell, *Enterprising Elite*; Jeremy, *Transatlantic Industrial Revolution*, 41; Bruland, *British Technology*, 18.

34. Bodmer, *Die Entwicklung der schweizerischen Textilwirtschaft*, 278; Meerwein, "Die Entwicklung," 25; Cameron, "The Diffusion of Technology," 220; Hau, *L'industrialisation de l'Alsace*, 366–70, 403ff.; Bernard Volger and Michel Hau, *Historie économique de l'Alsace: Croissance, crises, innovations: Vingt siècles de dévelopement régional* (Strasbourg: Éditions la nuée bleue, 1997), 146ff.; Dave Pretty, "The Cotton Textile Industry in Russia and the Soviet Union," in Van Voss et al., eds., *The Ashgate Companion to the History of Textile Workers*, 424; J. K. J. Thomson, "Explaining the 'Take-off' of the Catalan Cotton Industry," *Economic History Review* 58, no. 4 (November 2005): 727; Letter of Delegates of the Junta de Comercio, legajo 23, no. 21, fos. 6–11, Biblioteca de Catalunya, Barcelona; Herkner, *Die oberelsässische Baumwollindustrie*, 72ff.; Melvin T. Copeland, *The Cotton Manufacturing Industry of the United States* (Cambridge, MA: Harvard University Press, 1917), 9, 69, 70.

35. Mokyr, *Industrialization in the Low Countries*, 39; Adelmann, *Die Baumwollgewerbe Nordwestdeutschlands*, 89–90; Meerwein, "Die Entwicklung," 21; Konotopov et al., *Istoriia*, 79, 92; Lars K. Christensen, "Denmark: The Textile Industry and the Forming of Modern Industry," in Van Voss et al., eds., *The Ashgate Companion to the History of Textile Workers*, 144; Alexander Hamilton, "Report on the Subject of Manufactures, December 5, 1971," in Alexander Hamilton, *Writings* (New York: Library of America, 2001), 647–734; Samuel Rezneck, "The Rise and Early Development of Industrial Consciousness in the United States, 1760–1830," *Journal of Economic and Business History* 4 (1932): 784–811; Müller, "Die Textilindustrie des Raumes Puebla," 41.

36. Adelmann, *Die Baumwollgewerbe Nordwestdeutschlands*, 67; Herkner, *Die oberelsässische Baumwollindustrie*, 92, 95; Hau, *L'industrialisation de l'Alsace*, 209ff.; Oberlé, "La siècle des lumières," 164; Meerwein, "Die Entwicklung," 23, 28, 37, 68.

37. Bodmer, *Die Entwicklung der schweizerischen Textilwirtschaft*, 278; Tanner, *Spulen, Weben, Sticken*, 24, 33, 44.

38. Douglas A. Irwin and Peter Temin, "The Antebellum Tariff on Cotton Textiles Revisited," *Journal of Economic History* 61, no. 3 (September 2001): 795; U. S. Department of the Treasury, Letter from the Secretary of the Treasury, "Cultivation, Manufacture and Foreign Trade of Cotton," March 4, 1836, Doc. No. 146, Treasury Department, House of Representatives, 24th Congress, 1st Session (Washington, DC: Blaire & Rives, Printers, 1836); Jeremy, *Transatlantic Industrial Revolution*, 96; Mary B. Rose, *The Gregs of Quarry Bank Mill: The Rise and Decline of a Family Firm, 1750–1914* (New York: Cambridge University Press, 1986), 46.

39. Wright Armitage to Rev. Benjamin Goodier, Dunkinfield, March 2, 1817, in Box 1, Armitage Family Papers, Special Collections, New York Public Library, New York.

40. Temin, "Product Quality," 898; Dunham, "The Development of the Cotton Industry," 281; Meerwein, "Die Entwicklung," 43; United States Department of State, *Report on the Commercial Relations of the United States with Foreign Nations: Comparative Tariffs; Tabular Statements of the Domestic Exports of the United States; Duties on Importation of the Staple or Principal Production of the United States into Foreign Countries* (Washington, DC: Gales and Seaton, 1842), 534–35.

41. Paul Leuilliot, "L'essor économique du XIXe siècle et les transformations de la cité," in Livet and Oberlé, eds., *Histoire de Mulhouse*, 190; Dietsche, "Die industrielle Entwicklung," 56–57; Meerwein, "Die Entwicklung," 47, 51–52. For the importance of tariffs see also R. Dehn, *The German Cotton Industry*, 4; Kirchhain, "Das Wachstum," 185; Friedrich List, *National System of Political Economy* (New York: Longmans, Green, and Co., 1904), 169; Angel Smith et al., "Spain," in Van Voss et al., *The Ashgate Companion to the History of Textile Workers*, 455. There were many other states that charged high import duties; for a survey see United States Department of State, *Report in the Commercial Relations of the United States with Foreign Nations*, 534–35.

42. Temin, "Product Quality," 897, 898; Irwin and Temin, "The Antebellum Tariff," 780–89, 796. The 84 percent number (which is probably not entirely accurate) is taken from Hannah Josephson, *The Golden Threads: New England Mill Girls and Magnates* (New York: Russell & Russell, 1949), 30. For the role of the "Boston Associates" in the import of Indian cottons, see James Fichter, "Indian Textiles and

American Industrialization, 1790–1820" (unpublished paper, GEHN Conference, University of Padua, November 17–19, 2005, in author's possession).

43. Müller, "Die Textilindustrie des Raumes Puebla," 14, 16, 31, 35, 39, 43, 45, 48, 55; Rafael Dobado Gonzáles, Aurora Gómez Galvarriato, and Jefferey G. Williamson, "Globalization, De-industrialization and Mexican Exceptionalism, 1750–1879," National Bureau of Economic Research Working Paper No. 12316, June 2006, 5, 12, 13, 15, 35, 36, 40; see also Colin M. Lewis, "Cotton Textiles and Labour-Intensive Industrialization Since 1825" (unpublished paper, Global Economic History Network Conference, Osaka, December 16–18, 2004, in author's possession); Esteban de Antuñano, *Memoria breve de la industria manufacturera de México, desde el año de 1821 hasta el presente* (Puebla: Oficina del Hospital de S. Pedro, 1835); Esteban de Antuñano to Señor D. Carlos Bustamante, Puebla, December 4, 1836, as reprinted in Esteban de Antuñano, *Breve memoria del estado que guarda la fabrica de hildaos de algodon Constancia Mexicana y la industria de este ramo* (Puebla: Oficinia des Hospital de San Pedro, 1837), 4; David W. Walker, *Kinship, Business, and Politics: The Martinez del Rio Family in Mexico, 1824–1867* (Austin: University of Texas Press, 1986), 138; Camera de Disputados, *Dictamen de la Comisión de Industria, sobre la prohibición de hilaza y ejidos de algodón* (1835).

44. David W. Walker, *Kinship, Business, and Politics: The Martinez del Rio Family in Mexico, 1824–1867* (Austin: University of Texas Press, 1986), 149, 151, 161–62; Gonzáles, Galvarriato, and Williamson, "Globalization," 41. The number for India refers to the year 1887.

45. J. Thomson, *A Distinctive Industrialization*, 204; Daniel, "Entrepreneurship and the Russian Textile Industry," 8; W. Lochmueller, *Zur Entwicklung der Baumwollindustrie in Deutschland* (Jena: Gustav Fischer, 1906), 17; Hans-Werner Hahn, *Die industrielle Revolution in Deutschland* (Munich: R. Oldenbourg, 1998), 27. For a survey on the impact of states on European industrialization see Barry Supple, "The State and the Industrial Revolution, 1700–1914," in Carlo M. Cipolla, ed., *The Fontana Economic History of Europe*, vol. 3 (Glasgow: Collins, 1977), 301–57.

46. J. Thomson, *A Distinctive Industrialization*, 270; Jordi Nadal, "Spain, 1830–1914," in Carlo M. Cipolla, ed., *The Fontana Economic History of Europe*, vol. 4, part 2, 607; Smith et al., "Spain," in Van Voss et al., *The Ashgate Companion to the History of Textile Workers*, 453.

47. Thomson, "Explaining," 711–17.

48. Thomson, *A Distinctive Industrialization*, 274–75, 299. In 1793, Spanish producers were using 16.06 percent as much raw cotton as in Britain, by 1808 that percentage had fallen to 6–7.25 percent, and by 1816 to 2.2 percent; James Clayburn La Force Jr., *The Development of the Spanish Textile Industry, 1750–1800* (Berkeley: University of California Press, 1965), 16; Jordi Nadal, "Spain, 1830–1914," in Cipolla, *The Fontana Economic History of Europe*, vol. 4, part 2, 608.

49. Edward Baines, *History of the Cotton Manufacture in Great Britain* (London: H. Fisher, R. Fisher, and P. Jackson, 1835), 525; Wilma Pugh, "Calonne's 'New Deal,'" *Journal of Modern History* 11, no. 3 (1939): 289–312; François-Joseph Ruggiu, "India and the Reshaping of the French Colonial Policy, 1759–1789," in *Itinerario* 35, no. 2 (August 2011): 25–43; Alfons van der Kraan, "The Birth of the Dutch Cotton

Industry, 1830–1840," in Douglas A. Farnie and David J. Jeremy, eds., *The Fibre that Changed the World: The Cotton Industry in International Perspective, 1600–1990s* (Oxford: Oxford University Press, 2004), 285; Jan Luiten van Zanden and Arthur van Riel, *The Strictures of Inheritance: The Dutch Economy in the Nineteenth Century* (Princeton, NJ: Princeton University Press, 2004), 39–40; Mokyr, *Industry* 32, 103, 105, 107, 108.

50. Mokyr, *Industry*, 31, 34–35; Dhont and Bruwier, "The Low Countries, 1700–1914," 358–59.

51. Bodmer, *Die Entwicklung der schweizerischen Textilwirtschaft*, 290, 344–46; Bowring, *Bericht an das Englische Parlament*, 4. Tanner, "The Cotton Industry of Eastern Switzerland," 150. The German cotton industry, in similar ways, relied to an important extent on its ability to export, especially to North America; Dehn, *The German Cotton Industry*, 18; Dietrich Ebeling et al., "The German Wool and Cotton Industry from the Sixteenth to the Twentieth Century," in Van Voss et al., *The Ashgate Companion to the History of Textile Workers*, 208.

52. Mary Jo Maynes, "Gender, Labor, and Globalization in Historical Perspective: European Spinsters in the International Textile Industry, 1750–1900," *Journal of Women's History* 15, no. 4 (Winter 2004): 48.

53. Chapman, *The Cotton Industry*, 22; C. H. Lee, "The Cotton Textile Industry," in Roy Church, ed., *The Dynamics of Victorian Business: Problems and Perspectives to the 1870s* (London: George Allen & Unwin, 1980), 161; Adelmann, *Die Baumwollgewerbe Nordwestdeutschlands*, 153; Dunham, "The Development of the Cotton Industry," 288; Richard Leslie Hills, *Power from Steam: A History of the Stationary Steam Engine* (New York: Cambridge University Press, 1989), 117. These numbers are notoriously inaccurate and are just approximations. Chapman, *The Cotton Industry*, 29; Anthony Howe, *The Cotton Masters, 1830–1860* (New York: Clarendon Press, 1984), 6; *The Thirty-Fifth Annual Report of the Board of Directors of the Chamber of Commerce and Manufactures at Manchester, for the Year 1855* (Manchester: James Collins, 1856), 15.

54. Joseph E. Inikori, *Africans and the Industrial Revolution in England: A Study in International Trade and Economic Development* (New York: Cambridge University Press, 2002), 436; P. K. O'Brien and S. L. Engerman, "Exports and the Growth of the British Economy from the Glorious Revolution to the Peace of Amiens," in Barbara Solow, ed., *Slavery and the Rise of the Atlantic System* (New York: Cambridge University Press, 1991), 184, 188; Lee, "The Cotton Textile Industry," 165; Lars G. Sandberg, "Movements in the Quality of British Cotton Textile Exports," *Journal of Economic History* 28, no. 1 (March 1968): 15–19; Manchester Commercial Association Minutes, 1845–1858, record group M8/7/1, Manchester Archives and Library, Manchester.

55. For this argument, see also Jeremy Adelman, "Non-European Origins of European Revolutions" (unpublished paper, Making Europe: The Global Origins of the Old World Conference, Freiburg, 2010), 25.

56. Afaf Lutfi Al-Sayyid Marsot, *Egypt in the Reign of Muhammad Ali* (Cambridge: Cambridge University Press, 1984), 162; Robert L. Tignor, *Egyptian Textiles and British Capital, 1930–1956* (Cairo: American University in Cairo Press, 1989), 9; Joel Beinin, "Egyptian Textile Workers: From Craft Artisans Facing European Competition to Proletarians Contending with the State," in Van Voss et al., *The Ashgate Companion to the History of Textile Workers*, 174.

57. Tignor, *Egyptian Textiles*, 9; Marsot, *Egypt*, 166; Owen, *Cotton and the Egyptian Economy*, 23–24.

58. Jean Batou, "Muhammad-Ali's Egypt, 1805–1848: A Command Economy in the 19th Century?," in Jean Batou, ed., *Between Development and Underdevelopment: The Precocious Attempts at Industrialization of the Periphery, 1800–1870* (Geneva: Librairie Droz, 1991), 187; Owen, *Cotton and the Egyptian Economy*, 44.

59. Marsot, *Egypt*, 171, 181. By 1838, as many as thirty thousand workers might have labored in Egypt's cotton spinning mills. Colonel Campbell, Her Britannic Majesty's Agent and Consul-General in Egypt to John Bowring, Cairo, January 18, 1838, as reprinted in John Bowring, *Report on Egypt and Candia* (London: Her Majesty's Stationery Office, 1840), 186; Batou, "Muhammad-Ali's Egypt," 181, 185, 199; *Ausland* (1831), 1016.

60. Marsot, *Egypt*, 171; Colonel Campbell, Her Britannic Majesty's Agent and Consul-General in Egypt to John Bowring, Cairo, January 18, 1838, as reprinted in Bowring, *Report on Egypt*, 35; *Asiatic Journal and Monthly Register for British and Foreign India, China, and Australia*, New Series, 4 (March 1831): 133.

61. *Asiatic Journal and Monthly Register for British and Foreign India, China, and Australia*, New Series, 5 (May–August 1831): 62; *Asiatic Journal and Monthly Register for British and Foreign India, China, and Australia*, New Series, 4 (April 1831): 179, quoting an article from the *Indian Gazette*, October 5, 1830.

62. Rapport à Son Altesse Mehemet Ali, Vice Roi d'Égypt, sur la Filature et le Tissage du Cotton, par Jules Poulain, f78, Add. Mss. 37466, Egyptian State Papers, 1838–1849, Manuscript Division, British Library, London.

63. Marsot, *Egypt*, 169, 184; Beinin, "Egyptian Textile Workers," 177.

64. Batou, "Muhammad-Ali's Egypt," 182, 201–2; *Historical Dictionary of Egypt*, 3rd ed. (Lanham, MD: Scarecrow Press, 2003), 388; Marsot, *Egypt*, 177; Tignor, *Egyptian Textiles*, 8; Beinin, "Egyptian Textile Workers," 178; Joel Beinin, "Egyptian Textile Workers: From Craft Artisans Facing European Competition to Proletarians Contending with the State" (unpublished paper, Textile Conference IISH, November 2004), 6.

65. The existence of a vibrant proto-industry is rightly emphasized in John Dickinson and Robert Delson, "Enterprise Under Colonialism: A Study of Pioneer Industrialization in Brazil, 1700–1830" (working paper, Institute of Latin American Studies, University of Liverpool, 1991), esp. 52; see also Herculano Gomes Mathias, *Algodão no Brasil* (Rio de Janeiro: Index Editoria, 1988), 67, 83; Maria Regina and Ciparrone Mello, *A industrialização do algodão em São Paulo* (São Paulo: Editoria Perspectiva, 1983), 23; Stein, *The Brazilian Cotton Manufacture*, 2, 4, 20–21; Roberta Marx Delson, "Brazil: The Origin of the Textile Industry," in Van Voss et al., *The Ashgate Companion to the History of Textile Workers*, 75, 77, 934; Gonzáles, Galvarriato, and Williamson, "Globalization," 17.

66. Stein, *The Brazilian Cotton Manufacture*, 15.

67. Ibid., 7, 13; Eugene W. Ridings Jr., "The Merchant Elite and the Development of Brazil: The Case of Bahia During the Empire," *Journal of Interamerican Studies and World Affairs* 15, no. 3 (August 1973): 336, 337, 342–45.

68. Stein, *The Brazilian Cotton Manufacture*, 5–6, 51–52; Ridings Jr., "The Merchant Elite and the Development of Brazil," 344.

69. W. A. Graham Clark, *Cotton Goods in Latin America: Part 1, Cuba, Mexico, and*

Central America: Transmitted to Congress in Compliance with the Act of March 4, 1909 Authorizing Investigations of Trade Conditions Abroad (Washington, DC: Government Printing Office, 1909), 9.

70. Even an author who tries to show the importance of "southern industrialization" ends up providing ample evidence for the feeble nature of these efforts. See Michael Gagnon, *Transition to an Industrial South: Athens, Georgia, 1830–1870* (Baton Rouge: Lousiana State University Press, 2012); Broadus Mitchell, *The Rise of Cotton Mills in the South* (Baltimore: Johns Hopkins University Press, 1921), 21. In 1831, cloth output in the North was seventeen times as large as that in the slave states. See Friends of Domestic Industry, Reports of the Committees of the Friends of Domestic Industry, assembled at New York, Octber 31, 1831 (1831), 9–47. There is also a fundamental discontinuity between these mills and later southern industrialization.

71. Richard Roberts, "West Africa and the Pondicherry Textile Industry," *Indian Economic and Social History Review* 31, no. 2 (June 1994): 142–45, 151, 153, 158; Tirthankar Roy, "The Long Globalization and Textile Producers in India," in Van Voss et al., *The Ashgate Companion to the History of Textile Workers*, 266; Dwijendra Tripathi, *Historical Roots of Industrial Entrepreneurship in India and Japan: A Comparative Interpretation* (New Delhi: Manohar, 1997), 104, 105.

72. Howard F. Cline, "The Spirit of Enterprise in Yucatan," 138; Jorge Munoz Gonzalez, *Valladolid: 450 Años de Luz* (Valladolid: Ayuntamiento de Valladolid, 1993), 40; Ramírez, *Sociedad, Estructura Agraria*, 35.

73. Dale W. Tomich, *Through the Prism of Slavery* (Lanham, MD: Rowman & Littefield, 2004), 70.

74. Rosa Luxemburg, *The Accumulation of Capital* (New Haven, CT: Yale University Press, 1951), chapter 26.

CHAPTER SEVEN: MOBILIZING INDUSTRIAL LABOR

1. "Fragen eines lesenden Arbeiters," translated by M. Hamburger, *Bertolt Brecht: Poems, 1913–1956,* (New York and London: Methuen, 1976).

2. For the quotation, see forum post by "The Longford," March 9, 2009, http://www.skyscrapercity.com/showthread.php?t=823790, accessed March 8, 2013; Ellen Hootton's case is documented in House of Commons Parliamentary Papers, First Report of the Central Board of His Majesty's Commissioners for Inquiring into the Employment of Children in Factories, 1833, xx, D.i, 103–15. Her history has also been beautifully analyzed by Douglas A. Galbi, "Through the Eyes in the Storm: Aspects of the Personal History of Women Workers in the Industrial Revolution," *Social History* 21, no. 2 (1996): 142–59.

3. Maurice Dobb, *Studies in the Development of Capitalism* (New York: International Publishers, 1964), 272–73.

4. Mike Williams and Douglas A. Farnie, *Cotton Mills in Greater Manchester* (Preston, UK: Carnegie, 1992), 236; Stanley D. Chapman, *The Early Factory Masters: The Transition to the Factory System in the Midlands Textile Industry* (Newton Abbot, Devon, UK: David & Charles, 1967), 170.

5. Leone Levi, "On the Cotton Trade and Manufacture, as Affected by the Civil War in America," *Journal of the Statistical Society of London* 26, no. 8 (March 1863): 26.

6. Mary B. Rose, *Networks and Business Values: The British and American Cotton Industries Since 1750* (Cambridge: Cambridge University Press, 2000), 30; Günter Kirchhain, "Das Wachstum der Deutschen Baumwollindustrie im 19. Jahrhundert: Eine Historische Modellstudie zur Empirischen Wachstumsforschung" (PhD dissertation, University of Münster, 1973), 73; Gerhard Adelmann, "Zur regionalen Differenzierung der Baumwoll-und Seidenverarbeitung und der Textilen Spezialfertigungen Deutschlands, 1846–1907," in Hans Pohl, ed., *Gewerbe und Industrielandschaften vom Spätmittelalter bis ins 20. Jahrhundert* (Stuttgart: Franz Steiner, 1986), 293; Hans-Ulrich Wehler, *Deutsche Gesellschaftsgeschichte*, vol. 2 (Munich: Verlag C. H. Beck, 1987), 92; Michel Hau, *L'industrialisation de l'Alsace, 1803–1939* (Strasbourg: Association des Publications près les Universités de Strasbourg, 1987), 89; Jean-François Bergier, *Histoire économique de la Suisse* (Lausanne: Payot, 1984), 192. Another source estimated the number of cotton workers in the United States in 1830 as 179,000. See Letter from the Secretary of the Treasury, Cultivation, Manufacture and Foreign Trade of Cotton, March 4, 1836, Doc. No. 146, Treasury Department, House of Representatives, 24th Congress, 1st Session, in Levi Woodbury, *Woodbury's Tables and Notes on the Cultivation, Manufacture, and Foreign Trade of Cotton* (Washington, DC: Printed by Blaire & Rives, 1836), 51. On Russia, see A. Khromov, *Ekonomicheskoe razvitie Rossii v XIX-XX Vekah: 1800–1917* (Moscow: Gos. Izd. Politicheskoi Literatury, 1950), 32; Dave Pretty, "The Cotton Textile Industry in Russia and the Soviet Union," in Lex Heerma van Voss, Els Hiemstra-Kuperus, and Elise van Nederveen Meerkerk, eds., *The Ashgate Companion to the History of Textile Workers, 1650–2000* (Burlington, VT: Ashgate, 2010), 425, 428; Michael Jansen, *De industriële ontwikkeling in Nederland 1800–1850* (Amsterdam: NEHA, 1999), 149, 333–36; CBS, *Volkstelling 1849*, estimates by Elise van Nederveen Meerkerk, correspondence with the author, October 29, 2013. For Spain see Angel Smith et al., "Spain," in Van Voss et al., eds., *The Ashgate Companion to the History of Textile Workers*, 456; more than 90 percent of Spain's cotton industry was located in Catalonia. J. K. J. Thomson, *A Distinctive Industrialization: Cotton in Barcelona, 1728–1832* (Cambridge: Cambridge University Press, 1992), 262.

7. See Karl Polanyi, *The Great Transformation: The Political and Economic Origins of Our Time* (Boston: Beacon Press, 1957), 72; in chapter 6 Polanyi writes about land, labor, and money as fictitious commodities.

8. As cited in E. P. Thompson, *The Making of the English Working Class* (New York: Vintage, 1966), 190; see also S. D. Chapman, *The Cotton Industry in the Industrial Revolution* (London: Macmillan, 1972), 53.

9. Charles Tilly, "Did the Cake of Custom Break?" in John M. Merriman, ed., *Consciousness and Class Experience in Nineteenth-Century Europe* (New York: Holmes & Meier Publishers, 1979); Eugen Weber, *Peasants into Frenchmen: The Modernization of Rural France, 1870–1914* (Stanford, CA: Stanford University Press, 1976).

10. Robert J. Steinfeld, *Coercion, Contract, and Free Labor in the Nineteenth Century* (Cambridge: Cambridge University Press, 2001), 20.

11. Ibid., 47, 74–75, 317; "Gesetzesammlung für die Königlichen Preussischen Staaten, 1845," as cited in ibid., 245.

12. Marta Vicente, "Artisans and Work in a Barcelona Cotton Factory, 1770–1816," *International Review of Social History* 45 (2000): 3, 4, 12, 13, 18.

13. Employment Ledger for Dover Manufacturing Company, 1823–4 (Dover, NH), Dover-Cocheco Collection, Baker Library, Harvard Business School, Cambridge, MA.

14. Benjamin Martin, *The Agony of Modernization: Labor and Industrialization in Spain* (Ithaca, NY: ILR Press, 1990), 21; Georg Meerwein, *Die Entwicklung der Chemnitzer bezw. Sächsischen Baumwollspinnerei von 1789–1879* (PhD dissertation, University of Heidelberg, 1914), 21; Walter Bodmer, *Die Entwicklung der Schweizerischen Textilwirtschaft im Rahmen der übrigen Industrien und Wirtschaftszweige* (Zürich: Verlag Berichthaus, 1960), 220, 224, 227; L. Dunham, "The Development of the Cotton Industry in France and the Anglo-French Treaty of Commerce of 1860," *Economic History Review* 1, no. 2 (January 1928): 286; Robert Lévy, *Histoire économique de l'industrie cotonnière en Alsace* (Paris: F. Alcan, 1912), 1ff.; David Allen Harvey, *Constructing Class and Nationality in Alsace, 1830–1945* (Dekalb: Northern Illinois University Press, 2001), 56; Thomson, *A Distinctive Industrialization*, 259.

15. Robert Marx Delson, "How Will We Get Our Workers? Ethnicity and Migration of Global Textile Workers," in Van Voss et al., eds., *The Ashgate Companion to the History of Textile Workers*, 662, 665; G. Bischoff, "Guebwiller vers 1830: La vie économique et sociale d'une petite ville industrielle à la fin de la Restauration," *Annuaire de la Société d'Histoire des Régions de Thann–Guebwiller* 7 (1965–1967): 64–74; Elise van Nederveen Meerkerk et al., "The Netherlands," in Van Voss et al., eds., *The Ashgate Companion to the History of Textile Workers*, 383; Joel Mokyr, *Industrialization in the Low Countries, 1795–1850* (New Haven, CT: Yale University Press, 1976), 38.

16. Bodmer, *Die Entwicklung der Schweizerischen Textilwirtschaft*, 295, 298; Delson, "How Will We Get Our Workers?" 652–53, 666–67; Erik Amburger, *Die Anwerbung ausländischer Fachkräfte für die Wirtschaft Russlands vom 15. bis ins 19. Jahrhundert* (Wiesbaden: Otto Harrassowitz, 1968), 147.

17. Meeting of the Manchester Chamber of Commerce, 1st February 1826, Proceedings of the Manchester Chamber of Commerce, 1821–1827, Record Group M8, Box 2/1, Archives of the Manchester Chamber of Commerce, Manchester Archives and Local Studies, Manchester; Gary Saxonhouse and Gavin Wright, "Two Forms of Cheap Labor in Textile History," in Gary Saxonhouse and Gavin Wright, eds., *Technique, Spirit and Form in the Making of the Modern Economies: Essays in Honor of William N. Parker* (Greenwich, CT: JAI Press, 1984), 7; Robert F. Dalzell, *Enterprising Elite: The Boston Associates and the World They Made* (Cambridge, MA: Harvard University Press, 1987), 33.

18. For the information relating to the Dover Manufacturing Company see Payroll Account Books, 1823–1824, Dover Manufacturing Company, Dover, New Hampshire, in Cocheco Manufacturing Company Papers, Baker Library, Harvard Business School, Cambridge, MA; Barbara M. Tucker, *Samuel Slater and the Origins of the American Textile Industry, 1790–1860* (Ithaca, NY: Cornell University Press, 1984), 139.

19. Carolyn Tuttle and Simone Wegge, "The Role of Child Labor in Industrialization" (presentation, Economic History Seminar, Harvard University, April 2004), 21, 49; McConnel & Kennedy Papers, MCK/4/51, John Rylands Library, Manchester.

20. Terry Wyke, "Quarry Bank Mill, Styal, Cheshire," Revealing Histories, Remembering Slavery, accessed July 21, 2012, http://www.revealinghistories.org.uk/how-did-money-from-slavery-help-develop-greater-manchester/places/quarry-bank-mill-styal-cheshire.html; Mary B. Rose, *The Gregs of Quarry Bank Mill: The Rise and Decline of a Family Firm, 1750–1914* (Cambridge: Cambridge University Press, 1986), 28, 31, 109–10; George Unwin, *Samuel Oldknow and the Arkwrights: The Industrial Revolution at Stockport and Marple* (Manchester: Manchester University Press, 1924), 170–71; *Edinburgh Review, or Critical Journal* 61, no. 124 (July 1835): 464.

21. Tuttle and Wegge, "The Role of Child Labor in Industrialization," Table 1A, Table 2, Table 3a; Gerhard Adelmann, *Die Baumwollgewerbe Nordwestdeutschlands und der westlichen Nachbarländer beim Übergang von der vorindustriellen zur frühindustriellen Zeit, 1750–1815* (Stuttgart: Franz Steiner Verlag, 2001), 96; M. V. Konotopov et al., *Istorüa otechestvennoi tekstil'noi promyshlennosti* (Moscow: Legprombytizdat, 1992), 97; Meerwein, *Die Entwicklung der Chemnitzer*, 35; M. M. Gutiérrez, *Comercio libre o funesta teoría de la libertad económica absoluta* (Madrid: M. Calero, 1834); Wolfgang Müller, "Die Textilindustrie des Raumes Puebla (Mexiko) im 19. Jahrhundert" (PhD dissertation, University of Bonn, 1977), 279, 281; "Rapport de la commission chargée d'examiner la question relative à l'emploi des enfants dans les filatures de coton," in *Bulletin de la Société Industrielle de Mulhouse* (1837), 482, 493; Harvey, *Constructing Class and Nationality in Alsace*, 54; Marjatta Rahikainen, *Centuries of Child Labour: European Experiences from the Seventeenth to the Twentieth Century* (Hampshire, UK: Ashgate 2004), 133.

22. Maxine Berg, "What Difference Did Women's Work Make to the Industrial Revolution?" in Pamela Sharpe, ed., *Women's Work: The English Experience, 1650–1914* (London: Arnold, 1998), 154, 158; Mary Jo Maynes, "Gender, Labor, and Globalization in Historical Perspective: European Spinsters in the International Textile Industry, 1750–1900," *Journal of Women's History* 15, no. 4 (Winter 2004): 56; Payroll Account Books, 1823–1824, Dover Manufacturing Company, Dover, New Hampshire, Cocheco Manufacturing Company Papers, Baker Library, Harvard Business School, Cambridge, MA; Janet Hunter and Helen Macnaughtan, "Gender and the Global Textile Industry," in Van Voss et al., eds., *The Ashgate Companion to the History of Textile Workers*, 705.

23. Hunter and Macnaughtan, "Gender and the Global Textile Industry," 705; Maynes, "Gender, Labor, and Globalization in Historical Perspective," 51, 54; William Rathbone VI to William Rathbone V, Baltimore, May 13, 1841, in Box IX.3.53–82, RP, Rathbone Papers, Special Collections and Archives, University of Liverpool; William Rathbone VI to William Rathbone V, Boston, June 18, 1841, in ibid.

24. Hunter and Macnaughtan, "Gender and the Global Textile Industry," 710, 715; Berg, "What Difference Did Women's Work Make to the Industrial Revolution?" 154, 158, 168.

25. Maynes, "Gender, Labor, and Globalization in Historical Perspective," 55; Kenneth Pomeranz, "Cotton Textiles, Division of Labor and the Economic and Social Conditions of Women: A Preliminary Survey" (presentation, Conference 5: Cotton Textiles, Global Economic History Network, Osaka, December 2004), 20; Jack A. Goldstone, "Gender, Work, and Culture: Why the Industrial Revolution Came Early

to England but Late to China," *Sociological Perspectives* 39, no. 1 (Spring 1996): 1–21; Philip C. C. Huang, *The Peasant Family and Rural Development in the Yangzi Delta, 1350–1988* (Stanford, CA: Stanford University Press, 1990), 91 and 110ff.

26. J. Dhondt, "The Cotton Industry at Ghent During the French Regime," in F. Crouzet, W. H. Chaloner, and W. M. Stern, eds., *Essays in European Economic History, 1789–1914* (London: Edward Arnold, 1969), 21; Wallace Daniel, "Entrepreneurship and the Russian Textile Industry: From Peter the Great to Catherine the Great," *Russian Review* 54 (January 1995): 7; I. D. Maulsby, Maryland General Assembly, Joint Committee on the Penitentiary, *Testimony Taken Before the Joint Committee of the Legislature of Maryland, on the Penitentiary* (Annapolis, 1837), 31; Rebecca McLennan, *The Crisis of Imprisonment: Protest, Politics, and the Making of the American Penal State, 1776–1941* (New York: Cambridge University Press, 2008), 66; Dave Pretty, "The Cotton Textile Industry in Russia and the Soviet Union" (presentation, Textile Conference, International Institute of Social History, Amsterdam, November 2004), 7; M. L. Gavlin, *Iz istorii rossiiskogo predprinimatel'stva: dinastiia Knopov: nauchno-analiticheskii obzor* (Moscow: INION AN SSSR, 1995), 34–35; Wolfgang Müller, "Die Textilindustrie des Raumes Puebla (Mexiko) im 19. Jahrhundert," 298–99; Max Hamburger, "Standortgeschichte der Deutschen Baumwoll-Industrie" (PhD dissertation, University of Heidelberg, 1911); Andrea Komlosy, "Austria and Czechoslavakia: The Habsburg Monarchy and Its Successor States," in Van Voss et al., eds., *The Ashgate Companion to the History of Textile Workers*, 57.

27. Delson, "How Will We Get Our Workers?" 657–58, 660; "In our country" cited in Stanley J. Stein, *The Brazilian Cotton Manufacture: Textile Enterprise in an Underdeveloped Area, 1850–1950* (Cambridge, MA: Harvard University Press, 1957), 51; Jacqueline Jones, *Labor of Love, Labor of Sorrow: Black Women, Work, and the Family from Slavery to the Present* (New York: Basic Books, 1985), 30–31.

28. Delson, "How Will We Get Our Workers?" 655; Aleksei Viktorovich Koval'chuk, *Manufakturnaia promyshlennost' Moskvy vo vtoroi polovine XVIII veka: Tekstil'noe proizvodstvo* (Moscow: Editorial URSS, 1999), 311. The general story of disciplining workers to factory labor is told most powerfully by E. P. Thompson, "Time, Work-Discipline and Industrial Capitalism," *Past and Present* 38 (1967): 56–97; Time Book, Oldknow Papers, Record Group SO, Box 12/16, John Rylands Library, Manchester; Chapman, *The Cotton Industry in the Industrial Revolution*, 56.

29. Dietrich Ebeling et al., Die deutsche Woll- und Baumwollindustrie presented at the International Textile History Conference, November 2004, 32. Harvey, *Constructing Class and Nationality in Alsace*, 59; Angel Smith et al., "Spain," 460; Van Nederveen Meerkerk et al., "The Netherlands," in Van Voss et al., eds., *The Ashgate Companion to the History of Textile Workers*, 385; see also the brilliant article by Marcel van der Linden, "Re-constructing the Origins of Modern Labor Management," *Labor History* 51 (November 2010): 509–22.

30. Ebeling et al., "The German Wool and Cotton Industry from the Sixteenth to the Twentieth Century," 227; J. Norris to Robert Peel, Secretary of State, April 28, 1826, Manchester, Public Record Office, Home Office, Introduction of Power Looms: J. Norris, Manchester, enclosing a hand bill addressed to the COTTON SPINNERS of Manchester, 1826, May 6, HO 44/16, National Archives of the UK, Kew; Paul

Huck, "Infant Mortality and Living Standards of English Workers During the Industrial Revolution," *Journal of Economic History* 55, no. 3 (September 1995): 547. See also Simon Szreter and Graham Mooney, "Urbanization, Mortality, and the Standard of Living Debate: New Estimates of the Expectation of Life at Birth in Nineteenth-Century British Cities," *Economic History Review*, New Series, 51, no. 1 (February 1998): 84–112; Hans-Joachim Voth, "The Longest Years: New Estimates of Labor Input in England, 1760–1830," *Journal of Economic History* 61, no. 4 (December 2001): 1065–82, quote on 1065; Proceedings of 24 April 1822, 30 January 1823, 23 April 1825, Proceedings of the Manchester Chamber of Commerce, 1821–1827, Record Group M8/2/1, Manchester Archives and Local Studies, Manchester; Seth Luther, *Address to the Working Men of New England, on the State of Education, and on the Condition of the Producing Classes in Europe and America* (New York: George H. Evans, 1833), 11.

31. Jeff Horn, *The Path Not Taken: French Industrialization in the Age of Revolution, 1750–1830* (Cambridge, MA: MIT Press, 2006), 107, 109–10, 116, 120.

32. H. A. Turner, *Trade Union Growth Structure and Policy: A Comparative Study of the Cotton Unions* (London: George Allen & Unwin, 1962), 385–86; Andrew Charlesworth et al., *Atlas of Industrial Protest in Britain, 1750–1985* (Basingstoke: Macmillan, 1996), 42–46.

33. Howard F. Cline, "The Aurora Yucateca and the Spirit of Enterprise in Yucatan, 1821–1847," *Hispanic American Historical Review* 27, no. 1 (1947): 30; Max Lemmenmeier, "Heimgewerbliche Bevölkerung und Fabrikarbeiterschaft in einem ländlichen Industriegebiet der Ostschweiz (Oberes Glattal) 1750–1910," in Karl Ditt and Sidney Pollard, eds., *Von der Heimarbeit in die Fabrik: Industrialisierung und Arbeiterschaft in Leinen- und Baumwollregionen Westeuropas während des 18. und 19. Jahrhunderts* (Paderborn: F. Schöningh, 1992), 410, 428ff.; Bodmer, *Die Entwicklung der Schweizerischen Textilwirtschaft*, 295–96; Van Nederveen Meerkerk et al., "The Netherlands," 386.

34. John Holt, *General View of the Agriculture of the County of Lancashire* (Dublin: John Archer, 1795), 208.

35. Thompson, *The Making of the English Working Class*; Horn, *The Path Not Taken*, 91, 95, 97–98. In France, one thousand out of twenty-five thousand water frames were destroyed; John Brown, *A Memoir of Robert Blincoe, an Orphan Boy; Sent from the Workhouse of St. Pancras, London at Seven Years of Age to Endure the Horrors of a Cotton-Mill, Through His Infancy and Youth, with a Minute Detail of His Sufferings, Being the First Memoir of the Kind Published* (Manchester: Printed for and Published by J. Doherty, 1832), 2.

36. Turner, *Trade Union Growth Structure and Policy*, 382–85; W. Foster to Robert Peel, July 13, 1826, Manchester, Home Office, Introduction of Power Looms: J. Norris, Manchester, enclosing a hand bill addressed to the COTTON SPINNERS of Manchester, 1826, May 6, HO 44/16, National Archives of the UK, Kew; Aaron Brenner et al., eds., *The Encyclopedia of Strikes in American History* (Armonk, NY: M. E. Sharpe, 2011), xvii; Mary H. Blewett, "USA: Shifting Landscapes of Class, Culture, Gender, Race and Protest in the American Northeast and South," in Van Voss et al., eds., *The Ashgate Companion to the History of Textile Workers*, 536; Angel Smith et

al., "Spain," 457; Edward Shorter and Charles Tilly, *Strikes in France, 1830–1968* (New York: Cambridge University Press, 1974), 195; Hunter and Macnaughtan, "Gender and the Global Textile Industry," 721.

37. Steinfeld, *Coercion, Contract, and Free Labor*, 245, 319.

CHAPTER EIGHT: MAKING COTTON GLOBAL

1. Beiblatt zu No. 6 of the *Neue Bremer Zeitung*, January 6, 1850, 1.

2. Henry S. Young, *Bygone Liverpool: Illustrated by Ninety-Seven Plates Reproduced from Original Paintings, Drawings, Manuscripts and Prints* (Liverpool: H. Young, 1913), 36; James Stonehouse, *Pictorial Liverpool: Its Annals, Commerce, Shipping, Institutions, Buildings, Sights, Excursions, &c. &c.: A New and Complete Hand-book for Resident, Visitor and Tourist* (England: H. Lacey, 1844?), 143. In 1821, 3,381 ships arrived in the port. *The Picture of Liverpool, or, Stranger's Guide* (Liverpool: Thomas Taylor, 1832), 31, 75. For a history of waterfront working-class activities, see Harold R. Hikins, *Building the Union: Studies on the Growth of the Workers' Movement, Merseyside, 1756–1967* (Liverpool: Toulouse Press for Liverpool Trades Council, 1973).

3. Graeme J. Milne, *Trade and Traders in Mid-Victorian Liverpool: Mercantile Business and the Making of a World Port* (Liverpool: Liverpool University Press, 2000), 29; Captain James Brown to James Croft, New Orleans, March 16, 1844, in record group 387 MD, Letter book of Captain James Brown, 1843–1852, item 48, Shipping Records of the Brown Family, Liverpool Records Office, Liverpool; Captain James Brown to James Croft, New Orleans, October 18, 1844, in ibid.; Captain James Brown to James Croft, New Orleans, March 16, 1844, in ibid.

4. Thomas Ellison, *The Cotton Trade of Great Britain: Including a History of the Liverpool Cotton Market and of the Liverpool Cotton Brokers' Association* (London: Effingham Wilson, 1886), 168–70, 172; Samuel Smith, *My Life-Work* (London: Hodder and Stoughton, 1902), 16; Henry Smithers, *Liverpool, Its Commerce, Statistics, and Institutions: With a History of the Cotton Trade* (Liverpool: Thomas Kaye, 1825), 140; High Gawthrop, *Fraser's Guide to Liverpool* (London: W. Kent and Co., 1855), 212.

5. The art on page 202 is from Franklin Elmore Papers, Library of Congress (RASP Ser. C, Pt. 2, reel 3). Thanks to Susan O'Donovan for this source.

6. Vincent Nolte, *Fifty Years in Both Hemispheres or, Reminiscences of the Life of a Former Merchant* (New York: Redfield, 1854), 278; *De Bow's Review* 12 (February 1852): 123; *Merchants' Magazine and Commercial Review* 15 (1846): 537.

7. John R. Killick argues that the international trade aspect of cotton, in contrast to the history of cotton planting, has been nearly completely ignored. John R. Killick, "The Cotton Operations of Alexander Brown and Sons in the Deep South, 1820–1860," *Journal of Southern History* 43 (May 1977): 169.

8. See Robin Pearson and David Richardson, "Networks, Institutional Innovation and Atlantic Trade before 1800," *Business History* 50, no. 6 (November 2008): 765; Annual Profit and Loss Accounts of John Tarleton, 920 TAR, Box 2, Liverpool Records Office, Liverpool; Annual Profit and Loss Accounts of Messrs. Tarleton and Backhouse, 920 TAR, Box 5, in ibid.; Earle Collection, D/Earle/5/9, Merseyside Maritime Museum, Liverpool; Milne, *Trade and Traders in Mid-Victorian Liverpool*, 48.

9. Edward Roger John Owen, *Cotton and the Egyptian Economy, 1820–1914: A Study in Trade and Development* (Oxford: Clarendon Press, 1969), 34, 90; J. Forbes Royle, *On the Culture and Commerce of Cotton in India and Elsewhere: With an Account of the Experiments Made by the Hon. East India Company up to the Present Time* (London: Smith, Elder & Co., 1851), 80–81; Great Britain Board of Trade, *Statistical Abstract for the United Kingdom*, 1856–1870, 18th no. (London: Her Majesty's Stationery Office, 1871), 58–59; Jean Legoy, *Le peuple du Havre et son histoire: Du négoce à l'industrie, 1800–1914, le cadre de vie* (Saint-Etienne du Rouvray: EDIP, 1982), 256; Ellison, *The Cotton Trade of Great Britain*, Appendix: Table 2; 350,448 pounds is converted from 3,129 cwt (1 pound is equal to 112 cwt according to Elizabeth Boody Schumpeter, *English Overseas Trade Statistics, 1697–1808* (Oxford: Clarendon Press, 1968), 34. Also, to cite another example, the import of British-manufactured yarn and cloth into Calcutta increased by a factor of four in the seventeen years after 1834. See Imports of Cotton, Piece Goods, Twist and Yarn in Calcutta 1833/34 to 1850/51, in MSS Eur F 78/44, Wood Papers, Oriental and India Office Collections, British Library, London; Werner Baer, *The Brazilian Economy: Growth and Development* (Westport, CT: Praeger, 2001), 17; Patrick Verley, "Exportations et croissance économique dans la France des Années 1860," *Annales* 43 (1988): 80; Leone Levi, "On the Cotton Trade and Manufacture, as Affected by the Civil War in America," *Journal of the Statistical Society of London* 26, no. 8 (March 1863): 32; Stanley Chapman, *Merchant Enterprise in Britain: From the Industrial Revolution to World War I* (Cambridge: Cambridge University Press, 1992), 6; Douglas A. Irwin, "Exports of Selected Commodities: 1790–1989," Table Ee569–589, in Susan B. Carter et al., eds., *Historical Statistics of the United States, Earliest Times to the Present: Millennial Edition* (New York: Cambridge University Press, 2006); Douglas A. Irwin, "Exports and Imports of Merchandise, Gold, and Silver: 1790–2002," Table Ee362–375, in Carter et al., eds., *Historical Statistics of the United States.*
10. Verley, "Exportations et croissance économique dans la France des Années 1860," 80.
11. Stanley Dumbell, "Early Liverpool Cotton Imports and the Organisation of the Cotton Market in the Eighteenth Century," *Economic Journal* 33 (September 1923): 367; Stanley Dumbell, "The Cotton Market in 1799," *Economic Journal* (January 1926): 141.
12. Dumbell, "Early Liverpool Cotton Imports and the Organisation of the Cotton Market in the Eighteenth Century," 369–70; Nigel Hall, "The Business Interests of Liverpool's Cotton Brokers, c. 1800–1914," *Northern History* 41 (September 2004): 339; Nigel Hall, "The Emergence of the Liverpool Raw Cotton Market, 1800–1850," *Northern History* 38 (March 2001): 74, 75, 77; *The Liverpool Trade Review* 53 (October 1954), 318–19; Francis E. Hyde, Bradbury B. Parkinson, and Sheila Marriner, "The Cotton Broker and the Rise of the Liverpool Cotton Market," *Economic History Review* 8 (1955): 81.
13. Hall, "The Business Interests of Liverpool's Cotton Brokers," 339–43; Milne, *Trade and Traders in Mid-Victorian Liverpool*, 124, 150; Ellison, *The Cotton Trade of Great Britain*, 166–67, 171, 176, 200, 236, 257; Hyde et. al, "The Cotton Broker and the Rise of the Liverpool Cotton Market," 76; Ellison, *The Cotton Trade of Great Britain*, 175; Hall, "The Business Interests of Liverpool's Cotton Brokers," 340.

14. Daily Purchases and Sales Book, 1814–1815, George Holt & Co., in Papers of John Aiton Todd, Record group MD 230:4, Liverpool Records Office, Liverpool; Ellison, *The Cotton Trade of Great Britain*, 206.

15. Ellison, *The Cotton Trade of Great Britain*, 206.

16. Allston Hill Garside, *Cotton Goes to Market: A Graphic Description of a Great Industry* (New York: Stokes, 1935), 47, 51, 58; Dumbell, "The Cotton Market in 1799," 147; Jacques Peuchet, *Dictionnaire universel de la géographie commerçante, contenant tout ce qui a raport à la situation et à l'étendue de chaque état commerçant; aux productions de l'agriculture, et au commerce qui s'en fait; aux manufactures, pêches, mines, et au commerce qui se fait de leurs produits; aux lois, usages, tribunaux et administrations du commerce*, vols. 1–5 (Paris: Chez Blanchon, 1799); for example see separate entries on Benin (vol. 2, p. 800), the United States (vol. 4, p. 16), and Saint Vincent (vol. 5, pp. 726–27). Even though Harold Woodman suggests that standards only came about after the 1870s, in the wake of the creation of cotton exchanges, such standards have a much longer history. Harold D. Woodman, *King Cotton and His Retainers: Financing and Marketing the Cotton Crop of the South, 1800–1925* (Columbus: University of South Carolina Press, 1990), xvii; Dumbell, "The Cotton Market in 1799," 147. For the emergence of these categories in various markets see Arthur Harrison Cole, *Wholesale Commodity Prices in the United States, 1700–1861* (Cambridge, MA: Harvard University Press, 1938), 110–343; *The Tradesman*, vol. 2, 182; *The Colonial Journal* 3, no. 5 (1817): 549; *The London Magazine* 1 (1820): 593; see also the important article by Philippe Minard, "Facing Uncertainty: Markets, Norms and Conventions in the Eighteenth Century," in Perry Gauci, ed., *Regulating the British Economy, 1660–1850* (Burlington, VT: Ashgate, 2011), 189–90.

17. Carl Johannes Fuchs, "Die Organisation des Liverpoolers Baumwollhandels," in Gustav Schmoller, ed., *Jahrbuch für Gesetzgebung, Verwaltung und Volkswirtschaft im deutschen Reich* 14 (Leipzig: Duncker & Humblot, 1890), 111; Ellison, *The Cotton Trade of Great Britain*, 272; Stephen M. Stigler, *Statistics on the Table: The History of Statistical Concepts and Methods* (Cambridge, MA: Harvard University Press, 1999), 364; Minute Book of Weekly Meetings, Liverpool Cotton Brokers' Association, April 3, 1842, in record 380 COT, file 1/1, Papers of the Liverpool Cotton Association, Liverpool Records Office, Liverpool; Minute Book of Weekly Meetings, Liverpool Cotton Brokers' Association, February 18, 1842, in ibid.; Minute Book of Weekly Meetings, Liverpool Cotton Brokers' Association, August 13, 1844, in ibid.; Minute Book of Weekly Meetings, Liverpool Cotton Brokers' Association, October 23, 1846, in ibid. In 1857, the Bombay Cotton Dealers' Managing Committee similarly distributed uniform, printed contracts, demanding the uniform packing of cotton bales, and settling conflicts by arbitration. The Bombay Cotton Dealers Managing Committee is cited in M. L. Dantwala, *A Hundred Years of Indian Cotton* (Bombay: East India Cotton Association, 1947), 63.

18. Minutes of the meeting of the American Chamber of Commerce, Liverpool, October 14, 1848, in record 380 AME, vol. 2, American Chamber of Commerce Records, Liverpool Records Office, Liverpool; Woodman, *King Cotton and His Retainers*, xvii.

19. Stanley Dumbell, "The Origin of Cotton Futures," *Economic Journal*, Supplement

(May 1827): 259–67; Fuchs, "Die Organisation des Liverpooles Baumwollhandels," 115; Hall, "The Liverpool Cotton Market: Britain's First Futures Market," 102; Daily Purchases and Sales Book, 1814–1815, George Holt & Co., in Papers of John Aiton Todd, Record group MD 230:4, Liverpool Records Office, Liverpool; Milne, *Trade and Traders in Mid-Victorian Liverpool*, 114, 260; "List of Liverpool cotton importers and brokers," April 20, 1860, in Correspondence sent to Baring in London by the Baring firm in Liverpool, House Correspondence, 1 Jan.–19 Apr. 1860, ING Baring Archives, London; Kenneth J. Lipartito, "The New York Cotton Exchange and the Development of the Cotton Futures Market," *Business History Review* 57 (Spring 1983): 51; Robert Lacombe, *La Bourse de Commerce du Havre* (Paris: Recueil Sirey, 1939), 3; Claudie Reinhart, "Les Reinhart: Une famille de négociants en coton et café au Havre, 1856–1963" (PhD dissertation, Sorbonne, 2005), 304; Smith, *My Life-Work*, 17.

20. Dumbell, "The Origin of Cotton Futures," 261.

21. D. M. Williams, "Liverpool Merchants and the Cotton Trade, 1820–1850," in J. R. Harris, ed., *Liverpool and Merseyside: Essays in the Economic and Social History of the Port and Its Hinterland* (London: Frank Cass & Co., 1969), 192.

22. Hall, "The Business Interests of Liverpool's Cotton Brokers," 339; Dumbell, "Early Liverpool Cotton Imports and the Organisation of the Cotton Market," 362–63; Hall, "The Emergence of the Liverpool Raw Cotton Market," 69, 71; Williams, "Liverpool Merchants and the Cotton Trade," 183; *Universal British Directory of Trade, Commerce, and Manufacture*, vol. 3 (London: n.p., 1790–94), 646; Francois Vigier, *Change and Apathy: Liverpool and Manchester During the Industrial Revolution* (Cambridge, MA: MIT Press, 1970), 64; Chapman, *Merchant Enterprise in Britain*, 83; Thomas Kaye, *The Stranger in Liverpool: Or, an Historical and Descriptive View of the Town of Liverpool and Its Environs* (Liverpool: T. Kaye, 1820), 33.

23. Nigel Hall, "A 'Quaker Confederation'? The Great Liverpool Cotton Speculation of 1825 Reconsidered," *Transactions of the Historical Society of Lancashire and Cheshire* 151 (2002): 2; Williams, "Liverpool Merchants and the Cotton Trade," 187–90; "Materials Concerning the Business Interests of James Stitt, Samuel Stitt and John J. Stitt," folder 1, record D/B/115/1–4, Stitt Brothers Papers, Merseyside Maritime Museum, Liverpool; Killick, "The Cotton Operations of Alexander Brown," 171; Chapman, *Merchant Enterprise in Britain*, 86.

24. Williams, "Liverpool Merchants and the Cotton Trade," 195; Sheila Marriner, *Rathbones of Liverpool, 1845–1873* (Liverpool: Liverpool University Press, 1961), xi, 14, 228–29. Sometimes brokers also seem to have mediated between sellers (factors) and buyers (merchants); see Woodman, *King Cotton and His Retainers*, 26. For the doctor's income, see R. V. Jackson, "The Structure of Pay in Nineteenth-Century Britain," *Economic History Review*, New Series, 40 (November 1987): 563; for the value of the profits in contemporary pounds, see Lawrence H. Officer and Samuel H. Williamson, "Five Ways to Compute the Relative Value of a U.K. Pound Amount, 1270 to Present," Measuring Worth, http://www.measuringworth.com/ukcompare/, accessed August 9, 2012; R. G. Wilson and A. L. Mackley, "How Much Did the English Country House Cost to Build, 1660–1880?," *Economic History Review*, New Series, 52 (August 1999): 446.

25. Nolte, *Fifty Years in Both Hemispheres*, 275, 281; Ralph W. Hidy, *The House of Baring in American Trade and Finance: English Merchant Bankers at Work, 1763–1861* (Cambridge, MA: Harvard University Press, 1949), 77, 89.

26. Philip Ziegler, *The Sixth Great Power: Baring, 1762–1929* (London: Collins, 1988), 130, 145; Hidy, *The House of Baring*, 107, 359, 361.

27. Ziegler, *The Sixth Great Power*, 131; Hidy, *The House of Baring*, 3, 185, 298. For the quote see Baring Brothers Liverpool to Francis Baring, Liverpool, July 21, 1833, House Correspondence, record group HC3, file 35,1, in ING Baring Archive, London. For the importance of the Baring cotton operations see other letters in the same folder. For output per cotton plantation worker see David Elits, *Economic Growth and the Ending of the Transatlantic Slave Trade* (Oxford University Press, 1987), 287.

28. Sam A. Mustafa, *Merchants and Migrations: Germans and Americans in Connection, 1776–1835* (Aldershot: Ashgate, 2001), 118; Ludwig Beutin, *Von 3 Ballen zum Weltmarkt: Kleine Bremer Baumwollchronik 1788–1872* (Bremen: Verlag Franz Leuwer, 1934), 11, 16; Karl-Heinz Schildknecht, *Bremer Baumwollbörse: Bremen und Baumwolle im Wandel der Zeiten* (Bremen: Bremer Baumwollbörse, 1999), 8, 9; Friedrich Rauers, *Bremer Handelsgeschichte im 19. Jahrhundert* (Bremen: Franz Leuwer, 1913), 35–39.

29. Beutin, *Von 3 Ballen zum Weltmarkt*, 20; Schiffsbuch "Albers," in D. H. Wätjen & Co. Papers, record group 7, 2092, box 19, Staatsarchiv Bremen, Germany. See also records of the Ship Magdalena, from January 1, 1859, to Dec. 31, 1861, D. H. Wätjen & Co. Papers, record group 7,2092, box 20, Staatsarchiv Bremen.

30. G. Weulersse, *Le port du Havre* (Paris: Dunod, 1921), 67; Legoy, *Le peuple du Havre et son histoire*, 217, 255, 257; *Revue du Havre*, 1850.

31. *New York Times*, April 17, 1901; Legoy, *Le peuple du Havre et son histoire*, 217, 257; Reinhart, "Les Reinhart," 26, 39, 41.

32. Claude Malon, *Jules Le Cesne: Député du Havre, 1818–1878* (Luneray: Editions Bertout, 1995), 11–12, 15, 24; Beutin, *Von 3 Ballen zum Weltmarkt*, 21.

33. Alfred D. Chandler Jr., *The Visible Hand: The Managerial Revolution in American Business* (Cambridge, MA: Harvard University Press, 1977), 29; Chapman, *Merchant Enterprise in Britain*, 150; John Crosby Brown, *A Hundred Years of Merchant Banking* (New York: privately printed, 1909), 64, 184; Circular, Brown Brothers & Company, October 1825, as reprinted in Brown, *A Hundred Years of Merchant Banking*, 190; Circular by Brown Brothers, October 31, 1815, as reprinted in ibid., 191; John Killick, "Risk, Specialization, and Profit in the Mercantile Sector of the Nineteenth Century Cotton Trade: Alexander Brown and Sons, 1820–80," *Business History Review* 16 (January 1974): 13.

34. John A. Kouwenhoven, *Partners in Banking: An Historical Portrait of a Great Private Bank, Brown Brothers Harriman & Co., 1818–1968* (Garden City. NY: Doubleday, 1967), 39, 43, 63, 70; Killick, "The Cotton Operations of Alexander Brown," 173, 176–77, 179–80, 185; Brown, *A Hundred Years of Merchant Banking*, 255; Chandler, *The Visible Hand*, 29; Tim Schenk, "Business Is International: The Rise of the House of Brown, 1800–1866" (BA thesis, Columbia University, 1997), 30; Killick, "Risk, Specialization, and Profit," 15. That $400,000 figure equals about $8.3 million in

2011. The prices for yachts and carriages in the 1830s are from Scott Derks and Tony Smith, *The Value of a Dollar: Colonial Era to the Civil War, 1600–1865* (Millerton, NY: Grey House Publishing, 2005).

35. Killick, "The Cotton Operations of Alexander Brown," 183; Sven Beckert, *The Monied Metropolis: New York City and the Consolidation of the American Bourgeoisie, 1850–1896* (New York: Cambridge University Press, 2001), 271.

36. Philip McMichael, "Slavery in Capitalism: The Rise and Demise of the U.S. Ante-bellum Cotton Culture," *Theory and Society* 20 (June 1991): 325–28; W. Nott & Co., New Orleans, November 26, 1829, to Thomas Baring, House Correspondence, HCV 5.7.17, ING Baring Archive, London. See also W. Nott to Thomas Baring, Private, New Orleans, August 25, 1830, ibid.; W. Nott to Thomas Baring, Private, New Orleans, August 25, 1830, in ibid.

37. Woodman, *King Cotton and His Retainers*, 99; Ziegler, *The Sixth Great Power*, 76, 150. Forstall was also the principal supporter of the journal *The Southerner*. E. J. Forstall to Baring Brothers London, New Orleans, February 19, 1848, House Correspondence, HC 5, 7.5, ING Baring Archive, London; Hidy, *The House of Baring*, 95–96; President of the Consolidated Association of Planters, April 7, 1829, New Orleans to Messrs Baring Brothers and Company, House Correspondence, HCV 5.7.17, ING Baring Archive, London; Edmond Forstall to Baring Brothers London, Liverpool, July 29, 1830, House Correspondence, HC 5, 7.5, ING Baring Archive, London.

38. Woodman, *King Cotton and His Retainers*, 8, 12, 13, 30; Chandler, *The Visible Hand*, 21; Joseph Holt Ingraham, *The South-west: By a Yankee*, vol. 2 (New York: Harper & Brothers 1835), 91.

39. Woodman, *King Cotton and His Retainers*, 34, 41, 53, 160; Chandler, *The Visible Hand*, 23.

40. Smith, *My Life-Work*, 25; Killick, "The Cotton Operations of Alexander Brown," 176; Jerrell H. Shofner, *Daniel Ladd: Merchant Prince of Frontier Florida* (Gainesville: University Presses of Florida, 1978), 2, 24, 35, 38, 44, 45, 53, 91, 88.

41. Salomon Volkart to J. M. Grob, Winterthur, July 3, 1851, copy book, letters, vol. 1, Volkart Archive, Winterthur, Switzerland; record group 920 TAR, file 4, letters, Tarleton Papers, Liverpool Records Office, Liverpool; Milne, *Trade and Traders in Mid-Victorian Liverpool*, 51; for Le Havre see Legoy, *Le peuple du Havre et son histoire*, 228; Weulersse, *Le port du Havre*, 86.

42. Killick, "The Cotton Operations of Alexander Brown," 186; Schenk, "Business Is International," 31.

43. Minutes of the meeting of the American Chamber of Commerce, Liverpool, August 9, 1843, in record 380 AME, vol. 2, American Chamber of Commerce Records, Liverpool Records Office, Liverpool.

44. Ibid.; Bonnie Martin, "Neighbor to Neighbor Capitalism: Local Credit Networks & the Mortgaging of Slaves," in Sven Beckert and Seth Rockman, eds., *Slavery's Capitalism: A New History of American Economic Development* (Philadelphia: University of Pennsylvania Press, forthcoming).

45. Milne, *Trade and Traders in Mid-Victorian Liverpool*, 116; Chapman, *Merchant Enterprise in Britain*, 101; Hamlin and Van Vechten, to Messrs. G. V. Robinson, New York,

March 8, 1820, in Hamlin and Van Vechten Papers, Manuscript Division, New York Public Library, New York.

46. Marika Vicziany, "Bombay Merchants and Structural Changes in the Export Community, 1850–1880," in Clive Dewey and K. N. Chaudhuri, eds., *Economy and Society: Essays in Indian Economic and Social History* (New York: Oxford University Press, 1979), 163–64; Jonathan Duncan to Earl of Worrington, Bombay, March 22, 1800, in Home Miscellaneous, vol. 471, Oriental and India Office Collections, British Library, London; Letter to the Agricultural Horticultural Society of Bombay, as quoted in Dantwala, *A Hundred Years of Indian Cotton*, 33; Dantwala, *A Hundred Years of Indian Cotton*, 32.

47. "Report on the Private trade between Europe, America and Bengal from 1st June 1776 to 31st May 1802, General Remarks," in Bengal Commercial Reports, External, 1795–1802, record group P/174, vol. 13, Oriental and India Office Collections, British Library, London; "Report of Commercial Occurrences," March 6, 1788, in Reports to the Governor General from the Board of Trade, 1789, in Home Misc, vol. 393, Oriental and India Office Collections, British Library; "Minutes of Proceedings, April 15, 1800," in Minutes of Commercial Proceedings at Bombay Castle from April 15, 1800, to 31st December, 1800, Bombay Commercial Proceedings, record group P/414, vol. 66, Oriental and India Office Collections, British Library; B. K. Karanjia, *Give Me a Bombay Merchant-Anytime: The Life of Sir Jamsetjee Jejeebhoy, Bt., 1783, 1859* (Mumbai: University of Mumbai, 1998); List of Members, *Report of the Bombay Chamber of Commerce for the Year 1861–62* (Bombay: Chesson & Woodhall, 1862), 10–12; *Report of the Bombay Chamber of Commerce for the Year 1846–47* (Bombay: American Mission Press, 1847), 7.

48. Walter R. Cassel, *Cotton: An Account of Its Culture in the Bombay Presidency* (Bombay: Bombay Education Society's Press, 1862), 289, 292; Christof Dejung, "Netzwerke im Welthandel am Beispiel der Schweizer Handelsfirma Gebrüder Volkart, 1851–1930" (unpublished paper, in author's possession), 5; John Richards to Baring Brothers London, Bombay, October 24, 1832, House Correspondence, HC 6.3, India and Indian Ocean, vol. 5, ING Baring Archive, London.

49. H. V. Bowen, "British Exports of Raw Cotton from India to China During the Late Eighteenth and Early Nineteenth Centuries," in Giorgio Riello and Tirthankar Roy, eds., *How India Clothed the World: The World of South Asian Textiles, 1500–1850* (Boston: Brill, 2009), 130; Elena Frangakis, "The Ottoman Port of Izmir in the Eighteenth and Early Nineteenth Centuries, 1695–1820," *Revue de L'Occident Musulman et de la Méditerranée* 39 (1985): 149–62; Wolfgang Müller, "Die Textilindustrie des Raumes Puebla (Mexiko) im 19. Jahrhundert" (PhD dissertation, University of Bonn, 1977), 99–102.

50. Johannes Niederer to Salomon Volkart, Batavia, December 20, 1854, typed copy in copy book, letters, vol. 1, Volkart Archive, Winterthur, Switzerland; Chapman, *Merchant Enterprise in Britain*, 181, 185; Hall, "The Emergence of the Liverpool Raw Cotton Market," 80; Milne, *Trade and Traders in Mid-Victorian Liverpool*, 100; Alexander Brown to William Brown, October 27, 1819, reprinted in Brown, *A Hundred Years of Merchant Banking*, 68.

51. Chapman, *Merchant Enterprise in Britain*, 181, 183.

52. See letters in RP.XXIV.2.6., machine copies of William Rathone VI Correspondence in America, Rathbone Papers, Special Collections and Archives, University of Liverpool, Liverpool; Adam Hodgson to Rathbone, Hodgson, New York, November 2, 1819, in record group RP.XXIII.3.1–25, ibid.; Adam Hodgson to Messrs. Rathbone, Hodgson, & Co., New York, January 11, 1821, in record group XIII 3.20, ibid.; William Rathbone VI to William Rathbone V, New York, April 26, 1841, in record group RP.IX.3.53–82, ibid.; William Rathbone VI to William Rathbone V, Baltimore, May 13, 1841, in record group RP.IX.3.53–82, ibid.; machine copies of William Rathbone VI Correspondence in America, in record group RP.XXIV.2.6., ibid.; William Rathbone VI to Messrs. Hicks, New York, November 10, 1848, in record group RP.XXIV.2.4., ibid.; William Rathbone VI to Messrs. Rathbone, Baltimore, December 2, 1848, in record group RP.XXIV.2.4., ibid.

53. Hidy, *The House of Baring*, 95, 174; House Correspondence, HC3.35,1, ING Baring Archive, London; Ziegler, *The Sixth Great Power*, 144; Malon, *Jules Le Cesne*, 17–18; William Rathbone to William Rathbone Jr., Liverpool, December 11, 1850, in record group RP.IX.4.1–22, Rathbone Papers, Special Collections and Archives, University of Liverpool, Liverpool; Adam Hodgson to Rathbone, Hodgson, & Co., September 27, 1820, in record group RP.XXIII.3.1–15, in ibid.; William Rathbone VI to Messrs. Rathbone, New York, March 3, 1849, in record group RP.XXIV.2.4, ibid.; Adam Hodgson to Messrs. Rathbone, Hodgson, & Co., New York, January 10, 1821, in record group XIII 3.18, in ibid.

54. Milne, *Trade and Traders in Mid-Victorian Liverpool*, 154–55.

55. Menge & Niemann, Hamburg, to Phelps, Dodge, Hamburg, July 14, 1841, in Phelps, Dodge Papers, Box 4, Folder July 1841, New York Public Library, Manuscripts and Archives Division, New York.

56. Smith, *My Life-Work*, 30; Gisborne to Baring Brothers, Calcutta, August 7, 1846, House Correspondence, record group HC 6, file 3, ING Baring Archive, London; Shofner, *Daniel Ladd*, 37; Nolte, *Fifty Years in Both Hemispheres*, 275. See also one of Nolte's circulars, for example dated New Orleans, March 23, 1839, in Brown Family Business Records, B 40 f5, John Carter Brown Library, Providence, Rhode Island. Thanks to Seth Rockman for bringing this document to my attention.

57. Shofner, *Daniel Ladd*, 37; on the general question of how agricultural statistics came into being see Conrad Taeuber, "Internationally Comparable Statistics on Food and Agriculture," *Milbank Memorial Fund Quarterly* 27 (July 1949): 299–313; see also Lettres des Indes etc. de 1844/45 écrites par F. C. Dollfus, à Jean Dollfus président du Comité pour l'Export des Tissus Imprimés d'Alsace, no call number, Archives du Musée de l'Impression sur Étoffes, Mulhouse, France.

58. See for example sample books, vol. 1247 (1825) and 1239 (1819), in Archives du Musée de l'Impression sur Étoffes, Mulhouse, France.

59. William Rathbone VI to Messrs. Rathbone, New York, January 8, 1849, in record group RP.XXIV.2.4., Rathbone Papers, Special Collections and Archives, University of Liverpool, Liverpool.

60. *British Packet and Argentine News*, August 4, 1826, and thereafter, in National Library of Argentina, Buenos Aires; Reinhart, "Les Reinhart," 27; *Bremer Handelsblatt*, every

issue; *Hunt's Merchants' Magazine and Commercial Review* 12 (February 1845): 195; *Hunt's Merchants' Magazine and Commercial Review* 14 (April 1846): 380.

61. *Asiatic Journal and Monthly Miscellany*, Third Series, 2 (London: Wm. H. Allen & Co., 1844), 148, 156.

62. Carl Johannes Fuchs, "Die Organisation des Liverpoolers Baumnwollhandels," in Gustav Schmoller, ed., *Jahrbuch fuer Gesetzgebung, Verwaltung und Volkswirtschaft im deutschen Reich* 14 (Leipzig: Duncker & Humblot, 1890), 112; Ellison, *The Cotton Trade of Great Britain*, 180–81; Minute Book of Weekly Meetings, Liverpool Cotton Brokers' Association, January 28, 1842, in record 380 COT, file 1/1, Papers of the Liverpool Cotton Association, Liverpool Records Office, Liverpool; R. Robson, "Raw Cotton Statistics," *Incorporated Statistician: The Journal of the Association of Incoroporated Statisticians* 5 (April 1955): 191; André Corvisier, *Histoire du Havre et de l'estuaire de la Seine* (Toulouse: Privat, 1983), 164; Eugene W. Ridings, "Business Associationalism, the Legitimation of Enterprise, and the Emergence of a Business Elite in Nineteenth-Century Brazil," *Business History Review* 63 (Winter 1989): 766–67; List of Members, *Report of the Bombay Chamber of Commerce for the Year 1861–62* (Bombay: Chesson & Woodhall, 1862), 10–12. For a detailed history of the political activities of Manchester merchants see Arthur Redford, *Manchester Merchants and Foreign Trade, 1794–1858*, vol. 1 (Manchester: Manchester University Press, 1934).

63. Trust as a core prerequisite for the emergence of markets, and thus the dependence of markets on relationships not generated in the market itself, is also emphasized by Hartmut Berghoff, "Vertrauen als Ökonomische Schlüsselvariable: Zur Theorie des Vertrauens und der Geschichte seiner Privatwirtschaflichen Produktion," in Karl-Peter Ellerbrook and Clemens Wischermann, eds., *Die Wirtschaftsgeschichte vor der Herausforderung durch die New Institutional Economics* (Dortmund: Gesellschaft für Westfälische Wirtschaftsgeschichte, 2004), 58–71; M. C. Casson, "An Economic Approach to Regional Business Networks," in John F. Wilson and Andrew Popp, eds., *Industrial Clusters and Regional Business Networks in England, 1750–1970* (Aldershot, UK: Ashgate, 2003), 28; Olivier Pétré-Grenouilleau, "Les négoces Atlantique français: Anatomie d'un capitalisme relationnel," *Dix-huitième Siècle* 33 (2001): 38. See also Geoffrey Jones, "Multinational Trading Companies in History and Theory," in Geoffrey Jones, ed., *The Multinational Traders* (London: Routledge, 1998), 5. For an important case study of Boston's Perkins family see Rachel Van, "Free Trade and Family Values: Free Trade and the Development of American Capitalism in the 19th Century" (PhD dissertation, Columbia University, 2011).

64. Edward Baines, *History of the Cotton Manufacture in Great Britain* (London: H. Fisher, R. Fisher, and P. Jackson, 1835), 319; Milne, *Trade and Traders in Mid-Victorian Liverpool*, 151.

65. William Rathbone VI to William Rathbone V, New York, April 26, 1841, in record group RP.IX.3.53–82, Rathbone Papers, Special Collections and Archives, University of Liverpool, Liverpool; Adam Hodgson to Messrs. Rathbone, Hodgson & Co., New York, January 9, 1821, in record group XXIII 3/19, ibid.; Adam Hodgson to Messrs. Rathbone, Hodgson, & Co., New York, January 2, 1821, in record group XIII 3.17, ibid.; J. Anderegg, "Volkart Brothers, 1851–1976" (unpublished manuscript, Volkart Brothers Archives, Winterthur, Switzerland), vol. 1, 42; Salomon Volkart to "Freund

Heitz," Winterthur, February 3, 1851, Copy book, letters, vol. 1, in ibid.; John Richards to Baring Brothers London, Bombay October 24, 1832, House Correspondence, HC 6.3, India and Indian Ocean, vol. 5, in ING Baring Archive, London.

66. William Rathbone IV to Joseph Reynolds Rathbone, June 25, 1805, in record group RP. IV.1.112–151, Rathbone Papers, University of Liverpool, Special Collections and Archives, Liverpool; William Rathbone IV to Joseph Reynolds Rathbone, Greenbank, December 3, 1807, in record group RP. IV.1.112–151, in ibid.; Brown, *A Hundred Years of Merchant Banking*, 262, 265; Milne, *Trade and Traders in Mid-Victorian Liverpool*, 152; Reinhart, "Les Reinhart," 27, 30.

67. Leoni M. Calvocoressi, "The House of Ralli Brothers," handwritten manuscript, dated Chios 1852, in record group MS 23836, Guildhall Library, London.

68. See *Ralli Brothers Limited* (n.p.: n.p., 1951), in Ralli Papers, Historical Materials of the Firm, record group MS 23836, Guildhall Library, London. On the Rallis see also Chapman, *Merchant Enterprise in Britain*, 155.

69. Resat Kasaba, *The Ottoman Empire and the World Economy: The Nineteenth Century* (Albany: State University of New York Press, 1988), 21; Alexander Kitroeff, *The Greeks in Egypt, 1919–1937* (London: Ithaca Press, 1989), 1, 76, 82, 88; Christos Hadziiossif, "La colonie grecque en Égypte, 1833–1856" (PhD dissertation, Sorbonne, 1980), 118, 119.

70. John Foster, "The Jewish Entrepreneur and the Family," in Konrad Kwiet, ed., *From the Emancipation to the Holocaust: Essays on Jewish Literature and History in Central Europe* (Kensington: University of New South Wales, 1987), 25; Bill Williams, *The Making of Manchester Jewry, 1740–1875* (Manchester: Manchester University Press, 1976), 17–19, 22, 34; Thomas Fowell Buxton recounts a story told to him by Nathan Rothschild in a letter to Miss Buxton, February 14, 1834, reprinted in Charles Buxton, ed., *Memoirs of Sir Thomas Fowell Buxton* (London: John Murray, 1852), 289; S. D. Chapman, "The Foundation of the English Rothschilds: N. M. Rothschild as a Textile Merchant," *Textile History* 8 (1977): 101–2, 113; Niall Ferguson, *The House of Rothschild: Money's Prophets, 1798–1848* (New York: Viking, 1999), 53; Alexander Dietz, *Frankfurter Handelsgeschichte* (Glasshütten: Verlag Detlev Auvermann, 1970), 330–34.

71. Anderegg, "Volkart Brothers, 1851–1976," vol. 1, 23; Walter H. Rambousek, Armin Vogt, and Hans R. Volkart, *Volkart: The History of a World Trading Company* (Frankfurt: Insel Verlag, 1991), 41, 69, 72; on this point, see the excellent work by Christof Dejung, for example, Dejung, "Hierarchie und Netzwerk: Steuerungsformen im Welthandel am Beispiel der Schweizer Handelsfirma Gebrueder Volkart, " in Hartmut Berghoof and Jörg Sydow, eds., *Unternehmerische Netzwerke: Eine Historische Organisationsform mit Zukunft?* (Stuttgart: Kohlhammer, 2007), 71–96.

72. E. Rathbone to William Rathbone Jr., Greenbank, 1850 (no date given), in record group RP.IX.4.1–22, Rathbone Papers, Special Collections and Archives, University of Liverpool, Liverpool; Reinhart, "Les Reinhart," 43; Weulersse, *Le port du Havre*, 88.

73. Smith, *My Life-Work*, 16.

74. See also Charles Tilly, *Coercion, Capital, and European States, AD 990–1990* (Cambridge, MA: Basil Blackwell, 1990).

75. Milne, *Trade and Traders in Mid-Victorian Liverpool*, 66, 82; Chapman, *Merchant*

Enterprise in Britain, 103; *Bremer Handelsblatt*, 1851, 6, 7; Minutes of the Meeting of the American Chamber of Commerce, Liverpool, October 29, 1824, in record 380 AME, vol. 1, American Chamber of Commerce Records, Liverpool Records Office, Liverpool; Dantwala, *A Hundred Years of Indian Cotton*, 31, 39; Woodman, *King Cotton and His Retainers*, 188; Legoy, *Le peuple du Havre et son histoire*, 226; Daniel Lord Jr., "Popular Principles Relating to the Law of Agency," *Hunt's Merchants' Magazine* 1, no. 4 (October 1839): 338.

76. Lord, "Popular Principles Relating to the Law of Agency," 338.

77. Dantwala, *A Hundred Years of Indian Cotton*, 43–46; *Report of the Bombay Chamber of Commerce for the Year 1850–51* (Bombay: American Mission Press, 1851), 9. Defining markets as institutions has a long and distinguished history; Gustav Schmoller and Werner Sombart said as much in the nineteenth century, as summarized in Geoffrey M. Hodgson, *How Economics Forgot History: The Problem of Historical Specificity in Social Science* (New York: Routledge, 2001), as did John A. Hobson, *The Social Problem: Life and Work* (New York: J. Pott and Company, 1902), 144; see also Douglass North, "Markets and Other Allocations Systems in History: The Challenge of Karl Polanyi," *Journal of European Economic History* 6, no. 3 (1977): 710. Michel Callon has also argued that the state does not intervene in the market, but constitutes it; see "Introduction: The Embeddedness of Economic Markets in Economics," in Michel Callon, ed., *The Laws of the Markets* (Malden, MA: Blackwell Publishers/Sociological Review, 1998), 40.

78. Arthur Redford, *Manchester Merchants and Foreign Trade, 1850–1939*, vol. 2 (Manchester: Manchester University Press, 1956), 3–11; Minutes of the Meeting of October 22, 1821, Proceedings of the Manchester Chamber of Commerce, record group M8, box 2/1, Manchester Archives and Local Studies, Manchester; Minutes of the Meeting of February, 27, 1822, ibid.; Minutes of the Meeting of April 24, 1822, ibid.; *Fifth Annual Report of the Board of Directors of the Chamber of Commerce and Manufactures, Manchester, for the Year 1825* (Manchester: Robinson and Bent, 1825), 8; *Tenth Annual Report of the Board of Directors of the Chamber of Commerce and Manufactures, Manchester, for the Year 1830* (Manchester: Robinson and Bent, 1831), 4; *Fifteenth Annual Report of the Board of Directors of the Chamber of Commerce and Manufactures, Manchester, for the Year 1835* (Manchester: Henry Smith, 1836), 1; *The Thirty-Sixth Annual Report of the Board of Directors of the Chamber of Commerce and Manufactures at Manchester, for the Year 1856* (Manchester: James Collins, 1857), 10, 15; Legoy, *Le peuple du Havre et son histoire*, 226; John Benjamin Smith, "Reminiscences," typescript, dated August 1913, in John Benjamin Smith Papers, record group MS Q, box 923.2.S 33, Manchester Archives and Local Studies, Manchester.

79. Minutes of the Meeting of the Society of Merchants, August 19, 1794, in Papers of the Society of Merchants, record group M8, box 1/1, Manchester Archives and Local Studies, Manchester; Copy of the Minutes of the Deputation from the Manchester of Commerce, 1841, in John Benjamin Smith Papers, record group MS f, box 932.2.S338, Manchester Archives and Local Studies; Minutes of the Meeting of March 15, 1824, Proceedings of the Manchester Chamber of Commerce, record group M8, box 2/1, Manchester Archives and Local Studies; *Fifth Annual Report of the Board of Directors . . . for the Year 1825*, 5, 22. See also *Seventh Annual Report of*

the Board of Directors of the Chamber of Commerce and Manufactures, Manchester, for the Year 1827 (Manchester: Robinson and Bent, 1827), 3; *Eighth Annual Report of the Board of Directors of the Chamber of Commerce and Manufactures, Manchester, for the Year 1828* (Manchester: Robinson and Bent, 1829), 2; Proceedings of the Manchester Chamber of Commerce, 1821–1827, Record group M8, Box 2/1, Manchester Archives and Local Studies.

80. Minutes of the Meeting of the Society of Merchants, February 27, 1794, in Papers of the Society of Merchants, record group M8, box 1/1, Manchester Archives and Local Studies, Manchester; Minutes of the Meeting of the Society of Merchants, March 5, 1795, in ibid.; *Eighth Annual Report of the Board of Directors . . . for the Year 1828,* 4; Address, London March 5, 1803, in Scrapbook of William Rathbone IV, in record group RP.4.17, Rathbone Papers, Special Collections and Archives, University of Liverpool, Liverpool.

81. *Report of the Proceeding of the Board of Directors of the Manchester Chamber of Commerce from the Time of Its Institution in the Year 1820 to the End of 1821* (Manchester: C. Wheeler and Son, 1821), 6, 9; *Ninth Annual Report of the Board of Directors of the Chamber of Commerce and Manufactures, Manchester, for the Year 1829* (Manchester: Robinson and Bent, 1830), 5; *The Thirty-Ninth Annual Report of the Board of Directors of the Chamber of Commerce and Manufactures at Manchester, for the Year 1859* (Manchester: Cave and Sever, 1860), 19, 35; for the idea that economic thinking formats the economy, presented with much greater sophistication, see Michel Callon, "Introduction: The Embeddedness of Economic Markets in Economics," in Callon, ed., *The Laws of the Markets,* 2.

82. Martin Murray to Baring Brothers London, Bombay, September 15, 1846, House Correspondence, HC 6.3, 9, in ING Baring Archive, London; Martin Murray to Baring Brothers London, Bombay, March 2, 1847, HC 6.3, 9, in ibid.; Hadziiossif, "La colonie grecque en Egypte," 113; Ahmed Abdel-Rahim Mustafa, "The Breakdown of the Monopoly System in Egypt After 1840," in Peter Malcom Holt, *Political and Social Change in Modern Egypt: Historical Studies from the Ottoman Conquest to the United Arab Republic* (London: Oxford University Press, 1968), 291, 293, 296; Kenneth Cuno, *The Pasha's Peasants: Land, Society, and Economy in Lower Egypt, 1740–1858* (Cambridge: Cambridge University Press, 1992), 125; Owen, *Cotton and the Egyptian Economy,* 37, 57, 65–66, 67, 77; Vicziany, "Bombay Merchants and Structural Changes in the Export Community," 168, 170.

83. This has been very well argued for the Italian case. See Enrico Dal Lago, *Agrarian Elites: American Slaveholders and Southern Italian Landowners, 1815–1861* (Baton Rouge: Louisiana State University Press, 2005).

84. Beckert, *The Monied Metropolis,* 26.

85. John R. Killick, "Atlantic and Far Eastern Models in the Cotton Trade, 1818–1980," University of Leeds School of Business and Economic Studies, Discussion Paper Series, June 1994, 1, 16; Killick, "The Cotton Operations of Alexander Brown," 189, 191.

86. Eugene W. Ridings Jr., "The Merchant Elite and the Development of Brazil: The Case of Bahia During the Empire," *Journal of Interamerican Studies and World Affairs* 15 (August 1973): 336, 348; Stanley J. Stein, *The Brazilian Cotton Manufacture: Textile Enterprise in an Underdeveloped Area, 1850–1950* (Cambridge, MA: Harvard University Press, 1957), 6. The uniqueness of the United States in this regard is often over-

looked, but emphasized to good effect by Robin Einhorn, "Slavery," in *Enterprise and Society* 9 (September 2008): 498.

CHAPTER NINE: A WAR REVERBERATES AROUND THE WORLD

1. This chapter draws on Sven Beckert, "Emancipation and Empire: Reconstructing the Worldwide Web of Cotton Production in the Age of the American Civil War," *American Historical Review* 109 (Dec. 2004), 1405–38. J. B. Smith (Stockport) in *Hansard's Parliamentary Debates*, Third Series, vol. 167, June 19, 1862 (London: Cornelius Buck, 1862), 754; Élisée Reclus, "Le coton et la crise américaine," *La Revue des Deux Mondes* 37 (January 1865): 176. The global population estimate is for the year 1850 and from Part 1, Population Division, Department of Economic and Social Affairs, United Nations Secretariat, *The World at Six Billion* (New York, 1999), 5, accessed February 14, 2013, http://www.un.org/esa/population/publications/sixbillion/sixbilpart1.pdf; Dwijendra Tripathi, "A Shot from Afar: India and the Failure of Confederate Diplomacy," *Indian Journal of American Studies* 10, no. 2 (1980): 75; D. A. Farnie, *The English Cotton Industry and the World Market, 1815–1896* (Oxford: Clarendon Press, 1979), 180; *Merchants' Magazine and Commercial Review* 45, no. 5 (November 1861): 481; *Merchants' Magazine and Commercial Review* 44, no. 6 (June 1861): 676; Leone Levi, "On the Cotton Trade and Manufacture, as Affected by the Civil War in America," *Journal of the Statistical Society of London* 26, no. 8 (March 1863): 32; Elijah Helm, "The Cotton Trade of the United Kingdom, During the Seven Years, 1862–1868, as Compared with the Seven Years, 1855–1861; With Remarks on the Return of Factories Existing in 1868," *Journal of the Statistical Society of London* 32, no. 4 (December 1869): 429.

2. *Merchants' Magazine and Commercial Review* 45, no. 5 (November 1861), 480; Douglass C. North, *The Economic Growth of the United States* (Englewood Cliffs, NJ: Prentice Hall, 1961), 40. The value of all exports of "U.S. merchandise" in 1860 was $316 million, while raw cotton exports amounted to $192 million. See U.S. Department of Commerce, Bureau of the Census, *Historical Statistics of the United States* (Washington, DC: Government Printing Office, 1975), 885, 899; *The Economist*, January 19, 1861, 58; M. K. Rozhkova, *Ekonomicheskiie sviazi Rossii so Srednei Aziei: 40–60-e gody XIX veka* (Moscow: Izd. Akademii Nauk SSSR, 1963), 61; "Vliyanie Amerikanskoi Voiny na Khlopchatobumazhnoe delo v Rossii" (The Effect of the American War on the Cotton Business in Russia), *Moskva* 25 (1867), January 25, 1867; Kaiserliches Statistisches Amt, *Statistisches Jahrbuch für das Deutsche Reich, Erster Jahrgang, 1880* (Berlin: Puttkammer & Mühlbrecht, 1880), 87; U.S. Bureau of Statistics, Treasury Department, *Cotton in Commerce, Statistics of United States, United Kingdom, France, Germany, Egypt and British India* (Washington, DC: Government Printing Office, 1895), 29; the French numbers are for 1859, see Claude Fohlen, *L'industrie textile au temps du Second Empire* (Paris: Librairie Plon, 1956), 284, 514; M. Gately, *The Development of the Russian Cotton Textile Industry in the Pre-revolutionary Years, 1861–1913* (Ann Arbor, MI: Xerox University Microfilms, 1968), 45; on the importance of the United States to world cotton markets see Gavin Wright, "Cotton Competition and the Post-Bellum Recovery of the American South," *Journal of Economic History* 34,

no. 3 (1974): 610–35; Gavin Wright, *Old South, New South: Revolutions in the Southern Economy Since the Civil War* (New York: Basic Books, 1986).

3. *The Economist*, February 2, 1861, 117.

4. John Greenleaf Whittier, "The Haschish," *John Greenleaf Whittier: Selected Poems*, Brenda Wineapple, ed. (New York: Library of America, 2004), 43–44. Thanks to George Blaustein for bringing this poem to my attention.

5. Herman Merivale, *Lectures on Colonization and Colonies, Delivered Before the University of Oxford in 1839, 1840 & 1841* (London: Humphrey Milford, 1928), 301–2, 304–5; for a fascinating discussion of Merivale see Daniel Rood, "Herman Merivale's Black Legend: Rethinking the Intellectual History of Free Trade Imperialism," *New West Indian Guide* 80, no. 3–4 (2006): 163–89; see also Edward Atkinson, *Cheap Cotton by Free Labor* (Boston: A. Williams & Co., 1861), 4.

6. This point is also made by Sugata Bose, "Introduction: Beyond the General and the Particular," in Sugata Bose, ed., *South Asia and World Capitalism* (New Delhi: Oxford University Press, 1990), 1–13; Karl Marx and Friedrich Engels, *Aufstand in Indien* (Berlin: Dietz Verlag, 1978), 270, originally published in 1853; Reclus, "Le coton," 176, 187; Frank Lawrence Owsley and Harriet Chappell Owsley, *King Cotton Diplomacy: Foreign Relations of the Confederate States of America* (Chicago: University of Chicago Press, 1959), 19; *De Bow's Review* 30, no. 1 (January 1861): 75–76; James Henry Hammond, "Speech on the Admission of Kansas, under the Lecompton Constitution, Delivered in the Senate of the United States, March 4, 1858," in James Henry Hammond, *Selections from the Letters and Speeches of the Hon. James H. Hammond of South Carolina* (New York: n.p., 1866), 317.

7. Leone Levi, "On the Cotton Trade and Manufacture, as Affected by the Civil War in America," *Journal of the Statistical Society of London* 26, no. 10 (March 1863): 37ff.; J. E. Horn, *La crise cotonnière et les textiles indigènes* (Paris: Dentu, 1863), 10.

8. For "treacherous foundations" see *Fifth Annual Report of the Cotton Supply Association* (Manchester: John J. Sale, 1862), 5; for "not to be safely trusted," see *Cotton Supply Reporter* (May 15, 1861): 497; see also *Cotton Supply Reporter* (January 2, 1860): 7; John Gunn Collins, *Scinde & The Punjab: The Gems of India in Respect to Their Vast and Unparalleled Capabilities of Supplanting the Slave States of America in the Cotton Markets of the World, or, An Appeal to the English Nation on Behalf of Its Great Cotton Interest, Threatened with Inadequate Supplies of the Raw Material* (Manchester: A. Ireland, 1858), 5; Louis Reybaud, *Le coton: Son régime, ses problèmes, son influence en Europe* (Paris: Michel Levy Frères, 1863), 383; for similar concerns see "Cotton Cultivation in India," *Calcutta Review* 37, no. 73 (September 1861): 87; Jay Sexton, *Debtor Diplomacy: Finance and American Foreign Relations in the Civil War Era, 1837–1873* (New York: Oxford University Press, 2005), 75; *Westminster and Foreign Quarterly Review: October, 1849–January, 1850* 52 (London: George Luxford, 1852), 214.

9. For this argument see chapters 3 and 4 in Sven Beckert, *The Monied Metropolis: New York City and the Consolidation of the American Bourgeoisie, 1850–1896* (Cambridge: Cambridge University Press, 2001).

10. Quoted in *Times of India*, Overland Summary, March 12, 1863.

11. *Merchants' Magazine and Commercial Review* 44, no. 6 (June 1861): 675; for Lieber see *Merchants' Magazine and Commercial Review* 45, no. 5 (November 1861): 514;

Allen Isaacman and Richard Roberts, "Cotton, Colonialism, and Social History in Sub-Saharan Africa: Introduction," in Allen Isaacman and Richard Roberts, eds., *Cotton, Colonialism, and Social History in Sub-Saharan Africa* (Portsmouth, NH: Heinemann, 1995), 7.

12. Neil Ashcroft, "British Trade with the Confederacy and the Effectiveness of Union Maritime Strategy During the Civil War," *International Journal of Maritime History* 10, no. 2 (December 1998), 155–76; Sam Negus, " 'The Once Proud Boast of the Englishman': British Neutrality and the Civil War Blockade" (unpublished paper, Massachusetts School of Law, 2007, in author's possession); on the "cotton famine" see also, among others, William Otto Henderson, *The Lancashire Cotton Famine, 1861–65* (Manchester: Manchester University Press, 1934); *Jahresbericht der Handels- und Gewerbekammer Chemnitz* (1865), 6, as quoted in Michael Löffler, *Preussens und Sachsens Beziehungen zu den USA während des Sezessionskrieges 1860–1865* (Münster: LIT, 1999), 302; Matthew B. Hammond, *The Cotton Industry: An Essay in American Economic History* (New York: Macmillan, 1897), Appendix. Even the Bradford worsted industry discontinued the use of now much more expensive cotton warp. See Mary H. Blewett, "The Dynamics of Labor Migration and Raw Material Acquisition in the Transatlantic Worsted Trade, 1830–1930," in Donna R. Gabaccia and Dirk Hoerder, eds., *Connecting Seas and Connected Ocean Rims: Indian, Atlantic, and Pacific Oceans and China Seas Migrations from the 1830s to the 1930s* (Boston: Brill, 2011), 138–70.

13. *Liverpool Mercury*, January 14, 1861, 2; *Liverpool Mercury*, July 1862; Löffler, *Preussens*, 194–255.

14. Even though much of the literature emphasizes that in 1861 there was a glut of cotton in the markets, David G. Surdham has shown that stocks of raw cotton in Europe were not extraordinarily large. The stock held on December 31, 1861, equaled the mill consumption of 13.4 weeks. See David G. Surdham, "King Cotton: Monarch or Pretender? The State of the Market for Raw Cotton on the Eve of the American Civil War," *Economic History Review* 51 (1998): 113–32, esp. 119; on the glutted markets as a sign of crisis see for example *Liverpool Mercury*, October 6, 1863, 6; Farnie, *English Cotton*, 141–43; *Moskva*, February 1, 1867, the "organ of Moscow capitalists," in V. Ya. Laverychev, *Krupnaya Burzhuaziia V Poreformennoi Rossii: 1861–1900* (Moscow: Izd. Mysl', 1974).

15. Charles Francis Adams Jr. to Henry Adams, Quincy, Massachusetts, August 25, 1861, in Worthington Chauncey Ford, ed., *A Cycle of Adams Letters, 1861–1865*, vol. 1 (Boston: Houghton Mifflin, 1920), 33; Nigel Hall, "The Liverpool Cotton Market and the American Civil War," *Northern History* 34, no. 1 (1998): 154; *Merchants' Magazine and Commercial Review* 49, no. 6 (December 1863): 411; for the statistics see Thomas Ellison, *The Cotton Trade of Great Britain, Including a History of the Liverpool Cotton Market and of the Liverpool Cotton Brokers' Association* (London: Effingham Wilson, 1886), Appendix, Table 1; for the numbers see *Liverpool Mercury*, November 11, 1861, 3; *Liverpool Mercury*, February 22, 1864, 6; on the relief efforts in Lancashire see John Watts, *The Facts of the Cotton Famine* (London: Simpkin, Marshall & Co., 1866); *Liverpool Mercury*, February 22, 1864, 6; Manchester Chamber of Commerce, *The Forty-First Annual Report of the Board of Directors for the Year 1861* (Manchester: Cave

& Server, 1862), 20; John O'Neil, diary entry, April 10, 1864, as cited in Rosalind Hall, "A Poor Cotton Weyver: Poverty and the Cotton Famine in Clitheroe," *Social History* 28, no. 2 (May 2003): 243; "Memorial of the Unemployed Operatives of Stalybridge," received February 23, 1863, in Various documents relating to the distress in the cotton manufacturing districts during the American Civil War, HO 45: 7523, Home Office, National Archives of the UK, Kew; "Facilities Required for Public Workers for the Employment of able-bodied Cotton Workmen at Ordinary Wages," Minutes of the Central Executive Committee, May 25, 1863, in ibid.

16. See *Liverpool Mercury, March 25, 1863,* 7; undated report, in various documents relating to the distress in the cotton manufacturing districts during the American Civil War, HO 45: 7523, Home Office, National Archives of the UK, Kew; William Rathbone to William Rathbone Jr., Green Bank, March 5, 1862, in letters of William Rathbone, R.P.IX.4.1–22, Rathbone Papers, University of Liverpool, Special Collections and Archives, Liverpool; *Times of India*, Overland Summary, June 12, 1862, 2; see also *Times of India*, Overland Summary, September 27, 1862, 3, October 17, 1862, 3, October 27, 1862, 2. Indeed, by far the largest international contributions to the relief of the suffering of Lancashire workers came from Calcutta and Bombay respectively. See Watts, *Facts*, 164; Charles Wood to James Bruce, Earl of Elgin, May 2, 1863, in MSS EUR F 78, LB 13, Wood Papers, Oriental and India Office Collections, British Library, London; M. J. Mathieu, *De la culture du coton dans la Guyane française* (Epinal: Alexis Cabasse, 1861), 47.

17. Arthur L. Dunham, "The Development of the Cotton Industry in France and the Anglo-French Treaty of Commerce of 1860," *Economic History Review* 1, no. 2 (January 1928): 292–94; Lynn M. Case, ed., *French Opinion on the United States and Mexico, 1860–1867: Extracts from the Reports of the Procureurs Généraux* (New York: D. Appleton-Century Company, 1936), 123–25; Thomas A. Sancton, "The Myth of French Worker Support for the North in the American Civil War," *French Historical Studies* 11, no. 1 (1979): 59, 66; Claude Fohlen, "La guerre de sécession et le commerce franco-américain," *Revue d'Histoire Moderne et Contemporaine* 8, no. 4 (October–December 1961), 259–70; Alphonse Cordier, *La crise cotonnière dans la Seine-Inférieur, ses causes et ses effets* (Rouen, 1864), 8; Claude Fohlen, *L'industrie textile au temps du Second Empire* (Paris: Librairie Plon, 1956), 257–62; Stephen McQueen Huntley, *Les rapports de la France et la Confédération pendant la guerre de sécession* (Toulouse: Imprimerie Regionale, 1932), 222; Mathieu, *De la culture*, 1; Harold Hyman, ed., *Heard Round the World: The Impact Abroad of the Civil War* (New York: Alfred A. Knopf, 1969), 132; on the social impact of the crisis in France see A. S. Ménier, *Au profit des ouvriers cotoniers: Pétition au Sénat sur la détresse cotonnière* (Paris: E. Dentu, 1863).

18. Löffler, *Preussens,* 126, 147; Emerson David Fite, *Social and Industrial Conditions in the North During the Civil War* (New York: Macmillan, 1910), 84, 86; Gately, *Development,* 47. The amount of cotton imported across the European border, most of it from the United States, had fallen from nearly 2.5 million pounds to a little less than half a million pounds. Mariya Konstantinovna Rozhkova, *Ekonomicheskiie sviazzi Rossii so Srednei Aziei, 40–60-e gody XIX veka* (Moscow: Izd-vo Akademii nauk SSSR, 1963), 61–62; to my knowledge there are no statistics that would allow us to determine the precise percentage of U.S. cotton among these exports. Contemporary

observers, however, all agreed that most of it originated from the United States—a reasonable estimate would be somewhere between 80 and 90 percent. Charles J. Sundell to William H. Seward, Stettin, May 15, 1863, Despatches from United States Consuls in Stettin, as quoted in Löffler, *Preussens*, 110.

19. John Rankin, *A History of Our Firm: Being Some Account of the Firm of Pollock, Gilmour and Co. and Its Offshoots and Connections, 1804–1920* (Liverpool: Henry Young & Sons, Limited, 1921), 157; Baring Brothers Liverpool to Baring Brothers London, August 24, 1863, in HC 3:35, Part 23, House Correspondence, Baring Brothers, ING Baring Archive, London. Baring Brothers & Co. was also the banker of the United States in London; see letter of Frederick William Seward to Thomas Haines Dudley, Washington, March 26, 1864, in Seward Papers, Library of Congress, Manuscript Division, Washington, DC; *Merchants' Magazine and Commercial Review* 49, no. 5 (November 1863): 350; Liverpool Chamber of Commerce, *Report of the Council, 1863* (Liverpool: Benson and Holmes, 1863), 18; John D. Pelzer, "Liverpool and the American Civil War," *History Today* 40, no. 3 (1990): 49; Hall, "Liverpool Cotton," 161; Samuel Smith, *My Life-Work* (London: Hodder and Stoughton, 1902), 34; *Liverpool Mercury*, January 6, 1862, 6; *Lowell Daily Citizen and News*, January 9, 1862.

20. Quote from *Times of India*, October 6, 1863, 1; see also *Times of India*, Overland Summary, September 8, 1864, 2–3; *Times of India* Overland Summary reported negatively on the practice on September 29, 1863, 5–6; Pelzer, "Liverpool," 52.

21. Chamber de Commerce de Rouen, *Délibération de la chambre sur la formation de la Compagnie française des cotons Algériens* (Rouen: Ch.-F. Lapierre et Cie, 1862), 5, in F/80/737, Fonds Ministériels, Archives d'outre-mer, Aix-en-Provence, France; *Pétition à Sa Majesté l'Empereur Napoléon III, au sujet de la culture du coton en Algérie*, Senones, February 13, 1862, in ibid.; *Bulletin de la Société industrielle de Mulhouse* 32 (1862), 347, as quoted in Fohlen, *L'industrie textile*, 347–48; the Mulhouse Chamber of Commerce even created a commission to look into the possibility of growing cotton in Algeria; see *Bulletin de la Société Industrielle de Mulhouse*, vol. 32 (1862), 346; Antoine Herzog, *L'Algérie et la crise cotonnière* (Colmar: Ch. M. Hoffmann, 1864); letter to the editor in *L'Industriel Alsacien*, December 25, 1862; Antoine Herzog to La Majesté, l'Empereur des Française, January 6, 1863, in F/80/737, Fonds Ministériels, Archives d'outre-mer, Aix-en-Provence, France; petitions from many other cotton regions also were sent to the emperor; Pétition à Sa Majesté l'Empereur Napoléon III, au sujet de la culture du coton en Algérie, Senones, February 13, 1862, in F/80/737, Fonds Ministériels, Archives d'outre mer, Aix-en-Provence, France, contained in 15 *cahiers,* signed by manufacturers from all regions of France. For evidence on this pressure, see also at the same location letter of F. Engel-Dollfus, président de la commission d'encouragement à la culture du coton en Algérie, to Monsieur le Marechal Comte Randon Senateur, Ministre Secrétaire d'État au Departement de la Guerre, Mulhouse, April 8, 1862.

22. *Liverpool Mercury*, August 12, 1862, 7. There was a general obsession with this question; Gladstone, for example, received a letter in 1862 from Mrs. E. Tennyson in which she related an elaborate scheme in which a specially created fund would reimburse manufacturers for the rising costs of raw cotton, so that they

would be enabled to continue employing their workers; see "Memorandum by Mrs. E. Tennyson to Gladstone related to the cotton famine," in Add. 44399 f. 188, vol. 314, Gladstone Papers, British Library, London; *Liverpool Mercury*, January 22, 1861, 2; William Thayer to William H. Seward, London, July 11, 1862, private letter, U.S. Consulate, Alexandria, Despatches from U.S. Consuls in Alexandria, National Archives, Washington, DC; Löffler, *Preussens*, 111; see *Hansard's Parliamentary Debates*, Third Series, vol. 171 (London: Cornelius Buck, 1863), 1771–840; Hansard's Parliamentary Debates, Third Series, vol. 165 (London: Cornelius Buck, 1862), 1155–230.

23. Karl Polanyi, *The Great Transformation: The Political and Economic Origins of Our Time* (Boston: Beacon Press, 1957), 78; Henry John Temple, Lord Palmerston to John Russell, Broadlands, October 6, 1861, Box 21, 30/22, Lord John Russell Papers, National Archives of the UK, Kew; see the notes and reports, including report by unknown author, "Le coton à la côte occidentale d'Afrique," n.d.; Note on Siam, n.d.; draft article, n.a., n.d., on "La culture du coton à la Guyana"; all in GEN 56/Folder 547, in Fonds Ministériels, Archives d'outre-mer, Aix-en-Provence, France.

24. Manchester, *Forty-First Annual Report*, 21; for evidence of this pressure see also Manchester Chamber of Commerce, *The Forty-Third Annual Report of the Board of Directors for the Year 1863* (Manchester: Cave & Server, 1866), 6; Proceedings of the Manchester Chamber of Commerce, 1858–1867, M8/2/6, Archives of the Manchester Chamber of Commerce, Manchester Archives and Local Studies, Manchester; Bombay Chamber of Commerce, *Report of the Bombay Chamber of Commerce for the Year 1859–60* (Bombay: Chesson & Woodhall, 1860), xxxiii; for earlier efforts to increase cotton production in India see Anti-Cant, *India v. America: A Letter to the Chairman of the Hon. East India Company, On Cotton* (London: Aylott & Jones, 1850); John Briggs, *The Cotton Trade of India with a Map of India, Coloured to Indicate the Different Spots Whereon all the Varieties of Cotton which are Brought into the British Market have been Successfully Cultivated* (London: John W. Parker, 1840); Chapman, *The Cotton and Commerce of India; The Cotton Trade of India* (London, 1839); Thomas Williamson, *Two Letters on the Advantages of Railway Communication in Western India, Addressed to the Right Hon. Lord Wharncliffe, Chairman of the Great Indian Peninsula Railway Company* (London: Richard & John E. Taylor, 1846); John Briggs, *The Cotton Trade of India: Part I. Its Past and Present Condition; Part II. Its Future Prospects: with a Map of India* (London: John W. Parkter, 1840); Walter R. Cassels, *Cotton: An Account of Its Culture in the Bombay Presidency* (Bombay: Bombay Education Society's Press, 1862), 16–237; *The Economist*, February 2, 1861, 117.

25. Potter is quoted in Manchester, *Forty-First Annual Report*, 21; for evidence of this pressure see also Manchester, *Forty-Third Annual Report*, 6; Proceedings of the Manchester Chamber of Commerce, 1858–1867, M8/2/6, Archives of the Manchester Chamber of Commerce, Manchester Archives and Local Studies, Manchester; Reclus, "Le coton," 202; the British East Indies took a full 30.83 percent of all piece goods exported from the United Kingdom in 1860; see Ellison, *Cotton Trade*, 64; James A. Mann, *The Cotton Trade of Great Britain: Its Rise, Progress and Present Extent* (Lon-

don: Frank Cass & Co., 1968), 112; for the quote from Nagpore see anonymous letter
to the editor of the *Englishman*, Nagpore, July 31, 1861, reprinted in *Times of India*,
August 21, 1861, 3; Charles Wood to Sir Frere, October 30, 1862, Letterbook, July 3 to
December 31, 1862, MSS EUR LB 11, F 78, Wood Papers, Oriental and India Office
Collections, British Library, London.

26. *Cotton Supply Reporter* (June 15, 1861): 532; Arthur W. Silver, *Manchester Men and
Indian Cotton, 1847–1872* (Manchester: Manchester University Press, 1966), 187.

27. For an account of the meeting see *Liverpool Mercury*, September 20, 1861, 7; see also
Liverpool Mercury, September 23, 1861, 2; Charles Wood to Sir George Clerk, March
18, 1861, in MSS EUR F 78, LB 7, Wood Papers, Oriental and India Office Collections, British Library, London; Major E. K. Elliot, "Report Regarding the Cultivation of Cotton in Nagpore," reprinted in *Times of India*, July 30, 1861, 3–4; "Cotton
Cultivation in India," *Calcutta Review* 37, no. 73 (September 1861): 89.

28. On the general thrust of legal infrastructure construction in India, see the important
work by Ritu Birla, *Stages of Capital: Law, Culture, and Market Governance in Late
Colonial India* (Durham, NC: Duke University Press, 2009); on the contested his-
tory of law in colonial situations see the fabulous book by Lauren Benton, *Law and
Colonial Cultures: Legal Regimes in World History, 1400–1900* (New York: Cambridge
University Press, 2002); as to crop liens see Charles Wood to William Maine, Octo-
ber 9, 1862, Letterbook, July 3 to December 31, 1862, MSS EUR LB 11, F 78, Wood
Papers, Oriental and India Office Collections, British Library, London; Charles
Wood to William Maine, October 9, 1862, in ibid.; Proceedings of the Manchester
Chamber of Commerce, September 23, 1861, Archives of the Manchester Chamber
of Commerce, Record Group M8, folder 2/6, in Manchester Archives and Local
Studies, Manchester; for the quote "making penal" see Charles Wood to W. J. P.
Grant, May 9, 1861, in MSS EUR F 78, LB 7, Wood Papers, Oriental and India
Office Collections, British Library; for the efforts by manufacturers see Charles
Wood to William Reeves, March 18, 1861, Letterbook, 18 March to 25 May, in ibid.;
Charles Wood to James Bruce, Earl of Elgin, October 25, 1862, Letterbook, 3 July
to 31 December 1862, in MSS EUR LB 11, F 78, Wood Papers, Oriental and India
Office Collections, British Library; Letter from Messrs. Mosley and Hurst, Agents
to the Cotton Supply Association, to W. Greq, Esq, Secretary to the Government of
India, June 20, 1861, reprinted in *Times of India*, July 18, 1861, 3; Charles Wood to
W. J. Grant, May 9, 1861, in MSS EUR LB 7, F 78, Oriental and India Office Collections, British Library, London. On the debates on the passage of a law that made the
adulteration of cotton a crime, see the *Times of India* reporting in 1863, for example
on Overland Summary, February 12, 1863, 6–7; also *Times of India*, Overland Summary, March 27 1863, 1; for pressures to change Indian contract law see Manchester
Chamber of Commerce, *The Forty-Second Annual Report of the Board of Directors for
the Year 1862* (Manchester: Cave & Server, 1863), 13, 37; see Charles Wood to William
Maine, October 9, 1862, Letterbook, July 3 to December 31, 1862, in MSS EUR LB
11, F 78, Wood Papers, Oriental and India Office Collections, British Library; reprint
of a resolution of the Home Department, February 28, 1861, Supplement to the
Calcutta Gazette, March 2, 1861, in Papers relating to Cotton Cultivation in India,
106, Wood Papers, MSS EUR F 78, Oriental and India Office Collections, Brit-

ish Library; some of the mechanisms are related well in John Henry Rivett-Carnac, *Many Memories of Life in India, At Home, and Abroad* (London: W. Blackwood and Sons, 1910), 165–93; for the debate during the war between manufacturers and government officials see also Charles Wood to James Bruce, Earl of Elgin, October 25, 1862, in MSS EUR LB 11, F 78, Wood Papers, Oriental and India Office Collections, British Library; Charles Wood to William Maine, October 9, 1862, Letterbook, July 3 to December 31, 1862, in ibid.; *Hansard's Parliamentary Debates*, Third Series, vol. 167, June 19, 1862 (London: Cornelius Buck, 1862), 767; Manchester, *Forty-Third Annual Report*, 26; Manchester, *Forty-First Annual Report; Liverpool Mercury*, September 24, 1862, 6; Charles Wood to Sir George Clerk, March 18, 1861, in MSS EUR LB 7, March 18 to May 25, 1861, in F78, Oriental and India Office Collections, British Library; Peter Harnetty, "The Imperialism of Free Trade: Lancashire, India, and the Cotton Supply Question, 1861–1865," *Journal of British Studies* 6, no. 1 (1966): 75–76; Dwijendra Tripathi, "Opportunism of Free Trade: Lancashire Cotton Famine and Indian Cotton Cultivation," *Indian Economic and Social History Review* 4, no. 3 (1967): 255–63; Liverpool Chamber of Commerce, *Twelfth Annual Report of the Liverpool Chamber of Commerce* (Liverpool: Neson & Mallett, 1862), 6; M. L. Dantwala, *A Hundred Years of Indian Cotton* (Bombay: East India Cotton Association, 1947), 46–47; reprint of a resolution of the Home Department, February 28, 1861, Supplement to the *Calcutta Gazette*, March 2, 1861, in Papers relating to Cotton Cultivation in India, 106, Wood Papers, MSS EUR F 78, Oriental and India Office Collections, British Library.

29. Charles Wood to James Bruce, Earl of Elgin, October 25, 1862, in MSS EUR LB 11, F 78, Wood Papers, Oriental and India Office Collections, British Library, London; *Times of India*, Overland Summary, January 14, 1864, 3; Charles Wood to Sir Charles Trevelyan, March 9, 1863, in MSS EUR F 78, LB 12, Wood Papers, Oriental and India Office Collections, British Library; the connection between lower duties, greater imports of Lancashire goods, and the availability of more raw cotton is made explicitly in Manchester, *Forty-First Annual Report*, 24; it was also anticipated here that India would become an ever more important market for British-manufactured cotton goods—and that exports of raw cotton were to pay for these imports.

30. *Hansard's Parliamentary Debates*, Third Series, vol. 167, June 19, 1862 (London: Cornelius Buck, 1862), 767; on Wood's "incompetence" see Manchester, *Forty-Third Annual Report*, 26; Manchester, *Forty-First Annual Report; Liverpool Mercury*, September 24, 1862, 6; Charles Wood to James Bruce, Earl of Elgin, January 10, 1863, in MSS EUR 78, LB 12, January 1 to April 27, 1863, Wood Collection, Oriental and India Office Collections, British Library, London; Charles Wood to Viceroy Earl Canning, February 18, 1861, in MSS Eur F 78, LB 6, Wood Papers, British Library, Oriental and India Office Collections, British Library; Charles Wood to Sir George Clerk, March 18, 1861, in LB 7, March 18 to May 25, 1861, F 78, MSS EUR, Oriental and India Office Collections, British Library; Peter Harnetty, "The Imperialism of Free Trade: Lancashire and the Indian Cotton Duties, 1859–1862," *Economic History Review* 18, no. 2 (1965): 75–76; for debate as whole see Tripathi, "Opportunism," 255–63.

31. *The Economist*, October 4, 1862, 1093–94.

32. Harnetty, "Imperialism, 1859–1862," 333–49; Manchester, *Forty-Second Annual Report*, 11, 22; the superintendent is quoted in *Times of India*, February 12, 1863, 3; Silver, *Manchester Men*, 254.

33. U.S. Consulate General Calcutta to William H. Seward, Calcutta, October 28, 1864, in Despatches of the U.S. Consul in Calcutta to U.S. Secretary of State, National Archives, Washington, DC; *Times of India*, Overland Summary, February 12, 1862, 1, cites the following numbers of cotton exports from Bombay: In 1860 India exported 497,649 bales of cotton to Europe and 205,161 bales to China; in 1861 it shipped 955,030 bales to Europe and only 67,209 to China. See *Times of India*, October 3, 1862, 2; Harnetty, "Imperialism, 1861–1865," 92; Mann, *The Cotton Trade*, 103, 112; *Statistical Abstracts for the United Kingdom in Each of the Last Fifteen Years from 1857 to 1871* (London: George E. Eyre and William Spottiswoode, 1872), 48–49; Fohlen, *L'industrie textile*, 287, 514.

34. The importance of the integration of the "hinterland" into the global economy and the relative "lateness" of this process is also emphasized by David Ludden, "World Economy and Village India, 1600–1900," in Sugata Bose, ed., *South Asia and World Capitalism* (New Delhi: Oxford University Press, 1990), 159–77; see Register of Invoices from the Consulate by Sundry Vessels bound for Ports in the United States, September 1863, in S 1040 (m168) reel 2, Despatches from United States Consulate General, Bombay, 1838–1906, National Archives, Washington DC; on the adjustment of machines, see letter from Mr. Baker, Inspector of Factories, to the Secretary of State for the Home Department, on the Present State of the Cotton Districts, in various documents relating to the distress in the cotton manufacturing districts during the American Civil War, in HO 45: 7523, Home Office, National Archives of the UK, Kew; Neil Charlesworth, *Peasants and Imperial Rule: Agriculture and Agrarian Society in the Bombay Presidency, 1850–1935* (Cambridge: Cambridge University Press, 1985), 135; *Statistical Abstracts for the United Kingdom* (London: George E. Eyre and William Spottiswoode, 1872), 48–49; Reichsenquete für die Baumwollen und Leinen-Industrie, *Statistische Ermittelungen*, Heft 1, 56–58; Mann, *The Cotton Trade*, 103, 112, 132; *Times of India*, Overland Summary, February 12, 1862, 1; *Times of India*, October 3, 1862, 2; Harnetty, "Imperialism, 1861–1865," 287, 514; Bombay Chamber of Commerce, *Report of the Bombay Chamber of Commerce for the Year 1863–64* (Bombay: Pearse and Sorabjeem 1865), 1; Frenise A. Logan, "India: Britain's Substitute for American Cotton, 1861–1865," *Journal of Southern History* 24, no. 4 (1958): 476; see also Manchester Chamber of Commerce, *The Forty-Fourth Annual Report of the Board of Directors for the Year 1864* (Manchester: Cave & Server, 1865), 18; B. R. Mitchell, *European Historical Statistics, 1750–1970* (New York: Columbia University Press, 1976), E14; Frenise A. Logan, "India's Loss of the British Cotton Market After 1865," *Journal of Southern History* 31, no. 1 (1965): 40–50; *Cotton Supply Reporter* (April 15, 1861): 473, reprint of article from *The Standard*, Agra, March 6, 1861.

35. *Merchants' Magazine and Commercial Review* 46, no. 2 (February 1862): 166; Edward Atkinson, "The Future Supply of Cotton," *North American Review* 98, no. 203 (April 1864): 481. Atkinson is not identified as the author, but his authorship becomes clear from his correspondence with Charles E. Norton. See N 297, Letters, 1861–1864, Edward A. Atkinson Papers, Massachusetts Historical Society, Boston.

36. One observer argues that without the war, the rapid expansion of cotton production in Egypt would have taken half a century; see Edward Mead Earle, "Egyptian Cotton and the American Civil War," *Political Science Quarterly* 41, no. 4 (1926), 520–45, 522; for the conversion of cantars into pounds see E. R. J. Owen, *Cotton and the Egyptian Economy* (Oxford: Clarendon Press, 1969), 89, 382–83; I assumed here that one cantar equaled 100 pounds; see Atkinson, "Future Supply," 481.

37. *Estatísticas históricas do Brasil: Séries econômicas, demográficas e sociais de 1550 a 1988* (Rio de Janeiro: Fundação Instituto Brasileiro de Geografia e Estatística, 1990), 346; they were urged on by the Manchester Chamber of Commerce and Lord Russell himself; see Manchester, *Forty-First Annual Report*, 8; Stanley S. Stein, *The Brazilian Cotton Manufacture* (Cambridge, MA: Harvard University Press, 1957), 43. The table on page 257 is based on information from Government of India, *Annual Statement of the Trade and Navigation of British India and Foreign Countries and of the Coasting Trade between the Several Presidencies and Provinces*, vol. 5 (Calcutta: Office of Superintendent of Government Printing, 1872); Government of India, *Annual Statement of the Trade and Navigation of British India and Foreign Countries and of the Coasting Trade between the Several Presidencies and Provinces*, vol. 9 (Calcutta: Office of Superintendent of Government Printing, 1876); Owen, *Cotton*, 90; *Estatísticas históricas do Brasil*, 346.

38. Orhan Kurmus, "The Cotton Famine and its Effects on the Ottoman Empire," in Huri Islamoglu-Inan, *The Ottoman Empire and the World-Economy* (Cambridge: Cambridge University Press, 1987), 162, 164, 165, 169; "Note of the Ministère de l'Algérie et des colonies," Paris, December 23, 1857; Société anonyme, "Compagnie française des cotons algeriens" (Paris: Imprimé du corps legislatif, 1863), in F/80/737, Fonds Ministériels, Archives d'outre-mer, Aix-en-Provence, France; see also Ministère de l'Algérie et des colonies, Direction de l'Administration de l'Algérie, 2ème bureau, Paris Décret, 1859, in Colonisation L/61, 2, Gouvernement Général de l'Algérie, Centre des Archives d'outre-mer, Aix-en-Provence; "Culture du Coton," by [illegible], Paris, July 19, 1859, in ibid.; Alejandro E. Bunge, *Las industrias del norte: Contribucion al estudio de una nueva política economia Argentina* (Buenos Aires: n.p., 1922), 209–10; *Liverpool Mercury*, November 9, 1863, 6; Thomas Schoonover, "Mexican Cotton and the American Civil War," *Americas* 30, no. 4 (April 1974): 430, 435; William S. Bell, *An Essay on the Peruvian Cotton Industry, 1825–1920* (Liverpool: University of Liverpool, Centre for Latin American Studies, 1985), 80; *Liverpool Mercury*, January 3, 1865, 6; for the importance of Chinese raw cotton imports see also Manchester, *Forty-Fourth Annual Report*, 16; "Der Baumwollbau in Togo, Seine Bisherige Entwicklung, und sein jetziger Stand," draft article in R 1001/8224, Bundesarchiv, Berlin.

39. *Manchester Guardian*, May 13, 1861, 4; May 16, 1861, 3; May 17, 1861, 4; May 25, 1861, 5; Céleste Duval, *Question cotonnière: La France peut s'emparer du monopole du coton par l'Afrique, elle peut rendre l'Angleterre, l'Europe, ses tributaires: L'Afrique est le vrai pays du coton* (Paris: Cosson, 1864), 7; *Queensland Guardian*, April 3, 1861, as cited in *Cotton Supply Reporter* (July 1, 1861): 554; Bunge, *Las industrias*, 209–10; *Liverpool Mercury*, November 9, 1863, 6, January 3, 1865, 6; Manchester, *Forty-Fourth Annual Report*, 16; Donna J. E. Maier, "Persistence of Precolonial Patterns of Production:

Cotton in German Togoland, 1800–1914," in Allen F. Isaacman and Richard Roberts, eds., *Cotton, Colonialism, and Social History in Sub-Saharan Africa* (Portsmouth, NH: Heinemann, 1995), 75; Peter Sebald, *Togo 1884–1914: Eine Geschichte der deutschen "Musterkolonie" auf der Grundlage amtlicher Quellen* (Berlin: Akademie-Verlag, 1988), 30; O. F. Metzger, *Unsere alte Kolonie Togo* (Neudamm: J. Neumann, 1941), 242; "Der Baumwollbau in Togo."

40. Samuel Ruggles, in front of the New York Chamber of Commerce, reprinted in *Merchants' Magazine and Commercial Review* 45, no. 1 (July 1861): 83.

41. On these discussions see Henry Blumenthal, "Confederate Diplomacy, Popular Notions and International Realities," *Journal of Southern History* 32, no. 2 (1966): 151–71; Carl N. Degler, *One Among Many: The Civil War in Comparative Perspective* (Gettysburg, PA: Gettysburg College, 1990); Hyman, ed., *Heard Round the World*; Owsley and Owsley, *King Cotton*; Bernarr Cresap, "Frank L. Owsley and King Cotton Diplomacy," *Alabama Review* 26, no. 4 (1973); Charles M. Hubbard, *The Burden of Confederate Diplomacy* (Knoxville: University of Tennessee Press, 1998); D. P. Crook, *Diplomacy During the American Civil War* (New York: Wiley, 1975); Howard Jones, *Union in Peril: The Crisis over British Intervention in the Civil War* (Chapel Hill: University of North Carolina Press, 1992); Lynn M. Case and Warren F. Spencer, *The United States and France: Civil War Diplomacy* (Philadelphia: University of Pennsylvania Press, 1970), 79; Löffler, *Preussens*; for pro-Confederate sentiments see *Liverpool Mercury*, June 24, 1861, 3, August 12, 1861, 2, September 20, 1861, 6, October 8, 1861, 5, October 15, 1861, 5, December 18, 1861, 6, April 18, 1862, 6; for pressure to recognize the Confederate government see *Liverpool Mercury*, July 16, 1862, 5, November 19, 1862, 3. For a controversial debate on slavery see the letters to the editor to the *Liverpool Mercury* printed on February 7 and 9, 1863, both on page 3; *Liverpool Mercury*, May 21, 1863, 7; Pelzer, "Liverpool," 46; for material support for the Confederacy see copy of letter from Thomas Haines Dudley, U.S. Consulate Liverpool, to Charles Francis Adams, Liverpool, May 4, 1864, in Seward Papers, Library of Congress, Washington, DC; Thomas Haines Dudley to William H. Seward, Liverpool, September 3, 1864, in ibid.; *Liverpool Mercury*, May 3, 1864, 6. Fraser, Trenholm & Company, operating out of Liverpool, secured funds for the Confederacy, built warships, and participated in blockade running; see the Fraser, Trenholm & Company Papers, Merseyside Maritime Museum, Liverpool; Liverpool merchants went into business with agents of the Confederacy in trading cotton bypassing the federal blockade; Letter by W. Fernie, Liverpool, to Fraser, Trenholm & Co, B/FT 1/13, Fraser, Trenholm & Company Papers, Merseyside Maritime Museum, Liverpool. Also see *Liverpool Mercury*, February 4, 1863, 3; for Manchester see *Liverpool Mercury*, May 23, 1863, 6; October 6, 1863, 6; October 17, 1863, 3; February 1, 1864, 7; for working-class support see *Liverpool Mercury*, May 2, 1862, 7; August 9, 1862, 5. See also Manchester, *Forty-First Annual Report*, 21–22; Rapport de Bigorie de Laschamps, Procureur Général de Colmar, April 7, 1862, as cited in Case, ed., *French Opinion*, 258; Dunham, "Development," 294; on the importance of cotton in the forming of French public and official opinion see Case, ed., *French Opinion*, 257; Rapport de Bigorie de Laschamps, Procureur Général de Colmar, July 14, 1862, cited in Case, ed., *French Opinion*, 260; George M. Black-

bourn, *French Newspaper Opinion on the American Civil War* (Westport, CT: Greenwood Press, 1997), 114; Donald Bellows, "A Study of British Conservative Reaction to the American Civil War," *Journal of Southern History* 51, no. 4 (November 1985): 505–26; *Hansard's Parliamentary Debates*, Third Series, vol. 171 (1863), 1774; *The Porcupine*, November 9, 1861, 61; more seriously, the *Money Market Review* claimed in May 1861 that the Confederacy "has the sympathy of the business men of the United Kingdom"; quoted in *Liverpool Mercury*, May 17, 1861; in December 1862, the Liverpool Chamber of Commerce, after a long and acrimonious debate, passed a resolution in which it demanded changes in international law that would protect the private property of neutrals on the high seas, in effect undermining the blockade of southern ports; *Liverpool Mercury*, December 4, 1862, 5, December 11, 1862, 3; Tony Barley, *Myths of the Slave Power: Confederate Slavery, Lancashire Workers and the Alabama* (Liverpool: Coach House Press, 1992), 49; *Liverpool Mercury*, May 23, 1863, 6, October 6, 1863, 6, October 17, 1863, 3, February 1, 1864, 7; Liverpool Chamber of Commerce, *Report of the Council, 1862* (Liverpool: Benson and Mallett, 1862), 20; Brown Brothers and Company, *Experiences of a Century, 1818–1918: Brown Brothers and Company* (Philadelphia: n.p., 1919), 47.

42. British workers, especially the cotton operatives of Lancashire, however, by and large did not agree with the pro-Confederate sympathies of some merchants and manufacturers, and they frequently spoke in support of the Union, especially once Lincoln proclaimed the possibility of emancipation. Lincoln himself communicated his appreciation for the support of Lancashire workers in early 1863. This is strongly argued by Barley, *Myths*, 67–71; Philip S. Foner, *British Labor and the American Civil War* (New York: Holmes & Meier, 1981), and Jones, *Union in Peril*, 225; against this view, but now largely refuted, Mary Ellison, *Support for Secession: Lancashire and the American Civil War* (Chicago: University of Chicago Press, 1972).

43. Jones, *Union in Peril*; Owsley and Owsley, *King Cotton*; for the Confederacy, see W. L. Trenholm to Charles Kuhn Prioleau (Liverpool), New York, June 21, 1865, B/FT 1/137, Fraser, Trenholm & Company Papers, Merseyside Maritime Museum, Liverpool; on the importance of wheat imports to Britain, see for example William Thayer to William H. Seward, London, July 19, 1862, Seward Papers, Library of Congress, Washington, DC; *Hansard's Parliamentary Debates*, Third Series, vol. 171, June 30, 1863, 1795. For a far-flung debate on why not to recognize the Confederacy, see ibid., 1771–1842; *Hansard's Parliamentary Debates*, Third Series, vol. 167, June 13, 1862, 543; George Campbell, Duke of Argyll, to Lord John Russell, October 11, 1862, Box 25, 30/22, Lord John Russell Papers, National Archives of the UK, Kew; on the Prussian desire for a strong United States to counterbalance British influence, see Löffler, *Preussens*, 59; see also Martin T. Tupper to Abraham Lincoln, May 13, 1861 (support from England), in Series 1, General Correspondence, 1833–1916, Abraham Lincoln Papers, Library of Congress, Washington, DC; for European pressures on Lincoln, see Lord John Russell Papers, National Archives of the UK, Kew; Lord Richard Lyons to Lord John Russell, Washington, 28 July 1863, in United States, Washington Legislation, Private Correspondence, Box 37, 30/22, Lord John Russell Papers, National Archives of the UK, Kew; Charles Wood to James Bruce, Earl of Elgin, August 9, 1862, LB 11, Letterbook, July 3 to December 31, 1862, MSS EUR

F 78, Wood Papers, Oriental and India Office Collections, British Library, London. American diplomats too were frequently reminded of Europe's urgent need for cotton; Henry S. Sanford to William H. Seward, April 10, 1862, Seward Papers, Manuscripts Division, Library of Congress, Washington, DC, quoted in Case and Spencer, *United States and France*, 290; William Thayer to William H. Seward, London, July 19, 1862, Seward Papers; William L. Dayton to Charles Francis Adams, Paris, November 21, 1862, AM 15236, Correspondence, Letters Sent A-C, Box I, Dayton Papers, as quoted in Case and Spencer, *United States and France*, 371.

44. Sancton, "Myth of French Worker," 58–80; for concerns about social upheaval and plans to improve the situation of unemployed cotton workers, see Ménier, *Au profit*; on British workers' collective action see Hall, "Poor Cotton Weyver," 227–50; Jones, *Union in Peril*, 55, argues that both Gladstone and Lyons cited fears of social upheaval among textile workers as reasons to intervene in the American conflict; Address by William E. Gladstone on the Cotton Famine, 1862, Add. 44690, f. 55, vol. 605, Gladstone Papers, British Library, London; William E. Gladstone, Speech on the American Civil War, Town Hall, Newcastle upon Tyne, October 7, 1862, as quoted in Jones, *Union in Peril*, 182.

45. Jones, *Union in Peril*, 114, 123, 129, 130, 133; Lord Richard Lyons to Lord John Russell, Washington, July 28, 1863, in United States, Washington Legislation, Private Correspondence, Box 37, 30/22, Lord John Russell Papers, National Archives of the UK, Kew; Charles Wood to James Bruce, Earl of Elgin, August 9, 1862, in LB 11, Letterbook, July 3 to December 31, 1862, MSS EUR F 78, Wood Papers, Oriental and India Office Collections, British Library, London; Glyndon G. Van Deusen, *William Henry Seward* (New York: Oxford University Press, 1967), 330–31, Abraham Lincoln, "Annual Message to Congress," December 3, 1861, in John George Nicolay and John Hay, eds., *Abraham Lincoln: Complete Works, Compromising His Speeches, Letters, State Papers, and Miscellaneous Writings*, vol. 2 (New York: Century Co., 1894), 94; "The Cabinet on Emancipation," MSS, July 22, 1862, reel 3, Edwin M. Stanton Papers, Library of Congress, Washington, DC. Thanks to Eric Foner for bringing this source to my attention.

46. William Thayer to William H. Seward, London, July 19, 1862, Seward Papers, Manuscript Division, Library of Congress, Washington, DC; Henry S. Sanford to William H. Seward, April 10, 1862, Seward Papers; William L. Dayton to William H. Seward, Paris, March 25, 1862, Despatches, France, State Department Correspondence, National Archives, Washington, DC. Napoleon argued that social unrest would follow if cotton could not be secured. Thurlow Weed to William H. Seward, Paris, April 4, 1862, in ibid.; Imbert-Koechlim is quoted in *Industrial Alsacien*, February 2, 1862, as cited in Sancton, "Myth of French Worker," 76; William L. Dayton to Charles Francis Adams, Paris, November 21, 1862, in AM 15236, Correspondence, Letters Sent A-C, Box I, Dayton Papers, quoted in Case and Spencer, *United States and France*, 371, also see 374; Owsley and Owsley, *King Cotton*, 16–17.

47. Charles Francis Adams Jr. to Henry Adams, Quincy, Massachusetts, August 25, 1861, in Ford, ed., *A Cycle of Adams Letters*, 34–35, 36.

48. For this fascinating story see Ricky-Dale Calhoun, "Seeds of Destruction: The Globalization of Cotton as a Result of the American Civil War" (PhD dissertation, Kan-

sas State University, 2012), 99ff., 150ff.; William Thayer to William Seward, March 5, 1863, Alexandria, in Despatches of the U.S. Consul in Alexandria to Seward, National Archives, Washington DC. See also David R. Serpell, "American Consular Activities in Egypt, 1849–1863," *Journal of Modern History* 10, no. 3 (1938): 344–63; William Thayer to William H. Seward, Despatch number 23, Alexandria, November 5, 1862, in Despatches of the U.S. Consul in Alexandria to Seward, National Archives, Washington DC; William H. Seward to William Thayer, Washington, December 15, 1862, Seward Papers, Library of Congress, Washington, DC; Ayoub Bey Trabulsi to William H. Seward, Alexandria, August 12, 1862, in Despatches of the U.S. Consul in Alexandria to Seward, National Archives, Washington, DC; William Thayer to William H. Seward, April 1, 1862, in ibid.; for the dispatches to Seward on cotton see for example William Thayer to William H. Seward, Alexandria, July 20, 1861, in ibid.; William Thayer to William H. Seward, Despatch number 23, Alexandria, November 5, 1862, in ibid.

49. William H. Seward to William Thayer, Washington, December 15, 1862, Seward Papers, Manuscript Division, Library of Congress, Washington, DC. See also Ayoub Bey Trabulsi to William H. Seward, Alexandria, August 12, 1862, in Despatches of the U.S. Consul in Alexandria to Seward, National Archives, Washington, DC; William Thayer to William H. Seward, April 1, 1862, in ibid.

50. Baring Brothers Liverpool to Joshua Bates, Liverpool, February 12, 1862, in HC 35: 1862, House Correspondence, Baring Brothers, ING Baring Archive, London; Charles Wood to James Bruce, Earl of Elgin, August 9, 1862, in MSS EUR F 78, LB 11, Wood Papers, Oriental and India Office Collections, British Library, London; Dunham, "Development," 295; Rapport de Neveu-Lemaire, procureur général de Nancy, January 5, 1864, as cited in Case, ed., *French Opinion*, 285–86; similar reports came in from other districts as well.

51. *Liverpool Mercury*, January 4, 1864, 8; the general argument is also made by Tripathi, "A Shot," 74–89; William H. Seward, March 25, 1871, in Olive Risely Seward, ed., *William H. Seward's Travels Around the World* (New York: D. Appleton & Co, 1873), 401.

52. This is the impression from reading the Annual Reports of the Manchester Chamber of Commerce; for a sense of relief by cotton interests see Manchester, *Forty-Third Annual Report*, 17, 25; *Liverpool Mercury*, August 8, 1864, 7, August 9, 1864, 7, August 10, 1864, 3, August 31, 1864, 7, September 22, 1864, 7, October 31, 1864, 7. See also Owsley and Owsley, *King Cotton*, 137, 143; Atkinson, "Future Supply," 485–86; John Bright to Edward A. Atkinson, London, May 29, 1862, Box N 298, Edward A. Atkinson Papers, Massachusetts Historical Society, Boston.

53. *Bremer Handelsblatt* 12 (1862), 335.

54. *The Economist*, September 21, 1861, 1042; J. E. Horn, *La crise cotonnière et les textiles indigènes* (Paris: Dentu, 1863), 14; Leone Levi, "On the Cotton Trade and Manufacture, as Affected by the Civil War in America," *Journal of the Statistical Society of London* 26, no. 8 (March 1863): 42; Stephen S. Remak, *La paix en Amérique* (Paris: Henri Plon, 1865), 25–26; *Bremer Handelsblatt*, April 22, 1865, 142.

55. The importance of slaves to the struggle for emancipation has been beautifully analyzed by many historians; see especially Ira Berlin et al., *Slaves No More: Three Essays*

on Emancipation and the Civil War (New York: Cambridge University Press, 1992); Eric Foner, *Reconstruction: America's Unfinished Revolution, 1863–1877* (New York: HarperCollins, 2002); Steven Hahn, *A Nation Under Our Feet: Black Political Struggles in the Rural South from Slavery to the Great Migration* (Cambridge, MA: Belknap Press of Harvard University, 2003); Steven Hahn, *The Political Worlds of Slavery and Freedom* (Cambridge, MA: Harvard University Press, 2009); on the contradictions of southern state formation and the weaknesses it wrought in war see also Stephanie McCurry, *Confederate Reckoning: Power and Politics in the Civil War South* (Cambridge, MA: Harvard University Press, 2010).

56. *London Mercury*, September 22, 1863, 7; Ravinder Kumar, *Western India in the Nineteenth Century: A Study in the Social History of Maharashtra* (London: Routledge & K. Paul, 1968), 35, 59, 151, 161; Maurus Staubli, *Reich und arm mit Baumwolle: Exportorientierte Landwirtschaft und soziale Stratifikation am Beispiel des Baumwollanbaus im indischen Distrikt Khandesh (Dekkan) 1850–1914* (Stuttgart: F. Steiner, 1994), 58, 68, 114–15, 187; Alan Richards, *Egypt's Agricultural Development, 1800–1980: Technical and Social Change* (Boulder, CO: Westview Press, 1982), 55, 61; in Turkestan, many years later, the result would be quite similar; John Whitman, "Turkestan Cotton in Imperial Russia," *American Slavic and East European Review* 15, no. 2 (1956): 190–205; on economic change in the postbellum South see Foner, *Reconstruction*, 392–411; Gavin Wright, *The Political Economy of the Cotton South: Households, Markets, and Wealth in the Nineteenth Century* (New York: Norton, 1978), 166–76; Wright, *Old South*, 34, 107; Steven Hahn, *The Roots of Southern Populism: Yeoman Farmers and the Transformation of the Georgia Upcountry, 1850–1890* (New York: Oxford University Press, 1983).

57. W. H. Holmes, *Free Cotton: How and Where to Grow It* (London: Chapman and Hall, 1862), 18; Merivale, *Lectures*, 315; Report of the Select Committee of the House of Commons, dated July 25, 1842, as cited in Alleyne Ireland, *Demerariana: Essays, Historical, Critical, and Descriptive* (New York: Macmillan, 1899), 150; *The Economist*, December 9, 1865, 1487, emphasis in original.

58. Holmes, *Free Cotton*, 16, 18, 22; Commission Coloniale, Rapport à M. le Ministre de la Marine et des Colonies sur l'Organisation du Travail Libre, Record Group Gen 40, box 317, Fonds Ministérielles, Archives d'outre-mer, Aix-en-Provence, France; *Cotton Supply Reporter* (December 16, 1861): 722.

59. Holmes, *Free Cotton*; Auteur de la paix en Europe par l'Alliance anglo-française, *Les blancs et les noirs en Amérique et le coton dans les deux mondes* (Paris: Dentu, 1862).

60. The theme of "rehearsal for Reconstruction" is taken from Willie Lee Nichols Rose, *Rehearsal for Reconstruction: The Port Royal Experiment* (Indianapolis: Bobbs-Merrill, 1964); *Liverpool Mercury*, September 23, 1863, 6; this was also the conclusion of an increasing number of people in Liverpool, who by 1863 had sent an ever-increasing number of letters to the editor of the *Liverpool Mercury* to make their antislavery voices heard; see *Liverpool Mercury*, January 19, 1863, 6, January 24, 1863, 7; Edward Atkinson, *Cheap Cotton by Free Labor* (Boston: A. Williams & Co., 1861); Atkinson Papers, Massachusetts Historical Society, Boston; Manchester, *Forty-First Annual Report*, 33; Atkinson, "Future Supply," 485–86.

61. Already in 1862, Mr. Caird argued in the House of Commons, that "the advantages

which the Southern States had hitherto derived from slave cultivation would be to a great extent at an end." *Hansard's Parliamentary Debates*, Third Series, vol. 167 (1862), 791; see *Liverpool Mercury*, January 3, 1865, 6, April 25, 1865, 6, May 13, 1865, 6; for prices, see John A. Todd, *World's Cotton Crops* (London: A. & C. Black, 1915 (1924), 429–32; XXIV.2.22, RP, Rathbone Papers, Special Collections and Archives, University of Liverpool; Baring Brothers Liverpool to Baring Brothers London, July 19, 1865, in House Correspondence, HC 3 (1865), folder 35 (Correspondence from Liverpool House), ING Baring Archive, London.

62. *Bremer Handelsblatt*, June 17, 1865, 234–35; W. A. Bruce to Lord John Russell, May 10, 1865, in Letters from Washington Minister of Great Britain to Foreign Office, Earl Russell, 1865, in 30: 22/38, Lord John Russell Papers, National Archives of the UK, Kew; W. A. Bruce to Lord John Russell, May 22, 1865, in ibid.

63. August Etienne, *Die Baumwollzucht im Wirtschaftsprogramm der deutschen Übersee-Politik* (Berlin: Verlag von Hermann Paetel, 1902), 28; the theme of labor shortage was also an important subject in discussions on the expansion of Indian cotton production during the U.S. Civil War; see *Times of India*, October 18, 1861, 3, February 27, 1863, 6; *Zeitfragen*, May 1, 1911, 1; Protocol of the Annual Meeting of the Manchester Cotton Supply Association, June 11, 1861, reprinted in "The Cotton Question," *Merchants' Magazine and Commercial Review* 45 (October 1861): 379; *Liverpool Mercury*, June 12, 1861, 3; the superintendent of the Cotton Gin Factory in the Dharwar Collectorate reported in May 1862, "Although the cultivation of native cotton is capable of extension to an enormous degree, yet the amount of labour available is barely sufficient to clean the quantity now produced"; quoted in *Times of India*, February 12, 1863, 3; *Bengal Hurkaru*, May 11, 1861, as reprinted in *Bombay Times and Standard*, May 17, 1861, 3.

64. *Cotton Supply Reporter* (June 15, 1861): 530; Supplement to *The Economist*, Commercial History and Review of 1865, March 10, 1866, 3; *Bremer Handelsblatt*, April 22, 1865, 142; the institution of slavery itself, of course, thrived for a few more decades in places such as Cuba, Brazil, and Africa; by and large, however, cotton was no longer produced by slaves; see Suzanne Miers and Richard Roberts, *The End of Slavery in Africa* (Madison: University of Wisconsin Press, 1988).

65. Timothy Mitchell, *Rule of Experts: Egypt, Techno-Politics, Modernity* (Berkeley: University of California Press, 2002), 59–60; Mathieu, *De la culture*, 25.

66. *Bremer Handelsblatt*, October 14, 1865, 372.

67. *The Economist*, December 9, 1865, 1487–88; Eric Foner, *Nothing but Freedom: Emancipation and Its Legacy* (Baton Rouge: Louisiana State University Press, 1983), 27–28.

68. Berlin et al., *Slaves No More*, 1–76.

69. Reclus, "Le coton," 208.

70. Baring Brothers Liverpool to Baring Brothers London, February 4, 1865, in House Correspondence, HC 3 (1865), folder 35 (Correspondence from Liverpool House), ING Baring Archive, London; *Gore's General Advertiser*, January 19, 1865, as cited in Hall, "Liverpool Cotton," 163; *Indian Daily News*, Extraordinary, March 8, 1865, clipping included in U.S. Consulate General Calcutta to William H. Seward, Calcutta, March 8, 1864, in Despatches of the U.S. Consul in Calcutta to U.S. Secretary of State, National Archives, Washington, DC; Letter from Calvin W. Smith to "Dear

Friends at home," Bombay, April 23, 1865, in folder 13, Ms. N-937, Calvin W. Smith Papers, Massachusetts Historical Society, Boston; Samuel Smith, *My Life-Work* (London: Hodder and Stoughton, 1902), 35; Brown Brothers, *Experiences*, 49–50.

71. William B. Forwood, "The Influence of Price upon the Cultivation and Consumption of Cotton During the Ten Years 1860–1870," *Journal of the Statistical Society of London* 33, no. 3 (September 1870): 371.

72. Horn, *La crise*, 43.

CHAPTER TEN: GLOBAL RECONSTRUCTION

1. Frederick W. A. Bruce to Earl of Clarendon, British Secretary of State, Washington, DC, December 18, 1865, reprinted in *Cotton Supply Reporter* (February 1, 1866): 1795; Memorandum, W. Hickens, Royal Engineers, to Secretary of State, Washington, DC, December 18, 1865, in ibid.

2. Edmund Ashworth, as cited in *Cotton Supply Reporter* (July 1, 1865): 1675; Maurice Williams, "The Cotton Trade of 1865," *Seven Year History of the Cotton Trade of Europe, 1861 to 1868* (Liverpool: William Potter, 1868), 19. For more on Williams see Thomas Ellison, *The Cotton Trade of Great Britain: Including a History of the Liverpool Cotton Market and of the Liverpool Cotton Brokers' Association* (London: Effingham Wilson, 1886), 255.

3. Robert Ed. Bühler, "Die Unabhängigkeitsbestrebungen Englands, Frankreichs und Deutschlands in ihrer Baumwollversorgung" (PhD dissertation, University of Zürich, 1929), 3; *Cotton Supply Reporter* (June 1, 1865): 1658.

4. B. R. Mitchell, *International Historical Statistics: The Americas, 1750–2005* (New York: Palgrave Macmillan, 2007), 391, 467, 547–49; Elijah Helm, "An International Survey of the Cotton Industry," *Quarterly Journal of Economics* 17, no. 3 (May 1903): 417; Gavin Wright, "Cotton Competition and the Post-bellum Recovery of the American South," *Journal of Economic History* 34, no. 3 (September 1974): 632–33. Douglas A. Farnie and David J. Jeremy, *The Fibre That Changed the World: The Cotton Industry in International Perspective, 1600–1990s* (Oxford: Oxford University Press, 2004), 23, 25.

5. The graph on page 279 is based on the author's analysis of data on cotton spindles from nineteen countries (Austria, Belgium, Brazil, Canada, China, France, Germany, India, Italy, Japan, Mexico, the Netherlands, Portugal, Russia, Spain, Sweden, Switzerland, the United Kingdom, and the United States). Due to the dispersed and inconsistent nature of the sources, this is not more than an estimate. Some numbers have been extrapolated. For the numbers see Louis Bader, *World Developments in the Cotton Industry, with Special Reference to the Cotton Piece Goods Industry in the United States* (New York: New York University Press, 1925), 33; Amiya Kumar Bagchi, *Private Investment in India, 1900–1939*, Cambridge South Asian Studies 10 (Cambridge: Cambridge University Press, 1972), 234; Javier Barajas Manzano, *Aspectos de la industria textil de algodón en México* (Mexico: Instituto Mexicano de Investigaciones Económicas, 1959), 43–44, 280; Belgium, Ministère de l'Intérieur, *Statistique de la Belgique, Industrie* (Brussels: Impr. de T. Lesigne, 1851), 471; Pierre Benaerts, *Les origines de la grande industrie allemande* (Paris: F. H. Turot, 1933), 486; Sabbato Louis

Besso, *The Cotton Industry in Switzerland, Vorarlberg, and Italy; A Report to the Electors of the Gartside Scholarships* (Manchester: Manchester University Press, 1910); George Bigwood, *Cotton* (New York: Holt, 1919), 61; H. J. Habakkuk and M. Postan, eds., *The Cambridge Economic History of Europe*, vol. 6 (Cambridge: Cambridge University Press, 1965), 443; Kang Chao, *The Development of Cotton Textile Production in China* (Cambridge, MA: Harvard University Press, 1977), 301–7; Stanley D. Chapman, "Fixed Capital Formation in the British Cotton Industry, 1770–1815," *Economic History Review*, New Series, 23, no. 2 (August 1970): 235–66, 252; Louis Bergeron and Jean-Antoine-Claude Chaptal, *De l'industrie française: Acteurs de l'histoire* (Paris: Impr. nationale éditions, 1993), 326; Melvin Thomas Copeland, *The Cotton Manufacturing Industry of the United States* (New York: A. M. Kelley, 1966), 19; see years 1878–1920 in *Cotton Facts: A Compilation from Official and Reliable Sources* (New York: A. B. Shepperson, 1878); Richard Dehn and Martin Rudolph, *The German Cotton Industry; A Report to the Electors of the Gartside Scholarships* (Manchester: Manchester University Press, 1913); Thomas Ellison, *A Hand-book of the Cotton Trade, or, A glance at the Past History, Present Condition, and the Future Prospects of the Cotton Commerce of the World* (London: Longman Brown Green Longmans and Roberts, 1858), 146–67; Ellison, *The Cotton Trade of Great Britain*, 72–3; D. A. Farnie, *The English Cotton Industry and the World Market, 1815–1896* (New York: Oxford University Press, 1979), 180; Mimerel Fils, "Filature du Cotton," in Michel Chevalier, ed., *Rapports du Jury international: Exposition universelle de 1867 à Paris*, vol. 4 (Paris: P. Dupont, 1868), 20; R. B. Forrester, *The Cotton Industry in France; A Report to the Electors of the Gartside Scholarships* (London: Longman, Green and Co., 1921), 5; "Industrie textile," *Annuaire statistique de la France* (Paris, 1877–1890, 1894); Michael Owen Gately, "The Development of the Russian Cotton Textile Industry in the Pre-revolutionary Years, 1861–1913" (PhD dissertation, University of Kansas, 1968), 134; Statistisches Reichsamt, *Statistisches Jahrbuch für das Deutsche Reich*, vol. 24 (1913), 107; Aurora Gómez Galvarriato, "The Impact of Revolution: Business and Labor in the Mexican Textile Industry, Orizaba, Veracruz, 1900–1930" (PhD dissertation, Harvard University, 2000), 23, 45; Great Britain, Committee on Industry, and Trade, *Survey of Textile Industries: Cotton, Wool, Artificial Silk* (London: Her Majesty's Stationery Office, 1928), 142; International Federation of Master Cotton Spinners' and Manufacturers' Associations, *International Cotton Statistics*, Arno S. Pearse, ed. (Manchester: Thiel & Tangye, 1921), 1–32; International Federation of Master Cotton Spinners' and Manufacturers' Associations and Arno S. Pearse, *The Cotton Industry of India, Being the Report of the Journey to India* (Manchester: Taylor, Garnett, Evans, 1930), 22; International Federation of Master Cotton Spinners' and Manufacturers' Associations and Arno S. Pearse, *The Cotton Industry of Japan and China, Being the Report of the Journey to Japan and China* (Manchester: Taylor Garnett Evans & Co. Ltd., 1929), 18–19, 154; Italy, Ministero di Agricoltura, Industria e Commercio, "L'industria del cotone in Italia," *Annali di Statistica*, series 4, no. 100 (Rome: Tipografia Nazionale di G. Bertero E.C., 1902), 12–13; Italy, Ministero di Agricoltura, Industria e Commercio, *Annuario statistico italiano* (Roma: Tip. Elzeviriana), see years 1878, 1881, 1886, 1892, 1900, 1904, and 1905–6; S. T. King and Ta-chün Liu, *China's Cotton Industry: A Statistical Study of Ownership of Capital, Output, and Labor*

Conditions (n.p.: n.p., 1929), 4; Sung Jae Koh, *Stages of Industrial Development in Asia: A Comparative History of the Cotton Industry in Japan, India, China, and Korea* (Philadelphia: University of Pennsylvania Press, 1966), 324–66; Richard A. Kraus, *Cotton and Cotton Goods in China, 1918–1936* (New York: Garland, 1980), 57, 99; John C. Latham and H. E. Alexander, *Cotton Movement and Fluctuations* (New York: Latham Alexander & Co., 1894–1910); Maurice Lévy-Leboyer, *Les banques européennes et l'industrialisation internationale dans la première moitié du XIXe siècle* (Paris: Presses Universitaires de France, 1964), 29; S. D. Mehta, *The Indian Cotton Textile Industry, an Economic Analysis* (Bombay: Published by G. K. Ved for the Textile Association of India, 1953), 139; B. R. Mitchell, *Abstract of British Historical Statistics* (Cambridge: Cambridge University Press, 1971) 185; B. R. Mitchell, *International Historical Statistics: Europe, 1750–1993* (New York: Stockton Press, 1998), 511; Charles Kroth Moser, *The Cotton Textile Industry of Far Eastern Countries* (Boston: Pepperell Manufacturing Company, 1930), 50; National Association of Cotton Manufacturers, *Standard Cotton Mill Practice and Equipment, with Classified Buyer's Index* (Boston: National Association of Cotton Manufacturers, 1919), 37; Keijiro Otsuka, Gustav Ranis, and Gary R. Saxonhouse, *Comparative Technology Choice in Development: The Indian and Japanese Cotton Textile Industries* (Houndmills, Basingstoke, UK: Macmillan, 1988), 6; Alexander Redgrave, "Report of Factory Inspectors," *Parliamentary Papers* (Great Britain: Parliament, House of Commons, 1855), 69; J. H. Schnitzler, *De la création de la richesse, ou, des intérêts matériels en France*, vol. 1 (Paris: H. Lebrun, 1842), 228; Stanley J. Stein, *The Brazilian Cotton Manufacture: Textile Enterprise in an Underdeveloped Area, 1850–1950* (Cambridge, MA: Harvard University Press, 1957), 191; Guy Thomson, "Continuity and Change in Mexican Manufacturing," in Jean Batou, ed., *Between Development and Underdevelopment: The Precocious Attempts at Industrialization of the Periphery, 1800–1870* (Geneva: Librairie Droz, 1991), 280; John A. Todd, *The World's Cotton Crops* (London: A. & C. Black, 1915), 411; Ugo Tombesi, *L'industria cotoniera italiana alla fine del secolo XIX* (Pesaro: G. Frederici, 1901), 66; United States, Bureau of Manufactures, *Cotton Fabrics in Middle Europe: Germany, Austria-Hungary, and Switzerland* (Washington, DC: Government Printing Office, 1908), 23, 125, 162; United States, Bureau of Manufactures, *Cotton Goods in Canada* (Washington, DC: Government Printing Office, 1913), 33; United States, Bureau of Manufactures, *Cotton Goods in Italy* (Washington, DC: Government Printing Office, 1912), 6; United States, Bureau of Manufactures, *Cotton Goods in Russia* (Washington, DC: Government Printing Office, 1912), 9–11; United States, Bureau of the Census, *Cotton Production and Distribution: Season of 1916–1917* (Washington, DC: Government Printing Office, 1918), 88; United States, Bureau of the Census, *Cotton Production in the United States* (Washington, DC: Government Printing Office, 1915), 56.

6. The general point is also made by Herbert S. Klein and Stanley Engerman, "The Transition from Slave to Free Labor: Notes on a Comparative Economic Model," in Manuel Moreno Fraginals, Frank Moya Pons, and Stanley L. Engerman, *Between Slavery and Free Labor: The Spanish-Speaking Caribbean in the Nineteenth Century* (Baltimore: Johns Hopkins University Press, 1985), 260.

7. Commission Coloniale, Rapport à M. le Ministre de la Marine et des Colonies sur

l'Organisation du Travail Libre, p. 61, in Record Group Gen 40, box 472, Fonds Ministérielles, Archives d'outre-mer, Aix-en-Provence, France.

8. The persistence of coercion is also emphasized by Lutz Raphael, "Krieg, Diktatur und Imperiale Erschliessung: Arbeitszwang und Zwangsarbeit 1880 bis 1960," in Elisabeth Herrmann-Ott, ed., *Sklaverei, Knechtschaft, Zwangsarbeit: Untersuchungen zur Sozial-, Rechts- und Kulturgeschichte.* (Hildesheim: Olms, 2005), 256–80; Robert Steinfeld, *Coercion, Contract, and Free Labor in the Nineteenth Century* (New York: Cambridge University Press, 2001); Eric Foner, *Nothing But Freedom: Emancipation and Its Legacy* (Baton Rouge: Louisiana State University Press, 1983); Nan Elizabeth Woodruff, *American Congo: The African American Freedom Struggle in the Delta* (Cambridge, MA: Harvard University Press, 2003); Donald Holley, *The Second Great Emancipation: The Mechanical Cotton Picker, Black Migration, and How They Shaped the Modern South* (Fayetteville: University of Arkansas Press, 2000), 104–5; Charles S. Aiken, *The Cotton Plantation South Since the Civil War* (Baltimore: Johns Hopkins University Press, 1998), 101.

9. Barbara Fields, "The Advent of Capitalist Agriculture: The New South in a Bourgeois World," in Thavolia Glymph et al., eds., *Essays on the Postbellum Southern Economy* (College Station: Texas A&M University Press, 1985), 74; *Southern Cultivator*, February 26, 1868, 61.

10. Edward Atkinson, *Cheap Cotton by Free Labor* (Boston: A. Williams & Co., 1861); *Commercial and Financial Chronicle* (November 11, 1865): 611–12.

11. *Southern Cultivator*, January 24, 1866, 5; W. A. Bruce to Earl Russell, Washington, May 10, 1865, in Letters from Washington Minister of Great Britain top Foreign Office, Earl Russell, 1865 (Private Correspondence), 30/22/38, National Archives of the UK, Kew; J. R. Busk to Messrs. Rathbone Brothers and Co., New York, April 24, 1865, in Rathbone Papers, Record number XXIV.2.22, RP, Rathbone Papers, Special Collections and Archives, University of Liverpool; *Commercial and Financial Chronicle* (August 26, 1865): 258ff.; George McHenry, *The Cotton Supply of the United States of America* (London: Spottiswoode & Co., 1865), 25ff.; Bengal Chamber of Commerce, Reports, 1864–1866, 809, as cited in Frenise A. Logan, "India's Loss of the British Cotton Market After 1865," *Journal of Southern History* 31, no. 1 (1965): 47; G. F. Forbes to Under Secretary of State for India, August 16, 1866, Secretariat Records Office, as quoted in Logan, "India's Loss of the British Cotton Market," 49.

12. Bliss Perry, *Life and Letters of Henry Lee Higginson*, vol. 1 (Boston: Atlantic Monthly Press, 1921), 247, *Southern Cultivator*, May 26, 1868, 133, 135. For examples of this discussion see *Southern Cultivator*, February 25, 1867, 42; August 25, 1867, 258; October 25, 1867, 308; January 26, 1868, 12; May 26, 1868, 135; Joseph P. Reidy, *From Slavery to Agrarian Capitalism in the Cotton Plantation South: Central Georgia, 1800–1880* (Chapel Hill: University of North Carolina Press, 1992), 137; *Southern Cultivator*, February 27, 1869, 51; *Macon Telegraph*, May 31, 1865.

13. Contract dated Boston, December 23, 1863, in various letters and notes, file 298, Edward A. Atkinson Papers, Massachusetts Historical Society, Boston; Eric Foner, *Reconstruction: America's Unfinished Revolution, 1863–1877* (New York: Harper & Row, 1988), 53, 54, 58; Edward Atkinson to his mother, Washington, July 5, 1864, in various letters and notes, file 298, Edward A. Atkinson Papers, Massachusetts Historical Society.

14. *Macon Daily Telegraph*, May 31, 1865, 1; Joseph D. Reid Jr., "Sharecropping as an Understandable Market Response: The Post-bellum South," *Journal of Economic History* 33, no. 1 (March 1973): 107.

15. Contract of January 29, 1866, in Alonzo T. and Millard Mial Papers, North Carolina Department of Archives and History, as cited in Reid, "Sharecropping as an Understandable Market Response," 108; Susan Eva O'Donovan, *Becoming Free in the Cotton South* (Cambridge, MA: Harvard University Press, 2007), 127, 129, 131; James C. Cobb, *The Most Southern Place on Earth: The Mississippi Delta and the Roots of Regional Identity* (New York: Oxford University Press, 1992), 48–50.

16. Foner, *Reconstruction*, 103, 104. It has been argued that throughout the Americas, former slaves desired "control over their own labor and access to their own lands." See Klein and Engerman, "The Transition from Slave to Free Labor," 256; "A Freedman's Speech," *Pennsylvania Freedmen's Bulletin* (January 1867): 16.

17. Reidy, *From Slavery to Agrarian Capitalism*, 144.

18. Foner, *Reconstruction*, 108, 134; Reidy, *From Slavery to Agrarian Capitalism*, 125, 150, 152; Amy Dru Stanley, "Beggars Can't Be Choosers: Compulsion and Contract in Postbellum America," *Journal of American History* 78, no. 4 (March 1992): 1274, 1285; Cobb, *The Most Southern Place*, 51; U.S. Congress, House, Orders Issue by the Commissioner and Assistant Commissioners of the Freedmen's Bureau, 65, as cited in Stanley, "Beggars Can't Be Choosers," 1284.

19. *Commercial and Financial Chronicle* (November 11, 1865): 611–12; "A Freedman's Speech," *Pennsylvania Freedmen's Bulletin* (January 1867): 115.

20. O'Donovan, *Becoming Free*, 162, 189, 224, 227, 240; Foner, *Reconstruction*, 138, 140; Cobb, *The Most Southern Place*, 51; James C. Scott, *Weapons of the Weak: Everyday Forms of Peasant Resistance* (New Haven, CT: Yale University Press, 1985), xv.

21. Gavin Wright, "The Strange Career of the New Southern Economic History," *Reviews in American History* 10, no. 4 (December 1982): 171; Foner, *Reconstruction*, 174; Fields, "The Advent of Capitalist Agriculture," 84; Reidy, *From Slavery to Agrarian Capitalism*, 159; *Southern Cultivator* 25, no. 11 (November 1867): 358; Aiken, *The Cotton Plantation South*, 34ff. Cobb, *The Most Southern Place*, 55, 70; W. E. B. DuBois, "Die Negerfrage in den Vereinigten Staaten," *Archiv für Sozialwissenschaft* 22 (1906): 52.

22. Reid, "Sharecropping as an Understandable Market Response," 114, 116, 118; Grimes Family Papers, #3357, Southern Historical Collection, as cited in Reid, "Sharecropping as an Understandable Market Response," 128–29.

23. Wright, "The Strange Career," 172, 176. Cobb, *The Most Southern Place*, 102; Harold D. Woodman, "Economic Reconstruction and the Rise of the New South, 1865–1900," in John B. Boles and Evelyn Thomas Nolan, eds., *Interpreting Southern History: Historiographical Essays in Honor of Sanford W. Higginbotham* (Baton Rouge: Louisiana State University Press, 1987), 268; DuBois, "Die Negerfrage," 41; C. L. Hardeman to John C. Burns, December 11, 1875, John C. Burrus Papers, Mississippi Department of Archives and History, as cited in Cobb, *The Most Southern Place*, 63; Eric Hobsbawm, *The Age of Empire, 1875–1914* (London: Weidenfeld and Nicolson, 1987), 36.

24. Wright, "The Strange Career," 170, 172; John R. Hanson II, "World Demand for

Cotton During the Nineteenth Century: Wright's Estimates Re-examined," *Journal of Economic History* 39, no. 4 (December 1979): 1015, 1016, 1018, 1019.

25. *Southern Cultivator*, January 26, 1868, 13; Telegram, Forstall and Sons to Baring Brothers, London, September 16, 1874, in record group HC 5.2.6.142, ING Baring Archive, London; O'Donovan, *Becoming Free*, 117; Cobb, *The Most Southern Place*, 91, 104, 114; Woodman, "Economic Reconstruction," 173; Reidy, *From Slavery to Agrarian Capitalism*, 222, 225; Aiken, *The Cotton Plantation South*, 23.

26. Steven Hahn, "Class and State in Postemancipation Societies: Southern Planters in Comparative Perspective," *American Historical Review* 95, no. 1 (February 1990): 83, 84, 96.

27. David F. Weiman, "The Economic Emancipation of the Non-slaveholding Class: Upcountry Farmers in the Georgia Cotton Economy," *Journal of Economic History* 45, no. 1 (1985): 72, 76, 78.

28. Weiman, "The Economic Emancipation of the Non-slaveholding Class," 84; DuBois, "Die Negerfrage," 38; Ernst von Halle, *Baumwollproduktion und Pflanzungswirtschaft in den Nordamerikanischen Südstaaten, Zweiter Teil, Sezessionskrieg und Rekonstruktion* (Leipzig: Dunker & Humboldt, 1906), 518, 661ff.; Foner, *Reconstruction*, 394.

29. *Southern Cultivator*, June 29, 1871, 221; Cobb, *The Most Southern Place*, 110; Jerre Mangione and Ben Morreale, *La Storia: Five Centuries of the Italian American Experience* (New York: Harper Perennial, 1992), 185; Aiken, *The Cotton Plantation South*, 61; E. Merton Coulter, *James Monroe Smith: Georgia Planter* (Athens: University of Georgia Press, 1961), 9, 14, 17, 35, 37, 67–69, 84, 90.

30. Julia Seibert, "Travail Libre ou Travail Forcé?: Die 'Arbeiterfrage' im belgischen Kongo 1908–1930," *Journal of Modern European History* 7, no. 1 (March 2009): 95–110; DuBois, "Die Negerfrage," 44.

31. United States Department of Commerce, Bureau of the Census, *Historical Statistics of the United States, Colonial Times to the Present* (New York: Basic Books, 1976), 518, 899; United States Bureau of Statistics, Department of the Treasury, *Cotton in Commerce: Statistics of United States, United Kingdom, France, Germany, Egypt, and British India* (Washington. DC: Government Printing Office, 1895), 29; France, Direction Générale des Douanes, *Tableau décennal du commerce de la France avec ses colonies et les puissances étrangères, 1887–96* (Paris, 1896), 2, 108; Kaiserliches Statistisches Amt, *Statistisches Jahrbuch für das Deutsche Reich*, vol. 13 (Berlin: Kaiserliches Statistisches Amt, 1892), 82–83; *Statistical Abstracts for the United Kingdom in Each of the Last Fifteen Years from 1886 to 1900* (London: Wyman and Sons, 1901), 92–93.

32. Bombay Chamber of Commerce, *Report of the Bombay Chamber of Commerce for the Year 1865–66* (Bombay: Education Society's Press, 1867), 213; B. R. Mitchell, *International Historical Statistics: Africa, Asia and Oceania, 1750–2005* (Basingstoke, UK: Palgrave Macmillan, 2007), 354; F. M. W. Schofield, Department of Revenue and Agriculture, Simla, September 15, 1888, 10, in Proceedings, Part B, Nos 6–8, April 1889, Fibres and Silk Branch, Department of Revenue and Agriculture, National Archives of India, New Delhi; *Statistical Abstract Relating to British India from 1903–04 to 1912–13* (London: His Majesty's Stationery Office, 1915), 188; *Statistical Tables Relating to Indian Cotton: Indian Spinning and Weaving Mills* (Bombay: Times of India Steam Press, 1889), 59; Toyo Menka Kaisha, *The Indian Cotton Facts 1930* (Bom-

bay: Toyo Menka Kaisha Ltd., 1930), 54; Dwijendra Tripathi, "India's Challenge to America in European Markets, 1876–1900," *Indian Journal of American Studies* 1, no. 1 (1969): 58; *Bericht der Handelskammer Bremen über das Jahr 1913* (Bremen: Hauschild, 1914), 38; Bombay Chamber of Commerce, *Report of the Bombay Chamber of Commerce for the Year 1865–66* (Bombay: Education Society's Press, 1867), 213. The permanence of this change is also emphasized by Maurus Staubli, *Reich und Arm mit Baumwolle: Exportorientierte Landwirtschaft am Beispiel des Baumwollanbaus im Indischen Distrikt Khandesh (Dekkan), 1850–1914* (Stuttgart: Franz Steiner Verlag, 1994), 66; James A. Mann, *The Cotton Trade of Great Britain: Its Rise, Progress, and Present Extent* (London: Simpkin, Marshall, 1860), 132; *Statistical Abstracts for British India from 1911–12 to 1920–21* (London: His Majesty's Stationery Office, 1924), 476–77. There is an unfortunate tendency in much of the literature on the effects of the Civil War on India to limit one's view to the relationship between India and Britain, which entirely misses the more important trade in raw cotton between India and continental Europe as well as Japan. For the "Empire-centric" view, see for example Logan, "India's Loss of the British Cotton Market," and also Wright, "Cotton Competition." On the importance of continental European markets see John Henry Rivett-Carnac, *Report of the Cotton Department for the Year 1868–69* (Bombay: Printed at the Education Society's Press, 1869), 139; C. B. Pritchard, *Annual Report on Cotton for the Bombay Presidency for the Year 1882–83* (Bombay: Cotton Department, Bombay Presidency, 1883), 2. On the importance of the Japanese market, see S. V. Fitzgerald and A. E. Nelson, *Central Provinces District Gazetteers, Amraoti District*, vol. A (Bombay: Claridge, 1911), 192, in record group V/27/65/6, Oriental and India Office Collections, British Library, London. On increased imports of Indian cotton to Europe see Tripathi, "India's Challenge to America in European Markets, 1876–1900," 57–65; *Statistical Abstracts for the United Kingdom for Each of the Fifteen Years from 1910 to 1924* (London: S. King & Son Ltd, 1926), 114–15; John A. Todd, *World's Cotton Crops* (London: A. & C. Black, 1915), 45; for the reasons why Indian cotton found a ready market on the continent see "Report by F. M. W. Schofield, Department of Revenue and Agriculture, Simla, 15 Sept. 1888," in Department of Revenue and Agriculture, Fibres and Silk Branch, April 1889, Nos. 6–8, Part B, National Archives of India, New Delhi; A. J. Dunlop to the Secretary of the Chamber of Commerce, Bombay, Alkolale, June 11, 1874, Proceedings, Part B, June 1874, No. 41/42, Fibres and Silk Branch, Agriculture and Commerce Department, Revenue, National Archives of India; "Statement Exhibiting the Moral and Material Progress and Condition of India, 1895–96," 109, Oriental and India Office Collections, British Library.

33. Mitchell, *International Historical Statistics: The Americas*, 227, 316.

34. International Federation of Master Cotton Spinners' and Manufacturers' Associations, *Official Report of the International Congress, Held in Egypt, 1927* (Manchester: International Federation of Master Cotton Spinners' and Manufacturers' Associations, 1927), 28, 49; Arnold Wright, ed., *Twentieth Century Impressions of Egypt: Its History, People, Commerce, Industries, and Resources* (London: Lloyd's Greater Britain Publishing Company, 1909), 280; B. R. Mitchell, *International Historical Statistics: Africa, Asia and Oceania, 1750–2005* (Basingstoke, UK: Palgrave Macmillan, 2007), 265.

35. Between 1866 and 1905 the number of spindles in Brazil increased by a factor of fifty-three. The Brazil discussion is based on *Estatísticas históricas do Brasil: Séries econômicas, demográficas e sociais de 1550 a 1988* (Rio de Janeiro: Fundação Instituto Brasileiro de Geogralica e Estatística, 1990), 346; on the number of spindles see Stanley J. Stein, *The Brazilian Cotton Manufacture: Textile Enterprise in an Underdeveloped Area, 1850–1950* (Cambridge, MA: Harvard University Press, 1957), 191; E. R. J. Owen, *Cotton and the Egyptian Economy, 1820–1914: A Study in Trade and Development* (Oxford: Clarendon Press, 1969), 90, 123, 124, 197; the permanence of this change is also emphasized by Alan Richards, *Egypt's Agricultural Development, 1800–1980: Technical and Social Change* (Boulder, CO: Westview Press, 1982), 31; Ellison, *The Cotton Trade of Great Britain*, 91; International Federation of Master Cotton Spinners' and Manufacturers' Associations, *Official Report of the International Congress, Held in Egypt*, 125.

36. Rivett-Carnac, *Report of the Cotton Department for the Year 1868–69*, 13, 114, 131; Alfred Comyn Lyall, ed., *Gazetteer for the Haiderábád Assigned Districts Commonly called Barár* (Bombay: Education Society's Press, 1870), 161; Charles B. Saunders, *Administration Report by the Resident at Hyderabad; including a Report on the Administration of the Hyderabad Assigned Districts for the year 1872–73* (Hyderabad: Residency Press, 1872), 12.

37. On the telegraph see Laxman D. Satya, *Cotton and Famine in Berar, 1850–1900* (New Delhi: Manohar, 1997), 142, 152. India and Bengal Despatches, vol. 82, August 17, 1853, pp. 1140–42, from Board of Directors, EIC London, to Financial/Railway Department, Government of India, quoted in Satya, *Cotton and Famine in Berar*, 142. On the sources of funding see Aruna Awasthi, *History and Development of Railways in India* (New Delhi: Deep & Deep Publications, 1994), 92; General Balfour is quoted in Rivett-Carnac, *Report of the Cotton Department for the Year 1868–69*, 114. On the relationship between railroads and Manchester goods see ibid., 155; Nelson, *Central Provinces District Gazetteers*, 248; Report on the Trade of the Hyderabad Assigned Districts for the Year 1883–84, p. 2, in record group V/24, in Hyderabad Assigned Districts, India, Department of Land Records and Agriculture Reports, Oriental and India Office Collections, British Library, London; Jürgen Osterhammel, *Kolonialismus: Geschichte, Formen, Folgen*, 6th ed. (Munich: Beck, 2006), 10. The quote characterizing Khamgaon is from Satya, *Cotton and Famine in Berar*, 173. The information on merchants is from John Henry Rivett-Carnac, *Many Memories of Life in India, At Home, and Abroad* (London: W. Blackwood and Sons, 1910), 166, 169; *Times of India*, March 11, 1870, 193, 199; "Report on the Cotton Trading Season in CP and Berar," June 1874, record group Fibres and Silk Branch, No 41/42, Part B, Revenue, Agriculture and Commerce Department, National Archives of India, New Delhi.

38. *Journal of the Society of Arts* 24 (February 25, 1876): 260; Rivett-Carnac, *Report of the Cotton Department for the Year 1868–69*, 100; Satya, *Cotton and Famine in Berar*, 153.

39. Rivett-Carnac, *Report of the Cotton Department for the Year 1868–69*, 115.

40. Formation of a Special Department of Agriculture, Commerce a Separate Branch of the Home Department, April 9, 1870, 91–102, Public Branch, Home Department, National Archives of India, New Delhi; Douglas E. Haynes, "Market Formation in

Khandeshh, 1820–1930," *Indian Economic and Social History Review* 36, no. 3 (1999): 294; *Asiatic Review* (October 1, 1914): 298–364; report by E. A. Hobson, 11, in Department of Revenue and Agriculture, Fibres and Silk Branch, November 1887, Nos. 22–23, Part B, in National Archives of Inda, New Delhi. And indeed, by 1863 Charles Wood could observe that "the present state of things is diminishing the home spinning"; in Charles Wood to James Bruce, Earl of Elgin, June 16, 1863 in MSS EUR F 78, LB 13, Wood Papers, Oriental and India Office Collections, British Library, London; letter from A. J. Dunlop, Assistant Commissioner in Charge of Cotton, to the Secretary of the Chamber of Commerce, Bombay, dated Camp Oomraoti, November 6, 1874, in Revenue, Agricultural and Commerce Department, Fibres and Silk Branch, Proceedings, Part B, November 1874, No. 5, National Archives of India, New Delhi; Satya, *Cotton and Famine in Berar*, 146, 183; Nelson, *Central Provinces District Gazetteers*, 248; printed letter from A. J. Dunlop to the Secretary of the Government of India, Revenue, Agriculture and Commerce, Hyderabad, April 2, 1878, in Report on the Trade of the Hyderabad Assigned Districts for the Year 1877–78, p. 6, in record group V/24, in Hyderabad Assigned Districts, India, Department of Land Records and Agriculture, Reports, Oriental and India Office Collections, British Library.

41. Rivett-Carnac, *Report of the Cotton Department for the Year 1868–69*, 91; Charles Wood to Sir Charles Trevelyan, April 9, 1863, MSS EUR F 78, LB 12, Wood Papers, Oriental and India Office Collections, British Library, London.

42. Satya, *Cotton and Famine in Berar*, 136–37, 180; *Asiatic*, June 11, 1872, in MS. f923.2.S330, Newspaper clippings, Benjamin John Smith Papers, Manchester Archives and Local Studies, Manchester. Also in the Northwestern Provinces, total acreage under cotton increased from 953,076 in 1861 to 1,730,634 in 1864. See Logan, "India's Loss of the British Cotton Market," 46; George Watt, *The Commercial Products of India* (London: John Murray, 1908), 600; *Times of India*, December 10, 1867, as quoted in Moulvie Syed Mahdi Ali, *Hyderabad Affairs*, vol. 5 (Bombay: Printed at the Times of India Steam Press, 1883), 260.

43. Timothy Mitchell, *Rule of Experts: Egypt, Techno-Politics, Modernity* (Berkeley: University of California Press, 2002), 57.

44. Ibid., 66–71.

45. Ibid., 67, 70.

46. Ibid., 62–63, 67, 71, 73; Great Britain, High Commissioner for Egypt and the Sudan, *Reports by His Majesty's Agent and Consul-General on the Finances, Administration, and Condition of Egypt and the Soudan* (London: His Majesty's Stationery Office, 1902), 24; International Federation of Master Cotton Spinners' and Manufacturers' Associations, *Official Report: Egypt and Anglo-Egyptian Soudan* (Manchester: n.p., 1921), 66.

47. Mitchell, *Rule of Experts*, 55, 63, 66, 72, 73, 76.

48. Satya, *Cotton and Famine in Berar*, 85, 169; Nelson, *Central Provinces District Gazetteers*, 150. On the wastelands see Satya, *Cotton and Famine in Berar*, 78. Already Karl Marx understood that the core demand of the mill owners was directed toward infrastructure improvements in India, to remove cotton to the coast. See Karl Marx and Friedrich Engels, *Aufstand in Indien* (Berlin: Dietz Verlag, 1978 [1853]), 264; Sandip Hazareesingh, "Cotton, Climate and Colonialism in Dharwar, Western India, 1840–1880," *Journal of Historical Geography* 38, no. 1 (2012): 14.

49. *How to Make India Take the Place of America as Our Cotton Field* (London: J. E. Taylor, n.d., probably 1863), 7.

50. Thomas Bazley, as quoted in *Merchants' Magazine and Commercial Review* 45, no. 5 (November 1861): 483; Satya, *Cotton and Famine in Berar*, 34, 47, 59, 62, 87, 91, 95; Nelson, *Central Provinces District Gazetteers*, 147, 226; A. C. Lydall, *Gazetteer for the Haidarabad Assigned Districts, Commonly Called Berar* (Bombay: Education Society's Press, 1870), 96, in record group V/27/65/112, Oriental and India Office Collections, British Library, London; Hazareesingh, "Cotton, Climate and Colonialism in Dharwar, Western India, 1840–1880," 12; Arno Schmidt, *Cotton Growing in India* (Manchester: International Federation of Master Cotton Spinners; and Manufacturers' Associations, 1912), 22.

51. David Hall-Matthews, "Colonial Ideologies of the Market and Famine Policy in Ahmednagar District, Bombay Presidency, c. 1870–1884," *Indian Economic and Social History Review* 36, no. 3 (1999): 307; Satya, *Cotton and Famine in Berar*, 80–81; Meltem Toksöz, "The Çukurova: From Nomadic Life to Commercial Agriculture, 1800–1908" (PhD dissertation, State University of New York at Binghamton, 2000), 75; Francis Turner, "Administration Report of the Cotton Department for the Year 1876–77," in record group V/24/434, Cotton Department, Bombay Presidency, Oriental and India Office Collections, British Library, London.

52. Satya, *Cotton and Famine in Berar*, 80, 161; *Times of India*, Overland Summary, January 14, 1864, 3.

53. Christof Dejung, "The Boundaries of Western Power: The Colonial Cotton Economy in India and the Problem of Quality," in Christof Dejung and Niels P. Petersson, eds., *The Foundations of Worldwide Economic Integration: Power, Institutions, and Global Markets, 1850–1930* (Cambridge: Cambridge University Press, 2012), 149–50.

54. International Federation of Master Cotton Spinners' and Manufacturers' Associations, *Official Report of the International Congress, Held in Egypt*, 64; E. B. Francis, "Report on the Cotton Cultivation in the Punjab for 1882–1883," Lahore, 1882, in record group V/24/441, Financial Commission, Oriental and India Office Collections, British Library, London.

55. F. M. W. Schofield, Department of Revenue and Agriculture, Simla, September 15, 1888, in Proceedings, Part B, Nos. 6–8, April 1889, Fibres and Silk Branch, Department of Revenue and Agriculture, National Archives of India, New Delhi; Samuel Ruggles, in front of the New York Chamber of Commerce, reprinted in *Merchants' Magazine and Commercial Review* 45, no. 1 (July 1861): 83; Rivett-Carnac, *Many Memories*, 166, 168; Peter Harnetty, "The Cotton Improvement Program in India, 1865–1875," *Agricultural History* 44, no. 4 (October 1970): 389; Satya, *Cotton and Famine in Berar*, 156ff.

56. Alfred Charles True, *A History of Agricultural Experimentation and Research in the United States, 1607–1925* (Washington, DC: Government Printing Office, 1937): 41–42; 64, 184, 199, 218, 221, 251, 256; I. Newton Hoffmann, "The Cotton Futures Act," *Journal of Political Economy* 23, no. 5 (May 1915): 482; Julia Obertreis, *Imperial Desert Dreams: Irrigation and Cotton Growing in Southern Central Asia, 1860s to 1991* (unpublished manuscript, 2009), chapter 1, 66. Since 1899, the Agricultural School (in Egypt) published a magazine (*Magazine of the Society of Agriculture*) that

provided this information in Arabic. See *Magazine of the Society of Agriculture and Agricultural School* 1 (1899), in National Library, Cairo. See also *L'Agriculture: Journal Agricole, Industrial, Commercial et Economique*, published since 1891, mostly in Arabic, in National Library, Cairo; International Federation of Master Cotton Spinners' and Manufacturers' Associations, *Official Report of the International Congress, Held in Egypt*, 54.

57. F. M. W. Schofield, "Note on Indian Cotton," 12, Department of Revenue and Agriculture, Simla, December 15, 1888, in April 1889, Nos. 6–8, Part B, Fibres and Silk Branch, National Archive of India, New Delhi; Satya, *Cotton and Famine in Berar*, 155; C. N. Livanos, *John Sakellaridis and Egyptian Cotton* (Alexandria: A. Procaccia, 1939), 79; Harnetty, "The Cotton Improvement," 383.

58. Hazareesingh, "Cotton, Climate and Colonialism in Dharwar, Western India, 1840–1880," 7.

59. *Bremer Handelsblatt*, June 28, 1873, 229; W. F. Bruck, *Türkische Baumwollwirtschaft: Eine Kolonialwirtschaftliche und -politische Untersuchung* (Jena: Gustav Fischer, 1919), 99; E. S. Symes, "Report on the Cultivation of Cotton in British Burma for the Year 1880–81," Rangoon, Revenue Department, record group V/24/446, in Oriental and India Office Collections, British Library, London.

60. On cotton exports after the Civil War see "Cotton Production in Queensland from 1866 to 1917," in A 8510–12/11, Advisory Council of Science and Industry Executive Committee, Cotton Growing, Correspondence with Commonwealth Board of Trade, National Archives of Australia; *Adelaide Advertiser*, January 11, 1904; Memorandum from Advisory Council to Commonwealth Board of Trade, September 13, 1918, in A 8510, 12/11, Advisory Council of Science and Industry Executive Committee, Cotton Growing, Correspondence with Commonwealth Board of Trade, National Archives of Australia; Theo Price, President, Price-Campbell Cotton Picker Corporation, New York to Advisory Council of Science and Industry, May 15, 1917, in NAA-A 8510–12/33, Advisory Council of Science and Industry Executive Committee, Cotton, Cotton Picker, National Archives of Australia; *Sydney Evening News*, March 17, 1920. For the general argument see also Buehler, "Die Unabhängigkeitsbestrebungen Englands," 111.

61. See for example Rudolf Fitzner, "Einiges über den Baumwollbau in Kleinasien," *Der Tropenpflanzer* 5 (1901), 530–36; Bruck, *Türkische Baumwollwirtschaft*, 3.

62. See also Marc Bloch, "Pour une histoire comparée des sociétés européennes," *Revue de Synthèse Historique* 46 (1928): 15–50.

63. Michael Mann, "Die Mär von der freien Lohnarbeit: Menschenhandel und erzwungene Arbeit in der Neuzeit," in Michael Mann, ed., *Menschenhandel und unfreie Arbeit* (Leipzig: Leipziger Universitätsverlag, 2003), 19; Marcel van der Linden, *Workers of the World: Essays Toward a Global Labor History* (Boston: Brill, 2008), 18–32, 52–54.

64. Fields, "The Advent of Capitalist Agriculture," 74; Satya, *Cotton and Famine in Berar*, 95; Arnold Wright, ed., *Twentieth Century Impressions of Egypt: Its History, People, Commerce, Industries, and Resources* (London: Lloyd's Greater Britain Publishing Company, 1909), 281, 284; International Federation of Master Cotton Spinners' and Manufacturers' Associations, *Official Report of the International Congress, Held in Egypt*, 95; Arno S. Pearse, *Brazilian Cotton* (Manchester: Printed by Taylor, Garnett,

Evans & Co., 1921), 75, 81; Michael J. Gonzales, "The Rise of Cotton Tenant Farming in Peru, 1890–1920: The Condor Valley," in *Agricultural History* 65, no. 1 (Winter 1991): 53, 58; George McCutcheon McBride, "Cotton Growing in South America," *Geographical Review* 9, no. 1 (January 1920): 42; Toksöz, "The Çukurova," 203, 246; *Levant Trade Review* 1, no. 1 (June 1911): as quoted in Toksöz, "The Çukurova," 182.

65. A. T. Moore, Inspector in Chief, Cotton Department, Report, in Proceedings, Part B, March 1875, No. 1/2, Fibres and Silk Branch, Agriculture and Commerce Department, Revenue, National Archives of India, New Delhi; David Hall-Matthews, "Colonial Ideologies of the Market and Famine Policy in Ahmednagar District, Bombay Presidency, c. 1870–1884," *Indian Economic and Social History Review* 36, no. 3 (1999): 307; A. E. Nelson, *Central Provinces Gazetteers, Buldana District* (Calcutta: Baptist Mission Press, 1910), 228; Toksöz, "The Çukurova," 272; Bruck, *Türkische Baumwollwirtschaft*, 41, 67.

66. Klein and Engerman, "The Transition from Slave to Free Labor," 255–70. This was a different system of labor than the one that emerged in the global sugar industry after emancipation. There, indentured workers took on a prominent role. The difference is probably related to the fact that sugar production is much more capital-intensive than the growing of cotton, and, moreover, because there are efficiencies of scale in sugar that do not exist in cotton. For the effects of emancipation on sugar, see especially Rebecca J. Scott, *Slave Emancipation in Cuba: The Transition to Free Labor, 1860–1899* (Princeton, NJ: Princeton University Press, 1985); David Northrup, *Indentured Labor in the Age of Imperialism, 1834–1922* (New York: Cambridge University Press, 1995); Frederick Cooper, Thomas C. Holt, and Rebecca J. Scott, *Beyond Slavery: Explorations of Race, Labor, and Citizenship in Postemancipation Societies* (Chapel Hill: University of North Carolina Press, 2000).

67. *Cotton Supply Reporter* (June 15, 1861): 530; M. J. Mathieu, *De la culture du coton dans la Guyane française* (Épinal: Alexis Cabasse, 1861); *Le Courier du Havre*, September 19, 1862, in Gen/56, Fonds Ministériels, Archives d'outre-mer, Aix-en-Provence. See also *Cotton Supply Reporter* (July 1, 1861): 554; Stephen S. Remak, *La paix en Amérique* (Paris: Henri Plon, 1865), 25–26. On the issue of coolie labor see also Black Ball Line, Liverpool to Messrs. Sandbach, Tinne and Co., January 1, 1864, in Record Group D 176, folder A (various), Sandbach, Tinne & Co, Papers, Merseyside Maritime Museum, Liverpool; Klein and Engerman, "The Transition from Slave to Free Labor," 255–70; Alan Richards, *Egypt's Agricultural Development, 1800–1980: Technical and Social Change* (Boulder, CO: Westview Press, 1981), 55, 61.

68. William K. Meyers, *Forge of Progress, Crucible of Revolt: Origins of the Mexican Revolution in La Comarca Lagunera, 1880–1911* (Albuquerque: University of New Mexico Press, 1994), 4, 6, 33–34, 48, 51.

69. Ibid., 40, 116–17, 120, 346; Werner Tobler, *Die mexikanische Revolution: Gesellschaftlicher Wandel und politischer Umbruch, 1876–1940* (Frankfurt am Main: Suhrkamp, 1984), 70ff.

70. Meyers, *Forge of Progress*, 123–25, 131; for Peru, see Michael J. Gonzales, "The Rise of Cotton Tenant Farming in Peru, 1890–1920: The Condor Valley," *Agricultural History* 65, no. 1 (Winter 1991): 71; for Egypt, see Mitchell, *Rule of Experts*.

71. Toksöz, "The Çukurova," 99.

72. Manchester Chamber of Commerce, *The Forty-Second Annual Report of the Board of Directors for the Year 1862* (Manchester: Cave & Server, 1863), 22; Rosa Luxemburg, "Die Akkumulation des Kapitals," in Rosa Luxemburg, *Gesammelte Werke*, Band 5 (Berlin: Dietz Verlag, 1981), 311–12, 317; Karl Polanyi, *The Great Transformation* (Boston: Beacon Press, 1968), 72–75.

73. Jürgen Osterhammel and Niels P. Petersson, *Geschichte der Globalisierung: Dimensionen, Prozesse, Epochen* (Munich: C. H. Beck, 2003), 70.

74. Eric Hobsbawm, *The Age of Empire, 1875–1914* (London: Weidenfeld and Nicolson, 1987), 40, 42, 45, 54, 59, 62, 66, 67, 69; Osterhammel and Petersson, *Geschichte der Globalisierung*, 69. See also Sven Beckert, "Space Matters: Eurafrica, the American Empire, and the Territorial Reorganization of European Capitalism, 1870–1960" (article in progress); Charles S. Maier, "Consigning the Twentieth Century to History: Alternative Narratives for the Modern Era," *American Historical Review* 105, no. 3 (June 2000): 807–31; Oldham Master Cotton Spinners' Association, *Report of the Committee, for Year Ending December 31, 1901* (Oldham: Dornan, 1902), 5, in record group 6/2/1–61m, Papers of the Oldham Master Cotton Spinners' Association, John Rylands Library, Manchester; Giovanni Arrighi, *The Long Twentieth Century: Money, Power, and the Origins of Our Times* (New York: Verso, 1994), 11; Jan-Frederik Abbeloos, "Belgium's Expansionist History Between 1870 and 1930: Imperialism and the Globalisation of Belgian Business," Munich Personal RePEc Archive Paper No. 11295 (posted October 30, 2008), accessed July 9, 2009, http://www.mpra.ub.uni-muenchen.de/11295.

75. International Federation of Master Cotton Spinners' and Manufacturers' Associations, *Official Report of the International Congress, Held in Egypt*, 31; Commission Coloniale, "Rapport sur l'organisation du travail libre," in 317/Gen 40/472, Fonds Ministérielle, Centre des archives d'outre-mer; Procès verbaux des séances de la commission du travail aux colonies, 1873–1874, 1105/Gen 127/473, Fonds Ministérielle, Centre des archives d'outre-mer, "Régime du travail dans les colonies, rapport, 1875," in 1152/Gen 135/475, Fonds Ministérielle, Archives d'outre-mer; *Liverpool Mercury*, September 23, 1863, 6; Edward Atkinson, *Cheap Cotton by Free Labor: By a Cotton Manufacturer* (Boston: A. Williams & Co, 1861), 478. See also John Bright to Edward Atkinson, London, May 29, 1862, Box N 298, ibid. Note from the Ambassade d'Espagne à Paris, no date, 994/Gen 117/474, Fonds Ministérielle, Archives d'outre-mer; copy of a report by R. B. D. Morier to the Secretary of State, The Marquis of Salisbury, October 12, 1889, Compilations, Vol. 51, 1890, Compilation No. 476, "Establishment by the Russian Government of a Model Cotton Plantation in the Merva Oasis," Revenue Department, Maharashtra State Archive, Mumbai; Rinji Sangyo Chosa Kyoku [Special Department of Research on Industries], *Chosen ni Okeru Menka ni Kansuru Chosa Seiseki* [The Research on Cotton in Korea] (August 1918); No-Shomu Sho Nomu Kyoku [Ministry of Agriculture and Commerce, Department of Agriculture], *Menka ni Kansuru Chosa* [The Research on Cotton] (March 1913).

76. This was also the case in many other countries. In Peru, for example, tenant farming and sharecropping became the dominant forms of cotton production in the wake of the Civil War and the enormous expansion of output that resulted from it. See Vincent Peloso, *Peasants on Plantations: Subaltern Strategies of Labor and Resistance in the Pisco Valley, Peru* (Durham, NC: Duke University Press, 1999); Michael R. Haines,

"Wholesale Prices of Selected Commodities: 1784–1998," Table Cc205–266, in Susan B. Carter, Scott Sigmund Gartner, Michael R. Haines, Alan L. Olmstead, Richard Sutch, and Gavin Wright, eds., *Historical Statistics of the United States, Earliest Times to the Present: Millennial Edition* (New York: Cambridge University Press, 2006); Peter Harnetty, *Imperialism and Free Trade: Lancashire and India in the Mid-Nineteenth Century* (Vancouver: University of British Columbia Press, 1972), 99.

CHAPTER ELEVEN: DESTRUCTIONS

1. John R. Killick, "Atlantic and Far Eastern Models in the Cotton Trade, 1818–1980," University of Leeds School of Business and Economic Studies, Discussion Paper Series, June 1994, 1; Toyo Menka Kaisha, *The Indian Cotton Facts 1930* (Bombay: Toyo Menka Kaisha Ltd., 1930), n.p.

2. On the occasion of the opening of the line the British viceroy himself linked the new state of affairs explicitly to the American Civil War. "Opening of the Khamgaon Railway," *Times of India*, March 11, 1870, reprinted in Moulvie Syed Mahdi Ali, *Hyderabad Affairs*, vol. 4 (Bombay: Printed at the Times of India Steam Press, 1883), 199. On Khamgaon see also John Henry Rivett-Carnac, *Report of the Cotton Department for the Year 1868–69* (Bombay: Printed at the Education Society's Press, 1869), 98ff., 131; A. C. Lydall, *Gazetteer for the Haidarabad Assigned Districts, Commonly Called Berar* (Bombay: Education Society's Press, 1870), 230, in record group V/27/65/112, Oriental and India Office Collections, British Library, London.

3. Haywood to Messers. Mosley and Hurst, Manchester, May 15, 1861, as reprinted in *Times of India*, July 18, 1861, 3. Very similar also *Cotton Supply Reporter* (June 15, 1861): 530; "Cotton Districts of Berar and Raichove Doab," India Office, London, to Governor in Council Bombay, December 17, 1862, Compilation No. 119, Compilations, Vol. 26, 1862–1864, Revenue Department, Maharashtra State Archives, Mumbai; J. B. Smith (Stockport) in *Hansard's Parliamentary Debates*, Third Series, vol. 167, June 19, 1862 (London: Cornelius Buck, 1862), 761; *Cotton Supply Reporter* (January 2, 1865); Arthur W. Silver, *Manchester Men and Indian Cotton, 1847–1872* (Manchester: Manchester University Press, 1966), 179; printed letter from A. J. Dunlop to the Secretary of the Government of India, Revenue, Agriculture and Commerce, Hyderabad, April 2, 1878, Hyderabad Assigned Districts, India, Department of Land Records and Agriculture, Reports, 1876–1891, record group V/24, file 4266, Oriental and India Office Collections, British Library, London.

4. George Reinhart, *Volkart Brothers: In Commemoration of the Seventy-Fifth Anniversary of the Foundation* (Winterthur: n.p., 1926); The Volkart's United Press Company Limited, Dossier 10, Volkart Archives, Winterthur, Switzerland. For an account of the development of the Indian cotton trade from Volkarts' perspective, see Jakob Brack-Liechti, "Einige Betrachtungen über den indischen Baumwollmarkt aus älterer Zeit, 23.2.1918," Volkart Archives; Salomon Volkart to "Bombay," Winterthur, March 17, 1870, and Salomon Volkart to "Bombay," Winterthur, May 27, 1870, in Correspondence of Salomon Volkart, second copy book, Winterthur, 1865–1867, Volkart Archives.

5. Hyderabad Assigned Districts, Land Records and Agriculture Department, *Report on the Rail and Road-borne Trade in the Hyderabad Assigned Districts for the Year 1894–95* (Hyderabad: Residency Government Press, 1895), Appendix B; Laxman D. Satya, *Cotton and Famine in Berar, 1850–1900* (New Delhi: Manohar, 1997), 168; Hyderabad Assigned Districts, Land Records and Agriculture Department, *Report on the Trade of the Hyderabad Assigned Districts for the Year 1882–83* (Hyderabad: Residency Government Press, 1883), 4, record group V/24, Reports, Oriental and India Office Collections, British Library, London; Correspondence of Salomon Volkart, second copy book, Winterthur, 1865–1867, in Volkart Archives, Winterthur, Switzerland; The Volkart's United Press Company Limited, Dossier 10, Volkart Archives; "Chronology of Events in Bombay," in Dossier 3, Bombay 1:4, Volkart Archives; Walter H. Rambousek et al., *Volkart: The History of a World Trading Company* (Frankfurt am Main: Insel Verlag, 1991), 72; Kaisha, *The Indian Cotton Facts 1930*, 50–51; printed letter from A. J. Dunlop to the Secretary of the Government of India, Revenue, Agriculture and Commerce, Hyderabad, April 2, 1878, in Hyderabad Assigned Districts, Land Records and Agriculture Department, *Report on the Trade of the Hyderabad Assigned Districts for the Year 1877–78* (Hyderabad: Residency Government Press, 1878), 4, in record group V/24, Reports, Oriental and India Office Collections, British Library, London; Kagotani Naoto, "Up-Country Purchase Activities of Indian Raw Cotton by Tōyō Menka's Bombay Branch, 1896–1935," in S. Sugiyama and Linda Grove, *Commercial Networks in Modern Asia* (Curzon: Richmond, 2001), 199, 200.

6. Christof Dejung, "The Boundaries of Western Power: The Colonial Cotton Economy in India and the Problem of Quality," in Christof Dejung and Niels P. Petersson, eds., *The Foundations of Worldwide Economic Integration: Power, Institutions, and Global Markets, 1850–1930* (Cambridge: Cambridge University Press, 2012), 148.

7. Douglas E. Haynes, "Market Formation in Khandeshh, 1820–1930," *Indian Economic and Social History Review* 36, no. 3 (1999): 294; *Asiatic Review* (October 1, 1914): 294; C. A. Bayly, *The Birth of the Modern World, 1780–1914* (Oxford: Blackwell, 2004), 138; Dwijendra Tripathi, "An Echo Beyond the Horizon: The Effect of American Civil War on India," in T. K. Ravindran, ed., *Journal of Indian History: Golden Jubilee Volume* (Trivandrum: University of Kerala, 1973), 660; Marika Vicziany, "Bombay Merchants and Structural Changes in the Export Community 1850 to 1880," in K. N. Chaudhuri and Clive Dewey, eds., *Economy and Society: Essays in Indian Economic and Social History* (Delhi: Oxford University Press, 1979), 163–96; Marika Vicziany, "The Cotton Trade and the Commercial Development of Bombay, 1855–75" (PhD dissertation, University of London, 1975), 170–71.

8. Arnold Wright, ed., *Twentieth Century Impressions of Egypt: Its History, People, Commerce, Industries, and Resources* (London: Lloyd's Greater Britain Publishing Company, 1909), 285; Alexander Kitroeff, *The Greeks in Egypt, 1919–1937* (Oxford: Middle East Centre, Oxford University, 1989), 76, 86; *Cinquante ans de labeur: The Kafr-El-Zayat Cotton Company Ltd., 1894–1944*, in Rare Books and Special Collections Library, American University in Cairo; *Ekthesis tou en Alexandria Genikou Proxeniou tis Egyptou 1883–1913* (Athens: n.p., 1915), 169–70.

9. Meltem Toksöz, "The Çukurova: From Nomadic Life to Commercial Agriculture,

1800–1908" (PhD dissertation, State University of New York at Binghamton, 2000), 103, 106, 120, 125, 137, 174, 191, 193, 245; W. F. Bruck, *Türkische Baumwollwirtschaft: Eine Kolonialwirtschaftliche und -politische Untersuchung* (Jena: Gustav Fischer, 1919), 9; William K. Meyers, *Forge of Progress, Crucible of Revolt: Origins of the Mexican Revolution in La Comarca Lagunera, 1880–1911* (Albuquerque: University of New Mexico Press, 1994), 48; Charles S. Aiken, *The Cotton Plantation South Since the Civil War* (Baltimore: Johns Hopkins University Press, 1998), 60.

10. L. Tuffly Ellis, "The Revolutionizing of the Texas Cotton Trade, 1865–1885," *Southwestern Historical Quarterly* 73, no. 4 (1970): 479.

11. Harold D. Woodman, "The Decline of Cotton Factorage after the Civil War," *American Historical Review* 71, no. 4 (1966): 1220ff., 1236; Ellis, "The Revolutionizing of the Texas Cotton Trade," 505.

12. Woodman, "The Decline of Cotton Factorage after the Civil War," 1223, 1228, 1231, 1239; *Bradstreet's: A Journal of Trade, Finance and Public Economy* 11 (February 14, 1885): 99–100; John R. Killick, "The Transformation of Cotton Marketing in the Late Nineteenth Century: Alexander Sprunt and Son of Wilmington, N.C., 1884–1956," *Business History Review* 55, no. 2 (Summer 1981): 162, 168.

13. Killick, "Atlantic and Far Eastern Models in the Cotton Trade," 17; Thomas Ellison, *The Cotton Trade of Great Britain* (London: Effingham Wilson, 1886), 280.

14. See, for example, Albert C. Stevens, " 'Futures' in the Wheat Market," *Quarterly Journal of Economics* 2, no. 1 (October 1887): 37–63; Jonathan Ira Levy, "Contemplating Delivery: Futures Trading and the Problem of Commodity Exchange in the United States, 1875–1905," *American Historical Review* 111, no. 2 (April 2006): 314; Alston Hill Garside, *Cotton Goes to Market: A Graphic Description of a Great Industry* (New York: Stokes, 1935), 166. On the discussions that resulted in the introduction of futures trading in Bremen see W II, 3, Baumwollterminhandel, Archive of the Handelskammer Bremen, Bremen, Germany; *Frankfurter Zeitung*, February 4, 1914.

15. Alfred Chandler, *The Visible Hand* (Cambridge, MA: Harvard University Press, 1977), 214; Kenneth J. Lipartito, "The New York Cotton Exchange and the Development of the Cotton Futures Market," *Business History Review* 57 (Spring 1983): 54.

16. Lipartito, "The New York Cotton Exchange," 53; Garside, *Cotton Goes to Market*, 133, 166.

17. Garside, *Cotton Goes to Market*, 54–55, 68, 145.

18. Jamie L. Pietruska, " 'Cotton Guessers': Crop Forecasters and the Rationalizing of Uncertainty in American Cotton Markets, 1890–1905," in Hartmut Berghoff, Philip Scranton, and Uwe Spiekermann, eds., *The Rise of Marketing and Market Research* (New York: Palgrave Macmillan, 2012), 49–72; Michael Hovland, "The Cotton Ginnings Reports Program at the Bureau of the Census," *Agricultural History* 68, no. 2 (Spring 1994): 147; N. Jasny, "Proposal for Revision of Agricultural Statistics," *Journal of Farm Economics* 24, no. 2 (May 1942): 402; H. Parker Willis, "Cotton and Crop Reporting," *Journal of Political Economy* 13, no. 4 (September 1905): 507; International Institute of Agriculture, Bureau of Statistics, *The Cotton-Growing Countries; Production and Trade* (Rome: International Institute of Agriculture, 1922).

19. Sources for the data in the graph for the years 1820–1850 are: 1820—*Tables of Revenue, Population, Commerce, &c. of the United Kingdom and Its Dependencies, Part I, from*

1820 to 1831, Both Inclusive (London: William Clowes, 1833), 65, 67, 70; Richard Burn, *Statistics of the Cotton Trade: Arranged in a Tabular Form: Also a Chronological History of Its Various Inventions, Improvements, etc., etc.* (London: Simpkin, Marshall 1847), 1; Ellison, *The Cotton Trade of Great Britain*, 63–64; T. Bazley, "Cotton Manufacture," *Encyclopaedia Britannica*, 8th ed., vol. 7 (Edinburgh: Black, 1854), 453; Lars G. Sandberg, *Lancashire in Decline: A Study in Entrepreneurship, Technology, and International Trade* (Columbus: Ohio State University Press, 1974), 142, 145, 254–62; Andrew Ure, *The Cotton Manufacture of Great Britain; Systematically Investigated . . . with an Introductory View of Its Comparative State in Foreign Countries*, vol. 1 (New York: Johnson Reprint Corp., 1970), 65–70, 328; Andrew Ure, *The Cotton Manufacture of Great Britain; Systematically Investigated . . . with an Introductory View of Its Comparative State in Foreign Countries*, vol. 2 (New York: Johnson Reprint Corp., 1970), 328; I. Watts, "Cotton," *Encyclopaedia Britannica*, 9th ed., vol. 6 (Edinburgh: Black, 1877), 503–4.

20. Amalendu Guha, "The Decline of India's Cotton Handicrafts, 1800–1905: A Quantitative Macro-Study," *Calcutta Historical Journal* 17 (1995): 44; Table No. 29, "Value of the Principal Articles of Merchandise and Treasure Imported into British India, by Sea, from Foreign Countries, in each of the Years ended 30th April," in *Statistical Abstracts Relating to British India from 1840 to 1865* (London: Her Majesty's Stationery Office, 1867); Douglas A. Farnie, *The English Cotton Industry and the World Market* (New York: Oxford University Press, 1979), 101; Lars G. Sandberg, "Movements in the Quality of British Cotton Textile Exports, 1815–1913," *Journal of Economic History* 28, no. 1 (March 1968): 1–27.

21. Diary of Voyage to Calcutta, Record Group MSS EUR F 349, box 1, Richard Kay Papers, Oriental and India Office Collections, British Library, London; Diary and notebook, Allahabad, 1820, in Record Group MSS EUR F 349, box 3, Richard Kay Papers, Oriental and India Office Collections, British Library; *Asiatic Journal and Monthly Register*, New Series, 16 (January–April 1835): 125; *Report of the Bombay Chamber of Commerce for the Year 1852–53* (Bombay: Bombay Gazette Press, 1853), 23.

22. Elena Frangakis, "The Ottoman Port of Izmir in the Eighteenth and Early Nineteenth Centuries, 1695–1820," *Revue de l'Occident musulman et de la Méditerranée* 39, no. 1 (1985): 150; Joel Beinin, "Egyptian Textile Workers: From Craft Artisans Facing European Competition to Proletarians Contending with the State," in Lex Heerma van Voss, Els Hiemstra-Kuperus, and Elise van Nederveen Meerkerk, eds., *The Ashgate Companion to the History of Textile Workers, 1650–2000* (Burlington, VT: Ashgate, 2010), 176; Patricia Davison and Patrick Harries, "Cotton Weaving in South-East Africa: Its History and Technology," in Dale Idiens and K. G. Ponting, eds., *Textiles of Africa* (Bath: Pasold Research Fund, 1980), 189; G. P. C. Thomson, "Continuity and Change in Mexican Manufacturing," in I. J. Baou, ed., *Between Development and Underdevelopment* (Geneva: Librairie Droz, 1991), 275; Robert A. Potash, *Mexican Government and Industrial Development in the Early Republic: The Banco de Avío* (Amherst: University of Massachusetts Press, 1983), 27; H. G. Ward, *Mexico* (London: H. Colburn, 1829), 60; Robert Cliver as cited by Prasannan Parthasarathi, "Global Trade and Textile Workers," in Van Voss et al., eds., *The Ashgate Companion to the History of Textile Workers*, 570.

23. Gisborne to Joshua Bates, Walton, October 15, 1832, House Correspondence, HC 6.3, India and Indian Ocean, 1, ING Baring Archive, London; Ralph W. Hidy, *The House of Baring in American Trade and Finance: English Merchant Bankers at Work, 1763–1861* (Cambridge, MA: Harvard University Press, 1949), 104; Baring Brothers Liverpool to Baring Brothers London, August 1, 1836, House Correspondence, HC 3.35, 2, ING Baring Archive. The Brown Brothers engaged in the export of manufactured goods as well. D. M. Williams, "Liverpool Merchants and the Cotton Trade, 1820–1850" in J. R. Harris, ed., *Liverpool and Merseyside: Essays in the Economic and Social History of the Port and Its Hinterland* (London: Frank Cass & Co, 1969), 197; John A. Kouwenhoven, *Partners in Banking: An Historical Portrait of a Great Private Bank, Brown Brothers Harriman & Co., 1818–1968* (Garden City: Doubleday & Co., 1967), 41; see also *Report of the Bombay Chamber of Commerce for the Year 1852–53*, 24; Letterbook, 1868–1869, in Papers of McConnel & Kennedy, record group MCK, box 2/2/23, John Rylands Library, Manchester; Letterbook, May 1814 to September 1816, in Papers of McConnel & Kennedy, record group MCK, box 2/2/5, John Rylands Library; Dotter to Fielden Brothers, Calcutta, October 17, 1840, in Correspondence Related to Commercial Activities, May 1812–April 1850, in Record Group FDN, box 1/15, papers of Fielden Brothers, John Rylands Library.

24. Stephen Broadberry and Bishnupriya Gupta, "Cotton Textiles and the Great Divergence: Lancashire, India and Shifting Competitive Advantage, 1600–1850: The Neglected Role of Factor Prices," *Economic History Review* 62, no. 2 (May 2009): 285; Jim Matson, "Deindustrialization or Peripheralization? The Case of Cotton Textiles in India, 1750–1950," in Sugata Bose, ed., *South Asia and World Capitalism* (New York: Oxford University Press, 1990), 215.

25. Bombay Chamber of Commerce, *Report of the Bombay Chamber of Commerce for the Year 1852–53*, 23; J. Forbes Watson, *Collection of Specimens and Illustrations of the Textile Manufacturers of India (Second Series)* (London: India Museum, 1873), in Library of the Royal Asiatic Society Library of Bombay, Mumbai; Part A, No. 1, November 1906, 1, Industries Branch, Department of Commerce and Industry, National Archives of India, New Delhi. Very similar also R. E. Enthoven, *The Cotton Fabrics of the Bombay Presidency* (Bombay: n.p., 1897).

26. "Report on the Native Cotton Manufacturers of the District of Ning-Po" (China), in Compilations Vol. 75, 1887, Compilation No. 919, Revenue Department, Maharashtra State Archives, Mumbai; *The Thirty-Fifth Annual Report of the Board of Directors of the Chamber of Commerce and Manufactures at Manchester, for the Year 1855* (Manchester: James Collins, 1856), 10–11; Contract Book, George Robinson & Co. Papers, record group MSf 382.2.R1, in Manchester Archives and Local Studies, Manchester; Broadberry and Gupta, "Cotton Textiles and the Great Divergence," 285; Matson, "Deindustrialization or Peripherialization?" 215; Karl Marx and Friedrich Engels, *Aufstand in Indien* (Berlin: Dietz Verlag, 1978 [1853]), 2; Konrad Specker, "Madras Handlooms in the Nineteenth Century," in Tirthankar Roy, ed., *Cloth and Commerce: Textiles in Colonial India* (Walnut Creek, CA: AltaMira Press, 1996), 216; T.G.T., "Letters on the Trade with India," in *Asiatic Journal* (September–December 1832): 256, as quoted in Edward Baines, *History of the Cotton Manufacture in Great Britain* (London: H. Fisher, R. Fisher, and P. Jackson, 1835), 81–82. It is interesting to

note that Baines quotes these Bengal merchants approvingly. He does not give any source for this letter, nor does he give any of the names of these 117 merchants. See also Arno S. Pearse, *The Cotton Industry of India, Being the Report of the Journey to India* (Manchester: Taylor, Garnett, Evans, 1930), 20.

27. Guha, "The Decline of India's Cotton Handicrafts," 56; quoted in *Times of India,* Overland Summary, July 8, 1864, 4; *Times of India,* Overland Summary, October 29, 1863, 1; see also J. Talboys Wheeler, Assistant Secretary to the Government of India, "Memorandum on the Effect of the Rise in Cotton upon the Manufactured Article," December 15, 1864, as reprinted in *Times of India,* Overland Summary, January 13, 1865, 3.

28. A. J. Dunlop to the Secretary of the Chamber of Commerce, Bombay, Camp Oomraoti, November 6, 1874, 4, Proceedings, Part B, November 1874, No. 5, Fibres and Silk Branch, Agriculture and Commerce Department, Revenue, National Archives of India, New Delhi; V. Garrett, *Monograph on Cotton Fabrics in the Hyderabad Assigned Districts* (New Delhi: Residency Government Press, 1897), 3; Report by E. A. Hobson, in Proceedings, Part B, Nos. 22–23, November 1887, Fibres and Silk Branch, Department of Revenue and Agriculture, National Archives of India; Rivett-Carnac, *Report of the Cotton Department for the Year 1868–69,* 35.

29. *The Thirty-Ninth Annual Report of the Board of Directors of the Chamber of Commerce and Manufactures at Manchester, for the Year 1859* (Manchester: Cave and Sever, 1860), 22–23.

30. Nitya Naraven Banerjei, *Monograph on the Cotton Fabrics of Bengal* (Calcutta: Bengal Secretariat Press, 1898), 2, 8; "Final Report on the Famine of 1896/97 in the Bombay Presidency," in 1898, Compilations Vol. 8, Revenue Department, Maharashtra State Archives, Mumbai.

31. Donald Quataert, "The Ottoman Empire, 1650–1922," in Van Voss et al., eds., *The Ashgate Companion to the History of Textile Workers,* 480; on China see the brilliant piece by Jacob Eyferth, "Women's Work and the Politics of Homespun in Socialist China, 1949–1980," in *International Review of Social History* (2012): 9–10; D. C. M. Platt, *Latin America and British Trade, 1806–1914* (London: Adam & Charles Black, 1972), 16; Lars Sundström, *The Trade of Guinea* (Lund: Håkan Ohlssons Boktryckerei, 1965), 160; Part A, No. 1, November 1906, 1, Industries Branch, Department of Commerce and Industry, National Archives of India, New Delhi.

32. Specker, "Madras Handlooms in the Nineteenth Century," 185; Bombay Chamber of Commerce, *Report of the Bombay Chamber of Commerce for the Year 1852–53,* 27; Report, Part C, No. 1, March 1906, Industries Branch, Commerce and Industry Department, National Archives of India, New Delhi; Tirthankar Roy, "The Long Globalization and Textile Producers in India," in Van Voss et al., eds., *The Ashgate Companion to the History of Textile Workers,* 266; M. P. Gandhi, *The Indian Cotton Textile Industry: Its Past, Present and Future* (Calcutta: G. N. Mitra, 1930), 82.

33. Beinin, "Egyptian Textile Workers," 181; Quataert, "The Ottoman Empire, 1650–1922," 479–80; for Africa, see Marion Johnson, "Technology, Competition, and African Crafts," in Clive Dewey and A. G. Hopkins, eds., *The Imperial Impact: Studies in the Economic History of Africa and India* (London: Athlone Press, 1978), 267; Part A, No. 1, November 1906, 3, Industries Branch, Department of Commerce and Industry, National Archives of India, New Delhi.

34. Robert Cliver, "China," in Van Voss et al., eds., *The Ashgate Companion to the History of Textile Workers*, 111.

35. Letter to the Secretary of the Revenue Department, Fort St. George, November 21, 1843, Revenue Branch, Revenue Department, National Archives of India, New Delhi.

36. Petition of the Weavers of the Chingleput District Complaining against the Loom Tax in the Madras Presidency, June 8, 1844, Revenue Branch, Revenue Department, National Archives of India, New Delhi.

37. Roy, "The Long Globalization and Textile Producers in India," 259; Guha, "The Decline of India's Cotton Handicrafts," 55; Matson, "Deindustrialization or Peripheralization?" 215.

38. Papers relating to Cotton Cultivation in India, MSS EUR F 78, 106, Wood Collection, Oriental and India Office Collections, British Library, London. A similar story can also be found in *Times of India*, Overland Summary, August 24, 1863, 1. See also Memorandum by the Department of Agriculture, Revenue and Commerce, Fibres and Silk Branch, to the Home Department, Calcutta, June 24, 1874, in Revenue, Agriculture and Commerce Department, Fibres and Silk Branch, June 1874, No. 41/42, Part B, National Archives of India, New Delhi; *Times of India*, Overland Summary, April 27, 1864, 5, November 13, 1864, 3, and November 28, 1864, 1; Peter Harnetty, "The Imperialism of Free Trade: Lancashire, India, and the Cotton Supply Question, 1861–1865," *Journal of British Studies* 6, no. 1 (November 1966): 92; *Times of India*, July 5, 1861, 3; Edward Mead Earle, "Egyptian Cotton and the American Civil War," *Political Science Quarterly* 41, no. 4 (1926): 521; Timothy Mitchell, *Rule of Experts: Egypt, Techno-Politics, Modernity* (Berkeley: University of California Press, 2002), 66.

39. Orhan Kurmus, "The Cotton Famine and Its Effects on the Ottoman Empire," in Huri Islamoglu-Inan, *The Ottoman Empire and the World-Economy* (Cambridge: Cambridge University Press, 1987), 165, 166, 168; Alan Richards, *Egypt's Agricultural Development, 1800–1980: Technical and Social Change* (Boulder, CO: Westview Press, 1982), 55; Mitchell, *Rule of Experts*, 60–64.

40. Rivett-Carnac, *Report of the Cotton Department for the Year 1868–69*, 132; John Aiton Todd, *The World's Cotton Crops* (London: A. & C. Black, 1915), 429–32. David Hall-Matthews, "Colonial Ideologies of the Market and Famine Policy in Ahmednagar District, Bombay Presidency, c. 1870–1884," *Indian Economic and Social History Review* 36, no. 3 (1999): 303–33; Samuel Smith, *The Cotton Trade of England, Being a Series of Letters Written from Bombay in the Spring of 1863* (London: Effingham, Wilson, 1863), 12–13; Allen Isaacman and Richard Roberts, "Cotton, Colonialism, and Social History in Sub-Saharan Africa," in Allen Isaacman and Richard Roberts, eds., *Cotton, Colonialism, and Social History in Sub-Saharan Africa* (Portsmouth, NH: Heinemann, 1995), 32, 34; Meyers, *Forge of Progress*, 126; Jorge Raul Colva, *El "Oro Blanco" en la Argentina* (Buenos Aires: Editorial Calidad, 1946), 15.

41. Data taken from "Index Numbers of Indian Prices 1861–1926," No. 2121, Calcutta: Government of India Central Publication Branch, 1928, Summary Tables III and VI, Oriental and India Office Collections, British Library, London. On the new uncertainty introduced by world market integration see also A. E. Nelson, *Central Provinces District Gazetteers, Amraoti District*, vol. A (Bombay: Claridge, 1911), 226, in record group V/27/65/6, Oriental and India Office Collections, British Library,

London; Hall-Matthews, "Colonial Ideologies of the Market and Famine," 307, 313; Memo by the Department of Agriculture, Revenue and Commerce, Fibres and Silk Branch, to the Home Department, Calcutta, June 24, 1874, Proceedings, Part B, June 1874, No. 41/42, Fibres and Silk Branch, Agriculture and Commerce Department, Revenue, National Archives of India, New Delhi; Frenise A. Logan, "India's Loss of the British Cotton Market after 1865," *Journal of Southern History* 31, no. 1 (1965): 46; Iltudus Thomas Prichard, who quoted Sir Trevelyan as saying in his budget statement for 1863 that "demand for exported produce could only be met by diverting to its production a large proportion of the land which has been previously employed in raising grain," cited in Iltudus Thomas Prichard, *The Administration of India, From 1859–1868*, vol. 1 (London: Macmillan, 1869), 9; for Egypt see E. R. J. Owen, *Cotton and the Egyptian Economy, 1820–1914: A Study in Trade and Development* (Oxford: Clarendon Press, 1969), 159; for Brazil see Luis Cordelio Barbosa, "Cotton in 19th Century Brazil: Dependency and Development" (PhD dissertation, University of Washington, 1989), 31, 95–102, 105–8, 142; see also International Federation of Master Cotton Spinners' and Manufacturers' Associations, *Official Report of the International Congress, Held in Egypt, 1927* (Manchester: International Federation of Master Cotton Spinners' and Manufacturers' Associations, 1927), 99.

42. Rivett-Carnac, *Report of the Cotton Department for the Year 1868–69*, 52.

43. Barbosa, "Cotton in 19th Century Brazil," 105. The connection between famine and the extension of cotton agriculture is also emphasized by Sandip Hazareesingh, "Cotton, Climate and Colonialism in Dharwar, Western India, 1840–1880," *Journal of Historical Geography* 38, no. 1 (2012): 16. On famines in the late nineteenth century in general see also Mike Davis, *Late Victorian Holocausts: El Niño Famines and the Making of the Third World* (New York: Verso, 2001), 7; Nelson, *Central Provinces District Gazetteers, Amraoti District*, vol. A. "The scarcity of 1896–97 was caused by high prices and not by failure of crops," reported the deputy commissioner of the Akola District (in Berar) to the Indian Famine Commission. See Indian Famine Commission, "Appendix, Evidence of Witnesses, Berar," *Report of the Indian Famine Commission* (Calcutta: n.p., 1901), 43, 53. For the mortality figures see Indian Famine Commission, "Appendix, Evidence of Witnesses, Berar," *Report of the Indian Famine Commission*, 54, 213. Total mortality between December 1899 and November 1900 was 84.7 per 1,000; see also Sugata Bose, "Pondering Poverty, Fighting Famines: Towards a New History of Economic Ideas," in Kaushik Basu, ed., *Arguments for a Better World: Essays in Honor of Amartya Sen* (New York: Oxford University Press, 2009), 428.

44. Mitchell, *Rule of Experts*, 63–64; on the riots see Neil Charlesworth, "The Myth of the Deccan Riots of 1875," *Modern Asian Studies* 6, no. 4 (1972): 401–21; Deccan Riots Commission, *Papers Relating to the Indebtedness of the Agricultural Classes in Bombay and Other Parts of India* (Bombay: Deccan Riots Commission, 1876); *Report of the Committee on the Riots in Poona and Ahmednagar, 1875* (Bombay: Government Central Press, 1876); Roderick J. Barman, "The Brazilian Peasantry Reexamined: The Implications of the Quebra-Quilo Revolt, 1874–1875," *Hispanic American Historical Review* 57, no. 3 (1977): 401–24; Armando Souto Maior, *Quebra-Quilos: Lutas sociais no outono do império* (São Paulo: Companhia Editora Nacional, 1978). The pressure

of raising taxes was also felt by Egyptian peasants who lost in the process most of the profits that they had accumulated during the Civil War. See Owen, *Cotton and the Egyptian Economy*, 144; W. H. Wyllie, Agent of the Governor General in Central India, to the Revenue and Agriculture Department, September 9, 1899, in Proceedings, Part B, Nos. 14–54, November 1899, Famine Branch, Department of Revenue and Agriculture, National Archives of India, New Delhi; Wady E. Medawar, *Études sur la question cotonnière et l'organisation agricole en Égypte* (Cairo: A. Gherson, 1900), 16, 20–21; William K. Meyers, "Seasons of Rebellion: Nature, Organisation of Cotton Production and the Dynamics of Revolution in La Laguna, Mexico, 1910–1916," *Journal of Latin American Studies* 30, no. 1 (February 1998): 63; Meyers, *Forge of Progress*, 132–34.

45. The importance of the discourse on cotton to anticolonial politics can also be traced in File 4, Correspondence, G. K. Gokhale, 1890–1911, in Servants of India Society Papers, Nehru Memorial Library, New Delhi; Correspondence, Sir Pherozeshah Mehta Papers, Nehru Memorial Library.

CHAPTER TWELVE: THE NEW COTTON IMPERIALISM

1. Department of Finance, *1895, Annual Return of the Foreign Trade of the Empire of Japan* (Tokyo: Koide, n.d.), 310; Department of Finance, *1902, Annual Return of the Foreign Trade of the Empire of Japan* (Tokyo: Koide, n.d.), 397; Department of Finance, *1920, Annual Return of the Foreign Trade of the Empire of Japan*, Part I (Tokyo: n.p., n.d.), 397; Tohei Sawamura, *Kindai chosen no mensaku mengyo* (Tokyo: Miraisha, 1985), 112; Chosen ni okeru menka saibai no genzai to shorai, n.d., mimeograph, Asian Reading Room, Library of Congress, Washington, DC; a slightly different account of the beginnings of Japanese efforts to increase cotton growing in colonial Korea can be found in Carter J. Eckert, *Offspring of Empire: The Koch and Kims and the Colonial Origins of Korean Capitalism, 1876–1945* (Seattle: University of Washington Press, 1991), 134.

2. *Dai-Nihon boseki rengokai geppo* 173 (January 25, 1906): 1–2; *Annual Report for 1907 on Reforms and Progress in Korea* (Seoul: H.I.J.M.'s Residency General, 1908), 84; Eckert, *Offspring of Empire*, 134–5.

3. Eckert, *Offspring of Empire*, 134; *Annual Report for 1912–13 on Reforms and Progress in Chosen* (Keijo: Government General of Chosen, 1914), 153; Department of Finance, *1909, Annual Return of the Foreign Trade of the Empire of Japan* (Tokyo: Koide, n.d.), 629; Cotton Department, Toyo Menka Kaisha Lts., *The Indian Cotton Facts* (Bombay: n.p., n.d.), Japanese Cotton Spinners Association Library, University of Osaka.

4. Rinji Sangyo Chosa Kyoku [Special Department of Research on Industries], *Chosen ni Okeru Menka ni Kansuru Chosa Seiseki* [The Research on Cotton in Korea] (August 1918), 1; Eckert, *Offspring of Empire*, 134; No-Shomu Sho Nomu Kyoku [Ministry of Agriculture and Commerce, Department of Agriculture], *Menka ni Kansuru Chosa* [The Research on Cotton] (Tokyo: No-shomu sho noji shikenjyo, 1905), 1–3, 76–83, chapter 2; Chosen sotokufu norinkyoku, *Chosen no nogyo* (Keijyo: Chosen sotokufu norinkyoku, 1934), 66–73.

5. Nihon mengyo kurabu, *Naigai mengyo nenkan* (Osaka: Nihon mengyo kurabu, 1931), 231, 233; *Annual Report for 1912–13*, 145, 153; *Annual Report for 1915–16*, 107; *Annual Report for 1921–22*, 263; Department of Finance of Japan, *Monthly Trade Return of Japan Proper and Karafuto (Sagalien) with Chosen (Korea)* (Tokyo: n.p., 1915), 24–25.

6. For this shift of conceptions of sovereignty see Henry Sumner Maine, *Ancient Law: Its Connection with the Early History of Society, and Its Relation to Modern Ideas* (New York: Henry Holt and Company, 1864); for a very interesting discussion on these issues see also Doreen Lustig, "Tracing the Origins of the Responsibility Gap of Businesses in International Law, 1870–1919" (unpublished paper, Tel Aviv University Law School, May 2012, in author's possession). Resolution passed by the Manchester Cotton Supply Association, reprinted in *Merchants' Magazine and Commercial Review* 44, no. 6 (June 1861): 678; Arthur Redford, *Manchester Merchants and Foreign Trade, 1794–1858* (Manchester: Manchester University Press, 1934), 217, 227; Kolonial-Wirtschaftliches Komitee, *Baumwoll-Expedition*; New England Cotton Manufacturers' Association, *Transactions of the New England Cotton Manufacturers' Association*, vol. 73 (Waltham, MA: n.p., 1902), 182.

7. For the price increase and a very good exploration of these events and their import see Jonathan Robbins, "The Cotton Crisis: Globalization and Empire in the Atlantic World, 1901–1920" (PhD dissertation, University of Rochester, 2010), 41–54; see also Edmund D. Morel, *Affairs of West Africa* (London: William Heinemann, 1902), 191; Kolonial-Wirtschaftliches Komitee, "Unsere Kolonialwirtschaft in ihrer Bedeutung für Industrie, Handel und Landwirtschaft," Manuscript, R 8024/37, Kolonial-Wirtschaftliches Komitee, Various Letters, 1914, Bundesarchiv, Berlin; for the notion of a "second cotton famine" see Christian Brannstrom, "Forest for Cotton: Institutions and Organizations in Brazil's Mid-Twentieth-Century Cotton Boom," *Journal of Historical Geography* 36, no. 2 (April 2010): 169.

8. Morel, *Affairs*, 191; Edward B. Barbier, *Scarcity and Frontiers: How Economies Have Developed Through Natural Resource Exploitation* (New York: Cambridge University Press, 2011); John C. Weaver, *The Great Land Rush and the Making of the Modern World, 1850–1900* (Montreal: McGill–Queen's University Press, 2003).

9. Muriel Joffe, "Autocracy, Capitalism and Empire: The Politics of Irrigation," *Russian Review* 54, no. 3 (July 1995): 367; Rosen is quoted in Mariya Konstantinovna Rozhkova, *Ekonomich eskaia politika tsarskogo pravitel'stva na Srednem Vostoke vo vtoroi chetverti XIX veka i russkaya burzhuaziya* (Moscow: Izd. Akademii Nauk SSSR, 1949), 100; on earlier hopes for Central Asia as the cotton supplier to Russia see also Pavel Nebol'sin, *Ocherki torgovli Rossii s Srednei Aziei* (Saint Petersburg: Tipografia Imperatorskoi Akademii Nauk, 1855), 18, 22, 25, 27; textile manufacturer Aleksandr Shipov stressed as early as 1857 the importance of securing access to Central Asian cotton; see Aleksandr Shipov, *Khlopchatobumazhnaia promyshlennost' i vazhnost' eco znacheniia v Rossii*, otd I (Moscow: T.T. Volkov & Co., 1857), 49–50; see Charles William Maynes, "America Discovers Central Asia," *Foreign Affairs* 82, no. 2 (March/April 2003): 120; Mariya Konstantinovna Rozhkova, *Ekonomiceskie svyazi Rossii so Srednei Aziei, 40–60-e gody XIX veka* (Moscow: Izd-vo Akademii nauk SSSR, 1963), 54–55, tables 9–10.

10. Quote in Rozhkova, *Ekonomicheskiie*, 64–65, 150–52; a pood (or 35.24 pounds) of

Asian cotton was sold for 7.75 rubles in 1861, but by 1863 the price had increased to more than 22 rubles; P. A. Khromov, *Ekonomicheskoe razvitie Rossii v XIX-XX vekakh: 1800–1917* (Moscow: Gos. Izd. Politicheskoi Literatury, 1950), 183; in some regions, such as in the Erivan gubernia (in the Caucasus), cotton production during the Civil War increased nearly tenfold, from 30,000 poods in 1861 to 273,000 poods in 1870; K. A. Pazhitnov, *Ocherki istorii tesktil' noi promyshlennosti dorrevolyutsionnoi Rossii: Khlopchato-Bumazhnaya l'no-pen' kovaya i shelkovaya promyshlennost* (Moscow: Izd. Akademii Nauk SSR, 1958), 98; Rozhkova, *Ekonomiceskie*, 55–61; see, for a discussion of the expansion of cotton agriculture in Russian Central Asia, Joffe, "Autocracy," 365–88; Julia Obertreis, *Imperial Desert Dreams: Irrigation and Cotton Growing in Southern Central Asia, 1860s to 1991* (unpublished manuscript, 2009), chapter 1, 23; *Moskva*, February 1, 1867; on January 8, 1866, Czar Alexander II received a memorandum written by the minister of finance in favor of the exertion of greater influence on Central Asia, which listed among the supporters of such a project the names of a group of Russian capitalists, including owners of such prominent cotton ventures as Ivan Khludov & Sons, Savva Morozov & Sons, Vl. Tertyakov, and D. I. Romanovskii; see N. A. Khalfin, *Prisoedinenie Srednei Azii k Rossii: 60–90 gody XIX v* (Moscow: Nauka, 1965), 211; on the general debate about Russian imperialism, see Andreas Kappeler, *The Russian Empire: A Multiethnic Empire* (Harlow: Longman, 2001), 175, 193; Dietrich Geyer, *Der russische Imperialismus: Studien über den Zusammenhang von innerer und auswärtiger Politik, 1860–1914* (Göttingen: Vandenhoeck & Ruprecht, 1977); Thomas C. Owen, "The Russian Industrial Society and Tsarist Economic Policy," *Journal of Economic History* 45, no. 3 (September 1985): 598; Brigitte Loehr, *Die Zukunft Russlands* (Wiesbaden: Franz Steiner Verlag, 1985), 73; Joffe, "Autocracy," 372; Bruno Biedermann, "Die Versorgung der russischen Baumwollindustrie mit Baumwolle eigener Produktion" (PhD dissertation, University of Heidelberg, 1907), 106.

11. Shtaba L. Kostenko, *Sredni aia Aziia i Vodvorenie v nei Russkoi Grazgdanstvennosti* (Saint Petersburg: Bezobrazova i kom, 1871), 221; Thomas Martin, *Baumwollindustrie in Sankt Petersburg und Moskau und die russische Zolltarifpolitik, 1850–1891: Eine vergleichende Regionalstudie* (Giessen: Fachverlag Koehler, 1998), 213, 215; Scott C. Levi, *The Indian Diaspora in Central Asia and Its Trade, 1550–1900* (Leiden: Brill, 2002), 249; Jeff Sahadeo, "Cultures of Cotton and Colonialism: Politics, Society, and the Environment in Central Asia, 1865–1923" (presentation, American Association for the Advancement of Slavic Studies Annual Convention, Toronto, November 2003), 5; George N. Curzon, *Russia in Central Asia in 1889 and the Anglo-Russian Question* (London: Cass, 1967), 405–7; Biedermann, "Die Versorgung," 40–44; on irrigation see also Obertreis, *Imperial Desert Dreams*; John Whitman, "Turkestan Cotton in Imperial Russia," *American Slavic and East European Review* 15, no. 2 (April 1956): 194–95, 199; Moritz Schanz, "Die Baumwolle in Russisch-Asien," *Beihefte zum Tropenpflanzer* 15 (1914): 8.

12. Obertreis, *Imperial Desert Dreams*, Chapter 1, 74ff.; these conflicts are best described in regard to the question of irrigation; see Joffe, "Autocracy," 369, 387; Whitman, "Turkestan Cotton," 194, 198, 201; the territory devoted to cotton agriculture increased by a factor of five between 1887 and 1899 in Russian Turkestan, Bukhara,

and Khiva; Anlage zum Bericht des Kaiserlichen Generalkonsulats in St. Petersburg, December 26, 1913, R 150F, FA 1, 360, Bundesarchiv, Berlin; the "cotton colony" quote can be found in I. Liashchenko, *Istoriia Narodnogo Khoziaistva SSSR*, vol. 2 (Moscow: Gos. Izd. Polit. Literatury, 1956), 542; "Handelsbericht des Kaiserlichen Konsulats für das Jahr 1909," in *Deutsches Handels-Archiv*, Zweiter Teil: Berichte über das Ausland, 1911 (Berlin: Ernst Siegfried Mittler und Sohn, 1911), 168; Schanz, "Die Baumwolle," 11; Annette M. B. Meakin, *In Russian Turkestan: A Garden of Asia and Its People* (New York: Charles Scribner's Sons, 1915), v; Ella R. Christie, *Through Kiva to Golden Samarkand* (London: Seeley, Service & Co., 1925), 204; Karl Supf, "Zur Baumwollfrage," in Kolonial-Wirtschaftliches Komitee, *Baumwoll-Expedition nach Togo* (no date, but probably 1900), 4–6, file 332, record group R 150F, Fonds Allemand 1, Papers of the Administration of the German Protectorate Togo (L'Administration du Protectorat Allemand du Togo), Archives Nationales du Togo, Lomé, microfilm copy in Bundesarchiv, Berlin; Michael Owen Gately, "The Development of the Russian Cotton Textile Industry in the Pre-revolutionary Years, 1861–1913" (PhD dissertation, University of Kansas, 1968), 169.

13. August Etienne, *Die Baumwollzucht im Wirtschaftsprogramm der deutschen Übersee-Politik* (Berlin: H. Paetal, 1902), 35, 36, 37, 41; *Harper's Weekly* reported that "Uzbekistan can thank the American Civil War" for its strong dependence on cotton; see *Harper's Weekly*, April 2002, 42.

14. Etienne, *Die Baumwollzucht*, 28.

15. Ibid., 13.

16. Biedermann, "Die Versorgung," 12; "Cotton in British East Africa," *Imperial and Asiatic Quarterly Review*, Third Series, 24 (July–October 1907): 84; Robert Ed. Buehler, "Die Unabhängigkeitsbestrebungen Englands, Frankreichs und Deutschlands in ihrer Baumwollversorgung" (PhD dissertation, University of Zürich, 1929), 57.

17. Oldham Master Cotton Spinners' Association, *Report of the Committee, for Year Ending December 31, 1901* (Oldham: Dornan, 1902), 4, in Record group 6/2/1–61m, Papers of the Oldham Master Cotton Spinners' Association, John Rylands Library, Manchester; Buehler, "Die Unabhängigkeitsbestrebungen," 68; British Cotton Growing Association, *Second Annual Report, for the Year Ending August 31st, 1906* (Manchester: Head Office, 1906), 8, 10; Correspondence, File 1, Files Relating to the Cotton Industry, British Cotton Growing Association, 2/5, OLD, Papers of the Oldham Textile Employers' Association, 1870–1960, John Rylands Library, Manchester; Morel, *Affairs*; for an excellent review of the activities of the British Cotton Growing Association, see Jonathan Robins, " 'The Black Man's Crop': Cotton, Imperialism and Public-Private Development in Britain's African Colonies, 1900–1918," Commodities of Empire Working Paper 11, The Open University and London Metropolitan University, September 2009; Oldham Master Cotton Spinners' Association, *Report of the Committee, for the Year Ending December 31, 1901* (Oldham: Thomas Dornan, 1902), 4, John Rylands Library, Manchester; File Empire Cotton Growing Association, 2/6, OLD, Papers of the Oldham Textile Employers' Association, 1870–1960, John Rylands Library, Manchester; N. M. Penzer, Federation of British Industries, Intelligence Department, *Cotton in British West Africa* (London: Federation of British Industries, 1920); John Harris, Parliamentary Secretary of the Soci-

ety, to E. Sedgwick, Boston, November 10, 1924, Papers of the British and Foreign Anti-Slavery and Aborigines Protection Society, MSS. British Empire S22, G143, Bodleian Library of Commonwealth & African Studies, University of Oxford; John Harris to Maxwell Garnett, January 20, 1925, MSS. British Empire 522, G446, Papers of the British and Foreign Anti-Slavery and Aborigines Protection Society, Rhodes House Library, Oxford; D. Edwards-Radclyffe, "Ramie, The Textile of the Future," *Imperial and Asiatic Quarterly Review*, Third Series, 20 (July–October 1905): 47.

18. Frédéric Engel-Dollfus, *Production du coton* (Paris: Paul Dupont, 1867); as General Faidherbe argued in 1889, "La culture du cotonnier comme l'élément le plus puissant du succès de la colonisation"; see General Faidherbe, *Le Sénégal: La France dans l'Afrique occidentale* (Paris: Librairie Hachette, 1889), 102; Association Cotonnière Coloniale, *Annexe au Bulletin No 3: Les coton indigènes du Dahomey et du Soudan à la filature et au tisage* (Paris: Jean Ganiche, 1904); Charles Brunel, *Le coton en Algérie* (Alger: Imprimierie Agricole, 1910); for French interest in colonial cotton see also Ed. C. Achard, "Le coton en Cilivie et en Syrie," in *L'Asie Française* (June 1922), Supplement; Documents Économiques, Politiques & Scientifiques, 19–64; *Bulletin de l'Union des Agriculteurs d'Égypte* 159 (March 1925): 73–85; Catalogue of the Library of the Société Industrielle de Mulhouse, Mulhouse, France; *Zeitfragen: Wochenschrift für deutsches Leben*, May 1, 1911, 1.

19. Sven Beckert, *The Monied Metropolis: New York City and the Consolidation of the American Bourgeoisie, 1850–1896* (Cambridge: Cambridge University Press, 2001), 87–89; J. De Cordova, *The Cultivation of Cotton in Texas* (London: J. King & Co., 1858), 3, 9, 24; National Association of Cotton Manufacturers and Planters, *Proceedings of a Convention Held in the City of New York, Wednesday, April 29, 1868, for the Purpose of Organizing the National Association of Cotton Manufacturers and Planters* (Boston: Prentiss & Deland, 1868); New England Cotton Manufacturers' Association, *Transactions of the New England Cotton Manufacturers' Association,* vol. 73 (Waltham, MA: n.p., 1902), 187; New England Cotton Manufacturers' Association, *Transactions of the New England Cotton Manufacturers' Association*, vol. 75 (1903), 191; New England Cotton Manufacturers' Association, *Transactions of the New England Cotton Manufacturers' Association*, vol. 79 (1905), 159.

20. See also Henry L. Abbott, "The Lowlands of the Mississippi," *The Galaxy* 5 (April 1868): 452; National Association of Cotton Manufacturers and Planters, *Articles of Association and By-Laws Adopted by the National Association of Cotton Manufacturers and Planters, April 29, 1868* (Boston: Prentiss & Deland, 1968); National Association of Cotton Manufacturers and Planters, *Proceedings of the First Annual Meeting of the National Association of Cotton Manufacturers and Planters, Held in the City of New York, Wednesday, June 30, 1869* (Boston: W. L. Deland & Co., 1869), 17; F. W. Loring and C. F. Atkinson, *Cotton Culture and the South Considered with Reference to Emigration* (Boston: A. Williams & Co., 1869), 3; New England Cotton Manufacturers' Association, *Transactions of the New England Cotton Manufacturers' Association*, vol. 76 (1904), 104. On Africa see Allen Isaacman and Richard Roberts, "Cotton, Colonialism, and Social History in Sub-Saharan Africa," in Allen Isaacman and Richard Roberts, eds., *Cotton, Colonialism, and Social History in Sub-Saharan Africa* (Portsmouth, NH: Heinemann, 1995), 1; Records of the Togo Baumwollgesellschaft

mbh, Record Group 7, 2016, Staatsarchiv Bremen, Bremen, Germany; Laxman D. Satya, *Cotton and Famine in Berar* (New Delhi: Manohar, 1997), 55; Thaddeus Raymond Sunseri, *Vilimani: Labor Migration and Rural Change in Early Colonial Tanzania* (Portsmouth, NH: Heinemann, 2002); Sven Beckert, "From Tuskegee to Togo: The Problem of Freedom in the Empire of Cotton," *Journal of American History* 92, no. 2 (September 2005): 498–526; Edward Mead Earle, "Egyptian Cotton and the American Civil War," *Political Science Quarterly* 41, no. 4 (1926): 520; *Westminster Review* 84, American Edition (1865): 228; *Zeitfragen: Wochenschrift für deutsches Leben,* May 1, 1911, 1; Kolonial-Wirtschaftliches Komitee, *Deutsch-Koloniale Baumwoll-Unternehmungen 1902/1903* (Berlin: Kolonial-Wirtschaftliches Komitee, 1903), 5.

21. Moulvi Syed Mahdi Ali, ed., *Hyderabad Affairs*, vol. 3 (Bombay: n.p., 1883), 112, 404, 451; *Manchester Guardian,* June 30, 1882, 4; Earle, "Egyptian Cotton," 544; Edward Roger John Owen, *Cotton and the Egyptian Economy, 1820–1914: A Study in Trade and Development* (Oxford: Clarendon Press, 1969), 89, 130, 141, 213ff., 247.

22. Meltem Toksöz, "The Çukurova: From Nomadic Life to Commercial Agriculture, 1800–1908" (PhD dissertation, State University of New York at Binghamton, 2000), 204, 206, 228; Anthony Hall, *Drought and Irrigation in North-East Brazil* (Cambridge: Cambridge University Press, 1978), 4; Roger L. Cunniff, "The Great Drought: Northeast Brazil, 1877–1880" (PhD dissertation, University of Texas at Austin, 1970), 79, 83, 87, 88, 89, 91–95; International Institute of Agriculture, Statistical Bureau, *The Cotton-Growing Countries: Production and Trade* (Rome: International Institute of Agriculture, 1922), 125.

23. Michael J. Gonzales, "The Rise of Cotton Tenant Farming in Peru, 1890–1920: The Condor Valley," *Agricultural History* 65, no. 1 (Winter 1991): 53, 55; Oficina Nacional de Agricultura, *El algodón, instrucciones agrícolas* (Buenos Aires: Penitenciaria Nacional, 1897), 1; Alejandro E. Bunge, *Las industrias del Norte: Contribución al estudio de una nueva política económia Argentina* (Buenos Aires: n.p., 1922), 212ff.; Heinz E. Platte, "Baumwollanbau in Argentinien," *Argentinisches Tagblatt* 20, no. 1 (January 1924): 19.

24. Toksöz, "Çukurova," 99; Weaver, *Great Land Rush,* 4.

25. See in general, Jürgen Osterhammel, *Kolonialismus: Geschichte, Formen, Folgen,* 6th ed. (Munich: Beck, 2009), 10–11; on the specifics see Secretary of the Interior, *Agriculture of the United States in 1860: Compiled from the Original Returns of the Eighth Census* (Washington, DC: Government Printing Office, 1864), 185, accessed May 25, 2009, http://www.agcensus.usda.gov/Publications/Historical_Publications/1860/1860b -08.pdf; United States Department of Agriculture, National Agricultural Statistics Service, accessed April 28, 2009, http://www.nass.usda.gov/QuickStats/indexbysubject .jsp?Text1=&site/NASS_MAIN&select=Select+a+State&Pass_name=&Pass_group =Crops+%26+Plants&Pass_subgroup=Field+Crops; since there are no numbers available on the precise extent of the territory on which cotton was grown in 1860, I assumed constant productivity to estimate the additional land needed to grow the additional cotton. The area of the state of South Carolina is 20,484,000 acres.

26. Gavin Wright, *Old South, New South: Revolutions in the Southern Economy Since the Civil War* (Baton Rouge: Louisiana State University Press, 1996), 34ff., 57; Secretary of the Interior, *Agriculture of the United States in 1860: Compiled from the Original*

Returns of the Eighth Census (Washington, DC: Government Printing Office, 1864), 185, accessed May 25, 2009, http://www.agcensus.usda.gov/Publications/Historical _Publications/1860/1860b-08.pdf; United States Department of Agriculture, National Agricultural Statistics Service, accessed April 28, 2009, http://www.nass.usda.gov/Quick Stats/indexbysubject.jsp?Text1=&site?=NASS_MAIN&select=Select+a+State&Pass _name=&Pass_group=Crops+%26+Plants&Pass_subgroup=Field+Crops; Charles S. Aiken, *The Cotton Plantation South Since the Civil War* (Baltimore: Johns Hopkins University Press, 1998), 59; James C. Cobb, *The Most Southern Place on Earth: The Mississippi Delta and the Roots of Regional Identity* (New York: Oxford University Press, 1992), viii, 95, 99, 100; Gavin Wright, "Agriculture in the South," in Glenn Porter, ed., *Encyclopedia of American Economic History: Studies of the Principal Movements and Ideas*, vol. 1 (New York: Charles Schribner's Sons, 1980), 382; Devra Weber, *Dark Sweat, White Gold: California Farm Workers, Cotton, and the New Deal* (Berkeley: University of California Press, 1994), 17–21.

27. U.S. Department of Commerce, U.S. Census Bureau, *Statistical Abstracts of the United States, 1921* (Washington, DC: Government Printing Office, 1922), 375; Randolph B. Campbell, *Gone to Texas: A History of the Lone Star State* (New York: Oxford University Press, 2003), 306, 308, 311.

28. Ray Allen Billington, *Westward Expansion: A History of the American Frontier* (New York: Macmillan, 1967), 659, 666.

29. Howard Wayne Morgan, *Oklahoma: A Bicentennial History* (New York: Norton, 1977), 42, 81, 91, 48, 49, 58, 147; United States Department of Agriculture, National Agricultural Statistics Service, accessed April 28, 2009, http://www.nass.usda.gov/ QuickStats/indexbysubject.jsp?Text1=&site/NASS_MAIN&select=Select+a+State&Pass_ name=&Pass_group=Crops+%26+Plants&Pass_subgroup=Field+Crops; U.S. Department of Commerce, U.S. Census Bureau, "Agriculture, 1909 and 1910, Reports by States, with Statistics for Counties, Nebraska-Wyoming," *Thirteenth Census of the United States Taken in the Year 1910*, vol. 7 (Washington, DC: Government Printing Office, 1913), 381; Eric V. Meeks, "The Tohono O'Odham, Wage Labor, and Resistant Adaptation," *Western Historical Quarterly* 34, no. 4 (Winter 2003): 480; Daniel H. Usner, *Indian Work: Language and Livelihood in Native American History* (Cambridge, MA: Harvard University Press, 2009), 55.

30. For an exploration of this issue see Sven Beckert, "Space Matters: Eurafrica, the American Empire, and the Territorialization of European Capitalism, 1870–1940" (article in progress).

31. Günter Kirchhain, "Das Wachstum der deutschen Baumwollindustrie im 19. Jahrhundert: Eine historische Modellstudie zur empirischen Wachstumsforschung" (PhD dissertation, University of Münster, 1973), 29–30, 73; Wilhelm Rieger, *Verzeichnis der im Deutschen Reiche auf Baumwolle laufenden Spindeln und Webstühle* (Stuttgart: Wilhelm Rieger, 1909), 72; for different and slightly lower numbers, see Wolfram Fischer, *Statistik der Bergbauproduktion Deutschland 1850–1914* (St. Kathatinen: Scripta Mercaturae Verlag, 1989), 403; *Handbuch der Wirtschaftskunde Deutschlands*, vol. 3 (Leipzig: Teubner, 1904), 602; it is indeed fascinating that in many ways the more important cotton industry plays much less of a role in our historical memory of late-nineteenth-century Germany. See also Karl Supf, "Zur Baumwollfrage," in

Kolonial-Wirtschaftliches Komitee, *Baumwoll-Expedition nach Togo* (no date, but probably 1900), 4–6, file 332, record group R 150F, Fonds Allemand 1, Papers of the Administration of the German Protectorate Togo (L'Administration du Protectorat Allemand du Togo), Archives Nationales du Togo, Lomé, microfilm copy in Bundesarchiv, Berlin; Kaiserliches Statistisches Amt, *Statistisches Jahrbuch für das Deutsche Reich*, vol. 23 (Berlin: Puttkammer & Mühlbrecht, 1902), 24; in 1903 the Kolonial-Wirtschaftliches Komitee reported that 1 million workers in Germany were dependent on the cotton industry; see Kolonial-Wirtschaftliches Komitee, *Deutsch-Koloniale*, 5; the value of the cotton industry's production amounted by 1913 to 2.2 billion marks, making it one of Germany's most significant industries. See Andor Kertész, *Die Textilindustrie Deutschlands im Welthandel* (Braunschweig: F. Vieweg, 1915), 13. See also Kaiserliches Statistisches Amt, *Statistisches Jahrbuch für das Deutsche Reich*, vol. 22 (Berlin: n.p., 1901), 135; Thaddeus Sunseri, "The Baumwollfrage: Cotton Colonialism in German East Africa," *Central European History* 34, no. 1 (March 2001): 35; for import statistics see Reichs-Enquete für die Baumwollen-und Leinen-Industrie, Statistische Ermittelungen I, Heft 1, 56–58; Kaiserliches Statistisches Amt, *Statistisches Jahrbuch für das Deutsche Reich*, vol. 1 (Berlin: n.p., 1880), 87; Kaiserliches Statistisches Amt, *Statistisches Jahrbuch für das Deutsche Reich*, vol. 20 (Berlin: n.p., 1899), 91.

32. See, for example, Ernst Henrici, "Die wirtschaftliche Nutzbarmachung des Togogebietes," *Der Tropenpflanzer: Zeitschrift für tropische Landwirtschaft* 3 (July 1899): 320; Sven Beckert, "Emancipation and Empire: Reconstructing the Worldwide Web of Cotton Production in the Age of the American Civil War," *American Historical Review* 109, no. 5 (December 2004): 1427; C. A. Bayly, *The Birth of the Modern World, 1780–1914: Global Connections and Comparisons* (Malden, MA: Blackwell, 2004), 161–65; Kaiserliches Statistisches Amt, *Statistisches Jahrbuch für das Deutsche Reich*, vol. 15 (Berlin: n.p., 1894), 45; Kaiserliches Statistisches Amt, *Statistisches Jahrbuch für das Deutsche Reich*, vol. 20 (Berlin: n.p., 1899), 91.

33. R. Hennings, "Der Baumwollkulturkampf," in *Zeitschrift für Kolonialpolitik, Kolonialrecht und Kolonialwirtschaft*, vol. 7 (1905), 906–14; Sunseri, "Baumwollfrage," 32; "Die Arbeit des Kolonial-Wirtschaftlichen Komitees, 1896–1914," file 579, record group R 150F, Fonds Allemand 1, Papers of the Administration of the German Protectorate Togo (L'Administration du Protectorat Allemand du Togo), Archives Nationales du Togo, Lomé, microfilm copy in Bundesarchiv, Berlin; Sunseri, "Baumwollfrage," 49; on German demand for colonial cotton see also Verband Deutscher Baumwollgarn-Verbraucher an v. Lindequist, Reichskolonialamt, Dresden, October 22, 1910, file 8224, record group R 1001, Papers of the Deutsche Kolonialgesellschaft, Bundesarchiv, Berlin.

34. Buehler, "Die Unabhängigkeitsbestrebungen," 23, 39; Biedermann, "Die Versorgung," 9; *Bericht der Handelskammer in Bremen für das Jahr 1904 an den Kaufmannskonvent* (Bremen: H. M. Hausschild, 1905), 30.

35. Department of Finance, *1920, Annual Return of the Foreign Trade of the Empire of Japan*, Part I (Tokyo: n.p., n.d.), 397; Buehler, "Die Unabhängigkeitsbestrebungen," 31; Supf, "Zur Baumwollfrage," 8.

36. Supf, "Zur Baumwollfrage," 4–6, 8; E. Henrici, "Der Baumwollbau in den deutschen Kolonien," *Der Tropenpflanzer: Zeitschrift für tropische Landwirtschaft* 3 (Novem-

ber 1899): 535–36. On Henrici see Herrmann A. L. Degener, *Unsere Zeitgenossen, Wer Ist's?: Biographien nebst Bibliographien* (Leipzig: n.p., 1911); calls for economic autarky are also reflected in "Einleitung," *Beihefte Zum Tropenpflanzer* 16, no. 1/2 (February 1916): 1–3, 71–73, 175–77; Karl Helfferich, "Die Baumwollfrage: Ein Weltwirtschaftliches Problem," *Marine-Rundschau* 15 (1904): 652; Karl Supf, "Bericht IV, Deutsch-Koloniale Baumwoll-Unternehmungen, 1903–1904" (1904), reprinted in *Der Tropenpflanzer: Zeitschrift für tropische Landwirtschaft* 8 (December 1904): 615; "Die Arbeit des Kolonial-Wirtschaftlichen Komitees, 1896–1914."

37. Sunseri, "Baumwollfrage," 33; O. F. Metzger, *Unsere Alte Kolonie Togo* (Neudamm: Neumann, 1941), 242; "Bericht über den Baumwollbau in Togo," enclosure in Kaiserliches Gouvernement Togo, Gouverneur Zech to Reichskolonialamt Berlin, November 23, 1909, 1, 8223, record group R 1001, Papers of the Deutsche Kolonialgesellschaft, Bundesarchiv, Berlin; "Der Baumwollbau in Togo, Seine Bisherige Entwicklung, und sein jetziger Stand," undated draft of an article, 8224, record group R 1001, Papers of the Deutsche Kolonialgesellschaft, Bundesarchiv, Berlin, [illegible] to von Bismark, March 26, 1890, file 8220, record group R 1001, Papers of the Deutsche Kolonialgesellschaft, Bundesarchiv, Berlin; Tony Smith, *Pattern of Imperialism: The United States, Great Britain, and the Late-Industrializing World Since 1815* (New York: Cambridge University Press, 1981), 15, 35; Eric Hobsbawm, *The Age of Empire, 1875–1914* (New York: Pantheon, 1987), 34–55; Isaacman and Roberts, "Cotton, Colonialism," in Isaacman and Roberts, eds., *Cotton, Colonialism,* 8–9; Leroy Vail and Landeg White, " 'Tawani, Machambero!': Forced Cotton and Rice Growing on the Zambezi," *Journal of African History* 19, no. 2 (1978): 244.

38. Kendahl Radcliffe, "The Tuskegee-Togo Cotton Scheme, 1900–1909" (PhD dissertation, University of California, Los Angeles, 1998), 16; on Ferdinand Goldberg see "Baumwollen- und sonstige Kulturen im Togo-Gebiet," *Deutsches Kolonialblatt* 2 (1891): 320–21; more generally on German interests in colonial cotton see Donna J. E. Maier, "Persistence of Precolonial Patterns of Production: Cotton in German Togoland, 1800–1914," in Isaacman and Roberts, eds., *Cotton, Colonialism,* 81; Peter Sebald, *Togo 1884–1914: Eine Geschichte der deutschen "Musterkolonie" auf der Grundlage amtlicher Quellen* (Berlin: Akademie-Verlag, 1988), 433; for a more complete rendering of this story see Sven Beckert, "From Tuskegee to Togo: The Problem of Freedom in the Empire of Cotton, *Journal of American History* 92 (September 2005)," 498–526; for a list of these plantations see Kolonial-Wirtschaftliches Komitee to Handelskammer Bremen, Berlin, July 23, 1913, in "Baumwollterminhandel," record group W II, 3, Handelskammer Bremen, Bremen, Germany; Sunseri, *Vilimani,* 1–25; Gerhard Bleifuss and Gerhard Hergenröder, *Die "Otto-Plantage Kilossa" (1907–1914): Aufbau und Ende eines kolonialen Unternehmens in Deutsch-Ostafrika* (Wendlingen: Schriftenreihe zur Stadtgeschichte, 1993), 43, 59.

39. "Encouragement pour la Culture aux colonies, du cotton etc. (1906–1908)," 9 AFFECO, Affairs Économique, Archives d'outre-mer, Aix-en-Provence; for the quote, see Reseignements sur la Culture du Coton, 1917, in 9 AFFECO, Affairs Économique, Archives d'outre-mer; Marie Philiponeau, *Le coton et l'Islam: Fil d'une histoire africaine* (Algiers: Casbah Editions, 2009), 114; Thomas J. Bassett, *The Peasant Cotton Revolution in West Africa: Côte d'Ivoire, 1880–1995* (Cambridge:

Cambridge University Press, 2001), 51, 52; Richard Roberts, "The Coercion of Free Markets: Cotton, Peasants, and the Colonial State in the French Soudan, 1924–1932," in Isaacman and Roberts, eds., *Cotton, Colonialism*, 222; Vail and White, "Tawani, Machambero," 241; League of Nations, Economic Intelligence Service, *Statistical Year-book of the League of Nations 1930/31* (Geneva: Series of League of Nations Publications, 1931), 108, accessed August 3, 2009, http://digital.library.northwestern .edu/league/leo267ag.pdf; A. Brixhe, *Le coton au Congo Belge* (Bruxelles: Direction de l'agriculture, des forêts et de l'élevage du Ministère des colonies, 1953), 13, 15, 19; Secretary of the Interior, *Agriculture of the United States in 1860: Compiled from the Original Returns of the Eighth Census* (Washington, DC: Government Printing Office, 1864), 185, accessed May 25, 2009, http://www.agcensus.usda.gov/Publications/ Historical_Publications/1860/1860b-08.pdf.

40. Hutton, as quoted in Robins, "The Black Man's Crop," 15; Cyril Ehrlich, "The Marketing of Cotton in Uganda, 1900–1950: A Case Study of Colonial Government Economic Policy" (PhD dissertation, University of London, 1958), 12, 13; Buehler, "Die Unabhängigkeitsbestrebungen," 122; British Cotton Growing Association, *Second Annual Report, for the Year Ending August 31st, 1906* (Manchester: Head Office, 1906), 23; on the British Cotton Growing Association see Robins, "The Black Man's Crop"; British Cotton Growing Association, *Second Annual Report, for the Year Ending August 31st, 1906*, 32; League of Nations, Economic Intelligence Service, *Statistical Year-book of the League of Nations 1930/31* (Geneva: Series of League of Nations Publications, 1931), 108; Secretary of the Interior, *Agriculture of the United States in 1860: Compiled from the Original Returns of the Eighth Census* (Washington, DC: Government Printing Office, 1864), 185, accessed May 25, 2009, http://www.agcensus.usda .gov/Publications/Historical_Publications/1860/1860b-08.pdf.

41. Josef Partsch, ed., *Geographie des Welthandels* (Breslau: Hirt, 1927), 209; B. R. Mitchell, *International Historical Statistics: The Americas, 1750–1993* (Basingstoke, UK: Macmillan, 2007), 222, 224, 227, 228; John A. Todd, *The World's Cotton Crops* (London: A. & C. Black, 1915), 395ff. 421; Heinrich Kuhn, *Die Baumwolle: Ihre Cultur, Structur und Verbreitung* (Wien: Hartleben, 1892), 69; John C. Branner, *Cotton in the Empire of Brazil; The Antiquity, Methods and Extent of Its Cultivation; Together with Statistics of Exportation and Home Consumption* (Washington, DC: Government Printing Office, 1885), 23–27; National Association of Cotton Manufacturers, *The Year Book of the National Association of Cotton Manufacturers and Cotton Manufacturers Manual* (1922), 83, accessed August 3, 2009, http://ia311228.us.archive.org/1/items/ yearbookofnation1922nati/yearbookofnation1922nati.pdf; International Institute of Agriculture, Statistical Bureau, *The Cotton-Growing Countries: Production and Trade* (Rome: International Institute of Agriculture, 1922), 127; League of Nations, Economic Intelligence Service, *Statistical Year-book of the League of Nations 1939/40* (Geneva: Series of League of Nations Publications, 1940), 122; United Nations, Department for Economic and Social Affairs, Statistics Division, *Statistical Yearbook*, vol. 4 (New York: Department of Economic and Social Affairs, Statistical Office, United Nations, 1952), 72; United States Department of Agriculture, Foreign Agricultural Service, Table 04 Cotton Area, Yield, and Production, accessed August 3, 2009, http:// www.fas.usda.gov/psdonline/psdReport.aspx?hidReportRetrievalName=Table+04

+Cotton+Area%2c+Yield%2c+and+Production&hidReportRetrievalID=851&hid
ReportRetrievalTemplateID=1; Biedermann, "Die Versorgung," 3.

42. *Revue des cultures coloniales* 12–13 (1903): 302.

43. For Central Asia, see for example Richard A. Pierce, *Russian Central Asia, 1867–1917: A Study in Colonial Rule* (Berkeley: University of California Press, 1960), 135–36; Toksöz, "Çukurova," 1, 13, 37, 79; Osterhammel, *Kolonialismus*, 17ff.

44. Nebol'sin, *Ocherki torgovli Rossii*, 25; Kostenko, *Sredniaia Aziia*, 213.

45. Nebol'sin, *Ocherki torgovli Rossii*, 25; Rozhkova, *Ekonomicheskiie*, 68; Whitman, "Turkestan Cotton," 199, 200; Schanz, "Die Baumwolle," 88, 368; Biedermann, "Die Versorgung," 72; Sahadeo, "Cultures," 3.

46. Biedermann, "Die Versorgung," 45, 46, 59.

47. Handelsbericht des Kaiserlichen Konsulats für das Jahr 1909, in Deutsches Handels-Archiv, *Zweiter Teil: Berichte über das Ausland, Jahrgang 1911* (Berlin: Ernst Siegfried Mittler und Sohn, 1911), 168; Whitman, "Turkestan Cotton," 200; Biedermann, "Die Versorgung," 70; Schanz, "Die Baumwolle," 10, 50.

48. Whitman, "Turkestan Cotton," 200, 203; Schanz, "Die Baumwolle," 131.

49. "British and Russian Commercial Competition in Central Asia," *Asiatic Quarterly Review* (London) 8 (July–October 1889): 439; Whitman, "Turkestan Cotton," 202; E. Z. Volkov, *Dinamika narodonaselenija SSSR za vosem'desjat let* (Moscow: Gos. izd., 1930), 40, 198–99, 208.

50. Kolonial-Wirtschaftliches Komitee, *Baumwoll-Expedition*, 4; the following pages are based on and make extensive use of materials in Beckert, "From Tuskegee to Togo." See also James N. Calloway to Booker T. Washington, November 20, 1900, Booker T. Washington Papers, Manuscripts Division, Library of Congress, Washington, DC; Kolonial-Wirtschaftliches Komitee to Washington, October 10, 1900, and December 11, 1900, Booker T. Washington Papers. On the plans for the "Baumwoll-Expedition," see also Kolonial-Wirtschaftliches Komitee, Antrag des Kolonialwirtschaftlichen Komitees auf Bewilligung eines Betrages von M 10,000.- zur Ausführung einer Baumwollexpedition nach Togo, Berlin, May 14, 1900, Oktober 1898–Oktober 1900, Band 2, Kolonial-Wirtschaftliches Komitee, File 594/K81, record group R 8023, Papers of the Deutsche Kolonialgesellschaft, Bundesarchiv, Berlin; on the episode see also Booker T. Washington, *Workings with the Hands* (New York: Doubleday, Page & Company, 1904), 226–30; Louis R. Harlan, "Booker T. Washington and the White Man's Burden," *American Historical Review* 71, no. 2 (January 1966): 441–67, 266–95; Edward Berman, "Tuskegee-in-Africa," *Journal of Negro Education* 41, no. 2 (Spring 1972): 99–112; W. Manning Marable, "Booker T. Washington and African Nationalism," *Phylon* 35, no. 4 (December 1974), 398–406; Michael O. West, "The Tuskegee Model of Development in Africa: Another Dimension of the African/African-American Connection," *Diplomatic History* 16, no. 3 (Summer 1992): 371–87; Milfred C. Fierce, *The Pan-African Idea in the United States, 1900–1919: African-American Interest in Africa and Interaction with West Africa* (New York: Garland, 1993), 171–97; Maier, "Persistence," 71–95; Radcliffe, "Tuskegee-Togo"; Andrew Zimmermann, *Alabama in Africa: Booker T. Washington, the German Empire, and the Globalization of the New South* (Princeton, NJ: Princeton University Press, 2012).

51. For an account of this change see Beckert, "Emancipation," 1405–38.

52. Supf, "Zur Baumwollfrage," 8; Kolonial-Wirtschaftliches Komitee, *Baumwoll-Expedition*, 3; see for a similar assessment Hutton, as quoted in Robins, "The Black Man's Crop," 4; see, for other examples of African Americans traveling to colonial cotton projects, Jonathan Robbins, "The Cotton Crisis: Globalization and Empire in the Atlantic World, 1901–1920" (PhD dissertation, University of Rochester, 2010), 220; Booker T. Washington to Beno von Herman auf Wain, September 20, 1900, Booker T. Washington Papers, Manuscripts Division, Library of Congress, Washington, DC.

53. For the Calloway quote see James N. Calloway to Washington, April 30, 1901, Booker T. Washington Papers, Manuscripts Division, Library of Congress, Washington, DC. See also James N. Calloway to Kolonial-Wirtschaftliches Komitee, 12 March 1901, file 8221, record group R 1001, Papers of the Deutsche Kolonialgesellschaft, Bundes-archiv, Berlin; M. B. K. Darkoh, "Togoland under the Germans: Thirty Years of Eco-nomic Development (1884–1914)," *Nigerian Geographic Journal* 10, no. 2 (1968): 112; James N. Calloway to Kolonial-Wirtschaftliches Komitee, February 3, 1901, file 8221, record group R 1001, Papers of the Deutsche Kolonialgesellschaft; James N. Calloway to Washington, February 3, 1901, Booker T. Washington Papers; James N. Calloway to Kolonial-Wirtschaftliches Komitee, May 14, 1901, file 8221, record group R 1001, Papers of the Deutsche Kolonialgesellschaft; this general point, in different contexts, is also made by Melissa Leach and James Fairhead, *Misreading the African Landscape: Society and Ecology in a Forest-Savanna Mosaic* (Cambridge: Cambridge University Press, 1996); Kojo Sebastian Amanor, *The New Frontier: Farmer Responses to Land Degradation: A West African Study* (Geneva: UNRISD, 1994).

54. John Robinson to Booker T. Washington, May 26, 1901, Booker T. Washington Papers, Manuscripts Division, Library of Congress, Washington, DC; James N. Calloway to Kolonial-Wirtschaftliches Komitee, June 13, 1901, file 8221, record group R 1001, Papers of the Deutsche Kolonialgesellschaft, Bundesarchiv, Berlin; James N. Calloway to Mr. Schmidt, November 11, 1901, file 1008, record group R 150F, Fonds Allemand 3, Papers of the Administration of the German Protector-ate Togo (L'Administration du Protectorat Allemand du Togo), Archives Nation-ales du Togo, Lomé, microfilm copy in Bundesarchiv, Berlin; James N. Calloway to Mr. Schmidt, November 11, 1901, file 1008, record group R 150F, Fonds Alle-mand 3, Papers of the Administration of the German Protectorate Togo; James N. Calloway to Kolonial-Wirtschaftliches Komitee, September 2, 1901, file 8221, record group R 1001, Papers of the Deutsche Kolonialgesellschaft; John Robinson to Booker T. Washington, May 26, 1901, Booker T. Washington Papers; James N. Calloway to Kolonial-Wirtschaftliches Komitee, March 12, 1901, file 8221, record group R 1001, Papers of the Deutsche Kolonialgesellschaft; eventually, one source reports that a full 105 men were involved in moving the wagons to the plantations; see Kolonial-Wirtschaftliches Komitee, *Baumwoll-Expedition*, 24.

55. Kolonial-Wirtschaftliches Komitee, *Baumwoll-Expedition*, 4–5, 26, for the Cal-loway quote see 28–36; F. Wohltmann, "Neujahrsgedanken 1905," *Der Tropen-pflanzer: Zeitschrift für tropische Landwirtschaft* 9 (January 1905): 5; Karl Supf, Kolonial-Wirtschaftliches Komitee, to Kolonial-Abteilung des Auswärtigen Amtes, Berlin, August 15, 1902, file 8221, record group R 1001, Papers of the Deutsche Kolo-nialgesellschaft, Bundesarchiv, Berlin.

56. *Der Tropenpflanzer: Zeitschrift für tropische Landwirtschaft* 7 (January 1903): 9.

57. Isaacman and Roberts, "Cotton, Colonialism," 25; Kolonial-Wirtschaftliches Komitee, *Deutsch-Koloniale Baumwoll-Unternehmungen, Bericht XI* (Frühjahr 1909), 28, file 8224, record group R 1001, Papers of the Deutsche Kolonialgesellschaft, Bundesarchiv, Berlin; Sunseri, "Baumwollfrage," 46, 48; Kolonial-Wirtschaftliches Komitee, "Verhandlungen der Baumwoll-Kommission des Kolonial-Wirtschaftlichen Komitees vom 25. April 1912," 169; peasant resistance against colonial cotton projects in a very different context is also described in Allen Isaacman et al., " 'Cotton Is the Mother of Poverty': Peasant Resistance to Forced Cotton Production in Mozambique, 1938–1961," *International Journal of African Historical Studies* 13, no. 4 (1980): 581–615.

58. Thomas Ellison, *The Cotton Trade of Great Britain* (New York: A. M. Kelley, 1968), 95; "Cotton in British East Africa," *Imperial and Asiatic Quarterly Review*, Third Series, 24 (July–October 1907): 85; Ehrlich, "Marketing," 1; British Cotton Growing Association, *Second Annual Report, for the Year Ending August 31st, 1906* (Manchester: Head Office, 1906), 23.

59. Kolonial-Wirtschaftliches Komitee, "Verhandlungen," 169; Doran H. Ross, ed., *Wrapped in Pride: Ghanaian Kente and African American Identity* (Los Angeles: UCLA Fowler Museum of Cultural History, 1998), 126–49; Agbenyega Adedze, "Cotton in Eweland: Historical Perspectives," in Ross, ed., *Wrapped in Pride*, 132; the numbers are from Maier, "Persistence," 75; see also Sebald, *Togo 1884–1914*, 30; Metzger, *Unsere*, 242; "Der Baumwollbau in Togo, Seine Bisherige Entwicklung, und sein jetziger Stand," undated draft of an article, file 8224, record group R 1001, Papers of the Deutsche Kolonialgesellschaft, Bundesarchiv, Berlin; Freiherr von Danckelman, *Mittheilungen von Forschungsreisenden und Gelehrten aus den Deutschen Schutzgebieten* 3 (1890): 140–41; "Bericht über den Baumwollbau in Togo," Enclosure in Kaiserliches Gouvernment Togo, Gouverneur Zech, to Reichskolonialamt, Berlin, November 23, 1909, 1, file 8223, record group R 1001, Papers of the Deutsche Kolonialgesellschaft; Isaacman and Roberts, "Cotton, Colonialism," 12.

60. John Robinson quoted in Kolonial-Wirtschaftliches Komitee, *Deutsch-Koloniale Baumwoll-Unternehmungen*, 1902, 1903 (Berlin, 1903), 18; *Zeitfragen: Wochenschrift für deutsches Leben*, May 1, 1911, 1.

61. German cotton merchants in particular were active in creating these ginning and pressing operations, helped by the Tuskegee experts, and as early as 1902 the Deutsche Togogesellschaft established itself in Berlin as a private enterprise that was to build gins and cotton buying agencies in Togo. See "Prospekt der Deutschen Togogesellschaft," Berlin, April 1902, private archive, Freiherr von Herman auf Wain, Schloss Wain, Wain, Germany; Karl Supf, *Deutsch-Koloniale Baumwoll-Unternehmungen, Bericht IX* (Berlin: Mittler, 1907), 304. See also G. H. Pape to Bezirksamt Atakpame, April 5, 1909, file 1009, record group R 150F, Fonds Allemand 3 Papers of the Administration of the German Protectorate Togo (L'Administration du Protectorat Allemand du Togo), Archives Nationales du Togo, Lomé, microfilm copy in Bundesarchiv, Berlin. During the 1908–9 season they stipulated the minimum price for ginned cotton, delivered at the coast, to be 30 pfennige per pound. See Verhandlungen des Kolonial-Wirtschaftlichen Komitees und der Baumwoll-Kommission,

November 11, 1908, file 8223, record group R 1001, Papers of the Deutsche Kolo-nialgesellschaft, Bundesarchiv, Berlin; Kolonial-Wirtschaftliches Komitee, *Deutsch-Koloniale Baumwoll-Unternehmungen*, 1902, 1903 (Berlin, 1903), 17; Radcliffe, "Tuskegee-Togo," 103.

62. James N. Calloway to Kolonial-Wirtschaftliches Komitee, June 13, 1901, file 8221, record group R 1001, Papers of the Deutsche Kolonialgesellschaft, Bundes-archiv, Berlin. In 1903 John Robinson reported that transporting cotton from Tove to Lomé would take ten to twelve days; Kolonial-Wirtschaftliches Komitee, *Deutsch-Koloniale*, 21; Karl Supf, Kolonial-Wirtschaftliches Komitee, to Auswärtiges Amt, Kolonial-Abteilung, May 10, 1902, file 8221, record group R 1001, Papers of the Deutsche Kolonialgesellschaft.

63. German cotton interests appealed to the Kolonial-Abteilung of the Auswärtiges Amt that *Steuerträger*, in effect forced laborers, should carry the cotton from Tove to the coast without pay. See Karl Supf, Kolonial-Wirtschaftliches Komitee, to Auswärtiges Amt, Kolonial-Abteilung, Nov. 15, 1901, 8221, record group R 1001, Papers of the Deutsche Kolonialgesellschaft, Bundesarchiv, Berlin. See also note "Station Mangu No. 170/11, May 8, 1911, file 4047, record group R 150F, Fonds Allemand 3, Papers of the Administration of the German Protectorate Togo (L'Administration du Pro-tectorat Allemand du Togo), Archives Nationales du Togo, Lomé, microfilm copy in Bundesarchiv, Berlin; Supf, "Zur Baumwollfrage," 12.

64. Radcliffe, "Tuskegee-Togo," 107; Verhandlungen des Kolonial-Wirtschaftlichen Komitees und der Baumwoll-Komission, November 11, 1908, file 8223, record group R 1001, Papers of the Deutsche Kolonialgesellschaft, Bundesarchiv, Berlin; Metzger, *Unsere Alte Kolonie*, 245, 252. For further statistics on the export of cotton from Togo after World War I see "Togo: La production du Coton," in *Agence Extérieure et Colo-niale*, October 29, 1925. The expansion of cotton production continued throughout the twentieth century, and in 2002–3, Togo produced 80 million kilograms of cot-ton, about nineteen times as much as in 1938 and 160 times as much as in 1913. See Reinhart, "Cotton Market Report 44" (January 23, 2004), accessed January 30, 2004, http://www.reinhart.ch/pdf_files/marketreportch.pdf.

65. Maier, "Persistence," 77. Moreover, large areas of Togo were also sparsely settled, lack-ing surplus labor for cotton production. See G. H. Pape, "Eine Berichtigung zu dem von Prof. Dr. A. Oppel verfassten Aufsatz 'Der Baumwollanbau in den deutschen Kolonien und seine Aussichten,' " file 3092, record group R 150F, Fonds Allemand 3, Papers of the Administration of the German Protectorate Togo (L'Administration du Protectorat Allemand du Togo), Archives Nationales du Togo, Lomé, microfilm copy in Bundesarchiv, Berlin. On intercropping see also Bassett, *Peasant Cotton*, 57; "Bericht über den Baumwollbau in Togo," Enclosure in Kaiserliches Gouvernement Togo, Gouverneur Zech to Reichskolonialamt Berlin, November 23, 1909, 2, file 8223, record group R 1001, Papers of the Deutsche Kolonialgesellschaft, Bundesar-chiv, Berlin; Beckert, "Emancipation"; Etienne, *Die Baumwollzucht*, 39.

66. The Dutch merchant is quoted in Adedze, "Cotton in Eweland," 132; "Der Baum-wollbau in Togo, Seine Bisherige Entwicklung, und sein jetziger Stand," undated draft of an article, 8224, record group R 1001, Papers of the Deutsche Kolonialgesell-schaft, Bundesarchiv, Berlin.

67. Kolonial-Wirtschaftliches Komitee, *Baumwoll-Expedition*, 44; signed Agreement between Graf Zech and Freese (for the Vietor company), March 1, 1904, file 332, record group R 150F, Fonds Allemand 1, Papers of the Administration of the German Protectorate Togo (L'Administration du Protectorat Allemand du Togo), Archives Nationales du Togo, Lomé, microfilm copy in Bundesarchiv, Berlin; Vail and White, "Tawani, Machambero," 241; Roberts, "Coercion," 223, 231, 236; Bassett, *Peasant Cotton*, 66; Isaacman and Roberts, "Cotton, Colonialism," 16.

68. This was also a point made by Morel, *Affairs*, 192; see also A. McPhee, *The Economic Revolution in British West Africa* (London: Cass, 1926), 49; Marion Johnson, "Cotton Imperialism in West Africa," *African Affairs* 73, no. 291 (April 1974): 182, 183.

69. *Deutsch-Koloniale Baumwoll-Unternehmungen, Bericht XI* (Frühjahr 1909), file 3092, record group R 150F, Fonds Allemand 3, Papers of the Administration of the German Protectorate Togo (L'Administration du Protectorat Allemand du Togo), Archives Nationales du Togo, Lomé, microfilm copy in Bundesarchiv, Berlin; James Stephen as quoted in David Brion Davis, *Slavery and Human Progress* (New York: Oxford University Press, 1984), 218.

70. Supf, "Zur Baumwollfrage," 9, 12; Gouverneur of Togo to Herrn Bezirksamts-leiter von Atakpame, December 9 (no year), file 1008, record group R 150F, Fonds Allemand 3, Papers of the Administration of the German Protectorate Togo; "Massnahmen zur Hebung der Baumwollkultur im Bezirk Atakpakme unter Mit-wirkung des Kolonialwirtschaftlichen Komitees," Verwaltung des deutschen Schutz-gebietes Togo, file 1008, record group R 150F, Fonds Allemand 3, Papers of the Administration of the German Protectorate Togo; for the Governor of Togo see Kolonial-Wirtschaftliches Komitee, *Deutsch-Koloniale Baumwoll-Unternehmungen*, 57–59; "Baumwollinspektion für Togo," file 1008, record group R 150F, Fonds Alle-mand 3, Papers of the Administration of the German Protectorate Togo. John Rob-inson had already remarked in 1904 that the "habits [of the people of Togo] cannot be changed in a day"; see "Baumwollanbau im Schutzgebiet Togo, Darlegungen des Pflanzers John W. Robinson vom 26. 4. 1904 betr. die Vorausetzungen, Boden- und Klimaverhältnisse, Methoden und Arbeitsverbesserung, Bewässerung," Fragment, file 89, record group R 150F, Fonds Allemand 1, Papers of the Administration of the German Protectorate Togo.

71. Paul Friebel to Togo Baumwollgesellschaft, Atakpame, April 7, 1911, File 7,2016, 1, Papers of the Togo Baumwollgesellschaft mbH, Staatsarchiv Bremen, Bremen, Ger-many; the experience of the British Cotton Growing Association in Africa in many ways paralleled the German experience; for its history see Robins, "The Black Man's Crop."

72. See "Baumwollanbau im Schutzgebiet Togo, Darlegungen des Pflanzers John W. Robinson vom 26. 4. 1904 betr. die Voraussetzungen, Boden- und Klimaverhältnisse, Methoden und Arbeitsverbesserung, Bewässerung," Fragment, 13 and 49, file 89, record group R 150F, Fonds Allemand 1, Papers of the Administration of the German Protectorate Togo (L'Administration du Protectorat Allemand du Togo), Archives Nationales du Togo, Lomé, microfilm copy in Bundesarchiv, Berlin; Anson Phelps Stokes, *A Brief Biography of Booker Washington* (Hampton, VA: Hampton Institute Press, 1936), 13; John Robinson to Graf Zech, January 12, 1904, file 332, record group

R 150F, Fonds Allemand 1, Papers of the Administration of the German Protectorate Togo.

73. Bassett, *Peasant Cotton*, 55, 59; Julia Seibert, "Arbeit und Gewalt: Die langsame Durchsetzung der Lohnarbeit im kolonialen Kongo, 1885–1960" (PhD dissertation, University of Trier, 2012), 186–206; Isaacman and Roberts, "Cotton, Colonialism," 27; Vail and White, "Tawani, Machambero," 252, 253.

74. For an excellent survey see Isaacman and Roberts, eds., *Cotton, Colonialism*. German cotton experts were still envious of British successes in Africa; see O. Warburg, "Zum Neuen Jahr 1914," *Der Tropenpflanzer: Zeitschrift für tropische Landwirtschaft* 18 (January 1914): 9; Polly Hill, *The Migrant Cocoa-Farmers of Southern Ghana: A Study in Rural Capitalism* (Cambridge: Cambridge University Press, 1963); League of Nations, Economic and Financial Section, International Statistical Yearbook 1926 (Geneva: Publications of League of Nations, 1927), 72; League of Nations, Economic Intelligence Service, *Statistical Year-book of the League of Nations 1939/40* (Geneva: Series of League of Nations Publications, 1940), 122; National Cotton Council of America, accessed April 10, 2013, http://www.cotton.org/econ/cropinfo/cropdata/country-statistics.cfm; Etonam Digo, "Togo Expects to Meet Cotton Production Targets as Harvest Avoids Flooding," Bloomberg, October 29, 2010, accessed April 10, 2013, http://www.bloomberg.com/news/2010-10-29/togo-expects-to-meet-cotton-production-targets-as-harvest-avoids-flooding.html.

75. Isaacman and Roberts, eds., *Cotton, Colonialism*; Bassett, *Peasant Cotton*; Ehrlich, "Marketing," 28–33; on the Association Cotonnière Coloniale see Kolonial-Wirtschaftliches Komitee, *Deutsch-Koloniale Baumwoll-Unternehmungen*, 66–68, 69–71; as to the Sudan, see Booker T. Washington to Gladwin Bouton, May 6, 1915, and Leigh Hart to Booker T. Washington, February 3, 1904, Booker T. Washington Papers, Library of Congress, Washington, DC; Radcliffe, "Tuskegee-Togo," 3, 133, 135; Karl Supf, *Deutsch-Koloniale Baumwoll-Unternehmungen*, 295, 297; German colonial cotton activists often referred to the experiences of the French, British, and Russians, see for example, Kolonial-Wirtschaftliches Komitee, *Deutsch-Koloniale Baumwoll-Unternehmungen*, 66–71; "Anlage zum Bericht des Kaiserlichen Generalkonsulats in Saint Petersburg," December 26, 1913, sent to Reichs-Kolonialamt and the Governor of Togo, 360, record group R 150F, Fonds Allemand 1, Papers of the Administration of the German Protectorate Togo (L'Administration du Protectorat Allemand du Togo), Archives Nationales du Togo, Lomé, microfilm copy in Bundesarchiv, Berlin; copy of a report by R. B. D. Morier to the Secretary of State, The Marquis of Salisbury, October 12, 1889, Compilations Vol. 51, 1890, Compilation No. 476, "Establishment by the Russian Government of a Model Cotton Plantation in the Merva Oasis," Revenue Department, Maharashtra State Archives, Mumbai; Robins, "The Black Man's Crop," 16; Ministère des Affaires étrangères, Direction des Affaires politiques et commerciales, No. 88, Copie M, Verchere de Reffye, Consul de France à Alexandrie à M. Pincarem Alexandrie, August 30, 1912, and Dépêche de Consulat de France, Saint Petersburg, June 15, 1912, in 9 AFFECO, Affairs économquie, Fonds Ministeriels, Archives d'outre-mer, Aix-en-Provence; *The Fourth International Congress of Delegated Representatives of Master Spinners' and Manufacturers' Associations, Held in Musikvereinsgebäude, Vienna, May 27th to 29th, 1907* (Manchester: Taylor,

Garnett, Evans, & Co., 1907), 306; International Cotton Congress, *Official Report of the International Cotton Congress, Held in Egypt, 1927* (Manchester: Taylor Garnett Evans & Co. Ltd., 1927), 179–89.

76. On the Soviet Union's efforts at increasing cotton production, see Obertreis, *Imperial Desert Dreams*; Maya Peterson, "Technologies of Rule: Empire, Water, and the Modernization of Central Asia, 1867–1941" (PhD dissertation, Harvard University, 2011); Christof Dejung, "The Boundaries of Western Power: The Colonial Cotton Economy in India and the Problem of Quality," in Christof Dejung and Niels P. Petersson, eds., *The Foundations of Worldwide Economic Integration: Power, Institutions, and Global Markets, 1850–1930* (Cambridge: Cambridge University Press, 2012), 156; Rudolf Asmis and Dr. Zeller, Taschkent, April 10, 1923, mailing of colonial cotton brochures, Berlin, May 7, 1923; memo, Der heutige Stand der Baumwollkultur in Turkestan und das Problem einer deutschen Mitarbeit an ihrem Wiederaufbau; minutes of the meeting of the Baumwoll-Kommission des Kolonial-Wirtschaftlichen Komitees, June 28, 1923; minutes of the meeting of the Baumwollbau-Kommission, Diskonto Gesellschaft, Berlin, July 12, 1923, all in Kolonial-Wirtschaftliches Komitee, R 8024/25, Bundesarchiv, Berlin; *Ekonomitsceskaja Shisnj*, July 12, 1923, translated by the German embassy in Moscow, in Kolonialwirtschaftliches Komitee, R 8024/25, Bundesarchiv, Berlin; there are also documents in the file testifying to the execution of cotton experts in Central Asia who did not do enough to fight a locus plague.

77. In a very different context, Kären Wigen has told a similar story about the incorporation of particular regions of Japan into the national and global economy; see Kären Wigen, *The Making of a Japanese Periphery, 1750–1920* (Berkeley: University of California Press, 1995).

78. Buehler, "Die Unabhängigkeitsbestrebungen," 91; Bleifuss and Hergenröder, *Die "Otto-Plantage Kilossa,"* 39; Pierre de Smet, *Les origins et l'organisation de la filature de coton en Belgique. Notice publiée à l'occasion du 25ème anniversaire de l'Association Cotonnière de Belgique* (Brüssels, 1926), 1; Obertreis, *Imperial Desert Dreams*, chapter 1, 67; E. R. B. Denniss, "Government of the Soudan Loan Guarantee," *Parliamentary Debates*, Fifth Series, vol. 52, col. 428, April 23, 1913.

79. See chapter 10, note 5.

CHAPTER THIRTEEN: THE RETURN OF THE GLOBAL SOUTH

1. Kenneth L. Gillion, *Ahmedabad: A Study in Indian Urban History* (Berkeley: University of California Press, 1968), 69; Makrand Mehta, *The Ahmedabad Cotton Textile Industry: Genesis and Growth* (Ahmedabad: New Order Book Co., 1982), viii, 33–34, 43, 50, 53; Dwijendra Tripathi, *Historical Roots of Industrial Entrepreneurship in India and Japan: A Comparative Interpretation* (New Delhi: Manohar, 1997), 108; Sujata Patel, *The Making of Industrial Relations: The Ahmedabad Textile Industry, 1918–1939* (Oxford: Oxford University Press, 1987), 21–22.

2. Mehta, *The Ahmedabad Cotton Textile Industry*, 54, 57; *Times of India*, June 12, 1861.

3. Mehta, *The Ahmedabad Cotton Textile Industry*, 6, 8–9, 14, 20.

4. Ibid., 66, 67, 77ff., 80, 85–87, 96–102; Salim Lakha, *Capitalism and Class in Colonial India: The Case of Ahmedabad* (New Delhi: Sterling Publishers, 1988), 64–66; Patel, *The Making of Industrial Relations*, 13, 21, 22, 23, 24; Tripathi, *Historical Roots of Industrial Entrepreneurship in India and Japan*, 107; Irina Spector-Marks, "Mr. Ghandi Visits Lancashire: A Study in Imperial Miscommunication" (Honors Thesis, Macalester College, 2008), 23.

5. Stephan H. Lindner, "Technology and Textiles Globalization," *History and Technology* 18 (2002), 3; Douglas A. Farnie and David J. Jeremy, *The Fibre that Changed the World: The Cotton Industry in International Perspective, 1600–1990s* (Oxford: Oxford University Press, 2004), 23; Lindner, "Technology and Textiles Globalization," 4; John Singleton, *Lancashire on the Scrapheap: The Cotton Industry, 1945–1970* (Oxford: Oxford University Press, 1991), 11; Douglas A. Farnie and Takeshi Abe, "Japan, Lancashire and the Asian Market for Cotton Manufactures, 1890–1990," in Douglas Farnie et al., eds., *Region and Strategy in Britain and Japan, Business in Lancashire and Kansai, 1890–1990* (London: Routledge, 2000), 140, 147.

6. Farnie and Jeremy, *The Fibre That Changed the World*, 23; David L. Carlton and Peter A. Coclanis, "Southern Textiles in Global Context," in Susanna Delfino and Michele Gillespie, eds., *Global Perspectives on Industrial Transformation in the American South* (Columbia: University of Missouri Press, 2005) 153, 155; Gary R. Saxonhouse and Gavin Wright, "New Evidence on the Stubborn English Mule and the Cotton Industry, 1878–1920," *Economic History Review*, New Series, 37, no. 4 (November 1984): 519. It is important to note that Japanese spindles produced significantly more thread than Indian spindles.

7. Arno S. Pearse, *The Cotton Industry of India, Being the Report of the Journey to India* (Manchester: Taylor, Garnett, Evans, 1930), 3.

8. Pearse, *The Cotton Industry of India*, 101; Philip T. Silvia, "The Spindle City: Labor, Politics, and Religion in Fall River, Massachusetts, 1870–1905" (PhD dissertation, Fordham University, 1973), 7; Thomas Russell Smith, "The Cotton Textile Industry of Fall River, Massachusetts: A Study of Industrial Localization" (PhD dissertation, Columbia University, 1943), 21; William F. Hartford, *Where Is Our Responsibility?: Unions and Economic Change in the New England Textile Industry, 1870–1960* (Amherst: University of Massachusetts Press, 1996), 7–8, 54; John T. Cumbler, *Working-Class Community in Industrial America: Work, Leisure, and Struggle in Two Industrial Cities, 1880–1930* (Westport, CT: Greenwood, 1979), 54.

9. Hartford, *Where Is Our Responsibility?* 12, 28; Mary H. Blewett, *Constant Turmoil: The Politics of Industrial Life in Nineteenth-Century New England* (Amherst: University of Massachusetts Press, 2000), 183; Massachusetts Bureau of Statistics of Labor, *Thirteenth Annual Report* (Boston: Rand, Avery & Co., 1882), 195.

10. Cumbler, *Working-Class Community in Industrial America*, 105, 118; Dietrich Ebeling et al., "The German Wool and Cotton Industry from the Sixteenth to the Twentieth Century," in Lex Heerma van Voss, Els Hiemstra-Kuperus, and Elise van Nederveen Meerkerk, eds., *The Ashgate Companion to the History of Textile Workers, 1650–2000* (Burlington, VT: Ashgate, 2010), 227. The Massachusetts Bureau of Statistics of Labor estimated that a family needed a minimum of $400 a year for rent, fuel, food, and clothing. See Massachusetts Bureau of Statistics of

Labor, *Sixth Annual Report* (Boston: Wright and Potter, 1875), 118, 221–354, esp. 291, 372, 373, 441.

11. Hartford, *Where Is Our Responsibility?* 7–17, 29; Isaac Cohen, "American Management and British Labor: Lancashire Immigrant Spinners in Industrial New England," *Comparative Studies in Society and History* 27, no. 4 (October 1, 1985): 611, 623–24; Blewett, *Constant Turmoil*, 112; David Montgomery, *The Fall of the House of Labor: The Workplace, the State, and American Labor Activism, 1865–1925* (New York: Cambridge University Press, 1989), 163.

12. R. B. Forrester, *The Cotton Industry in France* (Manchester: Manchester University Press, 1921), 100; Claude Fohlen, *L'industrie textile au temps du Second Empire* (Paris: Librairie Plon, 1956), 412; David Allen Harvey, *Constructing Class and Nationality in Alsace, 1830–1945* (DeKalb: Northern Illinois University Press, 2001), 3, 64, 65.

13. Ebeling et al.,"The German Wool and Cotton Industry," 228; R. M. R. Dehn, *The German Cotton Industry* (Manchester: Manchester University Press, 1913), 71–72.

14. M.V. Konotopov et al., *Istoriia otechestvennoi tekstil'noi promyshlennosti* (Moscow: Legprombytizdat, 1992), 179; Dave Pretty, "The Cotton Textile Industry in Russia and the Soviet Union," in Van Voss et al., eds., *The Ashgate Companion to the History of Textile Workers*, 435–37, 439; Dave Pretty, "The Cotton Textile Industry in Russia and the Soviet Union" (presentation, Textile Conference, International Institute of Social History, Amsterdam, November 2004), 17, 33.

15. Andreas Balthasar, Erich Gruner, and Hans Hirter, "Gewerkschaften und Arbeitgeber auf dem Arbeitsmarkt: Streiks, Kampf ums Recht und Verhältnis zu anderen Interessengruppen," in Erich Gruner, ed., *Arbeiterschaft und Wirtschaft in der Schweiz 1880–1914: Soziale Lage, Organisation und Kämpfe von Arbeitern und Unternehmern, politische Organisation und Sozialpolitik*, vol. 2, part 1 (Zürich: Chronos, 1988), 456ff., 464; Angel Smith et al., "Spain," in Van Voss et al., eds., *The Ashgate Companion to the History of Textile Workers*, 465–67; Elise van Nederveen Meerkerk, Lex Heerman van Voss, and Els Hiemstra-Kuperus, "The Netherlands," in Van Voss et al., eds., *The Ashgate Companion to the History of Textile Workers*, 388.

16. T. J. Hatton, G. R. Boyer, and R. E. Bailey, "The Union Wage Effect in Late Nineteenth Century Britain," *Economica* 61, no. 244 (November 1994): 436, 449; Farnie and Abe, "Japan, Lancashire and the Asian Market for Cotton Manufactures," 134, 136; William Lazonick, *Competitive Advantage on the Shop Floor* (Cambridge, MA: Harvard University Press, 1990), 115, 136.

17. Charles Tilly, "Social Change in Modern Europe: The Big Picture," in Lenard R. Berlanstein, ed., *The Industrial Revolution and Work in Nineteenth-Century Europe* (New York: Routledge, 1992), 54–55; Elise van Nederveen Meerkerk, Lex Heerma van Voss, and Els Hiemstra-Kuperus, "Covering the World: Some Conclusions to the Project," in Van Voss et al., eds., *The Ashgate Companion to the History of Textile Workers*, 773–92.

18. Dehn, *The German Cotton Industry*, 94; Kathleen Canning, *Languages of Labor and Gender: Female Factory Work in Germany, 1850–1914* (Ann Arbor: University of Michigan Press, 2002), 261; Günter Kirchhain, "Das Wachstum der deutschen Baumwollindustrie im 19. Jahrhundert: Eine historische Modellstudie zur empirischen Wachstumsforschung" (PhD dissertation, University of Münster, 1973), 86; Patricia

Penn Hilden, "Class and Gender: Conflicting Components of Women's Behaviour in the Textile Mills of Lille, Roubaix and Tourcoing, 1880–1914," *Historical Journal* 27, no. 2 (June 1984): 378; Smith et al., "Spain," 468.

19. Dehn, *The German Cotton Industry*, 82; Kirchhain, "Das Wachstum der deutschen Baumwollindustrie," 159–60. The annual wages rose in real terms (expressed in 1913 marks) from 563.58 marks per year to 860 marks per year. See implicit deflator of net national product in Table A.5, Cost of Living Indices in Germany, 1850–1985 (1913 = 100), Appendix, in P. Scholliers and Z. Zamagni, eds., *Labour's Reward: Real Wages and Economic Change in 19th- and 20th-Century Europe* (Brookfield, VT: Edward Elgar Publishing, 1995), 226; if we assume twelve days of labor in a two-week span, daily wages in Alsace in 1870 amounted to between 2.51–3.00 francs per day in 1910 francs, and 5.42–6.25 francs per day for 1910. To calculate real wages, see Table H1, Wholesale Price Indices, in B. R. Mitchell, *International Historical Statistics: Europe, 1750–2005* (New York: Palgrave Macmillan, 2007), 955–56. Smith et al., "Spain," 469; Smith, "The Cotton Textile Industry of Fall River," 88. In the 1890s, doffers made (in 2011 dollars) $35.92 per day, and in 1920 $53.72 per day. Loom-fixers went up from $42.39 per day in 1890 to $81.92 per day in 1920. See Table III. Classified Rates of Wages per Hour in Each State, by Years, 1907 to 1912, in Fred Cleveland Croxton, *Wages and Hours of Labor in the Cotton, Woolen, and Silk Industries* (Washington, DC: Government Printing Office, 1913).

20. Harvey, *Constructing Class and Nationality in Alsace*, 82; Dehn, *The German Cotton Industry*, 94; Georg Meerwein, "Die Entwicklung der Chemnitzer bezw. sächsischen Baumwollspinnerei von 1789–1879" (PhD dissertation, University of Heidelberg, 1914), 94; Beth English, "Beginnings of the Global Economy: Capital Mobility and the 1890s U.S. Textile Industry," in Delfino and Gillespie, eds., *Global Perspectives on Industrial Transformation in the American South*, 177; Walter Bodmer, *Die Entwicklung der schweizerischen Textilwirtschaft im Rahmen der übrigen Industrien und Wirtschafts-zweige* (Zürich: Verlag Berichthaus, 1960), 397.

21. English, "Beginnings of the Global Economy," 176; W. F. Bruck, *Die Geschichte des Kriegsausschusses der deutschen Baumwoll-Industrie* (Berlin: Kriegsausschuss der Deutschen Baumwoll-Industrie, 1920), 11; John Steven Toms, "Financial Constraints on Economic Growth: Profits, Capital Accumulation and the Development of the Lancashire Cotton-Spinning Industry, 1885–1914," *Accounting Business and Financial History* 4, no. 3 (1994): 367; J. H. Bamberg, "The Rationalization of the British Cotton Industry in the Interwar Years," *Textile History* 19, no. 1 (1988): 85; M. W. Kirby, "The Lancashire Cotton Industry in the Inter-War Years: A Study in Organizational Change" *Business History* 16, no. 2 (1974): 151.

22. Kirchhain, "Das Wachstum der deutschen Baumwollindustrie," 95, 166; Gregory Clark, "Why Isn't the Whole World Developed? Lessons from the Cotton Mills," *Journal of Economic History* 47, no. 1 (March 1987): 145, 148; Hermann Kellenbenz, *Deutsche Wirtschaftsgeschichte*, vol. 2 (München: Beck, 1981), 406; Meerkerk et al., "Covering the World," 785.

23. Gisela Müller, "Die Entstehung und Entwicklung der Wiesentäler Textilindustrie bis zum Jahre 1945" (PhD dissertation, University of Basel, 1965), 49; *Deutsche Volks-*

wirtschaftlichen Correspondenz 42 (Ulm: Gebrüder Rübling, 1879), 8; Brian A'Hearn, "Institutions, Externalities, and Economic Growth in Southern Italy: Evidence from the Cotton Textile Industry, 1861–1914," *Economic History Review* 51, no. 4 (1998): 742; Jörg Fisch, *Europa zwischen Wachstum und Gleichheit, 1850–1914* (Stuttgart: Ulmer, 2002), 65; Tom Kemp, *Economic Forces in French History* (London: Dennis Dobson, 1971), 184; Auguste Lalance, *La crise de l'industrie cotonnière* (Mulhouse: Veuve Bader & Cie., 1879), 6.

24. Department of Commerce and Labor, Bureau of Manufactures, and W. A. Graham Clark, *Cotton Goods in Latin America: Part 1, Cuba, Mexico, and Central America* (Washington, DC: Government Printing Office, 1909), 6–7, 14; Jordi Nadal, "The Failure of the Industrial Revolution in Spain, 1830–1914," in Carlo M. Cipolla, ed., *The Fontana Economic History of Europe*, vol. 4, part 2, *The Emergence of Industrial Societies* (Great Britain: Fontana, 1973), 612–13; M. V. Konotopov et al., *Istoriia otechestvennoi tekstil'noi promyshlennosti* (Moscow: Legprombytizdat, 1992), 268–69; For Atkinson see Edward Atkinson, *Cotton: Articles from the New York Herald* (Boston: Albert J. Wright, 1877), 31.

25. As reflected, for example, in the Proceedings of the Manchester Chamber of Commerce; in M8/2/1/16, Proceedings of the Manchester Chamber of Commerce, 1919–1925, Manchester Library and Local Studies, Manchester.

26. *Times*, September 6, 1927, 13; see also James Watt Jr. to Richard Bond, Esq., July 7, 1934, in DDX1115/6/26, Liverpool Records Office, Liverpool; as quoted in Spector-Marks, "Mr. Ghandi Visits Lancashire," 44.

27. "Textile Shutdown Visioned by Curley: New England Industry Will Die in Six Months Unless Washington Helps, He Says," *New York Times*, April 15, 1935. The importance of wage costs to the geographic location of textile production is also one of the (three) core findings of a multiyear research project at the Institute for Social History in Amsterdam. See Meerkerk et al., "Covering the World," 774.

28. For this conflict between Europe and the United States see Sven Beckert, "Space Matters: Eurafrica, the American Empire and the Territorialization of Industrial Capitalism, 1870–1940" (article in progress).

29. Carlton and Coclanis, "Southern Textiles in Global Context," 160, 167ff.; Alice Carol Galenson, *The Migration of the Cotton Textile Industry from New England to the South, 1880–1930* (New York: Garland, 1985), 2; Timothy J. Minchin, *Hiring the Black Worker: The Racial Integration of the Southern Textile Industry, 1960–1980* (Chapel Hill: University of North Carolina Press, 1999), 9; Robert M. Brown, "Cotton Manufacturing: North and South," *Economic Geography* 4, no. 1 (January 1, 1928): 74–87.

30. Mildred Gwin Andrews, *The Men and the Mills: A History of the Southern Textile Industry* (Macon, GA: Mercer University Press, 1987), 1; Galenson, *The Migration of the Cotton Textile Industry*, 189–90; Carlton and Coclanis, "Southern Textiles in Global Context," 155, 156, 158; for the "labor agitation" quote see *Commercial Bulletin*, September 28, 1894, as quoted in Beth English, *A Common Thread: Labor, Politics, and Capital Mobility in the Textile Industry* (Athens: University of Georgia Press, 2006), 39; *Lynchburg News*, January 18, 1895, as cited in English, "Beginnings of the Global Economy," 176; Hartford, *Where Is Our Responsibility?* 54.

31. Elijah Helm, "An International of the Cotton Industry," *Quarterly Journal of Economics* 17, no. 3 (May 1903): 428; Galenson, *The Migration of the Cotton Textile Industry*, 186; Melvin Thomas Copeland, *The Cotton Manufacturing Industry of the United States* (New York: A. M. Kelley, 1966), 40, 46. See also Steven Hahn, *The Roots of Southern Populism* (New York: Oxford University Press, 1983); Gavin Wright, "The Economic Revolution in the American South," *Journal of Economic Perspectives* 1, no. 1 (Summer 1987): 169. The story of how the transformation of southern countryside is related to the emergence of wage workers in the American South is told by Barbara Fields, "The Nineteenth-Century American South: History and Theory," *Plantation Society in the Americas* 2, no. 1 (April 1983): 7–27; Steven Hahn, "Class and State in Postemancipation Societies: Southern Planters in Comparative Perspective," *American Historical Review* 95, no. 1 (1990): 75–88; *Southern and Western Textile Excelsior*, December 11, 1897, as cited in English, "Beginnings of the Global Economy," 188; English, *A Common Thread*, 116.

32. Galenson, *The Migration of the Cotton Textile Industry*, 141; Copeland, *The Cotton Manufacturing Industry*, 42; Katherine Rye Jewell, "Region and Sub-Region: Mapping Southern Economic Identity" (unpublished paper, 36th Annual Meeting of the Social Science History Association, Boston, 2011).

33. Geoffrey Jones and Judith Vale, "Merchants as Business Groups: British Trading Companies in Asia before 1945," *Business History Review* 72, no. 3 (1998): 372; on Portugal see Board Minutes, vol. 1, 1888–1905, Boa Vista Spinning & Weaving Company, Guildhall Library, London. On the Ottoman Empire see Necla Geyikdagi, *Foreign Investment in the Ottoman Empire: International Trade and Relations, 1854–1914* (New York: I. B. Tauris, 2011), 131; E. R. J. Owen, "Lord Cromer and the Development of Egyptian Industry, 1883–1907," *Middle Eastern Studies* 2, no. 4 (July 1966): 283, 289; Arno S. Pearse, *Brazilian Cotton* (Manchester: Printed by Taylor, Garnett, Evans & Co., 1921), 29; Speech at Konferenz der mitteleuropäischen Wirtschaftsvereine in Dresden, am 17. und 18. Januar 1916, Protokolle der Verhandlungen, Auswärtiges Amt, 1916–1918, Akten betreffend den mitteleurpäischen Wirtschaftsverein, Auswärtiges Amt, R 901, 2502, Bundesarchiv, Berlin; Michael Owen Gately, "Development of the Russian Cotton Textile Industry in the Pre-revolutionary Years, 1861–1913" (PhD dissertation, University of Kansas, 1968), 156; Bianka Pietrow-Ennker, "Wirtschaftsbürger und Bürgerlichkeit im Königreich Polen: Das Beispiel von Lodz, dem Manchester des Ostens," *Geschichte und Gesellschaft* 31 (2005): 175, 177, 178.

34. The importance of institutions to economic development, and thus politics, as well as the damaging effects of colonialism, are also emphasized by Daron Acemoglu, Simon Johnson, and James A. Robinson, "Reversal of Fortune: Geography and Institutions in the Making of the Modern World Income Distribution," *Quarterly Journal of Economics* 117, no. 4 (November 2002): 1231–94. However, the kinds of institutions that I emphasize here are different.

35. Samuel C. Chu, *Reformer in Modern China: Chang Chien, 1853–1926* (New York: Columbia University Press, 1965), 17, 45–46; Albert Feuerwerker, *China's Early Industrialization: Sheng Hsuan-Huai (1844–1916) and Mandarin Enterprise* (Cambridge, MA: Harvard University Press, 1958), 15; on Zhang see also Elizabeth Köll, *From*

Cotton Mill to Business Empire: The Emergence of Regional Enterprises in Modern China (Cambridge, MA: Harvard University Press, 2003), 56–62.

36. Yen-P'ing Hao and Erh-min Wang, "Changing Chinese Views of Western Relations, 1840–95," in John K. Fairbank and Kwang-Ching Liu, *The Cambridge History of China*, vol. 11, *Late Ch'ing, 1800–1911*, part 2 (Cambridge: Cambridge University Press, 1980), 142–201; Feuerwerker, *China's Early Industrialization*, 36–37; Associação Industrial, *Representação dirigida ao exmo. Snr. Ministro da Fazenda* (Rio de Janeiro, 1881), 5, 11, as quoted in Stanley J. Stein, *The Brazilian Cotton Manufacture: Textile Enterprise in an Underdeveloped Area, 1850–1950* (Cambridge, MA: Harvard University Press, 1957), 82; Manifesto da Associação Industrial, *O Industrial (Orgão da Associação Industrial)*, May 21, 1881, as quoted in Stein, *The Brazilian Cotton Manufacture*, 82; Stein, *The Brazilian Cotton Manufacture*, 83–84.

37. Byron Marshall, *Capitalism and Nationalism in Pre-war Japan* (Palo Alto: Stanford University Press, 1967), 15–16.

38. Carter J. Eckert, *Offspring of Empire: The Koch'ang Kins and the Colonial Origins of Korean Capitalism, 1876–1945* (Seattle: University of Washington Press, 1991), 30, 40; Pearse, *The Cotton Industry of India*, 3.

39. Pearse, *Brazilian Cotton*, 27–28; Stein, *The Brazilian Cotton Manufacture*, 114.

40. Stein, *The Brazilian Cotton Manufacture*, 66–67, 77, 82, 84–85, 98 100–1; Pearse, *Brazilian Cotton*, 40; the Englishman is quoted in Stein, *The Brazilian Cotton Manufacture*, 101.

41. Stein, *The Brazilian Cotton Manufacture*, 53, 54, 57, 62; Pearse, *Brazilian Cotton*, 32; Companhia Brazil Industrial, *The Industry of Brazil*, 17.

42. Stein, *The Brazilian Cotton Manufacture*, 99; Rafael Dobado Gonzalez, Aurora Gomez Galvarriato, and Jeffrey G. Williamson, "Globalization, De-industrialization and Mexican Exceptionalism, 1750–1879," National Bureau of Economic Research Working Paper No. 12316, June 2006, 40; Stephen Haber, Armando Razo, and Noel Maurer, *The Politics of Property Rights: Political Instability, Credible Commitments, and Economic Growth in Mexico, 1876–1929* (New York: Cambridge University Press, 2003), 128; Clark et al., *Cotton Goods in Latin America*, 20, 38; Wolfgang Müller, "Die Textilindustrie des Raumes Puebla (Mexiko) im 19. Jahrhundert" (PhD dissertation, University of Bonn, 1977), 63; Stephen H. Haber, "Assessing the Obstacles to Industrialisation: The Mexican Economy, 1830–1940," *Journal of Latin American Studies* 24, no. 1 (February 1992), 18–21; Stephen Haber, *Crony Capitalism and Economic Growth in Latin America: Theory and Evidence* (Palo Alto, CA: Hoover Institution Press, 2002), 66, Table 2.3; Mirta Zaida Lobato, "A Global History of Textile Production, 1650–2000 (Argentina), Textile Conference IISH, November 11–13, 2004; Lockwood, Greene & Co. to Carlos Tornquist, Boston, August 13, 1924, in Industrias 144–8271, Biblioteca Tornquist del Banco Central de la República Argentina, Buenos Aires; Producción, elaboración y consumo del algodón en la República Argentina, 1924, in Industrias 144–8271, Biblioteca Tornquist del Banco Central de la República Argentina, Buenos Aires; Carlos D. Girola, *El Algodonero: Su cultivo en las varias partes del mundo, con referencias especiales a la República Argentinia* (Buenos Aires: Compania Sud-Americana, 1910).

43. A. J. Robertson, "Lancashire and the Rise of Japan, 1910–1937," in S. D. Chapman, ed., *The Textile Industries*, vol. 2 (London: I. B. Tauris, 1997), 490.

44. W. Miles Fletcher III, "The Japan Spinners Association: Creating Industrial Policy in Mejii Japan," *Journal of Japanese Studies* 22, no. 1 (1996): 67; E. Patricia Tsurumi, *Factory Girls: Women in the Thread Mills of Meiji Japan* (Princeton, NJ: Princeton University Press, 1990), 35; Thomas C., Smith, *Political Change and Industrial Development in Japan: Government Enterprise, 1868–1880* (Stanford, CA: Stanford University Press, 1955), 27, 58.

45. On imports see Motoshige Itoh and Masayuki Tanimoto, "Rural Entrepreneurs in the Cotton Weaving Industry in Japan," (unpublished paper, in author's possession, May 1995), 6; Ebara Soroku, as cited in Fletcher III, "The Japan Spinners Association," *Journal of Japanese Studies*, 67.

46. Fletcher III, "The Japan Spinners Association," 68; Yukio Okamoto, *Meijiki bōseki rōdō kankeishi: Nihonteki koyō, rōshi kankei keisei e no sekkin* (Fukuoka: Kyōshū Daigaku Shuppankai, 1993), 157–58, 213–14; Tsurumi, *Factory Girls*, 42.

47. Takeshi Abe, "The Development of Japanese Cotton Weaving Industry in Edo Period" (unpublished and undated paper, in author's possession), 1; Masayuki Tanimoto, "The Role of Tradition in Japan's Industrialization," in Masayuki Tanimoto, ed., *The Role of Tradition in Japan's Industrialization: Another Path to Industrialization*, vol. 2 (Oxford: Oxford University Press, 2006), 9.

48. Naosuke Takamura, *Nihon bōsekigyōshi josetsu*, vol. 1 (Tokyo: Hanawa Shobō, 1971), 63; Naosuke Takamura, *Nihon bōsekigyōshi josetsu*, vol. 2 (Tokyo: Hanawa Shobō, 1971), 119; Tanimoto, "The Role of Tradition in Japan's Industrialization," 4, 12; Farnie and Abe, "Japan, Lancashire and the Asian Market for Cotton Manufactures," 119.

49. Fletcher III, "The Japan Spinners Association," *Journal of Japanese Studies*, 49–75; Fletcher III, "The Japan Spinners Association," in *The Textile Industry*, 66; Farnie and Abe, "Japan, Lancashire and the Asian Market for Cotton Manufactures," 118, 126.

50. Farnie and Abe, "Japan, Lancashire and the Asian Market for Cotton Manufactures," 121, 128; Takeshi Abe, "The Development of the Producing-Center Cotton Textile Industry in Japan between the Two World Wars," *Japanese Yearbook on Business History* 9 (1992): 17, 19; see also Hikotaro Nishi, *Die Baumwollspinnerei in Japan* (Tübingen: Laupp'schen Buchhandlung, 1911), 71, 88.

51. Takamura, *Nihon bōsekigyōshi josetsu*, vol. 1, 239. On shipping see William Wray, *Mitsubishi and the N.Y.K., 1870–1914: Business Strategy in the Japanese Shipping Industry* (Cambridge, MA: Council on East Asian Studies, Harvard University, 1984).

52. For a general statistical overview see Nishi, *Die Baumwollspinnerei in Japan*, 78, 84; Farnie and Abe, "Japan, Lancashire and the Asian Market for Cotton Manufactures," 136–37; Takeshi Abe, "The Chinese Market for Japanese Cotton Textile Goods," in Kaoru Sugihara, ed., *Japan, China, and the Growth of the Asian International Economy, 1850–1949*, vol. 1 (Oxford: Oxford University Press 2005), 74, 77.

53. Natsuko Kitani, "Cotton, Tariffs and Empire: The Indo-British Trade Relationship and the Significance of Japan in the First Half of the 1930s" (PhD dissertation, Osaka University of Foreign Studies, 2004), iii–v, 5, 49, 65; Department of Overseas Trade, *Conditions and Prospects of United Kingdom Trade in India, 1937–38* (London: His Majesty's Stationery Office, 1939), 170. See also Toyo Menka Kaisha, *The Indian Cotton Facts 1930* (Bombay: Toyo Menka Kaisha Ltd., 1930), 98.

54. See the book collection of the Japanese Cotton Spinners Association, which con-

tains numerous books on labor questions in the United Kingdom, United States, Germany, India, and elsewhere; Japanese Cotton Spinners Association Library, University of Osaka. On labor more generally see E. Tsurumi, *Factory Girls*; on the link between the countryside and urban wage labor see Johannes Hirschmeier, *The Origins of Entrepreneurship in Meiji Japan* (Cambridge, MA: Harvard University Press, 1964), 80; Toshiaki Chokki, "Labor Management in the Cotton Spinning Industry," in Smitka ed., *The Textile Industry and the Rise of the Japanese Economy*, 7; Janet Hunter, *Women and the Labour Market in Japan's Industrialising Economy: The Textile Industry Before the Pacific War* (London: Routledge, 2003), 69–70, 123–24; Farnie and Abe, "Japan, Lancashire and the Asian Market for Cotton Manufactures," 120; Janet Hunter and Helen Macnaughtan, "Japan," in Van Voss et al., eds., *The Ashgate Companion to the History of Textile Workers*, 317; Gary Saxonhouse and Yukihiko Kiyokawa, "Supply and Demand for Quality Workers in Cotton Spinning in Japan and India," in Smitka, ed., *The Textile Industry and the Rise of the Japanese Economy*, 185.

55. Hunter, *Women and the Labour Market*, 4; Jun Sasaki, "Factory Girls in an Agrarian Setting circa 1910," in Tanimoto, ed., *The Role of Tradition in Japan's Industrialization*, 130; Tsurumi, *Factory Girls*, 10–19; Nishi, *Die Baumwollspinnerei in Japan*, 141.

56. Hunter and Macnaughtan, "Japan," 320–21. See also Gary Saxonhouse and Gavin Wright, "Two Forms of Cheap Labor in Textile History," in Gary Saxonhouse and Gavin Wright, eds., *Techniques, Spirit and Form in the Making of the Modern Economies: Essays in Honor of William N. Parker* (Greenwich, CT: JAI Press 1984), 3–31; Nishi, *Die Baumwollspinnerei in Japan*, 143, 155; Farnie and Abe, "Japan, Lancashire and the Asian Market for Cotton Manufactures," 135.

57. Farnie and Abe, "Japan, Lancashire and the Asian Market for Cotton Manufactures," 125; Takamura, *Nihon bōsekigyōshi josetsu*, vol. 1, 308; for the extent (and limits) of Japanese spinners' collective action see W. Miles Fletcher III, "Economic Power and Political Influence: The Japan Spinners Association, 1900–1930," *Asia Pacific Business Review* 7, no. 2 (Winter 2000): 39–62, especially 47.

58. Saxonhouse and Kiyokawa, "Supply and Demand for Quality Workers," 186; Chokki, "Labor Management in the Cotton Spinning Industry," 15; Nishi, *Die Baumwollspinnerei in Japan*, 147.

59. The table on page 408 is based on information from Nishi, *Die Baumwollspinnerei in Japan*, 55, 84; Department of Finance, *1912: Annual Return of the Foreign Trade of the Empire of Japan* (Tokyo: Insetsu Kyoku, n.d.), 554; for 1913–15, Department of Finance, *1915: Annual Return of the Foreign Trade of the Empire of Japan*, part 1 (Tokyo: Insetsu Kyoku, n.d.), 448; Department of Finance, *1917: Annual Return of the Foreign Trade of the Empire of Japan*, part 1 (Tokyo: Insetsu Kyoku, n.d.), 449. Department of Finance, *1895: Annual Return of the Foreign Trade of the Empire of Japan* (Tokyo: Insetsu Kyoku, n.d.), 296; for 1902, Department of Finance, *December 1902: Monthly Return of the Foreign Trade of the Empire of Japan* (Tokyo: Insetsu Kyoku, n.d.), 65; Tōyō Keizai Shinpōsha, ed., *Foreign Trade of Japan: A Statistical Survey* (Tokyo: 1935; 1975), 229–30, 49.

60. On the expansion of that industry see also the survey in Sung Jae Koh, *Stages of Industrial Development in Asia: A Comparative History of the Cotton Industry in*

Japan, India, China, and Korea (Philadelphia: University of Pennsylvania Press, 1966); Takamura, *Nihon bōsekigyōshi josetsu*, vol. 2, 121; Nishi, *Die Baumwollspinnerei in Japan*, 1; Takeshi Abé and Osamu Saitu, "From Putting-Out to the Factory: A Cotton-Weaving District in Late Meiji Japan," *Textile History* 19, no. 2 (1988): 143–58; Jun Sasaki, "Factory Girls in an Agrarian Setting circa 1910," in Tanimoto, ed., *The Role of Tradition in Japan's Industrialization*, 121; Takeshi Abe, "Organizational Changes in the Japanese Cotton Industry During the Inter-war Period," in Douglas A. Farnie and David J. Jeremy, eds., *The Fibre That Changed the World: The Cotton Industry in International Perspective, 1600–1990s* (Oxford: Oxford University Press, 2004), 462; Farnie and Abe, "Japan, Lancashire and the Asian Market for Cotton Manufactures," 146; Johzen Takeuchi, "The Role of 'Early Factories' in Japanese Industrialization," in Tanimoto, ed., *The Role of Tradition in Japan's Industrialization*, 76.

61. François Charles Roux, *Le coton en Égypte* (Paris: Librairie Armand Colin, 1908), 296, 297; Robert L. Tignor, *Egyptian Textiles and British Capital, 1930–1956* (Cairo: American University in Cairo Press, 1989), 9, 10; Owen, "Lord Cromer and the Development of Egyptian Industry," 285, 288, 291, 292; Bent Hansen and Karim Nashashibi, *Foreign Trade Regimes and Economic Development: Egypt* (New York: National Bureau of Economic Research, 1975), 4.

62. Tignor, *Egyptian Textiles and British Capital*, 12–14; Joel Beinin, "Egyptian Textile Workers: From Craft Artisans Facing European Competition to Proletarians Contending with the State," in Van Voss et al., eds., *The Ashgate Companion to the History of Textile Workers*, 185; Hansen and Nashashibi, *Foreign Trade Regimes and Economic Development*, 3–4; for the quote see Robert L. Tignor, "Economic Planning, and Development Projects in Interwar Egypt," *International Journal of African Historical Studies* 10, no. 2 (1977): 187, 189.

63. *Statistical Tables Relating to Indian Cotton: Indian Spinning and Weaving Mills* (Bombay: Times of India Steam Press, 1889), 95; Misra Bhubanes, *The Cotton Mill Industry of Eastern India in the Late Nineteenth Century: Constraints on Foreign Investment and Expansion* (Calcutta: Indian Institute of Management, 1985), 5; R. E. Enthoven, *The Cotton Fabrics of the Bombay Presidency* (Bombay: n.p., approx. 1897), 4; Pearse, *The Cotton Industry of India*, 22. On the growth of the Indian cotton industry see also Department of Commercial Intelligence and Statistics, *Monthly Statistics of Cotton Spinning and Weaving in India Mills* (Calcutta: n.p., 1929); Atma'ra'm Trimbuck to T. D. Mackenzie, Bombay, June 16, 1891, Revenue Department, 1891, No 160, Maharashtra State Archives, Mumbai.

64. Enthoven, *The Cotton Fabrics of the Bombay Presidency*, 6; *Statistical Tables Relating to Indian Cotton*, 116; *Report of the Bombay Millowners' Association for the Year 1897* (Bombay: Times of India Steam Press, 1898), 3; Amiya Kumar Bagchi, *Private Investment in India, 1900–1939* (Cambridge: Cambridge University Press, 1972), 9; Helm, "An International Survey of the Cotton Industry," 432.

65. "Statement Exhibiting the Moral and Material Progress and Condition of India, 1895–96," 172, in 1895, SW 241, Oriental and India Office Collections, British Library, London. A slightly higher number is cited in *Imperial and Asiatic Quarterly Review and Oriental and Colonial Record*, Third Series, 58 (July–October 1904):

49. On the general points see Tirthankar Roy, "The Long Globalization and Textile Producers in India," in Van Voss et al., eds., *The Ashgate Companion to the History of Textile Workers*, 266–67. Toyo Menka Kaisha, *The Indian Cotton Facts 1930* (Bombay: Toyo Menka Kaisha Ltd., 1930), 162, Appendix A, Progress of the Cotton Mill Industry; Enthoven, *The Cotton Fabrics of the Bombay Presidency*, 7; Eckehard Kulke, *The Parsees in India: A Minority as Agent of Social Change* (Munich: Weltforum Verlag, 1974), 120–25.

66. Morris D. Morris, *The Emergence of an Industrial Labor Force in India: A Study of the Bombay Cotton Mills, 1854–1947* (Berkeley: University of California Press, 1965), 101, 103, 114; Manmohandas Ramji, Chairman of the Bombay Millowners' Association, at Its Annual General Meeting held on April 28, 1910, in *Report of the Bombay Millowners' Association for the Year 1909* (Bombay: Times of India Steam Press, 1910), v; Letter from the Officiating Secretary of the Government of India, Home, Revenue and Agricultural Department (Judicial), no 12–711, dated May 2, 1881, in Revenue Department, 1881, No. 776, Acts and Regulations, Factory Act of 1881, in Maharashtra State Archives, Mumbai; Shashi Bushan Upadhyay, *Dissension and Unity: The Origins of Workers' Solidarity in the Cotton Mills of Bombay, 1875–1918* (Surat: Center for Social Studies, July 1990), 1; Dietmar Rothermund, *An Economic History of India: From Pre-colonial Times to 1991* (London: Routledge, 1993), 51; M. P. Gandhi, *The Indian Cotton Textile Industry: Its Past, Present and Future* (Calcutta: Mitra, 1930), 67; *Report of the Bombay Millowners' Association for the Year 1906* (Bombay: Times of India Steam Press, 1907), ii; "Memorandum on the Cotton Import and Excise Duties," 5–6, in L/E/9/153, Oriental and India Office Collections, British Library, London.

67. Rothermund, *An Economic History of India*, 37.

68. Tripathi, *Historical Roots of Industrial Entrepreneurship in India and Japan*, 14, 139.

69. Albert Feuerwerker, "Handicraft and Manufactured Cotton Textiles in China, 1871–1910," *Journal of Economic History* 30, no. 2 (June 1970): 338.

70. Ramon H. Myers, "Cotton Textile Handicraft and the Development of the Cotton Textile Industry in Modern China," *Economic History Review*, New Series, 18, no. 3 (1965): 615; Katy Le Mons Walker, "Economic Growth, Peasant Marginalization, and the Sexual Division of Labor in Early Twentieth-Century China: Women's Work in Nantong County," *Modern China* 19, no. 3 (July 1993): 360; R. S. Gundry, ed., *A Retrospect of Political and Commercial Affairs in China & Japan, During the Five Years 1873 to 1877* (Shanghai: Kelly & Walsh, 1878), Commercial, 1877, 98; Feuerwerker, "Handicraft and Manufactured Cotton Textiles in China," 342; H. D. Fong, "Cotton Industry and Trade in China," *Chinese Social and Political Science Review* 16 (October 1932): 400, 402; United States Department of Commerce and Ralph M. Odell, *Cotton Goods in China* (Washington, DC: Government Printing Office, 1916), 33, 43; M. V. Brandt, *Stand und Aufgabe der deutschen Industrie in Ostasien* (Hildesheim: August Lax, 1905), 11. In 1902, 55 percent of the value of cotton imports into China originated from Britain, 26.8 percent from the United States, and just 2.7 percent from Japan. By 1930, Japan had captured 72.2 percent, with Britain now reduced to 13.2 percent and the United States to a minuscule 0.1 percent. See for these statistics Kang Chao, with Jessica C. Y. Chao, *The Development of Cotton Textile Production in China* (Cambridge, MA: Harvard University Press, 1977), 97.

582 Notes to Pages 414–417

71. Köll, From Cotton Mill to Business Empire, 36–37; James R. Morrell, "Origins of the Cotton Textile Industry in China" (PhD dissertation, Harvard University, 1977), 1, 147–75.

72. Myers, "Cotton Textile Handicraft and the Development of the Cotton Textile Industry," 626–27; Feuerwerker, "Handicraft and Manufactured Cotton Textiles in China," 346; Fong, "Cotton Industry and Trade in China," 348, 370–71, 411, 416; Shigeru Akita, "The British Empire and International Order of Asia, 1930s–1950s" (presentation, 20th International Congress of Historical Sciences, Sydney, 2005), 16; Shigeru Akita, "The East Asian International Economic Order in the 1850s," in Antony Best, ed., The International History of East Asia, 1900–1908 (London: Routledge, 2010), 153–67; Abe, "The Chinese Market for Japanese Cotton Textile Goods," 83; Robert Cliver, "China," in Van Voss et al., eds., The Ashgate Companion to the History of Textile Workers, 116; Ralph M. Odell et al., Cotton Goods in China, 158.

73. Feuerwerker, "Handicraft and Manufactured Cotton Textiles in China," 346; Loren Brandt, Commercialization and Agricultural Development: Central and Eastern China, 1870–1937 (Cambridge: Cambridge University Press, 1989), 6; Robert Cliver, "China," in Van Voss et al., eds., The Ashgate Companion to the History of Textile Workers, 116; Bruce L. Reynolds, "The Impact of Trade and Foreign Investment on Industrialization: Chinese Textiles, 1875–1931" (PhD dissertation, University of Michigan, 1975), 64; Chong Su, The Foreign Trade of China (New York: Columbia University, 1919), 304; Department of Overseas Trade and H. H. Fox, Economic Conditions in China to September 1, 1929 (London, 1929), 7, as quoted in Akita, "The British Empire and International Order of Asia," 17.

74. Odell et al., Cotton Goods in China, 161, 162ff., 168, 178, 179; Fong, "Cotton Industry and Trade in China," 376; Report of the Bombay Millowners' Association for the Year 1907 (Bombay: Times of India Steam Press, 1908), ii.

75. Fong, "Cotton Industry and Trade in China," 376; Jack Goldstone, "Gender, Work and Culture: Why the Industrial Revolution Came Early to England but Late to China," Sociological Perspectives 39, no. 1 (1996): 1; Robert Cliver, "China," in Van Voss et al., eds., The Ashgate Companion to the History of Textile Workers, 123–24.

76. Chu, Reformer in Modern China, 19, 22, 24, 28; Marie-Claire Bergere, The Golden Age of the Chinese Bourgeoisie, 1911–1937 (Cambridge: Cambridge University Press, 1989), 51–60; Cliver, "China," 126, 194; Albert Feuerwerker, China's Early Industrialization, 20, 28, 44; see Ching-Chun Wang, "How China Recovered Tariff Autonomy," Annals of the American Academy of Political and Social Science 152, no. 1 (1930): 266–77; Frank Kai-Ming Su and Alvin Barber, "China's Tariff Autonomy, Fact or Myth," Far Eastern Survey 5, no. 12 (June 3, 1936): 115–22; Kang Chao et al., The Development of Cotton Textile Production in China, 102; Abe, "The Chinese Market for Japanese Cotton Textile Goods," 96; Feuerwerker, "Handicraft and Manufactured Cotton Textiles in China," 343; Akita, "The British Empire and International Order of Asia," 20.

77. Farnie and Abe, "Japan, Lancashire and the Asian Market for Cotton Manufactures," 138, 139. Japanese mills in China were among the most efficient in the world; Hunter et al., "Japan," 316–17; United States Tariff Commission, Cotton Cloth, Report no. 112 (Washington: n.p., 1936), 157. For wage increases see also Takamura, Nihon

bōsekigyōshi josetsu, vol. 2, 209; Abe, "The Chinese Market for Japanese Cotton Textile Goods," 95; Charles K. Moser, *The Cotton Textile Industry of Far Eastern Countries* (Boston: Pepperell Manufacturing Company, 1930), 87; Fong, "Cotton Industry and Trade in China," 350.

78. Richu Ding, "Shanghai Capitalists Before the 1911 Revolution," *Chinese Studies in History* 18, no. 3–4 (1985): 33–82.

79. R. L. N. Vijayanagar, Bombay Millowners' Association, *Centenary Souvenir, 1875–1975* (Bombay: The Association, 1979), 29, in Asiatic Society of Mumbai; *Report of the Bombay Millowners' Association . . . 1909,* vi; *Report of the Bombay Millowners' Association . . . 1897,* 80; *Report of the Bombay Millowners' Association for the Year 1900* (Bombay: Times of India Steam Press, 1901), 52. See also *Report of the Bombay Millowners' Association for the Year 1904* (Bombay: Times of India Steam Press, 1905), 156; *Report of the Bombay Millowners' Association . . . 1907,* xiii; Resolution of the First Indian Industrial Conference held at Benares on December 30, 1905, in Part C, No. 2, March 1906, Industries Branch, Department of Commerce and Industry, National Archives of India, New Delhi; Morris, *The Emergence of an Industrial Labor Force in India,* 38; *Report of the Bombay Millowners' Association . . . 1907,* xiii.

80. Mehta, *The Ahmedabad Cotton Textile Industry,* 114; *The Mahratta,* January 19, 1896, February 2, 1896, February 9, 1896; "Memorandum on the Cotton Import and Excise Duties," 6, L/E/9/153, in Oriental and India Office Collections, British Library, London; Gandhi, *The Indian Cotton Textile Industry,* 66; G. V. Josji to G. K. Gokhale, File 4, Joshi Correspondence with Gokhale, Nehru Memorial Library, New Delhi.

81. *Report of the Bombay Millowners' Association for the Year 1901* (Bombay: Times of India Steam Press, 1902), 17–18.

82. *The Mahratta,* March 15, 1896; Mehta, *The Ahmedabad Cotton Textile Industry,* 117–19, 131; Tripathi, *Historical Roots of Industrial Entrepreneurship in India and Japan,* 115; A. P. Kannangara, "Indian Millowners and Indian Nationalism Before 1914," *Past and Present* 40, no. 1 (July 1968): 151. Bomanji Dinshaw Petit, a Bombay mill owner, argued that "the Japanese are fired with the spirit of Swadeshi and are equipped with the power to utilize the spirit to the uttermost extent and advantage." *Report of the Bombay Millowners' Association . . . 1907,* xii. For a different argument see Kannangara, "Indian Millowners and Indian Nationalism before 1914," 147–64. In contrast, see Sumit Sarkar, *Modern India, 1855–1947* (New Delhi: Macmillan, 1983), 132; *Report of the Bombay Millowners' Association . . . 1906,* iii.

83. *Sydenham College Magazine* 1, no. 1 (August 1919); *The Mahratta,* October 11, 1896, May 3, 1896; Draft of the Minutes of a Meeting of the Cotton Merchants held at Surat on April 13, 1919, in File No. 11, Sir Purshotamdas Thakurdas Papers, Nehru Memorial Library, New Delhi; Letter of Purshotamdas Thakurdas to the Ahmedabad Millowners' Association, March 22, 1919, in ibid.; *Report of the Bombay Millowners' Association . . . 1904,* 158. See also *Report of the Bombay Millowners' Association . . . 1907,* iv; *Report of the Bombay Millowners' Association . . . 1909,* iv; *Report of the Bombay Millowners' Association . . . 1907,* viii.

84. Gandhi, *The Indian Cotton Textile Industry;* Lisa N. Trivedi, *Clothing Gandhi's Nation: Homespun and Modern India* (Bloomington: Indiana University Press, 2007), 105. The link between the Indian mill owners and the nationalist movement can also

be traced in Sir Purshotamdas Thakurdas Papers, Nehru Memorial Library, New Delhi: for example, Letter of Sir Purshotamdas Tharkurdas to Ahmedabad Millowners Association, March 22, 1919, in Sir Purshotamdas Thakurdas Papers, File No. 11, Nehru Memorial Library; see also Draft of the Minutes of a Meeting of the Cotton Merchants held at Surat on April 13, 1919, in ibid.; "The Cotton Association," in *Sydenham College Magazine* 1, no. 1 (August 1919), in ibid.; Sir Purshotamdas Tharkurdas to Amedabad Millowners' Association, March 22, 1919, in ibid.

85. Gandhi, *The Indian Cotton Textile Industry*, 71, 123. For the connections to mill owners see Makrand Mehta, "Gandhi and Ahmedabad, 1915–20," *Economic and Political Weekly* 40 (January 22–28, 2005): 296. A. P. Kannangara, "Indian Millowners and Indian Nationalism before 1914," *Past and Present* 40, no. 1 (July 1968): 164; Visvesvaraya, *Planned Economy for India* (Bangalore: Bangalore Press, 1934), v, 203; Ding, "Shanghai Capitalists Before the 1911 Revolution," 33–82; on India see also Bipan Chandra, *The Writings of Bipan Chandra: The Making of Modern India rom Marx to Gandhi* (Hyderabad: Orient Blackswan, 2012), 385–441.

86. Bagchi, *Private Investment in India*, 5, 240, 241.

87. "The Cooperation of Japanese and Korean Capitalists," as cited in Eckert, *Offspring of Empire*, 48; Mehta, *The Ahmedabad Cotton Textile Industry*, 121; *Report of the Bombay Millowners' Association for the Year 1908* (Bombay: Times of India Steam Press, 1909), vi; Ratanji Tata to G. K. Gokhale, Bombay, October 15, 1909, in Servants of India Society Papers, File 4, correspondence, Gokhale, 1890–1911, Part 2, Nehru Memorial Library, New Delhi; File No. 24, Sir Purshotamdas Thakurdas Papers, Nehru Memorial Library; Dietmar Rothermund, *The Global Impact of the Great Depression, 1929–1939* (London: Routledge, 1996), 96; *A Brief Memorandum Outlining a Plan of Economic Development for India*, 1944, as reprinted in Purshotamdas Thakurdas, ed., *A Brief Memorandum Outlining a Plan of Economic Development for India*, 2 vols. (London: Penguin, 1945).

88. See Joel Beinin, "Formation of the Egyptian Working Class," *Middle East Research and Information Project Reports* 94 (February 1981): 14–23; Beinin, "Egyptian Textile Workers," 188–89.

89. Fong, "Cotton Industry and Trade in China," 379, 381; Hung-Ting Ku, "Urban Mass Movement: The May Thirtieth Movement in Shanghai," *Modern Asian Studies* 13, no. 2 (1979): 197–216.

90. Morris, *The Emergence of an Industrial Labor Force in India*, 105, 178, 183; R. L. N. Vijayanagar, Bombay Millowners' Association, *Centenary Souvenir, 1875–1975* (Bombay: The Association, 1979), 63, in Asiatic Society of Mumbai; Mehta, *The Ahmedabad Cotton Textile Industry*, 113; Makrand Mehta, "Gandhi and Ahmedabad, 1915–20," *Economic and Political Weekly* 40 (January 22–28, 2005): 298; Vijayanagar, *Centenary Souvenir, 1875–1975*, 29; Roy, "The Long Globalization and Textile Producers in India," 269.

91. Jacob Eyferth, "Women's Work and the Politics of Homespun in Socialist China, 1949–1980," *International Review of Social History* 57, no. 3 (2012): 13; Prabhat Patnaik, "Industrial Development in India Since Independence," *Social Scientist* 7, no. 11 (June 1979): 7; Paritosh Banerjee, "Productivity Trends and Factor Compensation in Cotton Textile Industry in India: A Rejoinder," *Indian Journal of Industrial Relations*

4 (April 1969): 542; Government of India, Ministry of Labour, *Industrial Committee on Cotton Textiles*, First Session, Summary of Proceedings, New Delhi, January 1948; Lars K. Christensen, "Institutions in Textile Production: Guilds and Trade Unions," in Van Voss et al., eds., *The Ashgate Companion to the History of Textile Workers*, 766; Hansen and Nashashibi, *Foreign Trade Regimes and Economic Development*, 7, 19–20.

92. Eyferth, "Women's Work and the Politics of Homespun," 21.

CHAPTER FOURTEEN: THE WEAVE AND THE WEFT: AN EPILOGUE

1. "Liverpool. By Order of the Liverpool Cotton Association Ltd., Catalogue of the Valuable Club Furnishings etc. to be Sold by Auction by Marsh Lyons & Co., Tuesday, 17th December 1963," Greater Manchester County Record Office, Manchester.

2. Douglas A. Farnie and Takeshi Abe, "Japan, Lancashire and the Asian Market for Cotton Manufactures, 1890–1990," in Douglas Farnie et al., eds., *Region and Strategy in Britain and Japan, Business in Lancashire and Kansai, 1890–1990* (London: Routledge, 2000), 151–52; John Singleton, "Lancashire's Last Stand: Declining Employment in the British Cotton Industry, 1950–1970," *Economic History Review*, New Series, 39, no. 1 (February 1986): 92, 96–97; William Lazonick, "Industrial Organization and Technological Change: The Decline of the British Cotton Industry," *Business History Review* 57, no. 2 (Summer 1983): 219. It was ironically also in the 1960s that British historians began to deemphasize the importance of the cotton industry to the Industrial Revolution.

3. John Baffes, "The 'Cotton Problem,'" *World Bank Research Observer* 20, no. 1 (April 1, 2005): 116.

4. For India, see Official Indian Textile Statistics 2011–12, Ministry of Textiles, Government of India, Mumbai, accessed on June 5, 2013, http://www.txcindia.com/html/comp%20table%20pdf%202011–12/compsection1%2011–12.htm. For Pakistan see Muhammad Shahzad Iqbal et al., "Development of Textile Industrial Clusters in Pakistan," *Asian Social Science* 6, no. 11 (2010): 132, Table 4.2, "Share of Textiles in Employment." On China see Robert P. Antoshak, "Inefficiency and Atrophy in China's Spinning Sector Provide Opportunities of Others," *Cotton: Review of World Situation* 66 (November–December 2012), 14–17.

5. National Cotton Council of America, "The Economic Outlook for U.S. Cotton, 2013," accessed September 17, 2013, http://www.cotton.org/econ/reports/loader .cfm?csModule=security/getfile&PageID=142203. See also United States Department of Agriculture, Foreign Agricultural Service, "Cotton: World Markets and Trade," Circular Series, April 2013; Oxfam, "Cultivating Poverty: The Impact of US Cotton Subsidies on Africa, 2002," accessed March 15. 2012, http://www.oxfamamerica .org/files/cultivating-poverty.pdf. On world cotton area see International Cotton Advisory Committee, *Cotton: Review of World Situation* 66 (November–December 2012), 5; International Cotton Advisory Committee, "Survey of Cotton Labor Cost Components in Major Producing Countries" (April 2012), foreword. The estimate of 350 million is from *Frankfurter Allgemeine Zeitung*, April 1, 2010. For the general points see Naoko Otobe, "Global Economic Crisis, Gender and Employment: The

Impact and Policy Response," ILO Employment Working Paper No. 74, 2011, 8; Clive James, "Global Review of Commercialized Transgenic Crops: 2001, Feature: Bt Cotton," *International Service for the Acquisition of Agri-Biotech Applications* no. 26 (2002), 59. David Orden et al., "The Impact of Global Cotton and Wheat Prices on Rural Poverty in Pakistan," *Pakistan Development Review* 45, no. 4 (December 2006): 602; John Baffes, "The 'Cotton Problem,' " *World Bank Research Observer* 20, no. 1 (April 1, 2005): 109.

6. Sabrina Tavernise, "Old Farming Habits Leave Uzbekistan a Legacy of Salt," *New York Times*, June 15, 2008; "Ministry Blames Bt Cotton for Farmer Suicides," *Hindustan Times*, March 26, 2012; David L. Stern, "In Tajikistan, Debt-Ridden Farmers Say They Are the Pawns," *New York Times*, October 15, 2008; Vivekananda Nemana, "In India, GM Crops Come at a High Price," *New York Times*, India Ink Blog, October 16, 2012, accessed April 2, 2013, http://india.blogs.nytimes.com/2012/10/16/in-india-gm-crops-come-at-a-high-price/?_r=0.

7. Amy A. Quark, "Transnational Governance as Contested Institution-Building: China, Merchants, and Contract Rules in the Cotton Trade," *Politics and Society* 39, no. 1 (March 2011): 3–39.

8. Nelson Lichtenstein, "The Return of Merchant Capitalism," *International Labor and Working-Class History* 81 (2012): 8–27, 198.

9. *New York Times*, April 1, 1946, 37; International Cotton Association, History Timeline, accessed April 15, 2013, http://www.ica-ltd.org/about-us/our-history.

10. John T. Cumbler, *Working-Class Community in Industrial America: Work, Leisure, and Struggle in Two Industrial Cities, 1880–1930* (Westport, CT: Greenwood Press, 1979), 139.

11. Kang Chao, *The Development of Cotton Textile Production in China* (Cambridge, MA: East Asian Research Center, Harvard University, 1977), 269.

12. Ibid., 267; Alexander Eckstein, *Communist China's Economic Growth and Foreign Trade: Implications for U.S. Policy* (New York: McGraw-Hill, 1966), 56.

13. See "China's Leading Cotton Producer to Reduce Cotton-Growing Farmland," *China View* (December 25, 2008), accessed September 10, 2013, http://news.xinhuanet.com/english/2008-12/25/content_10559478.htm; National Cotton Council of America, Country Statistics, accessed December 15, 2012, http://www.cotton.org/econ/cropinfo/cropdata/country-statistics.cfm; Zhores A. Medvedev, *Soviet Agriculture* (New York: Norton, 1987), 229ff.; Charles S. Maier, "Consigning the Twentieth Century to History: Alternative Narratives for the Modern Era," *American Historical Review* 105, no. 3 (June 1, 2000): 807–831; Carol S. Leonard, *Agrarian Reform in Russia: The Road from Serfdom* (Cambridge: Cambridge University Press, 2011), 75.

14. See Maier, "Consigning," 807–31.

15. Oxfam, "Cultivating Poverty: The Impact of US Cotton Subsidies on Africa, 2002"; *New York Times*, August 5, 2003, A18, September 13, 2003, A26. Over the past decade, U.S. government cotton subsidies have ranged from around $1 billion to over $4 billion a year. John Baffes, "Cotton Subsidies, the WTO, and the 'Cotton Problem,' " World Bank Development Prospects Group & Poverty Reduction and Economic Management Network, Policy Research Working Paper 566 (May 2011), 18; Michael Grunwald, "Why the U.S. Is Also Giving Brazilians Farm Subsidies," *Time*, April

9, 2010; Realizing Rights: The Ethical Globalization Initiative, "US and EU Cotton Production and Export Policies and Their Impact on West and Central Africa: Coming to Grips with International Human Rights Obligations" (May 2004), 2, accessed January 20, 2013, http://www.policyinnovations.org/ideas/policy_library/data/01155/_res/id=sa_File1/.

16. See Akmad Hoji Khoresmiy, "Impact of the Cotton Sector on Soil Degradation" (presentation, Cotton Sector in Central Asia Conference, School of Oriental and African Studies, London, November 3–4, 2005); International Crisis Group, Joint Letter to Secretary Clinton regarding Uzbekistan, Washington, DC, September 27, 2011, accessed January 20, 2013, http://www.crisisgroup.org/en/publication-type/media-releases/2011/asia/joint-letter-to-secretary-clinton-regarding-uzbekistan.aspx; International Crisis Group, "The Curse of Cotton: Central Asia's Destructive Monoculture," Asia Report No. 93, February 28, 2005, accessed January 20, 2013, http://www.crisisgroup.org/en/regions/asia/central-asia/093-the-curse-of-cotton-central-asias-destructive-monoculture.aspx.

17. See David Harvey, *The Geopolitics of Capitalism* (New York: Macmillan, 1985).

18. See Xi Jin, "Where's the Way Out for China's Textile Industry?" *Cotton: Review of World Situation* 66 (November–December 2012): 10.

19. See Eric Hobsbawm, *The Age of Extremes: A History of the World, 1914–1991* (New York: Vintage, 1994); for a similar argument see Aditya Mukherjee, "What Human and Social Sciences for the 21st Century: Some Perspectives from the South" (presentation at Nation Congress on "What Human and Social Sciences for the 21st Century?" at the University of Caen, France, on December 7, 2012).

20. See Environmental Farm Subsidy Database, 2013, accessed September 25, 2013, http://farm.ewg.org/progdetail.php?fips=00000&progcode=cotton.

21. On Chinese households in the 1950s see Jacob Eyferth, "Women's Work and the Politics of Homespun in Socialist China, 1949–1980," *International Review of Social History* 57, no. 3 (2012): 2. On current household expenditures see United States Department of Labor, Bureau of Labor Statistics, Consumer Expenditures 2012, released September 10, 2013, accessed September 17, 2013, http://www.bls.gov/news.release/pdf/cesan.pdf; *Frankfurter Allgemeine Zeitung*, November 13, 2009, 25.

Index

Pages 449–587 refer to endnotes. Numbers in italics refer to illustrations.

ILLUSTRATION CREDITS

149 By Camille Schlumberger, 1819, Portraits mulhousiens de la fin du XVIe siècle au commencement du XIXe siècle

149 National Institute of Historical Studies of the Revolutions of Mexico

151 John Rylands Collection

162 Caroline Hövemeyer, 1889, Heimatmuseum Reutlingen

162 Colección Estéban de Antuñano Cortina

162 John Lossing, *A History of the United States: For Families and Libraries* (1859), 369

167 Auguste Couder, oil on canvas, 1841, Palace of Versailles, France

175 © Hulton Archive/Getty Images

183 Dover Public Library

186–87 © Sven Beckert, based on data from Payroll Account Books, 1823–1824, Dover Manufacturing Company, Dover, New Hampshire, Cocheco Manufacturing Company Papers, Baker Library, Harvard Business School, Cambridge, MA

189 © Sven Beckert, based on data from McConnel and Kennedy Papers, MCK/4/51, John Rylands Library, Manchester

190 Roy Westall, *Wilmslow and Alderley Edge: A Pictorial History* (Shopwyke Manor Bank, UK: Phillimore, 1994)

199 Library of Congress, Washington, D.C.

202 Franklin Elmore Papers, Box 4, Library of Congress, Washington, D.C.

217 *Dictionnaire biographique comprenant la liste et les biographies des notabilités du Département de la Seine- Inférieure*, 1892

217 Georges Dubosc, *La Guerre de 1870–71 en Normandie*, 1905

217 National Portrait Gallery, London

234 © Kanton Zurich.

242 *Punch, or the London Charivari*, November 16, 1861

257 © Sven Beckert, based on data from Government of India, *Annual Statement of the Trade and Navigation of British India and Foreign* Countries (Calcutta: Office of Superindendent of Printing, 1872, 1876), vol. 5 and vol. 9; Roger Owen, *Cotton and the Egyptian Economy: A Study in Trade and Development* (Oxford: Clarendon Press, 1969), 90; Estatísticas *históricas do Brasil: Séries econômicas, demográficas e sociais de 1550 a 1988* (Rio de Janeiro: Fundação Instituto Brasileiro de Geogralica e Estatística, 1990), 346

259 École Nationale des Ponts et Chaussées, Paris, Folio 10975

260 Library of Congress Prints and Photographs Division, Washington, D.C.

262 Library of Congress Prints and Photographs Division, Washington, D.C.

274 Volkart Brothers Archive

279 © Sven Beckert, based on data in Sven Beckert, "Emancipation and Empire: Reconstructing the Worldwide Web of Cotton Production in the Age of the American Civil War," *American Historical Review* 109 (5), 1437

288 State Library of Louisiana

289 Lewis Hines

291 Mississippi Department of Archives & History, Jackson, MS

308 Archivo de la Casa Guillermo Purcell, Casa Purcell, San Pedro de las Colonias, Coahuila, Mexico

312 © Volkart Brothers Archive

315 © Volkart Brothers Archive

317 Walter H. Rambousek, Armin Vogt, and Hans R. Volkart, *Volkart: Die Geschichte einer Welthandelsfirma* (Frankfurt am Main: Insel Verlag, 1990), 81

318 Dimitri J. Zerbini, *Histoire d'un enterprise industrielle: The Kafr-El-Zayat Cotton Company, 1894–1956* (Alexandria: Sociéte de Publications Égyptienne, 1956)

321 Greater Manchester County Record Office, Manchester, B/10/10/3/719

322 Museum of the City of New York

325 © Sven Beckert, based on data referenced in chapter 11, note 19

326 Papers of B & S Astardjan, Manchester County Record-Office, Manchester, UK

327 © Volkart Brothers Archive

328 © Sven Beckert, based on data referenced in chapter 11, endnote 19

330 Rylands and Sons Archive, John Rylands Library, Manchester

337 George Lambert, *India, the horror-stricken empire: containing a full account of the famine, plague, and earthquake of 1896–7, including a complete narration of the relief work through the Home and Foreign Relief Commission* (Elkhart, IN.: Mennonite Pub. Co., 1898), 51

340 Kolonial-Wirtschaftliches Kommittee, "Baumwoll-Expedition nach Togo, Bericht, 1901," aus *Beihefte zum Tropenpflanzer* 3, 2 (1902), 338

342 Annual Report on Reforms and Progress in Chosen (Korea), 1912–13, compiled by Government-General of Chosen, Seoul, December 1914, Illustration 15, opp. 154

349 Imago Mundi, *Dictionnaire biographique,* "Faidherbe"

361 S. Ponjatovskij, *Opyt Izučenija Chlopkovodstva v Turkestaně i Zakaspijskoj Oblasti* (Saint Petersburg: Tipografija V.Y. Kirš'auma, 1913)

369 Bundesarchiv Berlin-Lichterfelde, R 1001, file 8223

370 Photograph by A. Vogt, Universitaetsbibliothek Frankfurt, Deutsche Kolonialgesellschaft/Bildarchiv, Nr. 101, 3–3501017

376 E. M. Mirzoev, "Agriculture," poster, 1937, International Institute of Social History, Amsterdam, Netherlands

379 Arno S. Pearse, *Brazilian Cotton: Being the Report of the Journey of the International Cotton Mission* (Manchester: International Federation of Master Cotton Spinners' & Manufacturers' Associations, 1921)

383 © Sven Beckert, based on data in "World's Consumption of All Kinds of Cotton," in Statistics of World Consumption of Cotton, 1910–1931, MD 230/44, Papers of John A. Todd, Liverpool Records Office, Liverpool

386 The Spinner Photographic Collection

396 Lewis Hine

397 © Armada Business Park

399 Library of Congress, Washington, D.C.

400 © Sven Beckert, based on data in Stephen Haber, ed., *How Latin America Fell Behind: Essays on the Economic Histories of Brazil and Mexico, 1800–1914* (Palo Alto, CA: Stanford University Press: 1997), 162

404 Kinsei Meishi Shashin, vol.2 (1934–35), National Diet Library, Tokyo, Japan

408 © Sven Beckert, based on data in Hikotaro Nishi, *Die Baumwollspinnerei in Japan* (Tübingen: Verlag der H. Laupp'schen Buchhandlung, 1911), 55; The Department of Finance, *1912: Annual Return of the Foreign Trade of the Empire of Japan* (Tokyo: Insetsu Kyoku, n.d.), 554; The Department of Finance, *1915: Annual Return of the Foreign Trade of the Empire of Japan,* part 1 (Tokyo: Insetsu Kyoku, n.d.), 448; The Department of Finance, *1917: Annual Return of the Foreign Trade of the Empire of Japan,* part 1 (Tokyo: Insetsu Kyoku, n. d.), 449; Hikotaro Nishi, *Die Baumwollspinnerei in Japan* (Tübingen: Verlag der H. Laupp'schen Buchhandlung, 1911), 84; The Department of Finance, 1895, *Annual Return of the Foreign Trade of the Empire of Japan* (Tokyo: Insetsu Kyoku, n.d.), 296; The Department of Finance, *December 1902: Monthly Return of the Foreign Trade of the Empire of Japan* (Tokyo: Insetsu Kyoku, n.d.), 65; Tōyō Keizai Shinpōsha, ed., *Foreign Trade of Japan: A Statistical Survey* (Tokyo: 1935; 1975), 229–30, 49

417 © Sven Beckert, based on data in Ownership of Spindles in Chinese Cotton Production; Peter Duus, "Zaikabō: Japanese Cotton Mills in China," in Michael Smitka, ed., *The Textile Industry and the Rise of the Japanese Economy* (New York: Garland, 1998), 82f

421 Photo by Vithalbhai Jhaveri at GandhiServe, 1925

422 © *Times of India*

425 *Bombay Industries: The Cotton Mills: A Review of the Progress of the Textile Industry in Bombay from 1850 to 1926 and the Present Constitution, Management and Financial Position of the Spinning and Weaving Factories* (Bombay: Indian Textile Journal, 1927), 487

427 © Reuters

430 © Noah Beckert

432 © Sven Beckert, based on data in indexmundi.com/agriculture/?-commodity=cotton&graph =production, U.S. Department of Agriculture

436 Institute for Social History